EXPLORING
MACINTOSH
Concepts in Visually Oriented Computing

EXPLORING MACINTOSH

Concepts in Visually Oriented Computing

KEN ABERNETHY / T. RAY NANNEY / HAYDEN PORTER

Furman University

Microsoft Works 2.0
Update Now Available!
(See page ix.)

WILEY

JOHN WILEY & SONS, INC.

New York   Chichester   Brisbane   Toronto   Singapore

Library of Congress Cataloging in Publication Data:

Abernethy, Ken.
   Exploring Macintosh: Concepts in Visually Oriented Computing

   Includes index.
   1. Macintosh (Computer)—Programming. I. Nanney, T. Ray. II. Porter, Hayden. III. Title.

QA76.8M3A23 1989 005.265   88-37874
                                                                              CIP

ISBN 0-471-61772-5

Printed in the United States of America

10 9 8 7 6 5 4 3

ACKNOWLEDGEMENTS

The authors have had support from a number of persons and organizations in the course of preparing this manuscript. While it is not possible to mention all of them in this short space we will mention some without whose help we could not have been successful. We would like to express our appreciation to our editor, Joe Dougherty, for his untiring assistance, good council, and keeping everything moving, given the tight production schedule. To the staff at Wiley, including Paul Constantine, Caren Parnes, Rita Warwell, Sandra Russell, Sheila Granda and Richard Koreto, we express our appreciation for a job well done in designing the book layout, the cover, and high-quality copyediting.

Our thanks also go to John Lippert of Apple Computer, Inc., for his support of our ideas and encouragement, and to Apple Computer, Inc. for providing a grant that in part allowed us to set up a laboratory where we could class–test our ideas for this book.

We also wish to express our appreciation to Microsoft Corporation for providing copies of Microsoft Word, and Microsoft Works, and Aldus for providing a copy of PageMaker.

Furman University Vice President for Academic Affairs and Dean, Dr. John Crabtree, Jr., receives our special thanks for his generous support of this project by providing funds to help establish a Macintosh computer laboratory, and by providing the resources necessary to produce the manuscript and duplicate materials. He also has assisted us by providing staff to help in typing revisions of the manuscript. Kathy Norris, our devoted departmental secretary, converted all chapters to the required styles for publication and was generally indispensable in helping meet all of the deadlines. Lynn Roosevelt helped in many valuable ways. We also acknowledge the enormous support of our families, especially our wives, Sherry, Lib, and Pat, who spent long hours without husbands and who also proofread willingly many revisions of each chapter. Finally, we thank all the Furman University students who gave us their frank and open reactions to the concepts presented in the initial offerings of the course CS16, Introduction to Computing for Non-Science Majors, for which this book was written.

PREFACE

This book is about using computers and a new generation of sophisticated applications software to solve information management problems. Solutions to information management problems include such activities as making calculations and presenting reports, tables, and graphs based on those calculations; collecting, storing, updating, and retrieving data; organizing and implementing methods for the effective display and interpretation of information; and producing multi-featured documents for the dissemination of information. Because such activities are central to almost any modern enterprise, the applicability of the methods presented here is exceptionally broad.

The book has a strong conceptual orientation. The emphasis throughout is on a mastery of the concepts necessary to use the computer as a problem-solving tool. Although specific software products are covered in detail, this coverage is made generic where possible so that the reader will be able to transfer the knowledge gained to other software packages. The development is self-contained, and no prior computer knowledge or experience is assumed or required.

A primary goal of this text is to provide the reader with the concepts and methods essential for attainment of computer competency in the most important areas of information management. As such, it should not be confused with the current flood of books available on the subject of computer literacy, most of which contain some material on some of the same kinds of software discussed here. While these books intend to give their readers a general overview of such software within the broader context of the study of many aspects of computer technology, it is our intent that the reader acquire the ability to use such software to construct computer solutions to real and significant problems. Additionally, this book makes no attempt to cover the broad areas of the history, diverse uses, and societal implications of general computer technology. Indeed, those readers who have completed a study of computer literacy should find very little overlap between that study and the coverage in this book.

Because the focus of this book is on problem solving as opposed to learning "about" computers, we have chosen to restrict the discussion to the Macintosh computer and its software packages. The reason for this choice is that the Macintosh–human interface is currently the most elegant and easy-to-use interface available on a personal computer. Its mastery requires much less time, effort, and preoccupation with the computer itself than other available interfaces and operating systems. As a consequence, the reader will be able to concentrate on learning the Macintosh as a tool for problem solving, instead of expending great energy solving the problem of learning to use the computer. An additional advantage of the Macintosh is the ease with which it allows integration of text, graphics, and sound, thus supporting more flexible and powerful document preparation methods than are available on other machines.

Some of the conceptual material included has not been presented before at this level, but the authors' experience has shown that beginning students can readily understand the material. In fact, they seem to learn the associated software more easily than students who have not been given this conceptual background. In addition, the conceptual material gives the reader access to a number of different software products. For example, on separate occasions, we have successfully used the conceptual database material to teach four quite different database software packages. Spreadsheets are introduced with considerable time being devoted to presenting the underlying concepts as opposed to considering only the details of a particular spreadsheet package. Once this conceptual base is in place, students are able to learn the use of particular packages quickly.

All the software packages studied are described from the viewpoint of a user trying to communicate to the computer what is to be done to solve some problem. The nature of the communication process is discussed, and using a software package is shown to involve learning the language of the package. This perspective draws on the reader's innate knowledge of language and communication to develop a deeper understanding of the use of software packages.

Part I of the book gives the concepts and techniques necessary for using the Macintosh, or any windows-oriented computer, effectively. Important topics discussed include the significance for computer problem solving of a visual orientation, a thorough description of the Macintosh interface, techniques for using the Macintosh desktop environment, the computer as a language interpreter, techniques for interacting with various computing contexts, and the hierarchical file system of the Macintosh. This part provides essential information for the remainder of the book.

In **Part II** the Microsoft Works® integrated software package is used for exploring word processing, spreadsheets, database systems, communications software, and the nature of integrated software packages. A thorough discussion is provided for each of the components of Microsoft Works. This package was selected because of its widespread use for information management problems, because the concepts and techniques used in it transfer readily to other software packages, and because the package makes available a wide range of capabilities for a reasonable cost. The topics in this section together with Part I may be sufficient for many 3 semester hour courses.

Part III contains optional topics that demonstrate that a mastery of the concepts and techniques of Parts I and II makes it relatively easy to learn and understand additional software packages and problem-solving capabilities. Part III may be omitted entirely or selected chapters from it may be covered in any sequence (except that Chapters 17 and 18 must be covered in order). Among the topics covered are: advanced document preparation techniques, demonstrated using Microsoft Word®; desktop publishing concepts, demonstrated using Page-Maker®; relational database system concepts, demonstrated using Reflex Plus®; advanced spreadsheet concepts, demonstrated using Excel®; the use of sound and animation, demonstrated using ConcertWare®, MacRecorder® and VideoWorksII®; and hypertext concepts using HyperCard®.

It is our hope that the book demonstrates that we are at the beginning of an exciting new phase of the computer era. During the next few years, truly remarkable qualitative changes will occur in the ways people use computers. These changes will be driven by new software concepts and products that deliver new problem-solving capabilities to computer users. Those users who make the commitment to master these new ideas and products will find them absolutely indispensable in their own creative and problem-solving tasks.

Ken Abernethy
T. Ray Nanney
Hayden Porter

NOTE ON SOFTWARE VERSIONS.

There is a large number of software packages discussed in the text. These packages were current releases at the time of writing. However, given the length of time between writing of the text and its publication some new releases of software will no doubt be available by the time you read this note. For completeness, we list here all version numbers of the software discussed in our book.

Software Package Name	Version Number
Microsoft Word	3.01
Microsoft Excel	1.04
Microsoft Works	1.1
MacPaint	1.5
VideoWorksII	2.0
Reflex Plus	1.01
HyperCard	1.0
Finder	6.0
System	4.2
MacRecorder	1.05
PageMaker	2.0 and 3.0
ConcertWare+Midi	4.0

SPECIAL NOTE.

A supplement covering the latest version of Microsoft Works® is now available at no extra cost to purchasers of this text. To obtain an individual copy of the supplement, please send a self-addressed mailer (large enough to hold an $8^1/_2$ x $5^1/_2$ inch booklet) to the address below. Instructors may obtain multiple copies for classroom use by writing on departmental letterhead to the following address or contacting their local address.

Mr. Joseph B. Dougherty
John Wiley & Sons, Inc.
605 Third Ave.
New York, NY 10158

CONTENTS

PART III   INVESTIGATING SOME ADVANCED CONCEPTS

PART I

MASTERING SOME ESSENTIAL SKILLS

CHAPTER 1

INTRODUCING VISUALLY ORIENTED COMPUTING

LEARNING OBJECTIVES

- To understand what is meant by visually oriented computing.
- To gain an introductory understanding of the Macintosh human-computer interface philosophy.
- To appreciate some of the computer applications possible using graphic visualization of data.
- To learn how visually oriented computing can enhance your ability for problem solving with the computer.

I n this chapter you will be introduced to the concepts of visually oriented computing. You will be given a brief introduction to the Macintosh human-computer interface philosophy and gain an appreciation for the ease of communicating with the computer in a visual mode. You will see some advantages of visualization of computer output and learn how such visualization has proved invaluable in many areas. Finally, you will explore how visually oriented computing has greatly enhanced the role of the computer as an aid to problem solving and how this enhancement will improve your own ability to use the computer.

1.1 NEW COMPUTING VISTAS

According to John Scully, chief executive officer at Apple Computer:

> We are on the verge of creating new tools, which, like the printing press, will empower individuals, unlock worlds of knowledge, and forge a new community of ideas.... These tools won't just take you to the doorstep of great resources as sophisticated computers do now; they will invite you deep inside to explore secrets, interpreting and explaining—converting vast quantities of information into personalized and understandable knowledge.

These aren't the words of a man who is *only* out to sell you a computer; they are the words of a man who is so genuinely excited about the new possibilities of computing that he has to share his feelings. It is an excitement about using technology to open doors to vistas of personal creativity and productivity that we could not have imagined 10 years ago. Because these new methods of computing allow anyone to collect, organize, manipulate, interpret, and disseminate information, in the coming years, they will directly affect nearly everyone in our society.

Over the past four or five years, new developments in computer hardware and software have made the computing environments of previous times appear as outdated as the horse and buggy. In yesterday's environments we were forced to work at "assembling jigsaw puzzles in the dark," to quote computer scientist Richard Weinberg. Indeed, not only were we assembling the puzzles in the dark, we were admiring our handiwork in, at best, a half-lit room. The new environments allow us to participate in the process of computing in a fully lit room.

What are the ideas that drive this kind of excitement? What developments are responsible for such a radical change in computing environments? How do the new environments enhance our abilities to use computers to solve problems in ways that were undreamed of just a few years ago? These are the central questions this chapter addresses.

VISUAL MODE COMPUTING.   The central idea contributing to the creation of the new computing vistas is the concept of **visually oriented computing.** By this phrase we mean the organization of computing environments so that the human–computer interaction takes place in visual ways. This allows you as a computer

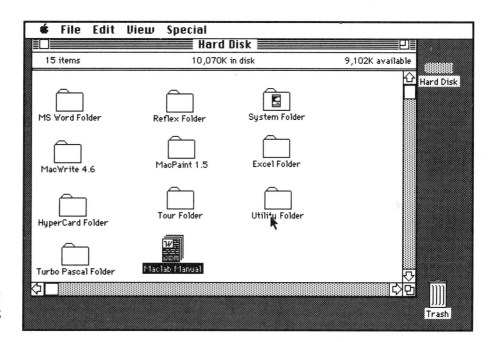

Figure 1.1 Macintosh starting screen, typical of that seen in a windowing environment.

user to *see* graphically the effects of your communications with the computer. Computers possessing these graphical forms of interaction are collectively called **windowing environments**. Consider as an example the contrast between the computer screens shown in Figure 1.1 and in Figure 1.2. Both of these are screens that would be presented to a user near the beginning of a computing session.

Because the Macintosh uses a windowing environment, communicating with it involves manipulating symbols such as the ones seen in Figure 1.1. Instead of being forced to remember long and sometimes complicated strings of symbols and commands to give instructions to the computer, you will be able to rely on your visual powers to help you remember and better understand the communication you establish with the computer. This improved communication is extremely important, for *communication* is at the heart of using computers for productive

```
RBASE    BAT          73    2-13-87     2:45p
12PLUS        <DIR>          3-03-86     1:18p
LETTER1  DOC         567    4-06-87    12:26p
INFSYS   EXE        2345    6-01-85     3:56a
DAVE2    DOC         765    4-12-88    11:54a
RBSYS         <DIR>          1-30-88    12:44a
RBBK     DAT          48    3-30-88    11:33a
         97 Files    1417216 bytes free

C>█
```

Figure 1.2 Typical starting screen for a traditional personal computer.

problem solving. The primary reason many people have been intimidated by computers is that even though they understand *what* they want the computer to do, they don't understand *how one communicates to the computer what is to be done*. Visually oriented computing in windowing environments will greatly increase our abilities to communicate with computers.

Understandably, not all of us have been excited by the prospect of learning an esoteric and unnatural computer language to communicate our ideas to a computer. But all of us are (or could easily become) excited about what the computer can do for us—provided using a computer becomes more natural and intuitive. We are rapidly reaching the point where we can tap this resource without having to become computer professionals. The ability to use your visual powers to manipulate graphical objects on the screen as a part of the communication process will make this possible.

USING VISUAL COMPUTER OUTPUT. Another important aspect of visually oriented computing concerns the communication from computer to human. Instead of getting the results of the computer's actions as a listing of text and/or numbers and then spending hours interpreting those results, we can have the computer output appear in more interpretable graphical forms. Consider, for example, the two computer printouts shown in Figure 1.3. The advantages of graphical data display are obvious and have been recognized for years, but we have just recently developed the technology to be able to produce such display routinely and painlessly.

Which of the two notes shown in Figure 1.4 is more likely to produce the desired result? The note on the left was produced using the program MacPaint® on a Macintosh (in about three minutes). Or consider a program that produces music as its output—not musical scores but *actual musical sounds*. And what about the spoken word? (HAL isn't here yet, but we're moving in that direction.)

On the other hand, we might prefer architectural drawings, or color-enhanced photographic images, that have been stored in the computer electronically as our program output. Indeed, not only photographic images, but music and other sound may be converted to a discrete or digitized electronic form and then stored in a computer to be manipulated and reproduced later. These ideas will be explored more fully when you learn about computer animation and music generation and manipulation software in Chapter 20.

The possibilities for productively using flexible and visual methods of presenting computer output are virtually unlimited. Later in this chapter, we con-

Category	Percentage
Food	25%
Rent	30%
Utilities	20%
Entertainment	10%
Other	15%

Figure 1.3 Comparing data listing and graphical output.

Figure 1.4 Making a visual impression.

sider some practical examples of how such methods have opened new doors to problem solving. You may be surprised to learn how many of these techniques are available to you as the user of a personal computer with a windowing environment like a Macintosh.

EVOLUTION OF TECHNOLOGY. What technological advances have made these revolutionary changes in computing environments possible? It was not so many years ago that the only computers available were large mainframe computers housed in highly structured centralized computer centers. Easy-to-use software of the kind discussed in this text was not available, and computer problem solving required the use of programming languages. The primary method for communicating programs and commands to these computers was by using a stack of punched computer cards, which had to be laboriously prepared using keypunch machines. A user had to give his card stack to a computer operator and wait (often for hours) for his stack to be processed in a "batch" consisting of many users' card stacks. No wonder there was no headlong rush by the general public to get involved with computing! Computing was reserved for the few brave souls whose need to use the computer was strong enough to induce them to jump through an unpleasant series of hoops!

Even as recently as 10 years ago, a computer's processing power was nearly completely reserved for *doing a user's job*, not for making that job easier to accomplish. The typical computing environment then consisted of large mainframe computers with terminals providing user access. Many users could concurrently access the computing resource through an arrangement called *time-sharing*. Because one computer was serving many individuals there was little computing power remaining to provide what was then considered conveniences for the user. After all, it was assumed that anyone using the computer had at least a reasonable amount of computer knowledge and hence needed only a minimum amount of assistance to make effective use of the machine.

With the advent of low-cost personal computers and self-contained computer workstations, this philosophy changed drastically. The typical personal computer user did not share computer processing power with other users. This allowed software vendors to concentrate on giving the user more control over the computing environment. However, the truly important advances in this area had to await further improvement in computing power.

Not only have computers become more powerful, but the cost of producing more and more powerful computer hardware has dropped dramatically in the last 10 years. In fact, many of the desktop microcomputers of today are actually far more powerful (faster, with more memory and graphics display capabilities) than earlier room-sized mainframe computers costing a hundred times more. As a consequence, today's microcomputer user has resources far in excess of those required for the solution of the majority of the problems for which a typical user seeks computer solutions. Hence, software designers have begun to take advantage of this excess computing power.

The first obvious benefits provided for the software user were some additional features that made using the software more interesting, more fun, and easier. For example, 10 years ago, using computer graphics for output was considered an interesting novelty but certainly not a necessity. Indeed, the graphics techniques available at that time appear extremely crude and uninteresting to us now. What has happened is the gradual realization that these user conveniences, especially graphics, can be used to enhance computer usage in a dazzling array of directions. Once this potential was recognized, computing had taken the first step toward a new age. We have really just begun this journey, but already there are some exciting milestones.

THE MACINTOSH.   The introduction of the Macintosh line of computers in 1984 is a significant event in the brief history of visually oriented computing. Although the Macintosh was not the first computer to provide a visual human-computer interface, it did launch the popularization and acceptance of such interfaces. These interfaces have had an important impact on the way people use computers.

The visual-graphical characteristic of windowing environments such as the Macintosh and IBM PS/2 interfaces has converted many people, who were not computer users, into productive and creative computer fanatics—not because the computer is the central aspect of their work, but because it provides a medium through which they can creatively explore their ideas and enhances the force with which they express them! Today this same kind of graphics-oriented interface is being adapted to larger computer systems, through an interface called X windows.

The major goal of this text is to help you become a productive and creative user of the computer, a user who is at least enthusiastic, if not fanatic. We think this will happen as you learn to use some high-productivity problem-solving software—spreadsheets, database management systems, word processors, and desktop publishing systems, to name some of the major categories. These software environments will allow you to explore *your* ideas naturally, intuitively, and visually. The use of a visual interface will enhance your ability to learn and use this software. In the next section, we explore the specific Macintosh implementation of human-computer communication and give a quick overview of some of the major features of the Macintosh interface. While this discussion is particular to the Macintosh, most of the concepts are applicable on any computer having a windowing environment.

Exercise Set 1.1

1. Describe what is meant by visually oriented computing.

2. What is meant by visual mode computing?

3. How does visual mode computing affect a computer user's ability to communicate with a computer?

4. List some advantages of graphical computer output over textual output. Give some examples (other than the ones in the text) of where this would be particularly useful.

5. Describe some of the changes that have taken place in computing environments over the past 10 years.

6. What do the authors claim as the major goal of this text?

1.2 OVERVIEW OF THE MACINTOSH INTERFACE

In this section you will be introduced to the major features of the Macintosh visual mode interface. This section is intended as a get-acquainted tour, not as formal instruction. All the ideas mentioned here will be expanded in the next few chapters, where you will be given a chance to practice using them.

THE OFFICE–DESKTOP METAPHOR.   The Macintosh human-computer interface is visually oriented and takes its primary ideas from the model of information organization in a noncomputerized office. The starting point for this organization is the **desktop**. The desktop is the displayed screen with which you work when communicating with the computer. On this desktop you will open **disks** (which you might think of as filing cabinet drawers), in which can be placed numbers of **files** and **folders** that contain various information.

A great variety of entities exist as files, including such things as word processing documents (such as this chapter) and charts. Folders are used to organize your files into related groups—just as you would do in your noncomputerized office. Folders can contain files as well as other folders. To view the contents of a folder or a disk, you open a **window** to that object. A window is a region on the screen that is associated with a particular disk, folder, or file. In this region information about the associated object can be displayed. Some examples follow shortly. You can have many windows open on your desktop at one time, but only one window can be active. Only the objects in the active window may be manipulated. There is also a **trash can** on the desktop—for disposing of unwanted files and/or folders.

OF MICE AND ICONS.   Disks, files, folders, and the trash can are all represented on the desktop screen by **icons**, or symbolic pictures, whose shapes suggest the kinds of objects they represent. The manipulation of files, folders, and windows associated with them is accomplished primarily through the use of a **mouse** (see Figure 1.5). The mouse has a contact ball on its underside that turns as you roll the mouse around a flat surface next to your computer. As the ball rolls, the **mouse pointer** (a bold arrow) is moved on the computer desktop screen. You may position this pointer to touch objects or areas of the screen—that is, to point them

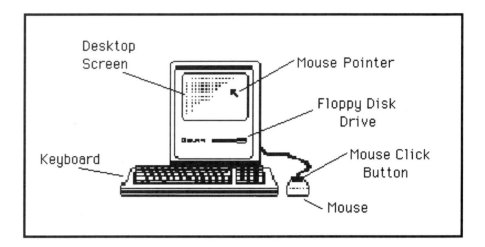

Figure 1.5 A Macintosh computer.

out to the computer. Actions on the objects touched by the pointer are accomplished through a **click button** on top of the mouse. By manipulating this button you can very easily open and close windows, resize and reposition windows, move files to the trash can or into different folders, and do many other useful tasks.

SOME EXAMPLE DESKTOPS. Figure 1.6 shows a Macintosh desktop with two disks present—the system's hard disk and a disk named *Letters*—and the trash can. (Disks are described more completely in Chapter 2.) Note carefully the shape of each of the icons. In the upper left part of the desktop you see the mouse pointer (just under the name **File**). The five items (of which **File** is one) in the row at the top of the desktop are names of menus. We will say more about menus shortly.

Recall that to display the contents of a disk or folder you open a window to the object. In Figure 1.7 the desktop of Figure 1.6 is shown after a window has been opened for the *Hard Disk*. Opening an object is accomplished by moving the mouse so that the mouse pointer is over the icon for the object and then clicking the mouse button twice in rapid succession (called *double-clicking*). Objects different from disks and folders may also be opened, but the action of opening them has a different meaning in these cases. (We postpone further discussion of this matter to Chapter 2.) Note that the hard disk contains various folders that are displayed in its window. Again, observe how the shape of the folder icon reminds you of the *kind* of object it represents. Recall that we expect each of the folders to contain additional information—files and/or other folders.

If you open the folder named *MS Word* shown in Figure 1.7, you get a desktop like that shown in Figure 1.8. Notice that on this desktop two windows appear— one showing the contents of the hard disk and the other showing the contents of the folder *MS Word*. Because we just opened the *MS Word* folder, its window is active. You can have many windows opened on our desktop at once. The active window is the one that appears on top of the others. It is easy to change the active window and thus switch the order of windows. For example, to make the *Hard Disk* window the active window (see Figure 1.8), you would position the mouse pointer anywhere in the *Hard Disk* window and click the mouse button. The active

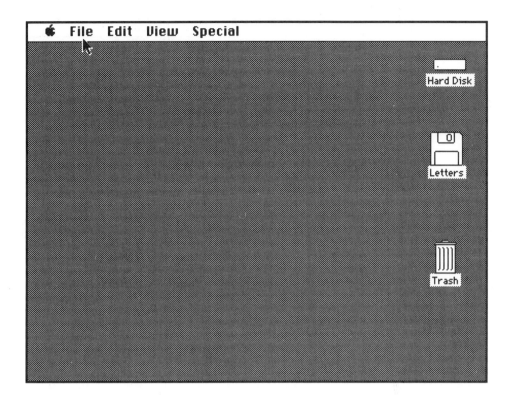

Figure 1.6 Macintosh desktop with two disks and the trash can.

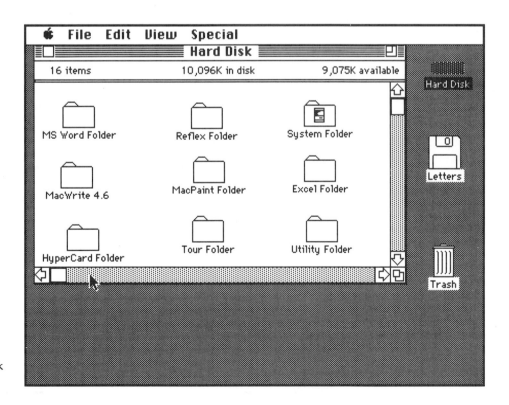

Figure 1.7 Desktop of Figure 1.6 with hard disk window opened.

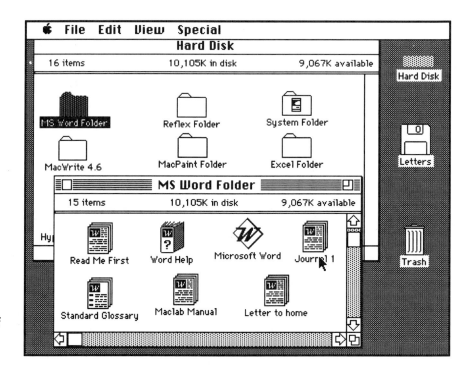

Figure 1.8 The desktop of Figure 1.7 with the *MS Word* folder opened.

window always has the horizontal bars in its top border and appears on top of the other windows being displayed. Note the icons in the *MS Word* folder. The icons shaped like pages of text represent documents produced by the MS Word® application program, which is represented by the diamond-shaped icon labeled *Microsoft Word*.

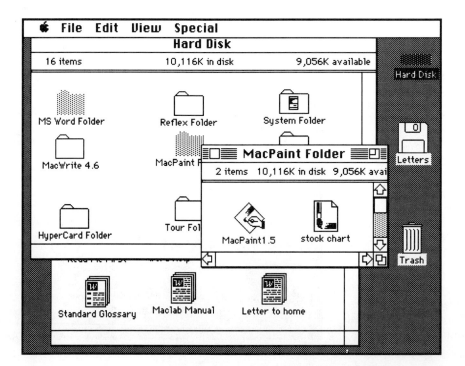

Figure 1.9 Desktop of Figure 1.8 with *MacPaint* folder opened.

Figure 1.9 shows the desktop of Figure 1.8 with the additional MacPaint folder opened. Note the shape of the two icons in this folder. The shape of the *stock chart* icon is meant to suggest a diagram or drawing that has been produced with the MacPaint® application program. All documents produced by the MacPaint program will have an icon of this shape. The icon labeled *MacPaint 1.5* is the actual MacPaint program itself. By opening this program you are able to run, or execute, the MacPaint application. You will see some effects of running this application shortly.

When you have several windows present at once on your desktop, it can become cluttered quickly. You can control this clutter by organizing your desktop as you desire (just as you would a real desktop). For example, you can resize and reposition windows at will. One possible reorganization of the desktop shown in Figure 1.9 is given in Figure 1.10. As you will see in Chapter 2, this transition can be done in a matter of a few seconds using the mouse.

USING APPLICATIONS.   Applications provide the means for creating and manipulating information on your computer. Let us now examine briefly some aspects of running a Macintosh application. The MacPaint application allows you to create drawings and paintings on an electronic canvas. If you open the MacPaint application, you are presented with the screen shown in Figure 1.11. You will notice on the left of the screen two columns of icons. These are the MacPaint *tools* available for your use. Along the bottom of the screen are a number of predesigned *fill patterns* that can be used to fill enclosed areas or as the patterns for such tools as the spray can. The icons on the left represent various drawing tools. The shapes of the icons suggest the functions that are available. For example, the spray can tool does just what its icon suggests—sprays paint (sounds

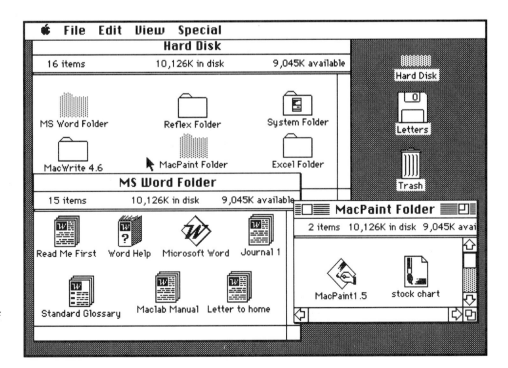

Figure 1.10 The desktop of Figure 1.9 with windows resized and repositioned.

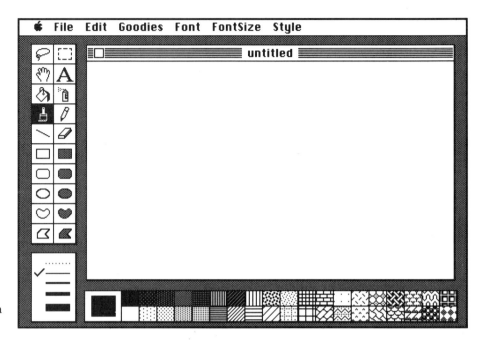

Figure 1.11 Starting screen for MacPaint.

like fun, doesn't it?). The window labeled *untitled* is an electronic canvas on which the drawings and paintings are produced.

Figure 1.12 demonstrates the results of using some of the tools. Note that some tools are used to create predesigned objects, like rectangles, ovals, circles, and so on, and other tools allow the construction of freehand objects, like the face. Each of these objects was created using the mouse. Various character sizes and styles are available for the insertion of text into your pictures and charts. In

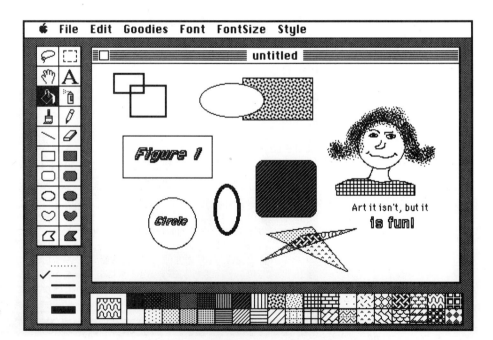

Figure 1.12 MacPaint screen with some sample constructions.

Chapter 2, you will work with MacPaint to produce some pictures and graphs, and in Chapter 3, the MacPaint application package will be described in detail.

One of the most advantageous features of the Macintosh interface is the extensive use of **dialog boxes** within most application packages. These boxes often require only that you make a selection by moving and clicking the mouse. On some occasions, a typed response is necessary (to name a document not previously named, for example), but generally actions with the mouse suffice. An example of a dialog box within the word processor MS Word (*MS* stands for *Microsoft*, the name of a major microcomputer software company) is shown in Figure 1.13. This box appears as a response to the user's request to "quit" or exit the MS Word program; the program wants to know whether the user wishes to save the modified document. Response is made by using the mouse to move the pointer to the appropriate response box and clicking. Such boxes can make the process of communicating your wishes to the computer very easy and natural.

Another feature that smooths the way for painless computer usage is the concept of **pull-down menus**. These are menus that can be accessed (pulled down) from the row of menu choices along the top of an application window by using the mouse. When a choice along that row is selected, a set of menu options appears automatically. The desired choice from the menu can then be selected using the mouse and without typing or having to remember what must be typed in to select that choice. Generally, *all* the options available to you are shown. Because you need to type *nothing*, you need to remember very little; thus, you can access the appropriate menu choice quickly and painlessly with the mouse. Pull-down menus are explained more fully in Chapter 2. A preview of some of the MacPaint pull-down menus is shown in Figure 1.14. Each of these options within a menu allows you to direct the computer to some kind of action. Once you have gained experience using these menus, you will have full control over your computer environment. Each option in a menu can be explored intuitively, by trying it out to learn its effects. The Macintosh invites exploration because it usually provides a graceful undoing of a selected operation.

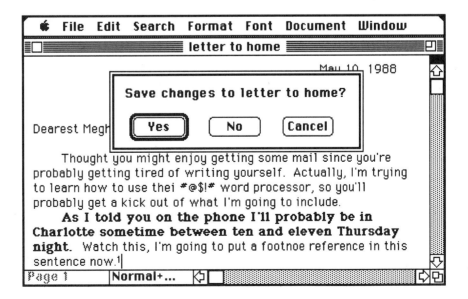

Figure 1.13 MS Word dialog box.

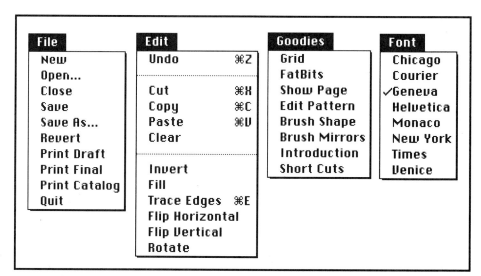

Figure 1.14 A preview of some MacPaint pull-down menus.

Before concluding our quick tour of the Macintosh interface we should not fail to mention one of the truly advantageous aspects of the Macintosh philosophy, the **consistency of the interface across different applications**. Learning a software application program is usually a nontrivial task. On many computers, learning two different software applications is roughly twice the amount of work as learning one application, because software applications have few common features and access methods. On the Macintosh, as in many windowing environments, this problem is addressed with the philosophy that *all* applications should take advantage of certain features of the interface. This consistency of interface across different applications is of tremendous benefit to the computer user. For example, all Macintosh applications will make extensive use of pull-down menus. Not only will pull-down menus be used, but most of them will appear and function similarly from application to application. In addition, many pull-down menu choices can also be executed directly from the keyboard if the user desires.

As an example, compare the **File** and **Edit** pull-down menus from the packages MS Word, MacPaint, and Excel® that are shown in Figure 1.15. As you will soon see, each option of the same name operates nearly identically in each different application. Once a single application has been mastered, new applications become easier to learn. The more you use the Macintosh, the more familiar you become with the "common" features, and the more natural the use of the computer becomes for an amazing variety of purposes. You will see this advantage in a dramatic way as you learn the various software packages discussed later in this text.

An additional advantage of pull-down menus is observed if you use an application infrequently. You will tend to forget specific access methods and commands of any infrequently used application (even though you will likely remember the functions and capabilities of the application). With pull-down menus giving you instant access to the commands available at any point within an application, you are not required to remember the specific commands. Remembering only that a certain function exists, you can very quickly search through the pull-down menus until you find it. You will likely recognize the

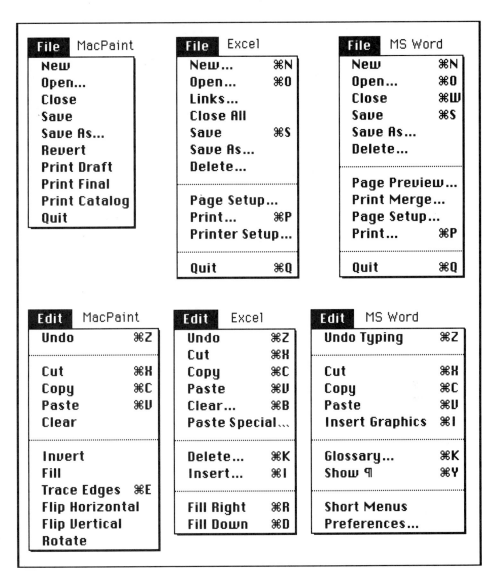

Figure 1.15 A comparison of pull-down menus from several application packages.

function when you see its menu name, even though you wouldn't be able to cite it from memory. The readily available menus quickly refresh your memory and make using the application as easy and natural as if you used it much more frequently. These same considerations also make it far easier to learn a new software application on the Macintosh than would be the case on a nonwindowing machine. In fact, because they are so intuitive, you will be able to begin the use of many software applications without even reading the user's manual! (You cannot fully appreciate this advantage, unless you have already tried to read some user's manuals.)

PERSPECTIVE. The use of windowing environments makes it much easier for you to learn to *use* a given type of software. Learning to use the appropriate software is one step in using the computer for problem solving, but it is not the only, or even the most important, step. The central issue in using the computer to solve problems (of whatever type) is that *you* are the problem solver, not the computer. The computer and its software are the tools and the medium that you use to facilitate your work *after* you have formulated the steps of the problem solution.

While windowing environments are excellent tools for a great variety of problem solving, you should never forget that you must master the concepts necessary for solving the problem and then translate your solution into a form that the computer can use to produce answers. The advantage of a windowing environment is that it makes that translation much easier than it was previously. In this text we will not only introduce you to a variety of software tools, but also help you learn some extremely important problem-solving skills—skills that transcend the computer environment.

Exercise Set 1.2

1. What is meant by the office-desktop metaphor?
2. What is a window?
3. What is the function of a mouse? How does it work?
4. What are icons and how are they used?
5. Where do the names of the pull-down menus appear on a Macintosh desktop?
6. How does a folder differ from a file?
7. How do you view the contents of a folder or a disk?
8. Can more than one window be open at once on the Macintosh desktop? Can more than one window be active at once?
9. What do the icons in the "palette" on the left side of the MacPaint application window represent?
10. What are dialog boxes?
11. Describe several advantages that pull-down menus provide.
12. Why is a consistent interface across applications so important to a Macintosh user?
13. What is the role of a computer and its software in the problem-solving process?

1.3. VISUALIZATION OF COMPUTER OUTPUT

As we noted in the first section of this chapter, visually oriented computing has two primary directions: communicating our desires to the computer in a visual or graphical mode and the graphical visualization of computer output. In the previous section you were introduced to some of the ways a windowing environment makes possible communicating with the computer in a visual mode. In this section, we briefly explore the second of these directions—**visualization of computer output** in a pictorial and/or graphical manner. Interest in visually oriented computing is large and growing; as a consequence, the scope of applications for the new methods for data visualization is astounding. We begin with some examples using the Macintosh and conclude the section with a sampling of some more generic examples that illustrate a few of the exciting kinds of problems being solved with these methods.

Again, remember that the purpose of this chapter is to give you a broad overview of many different ideas and concepts. As a consequence, you should not be concerned if you have less than a complete understanding of some of the topics discussed. Some are included here for illustrative purposes only; the ones that are more directly related to subsequent parts of the text are developed fully later on, when they are needed.

MACINTOSH EXAMPLES. In this text, our primary interest is in the use of visual mode computing for personal problem solving. The following examples will give you some indication of the variety of methods being used for visualization of data for several different kinds of problem solving on the Macintosh. It is not our intent to develop these ideas fully here; rather, we want to see what some of the possibilities are for using the visualization of data as a problem-solving technique on the Macintosh.

We have already seen in Figure 1.3 how the graphical display of data can enhance our ability to interpret and use the data. A number of software applications have as their central purpose the graphical display of data. For example, using the application Cricket Graph®, a user can manipulate data sets to produce many varieties of graphical output. Even applications whose primary purpose is not necessarily to display graphical output contain powerful graphical output features. Two outstanding examples are MS Works®—an integrated software application (so called because it includes a word processor, a spreadsheet, a database manager, and a communication module, each of which may exchange information)—and Excel (a sophisticated spreadsheet application); you will study both in detail in this text. The pie chart in Figure 1.3 was created in Excel with just several clicks of the mouse button. There are a variety of additional graphical display options in Excel. Some of these are illustrated in Figure 1.16, where an example data set is displayed in a variety of formats. All these graphs were created quite simply and quickly by using dialog boxes within Excel. The package MS Works has similar graphical display capabilities, many of which are explored in Chapter 10.

Visually reinforced operations are essential in a good word processing application. The applications MS Works and MS Word, which we will study in this text, have a consistent visually based set of methods for cutting and pasting text, deleting text, highlighting portions of text for special formatting, and so on. MS Word also provides a "Page Preview" feature that allows you to see (two pages at once) how your document will appear when printed on various devices with various page settings (margins, headers, etc.). The graphical feature that allows you to see what will actually be printed is called "What You See Is What You Get" (abbreviated WYSIWYG). This feature is a necessity when you are working on multipage documents. Figure 1.17 demonstrates its use to preview an early version of pages of this chapter (which was written using MS Word).

In problems where large volumes of information need to be stored and retrieved selectively—so-called database management problems—it is often nec-

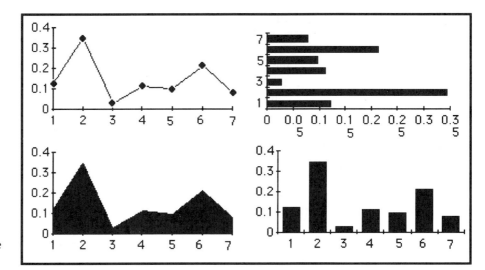

Figure 1.16 A data set displayed in various formats from the package Excel.

essary to store and retrieve information in separate files. To do this you must keep firmly in mind the file relation model that underlies your database. The database management system Reflex Plus®, which we study in a later chapter, provides a graphical method for defining such a relation model. Using this method, the files are defined in a database overview window and the relations among files are shown graphically. An illustration of this method is shown in Figure 1.18. In this way the underlying file model is made explicit, and this helps a user visualize the relationships inherent in the database. The importance of this capability will become more obvious to you when you learn about Reflex Plus.

In a later chapter, you will learn about Apple Computer's data organization tool called HyperCard®. With this tool a user organizes and links together a stack

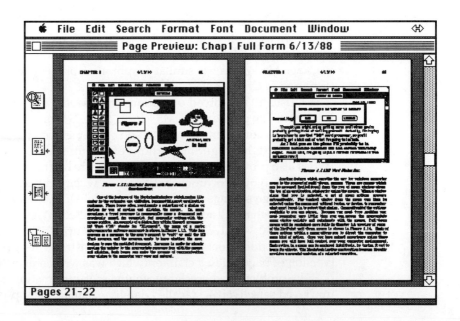

Figure 1.17 Page preview feature of MS Word.

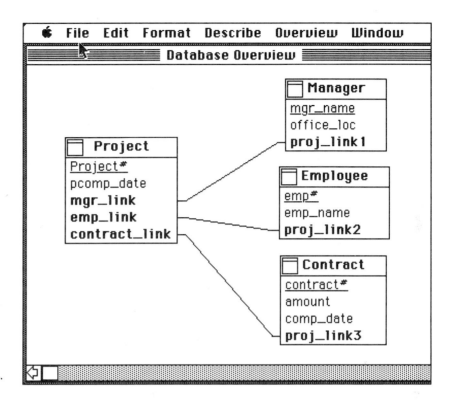

Figure 1.18 File relationships displayed graphically in Reflex Plus.

of cards that hold various categories of information. The starting point for searching through such a stack is called the *Home Card*. An example *Home Card* is shown in Figure 1.19; note its graphical format to help guide your interpretation.

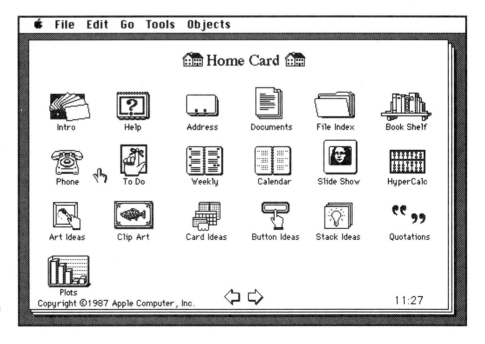

Figure 1.19 *Home Card* in a HyperCard stack.

If the telephone icon in the screen of Figure 1.19 is selected (by clicking the mouse with the mouse pointer positioned over the icon), the screen shown in Figure 1.20 appears. From this screen you can use a device called a modem to dial a number to connect your computer to another remote computer or network. You will learn more about these ideas in Chapters 3 and 13.

Consider the Macintosh screen shown in Figure 1.21. This screen is output from a database containing information about houses for a real estate office. Notice the incorporation of the floor plan drawing and an elevation sketch of the actual house. This particular output was produced using the database management application Helix®.

Figures 1.22 and 1.23 show screens presented in the application ConcertWare®. This application allows you to write musical scores in multiple voices and then play them. You can choose to hear all or any subset of the voices at a given time and control the tempo as well as the instrument used to perform each voice. You can view the musical composition in a variety of formats and make modifications to the score by using the mouse. This software can even control a music synthesizer and allow you to record notes played on a keyboard. Hence, sound is another medium over which the computer gives you control. More details about ConcertWare are given in Chapter 20.

There are a large number of Macintosh applications that we could mention. For example, the program TheaterGame allows its user to construct scenes from *Hamlet*, which are then displayed graphically on the screen. A number of available applications produce graphical models of the way atoms combine to form molecules. There are programs that graphically demonstrate Mendelian genetics; others produce dynamic models of plate tectonics in geology. In fact, you can probably find several programs that apply to a problem that currently interests you.

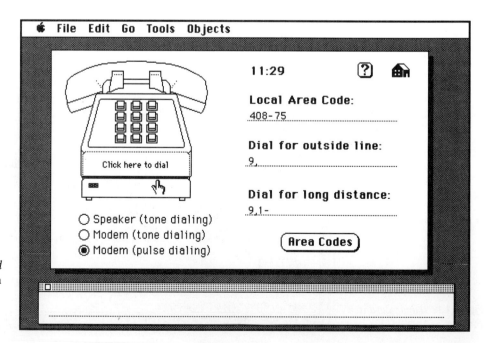

Figure 1.20 The *Phone Card* application accessed from the *Home Card* in the HyperCard application shown in Figure 1.19.

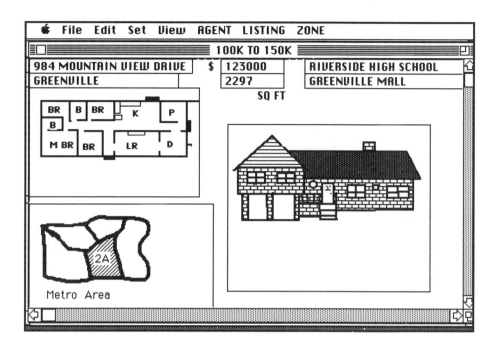

Figure 1.21 Example output from a real estate database in Helix.

In this book we cannot hope to discuss even a small percentage of the Macintosh software currently available. Instead, we shall concentrate on the categories of software that will provide you with a basic set of computer problem-solving skills. These basic software categories consist of word processors and desktop publishing tools, database management systems, spreadsheets (applica-

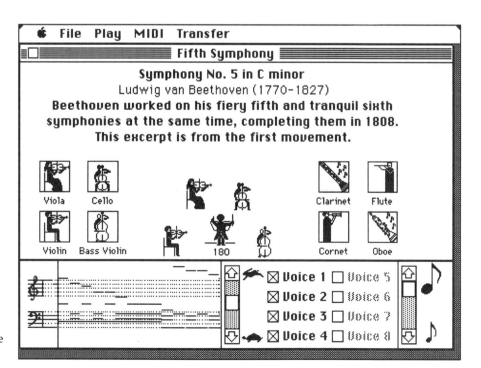

Figure 1.22 Window in the program ConcertWare.

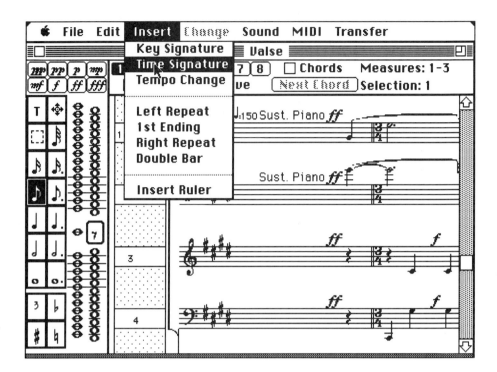

Figure 1.23 A pull-down menu in the program ConcertWare.

tions for computing numbers and graphing results), applications that allow you to organize and present information, and applications to communicate with computers and networks. With the skills you will master in studying these various types of Macintosh software, you will be ready to learn whatever software that is, or later becomes, important to you.

MORE GENERAL EXAMPLES.   One of the most promising directions in visually oriented computing is the development of so-called **hypertext systems**. Hypertext can be thought of as a completely new form of publishing and disseminating information. It delivers information in many different forms. Graphs, maps, charts, pictures, music, speech, and so on, are "embedded" in textual material. The reader of this material has the option of taking different paths through the linked structure of information. For example, while reading about Bach, the reader might like to listen to an excerpt from a piece of his music or see a map of the area in which he lived. Informational content is no longer bound by the organizational choices made by its author or editor. The user chooses his own organization. In the future, traditional methods for finding and displaying related information may seem unbearably awkward and inefficient. Chapter 21 explores some of the methods and consequences of hypertext systems more fully.

Scientists at the University of California at San Diego and at Emory University are converting images of brain neurons taken with electron microscopes into computer form by manually tracing contour lines. The computer then reconstructs surface images of the entire neuron. Neuron structure can then be studied from these constructed surface images using computer models, and the changes that occur in such tissue can be classified and analyzed. It is hoped that such methods will provide clues concerning the causes of Alzheimer's disease. For some time now, computers have been used to visualize brain tissue by scanning the brain using magnetic resonance imaging techniques. Information gained in this painless and safe way has replaced much of the need for exploratory brain surgery, which is often life threatening and might prove to have been unnecessary. Such computer visualization techniques have no doubt saved many lives.

At the University of Illinois, researchers are using computer-generated visual 3-D models of thunderstorms to attempt to understand better the dynamics that lead to the development of tornadoes, severe updrafts, and horizontal wind shears. Other meteorologists study more global weather patterns using color-coded computer generated weather maps. The graphical and coded display of such large amounts of information is indispensable to improve our abilities to interpret it. Such maps require large amounts of computing power and would be absolutely impossible to produce manually.

By modeling the physical effects of pulling or squeezing facial muscles, workers have been able to produce computer-simulated animations of various facial expressions. One objective of such simulation is to use the knowledge gained from this work to help teach lip reading to the hearing impaired. Another possible use is to predict and demonstrate muscle responsiveness and mobility that might result from various techniques of facial surgery.

The ability to produce detailed engineering and architectural drawings that can be easily modified has dramatically affected these fields. Modifications to drawings that used to take days can now be done in minutes. This capability has allowed engineers and architects to adopt "what if" strategies in the design of machines, systems, and structures. Some modeling programs allow the architect to produce a 3-D visualization of how a proposed structure would appear, even allowing the user to take a computer-simulated "walk" through the structure and gain a sense of its proportions and visual impact that would not be possible even using physical scale models of the structure.

Using computer visualization models, NASA scientists are able to create from satellite photographs color maps of the atmosphere that allow theories of such atmospheric processes as the formation of the protective ozone layer to be studied and verified. Of course, we are all familiar with the many spectacular computer-enhanced photographs of objects in our solar system sent back by NASA interplanetary probes. As another example, NASA engineers are able to test various winding patterns for the fiber-wound shell of solid rocket boosters. They use computers to simulate graphically the pattern to be tested and then use a computer-generated color code to determine various tensions imposed on the fiber by the winding pattern.

Graphics experts at George Washington University are working on an artist's computer "brush and canvas" system. With this system, an artist can choose from a variety of electronic brush shapes and then can apply these brushes using many different "touches." Once a painting is created on the screen, it can be modified in ways quite similar to those employed using actual canvas and real paint and brushes. Such a system has the potential to utilize millions of tints and shades of color. The artist must still supply the artistic talent, but the computer supplies a new medium for artistic expression.

We should be careful to differentiate between the kind of artistic medium provided by such computer systems as that described in the preceding paragraph and computer programs that do actually generate the artistic product. It may well be that these computer-generated products, which derive from human imagination coupled with the computer's abilities to calculate and iterate very rapidly, will eventually be looked upon as a completely new kind of art. You have no doubt enjoyed the special effects and alien landscapes produced by computer-generated animation in such films as *The Last Starfighter, Star Wars,* and *Star Trek II.* Certainly, films such as Pixar's *Red's Dream* and *Luxo, Jr.,* in which all scenes are generated and completely animated using computers, will promote the proposition that such electronic animation is indeed a new art form.

We could cite many more examples of interesting and important applications that depend heavily on the visualization of data for their effectiveness, and even for their existence. However, that would carry us too far afield from our major purpose in this text. The preceding examples have been offered to stimulate your appetite a bit and make you aware of some exciting developments in visually oriented computing.

Exercise Set 1.3

1. Give five examples of how Macintosh application software makes good use of data visualization. Explain each use briefly.

2. What is hypertext?

3. Describe four non-Macintosh applications where data visualization is essential to the application.

4. Discuss the two kinds of computer-aided "art" described in the text. Do you think either (or both) of these deserve to be called art?

5. Don't miss an opportunity to see either of the Pixar computer-animated films mentioned in the text!

1.4. ENHANCED PROBLEM SOLVING WITH VISUALLY ORIENTED COMPUTING

There is no doubt that people who use computers in visual modes have more fun than their traditional computer user friends. However, it is not just the fun of it that makes visual mode computing exciting and worthwhile. Visually oriented computing has actually advanced our problem-solving abilities significantly by placing a new problem-solving tool in our hands. Many of the example applications discussed in the previous section would not be feasible without sophisticated data visualization techniques. It is also true that even in areas where the kinds of problem solving taking place could be done without benefit of visual mode computing, problem-solving activities are greatly enhanced by the fact that they can be done in a visual mode. The reasons for this enhancement are many.

Perhaps the most important way in which visually oriented computing has enhanced, and will continue to enhance, problem solving is through its encouragement for many more people to become engaged in the computer problem-solving process. People without the time or the inclination to spend the many months that were required in the past to learn the effective use of computers for solving their problems can now use the computer as a problem-solving tool. Not only will these people use the computer, but they will use it creatively and productively. Doctors, lawyers, scientists, engineers, business managers, teachers, writers, advertisers, political analysts, musicians, artists, and a host of other professionals will discover new needs and methods for addressing those needs through their interaction with computers. The very fact that these people are using computers and buying software applications will encourage entrepreneurs to develop new and increasingly innovative software to enhance their computer usage.

New lines of communication will develop between the arts and the sciences. We are already seeing how the push for better data visualization techniques in the sciences has encouraged the development of new tools for graphic artists and perhaps even encouraged the development of a completely new art form. The interaction and common communication medium provided by visually oriented computing should provide even greater benefits in this direction in the future.

There are also significant advantages inherent in visually oriented computing for longtime computer users. The increase in productivity that is possible with a package like Excel over what would be possible with older software packages can be dramatic. Managers are better able to organize and present data supporting their decision making. Scientists are able to make "what if" calculations and see the results presented graphically without having to write computer programs. Using database management systems, businessmen, doctors, lawyers, librarians, collectors, and others can track information and make more meaningful and more efficient use of it. Word processing has already affected all of us; now we are able to incorporate graphics in our documents and lay out those documents so that they are indistinguishable from those produced by professional printing houses. Information can be disseminated in more attractive and more meaningful formats, and it will arrive and be responded to much more quickly. Electronic mail provides a new communication medium of great promise and usefulness. Hypermedia systems will provide new avenues for the expression of creativity for us all.

For more than 30 years, we have been engaged in using computers to solve problems. We have tackled these problems primarily with an analytic, "left-brain" approach. Indeed, we have often asked someone else to extract the solution to our problem from the computer, with the inevitable result that some of the problem itself got lost as we translated our requirements to the person who would communicate with the computer. We are now freed from these constraints. We can engage the right side of the brain in our computer problem solving in more meaningful and more exciting ways than we have in the past. Increasingly, we rely less on someone else to do our communicating to the computer. We are not only able to communicate for ourselves, but able to orchestrate computer solutions to our problems in creative and innovative ways that match our understanding of our own fields. These are indeed exciting times to be learning about problem solving using computers!

Key Concepts

Click button	Data visualization
Dialog box	Disk
File	Folder
Hypertext system	Icon

Interface consistency across applications
Mouse
Pull-down menu
Visually oriented computing
Windowing environments

Macintosh desktop metaphor
Mouse pointer
Trash can
Window

GETTING STARTED WITH THE MACINTOSH

LEARNING OBJECTIVES

- To gain an understanding of the basic components of any computer system.

- To become familiar with some standard configurations of the Macintosh.

- To learn how to start up and shut down the Macintosh.

- To learn the basic concepts and operations necessary for using the Macintosh desktop environment.

- To use the MacPaint drawing package to get a brief introduction to starting, using, and quitting a Macintosh application software package.

T his chapter gives a brief discussion of the components of a computer and the different kinds of Macintosh computers available. Then the fundamental operations for using the Macintosh interface are discussed. As you have seen in Chapter 1, it is this graphics-based interface that makes the Macintosh so intuitive and easy to use. Finally, the techniques for opening and closing a Macintosh application are illustrated with MacPaint, an application that makes it easy and fun to create drawings. If this is your first experience with a Macintosh, you should read the chapter carefully and perform the computer practice activities given in the chapter. If you already have experience with the Macintosh, you may wish to skim this chapter.

2.1 COMPUTER COMPONENTS

From a functional perspective all computers can be viewed as consisting of input devices, a central processing unit, memory units, and output devices as shown in Figure 2.1. The central processing unit receives information from the outside world by means of the input devices, manipulates the information based on the instructions stored in its memory, and sends the results to one or more of the output devices.

CENTRAL PROCESSING UNIT. Inside the **central processing unit** of the computer are two subunits, the **control unit** and the **arithmetic logic unit.** The control unit manages the activities of all the components that make up the computer. When

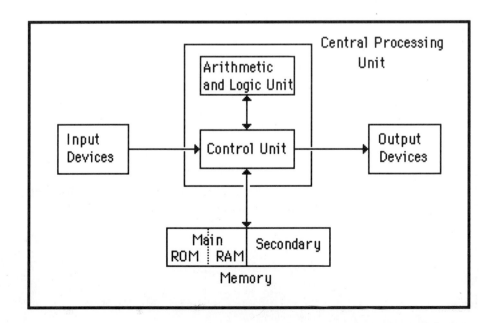

Figure 2.1 Functional organization of a computer.

manipulations of information are required, such as adding or subtracting numbers, the control unit routes the information to the arithmetic logic unit, where the actual operations on the information take place. Today all the circuitry necessary for the control unit and arithmetic logic unit functions can be created on one small piece of silicon called a **chip.** These silicon chips are about one eighth the size of your fingernail. A single-chip central processing unit is called a *microprocessor*. The term *microprocessor* is used not because the chip has low performance but because it is constructed using a technology that produces computers that are very small in their physical size.

Central processing units used to be a very expensive part of a computer. Today's microprocessor chips can be replicated hundreds of thousands of times at a very low cost. Hence, although they are very expensive to design, when they are produced in large quantities, these chips cost only several dollars each. Of course higher-performance microprocessors are generally more expensive than lower-performance ones.

Today's microprocessors can perform from about 1 to 8 million operations (additions, multiplications, etc.) per second. Microprocessor chips will soon be available that can perform at over twenty times these speeds. Thus, even more of a microprocessor's time can be expected to be devoted to software user conveniences, as we discussed in Chapter 1.

MAIN MEMORY.   When a program is being executed, data being used by the program itself and other information are all stored in the computer's **main memory**. Main memory is composed of chips that reside inside the computer's housing. Additional memory chips can often be added to a computer to expand the amount of memory it contains. It is convenient to think of main memory as consisting of cells, each of which has an address and can contain information. The amount of information that can exist in one cell of memory varies and depends upon the kind of computer considered.

The smallest unit of information used by any computer is called a **bit** (for binary digit). A bit can exist in only one of two distinct states, which are sometimes referred to as *on* and *off* and represented by the digits 1 and 0, respectively. Cells are composed of some number of bits grouped together. From these binary symbols (bits) are formed all characters, documents, pictures, music, and so on, that the computer manipulates. For all Macintoshes, except the Macintosh II, 16 bits are grouped together to form one cell. For the Macintosh II, 32 bits are grouped together for a cell. It might be helpful to think of memory cells as analogous to an array of post office boxes that have box numbers (i.e., addresses) and in each box are the cell's contents—a group of bits.

Computer memory used by application programs is called random access memory, or **RAM**, because the memory cells can be accessed in any sequence. The time taken to access any cell in RAM is the same no matter where it is located. RAM typically can be accessed several million times a second! Information may be transferred to and from RAM as dictated by the control unit. An essential feature of RAM is that it is *volatile*. This means that if the power to the computer is turned off for any reason, the contents of RAM will be forgotten—lost forever! Since the result of your working with the computer is often held (at least temporarily) in RAM, it is important to be sure to save your work occasionally during a work session to a more permanent and secure medium called secondary memory, which we discuss shortly.

Read only memory, or **ROM**, is computer memory in which cell contents can be read but not changed. ROM is nonvolatile; its contents are not lost when the power is turned off. Part of the **operating system**, which is a collection of programs that control the operation of the computer, is stored in ROM. When the computer is first turned on, the control unit causes the operating system program in ROM to be accessed automatically; it is through this program that you are able to initially communicate with the computer. The process of allowing the operating system to take control of your communication with the computer is called **booting** the computer.

The size of computer memory is given in terms of the number of bytes it contains. A **byte** is 8 bits, which is sufficient to store one alphabetic character (typewriter symbol), such as "A", "B", "/", and so on, in memory. Because computer memories consist of thousands to millions of bytes, memory sizes are usually measured using the units of K or M, which are defined as:

$$1K = 1024 = 2^{10} \text{ (approximately 1000)}$$

$$1M = 1024 \times 1024 = 1,048,576 = 2^{20} \text{ (approximately 1 million)}$$

For example, 512K bytes of computer memory contains 524,288 bytes (or characters). The unit K is sometimes called *kilo*, and the unit M is sometimes called *mega*.

SECONDARY MEMORY.   Computer main memory is expensive as well as volatile. For these reasons, **secondary memory** is used for inexpensive and more permanent storage of programs and data. The major secondary memory device used is the *disk drive*. These devices store information on magnetic **disks**—small circular metal or plastic disks that are coated with a magnetic material that stores bits of information. There are two kinds of magnetic disk drives, **hard disk drives** and **floppy disk drives**.

Hard disk drives generally have disks sealed inside the drive and you cannot see them or remove them. Floppy disk drives use a small cartridge that contains the actual disk. The cartridges are called *floppy disks* **(or** *diskettes***)** and they can be inserted and removed from the disk drive. A floppy disk for the Macintosh floppy disk drive is a 3.5-inch disk enclosed in a plastic case for protection. These disks are portable and hold 400K or 800K bytes of information, depending upon whether

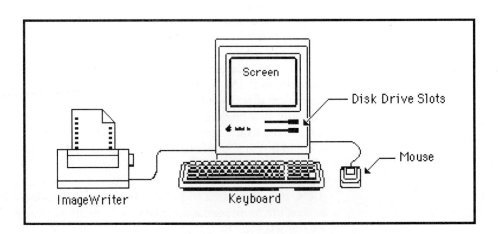

Figure 2.2 The Macintosh SE with printer.

one or both sides are used (remember that one byte can hold one character of text). Assuming that a page of text has 43 lines, each containing 65 characters, an 800K byte disk can hold about 293 pages of text. A floppy disk for the Macintosh costs approximately $2, and the price of such disks is continually decreasing. The same capacity of main memory costs hundreds of dollars.

Floppy disk drives may be internally or externally installed. The computer shown in Figure 2.2 has two floppy disk drives. A disk can be inserted into either of these drives. An external floppy disk drive, if connected, would be positioned beside the computer.

A hard disk drive may be installed within the computer case, or it may be attached externally. These drives can store much more information than can be placed on a floppy disk. Today 20M-byte to 80M-byte hard disks typically are used. Also, the operating speed of hard disk drives is much greater than that of floppy disk drives. If a hard disk drive is mounted internally in the Macintosh SE or Macintosh II computers, it takes up one of the slots normally occupied by a floppy disk drive. When an internal hard drive is activated, a small indicator light at the front of the disk drive slot indicates when it is being accessed. External hard disk drives are often placed under the Macintosh computer. Hard disk drives are very desirable and are actually required to run some software packages on a Macintosh. Their prices are decreasing rapidly and will soon be comparable to the cost of an external floppy disk drive.

Another kind of secondary memory device is the **optical disk drive,** which stores information optically rather than magnetically. Bits are created by literally burning pits into the surface of a reflective plastic disk. The state of the bit (on or off) can be sensed by determining the intensity of laser light reflected from the disk surface. Optical disks permit extremely high-density recording of information. One optical disk the size of an audio compact disk can hold 300 or 400 million bytes of data—the equivalent of several entire encyclopedias, including pictures! Such densely packed information is necessary to allow use of the hypertext concepts mentioned in Chapter 1, which will be discussed more completely in Chapter 21 of the text.

Regardless of the type of disk used, it will be divided into tracks as shown in Figure 2.3. A read-write head can move accurately and quickly to a position over the desired track to find requested information, as the disk itself spins under the read-write head. Several tracks are used to store the starting addresses of the programs and documents stored on a disk. These tracks are called the **directory** of the disk.

When a request is made for a program or a document, the read-write head moves to the directory tracks, determines the location of the requested item, moves to the location of the item, and reads it into RAM. This is approximately 10,000 times slower than retrieving information that is already in RAM. Disks represent a tradeoff between the need to store large amounts of information permanently and inexpensively and the time required to access the information.

INPUT DEVICES.   An example of an **input device** for the Macintosh is the *mouse* (see Figure 2.2), which is used to change the location of a pointer on the screen. The pointer may appear as an arrowhead or may have some other shape, depending upon the application being used. Recall from Chapter 1 that as the mouse is moved on a flat surface, a ball in the base of the mouse turns. This movement is converted

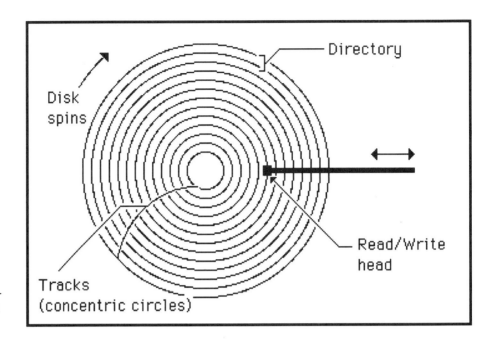

Figure 2.3 Disk organization showing tracks and directory.

into movement of the pointer on the screen. Details on the use of the mouse are given in Section 2.3.1. Through the use of the mouse you may easily communicate many commands to the computer.

Another common input device is the *keyboard*, which is used for typing information to be used by the computer. This information may consist of commands you wish the computer to perform, text for documents, or data for calculations.

A *scanner* is an input device that literally takes a computer "picture" of the object placed in front of it. Some scanners accept only pictures of objects or information typed on pages of paper. In some instances they not only generate a computer (electronic) image of a typewritten page but actually convert the images of letters into characters that can then be edited just as if you typed them in from the keyboard. Other scanners use TV cameras to input information and are therefore capable of entering scenes from the three-dimensional world into the computer. When continuous entities (such as a TV camera image) are converted to the discrete form necessary to store them in a computer's memory, we say that the entities have been *digitized*.

A *MIDI* (musical instrument digital interface) *keyboard* is an input device that allows you to enter music directly into the computer as you play it. It can provide for the musician-composer an electronic music editing facility similar to the electronic editing of words that word processors provide for the author.

OUTPUT DEVICES.   The *screen*, or *CRT* (for cathode ray tube), is the primary **output device** of the Macintosh and other personal computers. For all Macintoshes except the Macintosh II, it consists of a 9-inch diagonal monochrome CRT on which small black or white squares, called pixels or picture elements, are displayed. Each pixel has a dimension of 1/72 inch per side. A horizontal line on the screen contains 512 pixels, and there are 342 horizontal lines down the screen. The value of each pixel (it must be only white or black) is stored in computer memory, and changes in the stored memory values are reflected directly as changes in the display on the screen.

For the Macintosh II, the screen is larger, and a variety of values are available for each pixel. Thus, pixels on the Macintosh II can have shades of gray or colors. Currently, up to 256 different colors or shades of gray are possible. The 12-inch monochrome screen has 640 pixels per horizontal line, and there are 480 horizontal lines down the screen. Until very recently, graphics display screens having this resolution cost several tens of thousands of dollars—and that cost didn't include the computer!

Computer screens that display memory contents directly on them are called **bit-mapped graphics** screens. All text and graphics displayed on the Macintosh computers are drawn as bit-mapped graphics objects. This aspect of the Macintosh design means that text, graphics, pictures, and so on, can all be naturally integrated in a single document. Most personal computers do not use bit-mapped displays for both text and graphics, using instead one kind of display for text and another for graphics. As a consequence, it is more difficult for software applications on these computers to merge and integrate text and graphics within single documents.

The *ImageWriter*® printer is an output device that can print a dot for each pixel displayed on the screen. It prints pictures, graphics, or text with the same resolution as the monochrome screen on the Macintosh II and on the Macintosh 512, Plus, and SE. As mentioned earlier, text, graphics, and pictures can be easily mixed for output on the ImageWriter printer because all forms of data are converted to pixel form for output.

The Apple *LaserWriter*® printer, based on photocopy technology, is another popular output device for the Macintosh family of computers. This printer, which can print with a resolution of 300 pixels per inch, is often used for important correspondence and for desktop publishing. Like the ImageWriter, it can integrate text, graphics, and pictures. The LaserWriter printer can use Postscript, a special language that describes how pages of documents should appear. Access to this language allows very impressive desktop publishing output, as you will see later in the text.

A *MIDI-compatible synthesizer* is another output device that allows the computer to control a group of electronically synthesized instruments to play a musical score, much as a conductor would direct an orchestra.

A *modem* is both an input and an output device. It allows your computer to communicate with other computers over telephone lines.

Exercise Set 2.1

1. Draw a diagram that shows the functional units of a computer.
2. Define or describe the following.
   a. central processing unit
   b. mouse
   c. keyboard
   d. pixel
   e. bit-mapped screen displays
   f. ImageWriter
   g. RAM
   h. ROM

      i.   operating system
      j.   1K and 1M
      k.   floppy disk
      l.   disk tracks
      m. disk directory

3. Describe the resolution of the screen of the Macintosh SE in terms of pixels.

4. Assuming that a single bit in RAM is used to represent the state of a pixel on the screen and that all bits in a byte can be used for storing pixel states, compute the number of K bytes required to store the 9-inch monochrome screen display.

5. Where is the operating system program stored that begins the boot process for the Macintosh?

6. Compute the number of "average-sized words" that can be stored on an 800K-byte floppy disk, where an average-sized word is six characters long. Recall that 1 byte can store the code for one character.

7. Compute the approximate number of pages of text that can be stored on an 20M-byte disk. Assume that a page has 43 lines, each containing 65 characters.

8. Compute the approximate number of books of text that can be stored on an optical disk of 400M bytes. Assume that a book has 300 pages with each page the same size as that defined in problem 7.

2.2 MACINTOSH CONFIGURATIONS

A **computer's configuration** is the particular combination of peripheral devices, internal disk drives, and RAM and ROM associated with the computer. Table 2.1 lists the available configurations for various Macintoshes in the chronological order of their availability. The newest computers, the Macintosh SE and the Macintosh II, were introduced simultaneously in 1987. The configuration of the Macintosh ordinarily determines the kinds of work that can be done and the ease of operation of the system. For example, some software packages cannot be run on a Macintosh with less than 1M byte of RAM. It is also very inconvenient, if not impossible, to use some software with a single floppy disk drive Macintosh. The Macintosh Plus, SE, and II can be recognized by the name printed on the front of the computer. The Macintosh 512K has its name stamped on the back of the computer.

Type	Memory Size (bytes)		Maximum Internal Drives	Floppy Disk Storage Size
	RAM	ROM		
Macintosh	128K	64K	1	400K
Macintosh 512	512K	64K	1	400K
Macintosh Enhanced	512K/1M	128K	1	800K
Macintosh Plus	1M	128K	1	800K
Macintosh SE	1M	256K	2	800K
Macintosh II	1M	256K	2	800K

Table 2.1 Minimum Configurations for Various Macintoshes

Note that the Macintosh, Macintosh 512, Macintosh Enhanced, and the Macintosh Plus all have a single internal floppy disk drive that is accessed through a slot on the front of the computer. The disk drives that store 800K bytes use both sides of a 3.5-inch disk, whereas the 400K disk drives use only one side. The 400K and 800K disks are not interchangeable. An 800K disk drive can read and write 400K disks, but not conversely. Be aware of this difference if you work with both kinds of computers!

The Macintosh SE and Macintosh II each have two disk drive slots, and two floppy disk drives may be installed. However, one floppy drive is often replaced by a hard disk drive. Any of the computers may have additional external floppy or hard disk drives.

The Macintosh SE and Macintosh II can be customized to fit the needs of users by the addition of circuit boards that may be plugged into expansion slots within the computer. The SE has a single expansion slot for adding a circuit board, and the II has six expansion slots. Earlier Macintoshes do not have expansion slots. One very desirable device to add through an expansion slot is a full-page display screen. With such a screen you can see an entire page of a document displayed at one time. The II has a more powerful microprocessor than the other Macintoshes. It also has an arithmetic coprocessor for increasing its computational speed. The II is capable of performing some computations as much as 100 times faster than other Macintoshes.

A Macintosh may also be a member of a network. A network allows computers to share dot matrix printers, laser printers, network disk drives and other devices. Section 3.4 describes the use of the AppleTalk® network.

Additional devices for input, output, or secondary memory can be connected externally to the computer and are also part of its configuration. The electrical signals necessary for these connections are provided by connectors that are located on the back of the various Macintosh cases. There are some differences between the different Macintoshes, so you may need to read the description about each specific model to learn the purpose for each connector. We will describe three of the connectors that are commonly used and show you the icons that are stamped into the Macintosh case to identify them. This discussion should improve your understanding of some of the actions you will perform in the next two chapters.

Each Macintosh comes equipped with two serial RS422 interface connections located on the back of its case. These connections conform to an industry standard and may be used to connect your computer to a wide variety of printers, modems, plotters, MIDI synthesizers, or networks, including the AppleTalk network. Often the software application you are using must know to which of these two connections your printer, plotter, modem, or network is physically connected.

If you turn the computer around so that you are facing the back of the computer, the connector on the right side of the case (see Figure 2.4) has imprinted above it the icon of a telephone receiver with connecting wire. This connector is termed the *modem connector*. All the operations that relate to the modem port use this icon. Thus, if you have a plotter or a modem connected to the modem port, the wire from the device will plug into the rightmost connector—the one under the modem icon.

Just to the left of this connector is another one, identical in appearance, that has the icon of the printer imprinted over it. This connection is termed the *printer port*. Often either an AppleTalk network cable or an ImageWriter printer cable is

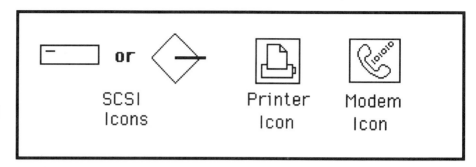

Figure 2.4 Icons imprinted over the SCSI, printer, and modem ports as viewed from the back of the Macintosh .

plugged into this connection. When the software running on your computer asks you to which port the printer, modem, and so on, is connected, just follow the cable from the device in question to the back of the computer case to see the icon under which it attaches. You will learn later how to select the icon presented by the computer.

Either of the preceding two ports can also be used to communicate with mainframe computers. In effect, your computer can imitate (or emulate) a mainframe computer terminal—the standard device used to communicate with mainframe computers. Software to perform this function on your computer is called terminal emulation software. This software will also ask you to determine which port should be used for communicating to the mainframe. Again, if you follow the wire coming from the mainframe computer to its connection on your computer, you will know which port to tell the software to use.

Another connector on the back of the case is the *SCSI* (small computer system interface—pronounced "scuzzy") port. The SCSI port is also an industry standard, and there are many devices available that can be attached to it. This one connector allows up to a total of six external high-speed devices, such as hard disk drives and optical scanners, to be connected to the Macintosh. Devices are "daisy-chained" together, that is, each new device added is connected by a cable to the one added before it. The first device is then connected directly to the computer through the SCSI connection on the back of its case. Through the SCSI connection you may add a very large amount of secondary memory to the computer. For example, an optical disk drive (or even several) could be added to this connection to allow you to experience and explore hypertext possibilities.

2.3 BASIC OPERATIONS

In this section we describe a number of fundamental operations that will allow you to start using the Macintosh. The full discussion of many operations will be delayed until later chapters, so do not be frustrated if you begin to realize that there are many things you do not yet know how to do. The goal of the discussion is to help orient you to how you will communicate with the computer using the mouse. Read this material first without trying to do the activities described. Later you will be asked to use the computer to practice what you have read.

2.3.1 Operations with the Mouse

The mouse is used to move the pointer on the screen and to gain access to the pull-down menus. These **mouse operations** will form the basis of much of your communication with the Macintosh. In this section we consider several of the most important techniques for operating the mouse. You will become familiar with the terminology associated with the use of the mouse. All the operations are simple and intuitive.

POINTING. The position of the pointer on the Macintosh desktop (i.e., the screen of the computer) can be controlled by moving the mouse on the *actual* desktop. Moving the mouse in any direction causes the pointer to move in exactly the same direction. We *point* to an icon on the desktop by positioning the pointer over the icon. This is a natural and intuitive action, and after some practice, moving the mouse to point to an icon becomes an automatic action.

CLICKING. A click of the mouse is a rapid press and release of the button found at the top of the mouse. To *select* an icon, point to the icon and then click; the selected icon will become highlighted.

PRESSING. The pressing operation consists of pressing and holding down (not releasing) the button on the mouse. The operation is normally used as part of the dragging operation.

DRAGGING. Dragging is a frequently used operation involving the following.

- The pointer is placed over an icon or over a name in the top line of the window, which is called the menu bar.

- The button on the mouse is pressed.

- The mouse is moved (without releasing the button on the mouse).

Dragging is used in moving one or more icons and in selecting commands from the pull-down menus.

DOUBLE CLICKING. Double clicking is performed by quickly pressing and releasing the mouse button twice. Double clicking is frequently used as a shortcut for other actions.

SHIFT CLICKING. Shift clicking consists of holding down the shift key while the mouse is repeatedly pointed to icons and clicked. In this way, each new icon is selected, becomes highlighted, and remains highlighted even as additional icons are selected. If the shift key is released and the mouse is pointed to another icon and clicked, the previously selected icons are deselected and hence are no longer highlighted. The operation of shift clicking is useful in selecting multiple icons to be treated as a unit, as, for example, when you want to move a group of icons together.

Exercise Set 2.3.1

1.   Define the following terms for the mouse.

    a.   pointing

    b.   clicking

    c.   pressing

    d.   dragging

    e.   double clicking

2.   Give a use for each of the terms in question 1.

2.3.2   Turning the Macintosh On and Off

The on-off switch for the Macintosh is on the back of the computer on the left side as you face the screen. As mentioned earlier, turning on the power to the computer and allowing it to read the part of its operating system stored in ROM is the first step in the process called **booting** the computer.

The completion of the booting process will be slightly different, depending upon what disk configuration you are working with. Suppose for a moment that you are using a Macintosh having only a floppy disk drive(s). After the computer is turned on, an icon of a disk containing a question mark flashes in the center of the screen, as in part (A) of Figure 2.5. This is an indication that the computer is working correctly and that a disk that contains the rest of the operating system's programs (stored in a folder called the **system folder**), should be inserted into a disk drive slot. The system disk that comes with the computer or any disk that has had the system folder copied to it will do. *The disk must always be inserted with the metal end toward the computer and the circular hole on the underside of the disk facing down.* Push the disk gently into the floppy disk drive slot; the computer will then snap it into place.

If the inserted disk does not have a copy of the system folder, the disk will be ejected automatically, and a flashing X will appear on the screen in the disk icon, as in part (B) of Figure 2.5. The computer may not be used until a disk with the system folder on it has been inserted in the drive, at which time the computer will display the smiling Macintosh shown in part (C) of Figure 2.5. The computer will then finish booting and you will be able to continue to communicate with it.

The Macintosh will always try to boot from a floppy disk drive before it tries to access any hard disk(s) connected to it. If you are using a Macintosh with a hard

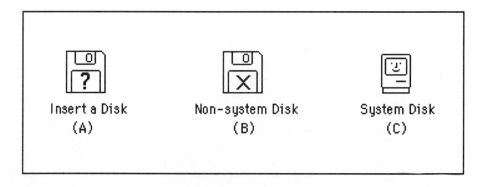

Figure 2.5 Macintosh startup icons.

disk drive, it is very likely that a system folder has been stored on the hard disk. If the hard disk is an internal drive, it will be powered up automatically when you turn on the power to your Macintosh. If no floppy disk is inserted in any of the system's floppy drives, the Macintosh will look automatically on the hard disk for a system folder. If none is found, you will receive the prompt shown in part (A) of Figure 2.5 and you must provide a system disk as discussed earlier. On the other hand, if your hard disk drive is externally connected, you must turn on the power to that drive—*before* turning on the Macintosh itself—for the system folder on the hard disk to be made available to the Macintosh.

When a system disk is inserted (or when the Macintosh finds a system folder on a hard disk), the smiling Mac icon shown in part (C) of Figure 2.5 will appear, a welcome message will flash briefly on the screen, and a desktop of the form shown in Figure 2.6 will be displayed. In the upper right-hand corner will be the icon of the startup disk, that is, the disk containing the system folder. In the lower right-hand corner will be the icon of a trash can, which is used to "throw away" or remove icons from a disk.

Turning on the computer causes the microprocessor to begin executing the part of the operating system program in ROM and to display the disk icon containing the flashing question mark. The ROM operating system program makes use of various programs that are stored in the system folder as discussed earlier. Access to this folder is necessary for the operating system to continue its work. For example, when the system folder is made available by inserting an appropriate disk, the operating system reads from it into computer memory a utility operating system program called the **Finder**, which serves as the primary intermediary between you and the computer.

The Finder allows you to organize and manage documents and applications. For example, it can be used to start an application such as a word processor. Inside the application many actions are controlled by the Finder program. When the application program completes its work, it returns control to the Finder on the desktop. The top line on the desktop, called the menu bar, contains the names of

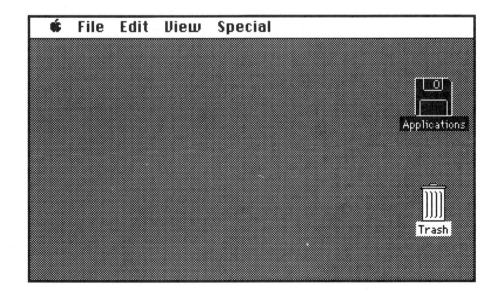

Figure 2.6 The starting desktop.

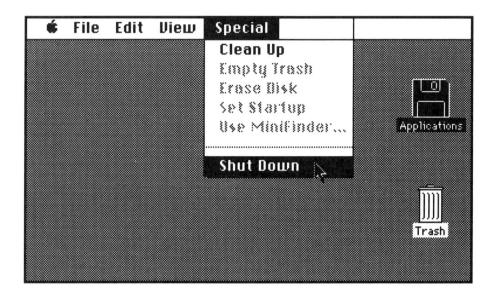

Figure 2.7 Selecting the *Shut Down* command.

the categories of Finder commands that can be performed by the computer's operating system at your request. We will discuss many of these commands later, but for now we mention a very important one—the command to shut down the computer.

To turn the power to the Macintosh off properly, the Finder **Special** menu must be available. The **Shut Down command** may be issued as follows. Point to **Special** and hold down the mouse button. When you do this, a menu will be displayed (or "pulled down") under **Special**. This technique can be used to look at the pull-down menu of any command category that is in the menu bar. Drag to the *Shut Down* command, as shown in Figure 2.7, and release the mouse button. The Finder will complete all pending actions and then display the box shown in Figure 2.8. The computer can now be turned off safely. Turning off your computer without using this procedure can result in a loss of work done and damage to the Finder program. On occasion you may be forced to turn off your machine without using this procedure (as when the machine is "hung" by a software package). *However, you should follow this procedure whenever possible.*

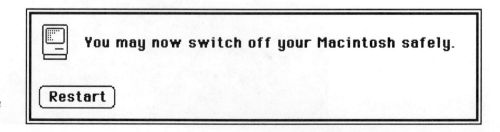

Figure 2.8 The *Shut Down* message box.

Exercise Set 2.3.2

1. What happens if you attempt to start a Macintosh using a nonsystem disk?
2. What is meant by a system disk?
3. Where on the startup desktop does the icon for the system disk appear?
4. What is the menu bar and what is contained in it?
5. What is the purpose of the Finder?
6. Describe the procedure for turning off the Macintosh. Why should this procedure normally be followed?

2.3.3 Initializing a New Disk

You will be using floppy disks to hold most of the data files and documents that you create using the Macintosh. Before a new disk can be used, it must be **initialized**. This process places address markers on each track so that they can be recognized, and it prepares a directory for the disk. Initialization also erases any information that was on the disk previously.

If you place an uninitialized *new* disk into a disk drive, the dialog box in Figure 2.9 will appear on the screen. Caution: An initialization dialog box will appear if you insert an already initialized 800K disk into a 400K disk drive. Note that if you proceed to initialize this disk, any information already stored on it will be lost. Assuming you do not wish to proceed, you can eject the disk by clicking the *Eject* button in the dialog box.

At the bottom of the dialog box the rectangles with rounded corners, called buttons, indicate the available choices. Assuming that your drive is an 800K drive, you would point to the *Two-Sided* button and click. For a 400K drive select *One-Sided*. For approximately a minute you will hear a quiet clicking noise as the disk is initialized. When you are asked, type a name for the disk that indicates its purpose and will thus help you to remember how you will use the disk. If you do not type a name, the disk will be given the name *untitled*. Of course, the name *untitled* will not help you later to recall the kinds of information you might have stored on the disk!

Note that if you are using a one-disk drive computer, you would have to eject the system disk with the *Eject* command of the **File** menu before you can insert the disk to be initialized. It will then be necessary for you to exchange the disks several times during this process at the times that the *Exchange Disk* message appears on

Figure 2.9 The initialization dialog box.

Figure 2.10 The *Exchange Disk* message.

the screen, as shown in Figure 2.10. The name of the disk in the *Exchange Disk* message will change to reflect the action needed. For a two-drive computer, with the disk to be initialized in one of the drives and the system disk in the other (or on a hard drive), no disk exchanging is necessary.

Exercise Set 2.3.3

1. What is the purpose of initializing a disk?
2. Why is special care needed when an initialized 800K disk is inserted into a 400K disk drive?

2.3.4 Opening Disks and Windows

Once your disks have information stored on them, you will, of course, want to be able to see what they contain. You may view the contents of a disk by **opening** it. Let us assume that a disk named *Applications* has been inserted into the disk drive and that the starting desktop has the form shown in Figure 2.6. Select the *Applications* icon by pointing to it and clicking. The icon will become highlighted as shown in Figure 2.11. Notice that the tip of the pointer is touching the center of the icon that is to be selected.

Opening a disk in the Macintosh desktop metaphor is analogous to opening the drawer of a filing cabinet to see its contents. Any disk whose icon is selected can be opened by pointing to the word **File** in the menu bar, dragging to *Open*, and then releasing the button. The process is illustrated in Figure 2.12, where the desktop is shown just before the *Open* command is to be issued by releasing the mouse button.

A shortcut for opening an object is to point to its icon and double-click. Opening an object always causes a window to be displayed, and in the case of the *Applications* disk, the window shown in Figure 2.13 is displayed. This window is a display of the contents of disk *Applications*.

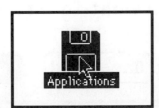

Figure 2.11 Icon selected for *Applications* disk.

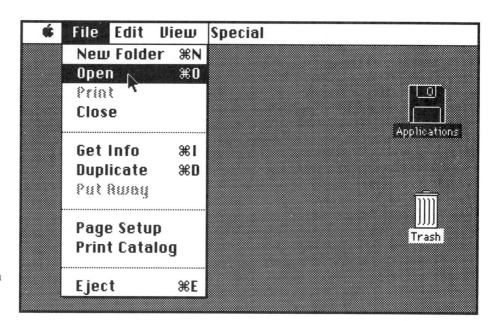

Figure 2.12 The **File** menu with *Open* command selected.

Note that icons are displayed for two application programs, *Microsoft Works* and *MacPaint 1.5*, and for three folders. Any of these objects could be opened by pointing to the appropriate icon, clicking, pointing to the **File** menu, dragging down the mouse to the *Open* command, and releasing the button (or alternately by pointing to the icon and double-clicking). If such an action were performed, a second window would be displayed. This situation is demonstrated in Figure 2.14 in which the folder *Paintings* has been opened. Contained inside *Paintings* are two paintings called *house* and *face*. Recall from Chapter 1 that the most recently

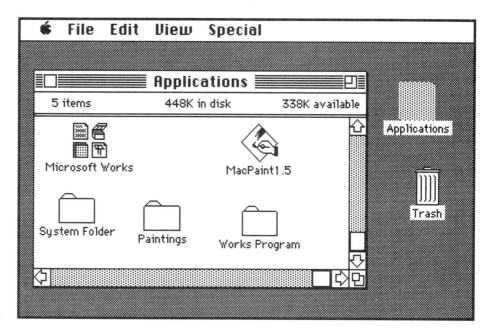

Figure 2.13 The desktop after opening *Applications*.

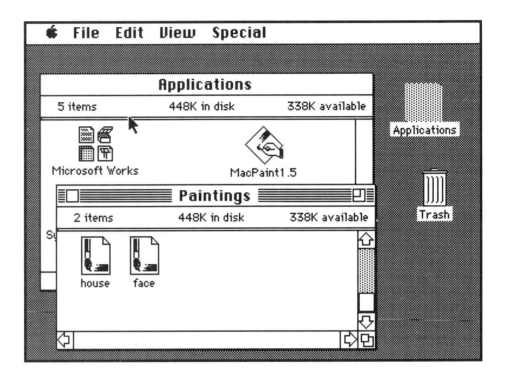

Figure 2.14 Two windows displayed.

accessed window is termed the *active window* and that it can be identified by the horizontal striping in its title bar (at the top of the window).

Commands issued using the mouse generally apply only to the icons in the active window. If there are two or more open windows and you would like to make a different window the active window so that you can work in it, move the pointer into the window of interest and click. This window becomes the active window and moves to the top of the stack of windows. For example, suppose in Figure 2.14 you want to make *Applications* the active window. You would move the pointer to any area in the *Applications* window and click. The result is shown in Figure 2.15.

Exercise Set 2.3.4

1. Give the steps for viewing a pull-down menu.
2. Give two methods for opening an icon.
3. What is the meaning of the term active window?
4. Give the method for changing to a new active window.

2.3.5 Common Features of Windows

You must feel comfortable manipulating windows on the desktop because much of your work will require moving windows, opening and closing them, and scrolling inside them. All Macintosh windows have many **features in common**, regardless of the particular environment or context in which they exist. Some of these features are identified in Figure 2.16. Techniques for using these features are quite valuable, because they can be applied to any window.

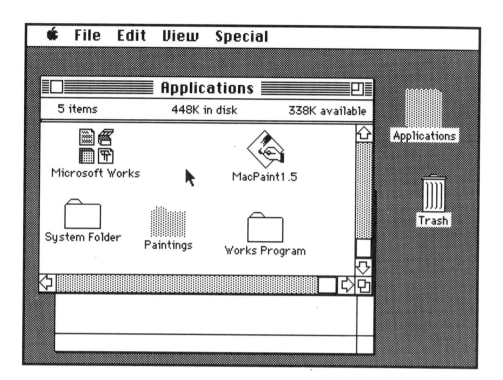

Figure 2.15 The desktop with a different active window.

CLOSE BOX.   The close box is used to *close* the window. Closing the window causes it to disappear from the screen. The procedure is to point to the close box and press the mouse button. As long as the button is pressed, a "star" appears in the close box. Releasing the button closes the window. If the pointer is moved from the close box before the mouse button is released, the window will not be closed. The

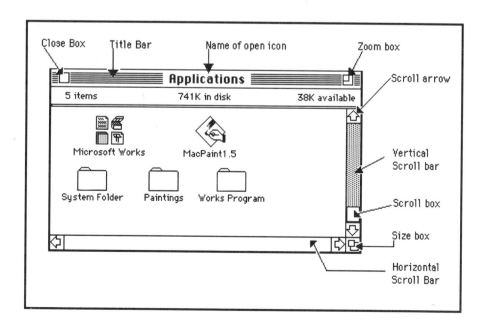

Figure 2.16 Common features of windows.

active window could also be closed by using the *Close* command in the **File** menu. You can always reopen a window using the steps discussed earlier.

TITLE BAR.   The title bar is the top line of the window, and it contains the close box, the name of the open object, and the zoom box, described below. Immediately below the title bar is a line that gives information about the number of items in the window and the space available on the disk as measured in bytes. The active window is always identified by a series of horizontal lines in its title bar. Inactive windows do not have this striping in their title bars.

NAME OF OPEN OBJECT.   The name of the open object is always displayed in the middle of the title bar. This feature is useful when several windows are displayed.

ZOOM BOX.   The zoom box, which is located in the right-hand corner of the title bar, is used to switch between a smaller or a larger version of the window. The zoom box is usually present in a window that shows icons, but it may be absent if the window has been opened for an application software package such as a word processing program.

SCROLL BARS.   A Macintosh window allows you to view part of a scene that may be so large that not all of it can be seen at once in the window. A scene may be, for example, a picture produced by a paint program, the folders on the desktop, or the words, lines, and pages of a word processing document. The scroll bars allow you to position the window so that you can see a different part of the scene. Elements in the *vertical scroll bar* allow you to move through the scene vertically. If the scene is a typed document produced by a word processing program, the vertical scroll bar is used to move to different lines and different pages in the document. Using the *horizontal scroll bar* elements, you may look at parts of the scene that are too wide to fit on the screen.

SCROLL ARROWS.   A window may have as many as four scroll arrows, two in the vertical scroll bar and two in the horizontal scroll bar. These arrows are used to move the window to a new location in the scene. In the vertical scroll bar, the upward pointing scroll arrow at the top of the bar can be used to move the window backward in the scene, for example, in a word processing document, to see previously typed lines. To use the scroll arrow, point to the arrow and click the arrow once for each line the window is to be moved. Alternatively, the mouse button can be pressed down and held until the window has been positioned as desired for viewing the scene. The downward-pointing scroll arrow is used in the same way to move the window down through the scene. For wide scenes the scroll arrows in the horizontal scroll bar move the window in the indicated direction.

SCROLL BOXES.   A scroll box shows the relative position of the window in the scene. Thus, if the scroll box is positioned at about the middle of the scroll bar, the window is in the middle of the scene. The scroll boxes can be used to move the window quickly through the scene. Point at the vertical or horizontal scroll box and drag the box to the desired part of the scene. Release the button when you are satisfied with the position of the window. Alternatively, you may move the window exactly one window width at a time by positioning the cursor above or below (or to the right or left of) the scroll box and clicking.

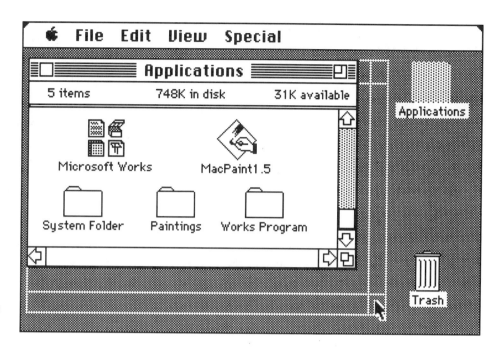

Figure 2.17 Using the size box.

SIZE BOX.   The size box is used to change the size of a window as it is displayed on the desktop. To change the size, drag the size box with the mouse. As the mouse (pointer) is moved, a dotted line will show the changing outline size of the window. When the desired size is obtained, release the mouse button and the window will assume that size. An example of enlarging a window is shown just before the release of the mouse button in Figure 2.17.

MOVING WINDOWS.   When you have several windows on your desktop at once, it is sometimes hard or impossible to "see" a window that you might want to use as your new active window, because that window is covered by other windows. Resizing windows will take care of this problem in some cases, but in others you may need to move some windows around on the desktop. The active window can be moved very easily by dragging its title bar to the desired new position on the desktop. By selecting new active windows and repeating this process, you should be able to find any desired window and position all windows so that you have access to them. Of course, in some cases, it may also be necessary to close some windows to reduce the desktop clutter.

Exercise Set 2.3.5

1.   Give the location and purpose of each of the following features of a window.
    a.   close box
    b.   title bar
    c.   zoom box
    d.   scroll bars
    e.   scroll arrows
    f.   scroll boxes
    g.   size box

Computer Practice 2.3

1. Turn on your Macintosh. Follow the instructions given in Section 2.3.2 that apply to your computer, and carefully go through the booting process.

2. If you have a disk available with the Macintosh *Tour Folder* on it, insert this disk and open this folder. Find and double-click on the icon labeled *Tour Engine*. From this point, simply follow the instructions, which will walk you through a set of basic mouse manipulation exercises.

3. Insert a new disk into (one of) your computer's floppy disk drive(s). Initialize this disk following the procedure given in Section 2.3.3.

4. Open the disk, which was initialized in step 3, by using the *Open* command of the **File** menu. Then close its window. Reopen the disk by double-clicking the disk icon.

5. Create a folder by selecting *New Folder* from the **File** menu. A new folder will appear in the active window. It will be named *Empty Folder* and will be highlighted. Rename the folder by immediately typing the new name, *Example*, then pressing the *Return* key.

6. Open the folder named *Example* by double-clicking on its icon. The resulting window will be empty.

7. Practice changing the size of the *Example* window using its size box. Also practice repositioning the window by dragging it by the title bar.

8. With *Example* as the active window (as it should be, when you finish step 5), create a second folder and name it *Inner*. Note that the new folder is inside the folder named *Example*. Open the folder *Inner*, which will be empty, by double-clicking it. You should now have both folder windows open.

9. If you can see the window *Example*, that is, if it is not completely hidden by the window for *Inner*, make *Example* the active window by clicking it. If needed, move the window *Inner* so that you may see the window *Example* and perform this operation.

10. Practice the process of moving the two windows *Inner* and *Example* around on the desktop, by dragging them by the title bar.

11. Close both windows by using the close box or by selecting *Close* from the **File** menu.

12. Shut down the computer by selecting the *Shut Down* command from the **Special** menu.

2.4 OPENING AND CLOSING A SAMPLE APPLICATION: MACPAINT

Opening an application or a document produced by an application has a different effect from opening a disk or a folder. This section illustrates how to open and close an application program, using as an example the application program MacPaint. In addition, MacPaint will be used to give you some feeling for how easy and intuitive it can be to use a Macintosh application. No attempt will be made to discuss the features of MacPaint in detail here. Even with this brief introduction, you will be able to have fun exploring painting with MacPaint. A more thorough discussion of MacPaint is given in Chapter 3.

Figure 2.18 The *MacPaint* icon.

Opening an application or a document produced by an application *starts*, or *runs*, that application. To open MacPaint or any application, first find the icon for it. The icon for MacPaint is shown in Figure 2.18. Notice how the icon gives an indication of the purpose of the application: It shows a hand using a paint brush. Next, select the icon by pointing to it and clicking. Finally, select the *Open* command from the **File** menu. Note that a shortcut for opening MacPaint, or any other application or document, is to double-click on the icon.

The opening MacPaint screen is shown in Figure 2.19. The window, which in this figure has the default name *untitled* (we will be able to rename it if we save it), is the Macintosh equivalent of a blank canvas on which a painting is to be made. As a Mac artist you can make paintings using any combination of a *pencil*, a *brush*, a *spray can*, a *paint can* (fill tool), or the geometric figure tools. An *eraser* can be used to remove unwanted parts of a painting. These tools are shown as icons in a rectangle to the left of the drawing window. Below the tool icons is a box that shows the possible widths of lines that can be drawn. Below the drawing window is a long rectangle that contains patterns that can be used to fill closed shapes or that can be sprayed by the spray can.

To select a tool, point to it and click. For example, if we point to the pencil and click, the pencil becomes highlighted. When the pointer is moved back over the canvas, it takes the shape of a pencil. By pressing down on the button you are

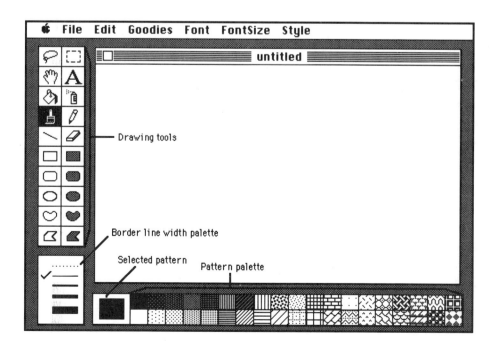

Figure 2.19 The opening MacPaint window.

Figure 2.20 Cartoon faces drawn using MacPaint.

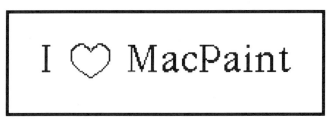

Figure 2.21 Using the text tool.

pushing the pencil against the canvas and movements of the mouse now leave a trail on the screen—just as a real pencil would. Release the button and the pencil is lifted from the canvas. Figure 2.20 shows cartoon faces drawn in this way.

The painting shown in Figure 2.21 was created by selecting the text tool, *A* (icon for alphabet), typing the first word, "I", skipping a few spaces by pressing the space bar, and typing the remaining word. The pencil was used to draw the heart in the spaces between the letters.

The line drawing of a house shown in Figure 2.22 was created in about three minutes using the pencil, the *straight edge* tool (located immediately below the

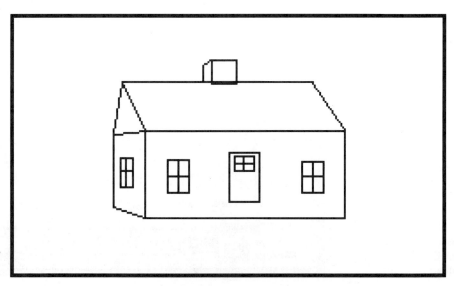

Figure 2.22 Line drawing of a house.

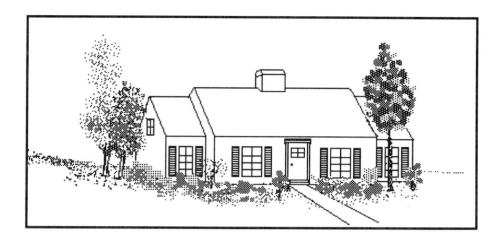

Figure 2.23 A more elaborate house.

brush in the drawing tools rectangle), and the *hollow rectangle* tool (located immediately below the straight edge tool). A more elaborate painting of a house in Figure 2.23 was created using the pencil, brush, straight edge, hollow rectangle, and spray can tools.

To **close** MacPaint, or any other application program, first close the application window by clicking the close box in the upper left-hand corner of the window. This will cause the dialog box shown in Figure 2.24 to be displayed if the painting has been changed since it was last saved. Currently, the painting exists only in RAM memory of the computer. If you do not save the painting document to the disk, then it will be lost forever!

Click the *Yes* box to save the contents of the window. Then the dialog box of Figure 2.25 will be displayed to allow the entering of the name for the saved document. After entering a name, click the *Save* button and the window will be closed. This procedure will save the document on the disk whose name appears above the *Eject* box in Figure 2.25. After the window is closed, the application may be closed by selecting the *Quit* command from the **File** menu. Note that if the *Quit* command in the **File** menu is selected without first closing the application window, the actions just described for saving the contents of the window will be automatically initiated if changes have been made to the painting since it was last saved.

Figure 2.24 Dialog box for closing a MacPaint window.

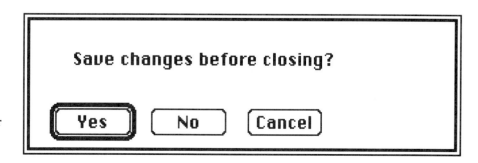

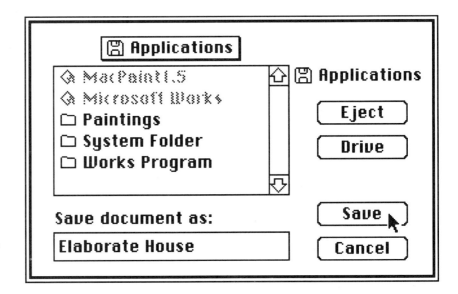

Figure 2.25 Dialog box for saving a MacPaint painting.

Exercise Set 2.4

1. How is an application opened?
2. How is an application closed?

Computer Practice 2.4

Explore the possibilities of MacPaint by opening the application and creating a picture that interests you. Use the pencil drawing tool. When you finish your drawing, save it or not as you desire, and then quit the MacPaint application. In the next chapter (Section 3.5), you will learn how to retrieve a saved painting if you wish to work on it later. That section also describes the use of all the MacPaint painting tools and explains how to print copies of your paintings.

Key Concepts

Arithmetic logic unit   Bit
Bit-mapped graphics display   Byte
Booting process   Central processing unit
Chip   Closing an application
Common window features   Computer configuration
Control unit   Disk directory
Finder program   Floppy disk drive
Hard disk drive   Initialization of disks
Input device   Main memory
Mouse operations   Open command
Opening an application   Operating system
Optical disk drive   Output device
RAM   ROM
Secondary memory   Shut Down command
Special menu   System folder

CHAPTER 3

INTERACTING WITH COMPUTING ENVIRONMENTS

LEARNING OBJECTIVES

- To view the computer as a language interpreter.
- To understand the difference between semantics and syntax of languages.
- To understand the hierarchy of language contexts necessary for communication with a computer.
- To view the computer as a part of a larger network of computers and devices.
- To use the MacPaint application language to create, save, retrieve, and print drawings and paintings.

In this chapter you will learn to view interacting with the computer as analogous to learning and conversing in several different languages. The very-high-level computer languages we will discuss are relatively simple, intuitive, and fun to learn; thus, you need not worry about having difficulty learning them! The choice of language to use will depend upon what you want the computer to do for you. You will see that your interaction with the computer can occur at a number of different language levels. In fact, depending upon the context in which it is issued, the same command can have very different meanings. You will also learn that your computer may exist in an extended environment called a network, which allows it to communicate with devices such as printers, plotters, shared disks, and other computers. Finally, you will see how to use the concepts presented in this chapter and the MacPaint drawing language to create, save, retrieve, and print your own drawings.

3.1 DISTINGUISHING AMONG DIFFERENT COMPUTER CONTEXTS

Although you may not have thought consciously about it at the time, in working through the hands-on exercises of Chapter 2, you experienced two very different views of the way the computer behaved. When you first started the computer, you were placed into a **context** of interacting with the computer at the level that we referred to as the desktop. While using the computer in the desktop context, certain kinds of operations were available to you. These included, for example, the abilities to move a folder from one position to another on the desktop, to open a folder to see what was in it, to create a new folder, to name a folder, and so on. For each of these actions you communicated commands to the computer through a series of manipulations of the mouse pointer position and appropriate pressing of the mouse button. For example, to move a folder, you pointed to it, pressed the mouse button, and then dragged it to the position you desired.

Later, when you opened the MacPaint application, you were able to draw simple figures by communicating your commands to the computer through a series of very similar manipulations of the mouse position and appropriate presses of the mouse button. For example, you could select the pencil and drag the mouse to draw freehand on the screen.

If you reflect for a moment, you will realize that the very different actions carried out by the computer in the preceding two contexts resulted from a very similar set of your actions of moving the mouse and pressing the mouse button. The context in which you gave the commands was different and led to very different results for the same actions. In one instance, the context in which the commands were issued was the desktop; in the other, the context was the MacPaint application.

This perspective brings us to a centrally important principle about communicating with computers. To have the computer do what you want, you must first *place the computer in the proper context*, so that it interprets your instruction the way you wish. For example, if you are in the desktop context, you cannot directly draw pictures on the screen. Rather, you must change the context to that of MacPaint. Recall that you can shift the Macintosh context to MacPaint by opening the MacPaint application icon. However, while you are in the MacPaint context you cannot move a folder around on the desktop or copy a document from one disk to another. These latter activities require that you be in the desktop context. To accomplish these activities, you must quit the MacPaint context and return to the desktop context by selecting the *Quit* option under the **File** menu.

Each different application that we study in this text has its own context associated with it, just as MacPaint and the desktop have their own unique contexts. To solve problems using any computer, it is necessary for you to understand which contexts are necessary to perform the actions that you desire, and how to place the computer into the context where the needed operations become available.

Before you can move effectively from one computer context to another, you must be able to recognize which context you are in at a given time. For example, if you did not recognize that you were in MacPaint, it could be very difficult to know how to get back to the desktop. Fear not! Each different application that we discuss has an easily recognized active window that it presents to you. Furthermore, as you close a context, a new active window (and hence a new context) will appear. In this way, the visual nature of the Macintosh helps you keep track of the context in which you are working. Indeed, this visually aided context identification is one of the more important advantages of the Macintosh interface in particular and of window-oriented environments in general on other computer systems. As you gain more experience with the Macintosh, you will become very competent in manipulating language contexts.

Exercise Set 3.1

1. Describe some ways in which the mouse commands given on the desktop behave differently from those same commands given in MacPaint. Give some examples in which they are the same.
2. Give some examples in the English language in which the same words can have entirely different meaning dependent upon the context in which they are interpreted.
3. Explain why you might expect context to be important for communication with computers.
4. Given your experience with the Macintosh so far, can you describe the kinds of problems that you would expect to solve using the commands available in the desktop context? Contrast with the MacPaint context.

3.2 APPLICATIONS VIEWED AS DEFINING A LANGUAGE

To understand communicating with the computer within a given context, it is valuable to think of each application as defining a language through which we communicate our wishes to the computer. A language consists of symbols and a set of rules as to how we can combine the symbols. For example, in our natural language we may think of the symbols as being words and the rules as being English grammar.

Whenever we learn a new language we must learn the symbols (*vocabulary*) and the rules of forming sentences (*grammar*). The rules that allow you to combine symbols together in a language are called collectively the **syntax** of the language. Note that symbols inherently have no meaning of their own. The symbol "Fox" has no intrinsic meaning. That is, the letters "F" followed by "o" followed by "x" do not by themselves intrinsically represent an animal. We have learned to associate the animal with this grouping of letters—this symbol. **Semantics** in language refers to the process of attaching meaning to symbols. Just as in learning a foreign language, to learn to use a computer application such as MacPaint to solve problems for us, we must learn both the semantics and the syntax of the language that MacPaint defines.

Let us examine in more detail what we mean by saying that the MacPaint application defines a language. A view of the MacPaint window is shown in Figure 3.1. Note that the labels appearing in the figure are for your information and do not appear in MacPaint. Recall from Chapter 2 that the symbols/icons in the large rectangle to the left of the drawing window are to be thought of as artists' tools that can be used to draw pictures.

Each of these icons is equivalent to a language command that communicates your wishes to the computer. By positioning the mouse pointer over any of these tool icons and clicking, we are communicating to the computer the exact instruction that we wish the computer to perform. These same instructions might have been issued by typing in some group of symbols as is typically done when using other kinds of computer interfaces; but consider how much easier and unambiguous this graphical form of communication is. As the user of the MacPaint language, you don't have to remember the syntax of any command or even the list of the commands you can issue. In other nonvisually oriented environments, these latter features of communicating with the computer prevent many people from using computers effectively; even though they know *what* they want to do, they

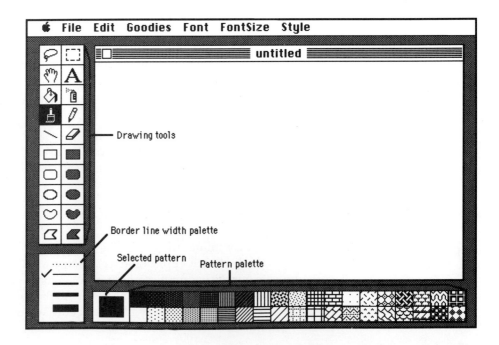

Figure 3.1 The MacPaint starting window.

don't know *how* to tell the computer to do it. They don't have the knowledge and mastery of the language that is necessary to communicate their wishes to the computer.

The selection of a MacPaint instruction is easy to communicate to the Macintosh. Furthermore, you are often able to understand the semantics, or meaning, of each instruction in the MacPaint application, because the form of the symbol representing the instruction is chosen to connote the effect it will have when executed. The semantic meaning of an instruction in a computer language is its effect—what it causes to happen. For example, selecting the spray can as a tool allows one to anticipate easily the effect that this instruction will produce when executed.

Actually, each MacPaint command requires you to give additional information before its execution can be completed. We may think of this information as being part of the syntax or form of the instruction being given. For example, if you select the spray can instruction, you must also specify where the spray can is to be positioned over the canvas, when you want to start spraying, and what kind of paint pattern you want the spray can to spray. To provide this additional information you must learn the allowed syntax of the additional mouse manipulations— positioning, clicking, and dragging—that are part of the spray can instruction.

Clearly, the mouse can be moved to position the spray can. Pressing and releasing the button would seem like a natural way to spray paint. And finally, the choice of a spray pattern from the pattern palette would be a natural way to select the kind of paint to be sprayed. Each of these ways for providing the additional information is the way MacPaint defines the actual syntax of the spray can instruction. In many instances the syntax of the command can be guessed intuitively, and tested, just by trying. If you try something that isn't possible for the Macintosh to carry out in its current context, it will usually beep and then let you try another action. If you actually cause it to execute something you didn't intend, it will usually allow you to undo the last instruction. So exploration using intuition is the common way to learn in the Macintosh environment.

In the Macintosh MacPaint environment, you are working with a pictorial language of icons in which the meaning of the commands is suggested by their symbols. The syntax of each command is intuitive and will involve interactions using the mouse. Actually, nearly every application used on the Macintosh will have elements of what we have discussed with regard to the MacPaint application. This discussion is not intended to explain features of MacPaint but rather to help you view learning a particular computer context-application as being equivalent to learning a new language. This language analogy is valid for learning the use of any computer, no matter what make or model, no matter whether you are learning to program it or to use it for high-level problem solving, as we will be doing later in this book.

In Figure 3.2 we summarize the aspects of communicating with the computer in any context. Here the human communicating with the computer must share the same language that the computer uses and must assume the same context that the computer uses in interpreting the meaning of the message sent.

As a concluding concept for this section, we note that if we were to collect all the commands that you gave to MacPaint as you drew a picture, in the order you gave them, we could call this collection a program. A **program** for a computer is nothing more than a list of instructions expressed in a language, such that when executed it solves a problem. Thus, as in Chapter 2, we might have stated that the

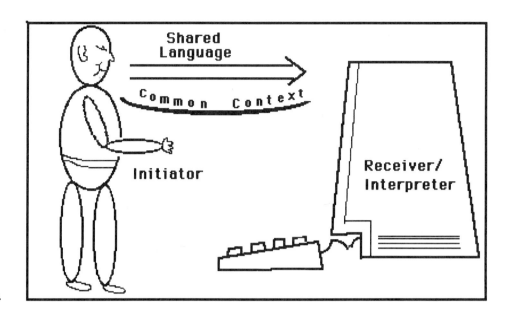

Figure 3.2 Human-computer communication viewed as language.

problem we were trying to solve was to draw a house. By collecting in the proper sequence the instructions we gave to MacPaint to draw a house, we would define a MacPaint program, whose execution would then reproduce the drawing of the house in Chapter 2.

As we will see later in this text, some applications allow you to record the sequence of commands you have entered and to give a name to this sequence. Then when that name is invoked, the entire sequence of commands is carried out by the computer. This process is referred to as creating **macros**, which are just short programs, written in an application language, that can be invoked when you need them.

Each of the applications we will study, such as MacPaint, is itself a program—a list of instructions in a language to solve a problem. The author of MacPaint, Bill Atkinson, wanted to write a program that would allow people using the Macintosh to draw pictures easily.

The high-level problem-solving environments and languages that we discuss in this book are very different from languages that are used to write applications software. These languages for writing applications are called third-generation languages. Examples are Pascal, C, FORTRAN, and BASIC. Third-generation languages can require years of study before a person can write a truly useful program. The time taken to develop a useful application such as MacPaint can be measured in years of one person's effort.

In contrast, by using the high-level problem-solving environments we discuss in this book, you will be able to solve meaningful problems using computers in only a few weeks. Only a few years ago these kinds of language environments did not even exist! Any use you wanted to make of computers would have required you to write a program in a third-generation language. Today you would write a program only if you need to use the computer to do something for which there is no readily available software package. Programming is an interesting and challenging activity, and those who master it have great flexibility in using the computer as a problem-solving tool. However, this book concentrates on the radically new ways in which people are now able to use computers without becoming programmers.

Exercise Set 3.2

1. Explain the difference between the syntax and sematics of a language.
2. Create your own example of a language that uses icons.
3. Comment about the ease of learning to use a computer when all the instructions are presented on a menu, as compared to one in which it is necessary to type in long strings of letters to tell the computer what you want to do.

3.3 NETWORKS OF COMPUTERS AND DEVICES

Thus far in our discussion, we have considered computers as isolated from each other and unconnected to any other devices, such as printers or plotters. A computer does not have to exist alone, unconnected to any other computers or auxiliary devices. In fact, in most Macintosh computer laboratory areas or office environments, printers are shared over a **network**. *Network* is the term used to describe interconnections of groups of computers and devices. A graphical representation of a network is shown in Figure 3.3. There are eight computers and four shared printers plus a special dedicated computer called a **file server**. All of these are connected by cables over which information can be exchanged.

When we say that a device is shared on a network we mean that any user connected to the network is able to **allocate** that device; that is, a user is allowed to treat that device as if it were controlled completely by the computer being used.

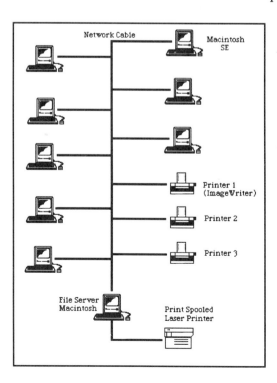

Figure 3.3 A typical Macintosh network.

For example, if a printer on the network is not currently being used by another user, you could allocate that printer for your use in printing a picture you drew in MacPaint. The activity of allocating a device on the network requires the use of commands in a language context in a way similar to our previous examples. For this reason we will term this context the *network context*. When you issue commands in the network context you are generally trying to communicate with computers or devices other than those that are attached directly to your computer.

It is also possible to have different kinds of printers available on the network. For example, many of you will have access to both dot matrix printers and laser printers on your network. The network context will allow you to select the kind of printer that you wish to use. Dot matrix printers provide graphical and textual output that is suitable for draft work of papers or general correspondence. In contrast, laser printers produce exceptionally professional appearing letters and drawings that are of nearly typeset quality. Often you will print early copies of your output on a dot matrix printer and the final version on a laser printer.

In addition to printer services, your network may provide a file server computer. Computer software can be very expensive. Many application packages cost $500 or more per copy. It is not possible for most organizations to provide large numbers of copies of such software. If a network provides a file server computer, then a user anywhere on the network can use applications stored on that computer's hard disk. The network provides the flexibility for you to gain access to the software at your own computer just as if it were stored on your own disk.

Additional features of networked file servers include providing storage for user files. For example, your instructor may ask you to turn in an assignment electronically by saving a copy of it on the network file server hard disk. Or perhaps you have a large paper to print and several other persons may also be waiting to obtain access to the networked printer. If the network provides **printer spooling**, it is possible to copy your output directly onto the network file server disk and turn your attention to other activities with your computer or to leave the computer laboratory altogether. The print spooler software will collect and manage the flow of documents to be sent to the printer. When your document's turn comes, it will automatically be printed whether you are there or not. Print spooling saves a lot of waiting for everyone concerned.

Often networks provide a service called **electronic mail**. When you access a network that provides electronic mail, one of the options provided will be the option to read your mail. You can exchange messages with other users of the network. These messages are stored on the file server disk and you may read yours at any time. Electronic mail is exciting to use, and interactive communication between message senders is also often possible. If a network extends beyond the locality of the campus, it may also be possible to send mail to persons all over the world! Ask your instructor what electronic mail services are provided on your campus.

So far in our discussion of networks, we have assumed that there was only one network. In fact, this may not be so. One computer can be tied into a very large number of different networks. Through the use of the network level language, it is possible to move from one network to another. Your computer can serve as a gateway to use other computers on other campuses, provided you have proper authorization to access these other environments.

Exercise Set 3.3

1.   What is a network?
2.   Name some ways that a network can affect your use of a computer.
3.   How do dot matrix and laser printers differ?
4.   What is meant by print spooling?
5.   Give two advantages to having file server services on a network.
6.   What is electronic mail?

3.4 ALLOCATING RESOURCES IN THE APPLETALK NETWORK

A number of different network environments are available for the Macintosh. In the discussion that follows we will assume that your installation has the AppleTalk® network and AppleShare® file server system available for your use. Other networks and file servers will function in a similar way, although the specific details of their use will differ.

In the Macintosh environment, access to networks and devices on the networks comes through use of the *Chooser* **option** under the **Apple** menu. The **Apple** menu is represented by the apple icon (with the "byte" taken out) positioned in the upper left-hand corner of the menu bar in any Macintosh application. Figure 3.4 shows an example of what the user sees in the network context. The example AppleTalk network we will be describing has three dot matrix printers (Apple ImageWriter printers), one laser printer (Apple LaserWriter) and one

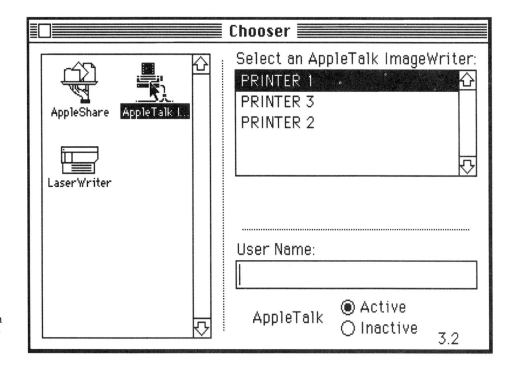

Figure 3.4 Selection of an AppleTalk ImageWriter in the network context.

file server with Apple LaserSpooler and AppleShare file server software. This network is the one diagrammed in Figure 3.3.

One of the most common uses of the *Chooser* is the selection of the printer that you want to use. In the hypothetical environment described earlier, you would have a choice of either one of the ImageWriter printers or the LaserWriter printer. Let us assume that you wish to select one of the ImageWriter printers on your network. First you must access the *Chooser* option under the **Apple** pull-down menu. A dialog box similar to that shown in Figure 3.4 will appear on the screen.

To select a networked printer, move the cursor to the icon for the printer shown connected to AppleTalk and click. The highlighted icon in Figure 3.4 is the one to use. Then move the cursor into the rectangle on the right and select the printer you wish to use by clicking on it. Finally, enter your name by typing it on the keyboard. Then click on the close box. You have now selected for your output the ImageWriter having the highlighted name.

You will need to familiarize yourself with your computer laboratory environment to determine the location of the printer with the name you chose. Clearly, you want to select one that is convenient for you. (Some may be in a different room or even on a different floor or in a different building!) Any application using the *Print* option under the **File** menu will now automatically route your output to the chosen printer. This printer name will also appear in the dialog box associated with a print command (to be discussed later). Thus, you can easily tell where your output will be directed at the time you request it to be printed.

The allocation of a networked LaserWriter printer also involves the use of the *Chooser* option. However, in this case you will want to select the icon for the LaserWriter rather than that for the ImageWriter. This is shown in Figure 3.5, where the LaserWriter icon is highlighted. In this case, for our hypothetical network configuration, there is only one LaserWriter available. For this network the LaserShare spooler software is also available. Hence, instead of seeing the name of a LaserWriter printer analogous to that which appeared in the

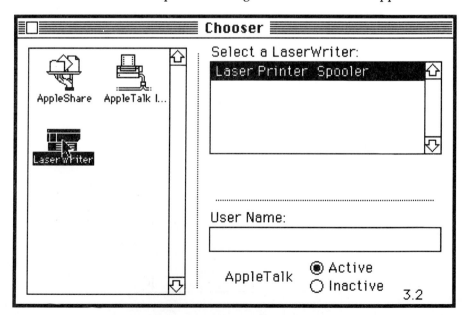

Figure 3.5 Selection of an AppleTalk LaserWriter in the network context.

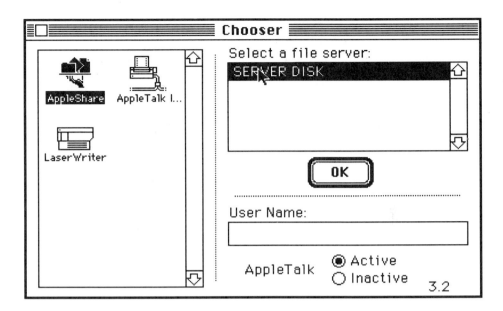

Figure 3.6 Selection of an AppleTalk file server in the network context.

ImageWriter selection, you now see the name of a spooler that allows many users to send output to the same LaserWriter. Enter your name into the lower rectangle by typing on the keyboard as before. Then close the dialog box. At this point you will have allocated the LaserWriter as your output device.

An important point should be mentioned. The output that is printed on the LaserWriter will not be identical to that produced on the ImageWriter in terms of the number of lines per page or number of characters per line. Thus, you may have to experiment with positions for the end of the page, for example, until you obtain the form you want your output to have. A nice feature of the Microsoft Word word processing application, as was mentioned briefly in Chapter 1, is that it allows you to preview the way your pages will appear on the printer you have selected.

Although the network environment is one you will likely encounter, you may be using a computer with a printer directly attached to it. In that case, whenever you wish to print a document, it will not be necessary for you to access the *Chooser* command from the **Apple** menu, provided your printer is attached to the printer port as discussed in Chapter 2. Instead you simply select the *Print* command from the **File** menu, and the output will be automaticaly directed to your connected printer.

As a final example of network usage, we show how the file server may be allocated. Repeat the selection of the *Chooser* option as described earlier. This will produce the dialog box of Figure 3.6. This time we select the AppleShare icon as shown highlighted in this figure. The available file server names are now displayed. For our hypothetical network just one file server is available, but there could be several. Each one of them would have a name, and you can allocate any number you desire. To allocate the file server or servers for your use, select from the file server names that you have authorization to use.

Selection of a file server name produces the dialog box of Figure 3.7. This dialog box allows you to sign on to the file server as either a registered user or a guest. As a registered user you must enter your password to gain access to the file

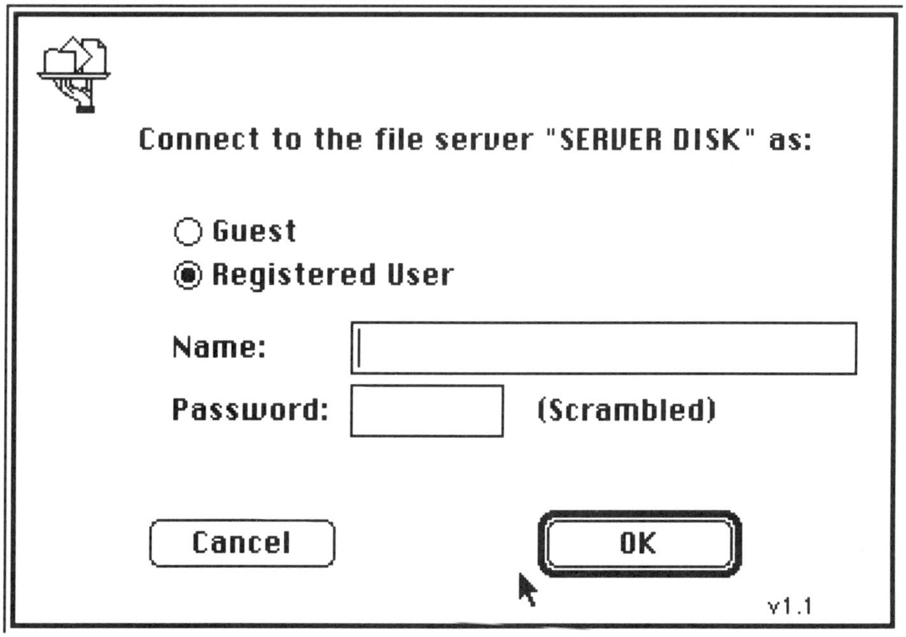

Connect to the file server "SERVER DISK" as:

○ Guest
◉ Registered User

Name: [   ]

Password: [   ] (Scrambled)

[Cancel] [OK]

v1.1

Figure 3.7 Sign-on dialog box for an AppleShare file server.

server. A guest does not need to have a password to use the file server. However, the level of access privileges is assigned by the file server, dependent upon how you sign on. Consequently, guests may not be able to use as many features of the file server as registered users. (*Note:* The preceding features may vary considerably from one environment to another.)

Once you have signed on to the file server, the desktop has a new icon in the disk area. This is shown in Figure 3.8. From now on you may use the file server disk just as you would use one of the disk drives attached to your computer. Note, however, that the kinds of operations you can perform depend upon the privi-

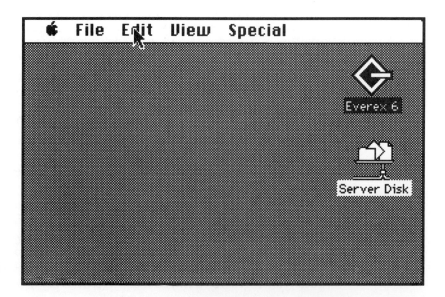

Figure 3.8 Filer server appears as a new disk on the desktop.

leges that have been assigned to you by the person who serves as the system manager for your file server. Normally, you will be able to execute applications on the file server by opening them just as you would for those applications on your own disks.

Exercise Set 3.4

1. What is the purpose of the *Chooser* command? How is it accessed?
2. Describe the method for selecting a printer on the AppleTalk network.
3. Describe the method for allocating a file server on the AppleTalk network.

3.5 EXPLORING THE MACPAINT LANGUAGE

As you already know, with MacPaint you can use the Macintosh to create sketches, drawings, and other graphics objects. In this section you will be given a more detailed description of the MacPaint language and contextual level. The purpose of this description is to provide the information necessary for you to explore MacPaint on your own, so that you can see how natural and intuitive its use is. During this exploration, you will also be practicing the use of, and movement between, different computer contexts. Descriptions and discussions are useful, but the way to learn and to master the ideas presented in this chapter is to experiment with an actual language and several different contexts. MacPaint allows you to do that and to have fun while you learn!

Read this section through without trying to carry out the described activities. At the end of the section, you will find several Computer Practice activities that allow you to explore at a leisurely pace the use of the tools and concepts you have read about.

As you read this material, continue to think of the actions that are being described as language commands. You will see that many of these commands require several steps on your part before they are completely understood by the Macintosh. However, as soon as the commands are completed, they are interpreted and executed. Hence you will see immediately whether the command you issued had the desired result. In this visually reinforced communication mode, it will be very easy to construct correct "programs." As soon as you issue an incorrect command, it will be obvious to you, and you can usually correct your mistake.

In Chapter 2 you saw how to run the MacPaint application by issuing commands within the desktop context. Recall that the opening MacPaint screen appears as shown in Figure 3.1. This window is the MacPaint equivalent of a blank page on which a sketch is to be made. As a "Mac artist," you can make paintings by using any combination of a pencil, brush, spray can, or many other tools. These tools are shown as icons in the rectangle to the left of the drawing window. Below the tool icons is a box that shows the possible widths of lines. Below the drawing window is a long rectangle that contains patterns that can be used to fill closed shapes. You were briefly introduced to the use of several of the tools in Chapter 2.

The **MacPaint tools**, shown with names in Figure 3.9, give the artist a wide range of options in producing a drawing. The tools *lasso* and *marquee* are used for selection and movement of all or part of a drawing; *scroll* moves the viewing

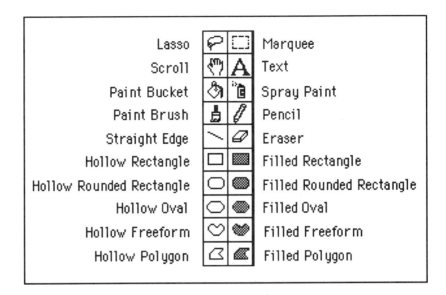

Figure 3.9 The MacPaint tools.

window around on the larger painting surface; *text* enters alphabetic characters; *paint bucket*, *spray paint*, *paint brush*, *pencil*, *straight edge*, and *eraser* are all painting tools; and the remaining tools are for painting frequently occurring shapes. Some techniques for using these tools are now covered in more detail.

3.5.1 The Painting Tools

The *paint bucket* is used to pour a pattern onto a closed portion of the painting. Click the *paint bucket* tool and the pointer assumes the shape of a paint bucket. Select the desired fill pattern from the pattern palette at the bottom of the MacPaint screen by positioning the pointer to the pattern desired and clicking. Note that the large square in the pattern rectangle changes to the selected pattern. Move the pointer to within the area to be filled. (The pointer is the tip of the outflowing paint.) Click the mouse, and the area will be filled. This procedure is illustrated in Figure 3.10. Be sure that the area to be filled is completely closed before you use the paint bucket. If the boundary of the area has any holes in it, the paint will leak out to cover the surrounding area. If this occurs, don't panic! By selecting the **Undo command** from the **Edit** menu, you can cancel the immediately preceding command.

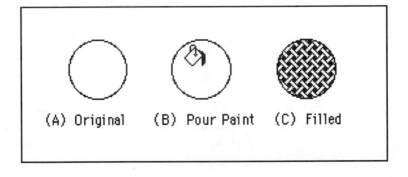

Figure 3.10 Using the paint bucket.

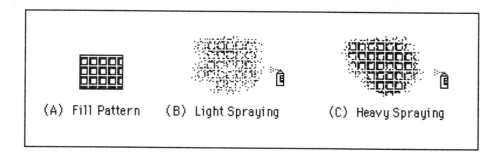

Figure 3.11 Using the spray paint can.

The *spray paint* can is used to spray a fill pattern on the painting. To use this tool, you click the can icon and the pointer will change into the spray paint can. Move the pointer to the area to be sprayed. Move the mouse as if it were the spray can, and use the mouse button as if it were a spray can nozzle button. The pattern will be sprayed just as if you were spraying paint. A sample is shown in Figure 3.11.

The *paint brush* can be used in painting any part of the page. Different shapes and sizes of brushes can be selected by using the *Brush Shape* command from the **Goodies** menu. The brush will always paint using the selected pattern from the pattern palette. The digits shown in Figure 3.12 were painted with different-shaped brushes (brush shapes can be rectangular, circular, angular lines, etc.) and different patterns.

The *pencil* is used to make drawings using the same techniques as those in normal drawing. If you click the pencil tool, the pointer assumes the shape of a pencil. Move the pointer to the desired location. Then hold down the mouse button and move the pencil to draw the desired figure. You will probably need considerable practice to be able to control accurately the motion of the mouse (and hence the pencil). If you make a mistake, you can use the *eraser* to remove part of the drawing or the *Undo* command to remove the part of the drawing made since you last completed another command. Note that if you release the mouse button at any point during a pencil drawing session, this counts as a completed command. To use the eraser, hold down the mouse button as you drag the eraser icon over the portion to be erased.

If you need finer control than can be achieved with the pencil and the eraser, using the *FatBits* command from the **Goodies** menu will allow you to work with the individual dots that make up a picture. A fast way to switch between regular and fatbits modes is to point to the area of interest using the pencil and then click while the *Command* (or *Clover*) key is depressed. Alternatively, first select a portion of the painting using the lasso or marquee (the use of these tools is

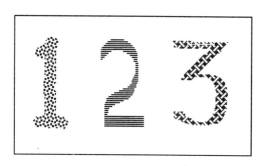

Figure 3.12 Painting using different brushes and patterns.

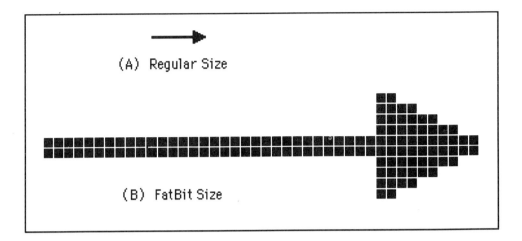

Figure 3.13 Regular size versus FatBit size.

discussed in the next section), then select the *FatBits* command and the picture will expand to show the individual dots. The difference in size is shown in Figure 3.13. The painting tools can be used with the fatbits object. For example, the pencil can be used with great accuracy to draw new lines; it can also be used to erase dots or even large areas of the painting. To use the pencil to erase, point at a drawn dot and click; moving the pencil without releasing the button after an erasure will continue to erase dots. When using the fatbits mode, you will see a small copy of the portion of the painting you are working on in the upper left of the window. To move back to regular mode, place the pencil in that area and click.

In the preceding operations, note how the context is shifting even within a given language environment. Within MacPaint, various actions are possible using exactly the same manipulations of the mouse. The actions that occur depend upon the command context in which the manipulations are carried out.

The *straight edge* tool can be used to draw a straight line between any two points. When this tool icon is clicked, the pointer becomes a small cross. Point to the first location, drag to the second location, keeping the button depressed, and then release the button to create a line between them. The pointer, now at the

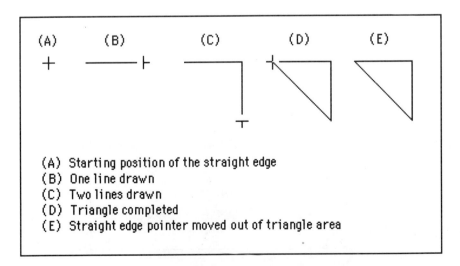

Figure 3.14 Use of the straight edge to draw a triangle.

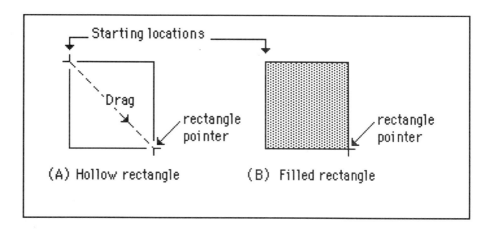

Figure 3.15 Painting hollow and filled rectangles.

second location, retains the cross shape, and moving the mouse will allow the cross to be repositioned to begin a new line segment. Notice that whenever the cross is touching a line, it is white. This feature allows you to line up separately created lines perfectly. The use of the straight edge to draw a triangle is shown in Figure 3.14.

The remaining painting tools make it easy to paint simple figures such as rectangles and ovals. For each type of figure there is a hollow tool and a filled tool. To paint a hollow rectangle (one which has no interior pattern), click the *hollow rectangle* tool and the pointer becomes a cross identical to that used for the straight edge. Place the tool at a location that is to be a corner of the rectangle, and drag to the diagonally opposite corner. Releasing the mouse button stops the drawing of the rectangle. Figure 3.15 illustrates this process. A filled rectangle is created in essentially the same way using the *filled rectangle* tool and a selected fill pattern.

The *text* tool allows you to type alphabetic characters into a painting. The size and style of these characters can be selected by choosing the appropriate option(s) under the **Font**, **Font Size**, and **Style** menus. The *Return* key moves the pointer to a position on the next line under the first character. The *Backspace* (or *Delete*) key erases preceding characters one by one, provided that you have not clicked the mouse button since starting to use the text tool. Once the mouse button is clicked, all editing must be done with the eraser or selection tools.

3.5.2 The Selection Tools

The tools *lasso* and *marquee* (also called the *selection rectangle*) allow the selection of portions of a painting for copying, erasing, moving, or fatbits expansion. In addition, the marquee can be used to stretch (or reduce) the selected portion of a painting. You will see that there is also an important difference in the way "background" is treated by these two tools when moving portions of paintings.

To use the *lasso*, select it from the set of tools by pointing to its icon and clicking. The pointer will then take the form of the lasso, with the tip of the pointer being the end of the lasso. If the mouse button is pressed and held and the lasso is moved by dragging the mouse, a line will appear on the screen to show the movement of the lasso. To *select* any object in a painting, drag the lasso around the object until the line made by the moving lasso crosses any portion of the lasso line drawn previously. Then release the mouse button. The lasso will automatically

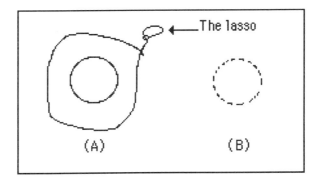

Figure 3.16 Selection using the lasso.

close about the selected object, and the boundary of the object will begin to blink. Figure 3.16(A) shows a line drawn by the lasso around a circle, and (B) shows the blinking circle after it is selected by releasing the mouse button. To *deselect* an object, point and click anywhere outside the object.

To *erase* the lasso-selected object, press the *Backspace* (or *Delete* key) in the upper right portion of your keyboard. If you decide you have made a mistake and really do not wish to erase the selected object, you can still recover the object by immediately selecting the *Undo* command from the **Edit** menu. Note that to accomplish the reversal of a command, you must select *Undo* from the **Edit** menu *before executing another command.* In other words, the *Undo* command applies only to the command issued immediately preceding it.

To *copy* the lasso selected object, select the **Copy command** from the **Edit** menu. A copy of the selected object is placed in a file called the **Clipboard**. (We usually say that we have placed such an object *on* the *Clipboard.*) Any object on the *Clipboard* can be *pasted* to a MacPaint figure by selecting the **Paste command** from the **Edit** menu. (More about the *Clipboard* file later.) When an object is pasted into a MacPaint painting, it is selected, and unless it is deselected, operations issued will be performed on it.

An alternative method for copying an object selected by the lasso without involving the *Clipboard* file is to hold down the *Option* key while you drag the object. In this case the original object will remain unchanged, and a copy of it will move as you perform the drag operation. Holding down both the *Option* and *Command* keys will let you make repeating copies. A simple painting constructed

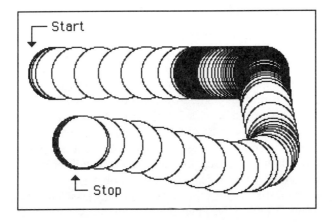

Figure 3.17 Effect of moving a circle at varying rates.

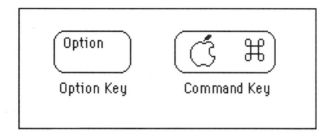

Figure 3.18 The *Option* and *Command* keys.

by moving a circle at a variable rate while pressing both the *Option* and *Command* keys is shown in Figure 3.17. The *Option* and *Command* keys are the leftmost keys on the bottom line of the keyboard; they have the appearance shown in Figure 3.18. On the Macintosh Plus and earlier computers only the clover icon is shown.

To *cut* a lasso-selected object, select the *Cut* command from the **Edit** menu. The object will be removed from the painting, and a copy of the object will be placed on the *Clipboard*. To *move* the selected object, drag it to the desired location. This operation is shown in Figure 3.19. Notice that the "clear" interior of a closed object (like the circle shown) is moved as a part of the figure. Don't forget that you can use the *Undo* command if you do not like the resulting figure.

To choose the *marquee* tool, point to it in the set of tools and click. The pointer will become a cross (+). The marquee can be used to select a portion of a painting that can be operated on just as we did with the lasso. To select with the marquee, move the cross to the desired portion of the painting and press and hold down the mouse button. Dragging the pointer will create a blinking rectangle that denotes the selected portion of the painting. Release the mouse button to complete the

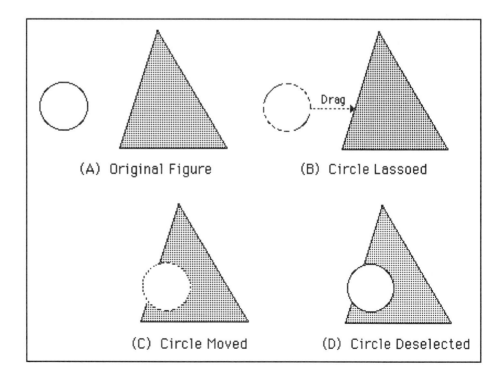

Figure 3.19 Using the Lasso to Move Objects.

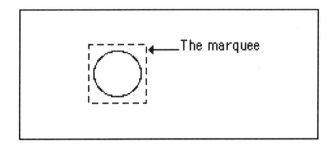

Figure 3.20 Selection using the marquee.

selection process. Clicking anywhere outside the marquee deselects the blinking area. You should keep this deselection process in mind because it may be necessary for you to make several attempts to select only the desired area.

All the operations described for the lasso can also be performed by the marquee, with two important differences. First, the *entire* area enclosed by the marquee is the portion of the painting to be moved, deleted, and so on, which implies that the marquee usually contains both an object and the background space around the object. For example, Figure 3.20 shows the selection of a circle using the marquee. Notice that the selected area includes some space outside the circle.

The result of using the marquee to select and move a circle is shown in Figure 3.21. Note that in this example, a portion of the filled triangle is erased when the circle is moved into it. The erased portion of the triangle corresponds to the area inside the marquee. Contrast this example with the similar example using the lasso shown in Figure 3.19.

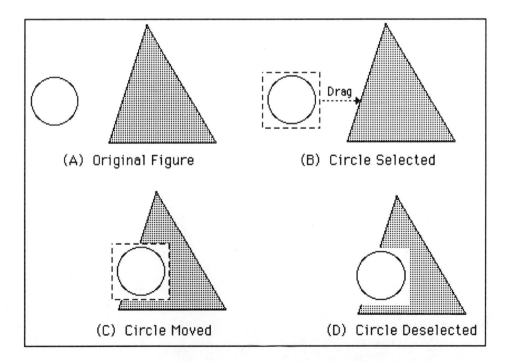

Figure 3.21 Using the Marquee to move an object.

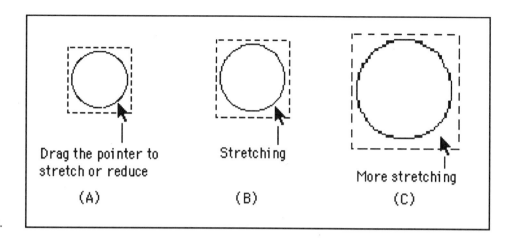

Figure 3.22 Stretching a circle using the marquee.

The second difference between the lasso and the marquee is that the marquee can be used to *stretch* (or reduce) parts of a painting. After a portion of the painting has been selected with the marquee, place the pointer inside the marquee. Finally, press the *Command* key shortly before pressing the mouse key, and drag the pointer in the direction of the desired change. This process is illustrated in Figure 3.22. The drawing can be stretched in the vertical and/or horizontal direction. Notice that some distortion occurs as the painting is stretched. Additionally, a marquee-selected portion of a drawing can be rotated 90 degrees left or right or flipped about its horizontal or vertical axis. These commands are found under the **Edit** menu.

3.5.3 The Scrolling Tool

The drawing window of MacPaint has dimensions of approximately 4.25 by 5.5 inches, which is considerably smaller than the 8- by 10-inch page that can be produced using MacPaint. Thus, the window allows the user to see only a portion of the page. To view a different part of the page, use the scroll tool that has the form of a hand. Click the *hand tool* (also called the *grabber*), and the pointer appears

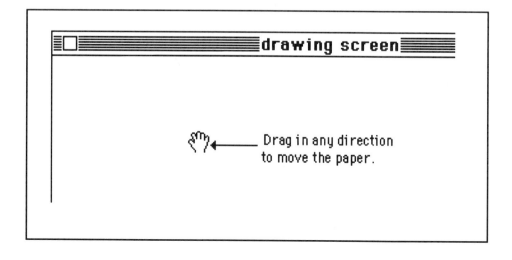

Figure 3.23 Using the scroll tool.

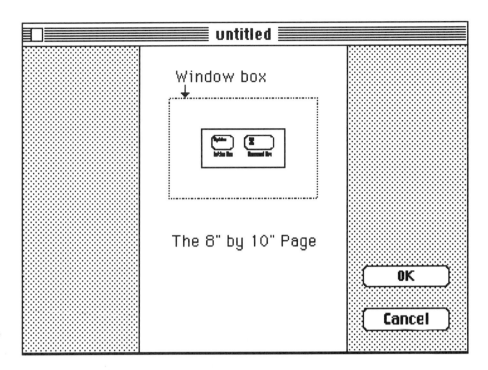

Figure 3.24 The *Show Page* command.

to be a hand as shown in Figure 3.23. Press the mouse button and drag the hand to move the page.

A reduced version of the entire page can be examined by selecting the *Show Page* command from the **Goodies** menu. The result is shown in Figure 3.24 for the case in which the *Option* and *Command* keys figure (3.18) is being displayed. Notice that in this version of the page the text cannot be read. If the pointer is inside the window box, which outlines the regular-sized window, dragging will move the window box. Clicking the OK box would then cause a different portion of the painting to be displayed. (The effect is the same as using the *hand tool* in the

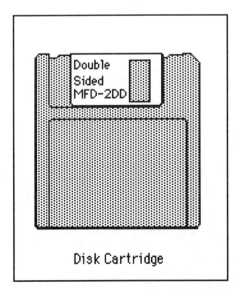

Figure 3.25 The Painting to be Constructed.

regular window.) If the pointer is outside the window box, dragging will move the contents of the page. However, this can be a *dangerous operation* as any portion of the painting moved off the page is lost unless the *Undo* command is given before any other action is taken.

3.5.4 An Example Painting Program

In this section we discuss a MacPaint program, or sequence of steps, for drawing a disk cartridge of the type shown in Figure 3.25. We have chosen this drawing because it is complex enough to demonstrate both a general problem-solving method and the use of a number of the MacPaint tools we have presented.

As with any nontrivial problem there are many possible approaches to designing and implementing a solution. The one shown for our drawing program

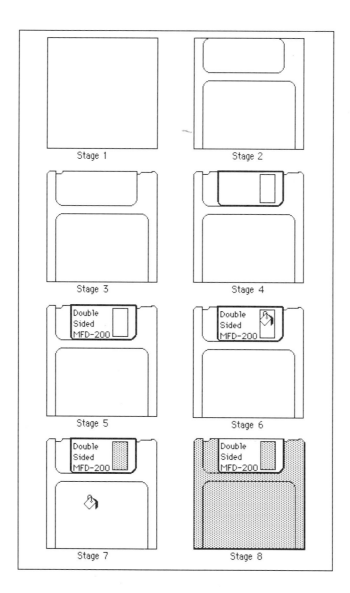

Figure 3.26 Stages in the painting of a disk cartridge.

has been chosen rather arbitrarily. If you believe that there is a simpler approach, try it out on your own. Our approach will demonstrate a general method for constructing problem solutions, which involves breaking a complex task up into a number of smaller and less complex tasks, then putting the solutions to these smaller tasks together in a sequence of steps that produces the overall solution we seek. This method, called **top-down problem solving**, can be used for a great variety of problem-solving tasks.

The major stages that we have planned for painting the disk cartridge are shown in Figure 3.26. The idea was to start with a rectangle of the correct size and then to modify it in a sequence of steps to obtain the desired result. Consult Figure 3.26 frequently as you read the following description of the program. For stage 1 the hollow rectangle was selected, and the rectangle was drawn.

To obtain stage 2, the rounded hollow rectangle was selected. The pointer was placed on the top line of the rectangle approximately 1/8 inch from the upper left-hand corner. The pointer was then moved diagonally until the upper rounded rectangle shown was obtained. Before the mouse button was released, several different-sized rounded rectangles were considered.

The lower rounded rectangle was then painted. This required placing the pointer on the left edge immediately below the left vertical line of the upper rounded rectangle. An extra vertical line was created using the fatbits feature between the existing upper rounded rectangle and the location for starting the lower rounded rectangle. This made possible the exact vertical alignment of the

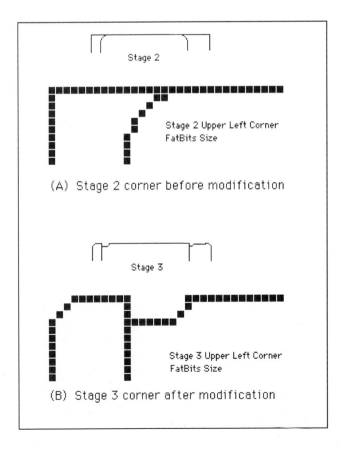

Figure 3.27 Modification of the top line using *FatBits*.

left sides of the rectangles. This extra line was erased after the second rectangle was drawn. The lower rectangle was extended to below the bottom line of the drawing so that right angles would be obtained at the bottom. The extra portion of the rounded rectangle below the drawing was erased. This completed stage 2.

Creating stage 3 required that the top line of the painting be modified to produce the slanted corners and indentations found on a disk cartridge. In addition, the upper rounded corners of the upper small rectangle needed to be changed to straight lines. All the work for this stage was done using the *FatBits* option to obtain increased control of the pencil. Figure 3.27 shows both the regular size of stages 2 and 3 and the fatbit size for the upper left-hand corner. Recall that pointing with the pencil to an existing dot and clicking will remove the dot and that pointing to a blank area and clicking will create a dot. Because of the large size of the dots in the fatbit size, it was easy to erase the appropriate dots and insert new dots.

Two actions were required to create stage 4. The slide was created in the fatbit mode by inserting extra dots on the inner edge of the existing upper rectangle, and an additional vertical line was inserted. The hole in the slide was created by using the hollow rectangle tool to draw a narrow vertical rectangle.

Stage 5 required only the use of the text tool to write information on the slide. Actually, some experimentation was required to obtain the correct placement of the words. For each unsatisfactory attempt, the *Undo* command in the **Edit** menu erased the words. The text pointer was then moved and another attempt was made.

Stages 6 through 8 involved pouring the selected fill pattern into all the areas of the painting except the slide. The paint can was placed in the rectangular opening of the slide, and the fill pattern was poured in. The can was moved to each of the other areas, and the pattern was poured.

3.5.5 Saving Your Paintings

Suppose you have finished making a drawing such as the one discussed in the previous section. It is natural to want to save that drawing so that it could be accessed later. In Section 2.4, we gave a very brief description of how to do this. In this section, we will explore this activity in some detail.

To save a painting, we need to issue commands within the desktop context. However, it would be more efficient to communicate our preferences about whether to save the painting *before* we quit the MacPaint application. In this way, if we do not desire to save our current work, the application can be closed without saving even a temporary copy. MacPaint, and all other Macintosh application packages, allows you to issue the desktop context commands necessary to save your work on whatever disk you choose. These commands are issued by way of a dialog box from within the application itself.

To gain access to the appropriate desktop context dialog box from within MacPaint (and most other applications), you may select one of the commands *Save*, *Save As*, *Close*, or *Quit* from the **File** pull-down menu. Each of these commands has a different interpretation.

If the painting being worked on is new and the ***Save* command** is issued, the dialog box shown in Figure 3.28 is displayed. Because the painting has no name (it is a new painting, and its window has the name *untitled*), we must first name it

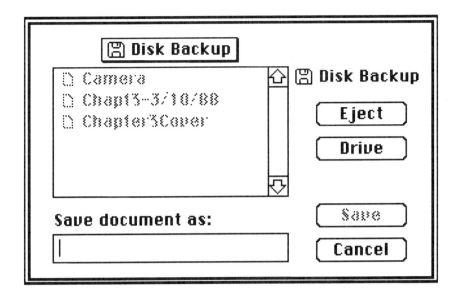

Figure 3.28 The *Save* dialog box in MacPaint.

before it can be saved. This is done by typing the name into the rectangle in the lower left of the dialog box. You will notice the name of the currently open disk above the *Eject* button in the dialog box. The name of the open folder that was in the active window before MacPaint was started (or the currently open disk name if the last active window was the disk window) appears above the scroll box to the left of the *Eject* button. If you wish to save your painting into the open folder, you do that by clicking the *Save* button.

However, if you wish to save your painting to another folder (on the same disk), you can change the folder by pointing to the folder icon in the rectangle where the currently open folder's name is displayed and by pressing and holding down the mouse button. When you do this, a pull-down menu of folders available at the current contextual level is displayed and you can choose one in the usual way. When you have chosen the desired folder, click the *Save* button.

To save your document to a different disk, you may click the *Drive* button to access a disk in a different disk drive (including the hard drive if one is available). Or you may wish to remove the current floppy disk and replace it with another. To do this, you would click *Eject*, then when your disk is ejected, you can insert another disk. From this point you would proceed to select the appropriate folder (if one is desired) before clicking the *Save* button.

Don't worry if the ideas in the previous several paragraphs seem a little unclear at the moment. In Chapter 4 these techniques are explained in much more detail in the discussion of hierarchical file systems.

The **Save As command** is commonly used when you are working on a painting that was previously saved and you now wish to save a modified version of it under a separate name or in a different folder or disk. In this case, if you simply issue the *Save* command, the painting (already having a name) will be saved automatically, with the new version *replacing* the old version under the same name. The only difference in the dialog box produced when you issue the *Save As* command, as opposed to the one in Figure 3.28, is that the old name will appear in the rectangle in the lower left of the box. You can save the new version under a different name by typing in the new name before clicking the *Save* button.

Note that saving the new version under a new name leaves the old version under the old name *unchanged*. You can also use the technique described in the previous two paragraphs to select a different folder or disk to which to save your painting.

When a painting is saved using either the *Save* or the *Save As* command, it is not closed. After either the *Save* or *Save As* command has been executed, you are returned to the working window, where you may continue working on your painting if you wish. *It is actually a good idea to save your work every 20 minutes or less, so that if for some reason the current work is compromised (by a power surge or failure, for example), you will have a recent copy of your work saved to disk.* If you do wish to stop work on the painting in your window after saving it, you may issue the *Close* **command** or the *Quit* **command**.

The *Close* command closes the painting window and then allows you to open another painting (or create a new one) if you desire. You'll see how to do this shortly. The *Quit* command not only closes your painting window, but also exits the MacPaint application and returns you to the desktop context. If either of these two commands is issued and you have not saved the painting in its current version, a dialog box will ask you whether you wish to save the changes (since the last saved version). If you click the *Yes* button and the painting is a new one that has not been saved yet, you will be given a dialog box like the one in Figure 3.28. If the painting was previously named and saved, then clicking *Yes* will result in the new version replacing the old version automatically as described earlier. When you issue either the *Close* or the *Quit* command, once you have taken care of saving (or not saving) the painting, execution of the original command is completed.

Let us assume that you saved the painting of the floppy disk constructed earlier on the disk named *Disk Backup*, by typing the name *DiskPainting* into the dialog box of Figure 3.28 and then clicking *Save*. Further suppose that you issued the *Quit* command from the **File** menu when you were returned to the MacPaint

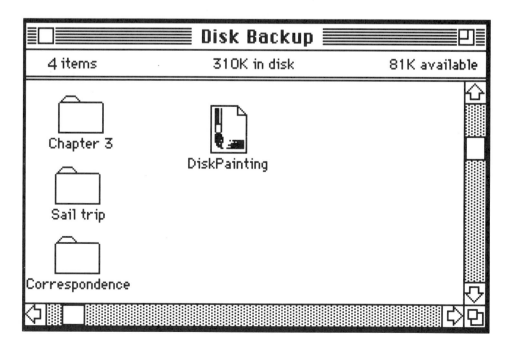

Figure 3.29 Desktop window after quitting MacPaint.

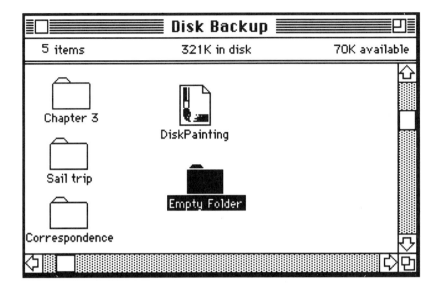

Figure 3.30 Disk window with a new folder.

window. Assuming further that you had opened the MacPaint application from this same disk, you would then be returned to the desktop context with a window for that disk opened as shown in Figure 3.29.

Because you may wish to construct other paintings later, it will reduce clutter in the disk window if you create a folder to hold this and future paintings. You can do this by issuing the *New Folder* command from the **File** menu. The result of the execution of this command is shown in Figure 3.30.

Notice that the folder is created in a selected state. You can name it by simply typing its name and then pressing the *Return* key. If you were to name it *Paintings* and then drag the icon for the painting *DiskPainting* to the folder, the disk window shown in Figure 3.31 would be produced. You could check your work by opening the folder *Paintings*. The result should be similar to that shown in Figure 3.32.

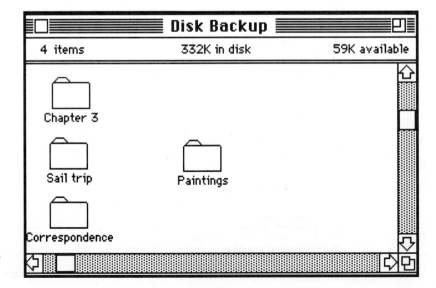

Figure 3.31 New folder named with *DiskPainting* placed in it.

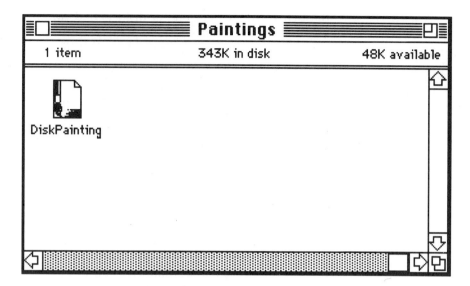

Figure 3.32 *Paintings* folder opened.

3.5.6 Opening a Saved Painting

There are two ways to open a saved painting in MacPaint. The easier way is to find and double-click on the icon for the painting itself. This command causes the MacPaint application to be started (even if it is in a different folder or on a different disk that is accessible) and then opens your painting within MacPaint.

A second way to accomplish this same task is to start MacPaint yourself by finding and double-clicking on the MacPaint icon. This command starts MacPaint and opens a new painting window (as shown in Figure 3.1). You can then close this "untitled" window by issuing the *Close* command from the **File** menu. Your painting may now be opened by issuing the ***Open* command** from the **File** menu. When this command is issued, you will be given a dialog box similar to the one shown in Figure 3.33. You can complete this command by finding your painting and clicking the *Open* button in the dialog box. Note that you may have to search

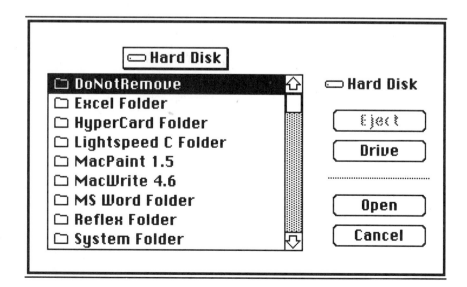

Figure 3.33 Dialog box for opening a painting from within MacPaint.

through several folders and/or disks to find your painting. If so, this process is identical to that described in the previous section for the *Save* command dialog box. Remember that this process is described again, and in more detail, in Chapter 4.

3.5.7 Printing a Painting

To print a painting, recall that if you are working in a networked environment, you need to select first a destination printer. This selection is done by issuing the *Chooser* command from the **Apple** menu, as described in Section 3.4. After a printer has been selected, the *Chooser* dialog box should be closed. If your computer is not connected to a network, then you must have a printer connected directly to your computer to print documents. In this case, you need not access the *Chooser* command but can go directly to the *Print* commands in the **File** menu as described earlier.

If the painting you want to print is currently open in MacPaint, you can print it by issuing the *Print Draft* or *Print Final* command from the **File** menu. (These produce different-quality paintings on the ImageWriter printer.) If the painting is not open, you must first open it before it can be printed. This can be done in one of two ways. You can open the painting directly (recall from the previous section that there are also two ways to do this—double-click the painting icon or first open MacPaint and then issue the *Open* command), or you can simply select (by single clicking) the painting and then issue the desired *Print* command from the **File** menu. With this latter method, the painting is automatically opened for you.

Exercise Set 3.5

1. Describe each of the MacPaint painting tools—*straight edge, paint brush, pencil, spray can,* and *paint bucket*—and give an example of how they are used.
2. Describe the use of the *lasso* and *marquee* tools in MacPaint. How do they differ?
3. Explain how to access the *FatBits* option in MacPaint. What is this option used for?
4. What is the *Undo* command used for in MacPaint? How is it accessed?
5. Explain the use of the *Save* and *Save As* commands for saving MacPaint paintings. How are the commands accessed? How do these commands differ?
6. Explain the use of the *Close* and *Quit* commands in MacPaint. How do they differ?
7. Describe two ways to open a saved MacPaint painting for modification.
8. Describe the process required to print a MacPaint painting.

Computer Practice 3.5

1. Start the MacPaint application. Create a line drawing of a house similar to that shown in Figure 2.22 in Chapter 2. You will need only the *straight edge* and *hollow rectangle* tools to do this. Practice the use of the *Undo* command and the *eraser*, even if you don't need them.
2. Save the painting that you created in step 1 under the name of *House1* on your disk. Quit the MacPaint application and then open your *House1* icon.
3. Print your painting *House1*.

4. While in MacPaint with your *House1* painting in the window (as in step 2), close the window. Now get a new screen by using the *New* command in the **File** menu.

5. Use the *pencil* to create some faces similar to those in Figure 2.20 in the new window you have invoked in step 3. Save this painting as *Faces1* on your disk.

6. Quit the MacPaint application. Create a new folder on your disk and name it *Paintings1*. Place the two paintings *House1* and *Faces1* in the folder *Paintings1*.

7. Open the MacPaint application directly using the MacPaint program icon. Close the "untitled" window that you are given. Now issue the *Open* command from the **File** menu. Find and open the painting *Faces1* using the *Open* dialog box you are given.

8. Make some changes to the painting in your *Faces1* window from step 7. Save these changes by issuing the *Save* command in the **File** menu. Now make more changes to the painting in the *Faces1* window. Issue the *Save As* command from the **File** menu, and proceed to save the changed *Faces1* painting under the name *Faces2* in your *Paintings1* folder.

9. Check your work in step 7 by quitting MacPaint and examining the contents of your *Paintings1* folder. If there is a problem, make sure you understand its source before proceeding. If needed, go back over some of the previous exercises.

10. Open the MacPaint application again and try to create the house drawing shown in Figure 2.23. You will need to use the *straight edge*, the *hollow rectangle*, the *paint can*, and perhaps some other tools. Save your painting as *House2*.

11. Practice the use of the *FatBits* option to refine your *House2* painting.

12. Close the *House2* painting (save the changes if you wish). Get a new painting screen. Use the *hollow tools* to create some closed figures on the screen. Use the *paint bucket* to fill some of your figures with various fill patterns.

13. Use both the *marquee* and and the *lasso* tools to move some of the figures you have created around on the screen.

14. By now, you should feel comfortable enough with the basic MacPaint tools and the methods for saving, retrieving, and printing paintings to explore MacPaint on your own.

Key Concepts

Allocating network resources	Chooser option
Clipboard	Close command
Copy command	Electronic mail
File server	Language Context
Language semantics	Language syntax
MacPaint tools	Macro
Network	Open command
Paste command	Printer spooling
Program	Quit command
Save As command	Save command
Top-down problem solving	Undo command

LEARNING MORE ABOUT THE MACINTOSH

L E A R N I N G   O B J E C T I V E S

- To understand basic computer resources in the Macintosh environment.
- To learn how disk and file manipulations may be conducted from the desktop context.
- To understand the hierarchical organization of files and folders used by the Macintosh.
- To learn how to navigate within file hierarchies both from the desktop context and from within application package contexts.
- To learn to manage basic printer and desk accessory resources.

I n this chapter you will learn in greater detail about the desktop (operating system) context of the Macintosh computer. The primary function of the desktop context is to allow you to manage the resources of your computer system. Using this context you will be able to rename files and folders, restructure the way information is placed into folders, copy files and folders from one disk to another, and remove files from a disk when necessary. You will explore the functions of a number of different menu operations that are present in the desktop context and that are commonly shared by many application packages. You will see that you can add to or delete from the font sets and/or sizes of fonts that the computer uses to display your information on its screen or on its printers. Finally, you will learn how to add to or delete from the system folder special programs, called desk accessories, to customize your computer to make your work easier.

4.1 RESOURCE MANAGEMENT FROM THE DESKTOP

To use a computer effectively, you must learn to manage the available **computer resources**. Because these resources exist beyond the scope of an application, most resource management operations must be performed from the desktop context of the computer. However, unlike many other computer systems, the Macintosh also allows access, using the **File** or the **Apple** menu, to some of the resource management operations within contexts other than the desktop. This section provides a brief overview of some different kinds of resources that are available within any computer system.

DISK RESOURCES.   Disk space is one of the most important computer resources. The organization of files and folders and the allocation of space for storage of information on a disk are both critical activities for the productive use of a computer. The need to manage disk resources is unavoidable, because disk storage is limited to 800K bytes on a floppy disk (400K on a single-sided disk), and you can easily store enough information on a single disk to run out of space. At the least, you will often need to restructure the way your information is stored on the disk so that you can access it more easily. Even when you first begin to use the Macintosh (or any other computer), a number of questions concerning disk resource management will quickly arise. For example:

- How do you copy a file from one disk to another—or perhaps one entire disk to another disk?
- How do you rename a file?
- How can you remove a file from your disk?
- How can you change the way in which folders and their contents are structured?
- How can you find a file whose name you know but whose location within a folder you have forgotten?

INPUT/OUTPUT RESOURCES.   The peripheral devices available to you, either those that are directly attached to your computer or those that can be allocated by you on a network, constitute another example of a resource. You have already learned to manage the printer resource in Chapter 3 by selecting the printer directly connected to your computer or a printer in a network, and in this chapter you will learn how to further manage the printer resource. For example, you can control the way a drawing or the pages of a document are oriented on the printed page. You can choose between having lines of text and/or a picture printed across the width of the page or along its length. You can also choose the paper size for the document and adjust the margins.

CLIPBOARD AND SCRAPBOOK RESOURCES.   The *Clipboard* and *Scrapbook* files are resources that you can control both in the desktop context and in application contexts. By using these resources, you can transfer data from one place to another within a given application context or between different application contexts. You can copy the *Clipboard* or *Scrapbook* files just as you would copy other files or folders.

CPU RESOURCE.   The microprocessor (central processing unit, or CPU) is an important resource of the computer whose use you can also control from the desktop. The process of opening an application causes the microprocessor's function to be controlled entirely by the application program. While the microprocessor is executing a given application, it may not be executing another one. (Future versions of the Macintosh operating system may change this, however.)

HUMAN–COMPUTER INTERFACE RESOURCE.   The human–computer interface can also be managed by changing the sensitivity of the mouse to your hand movements, changing the speed at which letters are repeated as you hold down a key, changing the background pattern on the desktop, and so on. You may even change the kind of interface that the computer presents to you by changing the operating system program that you use in communicating with the computer.

RESOURCE MANAGEMENT TOOLS.   The communication between you and the Macintosh computer is accomplished through a special component of the operating system called the Finder. Through the Finder you will issue many of the commands necessary to perform resource management operations. There are actually three versions of the human–computer interface—MiniFinder, Finder, and MultiFinder—and the nature of the interface is different for the three versions. Our discussions in this text always assume that you are using the Finder, but for the sake of completeness we describe briefly some features of the MiniFinder and the MultiFinder.

The MiniFinder program takes up much less space on a disk and in memory than the Finder, but it does not provide as many functions. It was developed so that computers with limited memory and disk storage would be able to execute some large software applications. You will normally need the MiniFinder only if you have a small amount of disk space (i.e., a single 400K byte disk drive) and 512K or less of RAM.

At the time of writing, the MultiFinder is the most recently released human-machine interface program available for the Macintosh. It provides a larger set of operations than does the Finder. One of the MultiFinder's most important features is the ability to change from one application context to another (or even to the desktop) without quitting an application. It also provides the ability to do some computation in the "backgound" (perhaps computing some complex formulas in a spreadsheet) while you continue working on some other activity such as word processing.

In the discussion that follows we will assume that you have installed on your computer system version 6.0 of the Finder. Most of the resource management operations that we describe will appear almost the same if you are using either the Finder or the MultiFinder. If you are using a version of the Finder that is earlier or later than 6.0, your menu options may appear slightly different from those discussed here.

To find out which version of the Finder you are using, select the *About the Finder* command from the **Apple** menu from within the desktop context, as shown in Figure 4.1. Note that your **Apple** menu choices will almost certainly be different from those shown in Figure 4.1. The reason is that commands can easily be added to or deleted from this menu, as you will see later.

After selecting the *About the Finder* command, a window like that shown in Figure 4.2 will be displayed. This window shows both the Finder version number and the System File version you are using. It also shows how much RAM is in your computer and how the memory is allocated between other operating system programs and the Finder.

Note that different versions of applications, such as MacPaint, are developed for use with certain System File and Finder versions and may not work with others. Hence, changing the System File or Finder can have important consequences and should be done only after careful consideration.

Figure 4.1 Getting information about the Finder version you are using.

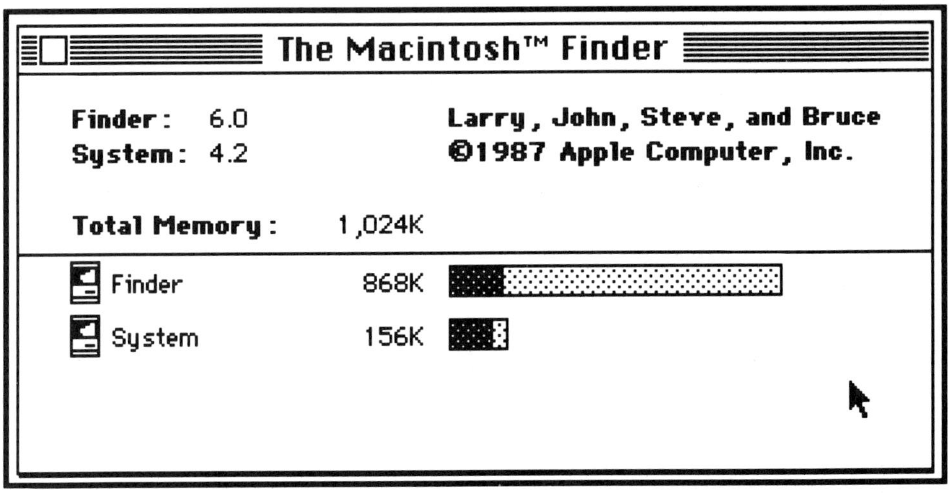

Figure 4.2 Determining Finder and System versions and RAM allocations.

If any of the following operations do not function as described, you may wish to ask your instructor to help you. It is possible that your computer is using different versions of the Finder and/or System File, and that may cause the steps described here (which are for the versions shown in Figure 4.2) to differ slightly from those you need to use on your computer.

You will soon learn to perform from the *desktop* all the resource management activities mentioned in this section and more, but it is also possible for some of the activities to be performed from *inside* application contexts such as MacPaint. Because of the uniformity of the way resource management commands are issued within various application packages, once you have learned about their function on the desktop, you will understand their function in essentially every other application context.

To find which resource management commands are available to use within an application, you need to consult the menu bar of the application that you are currently executing. If the desired command is present and displayed in bold type in a pull-down menu, its use is available within the application context. If the command is absent or dimmed, then you must set the context back to the desktop to perform the desired resource management operation.

Exercise Set 4.1

1. Give some examples of computer system resources.
2. Explain why you think it is important for you to learn to manage the resources you listed in exercise 1?
3. Which of the resource management capabilities described briefly in this section would you consider most important to know?
4. Describe the primary function of the Finder program.
5. Briefly tell how the MiniFinder and MultiFinder programs differ from the Finder program?
6. How can you find out which version of the Finder program and System File your computer has installed?

7. Suppose you have had your Macintosh for a while. Why might you not want to install the newest version of the Finder and System Files on your computer?

4.2 DISK MANIPULATIONS ON THE DESKTOP

In this section, you will learn some of the basic techniques for managing your disk collection. In particular, you will learn how to create a backup copy of a floppy disk by copying the contents of one entire disk to another disk. In addition, you will learn how to transfer all of the information on a floppy disk to a hard disk.

COPYING AN ENTIRE FLOPPY DISK TO ANOTHER FLOPPY DISK.   Occasionally, you will want to **copy one floppy disk to another**. For example, you should make a backup copy of each of the disks you receive when you purchase software and then use the backup disk. In the event the latter disk becomes corrupted and can no longer be read from or written to, you may make another copy of the original disk and begin again.

As with software applications, backup copies should always be kept of important work you are doing with the computer. When a floppy disk drive reads information from a disk, the disk read-write head of the drive is literally touching the disk surface. Eventually this contact will wear away the surface and the disk will become unreadable. Also on rare occasions a mechanical malfunction of the disk drive mechanism can occur that will destroy a floppy disk. Thus, you should never assume that information on a floppy disk is permanently stored or recoverable. Backup copies of anything valuable or important to you should always be made! This takes only a few moments and should become a habit. Consider the hours of time that you will invest in working with your computer and you will see why this is wise advice to follow!

COPYING DISKS ON A SINGLE–DISK–DRIVE COMPUTER.   Suppose you have a *one-disk-drive system* and wish to copy an entire disk. The disk to be copied should be placed in the floppy drive. After its icon appears on the desktop, use the *Eject* command in the **File** menu to remove the disk from the drive. Next place the disk that will receive the copy (the destination disk) into the drive. (Note that completing the copy process will overwrite any information currently on the destination disk.) Now you will have icons for two disks on the desktop. Drag the icon of the disk to be copied onto the icon of the disk to receive the copy. Be very careful that you do not confuse the icons for the source and destination disks!

For example, to copy the disk named *Chapter Two* to the disk named *Backup*, drag the *Chapter Two* disk icon onto the *Backup* disk icon as shown in Figure 4.3. Note that the line connecting the icon and its moved outline as shown in Figure 4.3 does not actually appear on the screen as you perform the drag operation; it is shown here only to indicate the direction of the movement of the icon. *Remember that the contents of the disk named* Backup *will be lost and be replaced with the contents of the disk named* Chapter Two.

An *Exchange Disk* message of the type shown in Figure 4.4 may be displayed a number of times during this copy process. You must follow these instructions to completion; otherwise you may lose information on *both* disks.

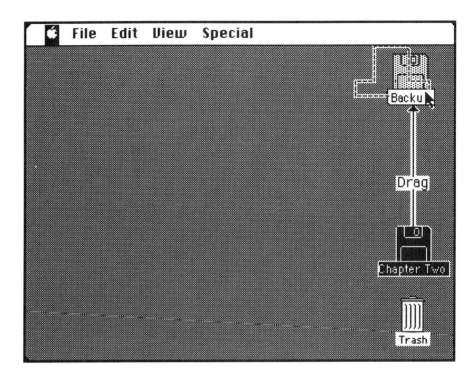

Figure 4.3 Copying an entire disk to a similar disk.

Once your pointer is over the *Backup* disk, its icon will darken. Release the button and the copying will begin. The copy operation will not occur until the *Backup* disk becomes highlighted. If you fail to move the cursor properly over the *Backup* disk, you simply move the *Chapter Two* icon to a different location on the desktop, and no copying will occur.

COPYING THE CONTENTS OF ONE DISK TO ANOTHER USING TWO FLOPPY DISK DRIVES. If you have two floppy disk drives available on your system, insert the disk to be copied in one drive and the disk that is to receive the copy in the other drive. Drag the icon of the disk to be copied over the icon of the disk to receive the copy as described earlier. Follow the instructions that appear on the screen. You may need to insert the disk containing the System File to complete the copy.

COPYING A FLOPPY DISK TO A HARD DISK. A special case arises when an entire **floppy disk is copied to a hard disk**. Often the hard disk is the system disk, and its icon, which is shown in Figure 4.5, is in the upper right-hand corner of the desktop. The process for dragging the icon of the disk to be copied is the same as that just described. However, because the hard disk has a much greater storage

Figure 4.4 The *Exchange Disk* message.

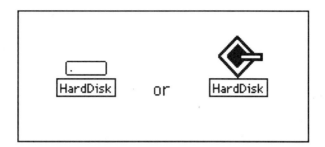

Figure 4.5 Forms of the *HardDisk* icon.

capacity than a 3.5-inch disk (perhaps 20 to 80 times as much capacity), there may be room for many of these smaller disks to be copied to one hard disk.

The Finder assumes that you do not intend to replace the *entire* contents of the hard disk with the contents of the floppy disk. Therefore, when a floppy disk is copied to the hard disk, none of the previous information on the hard disk will be removed. To keep the files of the floppy disk together, all the floppy disk's information is copied to the hard disk as the contents of a folder having the same name as the floppy disk. A message of the type shown in Figure 4.6 is displayed to remind you of this action.

Note that if you wish to copy one entire floppy disk to another floppy on a system having available one floppy disk drive and a hard disk, it will normally be faster to copy the floppy first to the hard disk and then to copy the disk folder from the hard disk to the second floppy.

ERASING A DISK.   At times, you may wish to remove all the information stored on a disk, often because you want to use the disk for other purposes and thus reclaim all the storage. This process is called **erasing**, or reinitializing, a disk. The most efficient way to erase a disk is to use the *Erase Disk* command in the **Special** menu, after selecting the disk to be erased. The message shown in Figure 4.7 will be displayed to give you an opportunity to change your mind. Read this message carefully to be sure that the name of the disk is the one you wish to erase. Once the erase process is started, *all* the information on the disk is lost. *There is no option to undo this command!* Click inside the two-sided button if your computer uses 800K floppy drives. Click inside the one-sided button if your system uses 400K floppy drives.

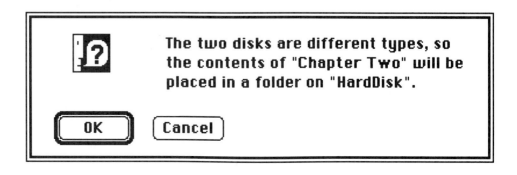

Figure 4.6 Copying to different disk types.

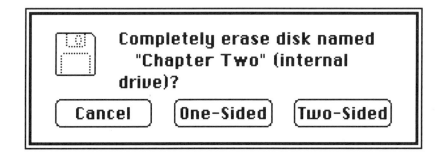

Figure 4.7 The *Erase Disk* message.

Exercise Set 4.2

1. Give two different reasons for wanting to copy an entire floppy disk to another floppy disk.
2. Describe the process for copying one floppy disk to another, assuming that you have a one floppy disk drive system.
3. Repeat exercise 2, assuming you have a two-floppy-disk-drive system.
4. How does copying a floppy disk to a hard disk differ from copying a floppy disk to another floppy disk?
5. How do you erase a disk?

Computer Practice 4.2

1. Locate the disk on which you stored the MacPaint paintings *House1*, *House2*, and *Faces1* in the folder *Paintings1* that you created in completing Computer Practice 3.5. If you did not complete that computer exercise, go back and complete it before proceeding with the computer exercises in this chapter.
2. Insert and initialize a second disk and name it *MyBackup*. Copy the first disk (with your paintings on it) directly to the new disk using the technique described in this section that is applicable to your computer system.
3. Open the disk *MyBackup* and verify that the copy procedure you employed in step 2 was successful. Close the disk window.
4. Select the disk *MyBackup* and reinitialize it using the *Erase Disk* command under the **Special** menu.
5. Open the disk *MyBackup* and verify that its contents have been erased.
6. Now, if your computer has a hard disk, copy the disk with your paintings to the hard disk. Open the hard disk and then find and open the folder that contains the contents of the disk you just copied to the hard disk in step 5. Finally, copy this folder to the disk *MyBackup*.

4.3 UNDERSTANDING HIERARCHICAL FILE SYSTEMS

Before we discuss resource management operations with files, it is important that you understand the nature of the **hierarchical file system** (HFS) that you will be using on the Macintosh computer. (*Note:* Older versions of the Macintosh do not support HFS—your instructor will provide information needed if you are using such a machine.) As we have seen in some of our prior examples, it is possible to have the desktop organized so that folders appear in other folders. Using this feature of file management, you will be able to build a hierarchy of file and folder organization, which allows for efficient and productive retrieval of information that you have stored on your disks.

Many computer systems make use of hierarchical file systems, including computers using the UNIX operating system and the popular MS-DOS operating system for the IBM PC and its compatibles. Although the Macintosh hierarchical system will be somewhat simpler to understand because of its direct analogy with a filing cabinet and its familiar folder filing system, what you learn here will be immediately applicable to a hierarchical file system of any computer, not just the Macintosh.

At the top of the hierarchy of the Macintosh file system is a disk. As you have already seen, there may be more than one disk drive attached to the computer, and certainly a floppy disk drive may have more than one disk used with it. Within a given disk, you may place files and folders. Each folder may in turn hold files and other folders. A typical arrangement is diagrammed in Figure 4.8. Here there are shown three disks named *Correspondence, Classes,* and *HardDisk.*

BUILDING A HIERARCHY WITH FOLDERS.   The steps necessary to build the hierarchical arrangement of files for the *Classes* disk in Figure 4.8 are now given. First the disk itself would be initialized and named *Classes* using the process described in Chapter 2. Next, with the *Classes* disk open and its window the active window, the command *New Folder* would be selected from the **File** menu. You would name the newly provided folder *Math.* A second new folder would be acquired and you would name it *Spanish.* Both folders would be at the top level in the *Classes* disk context, because the *Classes* window was the active window (or context) when the *New Folder* command was issued for acquiring each of these folders.

By opening the folder *Math* and then obtaining a new folder, the new folder can be created within the *Math* context. You would name this new folder *Calculus.*

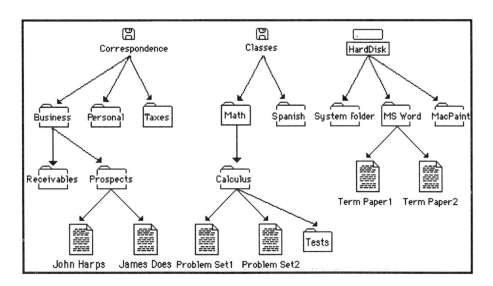

Figure 4.8 An example hierarchical file organization.

You now have added paths through the hierarchy shown in Figure 4.8 down to the *Calculus* folder. Next, after creating two documents called *Problem Set1* and *Problem Set2* (using some word processing application), those documents are placed at the level of the hierarchy shown in Figure 4.8 by placing them inside the *Calculus* folder. (You will see how to do this later.) Finally, while the *Calculus* folder is open and is the active window, a new folder is obtained and given the name *Tests*.

Exercise Set 4.3

1. Explain what is meant by a hierarchical file system.
2. Is the Macintosh the only computer that uses a hierarchical file system?
3. Describe briefly how you set up a file hierarchy on a disk for the Macintosh.
4. A Macintosh folder can hold individual files and other folders. Give an example in which this arrangement would be particularly useful.

4.4 FILE MANIPULATIONS ON THE DESKTOP

The Finder provides some very convenient ways to manage your disks' **file and folder hierarchies**. In this section we examine some of these disk resource management methods.

RESTRUCTURING A DISK'S FILE HIERARCHY.   After establishing a hierarchical file organization on a disk, you may easily change the structure of the hierarchy. This can be done by simply dragging the icon for a folder or file out of the folder whose window is active and then placing that icon into another folder's window, or over a different folder's icon. In this manner the file or folder whose icon was moved is placed at a different location in the hierarchy. Note that if a folder is moved in this way, all its contents (including other folders and their contents) are moved with it to the new location within the hierarchy.

For example, dragging the folder *Calculus* into any area of the window of the *Classes* disk changes the structure of that disk's hierarchy. In this case, *Calculus*, *Math*, and *Spanish* each would now be at the same level. This new hierarchy is shown in Figure 4.9.

Alternatively, it is just as simple to place a folder or file deeper into the hierarchy. As mentioned earlier, if a folder or file is dragged to a position over the icon of another folder, it will be inserted into the latter folder. By using the shift click method described in Chapter 2, several folders and/or files can be placed inside a folder at the same time.

You should practice using these tools for managing the resources of the file system. You will not feel comfortable using your computer until you have attained complete mastery of both setting up a file system hierarchy and "navigating" (moving up and down) within the hierarchy of a disk.

COPYING FILES AND FOLDERS FROM ONE DISK TO ANOTHER.   You have seen earlier in this chapter how to copy one entire disk to another. Often it is desirable to copy a file or a folder from one disk to another and position it in the new disk's file hierarchy.

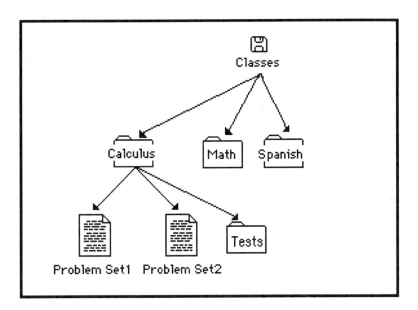

Figure 4.9 Changing the hierarchical structure.

The process of copying a file or folder from one disk to another is similar to the process just described for moving these objects within their own disk's hierarchy:

- Make sure that icons for both disks are displayed on the desktop. Recall that if you are using a single floppy disk drive system, this may require ejecting one disk and inserting the other.
- Place the disk that contains the file or folder that you wish to copy in a floppy disk drive.
- Open a window into the disk and open any folders as necessary so that the icon of the file or folder you wish to copy can be seen in the active window.
- If necessary, reposition the windows on the desktop so that you can see the icon of the destination disk.
- Select and drag the icon of the file or folder to be copied to a position over the icon of the destination disk. The latter will then be highlighted. When the mouse button is released, the copy process will begin.

If messages to exchange disks appear, follow them carefully as described before. There is an important difference in this process and the process for moving icons around on the same disk. At the conclusion of the copy process, *both disks* will contain the file or folder that is being copied. You may verify the presence of the icon on the new disk by opening a window into the disk. In Figure 4.10, the file *Chapter 2*, which is in the active window *Chapter Two*, is shown being copied to *HardDisk*.

   Just as in the case of moving folders on the same disk, when a folder is copied, all its contents (files and folders) are also copied to the new disk. Of course, once you have copied information to another disk, you may organize it in any way you like by opening that disk and then placing the copied information into folders.

   By properly opening folders on the disk to which you wish to copy, you may copy information *directly* into a folder on that disk. For example, if you wished to

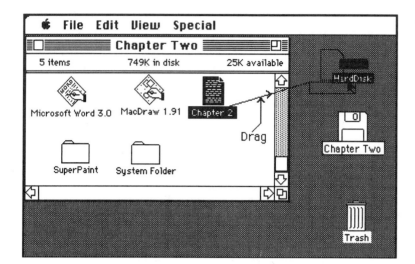

Figure 4.10 Copying a file to another disk.

copy the file *Chapter 2* from the disk *Chapter Two* to the folder *Book Chapters* on the hard disk, you would proceed almost as outlined earlier. The difference would be that before copying the file, you would have opened *HardDisk* and the folder *Book Chapters* on that disk. By positioning the associated windows carefully, it will then be possible to drag *Chapter 2* from the active window, *Chapter Two,* directly to the window *Book Chapters*. The result will be exactly the same as if you had first copied *Chapter 2* to *HardDisk* as described previously and then opened *HardDisk* and placed the copied *Chapter 2* into the folder *Book Chapters*, in the way we described earlier.

REMOVING A FILE. Removing a file, that is, deleting it from a disk, is accomplished by dragging the file icon into the *Trash* icon, normally found at the bottom right-hand corner of the desktop. If you make a mistake and discard a file that is still needed, the file can be recovered by opening the *Trash* icon and dragging the icon of the file back to the appropriate window—as long as neither you nor the Finder has emptied the trash. Figure 4.11 shows the document icon *Chapter 2* being dragged to the *Trash* icon.

The primary purpose of removing a file is to free additional space on a disk. Dragging the icon of a file to the trash does not free any space directly on the disk. The trash must be emptied before the space occupied by the file is returned to usable space on the disk. If the trash can contains unemptied icons, it will be bulging at its seams. (Note that this is not true for early Macintoshes.)

To empty the trash and thus recover needed space on the appropriate disk, select the *Empty Trash* command from the **Special** menu. The space formerly occupied by the files in the trash can will then be reclaimed, and the *Trash* icon will resume its normal shape. Once the Macintosh has emptied an icon from the trash, the associated file is lost and cannot be recovered; hence, placing icons into the trash should be done with considerable caution.

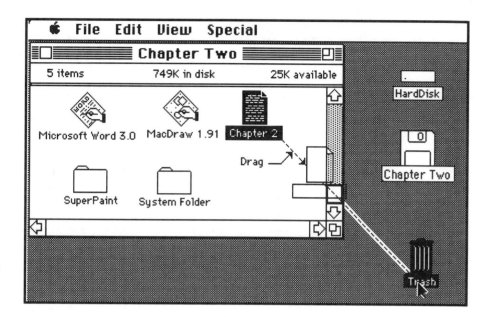

Figure 4.11 Removing an icon by dragging it into the *Trash* icon.

The operation of dragging the icon of a *disk* into the trash can does not discard the contents of the entire disk. Instead the disk is simply ejected from the disk drive and its icon is removed from the desktop. (On early Macintoshes, the disk icon is merely returned to its previous position.) To erase an entire disk you must use the *Erase Disk* command.

DUPLICATING A FILE.   It is a good idea to create a copy of any important file or folder. In that way if the original is accidentally altered, you will still have a copy. A copy may be made by first selecting the icon for the file or folder and then choosing the *Duplicate* command from the **File** menu. The file or folder will be duplicated and the name given the duplicate will be the original name, with the words *Copy of* prefixed, as shown in Figure 4.12 for the folder *mac book*.

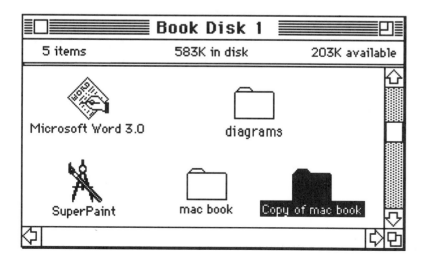

Figure 4.12 Duplicating a file.

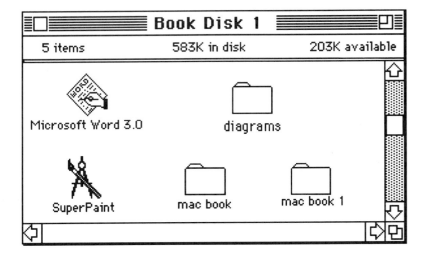

Figure 4.13 Renaming an icon that has been previously selected.

RENAMING AN ICON.   If you wish, you can rename an icon. For example, if you are making changes to a document and there is a reasonable possibility that you may want to revert to some earlier version, then you could rename each newly duplicated document to reflect the sequence of changes. To rename any icon, select the icon and type in the new name. Figure 4.13 shows the result of renaming the icon *Copy of mac book* to *mac book 1*.

EDITING THE NAME OF AN ICON.   Rather than retyping the entire name of the icon to change its name as described earlier, you can edit the name of the icon. By *edit* we mean delete, insert, or modify a few of the characters in the name.

To edit an icon name, first the icon should be selected. When the mouse pointer is moved to the line of text at the bottom of the icon, the pointer changes its shape into an *I-beam*. This change in shape is shown on the left side of Figure 4.14. The I-beam pointer can be moved anywhere in the line of text. If the mouse is clicked, a narrow line called the *text insertion pointer* appears at the current position of the I-beam pointer. If the I-beam pointer is moved away from the icon text line, the text insertion pointer will remain in its position, and the mouse pointer will revert to its usual arrow form. (See Figure 4.14.) Any characters typed from the keyboard at this time will be inserted starting at the position of this text insertion pointer, that is, between the *S* and the *a*. Each time the *Backspace* (or *Delete*) key is pressed, a character to the left of the text insertion pointer will be erased.

Figure 4.14 Editing of the name of a selected icon with the text insertion pointer.

If the I-beam pointer is positioned over the name and then dragged (while the button is depressed) along the name, a contiguous string of characters is selected (as shown by being highlighted) for modification. These characters will be replaced by any character string then typed from the keyboard. The *Backspace* (or *Delete*) key, if pressed while the text string is highlighted, will remove the selected characters from the name.

USING FIND FILE.   A hierarchical file system allows you to organize your files so that they are easy to find, even if you have hundreds of them. However, you must develop some conventions in structuring your folders and files. If you use no discipline in structuring them, you will soon become lost in a jumble of folders, and you will be unable to find anything!

If you have developed a reasonable organization method, you will usually have little difficulty finding what you need. However, on occasion, you may lose track of where in the hierarchy you have stored a file. Rather than hunting through folder after folder to locate it, there is a better way—if you can remember the name of the file. Under the **Apple** menu is a command *Find File* that can be used to show you the path that must be followed from the disk level down to where your file is located. For example, Figure 4.15 shows the result of performing *Find File* when the file name *Problem Set1*, from the example hierarchy of Figure 4.8, has been typed in. The search is started by selecting the "man running" icon. It may be stopped by selecting the "stop sign" icon. The *Find File* command will also find matches for parts of a file name. For example, by typing "set" instead of the complete file name *Problem Set1* in the preceding example, you could still locate the desired file.

It is possible (although not particularly advisable) for you to have two files with the same name, if they have been stored in separate folders. If this is the case for the file name you enter in the *Find File* command dialog box, there will be several lines in the rectangle in the middle of the box. In Figure 4.15 there is only one file whose name is *Problem Set1* on the disk *Classes*. Note the path to be followed in opening the disk and folders (as shown in the rectangle in the lower right-hand corner of the dialog box) agrees with that shown in Figure 4.8.

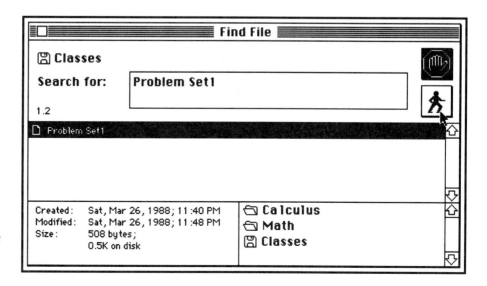

Figure 4.15 Using *Find File* to locate the path to a particular file.

The reason we can use the same file name for different files (in different folders) is that the Macintosh uses the path *plus* the name of the file to identify a file by its **complete path name.** To identify the file in Figure 4.15, the complete path name *Classes:Math/Calculus/Problem Set1* is actually used by the computer. Thus, we could have many files with the same simple name whose complete path names are quite distinct. The computer is not confused about which file we are looking for because we must always specify the path to the file. We can do this explicitly by making a selection from the *Find File* dialog box, or by opening the appropriate folders, and hence setting the context, until the file icon we desire is in the active window.

For example, to get to the file *Problem Set1,* you would need to navigate your way through the hierarchical file system opening the folders *Math* and *Calculus,* until the *Problem Set1* icon is shown in the active window. Because the computer is given the path to the file in this process, there is no ambiguity about which file you intended to use.

If you attempt to move two icons with the same name to the same folder within your hierarchy, you would be requesting the placement of two files with the same complete path name. This is not allowed. One of them would replace the other! If the message *Replace file of the same name* appears in a dialog box, you should understand that your requested operation has positioned two files having the same name with identical paths in the hierarchy. If you proceed, the file already in place within the folder to which you are moving a file will be replaced (and hence destroyed) as a result of your requested operation. There are many cases when you will wish exactly this action to be taken (when you are updating a file by moving a more recent copy to the folder, for example). However, it should be obvious that this is a procedure that should be done with caution.

Exercise Set 4.4

1. In what ways can a disk's hierarchical file organization be restructured?

2. Suppose folder C is placed within folder B, which is in turn within folder A on a disk. Describe the method for placing folder C at the same level in the disk's file hierarchy as folder A. Make a simple sketch to illustrate.

3. Referring to the original hierarchical structure described in exercise 2, suppose that folder D is a folder in the disk window (along with folder A). What steps are required to restructure the file hierarchy so that folder D will be found within the same context as folder C?

4. Describe carefully the procedure for copying folder B found within folder A, which is at the top hierarchical level disk, *Disk1*, to the top hierarchical level on the different disk, *Disk2*.

5. Describe two procedures for copying folder B of exercise 4 from *Disk1* into folder W, found at the top hierarchical level on *Disk2*.

6. How does the effect of dragging a file icon from one folder to another on the same disk differ from that of dragging the same icon from a folder on one disk to a folder on a different disk?

7. Describe the steps required to rename an icon.

8. Describe the process required to duplicate a file or folder.

9. How is a file or folder removed from a disk? Is the space on a disk occupied by a file or folder immediately available for reuse when that file or folder is removed from the disk? Explain.

10. Describe *all* the steps required to change the name of an icon from *Chap 2* to *Chapter 2*, if this is done by editing the name.

11. How is it possible for two files to have the same name and not be confused by the Macintosh operating system?

12. What is meant by a file's complete path name? Give a simple example.

13. Can the icons for two files with the same name be located within the same folder window? What happens if you attempt to move an icon to a folder where an icon by the same name already exists?

Computer Practice 4.4

1. Locate the disk containing the MacPaint paintings that you created as a result of Computer Practice 3.5. That disk (which we assume is named *MyDisk*) should have the following file hierarchy.

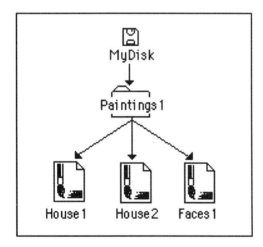

Create a second desktop folder on this disk and name it *Face Paintings*, generating the following hierachy.

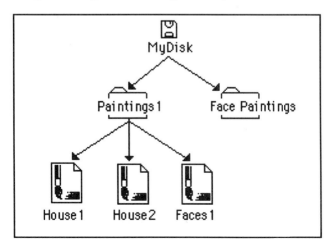

2. Move your painting *Faces1* inside folder *Face Paintings* using the techniques described in this section. After this is done, move the folder *Face Paintings* inside the folder *Paintings1* to create the following hierarchy.

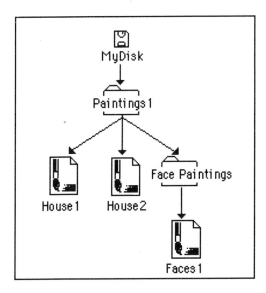

3. Close all windows open in *MyDisk*. Now open the appropriate folder windows and verify that your file–folder hierarchy matches the one shown in the previous figure.

4. Make the *Paintings* folder window the active window. Create a new folder and name it *House Paintings*. Move the two paintings *House1* and *House2* into this folder, creating the following hierarchy. Verify this hierarchy by closing all windows, then opening the appropriate windows one by one.

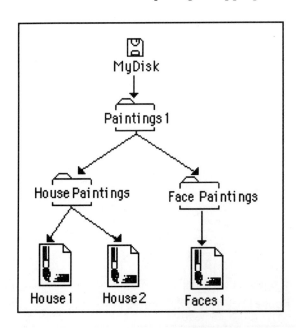

5. Close all windows and return to the desktop context. Create a new folder and name it *Weird Faces*. Next move this folder so that it is within the folder *Face Paintings*. Note that there are several ways to do this. You could first open the window for *Face Paintings* and move the new folder in directly. Or you could first move the new folder into the *Paintings1* folder, then open the *Paintings1* folder and drag the new folder to the folder *Face Paintings*. In either case, you will end up with the following hierarchy. Again, check this hierarchy. Leave your disk with this hierarchical structure because we will use this hierarchy again in the next computer exercise.

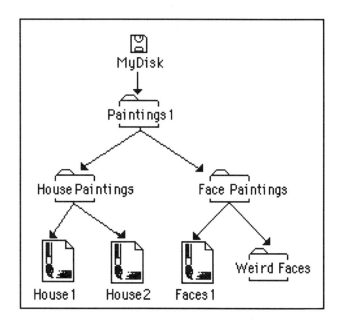

4.5 USING THE HIERARCHICAL FILE SYSTEM FROM WITHIN AN APPLICATION

In the previous section, we discussed in some detail the nature of the hierarchical file system that you will be using on the Macintosh computer, and you learned the basic techniques needed for managing and navigating within file hierarchies from the desktop context. To use application software packages, you will also need to understand how to navigate within this hierarchical file system when you are inside an application program.

When you are in the desktop context, you can often see windows for each of the open folders. However, from inside an application program, it will not be nearly as easy to visualize the relationships among various folders and files. You must rely upon an overview perspective of your file hierarchies (even for several disks at once), as illustrated in Figure 4.8. This doesn't mean that you must remember all the details of such a diagram—just the organization of the overall structure.

In the desktop context, you may move from one disk to another by selecting the icon of interest and then double-clicking to open a window to the disk to see its contents. When you are inside an application such as MacPaint, however, you cannot see the desktop. Thus, to manipulate documents in an application (e.g., to open them or to decide where in the file structure your work will be stored), you must use the **File** menu *Open, Save* or *Save As* commands, just as you did in the MacPaint exercises of Chapter 3.

These commands provide the same flexibility for **navigating within the file system hierarchy** as you have at the desktop context. However, you must manipulate the folders and disks in a slightly different way; that is, you must use a slightly different language. For example, to switch from one disk to another disk within an application, you must use the *Drive* option presented in the dialog box that results from either the *Open, Save* or *Save As* commands under the **File** menu.

The *Open, Save,* and *Save As* commands present slightly different dialog boxes. In the discussion and examples that follow, we will use the *Open* dialog box, but the ideas can be easily transferred to the other dialog boxes. Remember that the *Save* operation presents a dialog box only if the document has not been previously saved; that is, only if it is currently untitled. Finally, the dialog boxes for different applications are slightly different, but they have the same function that we describe here.

A typical *Open* dialog box is illustrated in Figure 4.16. The current context shown is the *Calculus* folder. This is equivalent to having the active window be the *Calculus* folder window. Note that the contents of the folder are listed in the rectangular area in the left center of the dialog box. (We shall call this area the *scroll window.*) Note also the name of the current disk, *Classes,* above the *Eject* button to the right of the scroll window.

We can pull down a menu that will show all the folders in the current complete path name for the folder that is "active." This is illustrated in Figure 4.17. (You will find it helpful to look back at Figure 4.8 frequently as you read this section to keep the example hierarchy clearly in mind.) By selecting a folder from this menu, you can get a new active folder.

If you select the *Math* folder as the new active folder, you will get the scroll window depicted in Figure 4.18. In that figure, the pull-down menu of folders in

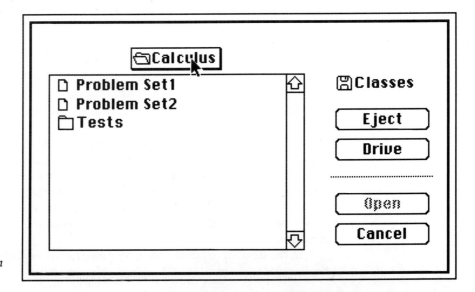

Figure 4.16 A typical *Open* dialog box.

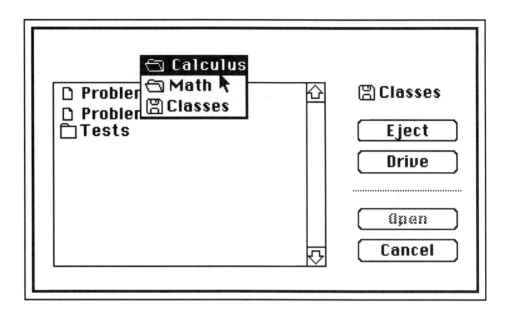

Figure 4.17 Viewing the path of folders to the *Calculus* folder.

the current complete path name is also shown. Because the *Math* folder is at the top of the disk hierarchy, only the folder itself and the disk *Classes* are shown in the menu.

If you now select the disk *Classes* as the new context, you will see a scroll window like the one shown in Figure 4.19. Note that the folder *Spanish* is now present for the first time in our discussion. It has not been visible before, because it was not accessible at the context levels within the hierarchy at which we were positioned.

To *Open* a document or perform a *Save As* into the *Spanish* folder, you could double-click on this folder displayed in the scroll window; this would put you immediately into its context. Hence, the diagram of Figure 4.8 illustrates all

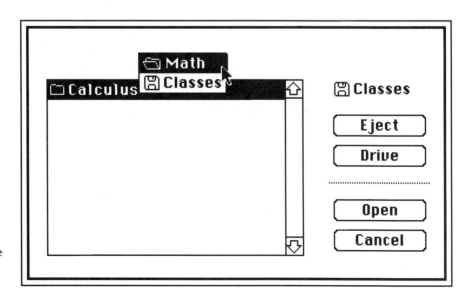

Figure 4.18 Moving up one level to the *Math* folder context.

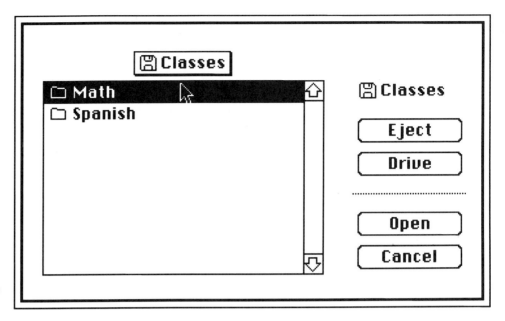

Figure 4.19 Moving up to the disk level in the *Classes* context.

possible paths by which you can move from the highest-level disk context, by opening in turn one folder at a time, to reach the folder that you wish to be active.

The *Drive* command within the *Open, Save,* or *Save As* command dialog boxes of any application allows you to choose the disk from which you will read your file or to which you will store your file. By successively clicking on the *Drive* button you can move horizontally across the diagram in Figure 4.8 at the highest level of the hierarchy to select *any* of the disk drives attached to the computer. Thus, the disks *Correspondence, Classes* and *HardDisk* will appear successively as the current context disk. The choices also would include network file server disks, if you had allocated them previously.

The *Eject* button in this dialog box allows you to exchange the disk in a floppy disk drive. Thus, you may choose which disk you will use from your entire collection of disks. The *Eject* button will be shown as dimmed text if a hard disk drive is the drive selected, as it is not possible to eject the disk of a hard disk drive.

Note that you may move at will up, down, and sideways in the overall hierarchical structure shown in Figure 4.8. When you wish to move up in the hierarchy, pull down the menu from the folder icon shown above the scroll window in the dialog box and select a folder at a higher level. All folders and files available in this context will be shown to you in the scroll window. When you wish to go deeper into the hierarchy, open a folder within the scroll window by double-clicking on its icon symbol. Any possible context within the entire file system hierarchy can be reached by issuing commands of these two kinds and by changing the active disk using the *Drive* command.

Exercise Set 4.5

1. When working within an application package, why is it important to have an overview of your file hierarchy?

2. How do you initiate a search for a file to be opened within an application package (without quitting the application)?

3. When searching for a file to open within an application package, describe carefully the method used to move upward in a disk's file hierarchy.

4. Describe carefully the method used to access a file that is embedded at a level lower than the currently displayed context in an *Open* dialog box.

5. How would you access, from within an application, a file that is in a different folder at the same level in the disk hierarchy as the currently active folder?

6. How do you change the disk context from an *Open* dialog box?

7. How many floppy disks can be accessed from within an application before you must quit the application and exchange floppy disks? Explain.

Computer Practice 4.5

1. Open the MacPaint application by double-clicking on the MacPaint icon. When you are given the blank screen *Untitled*, close this screen by choosing the *Close* command from the **File** menu. Next select the *Open* command from the **File** menu. You should see a dialog box that looks something like the following one. The various documents and folders shown are those on the hard disk from which MacPaint was accessed for this example. What you actually see will depend upon the particular disk or folder from which you access MacPaint on your computer.

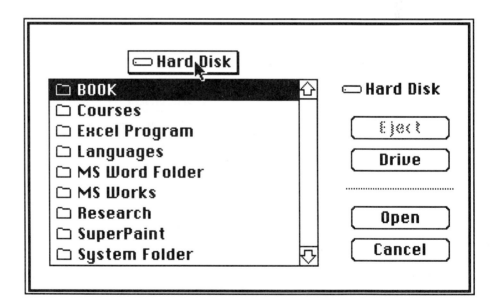

2. Insert the disk *MyDisk* that was configured in Computer Practice 4.4, step 5. If you already have a different disk inserted, click the *Eject* button in the preceding dialog box. When the inserted disk is ejected, insert the disk *MyDisk*. Then click the *Drive* button until a dialog box like the following one appears.

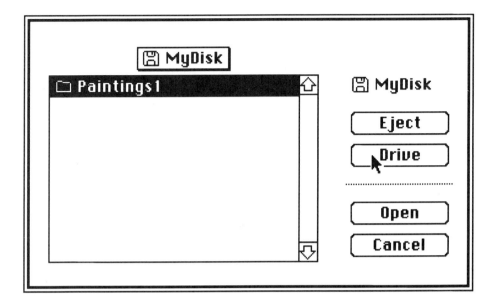

3. Open (by either double-clicking on its name or selecting the name and clicking the *Open* button) the folder *Paintings1* to generate the following dialog box. Notice how you are working down the hierarchy that we diagrammed in Computer Practice 4.4, step 5.

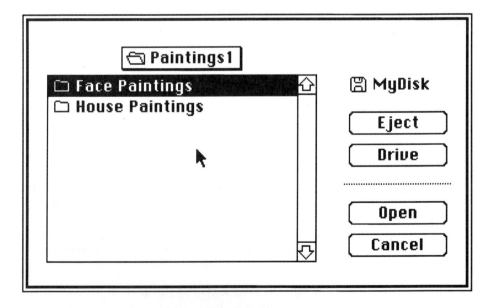

4. Next open the *Face Paintings* folder, to generate the following dialog box.

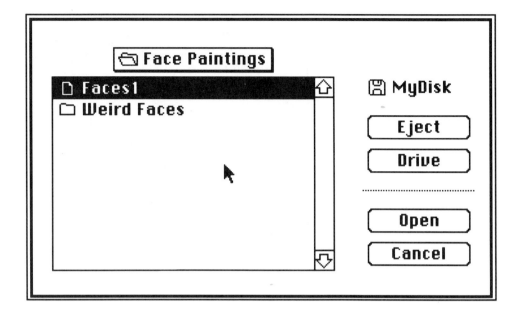

5. Now open the painting *Faces1*. Once this painting is opened in MacPaint, modify it by erasing the faces there and creating a "weird" face or two of your own. (perhaps something like the following one, which was created using various brush shapes).

When you have finished your painting, select the command *Save* As from the **File** menu. You should see a dialog box like the following one.

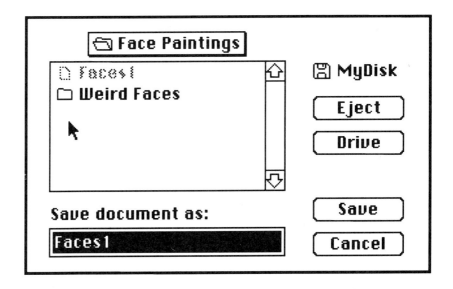

6. In the preceding dialog box, open the folder *Weird Faces*. Then rename your painting *Weird1* by typing the new name into the keyboard. (Note that the old name *Faces1* is already highlighted for replacement.) Your dialog box should then look like the one following.

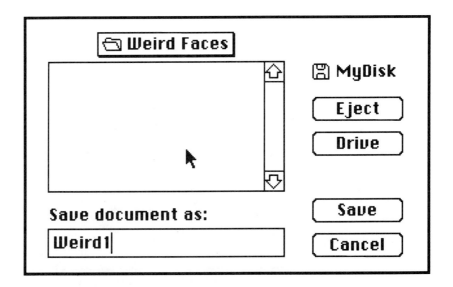

Clicking the *Save* button will save your modified painting as *Weird1* in the folder *Weird Faces*, leaving your disk structured as follows.

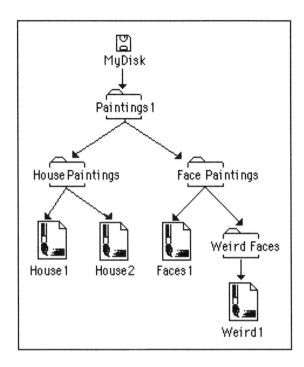

7. Quit the MacPaint application and return to the desktop context. Open your disk *MyDisk* and by opening the appropriate folders, verify that it has the preceding hierarchical structure.

8. Open the MacPaint application again and practice finding and opening the various paintings stored on the disk *MyDisk*. Do as many of these activities as is required to make you confident about navigating around your disk's hierarchy from within the MacPaint context. When you finish, quit the MacPaint application.

9. From the desktop context, use the *Find File* command from the **Apple** menu to locate the painting *Weird1*. Note carefully how the system generates the complete path to the painting.

4.6 MANAGING PRINTING RESOURCES

You learned in Chapter 3 how to allocate a printer to use for printing information, whether you were connected to a network or had a printer dedicated to your computer. In this section we discuss some related matters to allow you to have maximum flexibility using your printing resource.

PRINTER DRIVERS. To print on a printer the operating system program makes use of small programs called **printer drivers**. These programs convert the output from your application, such as MacPaint, into information that the printer needs to print the paintings you created. Your computer can use many different printers, and each one of them requires its own driver program.

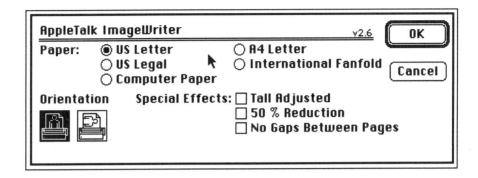

Figure 4.20 *Page Setup* command for the ImageWriter.

Driver programs for each printer must reside in the system folder. For example, the system folder usually has in it icons named *ImageWriter* and *LaserWriter*. These files contain the driver programs for the respective printers. If you do not have a *LaserWriter* icon in your system folder, you will not be able to print on the Apple LaserWriter printer, even if one is attached to your computer or an AppleTalk network to which you have access. All peripherals such as plotters, scanners, and so on, in addition to printers, must have drivers in the system folder to translate input or output for your application into meaningful instructions for use by the device.

DEFINING THE PAGE SETUP. Printers come in different sizes and are capable of printing on paper of different sizes and in different orientations. Specification of these available resources is normally done using the *Page Setup* command under the **File** menu. Figure 4.20 shows the result of selecting the *Page Setup* command from the desktop context when the ImageWriter has been previously selected using the *Chooser* command (from the **Apple** menu).

As shown in this screen image, a variety of paper size choices can be used. Some control can be exercised about the size of the output to be printed. For example, there is an option to use a 50 percent size reduction in the output by clicking on the square button so named.

In addition, the orientation of the text or painting on the page can be selected. In the lower left-hand side of the dialog box is shown the icons of a printer in which an image is printed across the narrow width of the paper, the usual orientation. Alternatively, the information may be printed oriented along the length of the page rather than the width. Pointing and clicking will choose between the two orientations. Finally, if desired, no spacing need be inserted at the end of a page. Thus, if the *No Gaps Between Pages* box is checked, the printer treats the paper as if it is a long, continuous roll. Very large banners and/or drawings can be produced in this manner.

A similar dialog box is produced if the printer previously selected, using the *Chooser* command, is the LaserWriter instead of the ImageWriter. An example of this dialog box is shown in Figure 4.21. You will note that a few added options are available.

One of the major differences between the LaserWriter dialog box in Figure 4.21 and the ImageWriter one in Figure 4.20 is that a variable degree of enlargement or reduction of the print size is possible. Font substitution may be used to produce higher-quality output than certain fonts selected in your application. Note that the orientation of the output on the page can be selected.

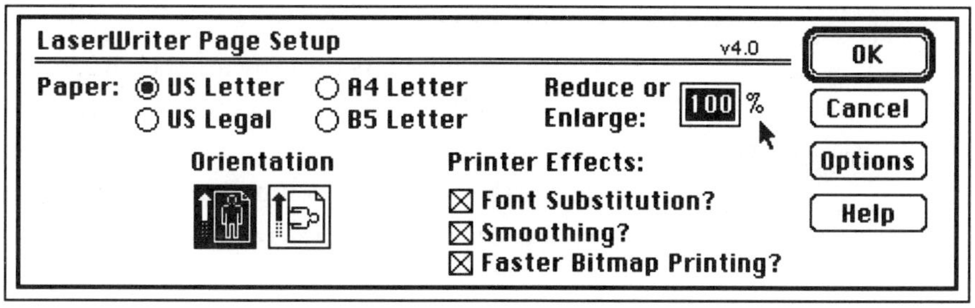

Figure 4.21 *Page Setup* command for LaserWriter.

Figure 4.22 shows the increased flexibility for controlling the output that is possible using the *Page Setup* **command** within the Microsoft Word application context. Many of the same options for controlling the printed output are available within the Microsoft Word word processing context as were available in the desktop context. Additional features specific to the word processing context also are provided, such as the ability to specify the margins within which the text will be printed. In Microsoft Word, the top, bottom, left, and right margin positions of the page are separately controlled. This allows precise formatting of the printed output. Here again, the orientation of the output on the page can be controlled: *Tall* means that the rows of the text are written across the narrower dimension of the paper; *Wide* means that the rows of text are oriented across the longer dimension.

The physical dimensions of a page can be independently specified. This allows the printer to produce normal letters, mailing labels, and so on. There is considerable control of the position of footnotes on the page as well as how these footnotes are numbered. Other kinds of applications provide similar features in the *Page Setup* command that will allow you to tailor printed output to your needs.

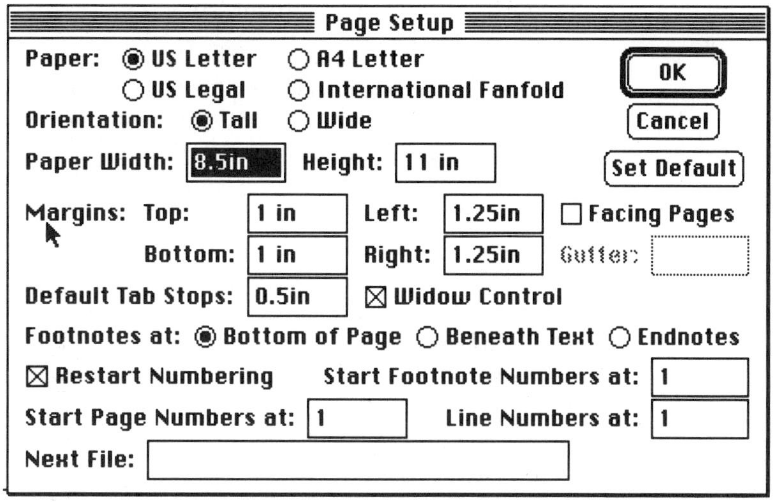

Figure 4.22 *Page Setup* command selected from the Microsoft Word context for the LaserWriter.

Exercise Set 4.6

1. What are printer drivers? Why are they important?

2. Where would you look to see what printer drivers are available for your Macintosh?

3. Where is the *Page Setup* command found? What is its purpose?

4. Describe some of the options available within the *Page Setup* command dialog box for the LaserWriter.

5. Give some differences in the options available for Page Setup for the Laser-Writer and the ImageWriter printers.

4.7 CLIPBOARD AND SCRAPBOOK RESOURCES

The *Clipboard* and the *Scrapbook* **files** are two very important resources that you control. You have seen examples of cutting or copying part of a picture in the MacPaint application. These same kinds of commands to *Cut, Copy*, and *Paste* pictures, drawings, and text exist in most other application contexts under the **Edit** menu. The Clipboard is essential for these commands, and the Scrapbook is very useful in conjunction with these commands for many applications.

The Clipboard and the Scrapbook serve an even more important function: They continue to exist outside of the contexts of any given application. This means that if you quit an application, the information that you have transferred into the Clipboard or the Scrapbook is not lost. As a result, if you open another application, the contents of the Clipboard or the Scrapbook that have been produced in a different application can be pasted into the working area of the new application. Hence, communication *between* different applications is not only possible in a Macintosh environment, but extremely easy. Because of the integration of text and graphics information possible with a bit-mapped display, a document produced by a word processing application can display pictures drawn in MacPaint or any other drawing or picture-producing environment. Columns of numbers or graphs produced by a spreadsheet may be easily copied into a word processing document using the Clipboard and/or Scrapbook.

MANAGING THE CLIPBOARD. The information contained in the Clipboard is determined by the most recent *Cut* or *Copy* command executed from within the **Edit** menu. This information is retained in the Clipboard until some other *Cut* or *Copy* command is carried out. There is an icon in the system folder named *Clipboard*, and this file is the current Clipboard. A *Paste* command issued from the **Edit** menu causes a copy of the information in the Clipboard to be entered into an application's context at the current cursor or pointer position. The *Paste* command does not empty the Clipboard, and any number of additional *Paste* commands may be performed transferring the same information each time. Note, however, that there is only one storage area associated with the Clipboard. The information stored there is lost as soon as another *Cut* or *Copy* command is issued. In contrast, the Scrapbook provides a storage area that can contain a large number of individual Clipboard images.

MANAGING THE SCRAPBOOK.   Information from the Clipboard may be retained on a disk for future reference. This is accomplished by first moving the information onto the Clipboard using a *Cut* or *Copy* command as discussed earlier. The information may then be pasted into the Scrapbook using the *Paste* command. The scrapbook is a file that is stored in the *System* folder. If you change the *System* folder for some reason, such as rebooting the computer from a new disk, the Scrapbook on the new disk will become the one used for all Scrapbook operations. Note that you can copy the Scrapbook from one disk to another because it is a file.

To paste information into the Scrapbook, select the *Scrapbook* command from the **Apple** menu. A window into the Scrapbook will appear (Figure 4.23). The scroll bar at the bottom of the window allows you to scroll through the different entries in the Scrapbook. At the left end of the scroll bar are shown two numbers separated by a slash. The number to the left of the slash is the number of the entry in the Scrapbook you currently are viewing. The number to the right of the slash shows the total number of entries currently in the Scrapbook. At the other end of the scroll bar is an indication of the kind of data format that is used to store the current entry. By selecting the *Paste* command from the **Edit** menu the current contents of the Clipboard can be inserted into the Scrapbook in a position *before* the currently displayed page.

To copy information from the Scrapbook into an application's context, it is first necessary to move the information into the Clipboard from the Scrapbook and then to copy the Clipboard into the application's context.

You can do this by first opening the Scrapbook by selecting the *Scrapbook* command from the **Edit** menu. The *Scrapbook* window will be displayed as the active window as shown in Figure 4.23. Next scroll through the Scrapbook using the scroll arrows until the information you wish to use is seen. Now select either the *Cut* or *Copy* command from the **Edit** menu. Note that *Cut* removes the entry

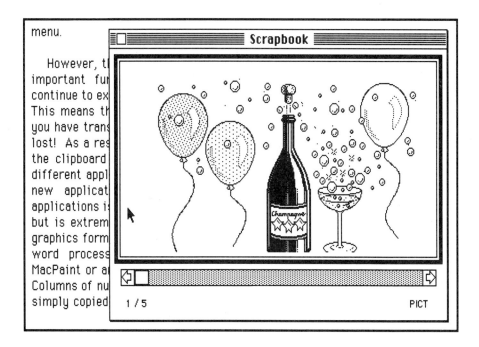

Figure 4.23 *Scrapbook* window activated from inside Microsoft Word.

from the Scrapbook when the information is transferred to the Clipboard. *Copy* copies the information to the Clipboard without removing it from the Scrapbook. At this point, the desired information is contained in the Clipboard.

Now make the application context the active window by either closing the *Scrapbook* window (by clicking in its close box) or clicking in the application window area. Finally, select the *Paste* command from the **Edit** menu. *Paste* will transfer the information from the Clipboard into the application context, as it is now the active context. Note that if you forget to deselect the Scrapbook, and hence leave its window as the active window, the contents of the Clipboard will simply be inserted into the Scrapbook again!

The Scrapbook can quickly become very large, particularly if you are copying numerous pictures into it. Because the Scrapbook is a file, it can use a very large amount of the space that you have available on a disk. To remove entries from the Scrapbook, it is necessary only to *Cut* them when the *Scrapbook* window is active. Because *Cut* removes an entry from the Scrapbook, each *Cut* operation decreases by one the number of entries in the Scrapbook. If desired, the entire Scrapbook can be emptied in this way—one at a time. Alternatively, you may drag the Scrapbook to the trash to remove it completely.

Exercise Set 4.7

1. What are the Clipboard and the Scrapbook?
2. Describe the use of the Clipboard for cutting and pasting operations.
3. How do the Clipboard and the Scrapbook differ?
4. Describe the method for storing information in the Scrapbook.
5. Describe the method for transferring information out of the Scrapbook.
6. Where are the Clipboard and the Scrapbook stored?

Computer Practice 4.7

1. Open the MacPaint application. Then open your painting *Weird1* by using the *Open* dialog boxes from within MacPaint, as you did in Computer Practice 4.5. Select part or all the open painting using the *marquee* tool. Choose the *Copy* command from the **Edit** menu to copy the *marquee*-selected part of your painting to the *Clipboard* file.

2. Close the painting *Weird1* and select the *New* command from the **Edit** menu. Now select the *Paste* command from the **Edit** menu. The part of the painting *Weird1* that you copied to the Clipboard in step 1 should now appear in the window *Untitled*.

3. Select the *Scrapbook* command from the **Apple** menu; the *Scrapbook* window should appear. Using the scroll bar located at the bottom of the *Scrapbook* window, examine some of the pictures in your *Scrapbook* file.

4. While the *Scrapbook* window is still open, select the *Paste* command from the **Edit** menu. Now scroll through the *Scrapbook* file and observe that the portion of the painting *Weird1* that you placed on the Clipboard has now been added to the Scrapbook, in a position immediately before the Scrapbook picture entry that was showing when you chose the *Paste* command.

5. While the *Scrapbook* window is still open, move the scroll box so that a picture other than your *Weird1* extract is showing. Select the *Copy* command from the **Edit** menu. You have now copied the displayed Scrapbook picture to the Clipboard. Close the *Scrapbook* window by clicking its close box.

6. You should now be returned to the *Untitled* painting. Select the *Paste* command from the **Edit** menu. You should see the Scrapbook picture that you copied to the Clipboard in step 5 appear in the Untitled window. This picture is selected already; you can move it around by dragging it.

7. Select the *Quit* command from the **File** menu and save the new painting by the name *Scrapcopy* in the folder *Paintings1* (but not inside either of the folders *House Paintings* or *Face Paintings*) by using the dialog boxes.

8. Once you have quit MacPaint, check to see that the painting *Scrapcopy* is in fact stored in the proper place in your file/folder hierarchy. When you have located the painting, drag it to the trash can.

4.8 MANAGING FONTS AND DESK ACCESSORIES

When you become more proficient in using your Macintosh, you will be interested in tailoring it to fit your own needs. Two major interests you will probably have are installing custom fonts into your System File and adding desk accessories to the **Apple** menu that are useful to you. In this section, we describe the process by which both of these activities can be done. If you are using the Macintosh for the first time, you may want to skip this section and read it later.

Because the Macintosh uses a bit-mapped screen to produce all its text and graphics, an extremely wide range of font size and style is available to the user. Fonts may include foreign alphabets, mathematical symbols, chemical symbols, and so on. Each of the symbols can be selected by typing a key on the keyboard after the appropriate font has been selected from the **Font** pull-down menu. A font size can also be chosen from this same menu.

Font sizes are shown in two ways in the **Font** menu. They appear to be either bold or outlined. Outlined fonts give the best possible output appearance when using the printers or when displayed on the screen. Exact patterns for these sizes are stored in the System File. Those sizes that are shown in bold type are interpolated from other sizes. They are *not* available in the System File. That is, the computer must make a guess about how each character should appear because no exact pattern is defined for it to use. Also, the styles of font that the computer can use are determined by the styles available in the System File. The computer cannot display fonts that are not contained in its System File.

Managing the fonts that are available in the System File is relatively easy. There is a utility program called Font/DA Mover (DA stands for Desk Accessory) that normally is stored in the Utilities folder of a system disk. This program is used to transfer font styles and sizes into or out of a System File. Each combination of style and size of a font takes up considerable disk space. Thus, you need to be able both **to add and to delete** fonts from the System File.

Execution of the Font/DA Mover utility program is carried out by finding the icon shown in Figure 4.24 and opening it. The Font/DA Mover utility program shows the screen of Figure 4.25 when it is executing. The program can be

Figure 4.24 *Font/DA Mover* icon (left), *Suitcase of Fonts* (center), and *Suitcase of Desk Accessories* (right).

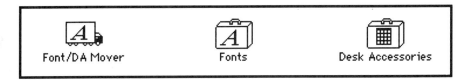

used to move either fonts or programs called desk accessories into the System File. You determine which action will be performed by clicking in the appropriate button at the top of the dialog box. For this example, the *Font* button has been selected. The System File into which the fonts are to be copied or deleted is shown on the left. It will be automatically opened if you have a system disk in a drive. The rectangle on the right is used to select the fonts to be entered into the System File from some other source, provided that you open such a source. Note that in the large rectangle at the bottom of the dialog box the style and size of any font selected are shown.

For example, the standard system disks sent from Apple along with a Macintosh computer contain a selection of fonts in addition to the ones already present in the System File. These fonts are contained in the suitcase icon labeled with the script "A" in Figure 4.24 and found in the *Utility* folder. In our example, if this source of fonts is opened, any of the fonts available in this file may be copied into the System File. Remember, however, that adding fonts increases the size of the System File. To copy a font set into the System File, click on the font name and size desired. The *Copy* button will become bold. Then click *Copy* and the font selected will be transferred.

Desk accessories are programs that can be executed by selecting their names under the **Apple** menu. These include such programs as *Calculator, Alarm Clock, Note Pad,* and so on. Many public domain desk accessory programs can be

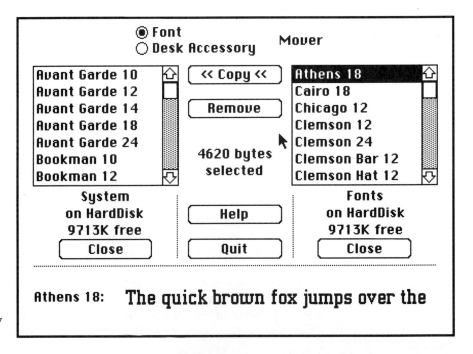

Figure 4.25 Active context for Font/DA Mover Utility program.

obtained at no cost and will perform certain functions you might require. For example, there are scientific calculator desk accessory programs that can compute the standard scientific functions in addition to performing arithmetic.

Once you have a source of desk accessories you may copy them into the System File using a method analogous to that used for the fonts mentioned earlier. Here select the *Desk Accessory* button in the Font/DA Mover utility program once you have opened it. Open the file having the source of desk accessories you wish to use—your System File will automatically be opened for you if it is available. Select each new desk accessory you wish to add by shift clicking. Then click on *Copy* and your selected desk accessories will be copied to the System File.

Once a new desk accessory has been copied into the System File, it may be executed by selecting it from the **Apple** menu. Desk accessories are usually available in application contexts.

Exercise Set 4.8

1. What are desk accessories?
2. How are desk accessories added to the **Apple** menu?
3. Describe the complete process for adding a new font to your Macintosh system.

Key Concepts

Adding and Deleting fonts
Complete path names for files
Copying floppy disk to floppy disk
Creating file and folder hierarchies
Erasing disks
Navigating in file hierarchies
Opening and saving files
  within applications
Printer drivers

Clipboard and Scrapbook files
Computer resources
Copying floppy disk to hard disk
Desk accessories
Find File command
Open, Save, and Save As... dialog
  box use
Page Setup command
Removing files

PART II

MASTERING PROBLEM-SOLVING USING MS WORKS

INTRODUCING INTEGRATED SOFTWARE CONCEPTS

L E A R N I N G   O B J E C T I V E S

- To learn what major components are included in typical integrated software packages.

- To gain an appreciation for the kinds of problems that can be solved using an integrated software package.

- To gain an overview perspective of the Microsoft Works integrated software package.

I n this chapter you will receive a brief overview of the software components that are usually a part of integrated software packages. These components typically include a word processor, a spreadsheet program, a database management system, and a communications module. By examining some simple examples, you will learn how such software can be used to help you solve a variety of problems. You will also be introduced to the integrated package, Microsoft Works, which you will be using throughout Part II of the text. Brief descriptions are given of the word processing, database, spreadsheet, and communications applications of Works. These descriptions are intended to provide a "road map" of Works.

5.1   INTRODUCTION TO INTEGRATED SOFTWARE PACKAGES

A typical integrated software package includes four basic components or modules: a word processor, a spreadsheet program, a database management system, and a communications module. Such packages are called integrated because of the ease with which data may be moved between the different modules within the packages.

Integrated software packages provide some very important conveniences and advantages. For example, it may be possible for you to have documents from several different kinds of applications software open at the same time, moving from one document to another by simply changing the active window. This ability provides a great advantage over having always to quit one application to access a different application. Additionally, with an integrated package, you are guaranteed a high degree of user interface consistency for all the applications included in the package. This can greatly reduce the learning time over that required to learn separate stand-alone packages for word processing, spreadsheet, database, and communications applications. Finally, the cost of an integrated package is considerably lower than the cost of the stand-alone packages required in its place.

Of course, as you might expect from the preceding comments concerning package costs, the number of features in each component of an integrated package is fewer than is typically available in a corresponding stand-alone package. Whether the additional features justify the increased costs and learning time of several stand-alone packages over an integrated package depends largely upon the use for which the software is being considered. As you will see, for a great many uses, an integrated package provides ample power and features.

5.1.1 Word Processors

The basic purpose of a **word processor** is to make possible the electronic creation, modification, and printing of documents. Any reasonably good word processor should have the basic features that allow you to do the following activities.

- Insert and delete characters, lines, paragraphs, and sections within your documents.
- Employ an automatic wordwrap feature to advance your text to the next line when necessary.
- Move sections of a document by cut-and-paste operations.
- Format paragraphs, controlling such parameters as spaces between lines, left and right margins, left and right justification of text, centering of text, tab settings, and indentation.
- Format characters and strings of characters by having them appear as bold, underlined, or italicized.
- Place text above or below the line as superscripts or subscripts.
- Insert page headers and footers, with automatic page numbering.
- Save, retrieve, and print created documents.

Additional features that a word processor *might* include would allow you to do the following activities.

- Use a variety of text font styles and sizes.
- Create footnotes that will automatically be numbered and placed on the page as required.
- Produce multiple-column documents, similar to newspaper or magazine copy.
- Preview full-page layouts before they are printed.
- Incorporate graphics objects within documents.
- Create style sheets that define paragraph formatting outside the text area proper.
- Check spelling and perform automatic hyphenation.
- Generate an index and table of contents.
- Create an integrated outline and text.
- Sort tables within a document.
- Merge separate documents.

As you will learn shortly, the Microsoft Works word processor provides all the preceding basic features and several of the additional features as well. When you study Microsoft Word later in this text, you will see that it provides all the preceding features (both basic and additional) as well as others.

You will find that the Microsoft Works word processor and MacPaint, together with the Macintosh Clipboard facility, provide enough capability to satisfy a great many of your document preparation needs. Mastering the Microsoft Works word processor will also allow you to upgrade your document preparation skills easily by learning more advanced word processing packages, such as Microsoft Word, as the need arises.

Exercise Set 5.1.1

1. What is the primary function of a word processor package?

2. List five features that would likely be included in any reasonably powerful word processor.

3. List five features that might be considered additional word processor features.

5.1.2 Spreadsheet Packages

Spreadsheet packages (or just "spreadsheets" for short) provide a framework within which many kinds of calculations can be performed with relative ease. These calculations can be "programmed" using the spreadsheet in a way that does not require the user to write computer programs. The spreadsheet worksheet (equivalent to the blank starting page of a word processor) is a rectangular table of cells as shown in Figure 5.1. Spreadsheet calculations are then performed by entering formulas into some of these cells. These formulas usually reference the contents of other cells as variables. An example of a simple formula calculation is demonstrated in Figure 5.2.

Even with such a simple example as that shown in Figure 5.2, we can illustrate some of the power of the spreadsheet as a computational tool. By changing values in cells that are referenced in **formulas**, you can automatically initiate the corresponding changes in the value computed by the formula. For example, if you were to change the value in cell A3 of Figure 5.2(b) to 100, then the value in cell A6 would be automatically adjusted to 150 by the spreadsheet.

The ability to adjust values and have the spreadsheet program automatically recalculate all its formulas allows you to perform quite easily what is often called *what if* **analysis**. For example, you might produce an amortization table that calculates your monthly principal and interest payments on a loan. You can then vary the interest rate used in your calculations by simply changing the value in one cell (the cell holding the interest rate). In this way, you can easily observe how your principal and interest payments change with the interest rate and thus answer questions of the form "*What if* the interest rate changes to. . . ?"

The variety of calculations that can be performed using a spreadsheet is very impressive. Most spreadsheets have built-in capabilities for calculating certain financial functions, standard statistical functions, trigonometric functions, logarithmic functions, and others. Of course, you can also calculate tables of values for a function that you enter as a formula.

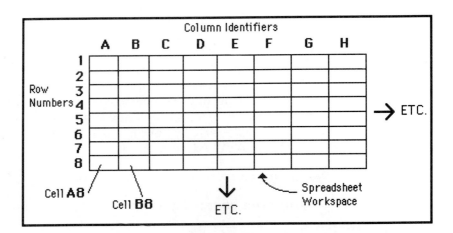

Figure 5.1 A typical spreadsheet program workspace.

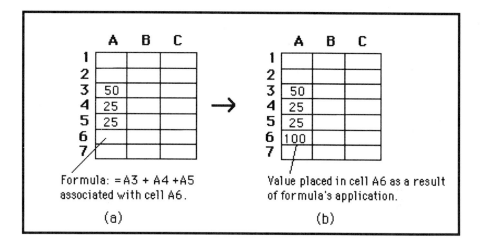

Figure 5.2 Spreadsheet calculation using a formula.

Another very valuable feature that most spreadsheets provide is the ability to present the results of calculations graphically. Often several types of graphs are available, including pie charts, bar charts, line graphs, and scatter plots.

An advanced feature provided by many spreadsheets is the ability to define **macro** programs (*macros* for short). Recall from Chapter 3 that macros are short programs that can be named and whose execution can be initiated by invoking their names. The ability to define and use macros allows you to tailor a spreadsheet application to your specific environment or needs. For example, you could write macros that create dialog boxes and data entry forms to streamline the use of your application for someone unfamiliar with using the spreadsheet.

A simple database facility is sometimes provided by a spreadsheet. This facility allows a user to search through sections of data within a spreadsheet's workspace, selecting only those rows that satisfy certain selection criteria. The combination of the calculational capabilities of a spreadsheet and some of the data selection capabilities of a database system provides great problem–solving power.

The Microsoft Works spreadsheet provides many of the capabilities discussed earlier, but it does not include macro and database capabilities. However, you will learn to use these capabilities if you study the stand-alone spreadsheet Excel discussed later in this text.

Exercise Set 5.1.2

1. What is the primary function of a spreadsheet package?
2. What is the appearance and organization of a spreadsheet program's basic workspace?
3. Calculations are usually performed in a spreadsheet by entering what into a cell?
4. Explain what is meant by *what if* analysis. How does a spreadsheet provide you with the capability to make such analysis?
5. Are spreadsheet calculations limited to business problems and budgets?

6. Why is the ability to define macros important for a spreadsheet user?

7. What kinds of graphical display capabilities are usually included in a spreadsheet?

8. What major capabilities are missing from the Microsoft Works spreadsheet?

5.1.3 Database Management Systems

The main purpose of a **database management system** is to allow a user to "manage" data or information. By "managing information," we mean the abilities to store information, update the stored information, and then retrieve that information at a later date.

As a user of a database management system, you must assume the responsibility of organizing your data in a manner that will allow the system to manage the data efficiently and flexibly. This means that you must decide what information is to be stored and the formats that will be used for its storage.

A **database file** is a unit of information storage designed to contain information about some fixed class of objects or entities. For example, a file might hold information about the books in your personal library, another file might contain information about the customers of your shop, and yet another file might store data about students enrolled at some college or university. It would make little sense, however, to attempt to store all these collections of information in a single file, because they are basically unrelated to each other. Generally, then, a database file should contain information about a *single class of entities* (such as customers, books, students, etc.).

Files are organized into smaller units called **records**. Once we decide what kinds of data are to be stored in a file to describe an entity, the actual data are placed in records within the file. Each record will hold one complete set of information about a *particular entity* in the entity class associated with the file. For example, if the file holds information about the entity class *Students*, then a record in that file holds information about some particular *Student* (Mary Smith, sophomore, etc.). The specific attributes representing the categories of information stored about a particular entity in each record are called the **fields** of the record. The file is composed of a collection of such records. The diagram of Figure 5.3 illustrates this organization for a hypothetical *Student* file.

Any database management system should include the capabilities to allow you to define database files, create and use data entry forms to enter and update data for those files, and retrieve data that has been previously stored. Most database systems will generate default data entry forms, which can then be

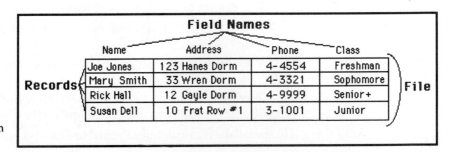

Figure 5.3 File organization illustrated.

modified if desired. Data retrieval capabilities should always include the abilities to select particular records from a single file that satisfy some simple selection criteria and to choose data from only certain fields for the records selected.

More advanced database systems allow related information to be retrieved from separate files. For example, we might choose a student's grades for last term from one file and that student's home address from another file. Most modern microcomputer database management systems that allow retrieval on separate files use the *relational database model*. This model will be discussed at length in later chapters of this text.

The database system component of Microsoft Works provides all the basic features mentioned earlier, with the exception of the ability to retrieve related information from separate files. In Chapter 18, you will study the relational database management system Reflex Plus, which provides methods for retrieving related information from multiple files.

Exercise Set 5.1.3

1. What is the main purpose of a database management system?
2. How does a database management system organize its data?
3. What kind of information is stored in a file?
4. How are files and records related? Give an example.
5. How are records and fields related? Give an example.
6. What major capability is missing from the Microsoft Works database system?

5.1.4 Communications Modules

A **communications module** is designed to allow your computer to communicate with another computer. The other computer can be in the next room or across the country, because computers can communicate by telephone. At one computer, a hardware device known as a *modem* converts the digital signals of the computer into a form for transmitting over a telephone line. At the other end of the telephone line, another modem reverses this conversion process for the receiving computer.

For a computer to communicate with another computer, both must use the same *protocol*. A protocol is an agreement between communicating parties about how the communication will be conducted, and it includes such rules as the form of the data and the actions to be taken when an error occurs. There are several computer communication protocols. Consequently, you will need to know what protocol is to be used for communicating with a particular computer, but you will not need to know the details of the protocol. The communications module must provide a means of setting your computer's protocol to that of the computer with which you wish to exchange data.

On-line *information services* such as CompuServe, Dialog, and Dow Jones News/Retrieval provide such services as bulletin boards on special topics, news, weather, sports, games, investment services, general reference materials, and many others. When you sign on to an information service, you will be asked to enter an account number and a password. Then you will be presented with a menu such as that shown in Figure 5.4.

```
┌─────────────────────────────────────────────────┐
│                                                  │
│   Universal On-line News and Services            │
│                                                  │
│   Enter the number of the desired service.       │
│                                                  │
│   1. Current News                                │
│   2. Stock Market Reports                         │
│   3. User Bulletin Boards                         │
│   4. Weather                                      │
│   5. Electronic Shopping                          │
│   6. Entertainment and Games                      │
│                                                  │
└─────────────────────────────────────────────────┘
```

Figure 5.4 A typical information service menu.

A communications module should have features to allow you to perform the following activities.

- Set values for the rate of data transfer, phone type, data size, and parameters that describe the modem.
- Transfer files between computers using several different protocols.
- Send blocks of text to save time in communicating with information services.
- Dial other computers automatically over the telephone.
- Instruct the modem to answer the phone if it rings.
- Use different types of modems.

In Chapter 13 you will learn how to use the MS Works communications module.

Exercise Set 5.1.4

1. What is the purpose of a communications module?
2. What is a modem? How many modems are required for communication between two computers?
3. What is a protocol?
4. What kinds of information can be obtained from the on-line information services?
5. List five features that are typically found in communications modules.

5.2 INTRODUCTION TO MICROSOFT WORKS

In this section we quickly preview some of the major features of the Microsoft Works program. These features and many others are treated in detail in subsequent chapters. For now, concentrate on thinking about what you might do with the components of Works to solve your problems.

Microsoft Works (also referred to as MS Works, or just Works) is an **integrated software package** that contains four types of application programs—a word processor, a spreadsheet package, a database management system, and a communications module. Each of the applications has an intuitive, easy–to–learn language to assist you in doing your work. Information can be transferred between the modules, which expands the usefulness of the package. This latter aspect of Works is discussed briefly at the end of this section.

The word processor has a sufficient number of features to meet most users' needs. With it you can create a document, correct errors, change the document format, and print the document. All the features needed for processing ordinary documents and even some complex ones are available.

Figure 5.5 shows a document produced by using the Works word processing module together with MacPaint. Such visually appealing combinations of text and graphics can be created with very little effort employing these packages.

The **mail merge** feature of Works combines records in the database with a word processing document. This can be used to produce automatically a copy of the letter in Figure 5.5 for each employee, personalized with the person's name and address. This could save much time if there were a large number of employees.

A Works database is a file of records on a disk that contain related information about a person, object, or any other entity of interest. It is important to realize that you can use the database to store any textual or numerical information that interests you.

With the Works database application, it is easy to design a file's records, modify the design of the records after the database has been created, enter data into the records, modify the contents of existing records, and retrieve information in formats that aid in answering questions about the data. You will learn to do all these processes and others later.

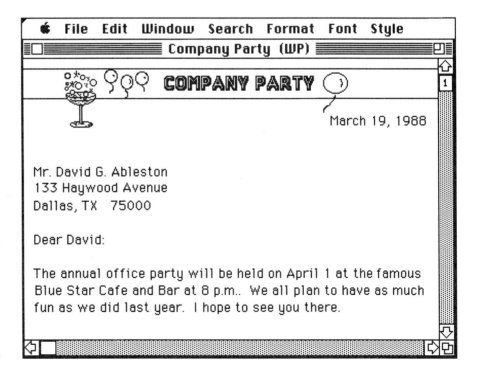

Figure 5.5 A sample word processing document using MS Works and MacPaint in combination.

```
┌──────────────────────────────────────────────────────────┐
│ ▣▤▤▤▤▤▤▤▤▤▤▤ Employee Names (DB) ▤▤▤▤▤▤▤▤▤▤▤ ⊡ │
├──────────────────────────────────────────────────────┬───┤
│ ┌──────────┬──────────┐                               │ ⇧ │
│ │Last Name │ Ableston │                               │   │
│ ├──────────┼──────────┤                               │   │
│ │First Name│ David    │                               │   │
│ ├──────────┼──────────┘                               │   │
│ │Initial │ G │                                        │   │
│ ├────────┴───┬──────────────┐                         │   │
│ │Department  │ Manufacturing│                         │   │
│ ├───────┬────┴─────────┐                              │   │
│ │Title  │ Inspector    │                              │   │
│ └───────┴──────────────┘                              │ ⇩ │
│                                                       │ ⊡ │
└──────────────────────────────────────────────────────┴───┘
```

Figure 5.6 A database form created using Works.

Works can be used to create a database form to allow input or display of a record. Alterations to the form design are easy to make. Figure 5.6 shows a simple form for an employee of a hypothetical company. It can be used for entering information that is to be stored in the database. Data on individual employees can also be retrieved and displayed using the form.

Information entered into the database using the form can also be viewed in a table format, which is more convenient for some situations. Figure 5.7 shows the table display format for several employees. Data for additional employees can also be entered into the file using the table form.

The Works spreadsheet can be used to perform almost any computation that is normally done using a calculator or computer program. Various accounting applications, such as accounts receivable, accounts payable, balance sheets, payroll, and profit and loss statements, are easy to do with a spreadsheet. Some other applications are inventory, grade calculations, budget modeling, simple statistics, and some scientific calculations.

The Works spreadsheet worksheet (to avoid this cumbersome duo of words, we refer to a spreadsheet worksheet as simply a worksheet from now on) is large—9999 rows by 256 columns. The language that you will learn in Chapter 10 for developing spreadsheets is intuitive and easy to learn. In fact, many beginners feel that using a spreadsheet is a natural extension of doing tabular calculations by hand. In the small sample spreadsheet of Figure 5.8 the values in the *Gross Pay* column were all computed by entering a single formula that described the calculation to be done.

A very important feature of spreadsheets is their graphics capability, the ability to present the worksheet data in a pictorial form, like that shown in Figure

```
┌──────────────────────────────────────────────────────────┐
│ ▣▤▤▤▤▤▤▤▤▤▤▤ Employee Names (DB) ▤▤▤▤▤▤▤▤▤▤▤ ⊡ │
├───────────┬───────────┬────────┬──────────────┬──────────┤
│Last Name  │First Name │Initial │Department    │Title     │
├───────────┼───────────┼────────┼──────────────┼──────────┤
│Ableston   │David      │G       │Manufacturing │Inspector │
│Highmaster │Jonathon   │A       │Marketing     │Salesman  │
│Jasper     │Thomas     │I       │Marketing     │Salesman  │
│Siththe    │Bernard    │R       │Grounds       │Gardener  │
│Zebbley    │Arthur     │P       │Accounting    │Clerk     │
├───────────┴───────────┴────────┴──────────────┴──────────┤
│ ◁ ▭ ░░░░░░░░░░░░░░░░░░░░░░░░░░░░░░░░░░░░░░░░░░ ▷⊡ │
└──────────────────────────────────────────────────────────┘
```

Figure 5.7 A portion of a table display for a database.

Figure 5.8 A sample Works worksheet.

	A	B	C	D	E	F	G
1	Last Name	First Name	Initial	Title	Rate	Hours	Gross Pay
2	Ableston	David	G	Inspector	$9.00	45	$405.00
3	Highmaster	Jonathon	A	Salesman	$7.50	55	$412.50
4	Jasper	Thomas	I	Salesman	$12.00	48	$576.00
5	Siththe	Bernard	R	Gardener	$6.25	40	$250.00
6	Zebbley	Arthur	P	Clerk	$7.30	42	$306.60
7							

Employee Pay (SS)

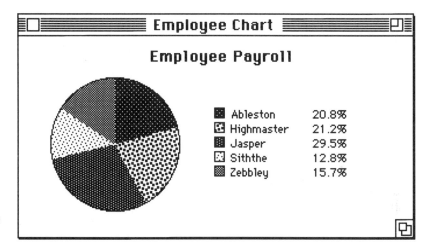

Figure 5.9 A pie chart of gross pay from the sample spreadsheet.

Employee Chart

Employee Payroll

■	Ableston	20.8%
▦	Highmaster	21.2%
▨	Jasper	29.5%
▢	Siththe	12.8%
▥	Zebbley	15.7%

5.9. Data tables and graphs produced from worksheets can be easily transferred to word processing documents.

Several Works windows can be open simultaneously, as shown in Figure 5.10. (The maximum number that can be open is 10.) The type of window is identified by the abbreviation in parentheses after the name of the window—(WP) word processing, (DB) database, and (SS) spreadsheet. *Employee Pay* (SS) is the active window.

Figure 5.10 Three open Works windows.

 File   Edit   Window   Select   Format   Options   Chart

Company Party (WP)

Employee Names (DB)

Employee Pay (SS)

	A	B	C	D	E	F	G
	st Name	First Name	Initial	Title	Rate	Hours	Gross Pay
	leston	David	G	Inspector	$9.00	45	$405.00
	ghmaster	Jonathon	A	Salesman	$7.50	55	$412.50
	sper	Thomas	I	Salesman	$12.00	48	$576.00
	ththe	Bernard	R	Gardener	$6.25	40	$250.00
	bbley	Arthur	P	Clerk	$7.30	42	$306.60

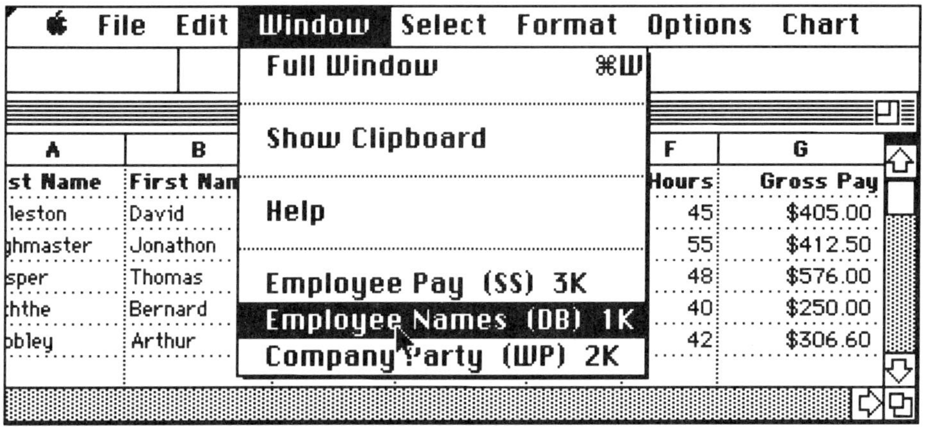

Figure 5.11 The **Window** menu with employee names selected.

These windows have been arranged so that a portion of each can be seen, but normally, one window would be covering the others. A special menu, **Window**, can be used to switch quickly between the open windows. This is shown in Figure 5.11, in which the *Employee Names* window has been selected. This feature makes it easy to examine and select information in a window for transfer to another window. For example, you might wish to transfer data from a database to a spreadsheet in order to do some complex calculations.

Finally, Works has a communications module that allows your computer to communicate with other computers. All of the features described earlier for communications modules are available in Works. The Works *Communications Settings* dialog box is shown in Figure 5.12. Clicking on various buttons in this dialog box will allow you to configure your computer to communicate with another computer. You will learn the meaning of some of these items in Chapter 13.

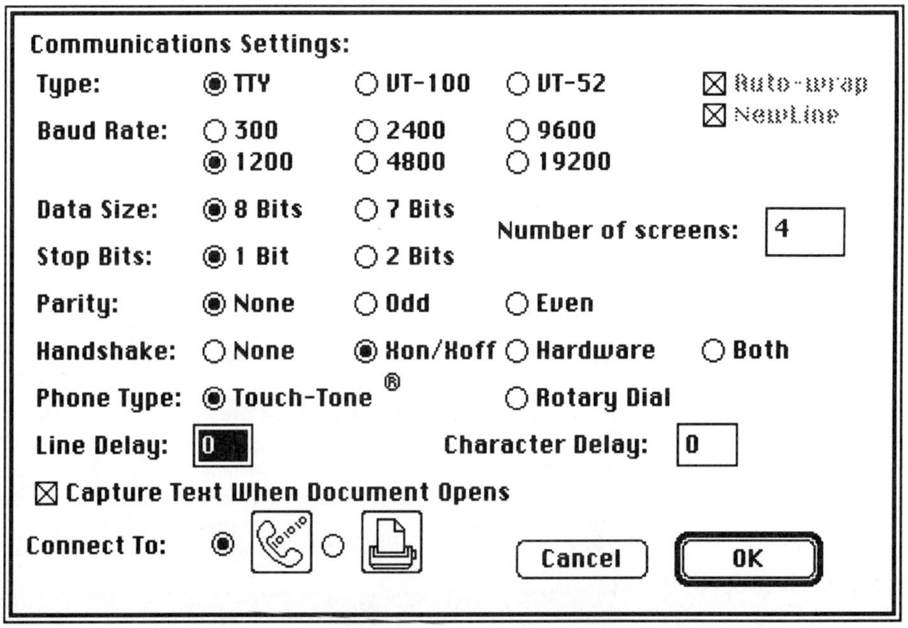

Figure 5.12 The *Communications Settings* dialog box.

Exercise Set 5.2

1. What modules does Works contain?
2. What is the mail merge feature?
3. Why is it desirable to be able to share information between two or more Works modules?
4. What are the two ways of viewing a Works database?
5. What is the maximum size of a Works spreadsheet?
6. What is the purpose of the **Window** menu?

Key Concepts

Communications modules
Database management system
Integrated software package
Mail merge
Spreadsheet formula
"What if" analysis
Word processor

Database file
Fields
Macros
Record
Spreadsheet packages
Window menu

CHAPTER 6

UNDERSTANDING TASKS COMMON TO WORKS MODULES

L E A R N I N G O B J E C T I V E S

- To learn how to create, save, and delete Works documents.

- To learn how to open and close existing Works documents.

- To learn how to use the the Works Help feature.

- To learn how to create and use document headers and footers.

- To learn how to print Works documents.

- To learn how to quit Works and use the Resume Works document.

I n this chapter you will learn how to start and quit MS Works. You will also learn how to accomplish a number of tasks that are common to all the modules of Works. These tasks include opening a document, creating a new document, using the Help feature, printing a document, using headers and footers, closing a document, and deleting a document. In addition, this chapter contains a summary of the menus and commands that are common to the Works modules.

6.1 ACCESSING WORKS DOCUMENTS

To start Works, find the Microsoft Works icon that is shown in Figure 6.1. Open Works by either double-clicking on this icon or selecting it and choosing the *Open* command of the **File** menu. Immediately the starting MS Works screen of Figure 6.2 will be displayed.

The icons at the top of the starting screen indicate the types of documents that can be produced in Works. Highlighting one of the icons by clicking it indicates that you are interested in that particular kind of document. For example, selecting the *Word Processor* icon causes the names of all documents of all previously created word processing documents to be displayed in the box in the lower left side of the window. Selecting the *Data Base* icon causes the names of data base documents to be displayed in the document box. Selecting the *All Works Types* icon causes the names of all files of any types created by Works to be displayed.

The name of the current folder (or disk) is displayed above a list of names of files of the selected type. If the document or folder of interest can be found in the scroll window, point to the name and double-click. If the file or folder is not found in the current scroll window, point to the name of the current folder or disk (shown above the scroll window), press the mouse button, and drag to the name of the desired folder and release the button. (Recall the discussion in Chapter 4 describing how to navigate through folders and disks.)

CREATING A DOCUMENT.   To **create a document,** proceed as follows.

- Return to the starting MS Works window (Figure 6.2) (if you are not already there) by selecting the *Open* command from the **File** menu.
- Select the icon for the type of document that you want to create.
- Click the *New* button.

A new document of the appropriate type will be opened, ready for data to be entered. The documents for the different types of applications have quite differ-

Figure 6.1 The Microsoft Works icon.

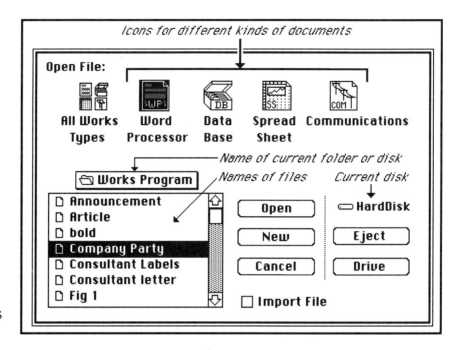

Figure 6.2 The starting MS Works window.

ent appearances: a blank sheet for a word processing document, a dialog box to enter a record field name for a database, a worksheet for the spreadsheet, and a settings dialog box for communications. In addition, the title bar of each document will contain one of the abbreviations (WP), (DB), (SS), or (CM) to identify the type of document. If you accidentally open a document of the wrong type, close the window by clicking the close box, and repeat the steps given earlier.

OPENING AN EXISTING DOCUMENT.   To open an existing document, perform the following.

- Select the disk and folder that contains the document of interest. It may be that information for the desired disk or document is already being displayed.

- Select the application type—word processor, database, spreadsheet, or communications. This causes the names of all documents of the selected type to be displayed in the document box.

- Select the document and open it by clicking the *Open* button. The document will then be displayed ready for additional work. As a shortcut, a document can be opened by double-clicking its name in the list of file names.

Suppose that you are working on a word processor document, that is, a word processing window is open and you are typing. Perhaps you realize that you should have modified another document (of any of the types) first. Select the *Open* command in the **File** menu. The starting MS Works window of Figure 6.2 will be displayed again. In fact, the starting window will always be displayed whenever you select the *Open* command. From the starting window you can open the document to be modified. At this point you would have two open windows, but only one would be active. Remember that you can switch between the two by accessing the **Window** menu.

At times you may want to open a document that was created using a program other than Works. This can be done by clicking the *Import File* box. Works imports documents from some programs, such as Microsoft Word and Excel, without any additional work by you. In some cases it will be necessary for you to use the non-Works program to save the file using the *text* option before it can be imported by Works.

Exercise Set 6.1

1. Describe the purpose of the various elements of the Works starting window.
2. What happens when the *All Works Types* icon is selected?
3. What happens when a module icon (e.g., Word Processor) is selected?
4. How do you open an existing Works document?
5. How do you create a new Works document?

6.2 SAVING A WORKS DOCUMENT

As you enter information into a document, it is stored in the volatile RAM memory of the computer. If there is a power failure or other malfunction, the information in RAM is lost. This can be very aggravating and in some cases disastrous. You can protect yourself by saving your work regularly. **Saving a document** causes a copy of it to be stored in nonvolatile magnetic form on a disk.

For particularly important documents it is a good idea to have a copy of the work on more than one disk. On infrequent occasions a power failure or a fluctuation in the power can cause information on a disk to be lost. Having several copies protects against this occurrence and a mechanical malfunction as well.

SAVING A DOCUMENT THE FIRST TIME.   To save a file the first time proceed as follows.

■ Select the *Save* or *Save As* command in the **File** menu. The *Save* dialog box shown in Figure 6.3 will be displayed.

■ Type the name of the document in the box titled *Save Document As*. You can edit the name in this box.

■ Click the *Export File* box if it is required to save the document in a form for use with applications other than Works.

■ Change the context, if desired, by selecting a different folder or disk, or both.

■ Click the *Save* box. The document will be saved in the desired context with the name that was entered, and the *Save* dialog box will disappear. The document window will remain open, and you can continue to work in it.

SAVING CHANGES TO AN EXISTING DOCUMENT.   After a document has been saved once, the latest stage of the work can be saved by proceeding as follows.

■ Select the *Save* command in the **File** menu. The document will be saved immediately. The dialog box will not be displayed because the name of the document is already known. The window for the document will remain open

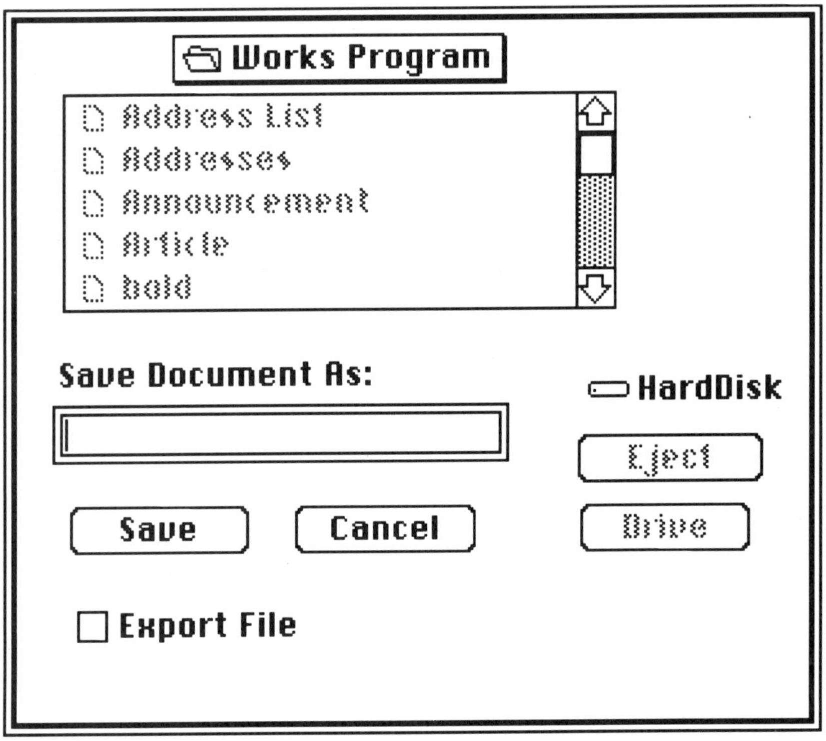

```
┌─────────────────────────────────────────────────┐
│              ╔═══════════════════════╗           │
│              ║  🗁 Works Program      ║           │
│           ┌──────────────────────────────┐       │
│           │ ▯ Address List           ⬆️ │       │
│           │ ▯ Addresses                 │       │
│           │ ▯ Announcement           ░░ │       │
│           │ ▯ Article                ░░ │       │
│           │ ▯ bold                   ⬇️ │       │
│           └──────────────────────────────┘       │
│                                                  │
│           Save Document As:      ▭ HardDisk      │
│           ┌──────────────────────┐               │
│           │▏                     │   ( Eject )    │
│           └──────────────────────┘               │
│           ( Save )   ( Cancel )     ( Drive )     │
│                                                  │
│           ☐ Export File                          │
└─────────────────────────────────────────────────┘
```

Figure 6.3 The dialog box for saving a document.

so that you can continue to work on the document. You should use this command frequently as you work on a document.

SAVING A DOCUMENT UNDER A DIFFERENT NAME.   Occasionally, you will find it desirable to save a copy of a document using a different name. For example, before starting extensive changes to a document, it is a good idea to work with a copy with a different name so that if the modifications are not satisfactory, you can return to use the original document. To accomplish this, proceed as follows.

- Select the *Save As* command from the **File** menu.
- Enter the new name in the dialog box.
- Select the context for saving the document.
- Click the *Save* button. The document is now saved with the new name and you are returned to the document. The document you are now working on is the newly named document.

CLOSING A DOCUMENT.   When you have finished work on a document, you should remove it from the desktop by **closing** it. This is done by performing the following.

- Select the *Close* command in the **File** menu or click the window close box. If any changes were made since the document was last saved, either of these actions will cause a dialog box to be displayed asking if you wish to save the changes made.

- Click the *Yes* button to save the changes before closing the document. Click the *No* button to close the document without saving the changes. Click the *Cancel* button to cancel the close command and to continue work on the document.

If you have documents open and attempt to quit Works, a dialog box similar to that previously described will be displayed successively for each of the open documents. This is a valuable safeguard against failing to save changes made to your documents.

Computer Practice 6.2

1. Open Works and click the *Word Processor* icon.
2. Click the *New* button.
3. Type your name and address in the word processing window.
4. Save the document for the first time by selecting the *Save As* command from the **File** menu, entering the name *Myaddress*, and clicking the *Save* button.
5. Write a short note about what you are going to do next weekend in the document which is still on the screen.
6. Save the altered document by selecting the *Save* command from the **File** menu.
7. Click the close box for the document, and the Works starting screen should be displayed.
8. Open your document again to verify that you were successful in creating and saving the document.
9. Select *Save As* again from the **File** menu and save the document under the name *Myaddress2*. Notice that the window you are returned to is now named *Myaddress2*.
10. Make some changes to your document and then select *Save* from the **File** menu. When you are returned to the document window, close the document.
11. Open both *Myaddress* and *Myaddress2* and observe where the changes you made in step 10 are recorded.
12. Quit Works by selecting the *Quit* command from the **File** menu.

6.3 USING THE HELP FEATURE

The **Help feature** of Works allows you to obtain quickly a short explanation of a command in any menu of the Works module you are using when you access the Help feature, or an explanation of some other feature of Works. Consequently, you will be able to use most of the commands without having to consult the reference manual. This feature is particularly valuable if you have experience with Works but have not used a command recently.

To use the Help feature proceed as follows.

- Select the *Help* command from the **Window** menu as shown in Figure 6.4. A *Help* window of the type shown in Figure 6.5 will be displayed. For this example, Help was executed from within the word processing module, so the *Help* window describes the word processor.

Figure 6.4 The *Help* command in the **Window** menu.

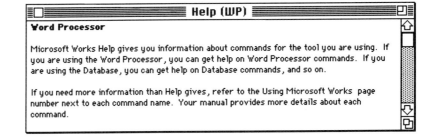

Figure 6.5 The *Help* window for the word processor.

■ Scroll through the window to find the information of interest.

If the pointer is moved outside the area of the *Help* window, it becomes a question mark, **?**, that can be used to access information rapidly about any command that appears in a menu. For example, if the pointer is moved to the **Search** menu in the word processor, dragged to the *Replace* command, as shown in Figure 6.6, and released, the *Help* window scrolls immediately to the explanation of the *Replace* command. The resulting *Help* window is shown in Figure 6.7.

Figure 6.6 Selecting the *Help* command for *Replace*.

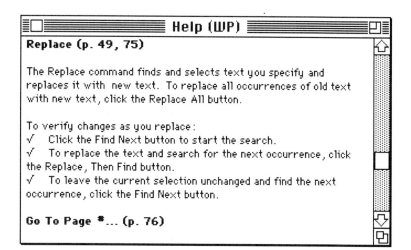

Figure 6.7 The *Help* window for the *Replace* command.

Computer Practice 6.3

1. Open Works and click the *Word Processing* icon.
2. Select the *Help* command from the **Window** menu. A *Help* window should be opened that resembles that of Figure 6.5.
3. Scroll through the window until you find the discussion of the *Save As* command.
4. Move the pointer outside the *Help* window so that it becomes a question mark. Point to the *Replace* command in the **Search** menu. Notice that a window resembling that of Figure 6.7 is displayed.
5. Use the question mark pointer to select the *Save As* command in the **File** menu. Notice that the same information is displayed in the *Help* window as you obtained by scrolling in step 3 of this exercise; however, the use of the question mark pointer was much faster than the scrolling method.
6. Click the close box of the *Help* window.
7. Select the *Quit* command from the **File** menu.

6.4 PRINTING A DOCUMENT

Printing any of the various kinds of Works documents involves the same steps. Proceed as follows.

- Use the *Chooser* command in the **Apple** menu to select the type of printer.
- Check the page settings by selecting the *Page Setup* command from the **File** menu. The window shown in Figure 6.8 will be displayed if the ImageWriter has been chosen. Note that you can set the paper type, orientation, and size. This ability is especially important for creating and printing mailing labels and other special forms. Give particular attention to setting the top, bottom, left, and right margins. Note that all these settings have default values that are satisfactory for most documents. If you know that the default settings are satisfactory, you can skip this entire step.

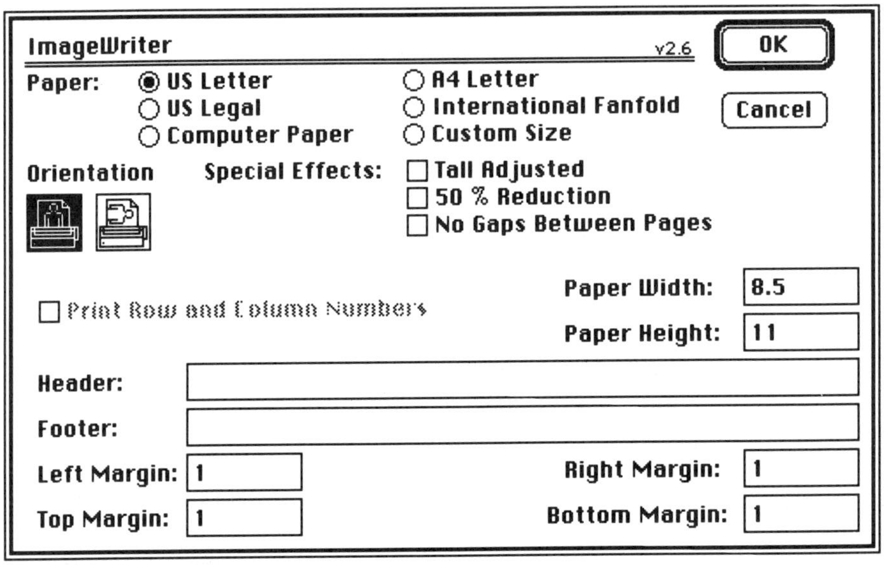

Figure 6.8 The *Page Setup* window for the ImageWriter.

- The **Page Setup window** for the LaserWriter is shown in Figure 6.9. The information in this window is very similar to that for the ImageWriter. The default *US Letter* refers to an 8.5- by 11-inch page. The *Reduce* or *Enlarge* box is set by default at 100% to prevent either reducing or enlarging. Again, note that the margin settings appear on this window.

- In both windows, boxes titled *Header* and *Footer* appear. The purposes of these boxes and the details of how to use them are presented in Section 6.5.

- Print the document by selecting the *Print* command from the **File** menu. Depending upon the printer selected, the *Print* dialog box of either Figure 6.10 or 6.11 will be displayed.

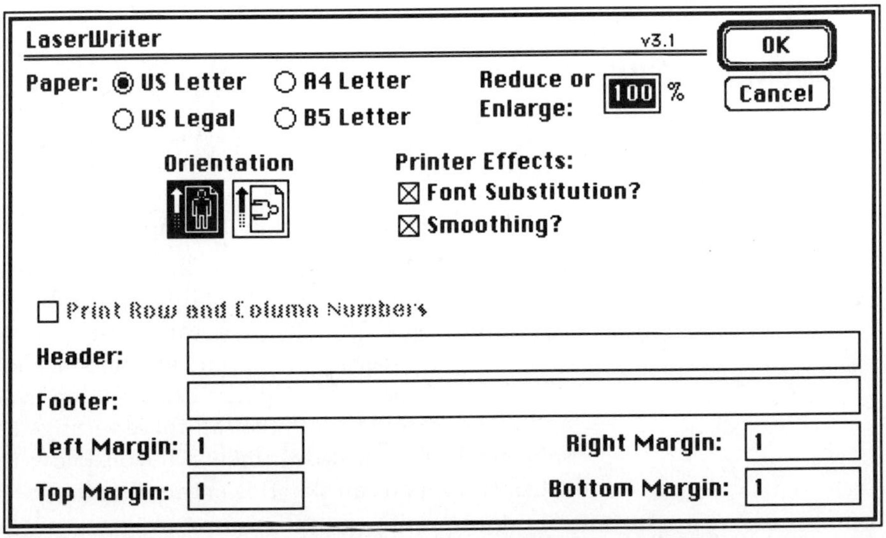

Figure 6.9 The *Page Setup* window for the Laser-Writer.

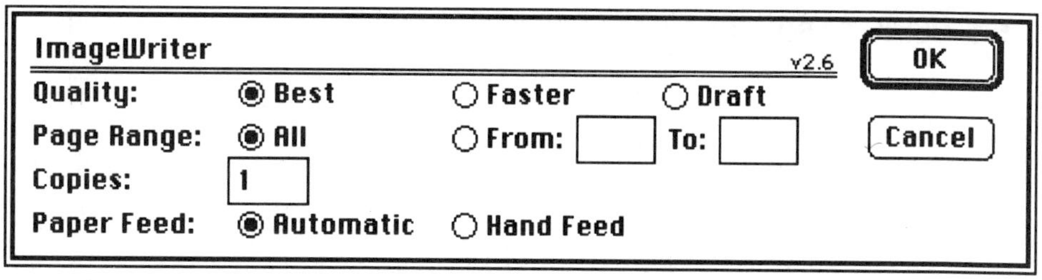

```
ImageWriter                                    v2.6    ( OK )
Quality:       ◉ Best        ○ Faster      ○ Draft
Page Range:    ◉ All         ○ From: [    ] To: [    ]   [ Cancel ]
Copies:        [ 1 ]
Paper Feed:    ◉ Automatic   ○ Hand Feed
```

Figure 6.10 *Print* dialog box for the ImageWriter.

For the ImageWriter, select the print quality by clicking the appropriate box. Note that the draft quality is fastest, but graphics, formatting information, fonts, and character styles are sacrificed to obtain printing speed, and so this option is seldom chosen.

For both printers a single page only or a given sequence of pages in the document can be printed by placing the pointer in the *From* box, entering the starting page number, tabbing to the *To* box, and entering the ending page number.

Computer Practice 6.4

1. Open Works and click the *Word Processing* icon.
2. Find your file, *Myaddress*, in the list of documents and select it.
3. Open the document by clicking the *Open* button or double-clicking on the document name.
4. Use the *Chooser* command in the **Apple** menu to select an ImageWriter printer if you have more than one kind of printer available.
5. Select the *Page Setup* command from the **File** menu.
6. Make sure that vertical orientation and *US Letter* are clicked. If paper width is not 8.5 inches and paper height is not 11 inches, change them. Set all margins to 1 inch.
7. Select the *Print* command from the **File** menu. Click the *Best* button, and then click the *OK* button. In a few seconds, your document should start printing.
8. Close the document by clicking the close box. Click the *No* button if you are asked whether you want to save changes to the document.
9. Quit Works by selecting *Quit* from the **File** menu.

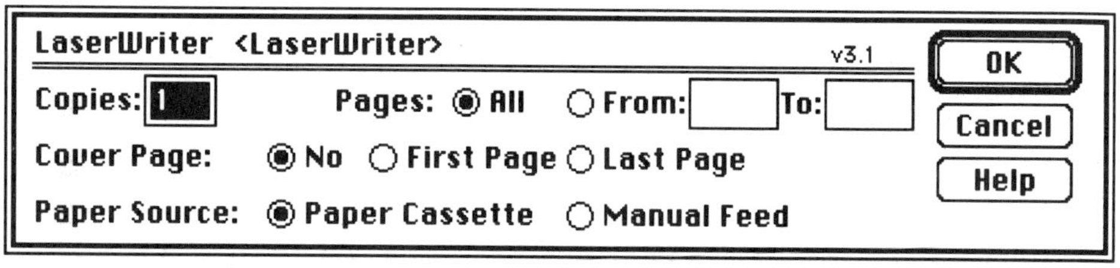

```
LaserWriter  <LaserWriter>                       v3.1    ( OK )
Copies: [ 1 ]        Pages: ◉ All  ○ From: [   ] To: [   ]   [ Cancel ]
Cover Page:     ◉ No  ○ First Page ○ Last Page              [ Help ]
Paper Source:   ◉ Paper Cassette   ○ Manual Feed
```

Figure 6.11 *Print* dialog box for the LaserWriter.

6.5 USING WORKS HEADERS AND FOOTERS

A **header** is a special line of text that appears as the top line of each page. A Works header appears in the area reserved for the top margin and does not reduce the area for entering text. It also does not show on the screen as a document is entered; it appears only on the printed document. A header may contain such information as a title, a page number, and a date. A **footer** is like a header except it is printed at the bottom of a page.

Recall that the *Page Setup* screens, Figures 6.8 and 6.9, contain blocks titled *Header* and *Footer*. Any information entered in these blocks will be treated as a header or a footer. Special sequences of characters starting with an **&** can be used to specify details of the format. The special formatting characters are elements of the language syntax and do not show when a header or footer is printed. Figure 6.12 shows the characters and their meanings.

To illustrate the use of the formatting characters, suppose that we have been asked to prepare a detailed proposal for a medical survey. To identify the pages of the proposal, we decide to use a header. Assume the following is entered in the *Header* box.

&L&BMedical Survey Proposal &C&D&RPage &P

The resulting header will appear as :

Medical Survey Proposal   **May 15, 1988**   **Page 1**

where the meanings of the parts of the header are

- &L causes the title to be left-justified.
- &B causes the title to be bold.
- *Medical Survey Proposal* is the title.

```
&L  Align at the left margin
&C  Center between the margins
&R  Align at the right margin

&P  Print the page number
&D  Print the current date
&T  Print the current time
&F  Print the document name

&B  Print in bold
&I  Print in italic
&&  Print an "&"
```

Figure 6.12 Formatting characters for Works headers and footers.

- &C causes the next item to be centered.
- &D causes the date to be printed.
- &R cause the next item to be right-justified.
- *Page* is to be printed.
- &P causes the current page number to be printed.

It is possible to prevent headers and footers from being printed on a document's first page. This is done by declaring the first page to be a title page. To do so, select the *Title Page* command in the **Format** menu. Then the header will be printed on the second and all following pages and the displayed page numbers, if included, will start with 2.

Computer Practice 6.5

1. Open Works and click the *Word Processing* icon.
2. Open your document, *Myaddress*.
3. Select the *Page Setup* command from the **File** menu.
4. Construct in the *Header* box a header that will print your name in bold at the left margin, the time centered on the line, and the date at the right margin. Click the **OK** button after you have entered the header. Save the document.
5. Print the document.
6. Quit Works by selecting the *Quit* command of the **File** menu.

6.6 DELETING A DOCUMENT

Deleting a document removes the document from a disk and makes the space used by the document available for use. To delete a file proceed as follows.

- Select the *Delete* command from the **File** menu. This causes the dialog box of Figure 6.13 to be displayed.
- Select the document to be deleted by scrolling until the name of the document is found and then clicking it. For example, suppose that the name *Article* is selected.
- Click the *Delete* button in the *Delete* dialog box. This causes the dialog box shown in Figure 6.14 to be displayed.
- Click the *OK* button in the dialog box to confirm that the document is really to be deleted. The document is now deleted, and the space it occupied on the disk is now available for other files. *Be careful using the Delete command because it cannot be undone.*

Of course, a document can also be deleted at the desktop context by dragging the document to the trash can and emptying the trash can.

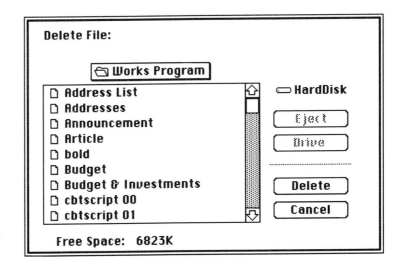

Figure 6.13 The *Delete File* dialog box.

Computer Practice 6.6

1. Open Works and click the *Word Processing* icon.
2. Select the *Delete* command from the **File** menu. When the *Delete File* dialog box is displayed, select your file *Myaddress*.
3. Click the *OK* button when you are asked to confirm the deletion.
4. Quit Works by selecting the *Quit* command from the **File** menu.

6.7 RESUMING WORKS

If the *Quit* command of the **File** menu is selected while there are documents on the desktop, Works saves the names of the documents on the desktop in a file named *Resume Works*. Later, opening the *Resume Works* file will restore the desktop to the form it had when the *Quit* command was given. To use this method proceed as follows:

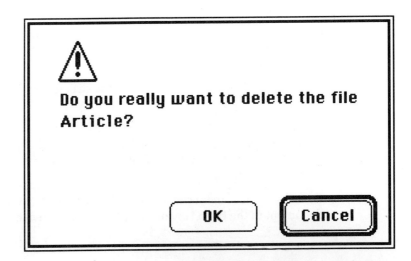

Figure 6.14 The *Confirm Deletion* dialog box.

- Select the *Quit* command from the **File** menu while there are documents on the desktop.
- Click the *Yes* button on the *Close* dialog box when it is displayed if you wish to save the changes to a document. Repeat this step for each document for which the *Close* dialog box is displayed.

When all documents on the desktop have been processed, you are returned directly to the Finder. Later you can open this desktop from within the Finder by double-clicking the *Resume Works* icon (Figure 6.15). You can, of course, start Works using the method described in Section 6.1.

The *Resume Works* document is not affected if you quit Works using a technique other than that just described. For example, if you close and save each document, and then select the *Quit* command, information about the desktop you were using is not saved in *Resume Works*. The *Resume Works* document is a convenient way to start Works with a group of commonly used documents already open and on the desktop in the relative positions that you desire.

Computer Practice 6.7

1. Open Works.
2. Select the word processor and create a new document. Save the empty document with the name *MyWordDoc*.
3. Repeat step 2 in turn for the database and spreadsheet modules. Name the documents *MyDataBase* and *MySpreadsheet*, respectively.
4. Remember the names of the documents and the relative location of their windows.
5. Quit Works by selecting the *Quit* command of the **File** menu. If *Close* dialog boxes are displayed, click the *No* box.
6. Find the *Resume Works* icon and double-click it. Works should start with the same documents open as was the case when the *Quit* command was executed. Note that you could select *Resume Works* in the scroll box with the same results.
7. Quit Works.

6.8 SUMMARY OF COMMON COMMANDS

The menus for Works common tasks are shown in Figure 6.16. In this section, we give a brief description of the commands in these menus.

Figure 6.15 The *Resume Works* icon.

File Menu

New. Creates a new document. Displays a dialog box to allow the creation of a new document of the desired type. Click the icon for the type of new document you want.

Open. Opens an existing document. Displays the opening Works window, Figure 6.2.

Close. Closes an open document. A dialog box will offer you the opportunity to save any changes not already saved before the document is closed.

Save. Saves a copy of the currently active document, replacing the previously existing copy of the document. Presents the same dialog box as *Save As,* for a document being saved for the first time.

Save As. Saves a copy of a document with a new name. The command causes the dialog box of Figure 6.3 to be displayed. It can be used interchangeably with the *Save* command to save a document for the first time.

Delete. Deletes a document. This command displays the *Delete* dialog box of Figure 6.13.

Page Setup. Controls the appearance of a printed page. Displays the appropriate dialog box, Figure 6.8 or Figure 6.9.

Print. Prints a document. Displays the appropriate dialog box, Figure 6.10 or Figure 6.11.

Print Window. Prints the contents of the active window as it appears on the screen, but without the title bar, scroll bar, and size box.

Eject Page. Ejects the current page in the ImageWriter printer and goes to the top of the next sheet of paper. This command is used to jump to the top of a new page on the ImageWriter after using *Print* Window. The command does not work for the LaserWriter.

Print Merge. Merges the contents of a word processing document and a database and prints a document for each record in the database. This topic is discussed in detail in Section 8.6.

Quit. Exits from the Works program and saves the names of the documents left open on the current desktop in the document *Resume Works.*

Edit Menu

Undo. Undoes the most recently executed editing command. The *Undo* command is dimmed if a command cannot be undone. *The* Delete *command and other commands in the **File** menu cannot be undone.*

Cut. Cuts (i.e., removes) the current selection from a document and saves a copy on the Clipboard.

Copy. Copies the current selection to the Clipboard. The selected text is unchanged in the document.

Paste. Pastes a copy of the contents of the Clipboard into the active document at the location of the insertion point. The contents of the Clipboard are unchanged.

Clear. Removes the current selection from a document, but does not place a copy of the selection on the Clipboard.

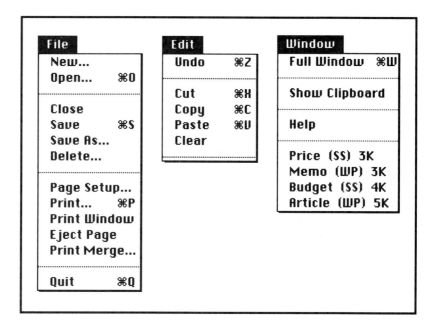

Figure 6.16 Menus that contain commands for common tasks.

Window Menu

Full Window/Small Window. Switches the active window between full size and small size. The size of the small window can be set by dragging the size box for the window. The size and position of a window are stored with the document when it is saved.

Show Clipboard. Opens the *Clipboard* window to display the contents of the Clipboard. The contents of the Clipboard cannot be edited. Click the close box of the *Clipboard* window to close it.

Help. Opens the *Help* window. This command was discussed in detail in Section 6.3.

Activate Window. This command does not occur explicitly in the menu, but it is implied for the names of the windows that are shown below the last dotted line in the **Window** menu. Selecting any of these names makes it the active window. For example, in Figure 6.16 the names *Price* (SS), *Memo* (WP), *Budget* (SS), and *Article* (WP) are the names of open documents, each of which has its own window. Selecting *Budget*, for example, will make it the active window. The name of the active window always appears first in the list.

Key Concepts

Closing a document   Creating a document
Deleting a document   Footers
Headers   Help feature
Page Setup window   Printing a document
Saving a document

CHAPTER 7

PREPARING DOCUMENTS

LEARNING OBJECTIVES

- To gain an overview of word processing concepts.

- To learn to create a document using the Works word processing module.

- To learn to edit a document using the Works word processing module.

- To learn how to format a document using the Works word processing module.

- To learn to search for text strings in a document using the Works word processing module.

I n this chapter you will learn to use the word processing component of Microsoft Works to prepare documents. As you will see, Works' word processor is powerful enough to satisfy many document preparation needs. In particular, you will learn to create a document, enter text into a document, modify a document, change the appearance of the document, save the document on disk, and print a copy of a document. Additionally, you will see how to enter pictorial or graphics data into the document.

7.1 DOCUMENT COMPLEXITY AND WORD PROCESSING

Suppose that you have the job of preparing a very important document. It does not matter what the document is; it could be a term paper, a quarterly sales report, a summary of a company's marketing strategy, or any other report that you know is important. Now consider that the quality of the report will have a significant impact on your future and that the time available to produce the report is too short.

If you have a good secretary, you might try dictating a first draft, getting the result typed, revising the draft, revising the second draft, and so on, until the result is satisfactory or you run out of time—whichever comes first. If you do not have a secretary or you do not dictate well, you will have to produce the first draft yourself. If you are only a so-so typist, the problem is even worse.

Word processing, the simplest of the document preparation tools, is a possible solution to your problem. With word processing it is easy to enter the document, to revise it as many times as appropriate, and to print a high-quality final copy. For the nonexpert typist the ease of correcting errors gives a sense of relaxation about the typing that lets the person concentrate on the document, its organization and content, rather than on the mechanics of the typing.

Document complexity varies greatly. Simple correspondence is not as complex as a report. A report is usually not as complex as a thesis or a book. Single-column documents are not as difficult to prepare as multicolumn documents. Documents having no graphical components are not as complex as documents containing drawings, charts, or photographs.

Preparing documents with page layouts of quality high enough for publication greatly increases the complexity of any of the cases described earlier. Until recent years, publishable documents, whether they were a company's annual report, a textbook, or a page of advertising copy, had to be prepared in final form by specialists. Desktop publishing, the extension of word processing to the production of publication-quality documents, is now available for direct use by those who need it. A computer such as the Macintosh, a laser printer, and an appropriate software package are required. Using desktop publishing software, very precise page layouts can be prepared. Often the text appearing in a desktop publishing document is written using a word processing system and then transferred to the desktop publishing software for production of the final document.

It is difficult for software designers to produce a document preparation program that is both easy to use and capable of handling the wide range in document complexity just described. For the Macintosh there are many word processor programs from which to choose, and to some extent the purchaser must make a choice between ease of use and the complexity of the document that the program can easily handle.

In this chapter we are going to survey the word processing features of the Works word processing module (hereafter called Works WP). The program is easy to use, and its operations are very intuitive. In Chapter 15 we are going to study Microsoft Word (hereafter called Word), which is one of the most feature-laden of the available Macintosh word processing systems. Because almost all that you learn here will transfer to Word, you will find Word easy to use. However, Word is capable of treating more complex documents than those that Works WP can handle.

Exercise Set 7.1

1. List several kinds of documents for which word processing would be valuable to you.
2. Why is a word processor particularly valuable to the nonexpert typist?
3. List five different types of documents arranged in increasing order of difficulty.

7.2 SOME WORD PROCESSING CONCEPTS

In this section we examine some word processing concepts that apply to any word processing system. You should note that there are many similarities between using a word processor and using a typewriter, but there are also many differences because of the flexibility that is possible with a computer. Working with a word processor can be divided into five major functions as follows:

- Creating and saving a document.
- Entering text.
- Editing text.
- Formatting text.
- Printing the text.

These functions will be discussed as if they were independent, but in practice you can jump back and forth between them in any sequence.

CREATING A DOCUMENT. Creating a document refers to giving a command, usually *New*, to create a disk file. This empty file is ready to receive the information that you enter through the keyboard or other input device. Because the information is normally stored in RAM as you work, it is essential that you frequently save a copy of the work to your disk. Because RAM is volatile, if the electrical power is interrupted before you have saved the work, it is lost. A good habit is to save the document whenever the amount entered would be troublesome to redo. The first time the document is saved, you will be asked to give it a name. Select a meaningful name, one that will help you remember the document's contents.

ENTERING TEXT.   Entering text involves using the keyboard to type the document. If you make an error during the typing and notice it immediately, you can use the *Backspace* (or *Delete*) key to erase the error. If you fail to notice the error, it can be corrected during the edit phase.

An important feature associated with entering text is **wordwrap**. When a word is typed that would extend beyond the right margin, it is moved (wrapped) to the beginning of the next line. In Figure 7.1, part A shows the word *demonstrating* extending beyond the right margin. Thus, it is moved to the next line as shown in part B. Actually, as soon as the *a* in *demonstrating* is typed, the partial word moves to the next line, because even the partial word will not fit on the line. Part C shows the appearance of the text after several lines have been entered. The *Return* (or *Enter*) key has not been pressed during the entry of these sentences. Note how this feature of a word processor differs from an ordinary typewriter, where you must use a carriage return at the end of each line. When using a word processor, you will press the *Return* key only when you wish to start a new paragraph.

A **paragraph** in a word processing document consists of the lines typed between pressing the *Return* key. That is, pressing the *Return* key ends a paragraph. It is very important that you follow this convention because paragraphs are automatically reformatted when, for example, margins are reset, line spacing is changed, text is added, or text is deleted. Hence, you will not want to have a carriage return embedded in what you think of as a single paragraph, because the word processor will treat such text as multiple paragraphs. The *Return* key is an element of the word processing language that must be well understood.

When the *Return* key is pressed, an **invisible character** (i.e., a character that does not show when the document is printed) is entered into the text to serve as a language symbol for the end of a paragraph. Many other invisible characters are entered to serve as signals that some action is to be taken. For example, pressing the *Tab* key, which in an ordinary typewriter moves the typing location to preset

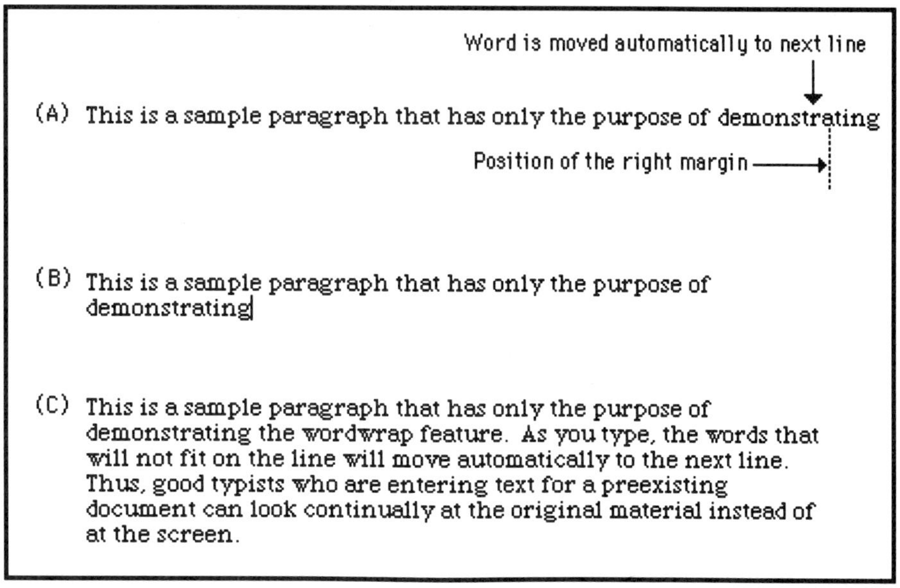

Word is moved automatically to next line

(A) This is a sample paragraph that has only the purpose of demonstrating

Position of the right margin ———▶

(B) This is a sample paragraph that has only the purpose of demonstrating

(C) This is a sample paragraph that has only the purpose of demonstrating the wordwrap feature. As you type, the words that will not fit on the line will move automatically to the next line. Thus, good typists who are entering text for a preexisting document can look continually at the original material instead of at the screen.

Figure 7.1 Illustration of the wordwrap feature.

column positions, enters an invisible character whose purpose is to position the text at some specified column position. In general, any action that causes a change in the formatted appearance of the text enters an invisible character.

Conversely, deleting an invisible character may change the appearance of the text. For example, deleting the blank space at the end of a paragraph removes the *Return* mark and causes the paragraph to become part of the next paragraph, assuming all the formatting of the next paragraph. Some word processors have a command to cause the invisible characters to be displayed in the text on the screen, which is valuable in many formatting situations. Finally, note that *a blank space between words is actually a character* and uses a unit of memory, just as do all other characters.

EDITING A DOCUMENT.   Editing a document is the process of modifying a previously entered document. New text can be entered in a document at any location by placing the insertion pointer at the desired location and then typing the text. Any text entered will take on the character formatting of the text at the insertion point. Existing text can be replaced by selecting the text (highlighting) and typing the new word as shown for the word *good* in part A of Figure 7.2. Part B shows the result of typing the word *excellent*. The method for selecting text depends on the word processor being used.

This example shows an important idea. To perform various operations during editing, the procedure is to *select and then do*. *Select* defines the object to be operated on. *Do* defines the operation to be performed. When editing is discussed for Works WP, you will see many applications of *select and then do*.

Copying is accomplished by selecting the text to be copied, using the *Copy* command that places a copy on the Clipboard, placing the pointer at the location where the copy is to be inserted, and giving the *Paste* command. Both the *Copy* and *Cut* commands place a copy of the selected text on the Clipboard. Details will be described when Works WP is discussed.

FORMATTING A DOCUMENT.   Formatting a document is the process of changing the appearance of the text. There are three kinds of formatting: character, paragraph, and section formatting. **Character formatting** is concerned with changing the appearance of an individual character or sequence of characters. A document can use different character **fonts**, **styles**, or **sizes** for emphasis or to create visual

(A)   This is a sample paragraph that has only the purpose of demonstrating the wordwrap feature. As you type, the words that will not fit on the line will move automatically to the next line. Thus, good typists who are entering text for a preexisting document can look continually at the original material instead of at the screen.

(B)   This is a sample paragraph that has only the purpose of demonstrating the wordwrap feature. As you type, the words that will not fit on the line will move automatically to the next line. Thus, excellent typists who are entering text for a preexisting document can look continually at the original material instead of at the screen.

Figure 7.2 Illustration of the selection process.

Figure 7.3 Sample character fonts.

```
Chicago
Courier
Geneva
New York
Venice
```

interest. Figure 7.3 shows examples of character fonts that can be used, Figure 7.4 shows character style names and corresponding examples, and Figure 7.5 shows character sizes and corresponding examples. Fonts are available for foreign alphabets such as Greek.

Character formatting is also used to create superscripts and subscripts. Superscript characters are raised above the normal position for a character in a line and are often used for footnote reference numbers (e.g., the 2 in $Totals^2$). Subscript characters are below the normal position for a character in a line (e.g., the i in V_i). Both superscripts and subscripts are used in mathematical notation.

You may customize paragraph margins, line spacing, justification (alignment of text along one or both margins), first line indenting, tabs, and other features for each paragraph using **paragraph formatting**. Thus, paragraphs with almost any desired appearance are possible.

To control the appearance of units of text consisting of one or more paragraphs, you use **section formatting**. For example, if some of the pages in a document are to be multicolumn but the rest are to be single-column, sections would be used to define the various parts of the document. Section formatting is considered an advanced feature, and consequently, not all word processors have it.

PRINTING.   Of course, all word processors provide ways to print documents. A document is not changed by printing. During the time that the document is being printed, you may not be able to use the computer for anything else. Some advanced word processors allow other work to be done during the printing. Also, if your network provides for spooling of the documents to be printed, once your

Figure 7.4 Sample character styles

Character Style	Example
Plain Text	wordwrap
Bold	**wordwrap**
Italic	*wordwrap*
Underline	wordwrap
Outline	wordwrap
Shadow	wordwrap

Character Size	Example
9 Point	wordwrap
10 Point	wordwrap
12 Point	wordwrap
14 Point	wordwrap
18 Point	wordwrap
24 Point	wordwrap

Figure 7.5 Examples of different sizes of characters.

document is spooled (i.e., copied to the file server), you will be able to continue work even though the printing may not be finished.

A *Page Setup* (or equivalent) command is used to set the major features of a page such as page height, page length, margins, and the locations of footnotes. The page margins and the paragraph margins, properly called the **paragraph indents**, have slightly different meanings. The page margin is set using the *Page Setup* command and is measured from the edge of the page. The paragraph indent is measured from the location of the page margin. In addition, the first line of a paragraph may also be indented. The situation is shown in Figure 7.6.

As you learn to use a word processor you will be learning to communicate to the computer what you want to do. You will be using a language for the communication process, and your effectiveness will depend in part on your ability to state your desires in word processing language. Each command in the language has consequences.

Part of the time you may not be aware that you are using a language. This is the result of the success of the designers of a word processor in translating normal actions with a typewriter into commands for the word processor. The most common action is entering text, and the command for this process should be as efficient as possible; pressing a key on the keyboard is all that is necessary. Features analogous to the physical cut and paste actions, with scissors and rubber cement, that are used in revising typewritten documents will normally appear as *Cut* and *Paste* commands in the **Edit** pull-down menu. Your intuition will often suffice for finding and using a word processing language command. Note that you do not have to master all features of a word processing language to use a word processor. As you write more complex documents, you can learn the necessary new commands to accomplish your goals.

Exercise Set 7.2

1. List and define the five major functions of word processing. In what order can the functions be done?
2. Why is it essential that a word processing document be saved frequently during processing?

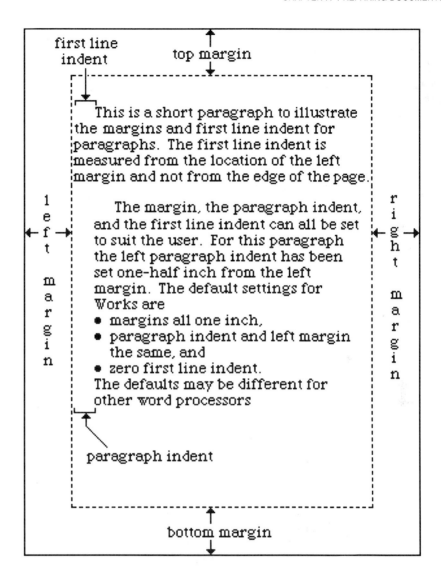

Figure 7.6 Organization of a word processing page.

3. What is wordwrap? Why is it so valuable?

4. What is a paragraph in word processing? Why would pressing the *Return* key at the end of every line be very poor word processing technique?

5. What is the purpose of the *Tab* key?

6. What are invisible characters and what is their significance in word processing documents? Why is having a command to display invisible characters valuable?

7. Describe the kinds of actions performed during the editing process. How is copying accomplished?

8. What is selection of text? Why is it important?

9. What is character formatting?

10. Explain the terms *font, style, size, subscript,* and *superscript* as they apply to character formatting.

11. What is paragraph formatting? List the kinds of document features controlled by paragraph formatting.
12. What is section formatting?
13. What effect does printing have on the contents of a stored document?
14. Why do you think learning a word processing language seems so easy and natural?
15. Describe the organization of a word processing page, giving particular attention to margins, paragraph indent, and first line indent.
16. Paragraph indent is measured from what page position?
17. First line indent is measured from what page position?

7.3 GETTING STARTED WITH WORKS WP

Works must already be running before you can start the word processor. Recall that once Works is open, the Works opening window will be displayed, and the icons for the various tools will appear at the top of the desktop, as shown in Figure 7.7. To start the Works WP, select its icon and either create a new WP document or open an existing WP document.

ENTERING TEXT. Let us assume that a new document has been created and that you are ready to enter text. The empty window, which has the appearance shown in Figure 7.8, contains two pointers: a blinking vertical line called the *insertion pointer*, which is the point at which text is entered, and the *I-beam pointer*, a nonblinking pointer whose position is controlled by the mouse. As text is entered, the insertion pointer will move along to indicate the new location for entering

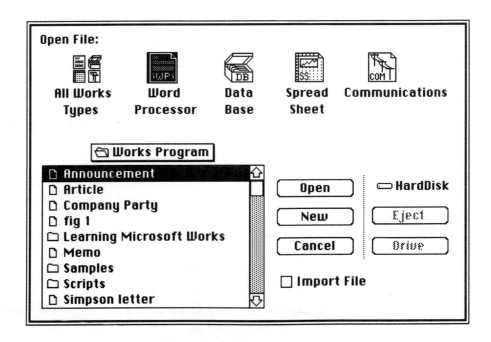

Figure 7.7 The Works opening window.

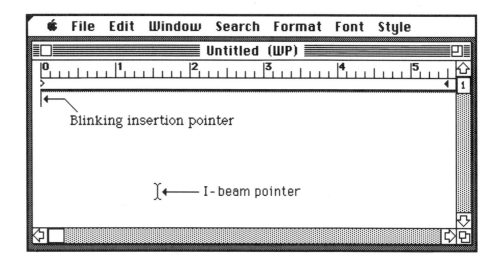

Figure 7.8 The empty Works WP window.

text. The I-beam is used to move the insertion pointer to any position in previously typed text. The I-beam pointer may not be visible initially, but it will appear as soon as you move the mouse.

At the top of the window is a picture of a **ruler** that shows the current format for paragraphs. A description of how to read a ruler and to modify its settings to structure paragraphs within your document is given in Section 7.5. Each paragraph has its own ruler that determines its indent settings and tabs. Rulers can be hidden by selecting the *Hide ruler* command from the **Format** menu. Hiding the rulers allows more text to be displayed in the window. For many purposes the default paragraph settings are satisfactory, and you can start typing immediately.

To enter information in the window, you would type just as you would with a typewriter. Remember that the *Return* key should be pressed *only* when you reach the end of a paragraph. To create a blank line between paragraphs, press the *Return* key twice at the end of a paragraph. Each additional pressing of the *Return* key will insert an additional blank line. Figure 7.9 shows a portion of a short letter. The blank lines were created as just described.

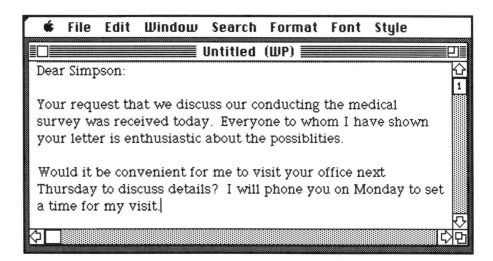

Figure 7.9 A short letter created with Works WP.

The title line of the document contains *Untitled (WP)*. This means that the document has not been saved, because saving a document requires that a name be given to it. The WP indicates that this is a word processing document as opposed to the other possible kinds of documents in Works. Selecting the *Save* or *Save As* command from the **File** menu allows you to save the document with whatever name you wish and causes the name to be displayed in the title bar in a way quite similar to the method used earlier with MacPaint.

Computer Practice 7.3

1. Open Works and start Works WP.
2. Create a new word processing document.
3. Type the information located in the box at the end of this practice into your document window. Type it exactly as you see it. Before starting, set the right indent marker (the black triangle on the right of the ruler) to 5.5 inches by pointing at the triangle and dragging it to the proper position. The left indent marker (the black triangle on the left of the ruler) should already be set to zero, but if it is not, drag it to that location.
4. Select the *Save As* command in the **File** menu, and save your document with the name *practice 7.3*. The document will be used again in the exercises of Section 7.4.
5. Quit Works.

```
Correcting a Document

A word processor such as that found in Works can change the way
that you think about writing a document. Creating a WP paper is less
trouble than ordinary typing because errors can be corrected properly
as they occur. It is however during the revising of a document that
word processing really shines. Revising becomes a satisfying
manipulating activity instead of a time-consuming retyping job.
Learning to use a word processor is well worth the time required. The
document can be modified in many ways, including:

1. Inserting new words, lines, or paragraphs.
2. Copying or moving blocks of information to new locations.
3. Changing the format of the entire document or the format of
various paragraphs.
```

7.4 EDITING TEXT

Editing text is the process of modifying text after it has been entered into a document. Almost all documents must be edited several times before the final version is obtained. Thus, learning the techniques for editing is very important to you. Recall that editing can be done at any time after text has been entered; it is not necessary to wait until the first draft has been completed. Errors should be corrected as soon as they are discovered.

To edit text, move the insertion pointer to the location of the text to be edited. First, find the desired page using scrolling. When the desired location is found, use the mouse to position the I-beam pointer at the position of interest and click the mouse. The insertion pointer moves to the new location. With the insertion pointer now in the proper location, a number of different editing operations can be performed.

INSERTING TEXT.   To **insert text**, type the text of interest. This can be as short as a single character or as long as many paragraphs.

Suppose that we notice that the word *Mr.* has been omitted in the letter to Mr. Simpson. Move the I-beam to just before the word *Simpson* in the salutation (see Figure 7.10) and click to move the insertion pointer there. Now type the missing word. We also note the the date for the proposed meeting has not been given. It is inserted after the word *Thursday*, as shown in Figure 7.11.

INSERTING PICTORIAL DATA.   In Figure 5.5 the visual impact of a letter for a company party was enhanced by adding a title that contained pictorial data. **Pictorial data insertion** is quite similar to insertion of ordinary text except that in many instances the picture is first prepared with a program such as MacPaint. To add pictorial data proceed as follows.

- Prepare the pictorial data using an application such as MacPaint.
- Copy the pictorial data to the Clipboard.
- Enter the Works document.
- Move the I-beam pointer to the location where the insertion is to occur.
- Click the mouse button to set the insertion point to this location.
- Paste the contents of the Clipboard into the document at the insertion point by selecting the *Paste* command of the **File** menu.

SELECTING TEXT.   The **selection of text** is a key process both for editing data and for formatting. Selection is the first step in the processes of replacing, deleting,

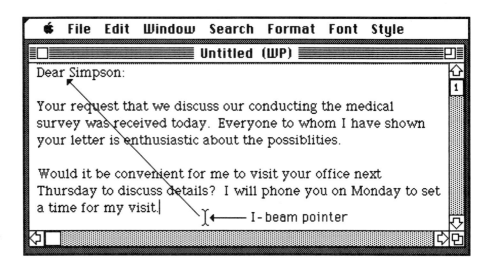

Figure 7.10 Moving the insertion pointer with the I-beam.

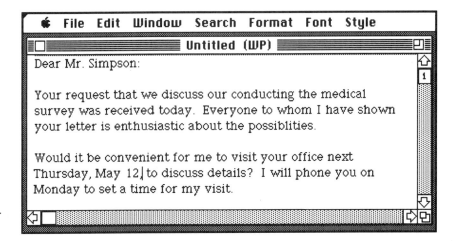

Figure 7.11 Example of inserting text.

copying, or moving text. The most general technique for selecting is dragging. In Works, selected text is highlighted. To select text by dragging, do the following steps.

- Using the I-beam, point to the beginning of the text to be selected.
- Drag the I-beam to the end of the text to be selected.
- Release the mouse button.

Figure 7.12 shows the result of selecting a phrase of text.

Any amount of text can be selected by dragging, from a single character to the entire document. To select large amounts of text, place the I-beam just before the beginning of the text to be selected and then drag the I-beam down the region between the left edge of the window and the left margin. As the I–beam moves down this region, the lines will be selected. When you reach the bottom of the window, the remaining text will scroll upward automatically and become selected. A common problem is to select more text than is desired, but don't panic if this happens to you. As long as you have not released the mouse button, the I-

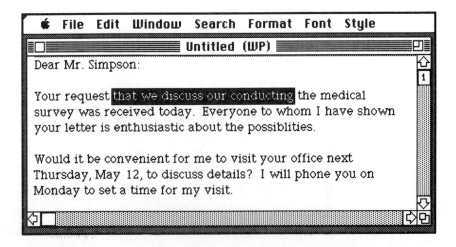

Figure 7.12 Selecting a phrase by dragging.

beam can be moved back up the window, deselecting lines. This method also works if you start within a line and drag down. Don't release the mouse button until you have selected exactly the text of interest. Figure 7.13 illustrates the method.

SELECTING TEXT RAPIDLY.   To select a word rapidly, point to the word of interest and double-click. The word will be highlighted. If you make a mistake and select the wrong word, click again to deselect the word.

The selection of a word can be extended to include as many additional words as you wish by pressing the *Shift* key and continuing to click words. Note that you must select the first word before pressing the *Shift* key. This method of extending the selection also works for the methods of rapid selection of lines and paragraphs that are discussed later. Recall that this method is called the *shift-click method*.

To select a line rapidly, move the I-beam pointer to the region between the left edge of the window and the left margin. The pointer will change to a left-pointing arrow. Locate the arrow beside the line to be selected and click.

You can select a paragraph rapidly by proceeding as just described for selecting a line, but double-click instead. The paragraph to the right of the arrow will be selected. By choosing the *Select All* command in the **Edit** menu, you can select the entire document at once.

DELETING TEXT.   The simplest way to **delete text** is to use the *Backspace* (or *Delete*) key when you make an error during typing. To delete text at any other time, you must first select the text using one of the methods discussed earlier. Then three methods are available for deleting the selected text.

- Method 1. Press the *Backspace* (or *Delete*) key. The text is deleted. If you have made a mistake, you can recover the deleted text by selecting the *Undo* command in the **Edit** menu. The *Undo* command works only if no other actions have been taken after the deletion.

- Method 2. Select the *Cut* command from the **Edit** menu. The selected text is deleted and a copy of it is saved on the Clipboard. This allows the text to be pasted into the document at another position.

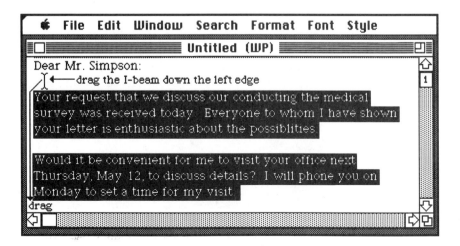

Figure 7.13 Selecting text by dragging.

■ Method 3. If you wish to **replace text** to be deleted with alternate text, you can type in or paste from the Clipboard the new text after selecting the text to be replaced. The selected text will be deleted automatically as you enter new text.

DELETING PICTURES.   As discussed earlier, pictures created using MacPaint or other graphics programs can be added to Works WP documents. To delete a picture, point to the interior of the picture and click. Then select the *Select Picture* command from the **Edit** menu. Finally, press the *Backspace* (or *Delete*) key or select the *Cut* command from the **Edit** menu, as appropriate for your goals.

MOVING TEXT.   In writing documents, it is often desirable to **move a block of text** to another location to achieve greater clarity, better visual impact, or better document organization. It is easy to move text using Works' cut and paste technique which is analogous to that done using scissors and tape with typed documents. Proceed as follows.

■ Select the block of interest using any of the selection methods.
■ Select the *Cut* command of the **Edit** menu. The selected text will be deleted from the document and a copy will be placed on the Clipboard.
■ Move the insertion pointer to the location where the text should be inserted.
■ Select the *Paste* command from the **Edit** menu. The text on the Clipboard will be pasted into the document immediately following the insertion point. The text is unchanged on the Clipboard, so it could also be pasted in other locations in the document.

Consider the example in Figures 7.14A and 7.14B. In the letter to Mr. Simpson we wish to interchange the first and second paragraphs. The second paragraph is selected, including an extra blank line. (Later this will be the space separating the two paragraphs.) Then the *Cut* command of the **Edit** menu is selected. The second paragraph disappears, but a copy of it is saved on the Clipboard. The I-beam pointer is moved to a point before the *T* in *Thank* and clicked to move the insertion pointer. Finally, from the **Edit** menu the *Paste* command is given to produce the result shown in Figure 7.14B.

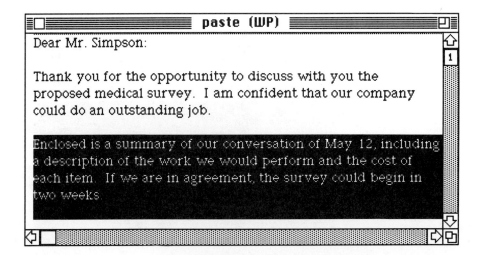

Figure 7.14A Paragraph selected for moving.

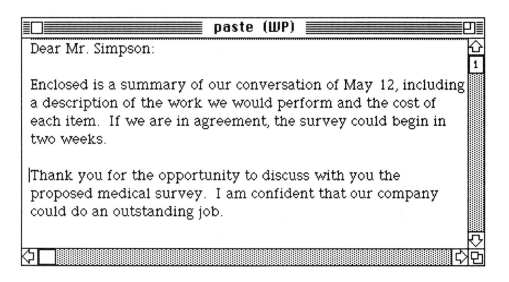

Figure 7.14B Paragraph after being moved.

COPYING TEXT.   Occasionally, you will wish to duplicate text in several parts of a document. This process is called **copying text**. To accomplish this, you proceed exactly as you would to move text, except that you use the *Copy* command instead of the *Cut* command in the **Edit** menu.

Exercise Set 7.4

1. What are the shapes and the purposes of the insertion pointer and the I-beam pointer?
2. Describe the process for inserting text into a document.
3. Describe the process for inserting pictorial data into a document.
4. Give several actions that can be performed on selected text.
5. Describe the following methods for selecting text:
   a. Dragging.
   b. Selecting a word rapidly.
   c. Selecting a line rapidly.
   d. Selecting a paragraph rapidly.
   e. Selecting the entire document.
   f. Selecting additional words by shift-clicking.
6. Give three methods for deleting text and indicate when each should be used.
7. Describe the process for deleting pictorial data.
8. Describe the process for moving text. In what way is the Clipboard involved in this process?
9. Describe the process for copying text. In what way is the Clipboard involved in this process?

Computer Practice 7.4

1. Start Works and open the document *practice 7.3* that you entered in Computer Practice 7.3.

2.   In line 4 change the word *properly* to the word *easily*.

3.   Move the word *easily*, which was just entered, before the word *corrected*, to produce the phrase *easily corrected*.

4.   In line 5 insert commas around the word *however*.

5.   In line 7 change the word *manipulating* to the word *creative*.

6.   In line 8 insert the words *and effort* immediately after the word *time*.

7.   Move the sentence starting in line 8 with the words *Learning to use* to the end of the document, and make it a new paragraph. A blank line should precede the new paragraph.

8.   Your document should now be identical to the text shown in the box at the end of this practice section. If your text is different, make appropriate corrections.

9.   After all the changes have been made and your document is identical to that in the box, use the *Save As* command of the **File** menu to save the document with the name *practice 7.4*. This document will be used for practice at the end of Section 7.5.

10.   Use the method described in Chapter 6 to print your document.

11.   Quit Works.

Correcting a Document

A word processor such as that found in Works can change the way that you think about writing a document. Creating a WP paper is less trouble than ordinary typing because errors can be easily corrected as they occur. It is, however, during the revising of a document that word processing really shines. Revising becomes a satisfying creative activity instead of a time-consuming retyping job. The document can be modified in many ways, including:

1. Inserting new words, lines, or paragraphs.
2. Copying or moving blocks of information to new locations.
3. Changing the format of the entire document or the format of various paragraphs.

Learning to use a word processor is well worth the time and effort required.

7.5 FORMATTING

This section gives the details for controlling the appearance of a document, its individual paragraphs, and the characters within the paragraphs. By using these features you will be able to create documents that have the desired visual impact.

PAGE FORMAT.   Recall from Chapter 6 that the page setup for all Works documents can be accomplished using the *Page Setup* command from the **File** menu.

Using this command and its dialog box, you can set the page margins, page size, headers, footers, orientation, and other special effects.

DOCUMENT FONT.   When you first start the Works WP, the font is set to Geneva. As you type the document, you can change to another font at any time by pointing to the **Font** menu and dragging to the desired font. The new font will apply only to the newly entered text—the previously typed text will not be affected. The font of previously entered text may also be changed by first selecting the text and then choosing a different font from the **Font** menu.

Figure 7.15 shows the form of several fonts. Note that the example sentence occupies different line lengths for different fonts. This is due to the difference in the design of the characters in different fonts. Also note that different fonts have quite different visual impact. You can use this feature to make documents convey your ideas more effectively.

PARAGRAPH FORMATTING AND RULERS.   **Rulers** are used to set the indents and tabs for individual paragraphs. *The settings displayed on a displayed ruler always refer to the paragraph in which the insertion point is located.* This formatting information is stored as invisible characters at the end of a paragraph. Thus, deleting the blank spaces at the end of a paragraph may change the format of the paragraph.

On a ruler two small black triangles show the locations of the left and the right indents. In addition, a smaller black rectangle shows how the first line of a paragraph will be indented. If all the lines of the paragraph have the same left indenting, both the left indent marker and the first line indenting marker will be at the same location. In this case, the first line indicator becomes a small white rectangle within the left indent marker. This situation is demonstrated in Figure 7.16A.

The three markers (left indent, right indent, and first line indent) can be moved along the ruler by dragging the marker to the desired location. In Figure 7.16B the first line indent marker has been moved to cause the first line to be indented 0.5 inch.

Marker settings that produce a **hanging indent** (left hanging first line) are shown in Figure 7.16C. Notice that the first line indent marker is to the left of the

Font	Sample Sentence
Chicago	**You may use different fonts in a document.**
Courier	You may use different fonts in a document.
Geneva	You may use different fonts in a document.
Helvetica	You may use different fonts in a document.
Monaco	You may use different fonts in a document.
New York	You may use different fonts in a document.
Times	You may use different fonts in a document.
Venice	*You may use different fonts in a document.*

Figure 7.15 A sample sentence using different fonts.

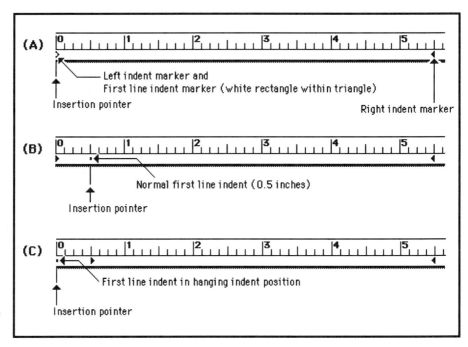

Figure 7.16 Examples of the ruler and its markers.

left indent marker. Figure 7.17 shows text entered with this technique. The *Return* key was not pressed during the typing of the text in the figure.

Tabs are placed by default every 0.5 inch across the ruler; these **default tabs** are invisible. If these locations of the tabs are not suitable, you can place a left tab at any location by pointing at the desired location on the ruler and clicking. Both left and right tabs are available, and both are illustrated in Figure 7.18. To enter a left tab, point at the ruler and click. Pointing at a tab and clicking changes a tab to the other tab type.

Left tabs fix the left edge of text at the position of the tab. Subsequent characters entered are to the right of the tab position. Notice in Figure 7.18 that the L in *Left* is at the location of the tab and that characters typed later are to the right of the tab.

Right tabs fix the right edge of text at the position of the tab. Notice in Figure 7.18 that the *p* in *stop* is at the location of the tab and that characters typed earlier have moved to the left. Right tabs are often used to align a column of digits.

An important feature of these tabs is that when you insert a new tab, invisible default tabs to the left of the entered tab are erased automatically. Erasure of the

This is an example of the hanging indent technique. The first line extends to the left of the rest of the paragraph, that is, it hangs over to the left. On the ruler the first line indent marker is 0.5 inches to the left of the left indent marker.

Figure 7.17 An example of the hanging indent technique.

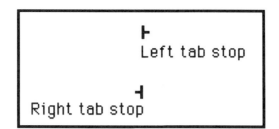

Figure 7.18 Right and left tabs.

default tabs may cause the text to be rearranged in a surprising manner, but if this happens, do not panic. Merely insert new tabs in the location of those erased by pointing at the desired locations on the ruler and clicking.

The use of tabs to create a table is shown in Figure 7.19. The tabs shown were used for entering each item name and its associated numerical data. Right tabs were used for positioning the columns of numbers. Note the location of the insertion pointer, and remember that the ruler displayed is always for the paragraph currently containing the insertion pointer. A series of left tabs in the ruler for the first paragraph was used for positioning the column headings.

LINE SPACING.   To change the line spacing in the paragraph in which the insertion pointer is located, select the *Spacing* command in the **Format** menu. The dialog box shown in Figure 7.20 will be displayed. Click the button for the desired line spacing; the paragraph will immediately have the indicated spacing. If you wish to change the spacing for several paragraphs, or perhaps for the entire document, select the text of interest and then proceed as described for a paragraph.

JUSTIFICATION OF TEXT.   The term *justification of text* refers to the alignment of the text in the paragraph along one or both of the indents. The **Format** menu contains four commands for controlling justification for the paragraph containing the insertion pointer or the selected paragraphs. *Left*, if selected, produces an aligned left indent with a jagged right indent. This is the justification style seen in most typewritten letters. *Justified* causes alignment of text at both the left and right

Item	Unit Cost	Number	Total
Micro disks	1.80	200	360.00
Printer ribbons	7.00	15	105.00
Paper, printer	21.10	6	126.60
Total			591.60

Figure 7.19 Using tabs for creating a table.

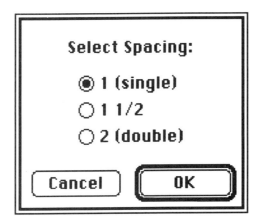

Figure 7.20 The *Spacing* dialog box.

indents. It is seen in books and other typeset documents. *Centered* causes text to be centered between the indents and is useful for titles. *Right* causes the text to be jagged along the left indent and smooth along the right indent, which is sometimes useful for special effects. Examples of the kinds of justification are given in Figure 7.21.

(A) Left justified, jagged right indent

Enclosed is a summary of our conversation of May 12, including a description of the work we would perform and the cost of each item. If we are in agreement, the survey could begin in two weeks.

(B) Justified, both indents even

Enclosed is a summary of our conversation of May 12, including a description of the work we would perform and the cost of each item. If we are in agreement, the survey could begin in two weeks.

(C) Centered

SUMMARY OF CONVERSATION
May 12

(D) Right justified, jagged left indent

Enclosed is a summary of our conversation of May 12, including a description of the work we would perform and the cost of each item. If we are in agreement, the survey could begin in two weeks.

Figure 7.21 Examples of the application of the *Justification* commands.

COPYING PARAGRAPH FORMATS. When the *Return* key is pressed, the current paragraph is ended and a new paragraph is started. All the formatting information of the first paragraph (e.g., indents, tabs, spacing, and justification) becomes associated with the new paragraph. This is valuable because adjacent paragraphs tend to have similar formats, and it would be inefficient to have to reset all the format parameters for each new paragraph.

Occasions arise when you need to use a format that is found in some other part of the document. One option is to reset all the format parameters manually, but it is usually faster to use the *Copy Format* command.

- Place the insertion pointer in the paragraph having the desired format.
- Select the *Copy Format* command of the **Format** menu.
- Place the insertion pointer in the paragraph that is to have the selected format.
- Select the *Paste Format* command of the **Format** menu.

If you wish to copy a format to a larger part of the document, select the portions of the document before giving the *Paste Format* command. You may also jump around in the document, pasting the format in various paragraphs.

CHARACTER FORMATTING. Interest and visual impact can be added to a document by character formatting in which the appearance of a portion of the text is made to be different from some other portion. The following three methods can be used independently or in combination:

- Changing the font.
- Changing character style.
- Changing the size of the characters.

To change the font of a portion of text, select the text; then in the **Font** menu, drag to the font of interest and release the mouse button. Illustrations of several fonts are given in Figure 7.15. Many fonts can be purchased and added to the **Font** menu to make them available in Works WP.

To change the style of a portion of text, select the text and then select the style from the **Style** menu. Figure 7.22 shows the styles available in Works WP.

The size of text is changed in the same way as the font or style except the appropriate size is selected from the **Style** menu. In Figure 7.5 the word *wordwrap* is shown in various sizes. The usual size for text is 12 points. You can experiment with the fonts, styles, and character sizes to see if they improve a document. If you cannot find a change that pleases you, converting the text back to its original format takes only a few seconds.

Normal Text	**Outline**
Bold	**Shadow**
Italic	**Superscript**
<u>**Underline**</u>	**Subscript**

Figure 7.22 Some styles available in Works WP.

PAGE BREAKS. As you type a Works document, the text is automatically divided into pages. The division between pages, or **page break**, is shown by a dotted line across the screen. The vertical scroll box contains the number of the page that is visible, as can be seen in Figure 7.19.

Occasionally the automatic page break produces an unsatisfactory result, such as when a short table is divided between two pages or when the last line of a paragraph is at the top of a page. You can override the automatic page break by using the *Page Break* command in the **Format** menu. To insert a manual page break, place the insertion pointer at the location of the desired page break and then select the *Page Break* command to insert the page break.

A manual page break will be signaled by a dashed line across the window instead of a dotted line. Once a manual page break is entered, Works WP will automatically reposition the page breaks for successive pages. To remove a manual page break, place the insertion pointer at the beginning of the line following the dashed line that represents the manual page break, and select the *Remove Page Break* command of the **Format** menu. This command only appears in the pull-down menu when the insertion pointer is properly positioned immediately following the manual page break line.

DRAWING LINES AND SHAPES. Selecting the *Draw* command of the **Edit** menu displays the dialog box shown in Figure 7.23 and switches the word processor into a mode for **drawing** simple figures. Point to any of the lines or shapes in the box and click. The selected shape will be highlighted, as is the case for the narrow straight line shown in the figure. Click the *OK* button to complete the selection. The word processing window will appear again, and the pointer will become a cross, +. Lines and shapes can then be drawn exactly as they are constructed in MacPaint. You will not be able to type again until you select the *Draw Off* command in the **Edit** menu.

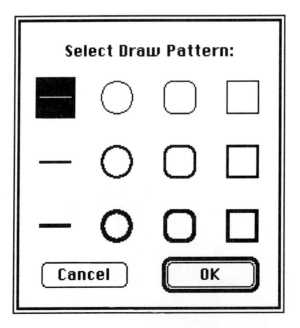

Figure 7.23 Shapes for drawing in the word processor.

Figure 7.24 shows two geometric shapes drawn as just described. The left shape was created by using the box with rounded corners. This command was executed three times, once for each component of the figure. The right shape is a rectangle with straight lines that connect the corners.

Drawing can be used to enhance or clarify a document. In Figure 7.25 a box has been drawn around the final total to emphasize it. If the table had been larger or more complex, vertical and horizontal lines could be used to make it easier to read. Text and drawings can overlay each other without obscuring the original information. For example, the box was drawn around the previously typed total value. *The text and drawings can also be moved or deleted independently.*

EDITING A FIGURE.   A figure can be edited using techniques similar to those used for text. A figure must first be selected using the *Select Picture* command in the **Edit** menu. Before the selection, place the pointer to the left of the figure. A selected figure will be highlighted and contained by a moving dashed line. A selected figure can be copied, cut, and pasted as if it were text. If the *Backspace* (or *Delete*) key is pressed while a figure is selected, the figure is deleted without placing it on the Clipboard. This action can be undone if no additional command has been given.

MOVING A FIGURE.   To move a figure, select it and move the pointer over it. The pointer will become a hand, as in MacPaint. When the hand is moved, the outline of the selected figure moves. Click when the figure is in the proper location. (*Note:* A figure may be composed of subfigures that must be manipulated independently. For example, the right object in Figure 7.24 is actually a rectangle and two straight lines. Thus, in that case, there are three figures to move or to edit.)

CHANGING THE SIZE OF A FIGURE.   To change the size of a figure, select it and move the pointer to any edge of the figure. The pointer will become a cross, +. Press the mouse button and drag the cross in any direction to change the size of the figure.

Exercise Set 7.5

1.   What is meant by formatting?

2.   Describe the process for setting paragraph indents.

3.   How do you change the font for the entire document?

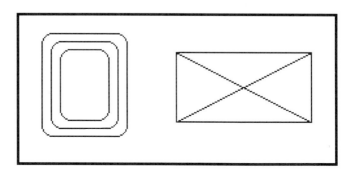

Figure 7.24 Geometric shapes created with the drawing feature.

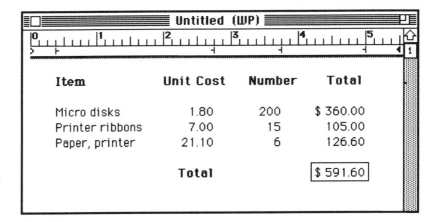

Figure 7.25 Enhancement of a document using the drawing feature.

4. Describe the procedure for displaying rulers and the procedure for hiding rulers.

5. To what part of a document does a ruler refer?

6. What is the purpose of a hanging indent? Describe the process for creating a hanging indent.

7. What is a default tab? Where are they located on a ruler? Can they be seen?

8. How is a tab stop inserted on a ruler? What happens to the default tabs to the left of the inserted tab?

9. How is a left tab stop changed to a right tab stop? What about the reverse change?

10. When is a right tab stop particularly valuable?

11. What is meant by the term *line spacing*? How is line spacing changed?

12. What is justification of text? What kinds of justification does Works have? How is a justification selection made?

13. Describe the process for copying a paragraph format.

14. Describe the kinds of character formatting that can be done in Works WP.

15. Describe how to insert and remove a manual page break.

16. Describe the drawing capabilities of Works WP.

17. Give the steps for drawing a triangle and for drawing two concentric circles.

18. Describe the steps for moving a figure drawn with Works WP.

19. Give the procedure for changing the size of a figure drawn with the word processor.

Computer Practice 7.5

1. Open Works and open the document *practice 7.4* that you saved in Computer Practice 7.4.

2. Center line 1 and make it bold.

3. Give the first paragraph a first line indent of 0.5 inches.

4. Make the first paragraph justified at both margins.

5. Give the numbered comments a hanging indent with the first line 0.5 inches from the margin and subsequent lines indented an additional 0.25 inches.

6. Give the final paragraph a first line indent of 0.5 inches and make it justified at both margins.

    Your document should now be identical to the text shown in the following box. If your text is different, make appropriate corrections.

7. After all the changes have been made and your document is identical to that given in the following box, use the *Save As* command of the **File** menu to save the document with the name *practice 7.5*.

Correcting a Document

A word processor such as that found in Works can change the way that you think about writing a document. Creating a WP paper is less trouble than ordinary typing because errors can be easily corrected as they occur. It is, however, during the revising of a document that word processing really shines. Revising becomes a satisfying creative activity instead of a time-consuming retyping job. The document can be modified in many ways, including:

1. Inserting new words, lines, or paragraphs.
2. Copying or moving blocks of information to new locations.
3. Changing the format of the entire document or the format of various paragraphs.

Learning to use a word processor is well worth the time and effort required.

---

8. Quit Works.

7.6 SEARCHING TEXT FOR SPECIFIC CHARACTER STRINGS

Suppose in a long document you needed to find a word or phrase that might occur in several locations. A manual search in which you read the document is both inefficient and error prone. Works provides a special feature for **searching text** to help with this problem. The **Search** menu, shown in Figure 7.26, has two search commands.

FIND COMMAND. The *Find* command is used to find occurrences of a word or phrase. For example, suppose that we needed to find all the occurrences of the word *Figure* in this chapter. Proceed as follows.

■ Select the *Find* command from the **Search** menu. This will cause the dialog box of Figure 7.27 (without the word *Figure* inserted) to be displayed.

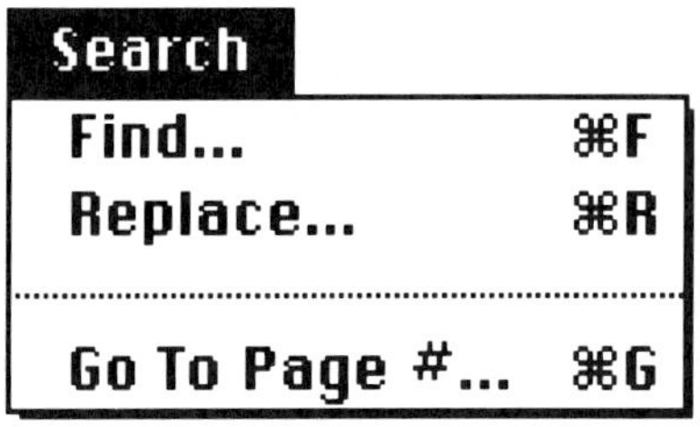

Search

Find...	⌘F
Replace...	⌘R
Go To Page #...	⌘G

Figure 7.26 The **Search** menu.

- Type the word or phrase of interest (*Figure*, in this case) in the long, rectangular box to the right of the words *Find What*. An entry in this box can be up to 80 characters in length.

- Click the box before *Match Whole Words Only* if you are interested only in whole words. For example, if you click this box, the word *Figures* would not be an exact match because of the *s* on the end, and it would not be found. It *would* be found if the box is not clicked.

- Click the box *Check Upper/Lowercase* if you want the case of the characters to be significant. For example, if the box is clicked, the word *figure* would not be found because its first character does not have the same case as the entered word *Figure*.

- Click the *Find Next* button to begin the search from the current location of the insertion pointer. When a match is found, the document is displayed with the word highlighted. The *Find* dialog box stays on the screen. If an occurrence is found that is not of interest, click the *Find Next* button again to continue the search. At the end of the document a message will be displayed that no more occurrences of the word could be found.

- Click the *Cancel* button to exit the *Find* command and return to work on the text. Normally, this will be done when an occurrence of the word has been found that needs modification. The *Find* dialog box will disappear from the screen, and the text containing the highlighted word will continue to be displayed.

REPLACE COMMAND. The operation of the *Replace* command is quite similar to the *Find* command except that the found word or phrase can be replaced with a new word or phrase. To use the command proceed as follows.

- Select the *Replace* command from the **Search** menu. The *Replace* dialog box of Figure 7.28 will be displayed (except for the information already in the *Find What* and *Replace With* boxes).

- Type the information in the *Find What* and *Replace With* boxes. Each entry may be as long as 80 characters. As an example, let us assume that a rather long

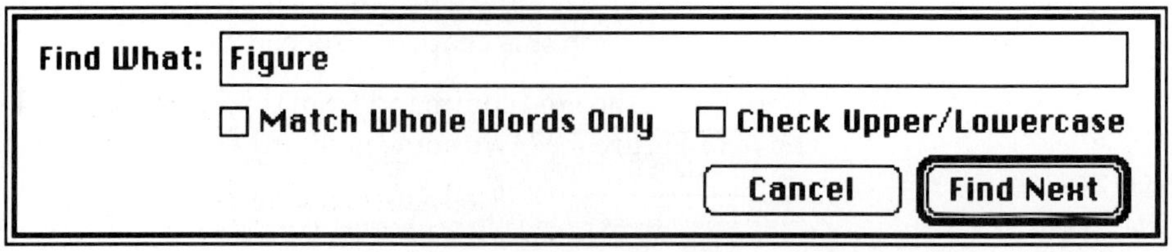

Find What: | Figure

☐ **Match Whole Words Only**   ☐ **Check Upper/Lowercase**

[Cancel] [**Find Next**]

Figure 7.27 The *Find* dialog box.

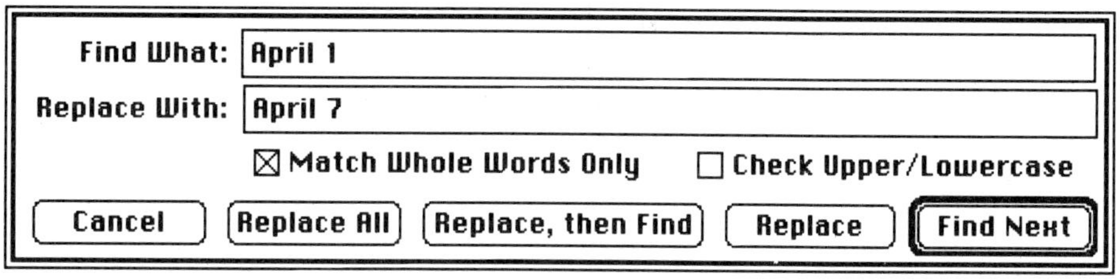

```
┌────────────────────────────────────────────────────────────────┐
│   Find What:  │April 1                                          │
│ Replace With: │April 7                                          │
│                 ☒ Match Whole Words Only    ☐ Check Upper/Lowercase │
│  ( Cancel )  (Replace All) (Replace, then Find)  ( Replace )  (Find Next) │
└────────────────────────────────────────────────────────────────┘
```

Figure 7.28 The *Replace* dialog box.

document mentions several times a meeting that is to be held on April 1. Then it is discovered that the meeting has been rescheduled for April 7, so this date must be changed throughout the document. In the *Find What* box, type *April 1*. In the *Replace With* box type *April 7*.

- Click the *Replace All* button to replace all occurrences of *April 1*. This is the command to use if you are certain that all occurrences of *April 1* refer to the meeting.

- Click the *Find Next* button if you are not sure that all occurrences of *April 1* refer to the meeting. When an occurrence of *April 1* is found, the search pauses with the phrase highlighted and the dialog box on the screen.

- Click the *Find Next* button to continue the search without changing the current occurrence of the phrase.

- Click the *Replace* button to replace only the current occurrence of the phrase. This does not terminate the processing, and you may select *Cancel* or another option as you wish.

- Click the *Replace, then Find* button to replace this occurrence of the phrase and then continue the search.

GO TO PAGE # COMMAND.   In long documents considerable time can be required using the scroll box to find the beginning of a page. An alternative and faster method is to use the *Go To Page #* command.

- Select the *Go To Page #* command from the **Search** menu. The dialog box of Figure 7.29 will be displayed.

- Type the page number in the box that follows the words *Go To Page #*.

- Click the *OK* button; the requested page will be displayed immediately.

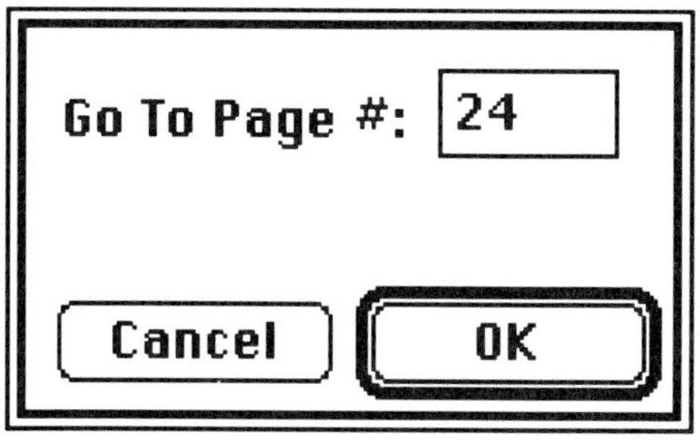

```
┌──────────────────────────────┐
│                              │
│  Go To Page #: │ 24      │   │
│                              │
│                              │
│   ( Cancel )     ( OK )      │
│                              │
└──────────────────────────────┘
```

Figure 7.29 The *Go To Page # dialog box.

Exercise Set 7.6

1. What commands are found in the **Search** menu?

2. What is the purpose of the *Find* command? How long a phrase can be used by the command?

3. What happens if the *Match Whole Words Only* box is not checked?

4. What is the purpose of the *Replace* command?

5. For the *Replace* command, explain the difference in the *Replace All*, the *Replace then Find*, and the *Replace* options.

Computer Practice 7.6

1. Start Works and open the document *practice 7.5* that was saved in Computer Practice 7.5.

2. Place the insertion pointer at the beginning of the document.

3. Select the *Find* command from the **Search** menu. Type the word *the* in the *Find What* box. Do not click the *Match Whole Words Only* button.

4. Click the *Find Next* button to start the search. Count the number of occurrences of *the*.

5. Repeat steps 3 and 4, but this time click the *Match Whole Words Only* button. What is the count for *the* this time?

6. Place the insertion pointer at the beginning of the document.

7. Select the *Replace* command from the **Search** menu. Type *the* in the *Find What* box and *THE* in the *Replace With* box. Do not click the *Match Whole Words Only* button. Click the *Replace All* button. Examine the document.

8. Using the *Replace* command, change the document back to its form before the steps in part 7 were executed.

9. Quit Works. Do not save the changes to the document on which you were working.

Key Concepts

Character formatting
Character style
Default tab
Document complexity
Editing text
Hanging indent
Invisible characters
Moving text
Page margins
Paragraph formatting
Pictorial data insertion
Ruler
Section formatting
Wordwrap

Character size
Copying text
Deleting text
Drawing in Works WP
Font
Inserting text
Justification of text
Page break
Paragraph
Paragraph indents
Replacing text
Searching text
Selection of text

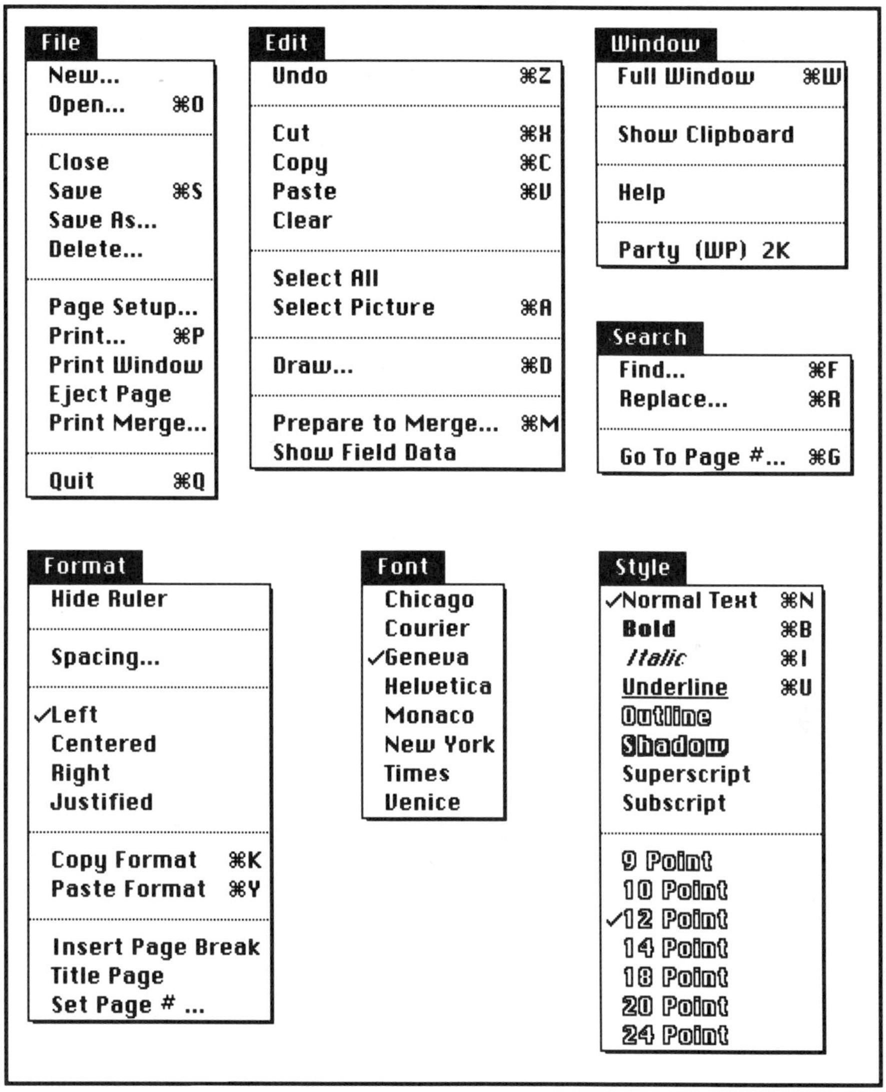

File
New...
Open...   ⌘O

Close
Save   ⌘S
Save As...
Delete...

Page Setup...
Print...   ⌘P
Print Window
Eject Page
Print Merge...

Quit   ⌘Q

Edit
Undo   ⌘Z

Cut   ⌘H
Copy   ⌘C
Paste   ⌘U
Clear

Select All
Select Picture   ⌘A

Draw...   ⌘D

Prepare to Merge... ⌘M
Show Field Data

Window
Full Window   ⌘W

Show Clipboard

Help

Party (WP) 2K

Search
Find...   ⌘F
Replace...   ⌘R

Go To Page #... ⌘G

Format
Hide Ruler

Spacing...

✓Left
Centered
Right
Justified

Copy Format   ⌘K
Paste Format   ⌘Y

Insert Page Break
Title Page
Set Page # ...

Font
Chicago
Courier
✓Geneva
Helvetica
Monaco
New York
Times
Venice

Style
✓Normal Text   ⌘N
Bold   ⌘B
Italic   ⌘I
Underline   ⌘U
Outline
Shadow
Superscript
Subscript

9 Point
10 Point
✓12 Point
14 Point
18 Point
20 Point
24 Point

Figure 7.30 The Works WP menus.

CHAPTER 8

KEEPING TRACK WITH DATABASES

L E A R N I N G   O B J E C T I V E S

- To understand what is meant by a database management system.
- To gain an introductory understanding of the relational database model.
- To learn how to create a Works database and enter data into it.
- To learn how to view, delete, and edit data in a Works database.
- To learn how to produce a merged database and word processing document in Works.

T his chapter introduces some of the basic ideas needed for understanding the use of a database management system. In particular, you will learn many of the fundamental concepts of the relational database model, which is by far the most widely used database model for microcomputer database management systems. You will see how to create a single-file database in the Works database module and how to enter data into that database. Additionally, you will learn several techniques for viewing and editing such data using various screen layouts and viewing modes. Finally, the use of a database for a print merge activity with the Works WP module will be examined.

8.1 BASIC DATABASE CONCEPTS

One of the most useful roles that computers serve is to solve information management problems. Information management problems are those problems in which there is a need to store, update, and retrieve data. Database management systems are software packages that make information management tasks easier and more natural than if specific third-generation language programs had to be written for each problem of this type.

Each **database management system** is constructed using some specific retrieval language and data model. In this chapter you will begin to explore the *relational database model*, which is used by a great many microcomputer database systems. Through this generic model, you will gain insight into how specific database management systems function. We begin with a study of some components of the relational model as they are defined in terms of the basic ideas of sets and operations on sets. You will then see how this model is implemented in the Works database component. In Chapter 17, you will extend your knowledge of this model to handle more complex data storage and retrieval problems. Once you understand the relational database model, you will be able to learn and use a great many different database management systems that are based on the model, including the system Reflex Plus, which is discussed in Chapter 18.

As mentioned earlier, a database management system is a software package designed to allow a user of the system to *manage*, or keep track of, a collection of related information, called a *database*. Within this context, we use the term *management* to mean the ability to specify an organization for our information storage and the ability to insert, delete, and retrieve information using that organization. The complexity of this management task depends directly upon the complexity of the structure of the data you wish to store and track.

In general, we will organize our information by first defining the entity classes about which we wish to collect information. An **entity class** is a collection of similar objects (called entities). For example, we might wish to keep information on the entity class of customers for our business or on the entity class of students enrolled at a university. Entities will possess a number of **attributes**, or characteristics, that will be of interest for our information problem. For example, we might want to collect information about a student's GPA (grade point average), hours completed, address, and phone number. We would then say that the entity class of students has attributes: GPA, hours completed, address, and phone number.

In some cases the database of information will be quite simple and can be thought of as a single **file** of identically formatted **records.** A record stores information about one member of the entity class. A file is a collection of information that we treat as a unit for disk storage. Typically, a file is organized into a sequence of smaller information units called records. For example, if we are interested in storing and retrieving information about the entity class consisting of customers of our business, we might organize a file with the following record format:

Name	Address	Phone	Credit-rating

The entity attributes *Name, Address, Phone,* and *Credit-rating* are called the **fields** of the record format. Our file would then consist of a list or sequence of records with the preceding field format. For example, the file itself might appear as in Figure 8.1.

In many cases the data we need to manage will be more extensive and have a more complex structure than the simple example in Figure 8.1. For instance, in addition to the customer information we described, we might wish to keep information about the products that we sell, the salesmen who sell to our customers, the suppliers of the products (or their components), the amounts and delivery dates of each particular sale, and so on. To keep track of this more complex set of information, we will need to consider a data organization scheme more complex than a single file of records. We will use a collection of related files rather than a single file, because to store all this information in a single file would be cumbersome and redundant. For example, each time we store information about a sale, we would not wish to store the entire personnel record for the salesman. A salesman may make hundreds of sales and this would mean his personnel record would be redundantly stored hundreds of times in our database. It would be much wiser to store the personnel record of each salesman once (in a separate file) and simply record the salesman's name or identification number with each of his sales.

If the information is scattered in several files, we have to consider how we will be able to retrieve related data from two or more files. In the preceding example, we may access a sale record and then wish to retrieve some information from the appropriate salesman's personnel record. The task of providing a data model and retrieval and management methods for a multiple-file data organization is exactly what a fully relational database management system is designed to accomplish.

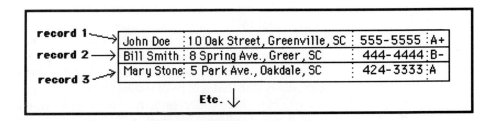

Figure 8.1 A file is composed of a sequence of records.

In this chapter, you will learn how to use the Works database module (hereafter called Works DB) to set up *single-file* databases. Because Works DB is not a fully relational database management system, we will postpone the consideration of related multiple-file databases until we discuss Reflex Plus in Chapter 18. In the meantime, Works DB will provide an excellent introduction to many of the basic ideas found in Reflex Plus as well as most other relational database management systems. Additionally, the capabilities within Works DB will be sufficient to solve completely many information management problems.

Exercise Set 8.1

1. What is a *database management system*?
2. What are *files*, *records*, and *fields*? How are they related?
3. Why is it often desirable to store information in several files as opposed to one file? Give an example different from the one in the text.

8.2 DATABASE MODELS

For you to interact with a database management system you must understand thoroughly the data model on which the system is based. Three major models have been successfully used in the construction of database management systems, and the user interface that a system presents depends directly upon which of these models has been chosen for its construction. The three models are the *hierarchical* model, the *network* model, and the *relational* model.

With all these models, data is stored in files with certain record formats. However, the user of a database management system needs only to understand the *overlying* model rather than the *underlying* file structure in order to use the system effectively. In fact, it is this insulation from the underlying file implementation details that allows you to become quite adept in using a database management system without your having to become a programmer. The extent of this insulation is quite different among the three major database models.

By far the most convenient and accessible of the three models is the relational model. For many applications, it does have the disadvantage of being the least efficient model in terms of the time required to generate responses to requests for certain types of information. Hence, in an application area where response time might be critical (airline reservation systems, emergency information systems, etc.), one of the other two models might prove superior. However, for most small business applications and other applications in which response times of a few seconds are acceptable, the relational model is the model of preference because of its ease of use and accessiblity to users not possessing computer programming skills. All leading microcomputer database management systems are based on the relational model, although the degree to which these products conform to the true conceptual relational model varies considerably from product to product.

For the reasons outlined previously, we will restrict our attention in this text to the relational database model. You will recall that Works DB is not a fully relational database system. As a consequence, we will study only the components of the relational model in this chapter needed for understanding Works DB. The extended relational model will be explored in Chapters 17 and 18.

Not all the relational model concepts are directly implemented either in Works DB or in Reflex Plus. However, a study of the complete model and its associated concepts, independent of a study of a particular software product, will greatly aid your understanding of Works DB, Reflex Plus, and the many other database management software products available on both the Macintosh and the IBM PC and compatible computers today.

Exercise Set 8.2

1. Name the three major database models.
2. Why is the choice of a database model important for a database user?
3. Which of the models will we study in this text? Why was this model chosen for emphasis?
4. Is Works DB a fully relational database system? Explain.

8.3 SETS AND CARTESIAN PRODUCTS

The relational database model is based on the mathematical concept of a **relation** and certain operators that can be applied to relations. In turn, these concepts are expressible using the ideas of **sets** and set operators. In this section, we discuss the concept of a set and the set operators that form subsets and Cartesian products of sets. Readers who are already familiar with these ideas may wish to skip to Section 8.4.

A **set** is simply a collection of objects, which are called its *elements*, or *members*. For example, the collection of all students in a given class is a set; the collection of desks in a classroom is a set; the collection of customer records that a given store keeps is a set; the whole numbers between 10 and 100 comprise a set. Notice that the members of a set may be any entities whatsoever: persons, desks, customer records, numbers.

The set A is said to be a **subset** of set B if it is true that every member of A is also a member of B. For example, the set of customers of a business with an A credit rating would be a subset of the set of all customers of a business. Similarly, the set of books about computers in your library is a subset of the set of all the books in your library.

TUPLES AND CARTESIAN PRODUCT SETS. An ordered **n-tuple** is a collection of n objects ordered in a particular way. For example, the names *Joe, John,* and *Mary,* in that order, form an ordered 3-tuple. The same n objects ordered in two different ways form two different n-tuples. We sometimes write an n-tuple using parentheses to enclosed the n objects, which are separated by commas. In the preceding example, we would write (Joe, John, Mary). Notice that each of the records we gave in Figure 8.1 can be thought of as an ordered list of four objects, or as a 4-tuple. Hence, the file of records could be thought of as a set of 4-tuples.

The following definition is basic to the study of the relational database model. Following the definition are several examples that illustrate the simplicity of the idea of a Cartesian product (named after the French philosopher/mathematican Descartes).

CARTESIAN PRODUCT OF *K* SETS.   Let $D_1, ..., D_k$ be any collection of k sets. The **Cartesian** (or **cross**) **product** of $D_1, ..., D_k$, written as $D_1 \times D_2 \times ... \times D_k$, is defined to be the set of all possible k-tuples $(d_1, d_2, ..., d_k)$, where for each $i = 1, ..., k$, the value d_i is taken from the set D_i.

Let us illustrate the situation with a simple example showing the Cartesian product of two sets. Suppose A = {Bill, Mary, Joe} and B = {manager, clerk}. Then the Cartesian product $A \times B$ = {(Bill,manager), (Bill,clerk), (Mary,manager), (Mary,clerk), (Joe,manager), (Joe,clerk)}.

Note that *all possible* pairs (or 2-tuples) of names from set A and job descriptions from set B are included in the product set $A \times B$. Because there are three elements in A and two elements in B, there are 3 x 2 = 6 elements in $A \times B$.

It probably occurs to you that not every one of these pairs is likely to be "meaningful" if our purpose is to model information about persons and their job descriptions. A more meaningful set of pairs could be written if we took a particular subset of the product set $A \times B$. For example, we might take the set {(Mary,manager), (Bill,clerk), (Joe,clerk)}. This last set could then be reasonably interpreted as relating each person to a job description. Such subsets of Cartesian products, called relations, are the basic data objects of the relational database model.

As a second example consider the sets ID# = {101,102,103}, NAME = {Smith, Jones}, and PAYRATE = {10.00,5.00}. Then the set ID# x NAME x PAYRATE would consist of the following 12 3-tuples:

{(101, Smith, 10.00), (101, Smith, 5.00), (101, Jones, 10.00), (101, Jones, 5.00), (102, Smith, 10.00), (102, Smith, 5.00), (102, Jones, 10.00), (102, Jones, 5.00), (103, Smith, 10.00), (103, Smith, 5.00), (103, Jones, 10.00), (103, Jones, 5.00)}

ID#	NAME	PAYRATE
101	Smith	10.00
101	Smith	5.00
101	Jones	10.00
101	Jones	5.00
102	Smith	10.00
102	Smith	5.00
102	Jones	10.00
102	Jones	5.00
103	Smith	10.00
103	Smith	5.00
103	Jones	10.00
103	Jones	5.00

Figure 8.2 Displaying a Cartesian product in table form.

ID#	NAME	PAYRATE
101	Smith	10.00
103	Jones	5.00

Figure 8.3 A semantically meaningful subset of the Cartesian product of Figure 8.2.

An equivalent, and perhaps more illustrative, way to display this information is to give it in table form as illustrated in Figure 8.2.

It is clear that the preceding Cartesian product taken as a whole contains tuples that do not hold meaningful information. Because we would commonly assume that a given person would have only one ID# and one PAYRATE, a more meaningful set might be some subset of the product set. For example, the set given in Figure 8.3 would be one that could be given a meaningful interpretation.

Exercise Set 8.3

Let $A = \{1,2\}$, $B = \{a,e\}$, and $C = \{a,1,d\}$. Write the following sets (in both tuple and table formats):

1. $B \times A$
2. $A \times C$
3. $A \times B$

Let NAME = {Joe, Dan, Sally}, GPA = {3.4, 3.5, 3.7, 1.2}, and ROOM = {E- 110, E - 144}.

4. Write the set NAME x GPA in table format. The table will have 12 rows.
5. Choose and display three different semantically meaningful subsets of the set NAME x GPA constructed in exercise 4.
6. Write the set NAME x GPA x ROOM in table form. The table will have 24 rows.
7. Choose and display three different semantically meaningful subsets of the set NAME x GPA x ROOM constructed in exercise 6.

8.4 RELATIONAL DATABASES

Drawing on the concept of a Cartesian product of sets, in the relational database model, we will think of our data as being organized into two-dimensional tables called **relational tables**. These tables contain rows of information, which consist of particular values for the various column headings in our table. We will think of a table holding information about some particular entity class, such as customers, employees, books, or experiments. The column headings will then represent some collection of the given entity class' attributes that we wish to keep information about. For example, the data about the entity class *Customer*, mentioned in Section 8.1, might be organized into a table with column headings *Name*, *Address*,

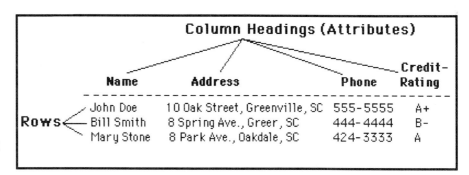

Figure 8.4 File of Figure 8.1 in table format.

Phone, and *Credit-rating.* An *instance* of this table would refer to an actual table with values for the attributes named in the column headings.

The organization of the preceding table is such that values in a given row of the table represent *related information.* In our example, that would mean that a row holds information about a *single* customer. In particular, the file structure that we illustrated in Figure 8.1 would translate directly into the instance table given in Figure 8.4.

Briefly, a **relational database** consists of a *collection* of tables, each of which is assigned a unique name. The columns of a table represent values for the various column headings (or attributes) associated with the entities that are being repre-sented in the table. A row in a table represents a related set of values, one value for each attribute, that corresponds to a *single* entity, such as a customer, an em-ployee, a sale, and so forth. A table then can be thought of as a collection of data relationships, each row representing a specific relationship (for some single entity) among the various attributes of the table.

RELATIONS. The preceding ideas can be expressed more precisely and suc-cinctly using the concept of a mathematical relation (from which the relational database model takes its name). It will prove advantageous for us to explore briefly this mathematical interpretation of the model. In our more formal discus-sion the terms *relation, attribute,* and *tuple* will replace the terms *table, column heading,* and *row,* respectively, that we used in our informal discussion earlier.

An attribute is a property or characteristic that an entity possesses or has associated with it. For example, the entity *Employee* might have the attributes *SS#(social security number), Name, Address, Department,* and *Salary.* Each attribute has a set of possible or allowable values; this set of allowable values for an attribute is called the **attribute domain.**

RELATION: Let A_1 , A_2 , ..., A_k be a set of k attributes, with respective domains $D_1, D_2, ..., D_k$. A *relation* over this set of attributes is any subset of $D_1 \times D_2 \times ... \times D_k$. Elements of a relation are called its *tuples.*

As an example, consider the two attributes *Name* and *Position* that have the domains D_1 and D_2:

$$D_1 = \{Jill, Mary, Bill\}$$

$$D_2 = \{manager, clerk\}.$$

Then the sets

$$R_1 = \{(\text{Jill,manager}), (\text{Mary,clerk}), (\text{Bill,clerk})\}$$

$$R_2 = \{(\text{Bill,manager}), (\text{Mary,manager}), (\text{Jill,clerk})\}$$

are examples of relations over the attributes *Name* and *Position.* Note also that the set

$$R_3 = \{(\text{Bill,manager}), (\text{Bill,clerk})\}$$

is a perfectly valid mathematical relation over these attributes, although we suspect that it violates some semantic "rule" about Bill being a manager and a clerk at the same time.

An important difference in the mathematical concept of relation and the database concept of relation is that in the mathematical definition of a relation, no mention is made of column names for attributes. Each component of a tuple in a mathematical relation takes its meaning from its *position* within the sequence of tuple components. However, for database relations we will agree to identify a component by the *name* of the column (or the attribute for which the component represents a value), rather than by its position relative to other components. We illustrate this difference with an example. Consider the two database relations R_1 and R_2 given here:

R_1:	Name	Position		R_2:	Position	Name
	John Doe	Clerk			Clerk	John Doe
	Jill Smith	Manager			Manager	Jill Smith
	Bill Jones	Salesman			Salesman	Bill Jones

We would readily agree that these two relations contain exactly the same information. However, from a mathematical point of view the two relations are, in fact, not equal, because writing them out, we have $R_1 = \{(\text{John Doe, Clerk}), (\text{Jill Smith, Manager}), (\text{Bill Jones, Salesman})\}$ and $R_2 = \{(\text{Clerk, John Doe}), (\text{Manager, Jill Smith}), (\text{Salesman, Bill Jones})\}$.

Clearly, these two sets are not equal (in fact, they have no elements in common), because the pairs in R_1 are not equal to the pairs in R_2. For these pairs to be mathematically equal, their *corresponding* (by relative position) components must be equal.

RELATIONAL SCHEMES.   For database relations we are more interested in informational content than mathematical structure. As a consequence, we will ignore differences such as those between R_1 and R_2 earlier and consider such relations to be equivalent. In other words, when we compare two relations for equality, we will always compare values of the same attributes (as identified by the same attribute *names*) and not worry at all about the relative positions in the attribute lists. To emphasize the dependence of a database relation on the names of its attributes, we will often indicate that R is a relation over a set of attributes—*Person* and *Job*, for example—by referring to the **relational scheme** for R as $R(Person, Job)$. With this notation, we would say that a relation R with scheme $R(A, B, C)$ and another relation S with scheme $S(B, C, A)$ over the same attributes in a different order have *equivalent relational schemes*.

Two relations are said to be *equal* if they have equivalent relational schemes *and* contain exactly the same tuple data. Relations with equivalent relational schemes are considered to be conceptually equivalent, although it is entirely possible that an *instance* of R could differ from an *instance* of S. That is, the relations R and S might contain different data and hence not be equal. But they are at least comparable, in that it makes perfectly good sense to ask if they are equal in data content, because they have equivalent relational schemes.

DATA TYPES.   An important characteristic of a relation is the kind of data that will be stored for each attribute, that is, the kind of objects contained in each attribute's domain set. When a relational scheme is defined for a relation R, it is assumed that the data types of each attribute are uniquely determined by the underlying attribute domain sets. Typical **data types** that we might use are text (strings of characters, such as names, addresses, and so on), integers (whole numbers—either positive or negative), real numbers (numbers with decimal parts), dates, time, and currency. Whenever a database table is constructed, it is essential to define the underlying data types because the computer will use different internal storage schemes for different data types. Thus, it will not be possible to have an attribute whose stored data is of more than one data type.

Exercise Set 8.4

1. What are *entities* and *attributes*? How are they related?
2. What is a *relation*?
3. How do database relations differ from their mathematical counterparts?
4. What can be said about the information in a single tuple (row) of a database relation?
5. What is meant by the *relational scheme* for a relation? Define what is meant when it is said that two relations have *equivalent* relational schemes?
6. What is an *instance* of a database relation?
7. When are two database relations *equal*?
8. What is meant by an attribute's *domain*? What is meant by an attribute's *data type*?

8.5 CREATING A DATABASE TABLE IN WORKS DB

In this section you will see how to create a Works DB table (all tables in Works DB are called *databases*), enter data into the table, view the data entered, and edit any

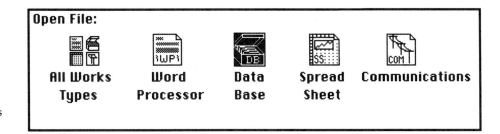

Figure 8.5 Module icons displayed after Works is opened.

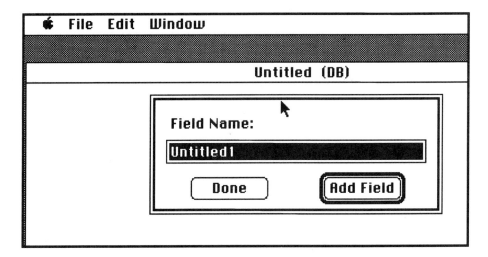

Figure 8.6 Startup screen for defining a Works database.

data that must be changed or corrected. The relation to be used as our example Works DB database is the customer information example from the previous sections.

DEFINING DATABASE TABLES.   To begin the process of creating a Works database, you must first open Works DB by double-clicking on its icon, which is highlighted in Figure 8.5. When you do this, the screen in Figure 8.6 will be displayed.

Using this dialog box, you can enter the names of your first attributes. Once you have entered the attribute names you will select each attribute in turn and then execute the *Set Field Attributes* command under the **Format** menu. This will produce the dialog box shown in Figure 8.7. Select the appropriate data type (*text* for all the attributes in our example) for the attribute just selected. Note that the default data type is text, and so it is not necessary for you to give the data type

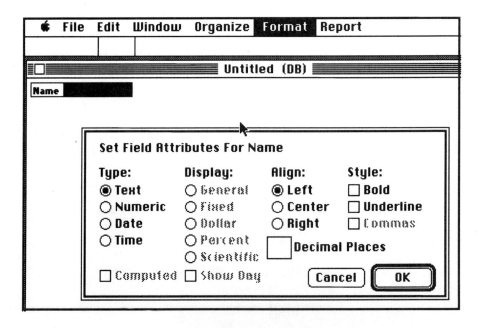

Figure 8.7 Dialog box for defining attribute data type.

explicitly for text attributes. You need to execute the *Set Field Attributes* command for text attributes only if you wish to change some of the other features shown in the dialog box. These features include setting the alignment of text to be either left-justified, right-justified, or centered, and setting the text style to bold and/or underline. The dimmed choices under *Display* and *Style* are for numeric data types. When you have finished setting the characteristics of the data field, click *OK*.

You are now in the untitled Works DB window, where you are given a dialog box like the one shown in Figure 8.6. Type in the name of the first attribute, *Name*. To add another field, click the *Add Field* button. Continuing in a similar manner, you can easily complete the definition of the database (relational table). When you have finshed entering the last field name, click *Done* when the dialog box of Figure 8.6 is presented. The resulting screen is shown in Figure 8.8. Select each attribute inturn and set its data type as described above.

ENTERING DATABASE DATA.   The screen shown in Figure 8.8 is called a *form*, and it can be used directly for data entry and display. If you desire, you can rearrange the positions of the attribute fields on this form. To do this, place the mouse pointer over an attribute name and it will turn into a hand symbol, as is shown in Figure 8.9. This feature functions just as its counterpart in MacPaint. You may drag attribute blocks freely around the form. Additionally, by dragging the lower right corner of an attribute block, you can stretch or shrink the block's size. Figure 8.10 shows one possible reorganization of the form.

In Figure 8.10, notice the number (1 in this case) in the upper left corner of the screen. This is the record number of the currently displayed record. In this case, this number tells you that the blank record on the screen is record number 1. You can now use the form to enter data. Select the *Name* data field by clicking anywhere inside it, and type in the name from the first row of data in Figure 8.4. Press *Return* and the *Address* data field will be selected and you can type in the appropriate address data from the first row of Figure 8.4. When you have entered a complete record and press *Return*, that record is stored in the database and a new blank record is presented for additional data entry. If you make a mistake

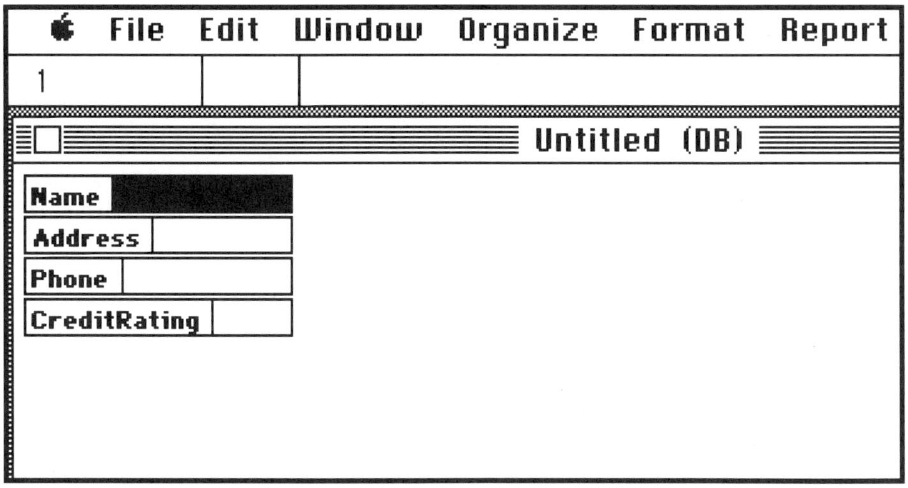

Figure 8.8: Definition of the customer database table completed.

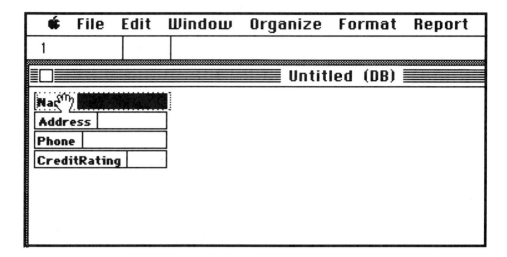

Figure 8.9 Preparing to move an attribute block within a form.

when typing and notice it before leaving a data field, you can simply backspace and correct. If you notice a mistake in a previously typed field, you can select that field (by clicking anywhere in it) and make your corrections in the data displayed in the bar at the top of the screen. The usual word processing functions of selecting by dragging, deleting and inserting text, and so forth, can be applied in this data display bar.

VIEWING DATA IN A FORM DISPLAY.   When you wish to move forward to the next data field for a record in a **form display**, you can press either the *Tab* key or the *Return* key. When you are in the last data field of a record and press either of these keys, you will move automatically to the first data field of the next record in the database; that record is then shown in place of the one you were previously viewing. To reverse the direction of your movement, hold down the *Shift* key while pressing either the *Return* or the *Tab* key. When you reach the first data field of a record in this manner, an additional *Shift* and *Return* (or *Tab*) will place you in the previous record in the database. Note that in a form display all fields for one record are shown.

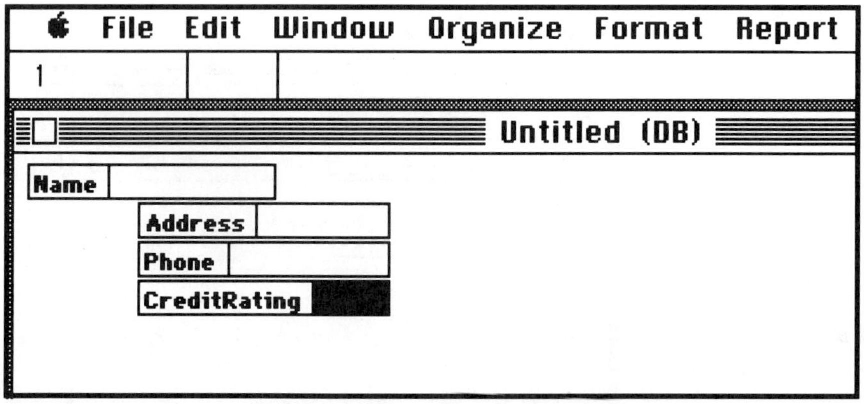

Figure 8.10 Reformatted form.

```
 File   Edit   Window   Organize   Format   Report

┌────────────────────────── Untitled (DB) ──────────────────────────┐
│ Name          │ Address           │ Phone     │ CreditRating      │
│───────────────┼───────────────────┼───────────┼───────────────────│
│ Bill Smith    │ 8 Spring Ave., Greer │ 444-4444 │ B-                │
│ John Doe      │ 10 Oak Street, Green │ 555-5555 │ A+                │
└────────────────────────────────────────────────────────────────────┘
```

Figure 8.11 Displaying data in list format.

VIEWING DATA IN A LIST DISPLAY.   There are many times when you would wish to view more than one record (row) of data at once. Works DB provides a **list display** for this purpose. By executing the *Show List* command from the **Format** menu you will access a display in the format shown in Figure 8.11. The list format may be used for data entry as well as for data display. By selecting the *Name* data field just below the data "John Doe" as shown in Figure 8.11, you can type in your next name. When you finish typing the name, press the *Tab* key (instead of the *Return* key as in the forms display) to move to the next data field. Holding down the *Shift* key and pressing *Tab* allows you to move back to the previous data field in a given row. The *Return* key will take you to the *next record* and leave you in the same attribute column. You can also use the mouse in the usual way to select new fields for entry by moving the pointer inside the field and clicking. To return to a form display, select the *Show Form* command under **Format.**

Notice in Figure 8.11 that John Doe's complete address is not shown, because there is not enough room for it in the space allocated for the attribute *Address*. This can be easily corrected by widening the data field space. To do this, move the mouse pointer to the dividing grid line between the *Address* and *Phone* data fields. You will notice that the pointer changes to a double horizontal arrow shape to suggest that you can now stretch (or reduce) the size of the *Address* data field. Click and drag the mouse to the right to expand the data space as desired. You can remove the grid lines shown in Figure 8.11 by executing the *No Grid* command under the **Format** menu. The list screen resulting from these actions is displayed in FIgure 8.12.

SORTING RECORDS.   **Sorting** is the process of arranging records in a desired sequence. In Works DB, records can be sorted by executing the *Sort* command of

```
 File   Edit   Window   Organize   Format   Report

┌────────────────────────── Untitled (DB) ──────────────────────────┐
│ Name         Address                      Phone       CreditRating │
│ Bill Smith   8 Spring Ave., Greer, SC     444-4444    B-           │
│ John Doe     10 Oak Street, Greenville, SC 555-5555   A+           │
└────────────────────────────────────────────────────────────────────┘
```

Figure 8.12 List format screen with no grid and expanded address data field.

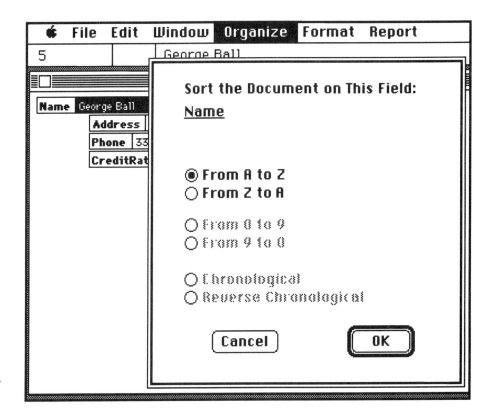

Figure 8.13 Dialog box for the *Sort* command.

the **Organize** menu. The first step is to select the name of an attribute by clicking it. Selecting the *Sort* command causes the dialog box of Figure 8.13 to be displayed. Data can be sorted in various orders, depending upon the sort attribute's data type. For example, suppose that *Name* is the attribute selected. Because *Name* is a text type, you have the choices "From A to Z" or "From Z to A." The *Sort* command can be used with either the form or list display. Note that this process can be repeated to sort a table by subcategories. In this case, the least significant attribute is sorted first, followed by progressively more significant attributes. Thus, for the database shown in Figure 8.14, to obtain a listing showing all people with the same credit rating, alphabetized according to name, we would sort on *Name* followed by sorting on *CreditRating*.

VIEWING DATA USING SPLIT SCREENS. It is often desirable to compare database records that are not located close to one another in our database organization. It is also often the case that database records are too long to fit on a screen. Works DB provides a very convenient and flexible method for viewing, comparing, and even editing data in different parts of a database. This is accomplished through the use of **split-screen displays.** To achieve a split screen, you need only click on and drag one of the small dark rectangles located at the top of the vertical scroll box and at the left of the horizontal scroll box in a list display screen.

Consider as an example the list display shown in Figure 8.14. In this display, the screen has been split horizontally into two separate list displays by dragging the split rectangle from the top of the original vertical scroll box. Notice that each display has its own scroll bar. These scroll bars are independent of each other, and

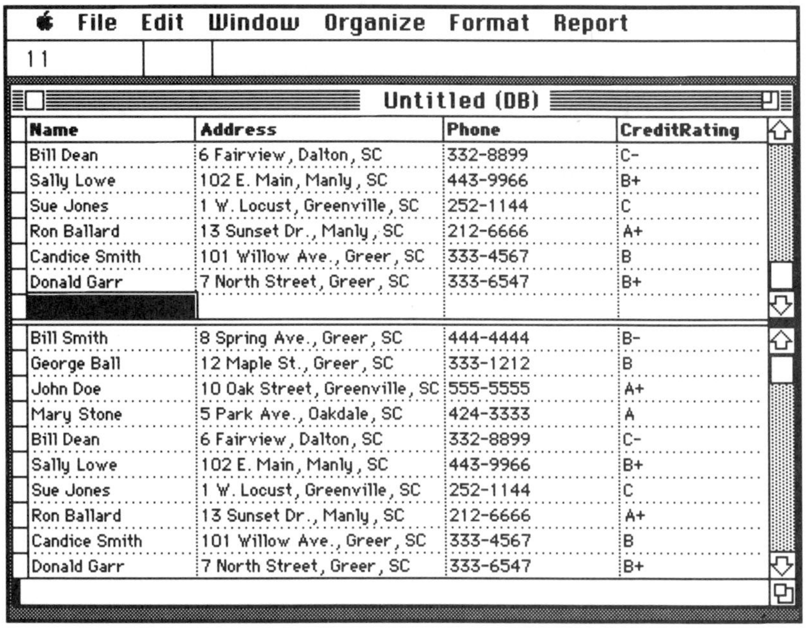

Figure 8.14 Horizontal split-screen database list display.

the *entire database* is available in each display. Hence, any two sections of the database can be viewed simultaneously using this technique.

In Figure 8.15, the screen has been split both horizontally and vertically into four scroll boxes. These boxes operate independently of each other in the sense that if you use one of the vertical screen scroll boxes, both the horizontal screens are scrolled on the approriate vertical side of the screen. Similarly, if you use a horizontal screen scroll box, both the vertical screens are scrolled in the appropriate horizontal side of the screen. This is done so that when you look at a row completely across the screen, you are always looking at data from the *same*

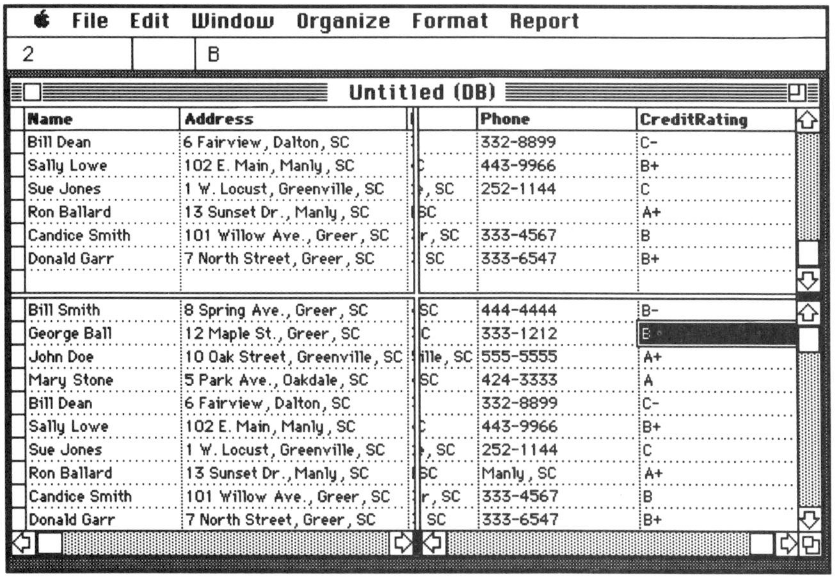

Figure 8.15 A four-display split screen.

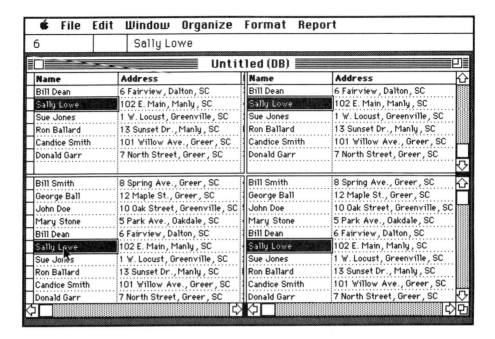

Figure 8.16 Viewing multiple copies of the same data.

original row in the database. In a similar manner, a column (even though it is split horizontally) always represents data for the *same* attribute. Notice in Figure 8.15 that the selected data is available for editing in the data display bar at the top of the screen, just as is the case when you are using a single screen display.

It is important to understand that with split-screen displays, the database data duplication that you are viewing is for display only. That is, the database itself is not duplicated. For example, if you consider the display shown in Figure 8.16, you will notice that the *Name* entry for record 6 ("Sally Lowe") appears in every display. When you select that data item, it is highlighted simultaneously in all four displays. Likewise, if you were to edit the data in the data display bar, the changes would be immediately reflected in all four displays.

DELETING RECORDS.   There are two methods for deleting an entire record from the database using a list display. You can select a whole record by dragging or by clicking in the box to the left of the first entry in a row. Once the row is selected, you can delete its data by executing the *Clear* command from the **Edit** menu. A blank record is left in the database. If the *Cut* command is executed instead, there is no blank record left behind. The *Cut* command places the removed information on the Clipboard. Either of these methods can be used on groups of contiguous selected records.

SAVING A DATABASE.   Quitting Works DB is accomplished in a manner completely analogous to that used to quit Works WP. Suppose you quit at this point and save the database you have created under the name *Customer*. Assuming you save the database in your MS Works folder, when you next open Works, you will see an icon for your database displayed as shown in Figure 8.17. You can then open the database and start Works DB by double-clicking that icon. Of course, you can also first open Works, select the Works DB icon, and then choose your

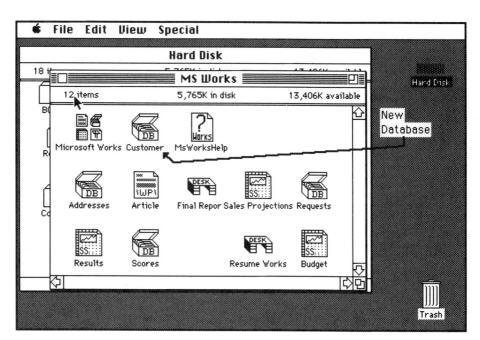

Figure 8.17 Saved customer database in MS Works folder.

database from the list of available databases in the scroll box that is subsequently displayed.

Exercise Set 8.5

1. Describe briefly the process used to define a Works DB table.
2. How can data be entered into a Works DB table? How does this differ, depending upon whether a forms or a list display is being used?
3. How can data in a Works DB table be edited?
4. Give two ways that data can be deleted from a Works DB table using a list display? How do these methods differ?
5. Why would you need a split-screen database display? Describe how to access such a display.
6. What is the difference between a *list* display and a *forms* display? How do you move from one display type to the other?
7. Describe how you can reorganize the appearance of a forms display.
8. Describe how data field areas can be expanded or reduced in a forms display. How is this done in a list display?

Computer Practice 8.5

1. Go through the construction of the *Customer* database table as described in this section. Complete all the activities referenced in the text description. Load into your database the data shown in the lower split screen displayed in Figure 8.14. Save the database on one of your disks for future use.

2. Suppose you wish to organize your LP record and cassette tape collection into a Works DB table. Identify the important attributes of records and tapes that you would wish to keep data about. (One such attribute might be whether the item is a record or a tape; others might be music category, artist, label, cost, etc.) Create a Works DB table to store the kind of information you have identified. Enter data for at least 25 records/tapes into the database. Try editing, viewing with split screens, and so on. Save your database on one of your disks for later use.

8.6 MERGING WORKS DATABASES AND WORD PROCESSING DOCUMENTS

It is possible to merge WP and DB documents. An example of merging DB into WP documents will now be presented. Read through this section without using the computer. At the end of the section, you will be asked to perform some similar exercises on your own.

Suppose you want to produce a word processing document that will list the customers in our example database, together with related information about them. The steps required to create such a document are as follows:

- Open Works WP to get a new word processing document.

- Using the *Open* command from the **File** menu, open the *Customer* database.

- Switch back to the word processing document by selecting its name under the **Window** menu.

- Execute the *Prepare to Merge* command under the **Edit** menu and you will be presented with the dialog box shown in Figure 8.18.

- Select a field name and click *Merge* to place that field in the word processing document at the position of the insertion pointer.

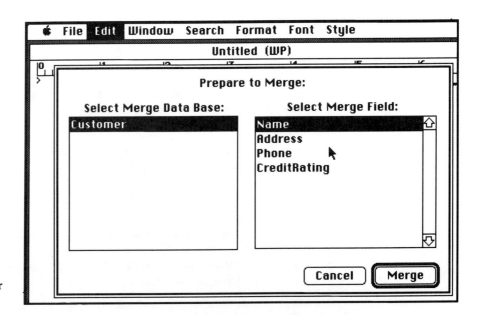

Figure 8.18 Dialog box for preparing a print merge.

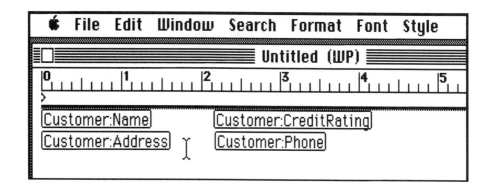

Figure 8.19 Data field names inserted and positioned within the word processing document.

- Repeat the previous two steps until you have entered all the database field names into your merged document.

Each of the selected field names will be placed in your word processing document at the position the insertion pointer occupies when you click *Merge*. However, once the field names are in the document they can be moved just as any word processing text. Figure 8.19 shows the word processing document after inserting all the field names from our *Customer* example database and then rearranging them. Notice the name of the database itself as a part of the field names. By using these complete path names, Works makes it possible to insert data from several different databases into the same word processing document.

By executing the *Show Field Data* command from the **Edit** menu, you can cause the data from the currently selected database record in *Customer* to be displayed, as is demonstrated in Figure 8.20. Executing *Show Field Names* in the **Edit** menu will return you to the situation shown in Figure 8.19.

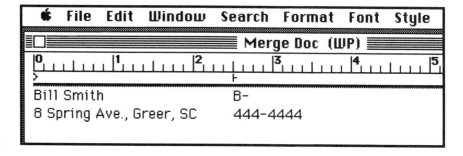

Figure 8.20 Displaying database data using the *Show Field Data* command.

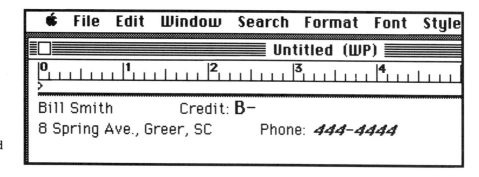

Figure 8.21 Formatted database data in the word processing document.

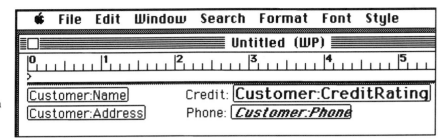

Figure 8.22 Field names with applied formatting indicated.

Once the field names are inserted and positioned, we can format the display of these items in all the ways that we can format other word processing text, such as use of italics, different fonts, various font sizes, and so on. We can also add descriptive labels. Figure 8.21 gives an example of such formatting. Notice in Figure 8.22 how the formatting shows up even after you have selected *Show Field Names* from the **Edit** menu.

For database information to be accessible to the word processing document, the appropriate database must be opened. If you should open the word processing document of Figure 8.22 (which has been saved as *Merge Doc*) without opening the database, you will receive error messages similar to those shown in Figure 8.23. Notice in that figure that the message "Customer:NOT ON DESK-TOP" for the *Credit* data field has wrapped to the next line. This action will not affect the way the data is displayed; it is simply a consequence of the length of the error message.

To print the word processing document with all the database data included, select the *Print Merge* command from the **File** menu. Both documents must be open for this command to execute successfully. *For each record in the database, a complete copy of the word processing document is printed.* It is possible to select only part of the database records for inclusion, as you will see in the next chapter. Additional merged WP/DB documents will be constructed in Chapter 14.

Exercise Set 8.6

1. Describe the process for merging data from Works DB with a Works WP document.
2. When a database and a word processing document are merged and printed, what is the relationship between records in the database and the output?
3. Can database information be formatted once it is merged into a word processing document?

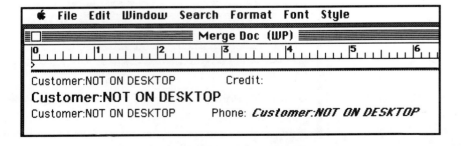

Figure 8.23 Attempting to access data from an unopened database.

4. What are the two forms in which database information is displayed in a merged document?
5. Describe the information on the *Prepare to Merge* dialog box.
6. Describe the procedure that might be followed for creating a word processing document to produce mailing labels from a database of names and addresses.

Computer Practice 8.6

1. Use the print merge activity described in this section to create a word processing document to produce mailing labels. Note that you will first need to create a database containing the mailing list of names and addresses. Experiment with formatting the fields in various styles and moving them around within the word processing document.
2. Print the merged document you created in step 1. How could the *Page Setup* command come in handy here to produce actual labels? (*Hint*: Think about page size.)
3. In this and the following practice exercises, you will construct a customer product registration custom form. An example of the form to be produced is shown in the following figure. The customer's name and address are to be supplied from a database.

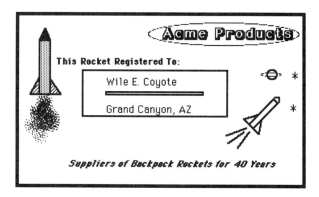

Begin by creating a merged document with the data fields from *Customer* positioned as shown in the next figure.

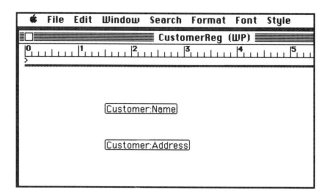

4. Select the area of the preceding document that includes the data fields (as shown in the following figure) and copy that area to the Clipboard. Quit Works and save your document as *CustomerReg*. Be sure to click the Yes box when asked if you wish to save the large Clipboard when you exit Works.

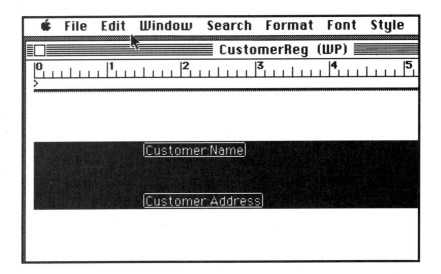

5. Open MacPaint and paste in the preceding area from the Clipboard. The resulting MacPaint screen should look like the following diagram. Notice that the field names are displayed in error format. Don't worry about that, because this occurs any time a merged document is copied to the clipboard.

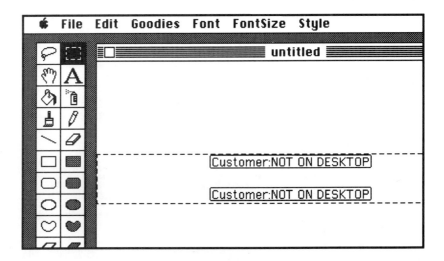

6. Using the appropriate MacPaint tools, create a form around the data field names similar to the one in the following figure.

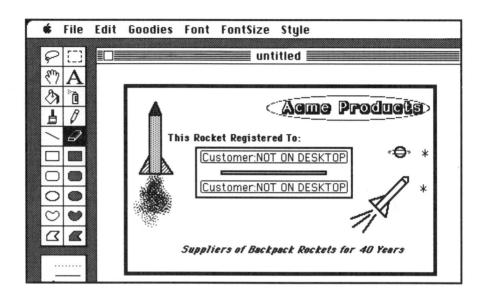

7. Use the eraser tool to erase both occurrences of the text "Customer:NOT ON DESKTOP" and its surrounding boxes in the preceding figure. Copy the resulting form (shown in the next figure) to the Clipboard and quit the MacPaint application. Save the MacPaint document as *RegForm*.

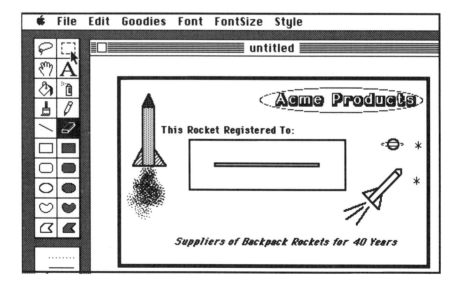

8. Open your Works WP document *CustomerReg* and your *Customer* database. Paste the form from the Clipboard into *CustomerReg*. Use the hand tool to position the picture as shown in the following diagram. Note that you will probably need to insert some *Returns* above your text to move it down a few rows to achieve the configuration shown.

9. Select *Show Field Data* under *Edit* to get a figure similar to the one shown at the beginning of this exercise. Print the merged document.

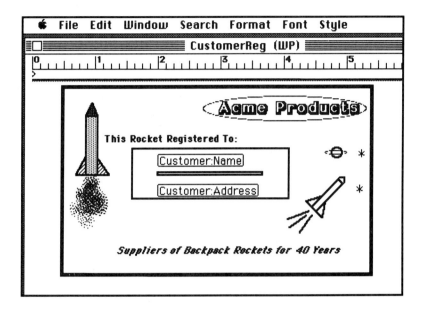

10. Save your work and exit MS Works.

Key Concepts

Attribute	Attribute domain
Cartesian (or cross) product of sets	Data type
Database management system	Entity class
Field	File
Form display	List display
N-tuple	Record
Relation	Relational database
Relational scheme	Relational table
Set	Split-screen display

CHAPTER 9

CREATING DATABASE REPORTS

L E A R N I N G   O B J E C T I V E S

- To begin a study of relational algebra.
- To learn how to use the select and project relational algebra retrieval operators.
- To understand how Works implements the select and project operators.
- To learn how to create customized database reports in Works.
- To learn how to include totals and subtotals in Works database reports.

T his chapter is about retrieving data from databases. In it you will be introduced to two of the five basic operators of the relational database retrieval language called relational algebra. You will see how those operators are implemented in the Works database system and how to use these operators to select the exact subset of information that you wish to extract from a database. Then you will learn how to display on the screen the subsets of the database that you have selected and how to create customized reports for viewing and/or printing the data you have selected. Finally, you will see how to include totals and subtotals in Works reports.

9.1 RETRIEVING DATABASE INFORMATION

Perhaps the most important characteristic of any database management system is the ease and flexibility with which it allows you to retrieve stored information. Because data retrieval is so central to database activities, all database models include both methods for modeling the storage of data and methods for retrieving the data once stored. For the purpose of data retrieval, the relational database model includes a *relational retrieval language*.

Actually, a number of quite different relational retrieval languages have been proposed and used in various relational database management systems. The language SQL (which stands for Structured Query Language and is pronounced "sequel") may eventually become the standard relational model retrieval language. In fact, IBM has announced that SQL will be embedded in the new OS/2 operating system for its PS/2 line of computers. However, at the time of this writing, many different relational database retrieval languages are available, and this situation is likely to continue for some time. We should note that the fundamental construct used in SQL is a modification of the **select** operator, which we discuss later.

Although no single language has become the standard relational retrieval language, a set of retrieval capabilities has been identified as highly desirable in any retrieval language. This set of capabilities, which is considered to be the minimum set of capabilities that any relational retrieval language ought to possess, is the language known as **relational algebra**. Any relational retrieval language that possesses at least the retrieval capability of relational algebra is said to be a *relationally complete* language. Many of the languages being used in relational database management systems are relationally complete. For example, the retrieval capabilities found in Reflex Plus and the language SQL are both relationally complete.

Relational algebra has *five basic operators* that are applied to existing database relations (or tables) to produce new relations. There are also other relational operators, called *derived operators*, that can be written as combinations of these five. Not all of the five basic relational algebra operators are implemented in Works; consequently, Works DB is not a fully relational system. Those operators that allow retrieval of related information residing in *two or more different* files are not present in Works DB, because Works DB does not allow such retrievals. In this section, we introduce the two of these five operators that are important for single file retrievals and explore their information retrieval capabilities using Works DB. The other three operators are discussed in Chapters 17 and 18.

THE SELECT OPERATOR. The **select operator** is applied to a single relation at a time. It produces a new relation with the same relational scheme (i.e., with the same attributes) as the original relation, but with a subset of the original relation's rows. Each row selected satisfies a given formula.

For a given relation R, a new relation, say S, selected from R on the basis of formula F, would be written as follows:

$$S = \text{select from } R \text{ where } F$$

Here F is some formula involving the attributes of R, so that the components of each row in R can be said either to satisfy formula F or not to satisfy it. An example from our *Customer* database of the previous chapter will help make this definition clear. Recall that that database has the following scheme: *Customer(Name, Address, Phone, CreditRating)*.

Suppose we want to produce a list of all the customers in the *Customer* database who have a credit rating of A. If we agree to name this list *CreditA*, the retrieval would be accomplished with the following use of the **select** operator:

$$CreditA = \text{select from } Customer \text{ where } CreditRating = A$$

Notice how the formula (*CreditRating* = A) is constructed to qualify exactly the rows in the database that we wish to extract. The syntax of the formula itself is quite simple. It includes the name of an attribute in our database scheme (*CreditRating*), followed by a comparison operator (=), followed by a value that the attribute is allowed to have (A). More examples will be given shortly.

THE PROJECT OPERATOR. The **project operator** is applied to a single relation at a time. It produces a new relation, whose relational scheme contains some subset of the attributes in the relational scheme for the original relation. The data for the new relation consists of all the rows from the original relation, dropping those attribute values for any attributes not in the relational scheme for the new projected relation.

For a given relation R with relational scheme $R(A, B, C, D)$ (remember that this simply means that relation R has attributes A, B, C, and D), a new relation, say P, projected from R could be written as follows:

$$P = \text{project } A, D \text{ from } R$$

Notice that A and D are attributes in the relational scheme for R. The new relation P includes all of the original data from R *except* that the columns representing attributes B and C have been removed. In addition, any duplicate rows are eliminated from P. You will see why this is necessary in some examples a little later. For now a simple example from our *Customer* database will illustrate the use of the **project** operator.

Suppose we want to produce a list of all our customers' names and addresses (omitting their phone numbers and credit ratings). This is accomplished quite easily with the **project** operator as follows:

AddressList = **project** *Name, Address* **from** *Customer*

In summary, the **select** operator is used to extract a subset of a relation that satisfies some condition(s), and the **project** operator is used to eliminate some attribute(s) in which we have no interest. We will now examine a few additional examples of the use of these operators.

SOME EXAMPLE RETRIEVALS.   Suppose we have a relation T with relational scheme T(*Name, Salary, Department, Position*) that contains the following data:

T:	Name	Salary	Department	Position
	Smith, J.P.	33,000	Sales	manager
	Kline, H.F.	14,000	Sales	clerk
	Jones, M.W	22,000	Marketing	designer
	Rand, G.J	26,000	Marketing	manager
	Wells, N.A.	15,000	Marketing	clerk
	King, R.A.	43,000	Marketing	manager

To retrieve the records for all the managers in the database, we would execute the following:

Mgr = **select from** T **where** *Position* = *manager*

This would produce the relation *Mgr* as follows:

Mgr:	Name	Salary	Department	Position
	Smith, J.P.	33,000	Sales	manager
	Rand, G.J	26,000	Marketing	manager
	King, R.A.	43,000	Marketing	manager

To retrieve the records for just those employees in the Marketing Department, we would execute the following:

$Mktg$ = **select from** T **where** *Department* = *Marketing*

This would produce the relation *Mktg* as follows:

$Mktg$:	Name	Salary	Department	Position
	Jones, M.W	22,000	Marketing	designer
	Rand, G.J	26,000	Marketing	manager
	Wells, N.A.	15,000	Marketing	clerk
	King, R.A.	43,000	Marketing	manager

To retrieve just the names and salaries for all records in the database, we would execute the following:

NameSalary = **project** *Name, Salary* **from** T

This would produce the relation *NameSalary* as follows:

NameSalary	*Name*	*Salary*
	Smith, J.P.	33,000
	Kline, H.F.	14,000
	Jones, M.W	22,000
	Rand, G.J	26,000
	Wells, N.A.	15,000
	King, R.A.	43,000

Suppose we want to retrieve the names and salaries for all employees in the Marketing Department. This retrieval requires both a **select** operator (to get only Marketing Department employees) and a **project** operator (to get only names and salaries). To accomplish it, we would execute the following two steps:

$$Mktg = \textbf{select from } T \textbf{ where } Department = \text{Marketing}$$

$$MktgSalary = \textbf{project } Name, Salary \textbf{ from } Mktg$$

These two retrievals would produce the relation *MktgSalary* as follows:

MktgSalary:	*Name*	*Salary*
	Jones, M.W	22,000
	Rand, G.J	26,000
	Wells, N.A.	15,000
	King, R.A.	43,000

Now suppose we wish to retrieve a list of position and department combinations that are represented in our database. To accomplish this, we would execute the following:

$$PosDept = \textbf{project } Position, Department \textbf{ from } T$$

Notice that in the **project** operator, we have reversed the order of the two attributes *Position* and *Department* from their order in the original relation *T*. This is perfectly acceptable and would initially produce the relation *PosDept* as follows:

PosDept:	*Position*	*Department*
	manager	Sales
	clerk	Sales
	designer	Marketing
	manager	Marketing
	clerk	Marketing
	manager	Marketing

Notice that in the preceding relation, we no longer can identify the employee that each row represented in the original relation. With this information no longer accessible, the fourth and sixth rows are equal. Because our interest is only in which position/department combinations are in our database, it is redundant to keep both of these rows. Hence, the **project** operator automatically eliminates such duplicate rows and produces the following for *PosDept*.

PosDept:	*Position*	*Department*
	manager	Sales
	clerk	Sales
	designer	Marketing
	manager	Marketing
	clerk	Marketing

Exercise Set 9.1

1. Define the **select** operator of relational algebra.
2. Define the **project** operator of relational algebra.

Using the relation *T* given in this section, write retrievals to produce the following:

3. A list of records for employees who are clerks.
4. A list of records for employees who make less than $20,000.
5. A list of the names of all the employees who are managers.

9.2 BUILDING COMPLEX SELECT RETRIEVALS

Often it is necessary to retrieve database information whose description is more complex than the simple descriptions we used in the examples of the last section. The **select** operator can be used directly to make many of these more complex retrievals. To do this, however, you need to have a knowledge of some basic arithmetic, comparison, and logical operators. In this section, we discuss the most important of these operators.

ARITHMETIC OPERATORS. The formulas used in **select** operator retrievals are generally allowed to contain arithmetic expressions and to use various comparison operators. The standard **arithmetic operators** and the symbols used to represent them are shown in Figure 9.1.

The order in which calculations involving several arithmetic operators are made is very important. For example, if x is computed by the formula $x = 3 + 4 * 6$, different answers are obtained, depending upon whether the addition or the multiplication is done first (we get 42 in the former case and 27 in the latter). To avoid such ambiguities, a convention or rule known as **precedence of operators** has been adopted. For the arithmetic operators the precedence rule is shown in Figure 9.2. Note that this rule implies that the correct answer for the preceding example is 27.

The precedence rule may not be adequate for all circumstances. For example, what is the correct order of evaluation of the operators in the following expression in which both operators have the same precedence level?

Operator	Symbol
addition	+
subtraction	-
multiplication	*
division	/
exponentiation	^

Figure 9.1 The standard arithmetic operators.

$$x = a - b + c$$

This ambiguity is resolved by the **left-to-right rule**, which states that if no other rule determines the precedence of operators, the operators should be applied in left-to-right order. Alas, as with all rules, there is an exception to this rule: *Exponentiation is performed right to left.*

Parentheses can be used to change the order of operator evaluation. In general, operators within parentheses are evaluated first, starting with the innermost nested parentheses and working outward. You have probably learned all these rules before, when you first learned to evaluate arithmetic expressions.

To illustrate these precedence and left-to-right rules, consider the evaluation of the following expression:

$$14 - 2 * 3 \wedge 2 / 2 + 3 * 4$$

Using the precedence rule, first evaluate $3 \wedge 2 = 9$, leaving

$$14 - 2 * 9 / 2 + 3 * 4$$

Next do all multiplication and division from left to right. The sequence is

$$= 14 - 18 / 2 + 3 * 4$$

$$= 14 - 9 + 3 * 4$$

$$= 14 - 9 + 12$$

Finally, do all addition and subtraction from left to right, yielding

Operator	Meaning	Precedence
^	exponentiation	highest
+, -	unary plus, unary minus	↕
*, /	multiplication, division	↕
+, -	addition, subtraction	lowest

Figure 9.2 Arithmetic operator precedence.

$$= 5 + 12$$

$$= 17$$

If you wish, you can make the precedence rules explicit by using parentheses and writing this expression as

$$(14 - ((2 * (3 \wedge 2)) / 2)) + (3 * 4)$$

Of course, the order of evaluation could be changed by placing the parentheses in different positions.

COMPARISON OPERATORS.   **Comparison operators** are combined with attribute names and expressions (which may use arithmetic operators) to make the formulas used in **select** retrievals. These comparison operators produce conditions that evaluate to either *True* or *False*. Just as the arithmetic operators take two numerical values and produce a single numerical value as a result, the comparison operators take two values (not necessarily numerical) and produce a logical result of *True* or *False*. The commonly used comparison operators and the symbols that are used to represent them are shown in Figure 9.3. The operators above the dotted line in that figure can be used to compare numbers, text strings, or dates; those below the line are used only in comparisons of text strings.

In conditions, the comparison operators can be thought of as asking a question. For example, the condition $x > y$ asks the question: *Is the current value of the variable* x *greater than the current value of the variable* y? The value of the condition is then *True* or *False* depending upon whether the answer to the question is *Yes* or *No*. When two text strings are compared, alphabetic (or dictionary) ordering is used for deciding the value of the condition.

If x and y have the following text string values (The quote marks are used to emphasize that string values—as opposed to variable names—are being used. *In general, the technique for writing string values depends upon the particular software package being used.*):

Operator	Symbol		
equal	eq	or	=
greater than	gt	or	>
less than	lt	or	<
greater than or equal	ge	or	>=
less than or equal	le	or	<=
not equal	ne	or	<>
--------	----	----	----
contains	none		
begins with	none		

Figure 9.3 Comparison operators.

$$x = \text{``shoes''}$$

$$y = \text{``table''}$$

then the value of $x > y$ is *False* because "shoes" would appear before "table" in a dictionary. Note also that the condition x *contains "oe"* is *True*, whereas the condition x *begins with "t"* is *False*.

Conditions can contain both arithmetic operators and comparison operators. In such cases the arithmetic operators take precedence (see Figure 9.7 for a summary of the precedence rules for all the operators we will use) and are always performed before the comparison operators are evaluated. For example, the following are all valid conditions:

$$x + y >= x * y$$

$$x * (y - z) <= (x - y)$$

$$(x + y) * (x + 10) < ((a + b) / (x + b))$$

If $x = 2$, $y = 4$, $a = 5$, and $b = 1$, the third condition would be evaluated as follows:

$$(2 + 4) * (2 + 10) < ((5 + 1) / (2 + 1))$$

$$6 * 12 < (6 / 3)$$

$$72 < 2$$

$$\text{False}$$

LOGICAL OPERATORS.   The **logical operators** NOT, AND, and OR can be used with arithmetic and comparison operators to produce complex conditions. The logical operator NOT takes a single condition (which evaluates to either *True* or *False*—this value is called the *truth value* of the condition) and reverses its truth value. The AND and OR operators combine truth values for two conditions to produce a truth value for the single combined condition. The way in which these operators combine truth values is given in Figure 9.4: the tables in that figure are called **truth tables**. Notice that AND is *True* only when both of its argument conditions are *True*, and OR is *True* when either (including both) of its argument conditions is *True*.

For complex conditions involving the combination of several logical operators, you can construct a truth table to find the value of the condition for all the possible values of the constituent conditions and/or logical variables. Consider the example given in Figure 9.5. Notice that because three logical variables are involved, there are eight different combinations of logical values.

Try making a table like the one in Figure 9.5 to evaluate the condition (x AND y) OR z. If you do this and compare the result with Figure 9.5, you will notice that the two conditions x AND (y OR z) and (x AND y) OR z have different evaluations. Hence, if we write the condition x AND y OR z without parentheses, it can be interpreted in two different ways, depending upon the order in which the operators are applied.

Just as with arithmetic operators, we can resolve the preceding ambiguity by using parentheses or by agreeing upon a precedence rule. The usual precedence rule for logical operators is given in Figure 9.6. However, this rule is not as universally applied as the arithmetic operator precedence rule. *Beware that some*

Operator	Truth Value of Result		

NOT x

x	NOT x
True	False
False	True

x AND y

x	y	x AND y
True	True	True
True	False	False
False	True	False
False	False	False

x OR y

x	y	x OR y
True	True	True
True	False	True
False	True	True
False	False	False

Figure 9.4 Truth tables defining the basic logical operators.

database and spreadsheet packages (including the spreadsheet in Works) use a left-to-right rule when evaluating combinations of the AND and OR logical operators. You should always check which rule is being followed before using combined logical operators in any software package. Works DB employs the rule of Figure 9.6.

Finally, we note that when arithmetic, comparison, and logical operators appear in the same condition, in the absence of parentheses, the order of precedence is arithmetic, comparison, then logical. This rule is summarized in Figure

Evaluating
x AND (y OR z)

x	y	z	y OR z	x AND (y OR z)
True	True	True	True	True
True	True	False	True	True
True	False	True	True	True
True	False	False	False	False
False	True	True	True	False
False	True	False	True	False
False	False	True	True	False
False	False	False	False	False

Figure 9.5 Evaluating a condition involving multiple logical operators.

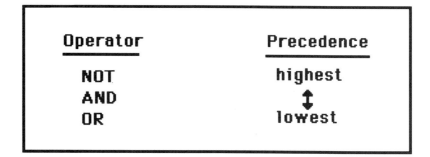

Figure 9.6 Logical operator precedence.

9.7. Although this rule is generally adhered to, it is not used in all software packages; so be cautious when using any package with which you are not familiar.

MULTIPLE-CONDITION RETRIEVALS. There are many cases when a data retrieval cannot be expressed as a simple formula involving only one attribute name, one comparison operator, and one value. For example, suppose a list of records is required for all employees in the Marketing Department whose salaries exceed $25,000. One possibility would be to execute the following pair of retrievals (the desired list is named *MktgSal25*):

> *Mktg* = **select from** *T* **where** *Department* = Marketing
>
> *MktgSal25* = **select from** *Mktg* **where** *Salary* > $25,000

These would produce the relation *MktgSal* as follows:

MktgSal:	*Name*	*Salary*	*Department*	*Position*
	Rand, G.J	26,000	Marketing	manager
	King, R.A.	43,000	Marketing	manager

Using the ideas of this section, we could write this retrieval using a single select operator as follows.

Operator	Meaning	Precedence
^	exponentiation	highest
+,-	unary plus, minus	
*,/	multiplication/ division	
+,-	addition/subtraction	
=,<>,<,>,<=,>=	comparison operators	
NOT AND OR	logical operators (caution with AND/OR)	lowest

Figure 9.7 Summary of usual operator precedence.

$MktgSal$ = **select from** T **where** $Department$ = Marketing

AND $Salary$ > \$25,000

For some information retrieval requirements, it is impossible to combine different **select** retrievals in a simple way to produce the desired result; in many of those cases a single **select** retrieval with a combined condition is easy to construct. For example, suppose we wish to retrieve a list of all employees who work in Sales *or* who earn more than \$25,000. This is accomplished with the following single **select** retrieval (call the list L):

L = **select from** T **where** $Department$ = Sales

OR $Salary$ > \$25,000

This retrieval will produce the relation L as follows. Notice that the record for employee J.P. Smith satisfies both the preceding constituent conditions. Because our use of OR is inclusive, such records are always included in such retrievals.

L:	*Name*	*Salary*	*Department*	*Position*
	Smith, J.P.	33,000	Sales	manager
	Kline, H.F.	14,000	Sales	clerk
	Rand, G.J	26,000	Marketing	manager
	King, R.A.	43,000	Marketing	manager

As a final example before we see how some of these ideas are implemented in Works DB, suppose we wish to produce a list of employees who are either in the Sales Department or (if not) in the Marketing Department and earn more than \$25,000. The following retrieval will produce such a list, N.

N = **select from** T **where** $Department$ = Sales OR

($Department$ = Marketing AND $Salary$ > \$25,000)

The N produced follows.

N:	*Name*	*Salary*	*Department*	*Position*
	Smith, J.P.	33,000	Sales	manager
	Kline, H.F.	14,000	Sales	clerk
	Rand, G.J	26,000	Marketing	manager
	King, R.A.	43,000	Marketing	manager

Notice carefully that the parentheses are not necessary in the preceding select retrieval, if we assume that AND has precedence over OR. However, without this assumption and without the parentheses, the first two conditions would be combined with the OR, and then that result and the last condition would be combined using AND. Check for yourself that such a retrieval produces a different list from that given above.

Exercise Set 9.2

Suppose that $x = 2$, $y = 3$, $w = 4$, $A = $ *False*, $B = $ *True*, and $C = $ *True*. Use the precedence rules given in this section to evaluate the following:

1. $x + y * w / 2 + y$
2. $x - y + w$
3. $x - y + w * x$
4. A AND B OR C
5. A AND (B OR C)
6. A OR B AND C
7. (A OR B) AND C
8. Give an example of truth values for A, B, and C so that the expressions in exercises 6 and 7 evaluate to *different* truth values.

Using the example relation T in the text, write the following retrievals using the **select** and/or **project** operators.

9. Retrieve a list of records for employees who either are clerks or earn less than $30,000.

10. Retrieve a list of records for employees who either are managers or are in Marketing and have a salary of less than $20,000.

11. Retrieve a list of names of all Sales Department employees who earn less than $20,000.

9.3 SELECTING AND DISPLAYING INFORMATION IN WORKS DB

In this section you will learn how to make retrievals using the **select** operator in Works DB. We begin by defining a new database that will be used for the examples in the remainder of this chapter.

EXAMPLE DATABASE. Suppose you are the program manager of radio station WWIN, which plays a variety of types of music during a week, with music sets grouped in many different ways. Hence, it is very desirable to automate your ability to select the various musical sets that you must program. You decide to place information about WWIN's sizable record collection in a Works DB database. Using this database, you can easily find what records of a given type are available in the station. In this way you can plan the week's music segments and have your assistant collect the appropriate records and deliver them to the appropriate D.J. in a timely manner.

Suppose you decide that the following attributes are important for your purposes: *Title, Artist, Label, Year Released, Highest Rating Attained on WWIN's Chart,* and *Music Type.* As a consequence, you might lay out the following record format:

Title	Artist	Label	YearRel	HighestR	Type

Let us suppose we have created such a Works DB database and placed your data into it. A sample list display from such a database is shown in Figure 9.8.

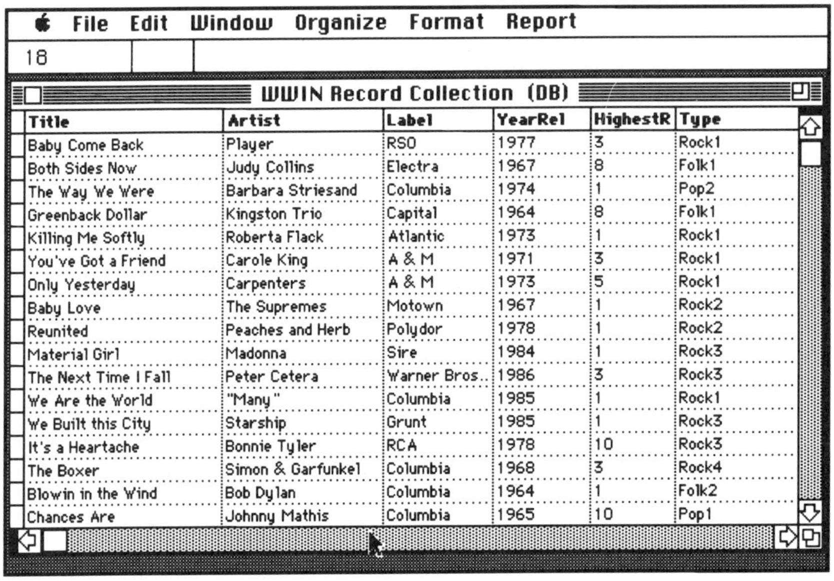

Title	Artist	Label	YearRel	HighestR	Type
Baby Come Back	Player	RSO	1977	3	Rock1
Both Sides Now	Judy Collins	Electra	1967	8	Folk1
The Way We Were	Barbara Striesand	Columbia	1974	1	Pop2
Greenback Dollar	Kingston Trio	Capital	1964	8	Folk1
Killing Me Softly	Roberta Flack	Atlantic	1973	1	Rock1
You've Got a Friend	Carole King	A & M	1971	3	Rock1
Only Yesterday	Carpenters	A & M	1973	5	Rock1
Baby Love	The Supremes	Motown	1967	1	Rock2
Reunited	Peaches and Herb	Polydor	1978	1	Rock2
Material Girl	Madonna	Sire	1984	1	Rock3
The Next Time I Fall	Peter Cetera	Warner Bros..	1986	3	Rock3
We Are the World	"Many"	Columbia	1985	1	Rock1
We Built this City	Starship	Grunt	1985	1	Rock3
It's a Heartache	Bonnie Tyler	RCA	1978	10	Rock3
The Boxer	Simon & Garfunkel	Columbia	1968	3	Rock4
Blowin in the Wind	Bob Dylan	Columbia	1964	1	Folk2
Chances Are	Johnny Mathis	Columbia	1965	10	Pop1

Figure 9.8 List display of the example database.

SELECTING RECORDS. Assume that you have opened the example database and are viewing the list display seen in Figure 9.8. To perform a **select** retrieval, you must construct a **record selection rule** by choosing the command *Record Selection* from the **Organize** menu. When this command is chosen, the screen shown in Figure 9.9 is displayed. Notice that the database attribute names are listed in the scroll rectangle to the left of the screen and the comparison operators in the scroll rectangle to the right. Values to be used in completing a record selection rule are entered into the rectangle labeled *Record Comparison Information*.

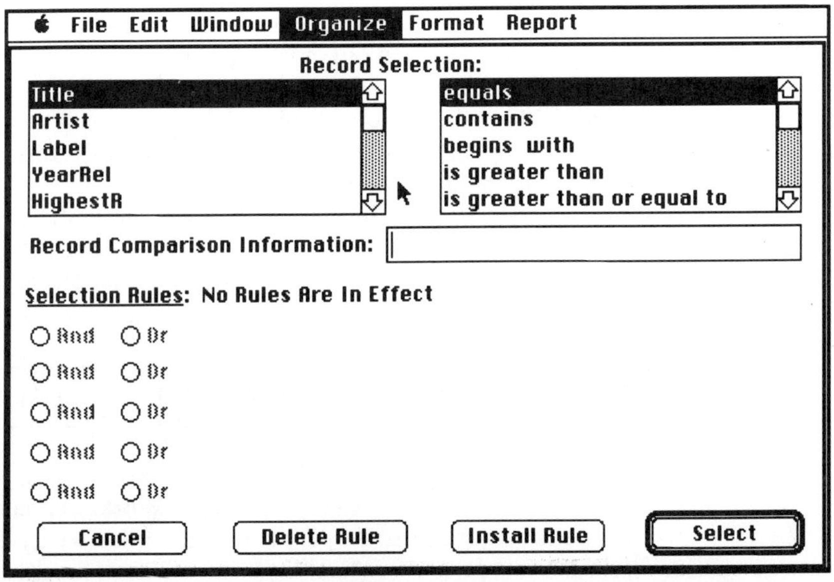

Figure 9.9 *Record Selection* dialog box.

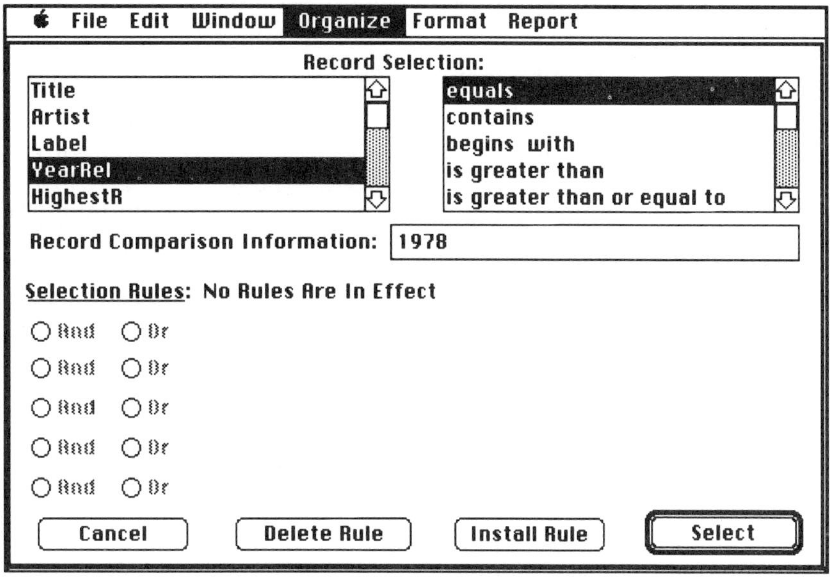

Figure 9.10 A simple **select** retrieval in Works DB.

Figure 9.10 shows the *Record Selection* dialog box with a simple **select** retrieval configured. By clicking the *Select* button, the information selected will be displayed (in either a list or form display, depending upon which of these was active when you accessed the *Record Selection* dialog box).

The resulting list display for the record selection of Figure 9.10 is shown in Figure 9.11. Because the example database is small, there are only two records with *YearRel* = 1978.

MULTIPLE-CONDITION RECORD SELECTIONS. To select the logical operators AND and OR, you first click on the *Install Rule* button to enter the rule being currently defined. Then you can click on either OR or AND and enter another rule. A combination rule built in this way can have *up to six constituent rules* (up to five logical operators). Remember that Works DB interprets these combination rules by giving AND precedence over OR. As a consequence, you must be careful when constructing a rule that involves both AND and OR to make sure your rule will be interpreted as you intend. Figure 9.12 shows the *Record Selection* dialog box with the following simple AND rule being constructed:

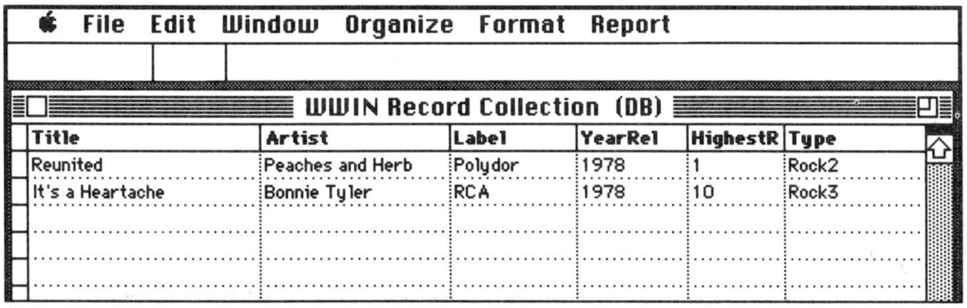

Figure 9.11 Display of results from retrieval of Figure 9.10.

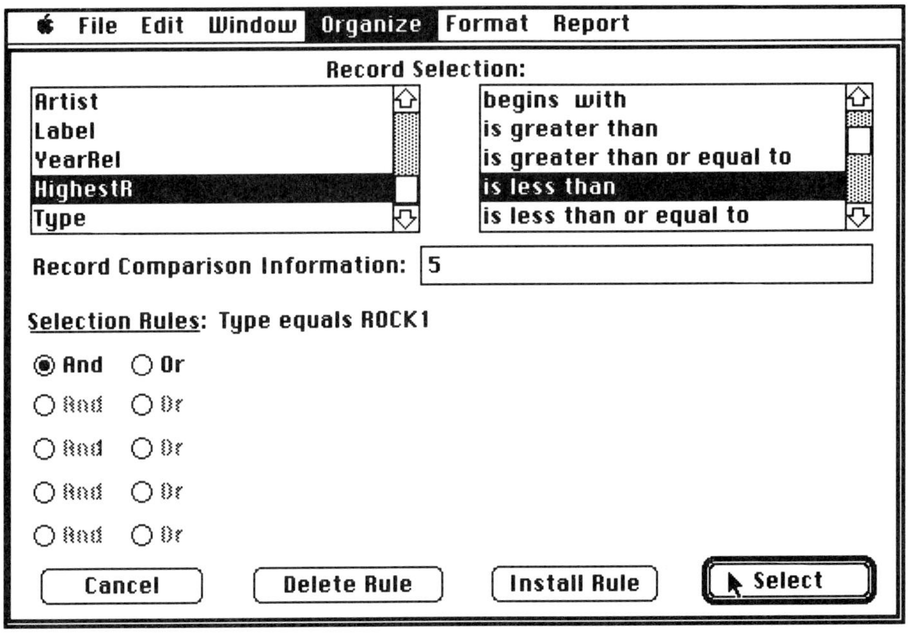

Figure 9.12 A simple AND rule being constructed.

select from *WWIN Record Collection* **where** *Type* = Rock1

AND *HighestR* < 5

The list display that results from clicking the *Select* button on the screen in Figure 9.12 is shown Figure 9.13. Check the records displayed to see that they satisfy the retrieval.

Now suppose we would like to produce a list of all the records that were released between 1975 and 1985 or achieved a number 1 WWIN rating no matter when they were released. The *Record Selection* dialog box shown in Figure 9.14 will produce such a list. Note that we are executing the following **select** retrieval. Also consider how the AND precedence over OR is being used.

select from *WWIN Record Collection* **where**

YearRel >= 1975 AND *YearRel* <= 1985 OR *HighestR* = 1

Note that the following retrieval *would not produce the correct result* if a left-to-right rule were applied in which AND and OR had the same precedence level:

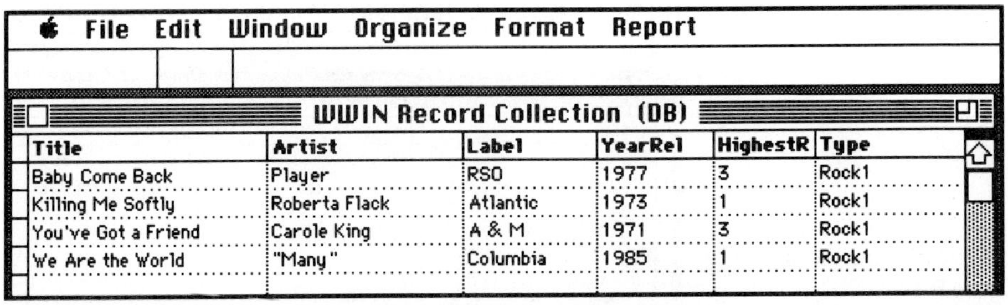

Figure 9.13 The list display of records selected in Figure 9.12.

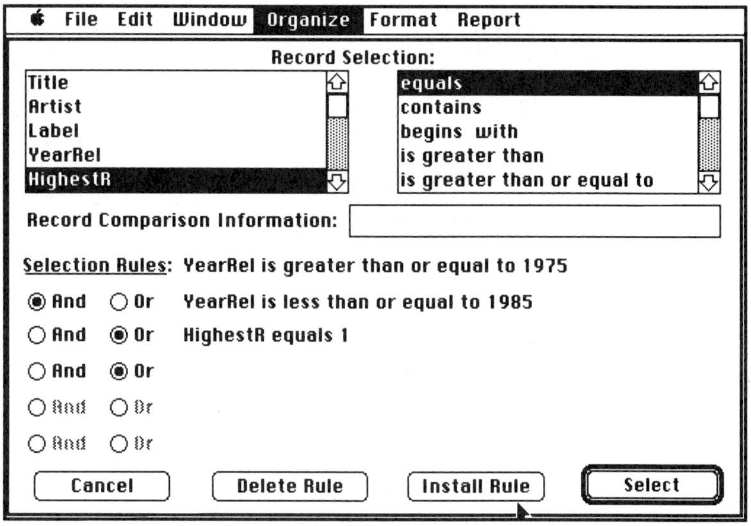

Figure 9.14 Selection with an AND and an OR condition.

select from *WWIN Record Collection* **where**

HighestR = 1 OR *YearRel* >= 1975 AND *YearRel* <= 1985

The list display produced by the selection made in Figure 9.14 is shown in Figure 9.15. Verify that the information is correct by manually selecting the appropriate records from the database shown in Figure 9.8.

As a final example in this section, consider the problem of producing a list of all Rock1 type records whose highest rating was either 1 or 3. The attempt to do this with the selection criteria shown in Figure 9.16 will fail. Can you see why?

The retrieval in Figure 9.16 is equivalent to the following retrieval because of the precedence of AND over OR.

select from WWIN *Record Collection* **where**

(*Type* = Rock1 AND *HighestR* = 1) OR *HighestR* = 3

Look at the preceding retrieval closely to see why it does not produce the desired list. The list that it does produce is shown in Figure 9.17. Verify by manually

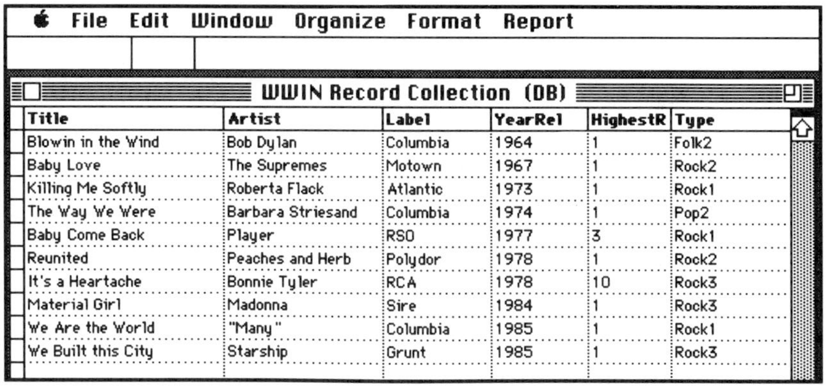

Figure 9.15 List display of records selected in Figure 9.14.

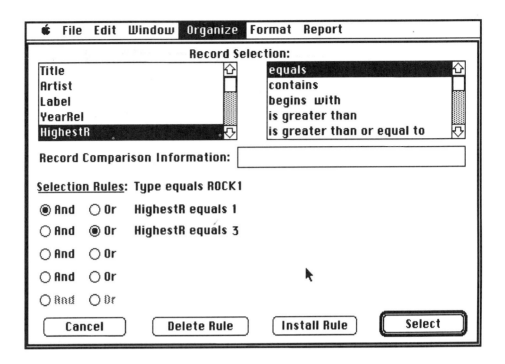

Figure 9.16 An incorrect **select** retrieval for all Rock1 type records whose highest rating was 1 or 3.

checking the database in Figure 9.8 that the data shown there is that produced by the preceding **select** operator. Notice that it is not the list we desired, because it includes some records that are not of type Rock1.

The correct retrieval is given in Figure 9.18. It is equivalent to the following (again because of the precedence of AND over OR).

select from *WWIN Record Collection* **where**

($Type$ = Rock1 AND *HighestR* = 1)

OR

($Type$ = Rock1 AND *HighestR* = 3)

The alternate correct retrieval

select from *WWIN Record Collection* **where**

$Type$ = Rock1 AND (*HighestR* = 1 OR *HighestR* = 3))

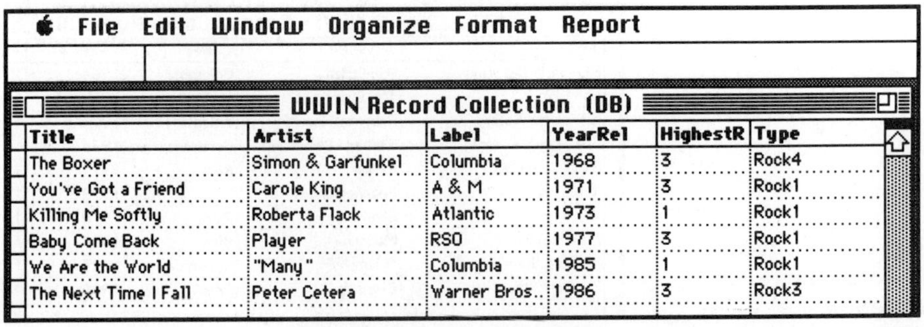

Title	Artist	Label	YearRel	HighestR	Type
The Boxer	Simon & Garfunkel	Columbia	1968	3	Rock4
You've Got a Friend	Carole King	A & M	1971	3	Rock1
Killing Me Softly	Roberta Flack	Atlantic	1973	1	Rock1
Baby Come Back	Player	RSO	1977	3	Rock1
We Are the World	"Many"	Columbia	1985	1	Rock1
The Next Time I Fall	Peter Cetera	Warner Bros.	1986	3	Rock3

Figure 9.17 List display produced by the **select** retrieval of Figure 9.16.

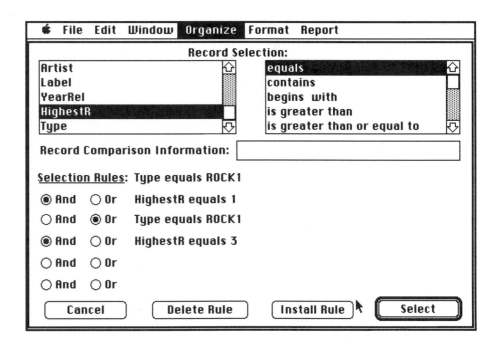

Figure 9.18 Correct version of retrieval attempted in Figure 9.16.

cannot be entered as a record selection rule because parenthese are not allowed in Works DB.

The records displayed in response to the retrieval written in Figure 9.18 are shown in Figure 9.19. Once again you should verify the data manually.

SAVING SELECTED SUBSETS.   Works allows you to **save any selected subset** of records as a database with its own name. In fact you can also delete some attributes from the selected subset of records before saving it. In other words, you can apply a **project** operator to the relation selected. To delete a field, display the subset of records on the screen and then select the field to be deleted by clicking on any entry in its column. *(Caution: You should not delete a field that is used in the select condition; if you do, the record selection will be canceled.)* Assuming you have chosen a field that is not included in the select condition, choose the *Delete Field* command from the **Edit** menu. You can delete as many such fields as you choose in this manner and thus construct the **project** operator that is desired. Note that any duplicate rows created in this way are not deleted.

Figure 9.19 List display for the **select** retrieval of Figure 9.18.

File	Edit	Window	Organize	Format	Report

WWIN Record Collection (DB)

Title	Artist	Label	YearRel	HighestR	Type
Baby Come Back	Player	RSO	1977	3	Rock1
Killing Me Softly	Roberta Flack	Atlantic	1973	1	Rock1
You've Got a Friend	Carole King	A & M	1971	3	Rock1
We Are the World	"Many"	Columbia	1985	1	Rock1

When you are ready to save the subset database, choose the *Save As* command from the **File** menu, name your new database, and check the *Save Selected Records Only* option. Be sure to give the new database a name different from that of your original database. When a subset database is saved, the original database is left intact, as long *as you do not save the changes to your original database when you exit Works DB.* You will need to be very cautious when extracting and saving subsets of databases to ensure that the original database remains unchanged. In fact, it is a good idea to use the *Save As* command to save a duplicate of the original database before you begin the construction of a subset database.

Exercise Set 9.3

1. How is the **select** operator of relational algebra implemented in Works DB? Give two examples using the example database of this section.

2. Give an example of one way the **project** relational algebra operator can be performed in Works DB. (You will see an additional method in the next section.)

3. How many conditions can be combined with the logical operators AND and OR in a Works DB selection rule?

4. Why is caution required in saving subsets of a database?

Computer Practice 9.3

1. Create the *WWIN Record Collection* database of this section and put the data shown in Figure 9.8 into it.

2. Try the example record selections described in Figures 9.10, 9.12, 9.14, 9.16, and 9.18.

3. Write a record selection rule to retrieve database records for all songs released during the 1970s that were rated number 1.

4. Write a record selection rule to retrieve database records for all songs that were rated number 1 and that were on either Motown or Columbia labels.

5. Write a record selection rule to retrieve database records for all songs that were rated number 1 or that were released on the Columbia label before 1970.

6. Write a record selection rule to retrieve database records for all songs released between 1975 and 1985 (inclusive) whose highest ratings were either number 1 or number 3.

7. Try some record selections of your own design from the WWIN database. Be sure to check the results manually for correctness using the database contents shown in Figure 9.8.

8. Save your database for later use.

9.4 CREATING WORKS DB REPORTS

It is very easy to create **database reports** that incorporate both the **select** and **project** relational algebra operators. Report specifications that are created during a session are automatically saved if changes to the database are saved when exiting the session. Saved report specifications will allow the report to incorporate any updated information in the database at a later time. The maximum number of reports that can be saved is eight. When you have eight report specifications saved and wish to save an additional report, one of the eight must first be deleted.

You will now see how to create Works DB reports. Suppose the database of interest is open. The **select** operator is applied just as in the previous section. When the appropriate records have been selected, execute the *New Report* command from the **Report** menu. A screen similar to the one shown in Figure 9.20 will be displayed. Notice the presence of a new menu, **TotalsPage,** on the menu bar. You will understand its purpose shortly.

The selection rules that have been entered are displayed on the reports definition screen. At the bottom of the reports definition screen (notice the database list display window is in the background in Figure 9.20) are shown the first three records that will appear in the report. The small triangle at the left edge of the field name bar marks the left margin of the report. A similar symbol also marks the right margin, but it cannot be seen on the screen in Figure 9.20 because the right margin is off the screen. The margins are controlled in the *Page Setup* dialog box, which can be accessed under the **File** menu.

To execute a **project** operator, fields that are not wanted in the report are moved to the right of the right margin marker. In Figure 9.21, the field *Label* is shown being moved to the right. This is done by moving the pointer over the field name so that it takes the shape of a hand and then dragging the field name to the right.

After moving all the unwanted fields to the right of the *Report Definition* screen, you can complete the **project** operator by adjusting the right margin using the *Page Setup* command so that only the fields you wish to include are in the

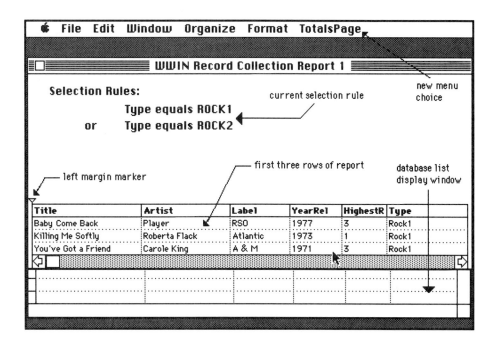

Figure 9.20 A *report definition* screen.

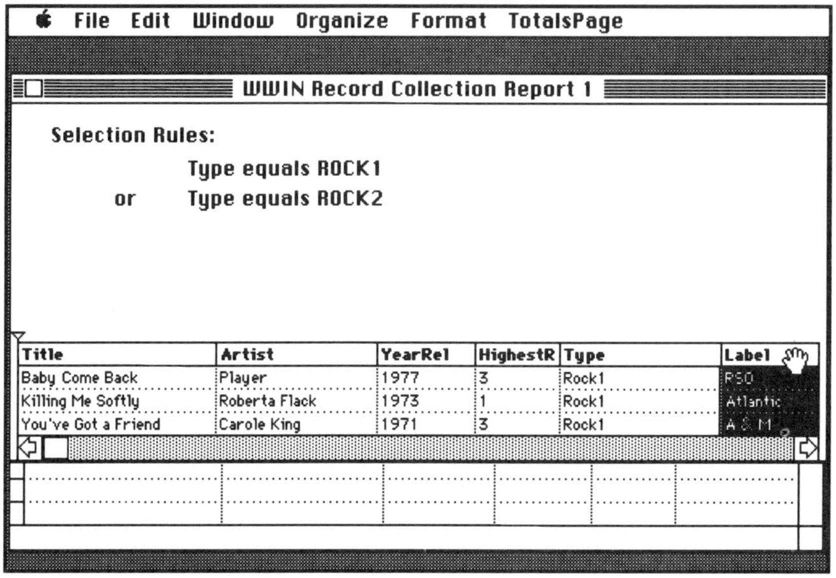

Figure 9.21 Moving a field to the right.

report. Some resizing of field widths will make this easier to achieve. Try placing the right margin and then adjusting field widths. The example shown in Figure 9.22 is a report definition that excludes the *Label* field. Notice also that in Figure 9.22 the report we are working on has a different name. Reports can easily be renamed by selecting the *Change Report Title* command from the **Edit** menu when a report window is active. The report *Rock1/Rock2 Report* is now ready to be printed. When it is printed, it will appear just as the first three data rows and the field title row that are displayed in Figure 9.22 between the margin markers.

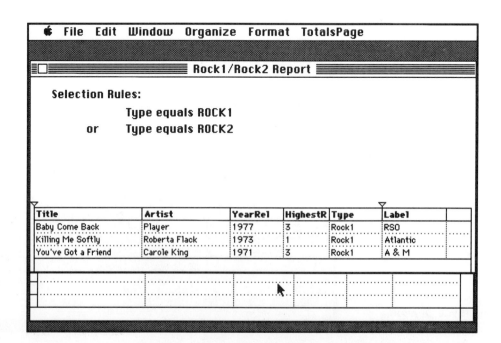

Figure 9.22 A report definition with the field named *Label* excluded.

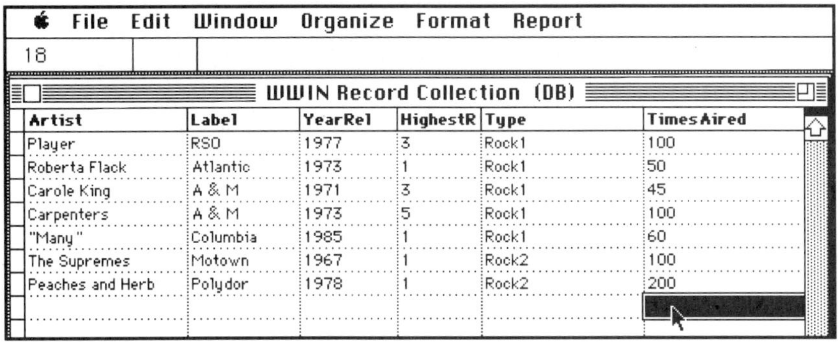

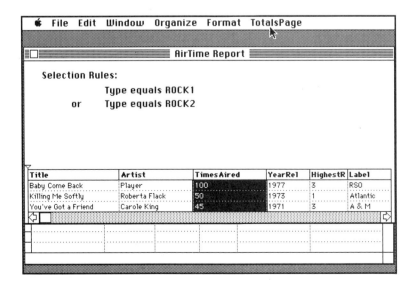

Figure 9.23 Adding a new field to a database.

TOTALS AND SUBTOTALS. To demonstrate the ability of Works DB to calculate **automatic totals and subtotals,** it will be necessary to add a data field that could be meaningfully summed. Let us suppose that you have notes indicating how many times a given record has been played on the air. Let us add to our database a field to contain this information. Return to the database list display by clicking on the portion of its window that can be seen at the bottom of the screen or by accessing it under the **Window** menu. Notice that the record selection rule is still in effect.

Next select the command *Add New Field* under the **Edit** menu. Name the new field *TimesAired* and it will be added to the database. The screen in Figure 9.23 shows the new field just after we have added data to it.

Choose the *New Report* command from the **Report** menu. We will use the same selection rule as in the previous report; however, we now move the *Times-Aired* field as shown in Figure 9.24. Next we select the *TimesAired* field and choose *Sum This Field* from the **TotalsPage** menu. If we print this report, Works DB will calculate a total for the attribute *TimesAired.*

To preview the report, you can choose the *Copy Totals* command under **Edit**. This command copies a portion of the report (the whole report if it is small) to the

Figure 9.24 Preparing to choose *TimesAired* for summing.

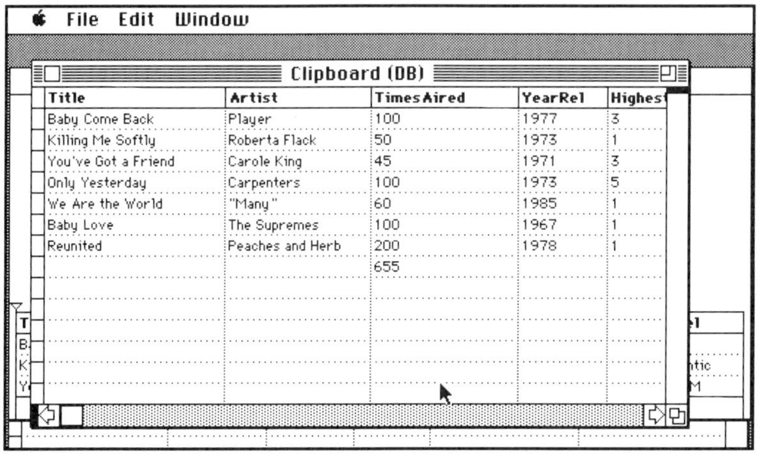

Figure 9.25 Preview of totals for the report that sums *TimesAired*.

Clipboard so that you can check the totals calculated for correctness. If *Copy Totals* is executed and the *Show Clipboard* command under **Window** is chosen, the screen shown in Figure 9.25 is displayed.

Figure 9.26 shows a second report that also sums the number of times records are aired. However, by selecting the field *Type* and executing the command *Total on Field Change* under the **TotalsPage** menu, you can force the calculation of a subtotal each time the entry in field *Type* changes. Of course this arrangement will make little sense unless you have sorted the database on the field *Type* so that equal *Type* entries appear together in sequence.

You can preview the subtotals and totals by using the *Copy Totals* and *Show Clipboard* commands. The result of these actions is shown in Figure 9.27. Notice that only the first record of each of the distinct categories in the *Type* field is shown and the *TimesAired* entries for those records are actually the calculated subtotals. If you print the report, you will see all the selected database entries, with subtotals and totals appearing on a separate line.

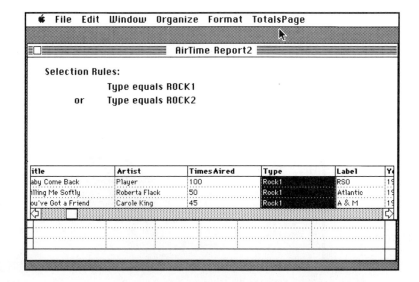

Figure 9.26 Preparing to define a report with subtotals for each different value of the field *Type*.

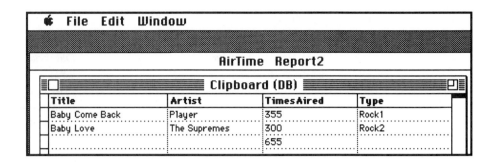

Figure 9.27 Previewing subtotals and totals for a report.

Exercise Set 9.4

1. Describe the method for creating a Works DB report.
2. How is the **project** relational algebra operator related to Works DB reports?
3. How is the **select** relational algebra operator related to Works DB reports?
4. Describe the steps for adding attribute totals to a Works DB report.
5. Describe the steps for adding subtotals to a Works DB report.
6. How is a data field added to a previously existing Works database?

Computer Practice 9.4

1. Using your WWIN database from Computer Practice 9.3, create and print the *Rock1/Rock2 Report* described in this section.
2. Modify the database you saved in Computer Practice 9.3 by adding the field *TimesAired*. Add the data shown in Figure 9.25 to your database. Now make sure you have all the database records displayed in a list window (if necessary, choose the command *Select All Records f*rom the **Organize** menu to do this) and then add data for all those records having blank entries for the field *TimesAired*. You are to supply the numbers.
3. Create and print the *AirTime Report* of this section.
4. Create and print the *AirTime Report2* of this section.
5. Create and print a report consisting of *Artist* and *Title* for all songs rated number 1.
6. Create and print a report consisting of *Artist*, *Title*, and *HighestR* for all songs released between 1975 and 1979 (inclusive) that were played more than 100 times.
7. Create and print a report consisting of *Artist*, *Title*, and *TimesAired* for all songs on the Columbia label. Include in your report the total of the *TimesAired* column.
8. Create and print a report consisting of *Artist, Title, Label,* and *TimesAired* for all songs. In your report, show subtotals for TimesAired for each different label—remember to sort on the *Label* field before specifying the report.

Key Concepts

Arithmetic operators
Comparison operators
Left-to-right rule
Precedence of operators
Record selection rule
Saving subsets of a database
Truth tables

Automatic totals and subtotals
Database reports
Logical operators
Project operator
Relational algebra
Select operator

CHAPTER 10

CALCULATING AND CHARTING WITH SPREADSHEETS

LEARNING OBJECTIVES

- To understand how a generic spreadsheet screen is organized.

- To understand the primary generic spreadsheet objects.

- To learn the use of some fundamental generic spreadsheet operators.

- To learn how the generic spreadsheet concepts are implemented in the Works spreadsheet module.

- To learn how to create and edit Works spreadsheets and to use them to perform some simple calculations.

- To learn how to produce charts and graphs that display the results of MS Works spreadsheet calculations.

I n this chapter you will learn about the kinds of elementary operations that you can perform with most spreadsheets and how these operations can be used to solve a very wide range of problems involving numerical calculations. In fact, modern spreadsheets are so powerful they can be used to solve problems that only a few years ago would have required writing complex computer programs. Basic spreadsheet concepts are first presented conceptually and then their specific implementation in the integrated package Works are studied. You will learn how the spreadsheet component of Works can be used to solve some simple problems that require the computing of numerical values and to chart and/or graph the results.

10.1 USE OF SPREADSHEET PACKAGES

The purpose of a spreadsheet is to provide the same ease of performing, altering, and graphically displaying mathematical calculations as the word processor provides for manipulating text in reports or documents or as a database management system provides for storing and retrieving information. Calculations that would be tedious and time-consuming using a calculator can be quickly carried out, structured in an easy-to-read tabular form, and graphed and/or charted using a spreadsheet. Thus, someone needing to perform mathematical calculations would find the spreadsheet as useful and necessary to them as the writer of a report would find the use of a word processor.

Spreadsheets are also often used for investigating *what if* kinds of questions. Many computations depend on a small set of values each of which may be either subject to change or not accurately known. For example, the decision about whether or not a company should borrow money will depend upon the interest rate at which money can be borrowed. Henceforth we will call such a value (i.e., one that is likely to change and upon which the result of a computation depends) a *parameter* of the problem being solved. In a well-designed spreadsheet, the parameters of a computation may be changed easily and the effects of the changes displayed rapidly in the tables and graphs produced. Consequently, the spreadsheet user may experiment with several alternative sets of parameter values to learn their effect on decisions that need to be made. This process of changing parameters to see their influence on the resulting decision is referred to as *what if* analysis. In many organizations the spreadsheet has made possible the use of a quantitative management approach rather than a qualitative one by allowing the development of spreadsheet models and exploration of results obtained from these models using *what if* analysis.

Spreadsheet software originated with the development of the VisiCalc program in 1979 for the Apple II computer. Very quickly after VisiCalc's introduction, a sizable group of spreadsheet users developed who generally had relatively little computer experience and certainly no programming background. Nonetheless, they were able to save substantial time and effort by adopting the spreadsheet for business problem solving. The usefulness of and enthusiastic reception received by spreadsheet programs helped to give credibility to the notion that personal computers could improve personal productivity and was a major factor for the introduction of personal computers into business and educational environments.

Not only do spreadsheet environments allow you to perform simple arithmetic operations such as addition, multiplication, and so on, but they also can be used to compute the kinds of functions that are important for many financial or scientific calculations. Such functions include the future value of an investment, the rate returned on an investment, time series analysis, trend analysis, the determination of the equation of a line that best fits a set of points, the mean and standard deviation of a set of numbers, and trigonometric, exponential, and logarithmic functions.

Graphs and charts produced by a spreadsheet can be easily incorporated into documents and/or reports prepared using a word processor or desktop publishing package. Similarly, data selected from a database can be imported into a spreadsheet to serve as input to the spreadsheet model, which then can generate graphs and/or tables to be incorporated into a report. Thus, considerable flexibility exists in the way spreadsheets can be used in problem areas that require computations.

The Works spreadsheet module (which we will name Works SS in further discussion) is described in depth in this and the following two chapters. It is well designed and provides an easily learned interface that will allow even an occasional Works SS user to explore its calculational properties intuitively—usually without the need for consulting the Works reference manual.

The spreadsheet environment is closer conceptually to a programming language than are the other software application contexts that are discussed in this book. Thus, the spreadsheet exhibits some of the power and complexity of a programming language such as BASIC. Consequently, the effective use of a spreadsheet will require you to understand in more detail certain aspects of how computers operate. In particular, you will need to master the *syntax for entering formulas* into a spreadsheet cell and how to *debug formulas* (find errors in logic in a syntactically correct formula you have entered). Also a number of other concepts will require precise mastery before the full power inherent in a spreadsheet can become accessible to you.

Finally, before you begin to take a detailed look at the Works SS, it is important to realize that spreadsheet programs were not developed from the perspective of a formal computational model but evolved instead as ad hoc models of computation to emulate the way accountants use paper and pencil for bookkeeping. Consequently, no completely satisfactory model exists that can serve as the basis from which to discuss spreadsheet environments.

Nonetheless, the concepts that make available the power and flexibility of a spreadsheet environment can be readily mastered by any serious student. Mastery of these concepts will pay you many dividends, as is aptly demonstrated by the rapid adoption of this software by the business community (and an increasing number of mathematicians and scientists!).

The approach taken in this and subsequent chapters on spreadsheets consists of an overview of a concept followed by examples of the concept as it is implemented in Works SS. *Our purpose in this approach is to separate the general problem-solving concepts from the details employed in the implementation of a particular package.*

Through our approach, you are spared the difficulty of trying to separate *what* you can accomplish in general in a spreadsheet environment from *how* you can accomplish it in a specific spreadsheet package. As a result, you should find it much easier to use later any new spreadsheet package such as Excel, Lotus 1-2-3, Multiplan, or even the next generation of spreadsheet environments.

Exercise Set 10.1

1. What is the purpose of a spreadsheet package?
2. When was the first spreadsheet software package marketed?
3. How does the spreadsheet differ from the word processing and database environments discussed so far?
4. Describe *what if* analysis.
5. What is a parameter? Give an example.

10.2 OVERVIEW OF GENERIC SPREADSHEET COMPOSITION

SIMPLE STRUCTURE. The basic **worksheet structure** is a rectangular grid of cells organized as a two-dimensional table as shown in Figure 10.1. Each cell is delimited by enclosing lines. This entire group or collection of cells we will term a *worksheet*, and a worksheet is given a *name*. Through the use of the name, the entire worksheet can be referenced. Consequently, when a worksheet is saved to or retrieved from disk, its name distinguishes it from all the other worksheets you have created.

CELL NAMES. The objects that make up a worksheet are called *cells*. Cells are the objects through which calculations are carried out and the results of computations are displayed. Just as it is important to name a worksheet as a whole to be able to select or reference the worksheet, it is also necessary to give a **cell name** to specify which *unique* cell is being selected or referenced out of all the cells that make up a worksheet. Default names for cells are provided by the *coordinates* of a cell in the table.

By convention in nearly all spreadsheet packages, the coordinates of a cell are the column label of a cell followed by the row label of a cell. Works SS adopts the convention, as shown in Figure 10.1, that columns in the table are labeled with capital letters (A,...,Z,AA,...,AZ,BA,...) and rows in the table are sequentially labeled with positive integers. Consequently, the default name, A1, references the cell in the upper left-hand corner of the table. Thus, to find the location of a cell whose default name is specified, find the position where the column and row coordinates of a cell intersect. For example, to find the location of cell C2, draw an imaginary line down the middle of the column named C and draw another imaginary line across the middle of the row named 2. The place where these two imaginary lines cross is the location of the cell C2.

The default name of a cell (its column and row position) tells you *where* the cell is in the worksheet. Some spreadsheets (not Works SS, however) allow you to attach other names to cells that make it easier to understand the purpose of a cell in a complex computation. For example, in Excel you can give a cell the name *interest rate* and refer to the cell by this name rather than by its default name.

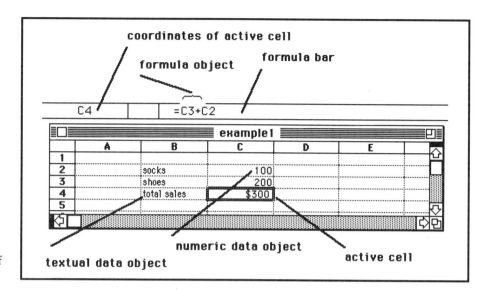

Figure 10.1 Components of a generic worksheet.

Note that the name of a cell is distinct from its contents. Think of the name of a cell as being like the address of a mail box. The address (name of the cell) tells you which mailbox (cell of the table) is being referenced. Clearly, however, the address alone tells you nothing about the letters/packages (contents) that are inside the box. To determine the latter you must go to the mailbox in question and open it up.

CONTENTS OF CELLS.   Cells themselves are structured objects. This means that a cell can contain more than one kind of object at the same time. A formula object and/or a data object will be contained in a cell into which information has been entered.

DATA OBJECT.   You should think of the **data object** of a cell as holding the data/information that is displayed by the cell. Data in a spreadsheet is similar to the kind of information that can be entered into a field of a database table. In the case of the worksheet it is information that often will be used in a computation. You learned in connection with the database discussion in Chapter 8 that you must distinguish between textual and numerical kinds of information. This is because the computer stores each of these kinds of information differently and must choose to operate on the information consistent with how it is stored.

DATA TYPE.   In a spreadsheet there are also different kinds of internal representations of information. Recall that each distinct kind is called a *data type*. Principal spreadsheet data types include:

- Textual data—any string of characters typed in from the keyboard.
- Numerical data—items that are in the form of numbers (i.e., a list of numerical digits that may include a dollar sign, unary minus sign, or decimal point).
- Logical data—the values of *True* or *False* only, which are represented in the Works SS as 1 for *True* and 0 for *False*.

For most spreadsheets, the data type of the data object is not specified at the time the data is entered into a cell. Instead, the spreadsheet interprets a cell's data type according to the way a cell is used in a calculation. Thus, a worksheet cell is said to be *implicitly* typed, in contrast to the *explicit* typing that is used in a database. The cell B4 in Figure 10.1 contains the textual data *total sales*. This data could never be interpreted as a numerical value. In contrast, the cell C4 contains *$300*. This latter data can be interpreted as either a textual or a numerical data type, depending upon the context in which it is used.

FORMATTING DATA OBJECTS. By convention in all spreadsheets, the value displayed at a cell's location (unless you explicitly instruct the spreadsheet to do otherwise) is the value of its data object. It is possible to tell the computer the form to use in displaying the data object of a cell. This process is called **formatting the cell's data object**. Thus, for example, it is possible to describe how many digits are to be displayed after the decimal point of a number, whether a dollar sign is to be used in the display of a number, whether commas are to be inserted in a number, whether scientific notation should be used to display a number, and so on.

FORMULA OBJECTS. A **formula object** contains an algebraic formula entered using a syntax specific to a given spreadsheet package. The formula entered describes how to compute the value of the data object in that same cell. Consequently, if a formula object is entered in a cell, the data object value is obtained by evaluating the formula in the formula object of the cell.

Formula objects may refer to other cells in a worksheet using arithmetic operations, such as addition, subtraction, multiplication, and so on, and to special functions that are built into the spreadsheet program. As a result, an extremely wide range of computations can be carried out by specifying a formula object. In the example of Figure 10.1, the formula object for cell C4 has the value =C3+C2, as shown in the top line of the spreadsheet. Thus, the data object for cell C4 will be obtained by adding the data object of cell C3 to the data object of cell C2. The value displayed at the location C4 is 300, which is calculated by adding the contents of cell C3 (the value 200) to the contents of cell C2 (the value 100).

The syntax for entering a formula is specific to each spreadsheet package and is checked as you enter the formula into a cell's formula object. If an entered formula has incorrect syntax, an error message will be displayed. Typically, the spreadsheet will not assign the formula to the formula object until the formula syntax has been corrected.

However, a formula may be entered as a syntactically correct formula—one that obeys the rules of the language—but that makes no sense when it is executed. For example, we might attempt to insert the formula =B2+C3 into the worksheet of Figure 10.1. In this case an error in evaluation arises because cell B2 has the data object value *socks*, which is a textual data type and not a numerical data type and hence should not be involved in an addition operation. Unfortunately, Works SS simply evaluates this expression assuming that cell B2 has the value 0 and let us know nothing. We will have more to say about this point in Chapter 12.

Exercise Set 10.2

1. Describe the structure of a worksheet.
2. What is the form of the default name of a worksheet cell?

3. Describe how to find cell A3 in Figure 10.1.

4. What does cell B3 contain in Figure 10.1?

5. How does a cell's data object differ from a cell's formula object?

6. Must a cell have both a data object and a formula object? Explain.

7. Explain the meaning of the formula object =C5+D8.

8. What is meant by formatting a cell's data object?

9. Why would you wish to format a cell's data object?

10. How does the term *syntax* apply to spreadsheet formulas?

10.3 GENERIC OPERATIONS ON WORKSHEET OBJECTS

Operations on spreadsheet objects form a hierarchy that conveniently can be broken down into those that involve the contents of a cell (the data object or the formula object) and those that alter the arrangement of the cells on the worksheet itself. We will term the former **cell-level operations** and the latter **sheet-level operations**. The former can be further broken down into cell-level editing operations and data-object operations, as illustrated in Figure 10.2.

Cell-level editing operations allow altering either the value of a data object or the form of the formula contained by the formula object of an individual cell. These operations are analogous to those provided in a word processing environment to edit text.

In contrast, **data-object operations** are used to construct mathematical formulas (using a spreadsheet defined syntax) from arithmetic, logical, and comparison operators, and built-in functions. These formulas may reference the data-object values of other cells and are used to produce a new data-object value in a cell containing the formula. The power of using a spreadsheet comes from your ability to build up strings of individual computations that reference each other. Learning to use these data-object operators is somewhat similar to learning how to write a program in a programming language. The major advantage in learning a spreadsheet instead of a programming language is that the syntax will be much more natural and therefore easier and faster to learn. Of course, you will not have the full problem-solving flexibility that you would have from a programming language.

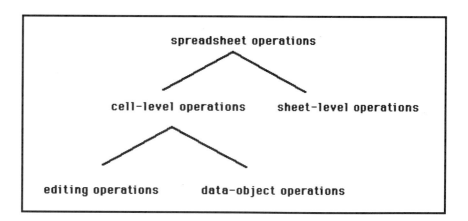

Figure 10.2 Hierarchy of spreadsheet operations.

Sheet-level editing operations are used to change the position of a cell or a group of cells on the worksheet and to copy formulas into entire columns and/or rows of cells at one time. However, because one cell may reference one or more other cells on a worksheet, complications can arise about which cell should be referenced by other cells when a given cell is repositioned (and consequently renamed!) in the worksheet. We will discuss this topic at greater length in the next chapter.

Exercise Set 10.3

1. List and define the different operations that can be performed on spreadsheet cells.
2. Draw a diagram of the hierarchy of the spreadsheet operations you listed in exercise 1.
3. How does a spreadsheet provide you with the ability to solve computational problems?
4. Why is a spreadsheet easy to learn?

10.4 GENERIC CELL-LEVEL EDITING OPERATIONS

The following short discussion describes in general terms the appearance of essentially any spreadsheet program as you interact with it. The "feel" or user friendliness of a spreadsheet package is dictated by the intuitiveness of the cell-level editing operations. Cell-level editing operations allow selection of an individual cell on the worksheet and subsequent alteration of the contents of the cell selected. A cell selected for editing is called the *active cell*. Only the contents inside the active cell can be altered directly by a cell-level editing operation.

The active cell on a sheet is usually shown highlighted or drawn with a box surrounding it to distinguish it from other cells. Cell C4 is the active cell in Figure 10.1. Consequently, when operations to modify the contents of a given cell are performed, this highlighting or outlining of a cell demonstrates the context within which you are working.

Various means are provided to move around on the worksheet to give you full control over selecting the cell of interest. Positioning on the worksheet is usually performed using the cursor control keys on a traditional computer or the mouse and/or cursor control keys on the Macintosh.

As shown in Figure 10.1, when a cell becomes the active cell, its coordinates are displayed in the left area of the formula bar. If the cell contains a formula object, the active cell's formula is displayed in the area to the right. If the active cell contains no formula object, then the data object of the selected cell is displayed in the right area of the formula bar. Before a formula or value has been entered into the active cell, its data object and formula object are empty and will display as "blank."

DATA-OBJECT ENTRY. Once a cell is selected as the active cell, data can be entered into its data object from the keyboard; we term this process **data-object entry**. Thus, for example, if B3 is the active cell and 200 is typed, 200 becomes the value of the data object of this cell and is displayed both in the formula bar and in the cell's location. Keyboard input is assigned by default to the data object of a cell. Essentially all spreadsheets work in this way. Thus, something special must be done to indicate to the spreadsheet that you wish to access the formula object of a cell rather than the data object.

FORMULA-OBJECT ENTRY.   The process of entering a formula into a cell we term **formula-object entry**. There are special symbols that when entered as the *first character* in a cell indicate the presence of a formula rather than a cell data object. We will use the = symbol as this special symbol/character in the following discussion. The = symbol is used for this purpose both in Works and Excel. Other spreadsheet programs might use +, -, and so on, as this special symbol. Hence, entering the characters =C3+C2 into cell C4 would be interpreted as assigning a formula to the formula object of cell C4.

Note in Figure 10.1 that the formula-object value =C3+C2 is displayed in the formula bar, and the data-object value that results from evaluating the formula (i.e., adding the value of cell C3 to the value of cell C2) is displayed in cell C4. This is a general feature of most spreadsheets and allows both the data-object value and the formula-object value of the selected cell to be displayed simultaneously. The $ appearing in cell C4 is present because the cell has been *formatted*—given a form with which to display the data-object value. The $ was not typed at the keyboard.

OTHER CELL-LEVEL EDITING FEATURES.   In addition to being able to enter information into a cell, it is possible to perform other kinds of editing operations. For example, the entire contents of a cell may be erased (both the data and formula objects), a single character or group of characters may be deleted or replaced, a single character or group of characters may be inserted, cutting and pasting similar to that done in a word processing environment may be performed in a given cell to alter its contents. Thus, the editing features *within* a cell are quite similar to those available in text editing in a word processing environment, and they allow great speed and flexibility in changing the contents of a given cell.

Exercise Set 10.4

1. What is the purpose of a cell-level editing command?
2. What is the active cell? Can cell-level editing commands be used on any cells besides the active cell?
3. What means are provided for you to position the cursor to make a cell the active cell?
4. What is displayed in the formula bar of the worksheet when a cell is selected as the active cell? Explain, dependent upon whether or not the cell contains a formula.
5. How do you enter a data object into a cell?
6. How do you enter a formula object into a cell?
7. How is learning to use a word processor of help in editing the contents of worksheet cells? Give examples.

10.5 CELL-LEVEL EDITING OPERATIONS USING WORKS

Having discussed the components of a worksheet in a generic spreadsheet environment and the kinds of cell-level editing operations that are available, we will now examine these features in Works.

BEGINNING A WORKS SPREADSHEET SESSION. You will recall from Chapter 5 that the Works integrated package is started by double-clicking the Works icon. You can then execute the Works SS module by double-clicking on its icon (shown in Figure 10.3) or on a worksheet whose name appears in the file window when the Works SS module is selected.

If the Works SS icon is double-clicked, you are presented with an *Untitled* worksheet, as shown in Figure 10.4. If instead an existing worksheet document is opened, then the contents of the worksheet will not appear empty as seen in Figure 10.4 but will contain all the data and formulas you have previously entered.

As you see from Figure 10.4, the Works SS is very similar to the model spreadsheet shown in Figure 10.1. Columns are labeled by letters and rows by positive integers. In the Works SS there are 256 columns labeled A, B, ..., AA, AB, ..., AZ, ..., IU, IV. There are also 9999 rows labeled 1 to 9999. This gives you approximately 2.56 million cells to work with to solve problems—provided your computer has sufficient memory to hold all this information!

The top line of the spreadsheet contains the menu bar from which the commands to work on the worksheet can be issued. These commands include cell-level and sheet-level commands. All menu commands are accessed as you have done in the previous Works applications. Thus, the desired menu name is pulled down and the mouse pointer dragged to select the command of interest. Commands available from the main menu bar are shown in Figure 10.5. Not only

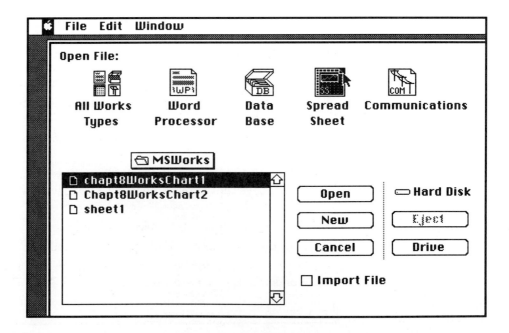

Figure 10.3 Opening the Works SS module.

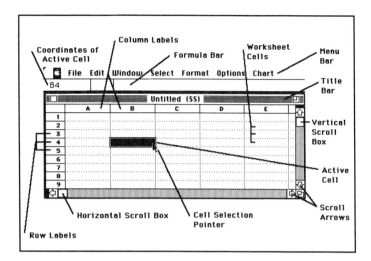

Figure 10.4 Features of Works SS.

will the menu commands in **File** behave like those you have learned previously, but the cell-level editing commands under the **Edit** menu, such as *Cut*, *Paste*, *Copy*, and so on, will be consistent with text editing commands you used in the Works WP and Works DB contexts.

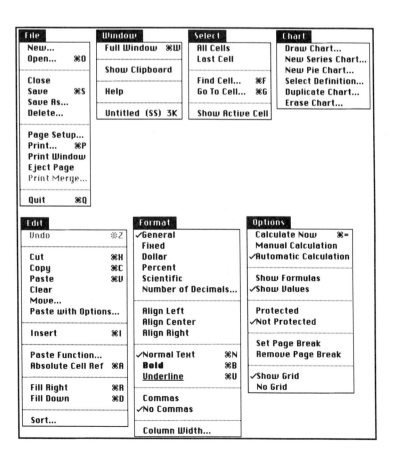

Figure 10.5 Menus in the Works SS environment.

The Macintosh screen is not large enough to display a full Works SS worksheet at one time. You should imagine, as with other application programs you have learned, that the screen is a window through which you view only a portion of the entire worksheet. The scroll boxes and scroll arrows are used to move the window about on the worksheet just as you have learned to move the window about in a document produced by the Works WP and Works DB modules. The orientation of the scroll arrow indicates the direction of the window motion within the application. Note that the spreadsheet provides both horizontal and vertical scroll bars and thus allows window movement in two directions.

Other window positioning commands can be found in the **Select** menu. Here the option *Find Cell* allows you to enter the value of the cell you wish to find just as you can enter a text string in the *Find* option of the **Search** menu in the Works WP component. Hence, by entering *10* in the dialog box that results from execution of this command, the window will be repositioned to show successively each cell whose data-object is equal to 10.

In a similar manner, the *Go To Cell* command provides you with the option to enter the coordinates of the cell whose position you would like to see appear in the window. Also, if you have used the scroll box or scroll arrows to reposition the window and have lost track of the position of the active cell, the command *Show Active Cell* will reposition the window to show the active cell in the window.

ACTIVE CELL.   In Works SS there is never more than one cell active at a time when performing cell-level editing operations. The **active cell** is the *only* cell on which the cell-level editing commands are being performed. It is easily distinguishable from the other cells because it is highlighted as shown in Figure 10.4. The coordinates of the active cell are always displayed in the active cell coordinate area within the formula bar, shown in Figure 10.4 just below the menu bar and above the upper left-hand corner of the worksheet. Thus, for example, cell B4 is the active cell in Figure 10.4.

SELECTION OF ACTIVE CELL LOCATION.   Selection of the location of the active cell is accomplished using the mouse. As you can easily verify, movement of the mouse causes a corresponding motion of the *cell-selection pointer*, which has the form of an arrow as shown in Figure 10.4. By positioning the tip of the arrow over a cell and clicking, the cell under the arrow is selected as the active cell and its location is displayed in the active cell coordinate area in the formula bar. Once a cell is made active, any information typed in from the keyboard or pasted using the **Edit** pull-down menu will be entered into it. All information entered into the active cell will be displayed in the formula bar as it is entered. The cell will continue to take information typed from the keyboard until you indicate that data entry is complete (or you have entered 238 characters!).

DATA ENTRY TERMINATION.   There are several ways to indicate **data entry termination** to the Works SS.

- Press the *Tab* key.
- Press the *Return* or *Enter* key.
- Select a new active cell by clicking.
- Select the *Check* button that appears in the space just left of the formula bar when data is entered.

■ Use the cursor control keys, if available, to move the pointer to a new cell.

The choice of the method to use will depend upon which is the most natural action to set up the next activity you want to perform. If you decide that the data you entered is *not* what you intended, you can restore a cell to its original state by selecting the *Undo* command from the **Edit** pull-down menu or selecting the X button that appears in the area just left of the formula bar when a cell is active and data is being entered.

FORMULA-BAR EDITING.   As noted earlier, each keystroke entered is displayed in the **formula bar**. You can think of the formula bar as being like a one-line document in the Works WP component. The editing commands you learned for word processing are available to operate on the information in the formula bar, a process termed **formula-bar editing.** Recall in this connection the function of the insertion pointer and the I-beam pointer. As information is typed into the formula bar, the position at which characters are inserted is indicated by | , a blinking vertical line—the insertion pointer. The position of the insertion pointer can be controlled by moving the I-beam pointer to the position desired in the formula bar and clicking, just as was done in the word processing component.

To invoke the I-beam pointer it is only necessary to move the cell-selection pointer into the area of the formula bar by suitable manipulation of the mouse. The cell-selection pointer changes into the I-beam pointer, and all the word processing actions, such as cut, paste, click and drag to select, and so on, are now available for you to use *within* the formula bar.

EDITING DATA OBJECTS AND FORMULA OBJECTS.   In the Works SS, cell-level editing commands are used to manipulate either the data-object value or the formula-object value of a cell. As noted earlier in this chapter, the distinction between a data-object value and a formula-object value is indicated by the presence of the = sign as the first character in the formula bar. If a cell contains no formula-object value (i.e., the first character in the formula bar is *not* an = sign), then any editing that is done directly alters the data-object value of the cell.

On the other hand, if the cell contains a formula, then any editing done alters the formula-object value. Such editing can only *indirectly* change the data-object value. That is, if a formula gives the result 103, you cannot select the 3 and change it to a 4. The following rule should be remembered.

> The data-object value displayed in a cell containing a formula is always determined by the evaluation of the formula. Therefore, it is impossible to edit a data object directly in a cell containing a formula.

CELL-SELECTION POINTER FUNCTIONS: DATA OBJECT VS. FORMULA OBJECT.   The operation of the cell-selection pointer is quite different, depending upon whether a data object or a formula object is being entered into the active cell. If a data-object value is being entered, moving the cell-selection pointer to a new cell and clicking will terminate the entry of the information shown in the formula bar for the first cell and then make the newly selected cell the active cell.

In contrast, if a formula object is being entered into the active cell, then moving the cell-selection pointer to a new cell and clicking will cause the *coordinates* of that new cell to be entered into the formula in the first cell and the first cell *will remain* the active cell. This feature allows you to enter formulas conveniently by clicking on the cells whose values you wish to reference. Works SS then enters those cell references automatically into the formulas for you. To complete the entry of the formula, use either the *Tab, Return,* or *Enter* key or click on the checkmark just to the left of the formula bar.

Cell references can be directly typed instead of using the cell-selection pointing method. The advantage of letting Works SS do it for you is that you are less likely to make an error in entering the cell location. Consequently, your formulas are more likely to compute the correct values.

EXAMPLE WORKS SS DATA-OBJECT ENTRY.   In the following we demonstrate the use of Works SS cell-level editing features to enter information into a cell. To make the example simple, we will construct a row of the worksheet shown in Figure 10.1. Read through this example first; then, if possible, carry it out using a Macintosh. An extension of this example is provided in problem 1 of the computer practice for this section.

Open Works and then double-click on the Works SS icon to open a worksheet as discussed earlier. Next, by moving the mouse, position the cell pointer in the center of cell B2 and click. This cell will be highlighted to indicate that it is the active cell. Type *socks* and the press the *Tab* key. This causes *socks* to be entered as the data object of cell B2, and cell C2 then becomes the new active cell. Next type *100* then move the cursor to point to the check box and click. You will now have entered the top row of the worksheet.

RANGE SELECTION.   The process of entering information, selecting a different cell, entering information into that cell, selecting a new cell, and so on, can be very awkward if a large number of cells are involved. Works SS provides a very convenient way to mark a rectangular group of cells, called a **cell range,** each cell of which is to be used successively to receive information. This process of marking contiguous groups of cells is called *range selection*.

A range of cells is selected by moving the cell-selection pointer to a corner of the rectangle of cells you wish to select. Drag the mouse. A darkened rectangular area will be highlighted. The proportions of this highlighted area can be controlled by positioning the mouse. When this highlighted area is satisfactory for your purposes, release the button. The area remains highlighted and the first cell selected is the initial active cell.

Once a range of cells is selected, typing causes information to appear in the initial active cell's formula bar. Pressing the *Tab* key or *Return* key inserts the information into the cell and automatically causes the cell in the next position of the darkened area to become active. The desired information can then be typed in for this new cell. Pressing the *Tab* key or *Return* key for this cell enters the information and another position in the darkened area becomes active. The difference between pressing the *Tab* and *Return* key for entering the data is that *Tab* moves across a row before starting the next lower row, whereas *Return* moves down a column before moving to the next column to the right in the highlighted area.

If the cell-selection pointer is used at any time to select a new cell while a range is active (indicated by the darkened rectangular area) *and a data object* is being assigned to the active cell, then the range of cells is deactivated and the cell selected becomes active. If a formula object is being assigned to the active cell, then the coordinates of that selected cell are entered into the current active cell, as discussed earlier. In this latter case, the cell remains the active cell open for additional data entry, and the range selection is still valid.

EXAMPLE OF RANGE SELECTION DATA ENTRY. To illustrate range selection we explain how to enter two rows of the worksheet in Figure 10.1. This example is further extended in problem 1 of the computer practice for this section. Read through this example first then perform it on a Macintosh, if possible.

Open Works. Once inside Works, open Works SS to obtain a new worksheet. Move the cell-selection pointer to cell B2 and drag the mouse to highlight the four cells B2, C2, B3, and C3. This range of cells is denoted by B2:C3, where B2 represents the upper left-hand corner cell and C3 represents the lower right-hand corner cell of the rectangular group of cells selected. A range of cells can always be represented using this syntax in a Works SS formula.

Looking closely, you will observe that cell B2 is the active cell. Type *socks* and press *Tab*. Note that C2 now becomes active. Type *100* and press *Tab*. Note that B3 now becomes active. Type *shoes* and press *Tab*. Now C3 becomes active. Type *200* and press *Tab*. Note that cell B2 now becomes active again. Thus, the cursor remains within the range selected.

SHIFT-CLICK RANGE SELECTION. Another method can be used to highlight a large rectangular area in Works SS. This method is the shift-click method, discussed in Chapter 2. First, position the cell-selection pointer over the upper left-hand corner of the rectangular area you wish to select and click. Next, using the scroll boxes and/or scroll arrows, position the cell-selection pointer over the cell in the lower right-hand corner of the rectangular area you wish to be selected. Finally, while holding the *Shift* key down, click the mouse button. The entire rectangle should now be highlighted.

Using the commands described previously, you can enter and edit data in any cells you desire while using the Works SS. The computer practice exercises at the end of this section will give you experience in working with cell-level editing operations and will allow you to become confident about entering any information you desire into a worksheet cell.

Exercise Set 10.5

1. Describe how you begin a session with Works SS.
2. How many rows and columns are provided in Works SS?
3. Is it likely that you can use all of Works SS rows and columns on a Macintosh with 1 megabyte of memory? Explain.
4. Explain how you can use the scroll arrows to position the Works SS window to the area of the worksheet you are interested in viewing.
5. Once you have scrolled to another area of the worksheet, how can you return to view the active cell location easily?
6. Explain how you can locate all the cells that contain the value 32.
7. Describe the appearance of the active cell in Works SS.
8. Describe how you make a cell the active cell in Works SS.

9. Describe how you select a range of cells in Works SS.

10. What are the ways to terminate the entry of information in the active cell?

11. Describe the different effects that clicking in a new cell has on the active cell when you enter a data object and formula object.

12. Can you change the data object of a cell when that cell contains a formula? Explain.

13. Explain how you could use the shift-click method to highlight the cells in the rectangle with cell A1 as the upper left-hand corner and cell H16 as the lower right-hand corner.

14. Describe how to perform the same selection as that in exercise 13 using only the mouse.

15. Explain why range selection is useful for data entry into a worksheet.

Computer Practice 10.5

1. a. Set up a worksheet using Works SS that will reproduce the results shown in Figure 10.1 of the text. Enter the labels for each data item by positioning the cursor to cell B2 and dragging to cell B4 to highlight cells in this column. Next type in the values *socks*, *shoes*, and *total sales*. Each cell entry should be terminated by pressing the *Tab* key or the *Return* key to move to the next cell. Should you enter a value incorrectly and notice it before you have pressed *Tab* or *Return*, press the *Backspace* (or *Delete*) key to erase the error and retype. Otherwise, continue until all values have been entered. After all values have been entered and you notice an error, select the cell whose entry is incorrect and use the editing features analogous to those in Works WP to correct it.

    b. When the preceding three entries have been made, select the range from C2 to C4, again by dragging. Enter *100*, *200*, and *=C3+C2* into these three cells. Terminate each entry by pressing either the *Tab* key or the *Return* key as before. Note that the value 300 appears automatically when you terminate the entry to cell C4.

    c. Finally, to format cell C4 to display its data object using a dollar sign, make C4 the active cell, then choose *Dollar* under the **Format** menu. Then select *Number of Digits* in the **Format** menu and type *0* in the dialog box.

    d. Save your worksheet with the name *Example1* using the *Save* or *Save As* command from the **File** menu. This command will operate just as it did for Works WP and Works DB.

2. Set up your own simple worksheet that will compute the sum of two numbers x and y. Use the *Example1* worksheet as a model. Label three cells in a column with x, y, and z, respectively. Enter numerical values for x and y in the column next to the one where the labels for x, y, and z appear—just as was done in computer practice problem 1. Enter a formula that will add the x and y values and place the result in the cell in the column to the right of where the label for z is entered. Experiment with changing values of x and y to see how the results for the computation of z are altered.

3. The operator - is used for subtraction, * for multiplication, and / for division in the Works SS. Set up a worksheet to compute the value $z = (x * y - 8)/2$. Note

that parentheses can also be entered into a worksheet formula and used just as they are in algebra.

10.6 CHARTING AND GRAPHING FEATURES IN WORKS SS

Before going on to examine the more powerful computational features of Works SS, we will briefly explore some charting/graphical features available in the spreadsheet environment. This will allow you to see graphically the results computed in a worksheet. You should read over this section first and then work through the discussion presented using a Macintosh.

As you will soon see, it is easy to generate a vast amount of computational data in a short time using a spreadsheet. However, it can be very difficult to make sense of a table of hundreds or even thousands of numbers. Graphical display of data is often essential to understand or interpret results of computations, and the Works SS provides several convenient charting/graphical display methods that can assist in the interpretation process.

The tables of data for which line or bar charts can be created must be row organized in Works SS. This means that the independent and corresponding dependent variables each must be arranged across a row of the table. To create such a table, first select an area of the worksheet as shown in Figure 10.6, where you will enter the independent values. Select the range A1:F1 for this purpose.

Now let us assume that we wish to graph the function

$$y = x^2$$

To graph this function you will require a series of values for x, the independent variable, that are evenly spaced (i.e., the difference between any adjacent values of x is the same). For our example, we use the series 1, 5, 9, 13, and 17 for x. To indicate that the first row corresponds to the x value, you will label the first cell with the value x. Do this by entering an x in cell A1. Note that to the computer there is nothing special about the value x. You are entering x to remind *yourself* when you see this table what values appear in the first row of the table. Cell values that serve this purpose of helping you to recall the meaning of some data entered in the worksheet are usually called **cell labels**.

Once the *Tab* key is pressed, cell B1 becomes the active cell. Type in *1* for this cell, press *Tab;* enter *5* for the next cell, C1; press *Tab;* and continue entering each of the values you wish x to take on—up to the last value of 17, which will be entered in cell F1. Rather than pressing *Tab* to enter this last value, either select the

	File	Edit	Window	Select	Format	Options	Chart
A1							

	A	B	C	D	E	F
1						
2						
3						

Figure 10.6 Highlighting row 1 of the worksheet.

Check box to the left of the formula bar or use the *Enter* key on the numeric keypad. Your worksheet should now appear as shown in Figure 10.7.

Now you are ready to enter the formulas that will allow the computation of the values of x^2. First, select the range of cells from A2 to F2. Because A2 is the active cell, typing $f(x) = x^2$ and pressing *Tab* will enter this label into the cell A2. This label will remind you that the function being computed is $f(x) = x^2$. (Here $\wedge$ is the symbol for exponentiation in Works SS formula syntax.)

Next type $=B1^2$ into cell B2 and press the *Tab* key. Because the first symbol entered into the cell is an equals sign (=), you are entering a formula into the formula object of the active cell. When the *Tab* key is pressed, the formula is entered, and the value 1 is computed and assigned to cell B2's data object. Note that the meaning of this formula is to compute the value of cell B1 (B1 contains 1) raised to the power of 2 (i.e., multiply the value in cell B1 times itself).

Because you pressed the *Tab* key, cell C2 has become the active cell. By typing $=C1^2$, you will now enter a formula in cell C2 to compute the value in cell C1 raised to the power of 2. Pressing the *Tab* key enters the formula in cell C2 and causes cell D2 to become active. Type in each corresponding formula until you have entered the corresponding formula in cell F2. Now, rather than pressing *Tab*, click on the check box just to the left of the formula bar. At this point your worksheet should appear as shown in Figure 10.8.

If the entry of these formulas seems tedious, it is! In fact, you can imagine how awkward this could become if you had a few hundred values to compute. Shortly you will learn how to direct Works SS to replicate formulas automatically for you. Replicating a formula means to copy it from one cell to the next throughout portions of rows or columns of the worksheet. Of course, such copying must reference the correct cells from which each formula's value should be taken. The adjustments necessary to assure this can be done automatically by the spreadsheet, provided you enter the formula in an appropriate manner. The topic of formula replication is discussed in Chapter 11.

Next, you will create a *Series Chart* of the function values. You first indicate to Works SS that you wish to create a chart. Do this by selecting *New Series Chart* from the **Chart** menu as shown in Figure 10.9. Note that you could have chosen the *New Pie Chart* option in this same manner. When the button is released, the dialog box in Figure 10.10 will appear. Through this dialog box you will specify the location of the data to be charted, the kind of chart to be drawn, the kind of vertical scale to use, and so on.

For the purposes of this graph choose a **line chart** by clicking on the button to the left of the picture of the line chart. The column labeled *Values to be Plotted* is used to tell the charting operation the location of the dependent and independent

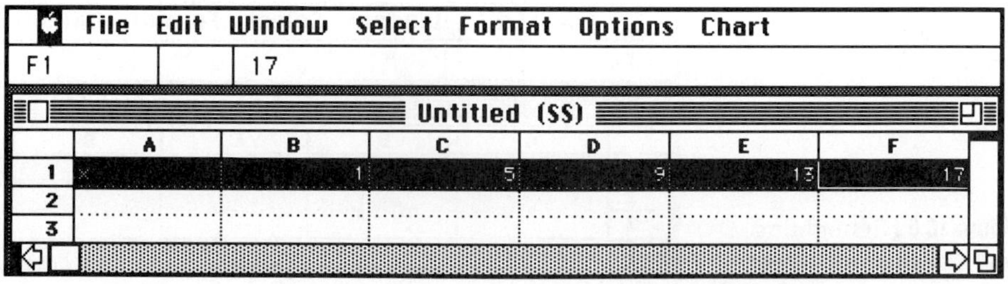

Figure 10.7 Entering the *x* values in row 1.

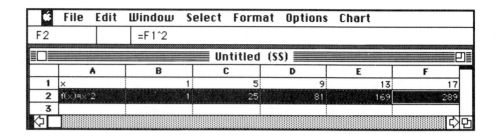

Figure 10.8 Results after computing function values.

variables on the worksheet. Because the function values are in row 2 of the worksheet you should enter 2 in the box to the right of the label *1st Row*.

Note that for this example there is only one function to plot, so that all other *Row* box values should be made blank. Do this by selecting and dragging across each one that is not empty and pressing the *Backspace* or *Delete* key. If more than one function was computed, it would be possible to chart each one (up to a total of four) on the same chart by entering the row location for each function's values. Also you must specify the starting column and ending column over which the values to be plotted extend. In our case the values start in column B and end in column F, so enter these values as shown in Figure 10.10.

Next, you will need to specify the location of the data legends. In this case the label $f(x)=x^2$ is listed in column A; thus, you will need to specify column A as the location of the label used for the data legend. Finally, it is necessary to locate the independent variable values (or horizontal titles). For this chart the location of the *x*'s is in row 1.

Note that in a strict sense Works SS charts are not really graphs, since the independent variable values are just labels that are attached at equal distances on the abscissa. In other words, even if your *x* values were not at equal distances, Works SS would place them on the graph as if they were. No method is available to you to circumvent this restriction. Although full-featured spreadsheet packages such as Excel or Lotus 1-2-3 provide true graphing, so that the independent variables can be at arbitrary distances, Works SS does not. For function computation this is rarely a problem because you can choose which *x* values you wish to use. For data obtained from other sources, however, you must use the data available to you, and this restriction becomes important.

The boxes at the bottom of the dialog box allow you to specify the chart title, vertical scale title, and horizontal scale title. For this example choose the values shown in Figure 10.10 and note the location where each of these appears in the final chart. You also have control over whether a linear plot or semi-logarithmic plot is to be made. For this example choose linear plot (numeric scale). Selection of

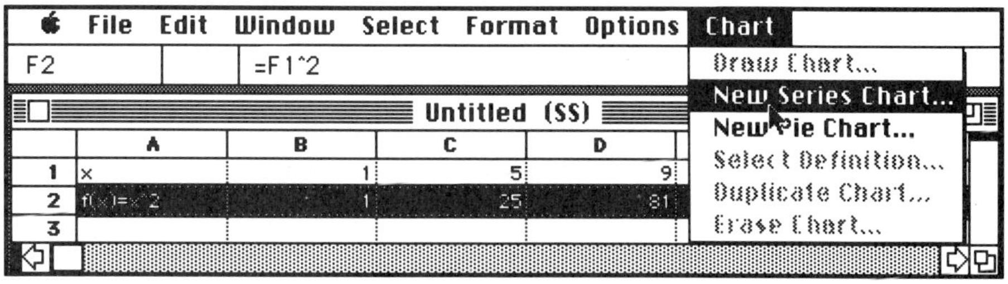

Figure 10.9 Selecting a new series chart from the **Chart** menu.

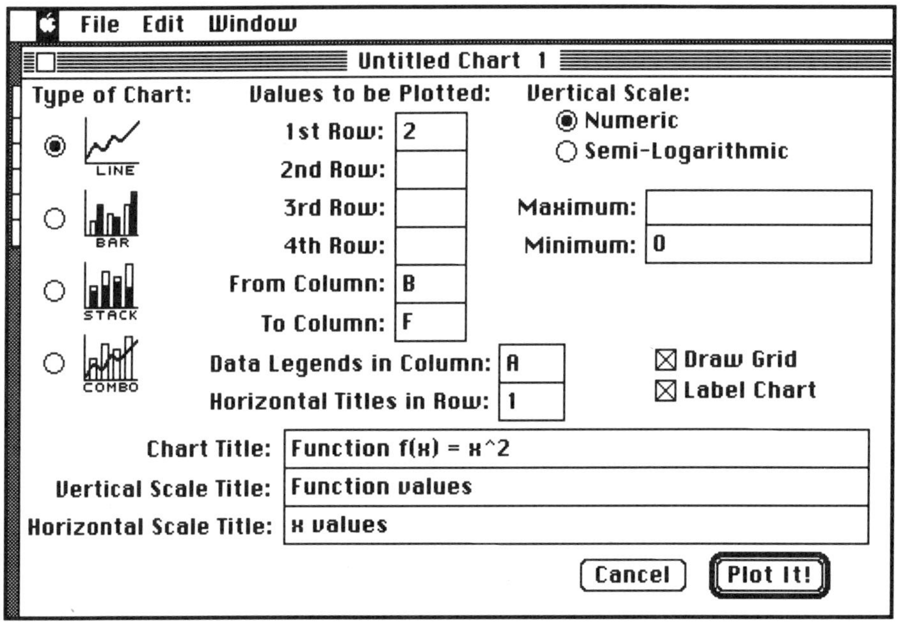

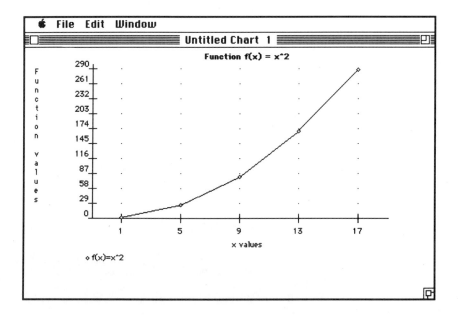

Figure 10.10 Selecting location of data to be charted.

semi-logarithmic scale would cause the logarithm of the function values to be taken and the chart drawn using a logarithmic scale for the vertical axis. If you wish you may specify the maximum and minimum values to be used on the vertical axis by filling in the boxes so labeled on the right-hand side of the dialog box. In certain cases the range of values to be graphed may be so large that you cannot see details of the graph. By changing the maximum and minimum values you will be able to observe the values of interest. If you enter nothing here, Works SS will compute these values for you according to the range of values present in the data to be graphed.

Figure 10.11 Resulting graph from Works SS for $f(x) = x^2$.

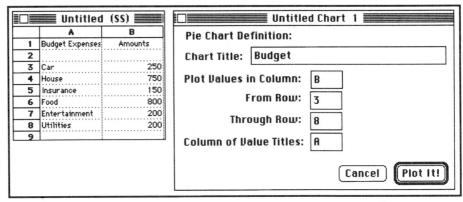

Figure 10.12 Worksheet (left) and *Pie Chart Definition* dialog box (right).

Finally, the boxes for *Draw Grid* and *Label Chart* allow you to decide if you wish to have a grid of lines drawn through the chart and if you wish to have the labels appear on the chart. For this example make sure that each box is checked. Once you have selected all of the entries as shown in Figure 10.10, click the *Plot It!* button. A chart identical to that shown in Figure 10.11 should appear.

Once a chart has been created you can gain access to the *Chart Definition* dialog box by choosing *Select Definition* from the **Chart** menu. Alternatively, you can double-click in the chart display area. When the *Chart Definition* dialog box appears, you can alter the choice of items you used in creating the first chart. For example, the line chart could be quickly altered to a **bar chart** if desired by clicking on the *bar chart* button in the dialog box shown in Figure 10.10.

In addition to line charts and bar charts that can be drawn within the *New Series Chart* command, Works SS allows you to construct **pie charts.** Pie charts are a very effective way to display data that consists of parts of a whole. For example, in your personal budget you might show the fractions of your income that go into house payments, car payments, insurance payments, food, and so on.

As a simple example, we show on the left of Figure 10.12 a sample home budget worksheet designed to illustrate the use of the pie chart. Here the relevant budget item categories have been entered in column A, and the amount of the budget for each corresponding category has been entered in column B. The pie chart that results is shown in Figure 10.13.

To create a pie chart it is necessary to select the *New Pie Chart* option from the **Chart** menu. When selected, the dialog box shown in the right of Figure 10.12 will be displayed. Note that unlike the line/bar chart discussed earlier, where the data was row organized, for the pie chart the data must be column organized. Thus, the data for the pie chart must be positioned down a single column, starting at a given initial row number and continuing to some final row number. These parameters, the column label, the starting row, and the ending row must be supplied to the *Pie Chart Definition* dialog box. You must also specify the column where the labels for each of the pie chart data values are listed. Figure 10.12 shows the entries used to construct the pie chart shown in Figure 10.13 from the worksheet values as arranged in Figure 10.12.

There is a limit of eight chart definitions that can be active at one time during a Works SS session. If you exceed this number of chart definitions, it will be necessary to erase some of these definitions and their corresponding charts before

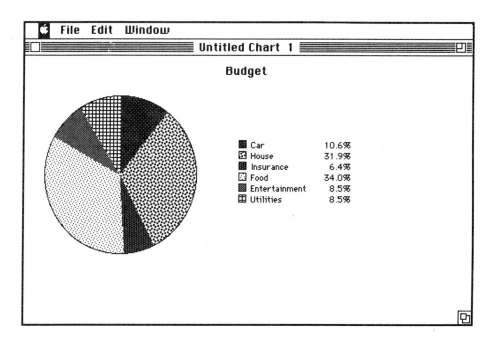

Figure 10.13 Pie chart produced from worksheet in Figure 10.12.

any additional charts can be constructed. This is accomplished by selecting the *Erase Chart* command from the **Chart** menu. A dialog box will appear that will allow you to select the name of the chart you wish to erase. Active charts are saved automatically with the worksheet.

The command *Draw Chart* in the **Chart** menu is used to draw a previously defined chart. Selection of this command will cause a dialog box to be displayed in which the name of a given chart can be selected and subsequently drawn.

By properly sizing and positioning your worksheet and charts you alter the worksheet and simultaneously observe the effect on the charts produced from the worksheet. For example, the window size for the preceding pie chart could be greatly reduced to provide room to position the budget worksheet alongside it. By clicking in the worksheet to make it the active window and changing budget entries, you will observe that the pie chart is automatically updated to reflect the worksheet changes.

Exercise Set 10.6

1. Under what main-level Works SS menu are charting operations available?
2. Describe the process of producing a line or bar chart in Works SS.
3. Describe the purpose of each element in the dialog box shown in Figure 10.10.
4. Describe the process of producing a pie chart in Works SS.
5. Describe the purpose of each element in the dialog box shown in Figure 10.12.
6. What is the maximum number of charts that can be active at one time in Works SS? If you exceed this number how can you make additional room?

Computer Practice 10.6

1. Create a worksheet that will allow you to display graphs of both $y = x^2$ and $y = x^3$ on the same graph. Do this by adding a new row to the table of the first

example in this section. Label this row by entering into cell A3 the label $y = x$^3 in analogy with the label $y = x$^2 done previously. Next, you will need to enter formulas to compute function values for the range B3 to F3. The formula to be entered into cell B3 is =B1^3. Fill in the other formulas as required. Finally select *New Series Chart* from the **Chart** menu and proceed as discussed in the first example of this section. You will now need to specify two rows for the computed values rather than one as used earlier. Print out a copy of your chart by selecting *Print* from the **File** menu.

2. Make up a sample budget for your college expenses organized by categories. Enter these categories as was done in the second example of this section. Plot a pie chart of your budget that you can send home. (Presumably this will show your parents that you do very little entertaining!)

3. Look up the populations of each of the states in your region of the country. Make a pie chart of the result.

4. Look up the total amount of goods and services produced by each state in your region. Make a pie chart of the results.

5. Set up a table of your monthly expenses. Make a bar chart of these expenses according to each month.

6. Estimate the number of miles that you have driven your car in each of the last four years. Draw a line chart of the number of miles as a function of the year.

7. Find average weekly values for your favorite stock over the last several weeks. Also compute the weekly average value of the Dow Jones industrial average for this same period. Plot a line chart that shows how your stock compares with the Dow Jones average for each week.

Key Concepts

Active call
Cell labels
Cell-level operations
Data entry termination
Data-object entry
Formatting a cell's data object
Formula-bar editing
Formula-object entry
Pie chart
Worksheet structure

Bar chart
Cell name
Cell range
Data object
Data-object operations
Formula bar
Formula object
Line chart
Sheet-level operation

CHAPTER 11

CONSTRUCTING SPREADSHEET FORMULAS

L E A R N I N G   O B J E C T I V E S

- To understand how spreadsheets use formulas similar to those in algebra.

- To learn how to approach solving a spreadsheet problem by developing both a problem description and the formulas necessary to solve the problem.

- To understand the sheet-level commands that allow cells to be moved about on the worksheet.

- To learn how to reference cells in formulas so that formulas can be easily and correctly replicated.

This chapter will teach you more about how to use spreadsheets for problem solving. You will learn to construct formulas using data object operators and see how this process is similar to developing a function in algebra. You will be introduced to a method to help you design a solution to a complex spreadsheet problem. In addition, you will learn how to choose between the use of relative and absolute references to a cell, so that cell formulas can be easily replicated. This knowledge will help you to construct numerous computations rapidly in a worksheet. Finally, some Works SS examples will demonstrate the use of many of these features.

11.1 FUNCTIONS

In the last chapter you learned some elementary concepts that are necessary to use a spreadsheet for problem solving. In this chapter you will learn additional concepts that will allow you to master the use of Works SS. Our approach will build upon an understanding of the concepts you learned in high school algebra. As you will see, an understanding of the concept of a function is essential if you are to utilize fully the computational power of the spreadsheet. In fact, any serious use of a spreadsheet requires you to develop functions to perform the computations of interest to you.

Recall from high school algebra that a *function*, *f*, of one variable, *x*, is denoted by the form $f(x)$ and is simply a *rule* for assigning a unique value to *f*, given a value for its argument, *x*. Thus, for each *x* value, there is one and only one value for *f*. The **domain of a function** is defined as the set of values from which the value of *x* may be chosen. The **range of a function** is the set of values that result from inserting into the function all values of *x* chosen from its domain.

As a simple example consider the function from the last chapter:

$$f(x) = x^2$$

The rule for computing the value of *f* in this example can be stated as taking the value of the argument *x* and multiplying it times itself. The values that *x* can take on (the domain) are all the real numbers. The values that can be computed by *f* (the range of *f*) given this domain are all nonnegative real numbers (i.e., the positive real numbers and zero).

Functions may have more than one argument. For example, we might have a function of two arguments $f(x,y)$ where

$$f(x,y) = x + y$$

The rule for computing the value of this function is to take the value of the argument *x* and add to it the value of the argument *y*. Note that there is one and only one value of *f*, given any pair of values for the arguments *x* and *y*.

In each preceding case, a function has been formed by operating on variables using well-known rules. In the first example the rule was multiplication. In the second example, the rule was addition. We may generalize from these examples by stating that useful functions are built from basic predefined operations on variables. In the next section we will examine several kinds of basic operators from which functions can be constructed to perform spreadsheet computations. Note, therefore, that the formulas we discussed in the last chapter may be thought of as examples of functions we constructed to perform calculations for us. Viewed in this way, the formula defines the rule to be used to compute the unique value of a data object for a cell, given a set of input values for the data objects of the other cells referenced in the formula.

Exercise Set 11.1

1. What is a mathematical function?
2. What is the domain of a function?
3. What is the range of a function?
4. How is a spreadsheet formula similar to a function?

11.2 GENERIC CELL-LEVEL OPERATORS ON DATA OBJECTS

In this section we discuss the generic features of spreadsheets that allow you to construct functions using arithmetic, logical, and comparison operators. These features are really part of a spreadsheet language syntax that you must learn in order to enter formulas that the spreadsheet can understand. The syntax of the language is very similar to that which you learned in algebra. Consequently, once the proper relationship between algebraic formulas and spreadsheet formulas is shown to you, entry of formulas should become very intuitive and natural. Spreadsheet environments, including Works SS, provide at least the features we describe in this section. In the next section you will learn how these features are implemented in the particular spreadsheet Works SS.

A PROBLEM-SOLVING STRATEGY. To **design a worksheet solution** to develop a worksheet to solve a computational problem, first write down on paper a description of *what* you want to do and the formulas you need to compute the answer to the problem. When necessary, you should describe how the value computed from one formula needs to be used by another formula.

The hardest part of problem solving is deciding *what* you want to do. During this step you should not be concerned at all with how it will be done on the computer—focus instead on trying to articulate carefully what steps are required to solve the problem by hand or with a calculator. For this purpose it is often desirable to give a high-level statement of the problem and then to try to break this high-level statement down into subsequently more and more refined descriptions of what is required. Your approach should be much like outlining a paper. Make the outline more and more detailed until all the steps necessary to solve the problem become clear. Recall that we used this process with MacPaint in Chapter 3 to construct a complex drawing. This approach is a useful problem-solving method for many kinds of problem areas.

Once you have decided the *what*, it is relatively easy to translate your description into a spreadsheet solution that describes *how* the computer is to carry out the solution for you. Toward this end you also will need to lay out how your computation will appear on the worksheet; that is, you will need to decide the number of cells that are to be used (this should be clear from your high-level description of the problem) and what purpose each cell will serve (whether it will hold an interest rate, for example). Then using your spreadsheet layout, translate your hand-written formulas into a spreadsheet syntax that has the same semantic meaning as your original natural language description of the problem. This latter step is used to tell the computer how to do the computation. Note that if *you* do not understand what you want to accomplish, there is absolutely no way to have the computer do it for you!

As a simple example, suppose that you decide to compute the formula $z=x+y$, for various values of x and y. Recall from algebra that the variables x, y, and z are just names. Also recall that before you can compute a value for z you must first substitute actual numerical values for x and y. For this simple example, the natural language statement of the problem is *add values of* x *and* y *to obtain the value of* z. This statement needs no further subdivision because it is already sufficiently precise to allow you to solve the problem.

Next, you lay out the worksheet. Any formula, such as the preceding one, can be directly **translated from algebra into a worksheet** computation by applying the following interpretation. First, you may think of a cell name in a worksheet as being like the variable name in a formula. Second, you may think of the data-object value in a cell as being like the value assigned to a variable in a formula. Thus, you may always pair a spreadsheet cell with a variable name appearing in an algebraic formula. Any desired pairing of cells and variable names can be chosen. Thus, we may arbitrarily choose a layout of cells in the spreadsheet to hold the actual values for x, y, and z. It is advantageous to label cells to remind yourself what the numbers in the cells represent.

Suppose, for example, that cell C2 is paired with x, cell C3 with y, and cell C4 with z. To make the data-object value of cell C4 always equal to the value of z in the algebraic formula you would enter the formula =C3+C2 into cell C4. Here + is an arithmetic operator whose semantic meaning is to add the values of the data objects of cells whose names are C3 and C2. That is, this operator operates on the data-object values in spreadsheet cells just like the algebraic operator + operates on algebraic variables. In fact, each of the operators listed in Figure 9.1 operates on spreadsheet cells analogous to its algebraic equivalent and with the same syntax for its use. Note that the symbols C3 and C2 are not valid numeric data but are instead the names of two cells that have values associated with them—just as x and y are names and not the actual data values to be used.

To label the cells to remind us what we are computing, we enter the symbols x, y, and z into cells B2, B3, and B4, respectively. See Figure 11.1. This completes the design of the simple worksheet.

SIMPLE ARITHMETIC OPERATORS. A data object that is consistent with a numerical data type can be operated on to produce a new numerical data object using the standard **arithmetic operators.** Review in Figure 9.1 the arithmetic operators and the symbols used to represent them. It is through these operators and the identification of variables with cell names as discussed earlier that algebraic formulas can be constructed.

OTHER FORMULA REFERENCES. All spreadsheets treat cell names as the location of the actual data to be used. Data values can be used directly in formulas, however, without requiring a cell name, just as numbers can appear in formulas in algebra without using a variable name. Suppose the algebraic formula we desired was $z=100 + y$. Then the formula entered in cell C4 is =100+C3. The + operation again means to add two numerical values. In this case, 100 is already a valid numerical data type and will be interpreted as the numerical value 100. Thus, 100 is not treated as the *location* of the data value but is instead the data value itself. This occurs because 100 is not a valid cell name—it does not begin with the necessary capital letter of a column label. Thus, there is no ambiguity about how to interpret it. C3, however, must be treated as a cell name, as discussed earlier. If the value of C3 is 200, then the value assigned to the data object of cell C4 will be 300.

SIMPLE LOGICAL OPERATORS. To perform certain computations in a spreadsheet it is necessary to use **logical operators.** These operators are already familiar to you from the discussion of Chapter 9. They are the operators AND, OR, and NOT. Recall that logical operators have logical values (*True* or *False* only) as input and they return a logical value as their result.

Logical operators are often used to incorporate a set of conditions into a spreadsheet computation. Suppose, for example, that a bonus should be awarded to a salesman only if his total sales were greater than $100,000 *and* his current salary was less than or equal to $50,000. That is, both of these conditions must be *True* before a bonus is given. On the other hand, if either or both conditions are false, then no bonus is given.

In English usage we may think of the term *and* as coupling two conditions together to produce a new condition that itself is either *True* or *False*. The new condition produced is the answer to the question whether or not to grant a bonus. Thus, the use of the AND operator allows us to combine two independent conditions (each of which is either *True* or *False*) into the result as to whether to grant a bonus—itself a *True* or *False* value.

You will find that building logical decisions based on the use of a hierarchy of these logical operators in spreadsheet formulas is an essential part of using a spreadsheet to solve most useful problems.

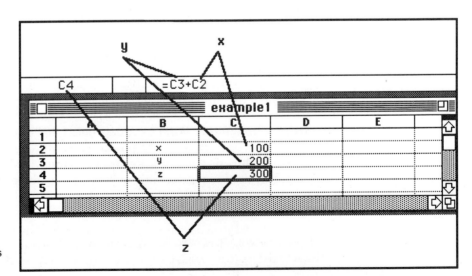

Figure 11.1 Interpretation of an algebraic formula as a worksheet formula.

COMPARISON OPERATORS. In addition to the simple arithmetic operators and logical operators discussed earlier, spreadsheets include another class of simple operators that operate on the values of data objects in formulas. These operators form a class called the **comparison operators.**

Recall from Chapter 9 that comparison operators take two values of a given data type and produce a logical value as a result. In spreadsheet usage the comparison operators are interpreted as asking a question. For example, $x > y$ asks the question: Is the value of the variable named x greater than the value of the variable named y? The answer to the question posed by a comparison operator is always a logical value (i.e., can only be *True* or *False*).

In worksheets it is often desirable to assign to a cell's data object the answer to a question posed by a comparison operator. We can assign the answer through a formula, just as we assign the result of a numerical operator using a formula. For example, suppose that we pair C1 with x and C2 with y in the preceding formula. Then the worksheet formula =C1>C2 entered into the cell C3 would cause the data object in cell C3 to be assigned the logical value *True* if the data-object value of the cell named C1 exceeded the data-object value of the cell named C2 and *False* otherwise. Explicitly, if C1 contained 100 and C2 contained 50, then C3 would be assigned *True*. If, on the other hand, C1 contained 50 and C2 contained 100, then C3 would be assigned *False*.

In many spreadsheet programs, any two values chosen from the same data type can be compared using a comparison operator. If C1 contained *shoes* and C2 contained *table*, then C3 would be assigned *False*. This occurs even though the values in these cells are not numerical but textual. When two textual values are compared, alphabetical order rather than numerical order is used to decide the answer to the question posed by the comparison operator. By alphabetical order we mean that strings of characters are ordered as they would be if they were entries in a dictionary. Because *shoes* appears before *table* in the dictionary, *shoes* is considered to be less than *table* in a comparison of text values.

The situation is actually slightly more complex than just the distinction between alphabetical and numerical order. The *&* is a valid text character. So are *?*, *#*, and so on. Each of the characters available on the computer keyboard can be thought of as belonging to a generalized alphabet, just as the letters A - Z belong to the ordinary alphabet. The order of the characters in this generalized alphabet is called the **collating sequence** of the computer and determines how the answers come out with respect to the questions asked by the comparison operations.

Note that the collating sequence on different computers or even in different spreadsheet packages can differ. However, it is generally true that when text values of the same case (all upper case or all lower case) are considered, the collating sequence preserves alphabetical order. Surprises can occur when text strings are compared that contain symbols other than strings of letters in the same case, however. In the event such strings need to be compared, it is wise to determine the collating sequence for the particular software package of interest, so that predictable results can be obtained.

OPERATOR PRECEDENCE. Spreadsheets have their own conventions about the order that is used to evaluate operators. Recall that **operator precedence** is the convention that is used to decide the order in which various operators are evaluated. In Works SS and Excel the hierarchy for operator precedence is given in Figure 9.7. *However, notice that AND and OR have equal precedence, in contrast to the way they are used in Works DB, where AND has precedence over OR.*

In expressions that include arithmetic, comparison, and logical operators, the arithmetic operators are evaluated first, followed by the comparison operators and then the logical operators. For example, the spreadsheet formula =2*3+1>3+2 AND 3<4*6 evaluates to *True*.

In the first step of the preceding evaluation, all the arithmetic operations are carried out. In the expression 2*3+1, the multiplication is carried out first, followed by the addition. This yields the following expression =7>5 AND 3<24. Then each comparison operation is carried out. This yields =*True* AND *True*. The logical AND operation is then carried out to give the final result *True*.

As a final note regarding the order of evaluation of operations in formulas, parentheses may be used in spreadsheet formulas to define the order of operations just as in algebra. Parentheses *always* have the highest level of precedence in evaluation. The innermost level of parentheses is evaluated first, working successively outward. Within a given level of parentheses, the rules of operator precedence apply as discussed above. The use of parentheses is well advised. There is no ambiguity in the order of evaluation of an expression if levels of parentheses are used to define a formula. Clarity for the spreadsheet user helps to prevent insidious errors from appearing in the computations produced by the worksheet. Additionally, a formula that uses parentheses is forced by its syntax to be evaluated by the computer in precisely the same way its author intended.

Exercise Set 11.2

1. Explain the importance of understanding the precedence of the operators listed in Figure 9.7 in connection with developing spreadsheet formulas.

2. How do numerical operators differ from logical and comparison operators?

3. How do logical operators differ from comparison operators?

4. In what way is the syntax used to specify a formula in a spreadsheet similar to the way a formula is specified in algebra? Why does this make using a spreadsheet very intuitive?

5. Write down a spreadsheet formula that could be used to compute the function $w = x * y + x / y * z \wedge x + y$. Show a drawing of a spreadsheet to compute this formula that has labels for each cell. Assume that the initial values of the variables are $x = 2$, $y = 3$, and $z = 5$.

6. Show, by inserting levels of parentheses, the operator precedence that would be applied in the evaluation of the function in exercise 5. What value is produced?

Let $x = 2$, $y = 3$, $z = 5$, $m = True$, $k = False$, $q = 3.5$ for the following.

7. Evaluate $w = x > y$.

8. Evaluate $w = m$ AND k OR NOT m.

9. Evaluate $w = x > y$ AND NOT $z <= y$.

10. Evaluate $w = x / z + - y \wedge x * q$.

11. Describe the steps suggested for solving a problem using a spreadsheet.

12. A company has three automobiles that it uses in its business. Each costs a certain amount to drive each year based upon the total number of miles driven. Assume that each automobile costs the company 25 cents per mile. Find the cost to drive each automobile and the total cost for driving all automobiles. Explain how to set up a spreadsheet solution to this problem using the steps you outlined in exercise 11. What are the parameters (see Section 10.1) for this problem.

13. Refer to exercise 12. Suppose that car 1 costs 25 cents per mile driven, car 2 costs 30 cents per mile driven, and car 3 costs 15 cents per mile driven. Construct a spreadsheet to answer the same questions as those in exercise 12.

11.3 WORKS SS OPERATORS

The operators defined in Works SS generally follow the generic rules discussed in the previous section, with the exception of a few relatively minor differences. First, note that the arithmetic operators, comparison operators, and logical operators in Works SS follow the *exact* precedence order as stated in Table 9.7, *where, however, AND and OR have the same level of precedence.* The differences in Works SS from the preceding generic discussion will now be discussed.

Comparison operators in Works SS are defined only for numerical values. Consequently, it is not possible to compare two textual data objects using the comparison operators in Works SS. (Note that textual comparisons can be made using Works DB, however.) The value computed from the use of the comparison operators in Works SS is a logical value just as defined for the generic operators discussed earlier, however, the logical values in Works SS are defined to be the number 0 for *False* and any other number for *True*. However, the *result* of a comparison operator will always yield a numerical value of either 0 or 1.

Logical operators in Works SS are defined as functions rather than as operators. Thus, when a generic operator of the form x AND y is used, it would be translated into Works SS as AND(x, y). The value of this function is the same as would be obtained if the operator AND had been applied to the values of x and y. Similarly, the OR function of Works SS has the form OR(x, y) and evaluates exactly the same as the OR operator shown in Figure 9.4. Finally, the NOT function of Works is defined to be NOT(x) and evaluates in the same way as the operator NOT defined in Figure 9.4. We note here again that arguments for the logical functions in Works SS take values that are 0 to represent *False* or any other number to represent *True* and the functions AND, OR, NOT each return a value or either 0 or 1 only.

One reason that AND and OR are often defined as functions in spreadsheets is that they can be easily generalized to have more than two arguments. For example, the function AND($V1, V2, ..., VN$), where there are now N arguments, each taking on a value of *True* or *False*, can be naturally defined as an extension of the two-argument AND function such that the N-argument AND function evaluates to *True* only if *each* of its arguments $V1, ..., VN$ is *True*. If one or more of the arguments $V1, ..., VN$ is *False* then the N-argument AND function evaluates to *False*. Clearly, this definition for two arguments reproduces the AND operator truth table of Figure 9.4.

A natural generalization also exists for the *N*-argument OR function. Here the function OR(*V1, V2, ..., VN*) evaluates to *False* only if all of its *N* arguments are *False*. If one or more of the *N* arguments is *True* then the *N*-argument OR function evaluates to *True*. This generalization reproduces the truth table for the two-argument OR operator in Figure 9.4. When computations depend on various conditions to decide which of several formulas need to be used to compute the final results, it is very desirable to have access to AND and OR functions with more than two arguments.

Exercise Set 11.3

1. Rewrite each of the AND, OR, and NOT operators in exercises 8 and 9 of Exercise Set 11.2 in terms of Works SS functions AND, OR, and NOT.
2. Write down the truth table for the function AND(*V1, V2, V3*).
3. Write down the truth table for the function OR(*V1, V2, V3*).
4. Construct a logical decision that would require the use of a three argument AND function.

11.4 GENERIC SHEET-LEVEL EDITING OPERATIONS

In addition to the cell-level editing features discussed in Chapter 10, which allow the information inside a selected cell to be modified, spreadsheets provide sheet-level editing operations, such as altering the position of a cell in the sheet; inserting or deleting a column, row, or group of selected cells; replicating the contents of a cell into a group of selected cells, and so on. These sheet-level editing operations are provided to make more convenient the maintenance of the worksheet as a whole. Consequently, the arrangement of cells on the worksheet and their interrelationships should be viewed as changeable.

Once a worksheet has been developed to solve a particular problem, it is often later rearranged. This may be done for the purpose of solving a related problem or altering the appearance of the report produced from the worksheet. Restructuring the worksheet alters the positions of some cells in the worksheet. Changes in the position of a cell alter its default name because the row and column position of the cell is altered. Because of such changes, a formula in a cell can inadvertently reference the wrong data for a computation unless the name of each cell repositioned is properly updated in *each* formula that references it.

Spreadsheet designers have anticipated these kinds of problems and have provided sheet-level editing commands that not only move cells on the worksheet but also update cell formulas in two different ways. The method of updating a cell reference in a formula depends upon whether **absolute reference** or **relative reference** has been used. In copying, moving, inserting, or deleting cells, the effect on the worksheet will depend upon the types of references employed in the formulas.

Cell references that give the locations of cells relative to the origin of the table are defined as absolute reference. Thus far, in all of our discussions about formulas in cells, we have been implicitly assuming that we have been using absolute reference to cells.

You can think of the origin of the table as the upper left-hand corner cell, whose location is A1. Using the table origin, cell B1 would be in row 1 and column B and cell A2 would be in row 2 and column A—just as we discussed before. Absolute cell references are particularly easy to understand and convenient to use to build formulas, as we have seen. However, such references can cause problems when worksheets are restructured. *By definition, in sheet-level editing commands, parts of formulas containing absolute references are not altered if replication or cutting and pasting of the formula occurs.*

To be in better agreement with the syntax adopted by the most popular spreadsheets (including Works SS and Excel), we will use a $ sign in front of a column or row label to indicate when a reference is absolute. Thus, the formula =$A$2 entered, say, into cell D10 of a Works SS worksheet means an absolute reference to the cell A2. Consequently, if this formula is replicated or alternatively is cut and then pasted into another cell, the reference will remain $A$2.

Relative reference, on the other hand, means that the cell in which a formula is contained becomes the *origin* from which the cell locations referenced in its formula are determined. Thus, for example, the formula =$C$3+$B$2 entered into cell A4 as an *absolute* reference might be written in the form =r2u1 + r1u2, expressed as a *relative* reference. In this hypothetical syntax, r2 means move right two columns from this cell's column, u1 means move up one row from this cell's row position, and so on. Hence, r2u1 applied to the cell address A4 would mean use the cell whose column is two to the right of A and whose row is one above 4. Thus, cell C3 is being referenced. This relationship is depicted in Figure 11.2. *When using sheet-level editing commands, if relative reference is used then the relationship is preserved between the formula in each cell and the cells that each formula references even when the cells are repositioned.*

This later statement has two important consequences. First, if cells are moved on the worksheet relative to one another, then each relative cell reference employed in each formula will be updated to reflect the *new* position of a cell after it is repositioned. In other words, the same data objects will be used in the parts of formulas employing relative reference even after the cells have been repositioned (renamed) on the worksheet.

Second, when replication (copying) of a formula is attempted from one cell to another, the spatial relationship between that cell and the other cells it references is identified for each relative reference employed in each formula—just as shown in Figure 11.2. This spatial relationship is used to form a *template* that describes

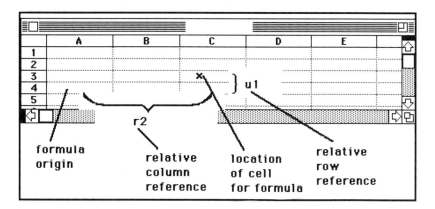

Figure 11.2 Use of relative coordinates to find a cell referenced in a formula.

how far away and in which direction each cell appearing in the formula is located from the current cell. This template is then applied to each cell in which the formula is to be copied and determines where the formula references are located—using the new cell as the origin. Some illustrations of these important concepts will now be given.

REPLICATING FORMULAS USING ABSOLUTE AND RELATIVE ADDRESSING. Relative reference is used to great advantage in **replication of formulas**—that is, the copying of a cell's formula to other cells. Suppose that the results of a spreadsheet computation produce two columns of 12 numbers each. One column contains the gross profits of a company for each month. The other contains the gross expense for each month. Further, suppose that we want to compute the net profit for each month. Define z as the net profit for a month. If x is the gross profit for a month and y is the gross expense for each month, then the formula relating x, y, and z, is $z = x - y$.

Now let us suppose that cells C30 to C41 and D30 to D41, respectively, contain the gross profit and gross expense for each month. Then 12 formulas need to be entered to compute each month's net profit. Each of these formulas will be of the form just given for z. Let's choose cells A45 to A56 to hold these 12 formulas and their resulting values. A picture of this arrangement is shown in Figure 11.3. Clearly, the formula to be entered into A45 would be =$C$30-$D$30 if absolute reference were used or =r2u15-r3u15 if relative reference were used. Conveniently, if relative referencing were used, instead of typing each of the remaining 11 formulas, it is possible to replicate (copy) the formula of cell A45 into each of the remaining cells A46 to A56.

If relative reference is used to replicate the formula in the preceding paragraph, then the spatial relationship between cells will be preserved in the replicated formulas. In other words, if relative reference is specified in the formula, then each of the cells A46 to A56 will receive the *same* formula, =r2u15-r3u15, *but these references are applied relative to the cell containing the formula*. Consequently, the net profit for the second month will be computed for cell A46 using cells C31 and D31, that for the third month will be computed from C32 and D32, and so on. Thus, relative reference in a formula allows the convenient entry of many formulas, each of which expresses the same relationship between a group of cells.

As discussed earlier, we may view relative reference in a formula as defining a **formula template** that fixes the positions of cells used by the formula relative to the cell containing the formula. This template may then be positioned over any new cell and shows the cells whose values are to be used in the formula for calculating a value for this new cell. An illustration of this template concept is shown in Figure 11.3.

If we reconsider this example using absolute reference (i.e., the formula in cell A45 is =$C$30-$D$30), then the replication produces a completely different result. Because cell addresses are *not modified* when using absolute reference, each cell A46 to A56 will receive the formula =$C$30-$D$30, and no reference to any of the cells C31 to C41 or D31 to D41 will occur in any formula. The monthly net profits will all be the same as the January net profit, assuming it is the one computed in cell A45.

In practice, it is not convenient for you to add and/or subtract cell addresses to find the relative coordinates of various cells, as would be required by this

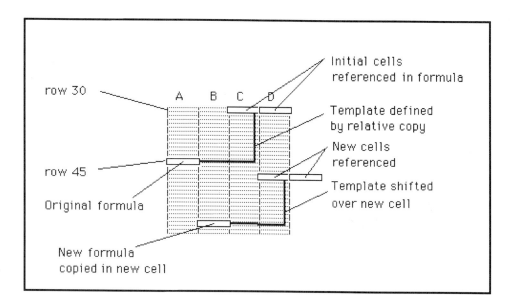

Figure 11.3 Template formed for relative reference.

hypothetical relative reference syntax. In fact, if this task were left up to you, it would often be true that errors would be made as you entered the relative coordinates of different cells into a formula. Furthermore, it is not convenient to show a relative address in a cell formula, because you have to add offsets to the current cell coordinates to find the locations of cells that are actually being referenced!

For most spreadsheets a different syntax is used for specifying relative addresses. *To indicate relative reference in Works SS and many other spreadsheets, the syntax used is to omit the $ in each column/row location component of the cell name.* Thus, if the formula =C1 were entered into cell A2 in a Works SS worksheet, then the type of reference would be understood to be relative reference, and would work just as if the formula =r2u1 of our preceding hypothetical syntax had been entered.

As a second example, consider the template formed in Figure 11.3. The formula required to form this example template for cell A45 on a Works SS worksheet is =C30 - D30. Consequently, if this formula were entered into cell A45 in Works and replicated down as in our earlier example, then, since relative addressing is being specified, the effect would be identical to that for the hypothetical syntax =r2u15 - r3u15. By always showing the table coordinates of the cell being referenced, as in Works, it is much easier for you to locate the actual cell of interest. In addition, when you enter a formula, you can reference the cell using its table coordinates and let the computer figure out its relative coordinates—a great simplification.

Because formula replication or cut and paste commands update cell formulas differently, depending upon the kind of reference employed, it is essential for you to understand fully the difference between absolute and relative references. It is also important to understand the effect of replicating cells when their formulas employ combinations of relative and absolute references in a spreadsheet.

INSERTING ROWS OR COLUMNS. Let us consider an example of the way that relative and absolute references work when using sheet-level editing. In this example we will insert a row into a worksheet. Recall that when absolute reference is chosen for a cell reference, no updating of that reference occurs when formula replication or cut and paste operations are performed. Consider the earlier computation of $z = x + y$, shown in Figure 11.1, where we paired the cells C2, C3, and C4 with the variables x, y, and z, respectively. Assume that the formula =$C$3+$C$2 was entered in cell C4.

Now suppose for some reason that it is necessary to insert a new row of cells in the worksheet between row 2 and row 3. That is, we picture the sheet being cut apart between the bottom of row 2 and the top of row 3. Next, the bottom part of the worksheet, containing rows numbered 3 and higher, is moved down to provide enough room to add a new row of cells. Clearly, in this process the cells in rows 1 and 2 are not moved, but all cells in rows 3 and higher are moved down the space of one row to make room for the new row to be added. We then add the row of empty cells.

To maintain the continuity of the cells on the sheet, the new row of cells that has been inserted must be named row 3. Consequently, the old row 3 must become row 4, the old row 4 must become row 5, and so on. Now if only this renumbering is done and the formulas in cells are not altered, the old cell C4 (which is now named cell C5) contains the formula =$C$3+$C$2.

The change in position of the cells could have a disastrous effect on the results computed from the formula. Cell C3 on the altered worksheet, which was referenced by the formula, should contain the value of y. However, because cell C3 is now one of the new cells inserted by the editing process, it has had no value assigned to it and the result obtained from the formula would be incorrect. Fortunately, all modern spreadsheets provide safeguards against these kinds of effects. Whenever sheet-level editing commands are performed that insert or delete rows or columns, the absolute addresses in formulas are updated so that the formulas continue to compute correct results.

Let's consider now the effect of the row insertion on a relative reference formula. Suppose the relative reference formula =C3+C2 is entered into cell C4. In relative coordinates, using our preceding hypothetical syntax, this formula would read =r0u1+r0u2. Thus, the cells currently being referenced are located one and two rows, respectively, above the current cell, and each is in the same column as the current cell.

Now if a row is added between rows 2 and 3, then by the definition of relative reference, the formulas in each cell are updated to preserve the relationship of the cells. In this case each relative reference in the formula for the old cell C4 (now cell C5 after editing) is checked to see if it needs to be altered. Note that the old cell C3 (now cell C4 after editing) still lies at position r0u1 relative to the formula cell. Thus, this reference requires no alteration. The old cell C2 (still cell C2 after editing), however, is now at position r0u3, because a row was added between its position and the cell containing the formula. This part of the formula must be updated. Consequently, the formula in cell C5 on the edited worksheet contains =r0u1+r0u3. Note that this altered formula would now be expressed as =C4+C2 in Works SS syntax, and it will evaluate properly to the *same* value as before the editing was done. Note also that deleting a row or a column will cause formulas to be updated as described for adding rows or columns. However, if the row or column deleted contains a referenced cell, then there is no valid method for updating the affected cell formulas. Many spreadsheets will identify this occurrence by writing an error message.

COMBINATIONS OF ABSOLUTE AND RELATIVE REFERENCE. We note in closing this section that combinations of absolute and relative reference are possible in defining formulas. For example, the formula =$A1 entered in cell D3 means that the column label is treated as absolute, but the row label is treated as relative. If the formula is replicated, the row reference will be updated, but the column reference will be unchanged. If a new column of cells were inserted before column A, then the formula in cell D3 would change to $B1. Instead of adding a new column before A, suppose we insert a new row before row 1. Because the row location was relative in the formula, it will be altered to preserve the row location of the two cells. Consequently, the formula in cell D4 (one new row was added) becomes =$A2. Clearly, the result computed from this formula will be the same value as before a row was added.

Use of a mixture of absolute and relative reference in one cell address can be helpful in generating a table in which two variables are used for computation. You will explore such usage in the exercises of the next chapter.

Exercise Set 11.4

1. Explain the term *relative reference* to a cell. Describe the syntax that Works SS uses for relative reference. Describe the hypothetical syntax that is discussed in this section for relative reference.
2. Explain the term *absolute reference* to a cell. Describe the syntax that is used by Works SS to represent an absolute reference to a cell.
3. What is a *formula template*?
4. Explain why repositioning a cell on the worksheet can cause formulas in other cells to become incorrect.
5. How do cell data-object operators differ from sheet-level operators?
6. Suppose that the cell C6 contains the formula =A7+B4*F5. If this formula is replicated in cell H5 what will its form be? Use Works SS syntax as discussed in this section. (*Note*: It will be helpful for you to sketch an example worksheet.)
7. Suppose that the cell C6 contains the formula =$A$7+$B$4*$F$5. If this formula is replicated in cell H5, what will its form be? Use Works SS syntax.
8. Suppose that the cell C6 contains the formula =$A$7+B4*$F$5. If this formula is replicated in cell H5, what will its form be? Use Works SS syntax.

11.5 WORKS SS SHEET-LEVEL EDITING OPERATIONS

Recall that sheet-level editing operations cause a restructuring (repositioning of cells) of the worksheet and/or affect the contents of more than one cell at a time. These operations are normally performed after some information already has been entered into the worksheet. At that point you might discover either that cells need to be rearranged to make room for additional information or that a formula needs to be replicated among a number of cells. The sheet-level operations we discuss are found under the **Edit** pull-down menu. These operations include *Undo, Cut, Copy, Paste, Clear, Move, Paste with Options, Insert, Paste Function, Fill Right, Fill Down*, and *Sort*.

In using sheet-level operations, two things need to be kept in mind. The first of these relates to the use of formulas that reference cells whose locations are altered as a result of a sheet-level operation. Recall from the last section that the part of a formula that employs an absolute cell reference is not altered if the formula is replicated or if a cut and paste operation occurs. In contrast, those parts of a formula that do employ relative reference or refer to cells where positions are changed by row or column insertions or deletions are updated to reflect each cell's new location. *It is extremely important when you enter a formula that you choose the proper mode of reference for each cell.*

Second, because a worksheet is a grid structure, if you add or delete a row or column of cells, the worksheet will be rearranged. Cells throughout the entire sheet will be relocated when an insertion or deletion occurs. *Consequently, one apparently small change in a worksheet can have a major effect on the overall form of the worksheet.*

If the effect of a sheet-level operation is not what you intended and you haven't as yet performed another operation, selection of the *Undo* operation will restore the worksheet to its previous state. *Undo* can save you a lot of typing, trying to restore part of a worksheet that was inadvertently altered.

INSERTING/DELETING ROWS AND COLUMNS OF CELLS.   The operations of *Insert* and *Cut* allow, respectively, a row or column of cells to be added or deleted from the worksheet. Clearly, to *Insert* or *Cut* it is necessary to indicate where a row or column of cells is to be added or deleted. Works SS makes use of the point and click feature to select a row or column where the operation will occur. To select a column (row), move the cell-selection pointer into the column (row) label area, point to the column (row) of interest, and click. The entire column (row) will be highlighted. By pulling down the **Edit** menu and selecting *Insert,* an entire new column (row) will be inserted in the worksheet before the column (row) selected. Because cell positions will be altered as the result of adding the new column (row) addresses of cells referenced in formulas will be automatically updated. To use *Insert* on a row, it is not necessary to highlight the entire row. In fact, if only one cell is highlighted and *Insert* is selected, then an entire row is automatically added to the worksheet.

When an entire column (row) is selected, *Cut* will cause the highlighted column (row) to be removed from the worksheet. That is, *Cut* works similarly to *Insert* in that the entire column (row) is altered. However, if one cell or a group of cells (but not a row or column) is highlighted, then *Cut* only removes the *contents* of the cells and places them on the Clipboard.

COPY/PASTE.   One way that Works SS provides the operation of replicating a formula is through the *Copy* and *Paste* operation sequence accessed through the **Edit** pull-down menu. While replication using this method will seem most natural to you at first because you have used it for other application environments, the *Fill Right* and *Fill Down* operations, which we discuss shortly, are better for most uses.

The operation of the *Copy* and *Paste* sequence for cell replication is similar to what you learned previously in Works WP to copy text into other parts of a document. First, the range of cells whose formula or data objects are to be copied must be selected. This selection is usually performed using the cell-selection pointer to point to the initial cell of the range and drag. Next, *Copy* is selected from the **Edit** menu. Then the range of cells to which you wish to copy must be defined. The selection of the range to which the formulas are to be copied is carried out by dragging. The range of cells selected then is highlighted in black. The range is also displayed in the active cell location descriptor of the worksheet. Finally, the *Paste* operation is selected from the **File** menu. At this time, replication of the contents of the initial cells is carried out. In the process of replicating formulas using *Copy*, where relative references to cells have been specified, a template is set up analogous to the discussion earlier in this chapter and is used to determine the location of each cell referenced in the replicated formula.

Note that a *Copy* and *Paste* sequence will always produce the same number of cells in the *Paste* operation that were highlighted during the *Copy* operation.

MOVE VERSUS CUT. The *Move* operation is not identical to *Cut* in Works SS. First and most important, a *Move* operation retains the *original* cell references in formulas. Thus, in this instance *no* template is formed to use for determining cell references, no matter what kind of cell reference is used in the formula. The formula placed in the new cell references the same cells as the original cell. *Move* is used, as its name suggests, to reposition a cell on the worksheet while leaving its formula intact.

In contrast, the *Cut* operation followed by *Paste* causes a template to be formed and all relative references are updated according to the new origin of the cell after it is pasted into position.

As a final note regarding pasting operations, we point out that there is another operation in Works SS called *Paste with Options* that is available from the **Edit** pull-down menu. Choosing *Paste with Options* allows only a portion of a cell to be copied. For example, perhaps we wish only to copy the data-object value from a cell instead of a cell's formula. If *Paste with Options* is chosen rather than *Paste*, then one of the options available in the form of a button is *Values*. Selection of this option means only the value of the data object is copied—not the formula.

FILL RIGHT/FILL DOWN. Works SS provides a more convenient operation than *Copy* and *Paste* for replicating cell formulas. **Fill Right** and **Fill Down** allow one formula to be replicated in an entire range selected in a row or column, respectively, whereas *Copy* and *Paste* can replicate a formula into one cell at a time. A formula replicated using *Fill Right* or *Fill Down* defines a template for cell references just as described in connection with *Copy*. Consequently, relative references in the formula being replicated will cause a template to be constructed and new formulas will be produced in each cell according to the template. Such a procedure can be highly advantageous.

Consider the example shown starting with Figure 11.4, where a table of information is to be prepared. We have entered the current year's total salaries for several departments. Also in cell C10 we have computed the total salaries for all departments using the formula =C4+C5+C6+C7+C8. Suppose that we wish to project salaries for various departments from one year to the next using the formula

next year's salary = current salary * 1.06

Then we may easily construct the formulas required in two steps. First, we enter the formula to compute the Lingerie Department's salary for 1988 from the same

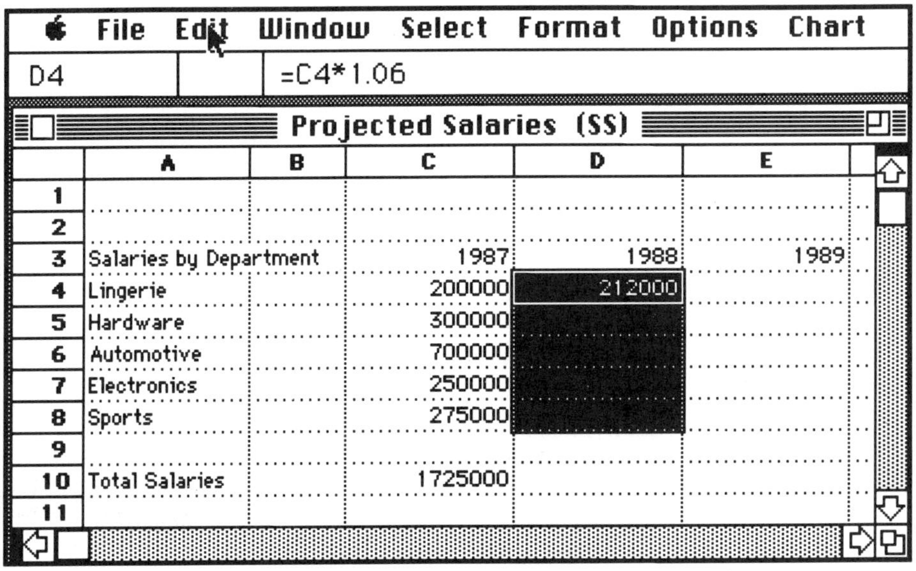

Figure 11.4 Use of selection of cells for formula replication.

department's salary in 1987. Thus, we enter in cell D4, the formula =C4*1.06. This is shown in the formula bar of Figure 11.4. We select the range of cells D4:D8, the darkened area in the figure.

Next, we choose *Fill Down* from the **Edit** menu. This causes the formula in cell D4 to be replicated into all cells below it, as shown in Figure 11.5. Now, having replicated all the formulas down column D, we can replicate the formulas into the cells to the right. Select the range D4:E8 and choose *Fill Right* from the **Edit** pull-down menu to produce the final form for the table shown in Figure 11.6.

Consequently, we obtained the entire table with only two fill operations. Producing this table using *Copy* and *Paste* would have worked, but it would have been more time-consuming. (We would begin by copying a single cell to another,

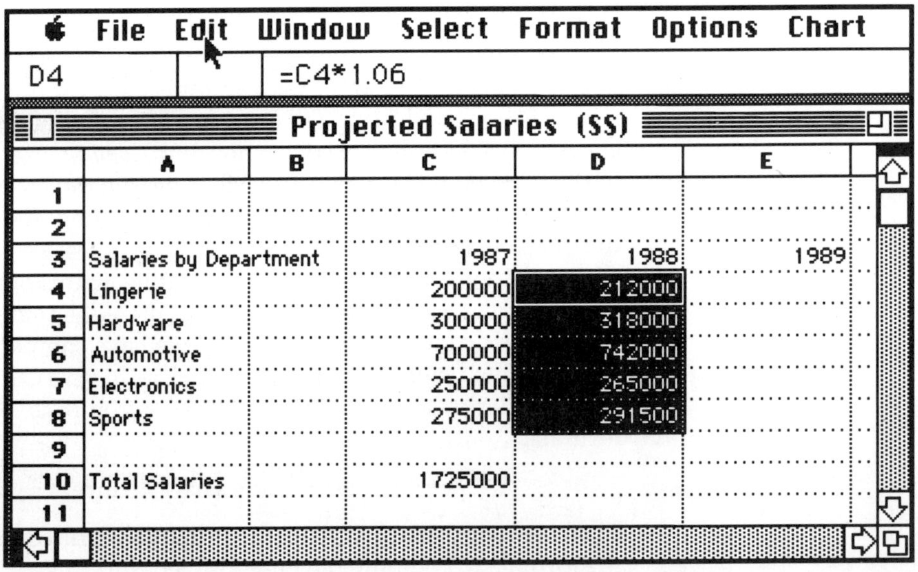

Figure 11.5 Use of *Fill Down* for formula replication in first column.

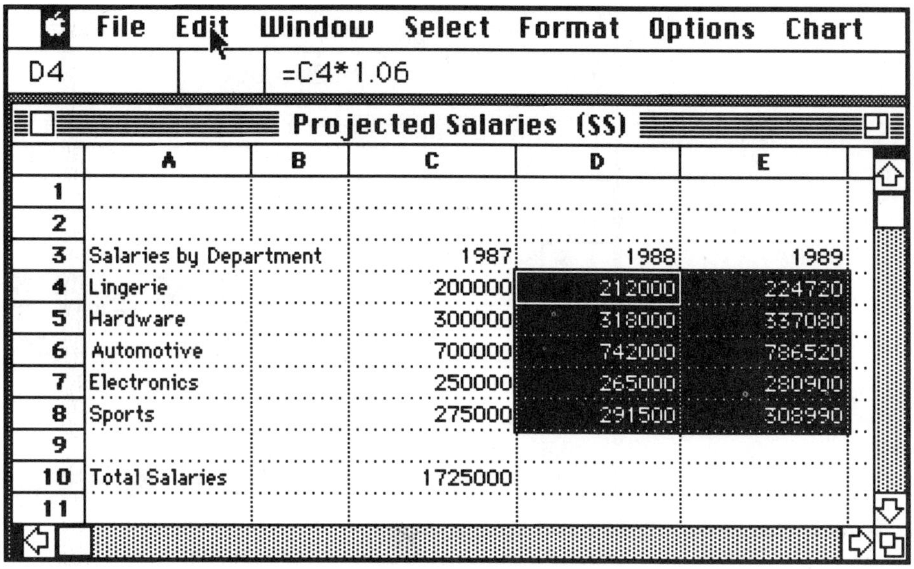

Figure 11.6 Use of *Fill Right* for replication of remaining formulas.

then another cell to another, and so on.) To complete the *Total Salaries* line in the table select the range C10:E10 and execute a *Fill Right* operation. The result is shown in Figure 11.7.

In Figure 11.8, we show the use of the **Format** menu to create an easier-to-read table. First, the range C4:E10 is selected (as shown highlighted). Then the *Comma* option is chosen from under the **Format** menu. Next, the *Dollar* option is chosen from under the **Format** menu. Finally, the *Number of Digits* option from the **Format** menu is set at zero. This sequence produces the display of Figure 11.8.

CLEAR. *Clear* has as its function the removing of information in a cell without deleting the actual cell from the worksheet. Thus, if the contents of a cell or group of cells is not what you desire, you can select the range desired and select the *Clear*

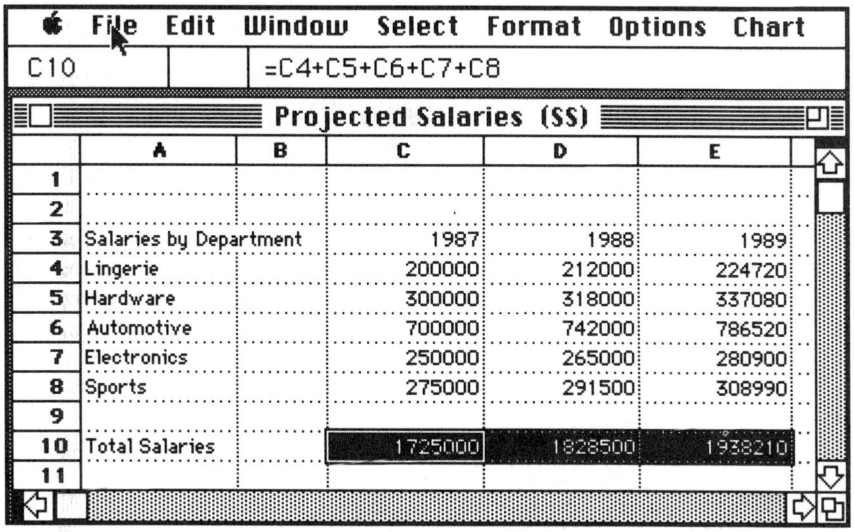

Figure 11.7 Using *Fill Right* for the total salaries.

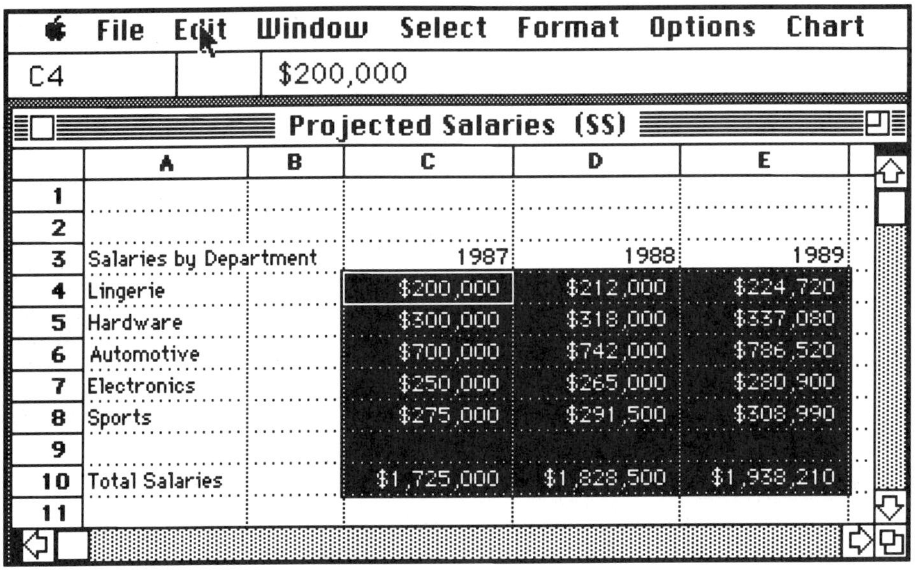

Figure 11.8 Using the **Format** menu for style.

operation from the **Edit** pull-down menu. *Clear* is similar to *Cut* except that nothing is placed on the Clipboard.

SORT.   Just as you were able to sort a table in the Works DB, Works SS allows you to sort *rows* in a spreadsheet. As an example of the use of the *Sort* option in the **Edit** menu, we consider the *Projected Salaries* worksheet example from the preceding discussion. In this example let us suppose that we wished to alphabetize the list of departments to make it easier to find a given department in the worksheet. First, the area to be sorted must be selected. As shown in Figure 11.9, the range A4:E8 is selected. *Note that only those items within the selected area are sorted.* Next, the *Sort* option is selected from the **Edit** menu.

A dialog box such as that shown in Figure 11.10 will be displayed. You now select the column position that is to be used for each level of the sort. Because we wish to sort according to alphabetical order on department, we specify column A,

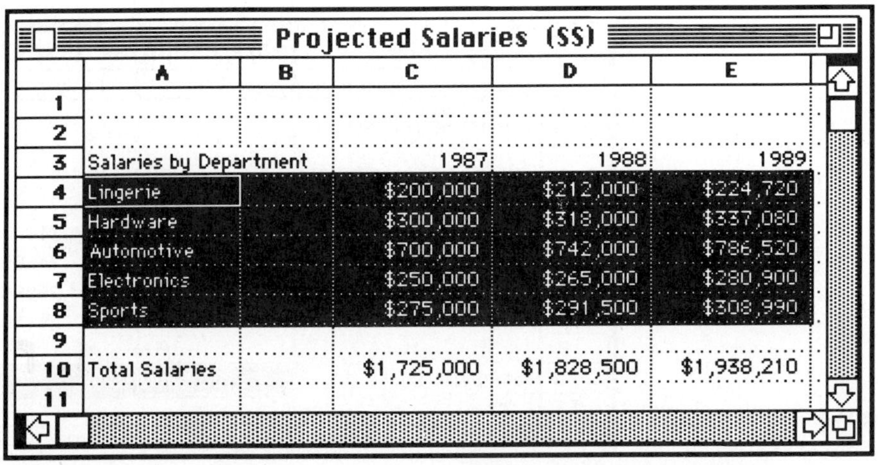

Figure 11.9 Selecting the range for the *Sort* operation.

where the departments are listed. Also ascending order is chosen because we wish to have the departments appear in alphabetical order—Automotive first, Electronics next, and so on. Then click on the *OK* button.

The result of this sort is shown in Figure 11.11. Note that the departments now appear in alphabetical order in the first column and the other columns have been altered so as to keep the salaries for each of the departments with the corresponding department name.

It is important to emphasize that if we had only selected column A, that is, highlighted the range A4:A8 and performed the sort, then the department column would have been sorted but the remaining columns would have been unchanged. Consequently, Automotive would have shown a 1987 salary of 200,000 rather than the correct value as shown in Figure 11.11! For this reason be very careful when using the *Sort* option.

We could have sorted the worksheet table by the value of salary instead of alphabetizing by department. This would be accomplished by selecting the range A4:E8 and choosing column C for the sort rather than column A as done earlier.

Finally, the sort may be performed up to three levels deep. We might imagine a situation in which we have columns containing states, cities, and last names. We might sort the table by states as the outer level, then within the same state sort next by cities, then sort within the same state and city according to last name. This is the origin of the terms *1st Key Column, 2nd Key Column*, and *3rd Key Column* in the dialog box of Figure 11.10. The term *1st Key Column* refers to the outermost level of the sort, *2nd Key Column* to the next level, and so on.

SETTING THE COLUMN WIDTH.   In many instances it is desirable to adjust the column widths in the worksheet. When the pointer is positioned inside the column label area and intersects one of the lines demarking the edge of a column, the pointer will change into two oppositely directed connected arrows that are

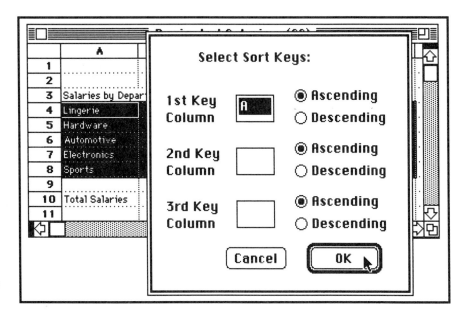

Figure 11.10 Choosing the columns for the sort.

	A	B	C	D	E
	Projected Salaries (SS)				
1					
2					
3	Salaries by Department		1987	1988	1989
4	Automotive		$700,000	$742,000	$786,520
5	Electronics		$250,000	$265,000	$280,900
6	Hardware		$300,000	$318,000	$337,080
7	Lingerie		$200,000	$212,000	$224,720
8	Sports		$275,000	$291,500	$308,990
9					
10	Total Salaries		$1,725,000	$1,828,500	$1,938,210
11					

Figure 11.11 Result of Sorting by Department.

pointed in the directions of the left and right sides of the screen, as shown in Figure 11.12.

If the button is held down and the mouse moved left or right, then the position of the column boundary will follow the mouse. Thus, drag operations can be used to increase or decrease the width of the column whose right boundary is delimited by this line. The widths of other columns are not affected by this operation. Hence, using this method you can easily set each column to the width you desire for display purposes. Notice that this is quite similar to the method used to adjust the data field widths in the Works DB list display. In Works SS there is no option to alter the height of a row of cells in the worksheet.

Changing the width of a column can affect the value displayed in a cell. As long as there is sufficient room to display the numerical value in a cell, Works SS will not complain, it will simply display the value. If, however, the width of a cell becomes too small for a numerical value to be displayed properly, Works SS displays the string of symbols #### across a cell, as shown in cell B2 at the bottom of Figure 11.12. For the display of text, there is spillover into the next cell if it is not occupied.

The form of this "error" display is chosen to protect you from inadvertently misinterpreting the numerical value in the cell. Works SS still retains the correct numerical value of this cell and the correct value will be used in any formula that references this cell. Note, however, that if Works SS were to display only a few of the digits of the number in a cell instead of the error symbols, *you* would not know that only part of the number was displayed. You would naturally assume that the digits displayed represented the *entire* number and would, therefore, interpret the value displayed incorrectly. To see the correct value, simply increase the column width sufficiently and the number will reappear.

Exercise Set 11.5

1. How does the *Move* option differ from the *Cut* and *Paste* operation sequence?
2. Describe the function of *Fill Down* and *Fill Right* sheet-level operations. Why are they useful?

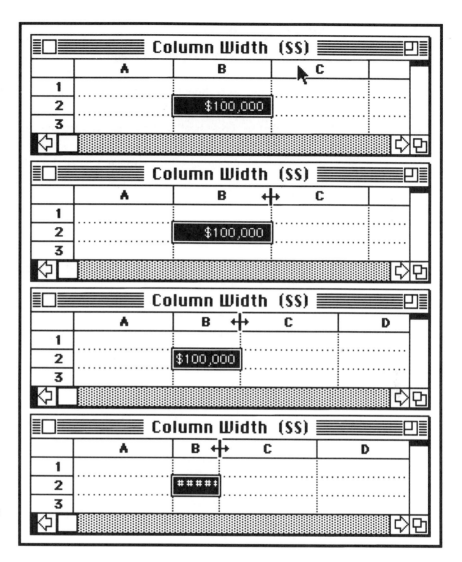

Figure 11.12 Changing the column width by dragging.

3. How do the *Fill Down* and *Fill Right* sheet-level operations differ from the *Copy* and *Paste* operation sequence in Works SS.

4. How do you insert a new row or column in the worksheet?

5. How do you remove a row or column from the worksheet?

6. How do the operations *Clear* and *Cut* differ?

7. How do the operations *Paste* and *Paste with Options* differ?

8. Explain how you can alter the width of a column in the worksheet.

9. Is it possible to change the height of a row in Works SS?

10. Explain how you can sort a table of information in the Works SS.

Computer Practice 11.5

1. Construct the worksheet for the *Projected Salaries* example worked out in this section.

2. Using the worksheet for exercise 1, sort the table according to department, as done in the example of this section.

3. Using the worksheet for exercise 1, sort the table according to increasing departmental salaries.

4. Using the worksheet for exercise 1, sort the table according to decreasing departmental salaries. Make a pie chart of salaries for the year 1988. Make a pie chart of salaries for the year 1989.

5. Using the worksheet for exercise 1, make one line chart showing how the salaries for the Lingerie, Hardware, and Sports Departments vary from year to year.

6. Using the worksheet for exercise 1, extend the table out to the year 2000. To do this use a formula to compute the year number from the previous year number and replicate the formula using the *Fill Right* command. This will remove the necessity of your entering each year number by hand. Next, think carefully about how you can replicate existing worksheet formulas to compute the required salaries.

7. Using the worksheet for exercise 6, compute the ratio of salaries in the year 2000 to those in 1987. Place these values in the column after the year 2000 and label the column appropriately.

8. Assume that the inflation rate for the year changes according to the following table.

1988	1989	1990	1991	1992	1993	1994	1995	1996	1997	1998	1999	2000
5.0	5.5	6.0	7.0	6.0	5.0	4.5	5.0	5.5	6.0	6.5	6.8	7.5

Set up a separate section on your worksheet to find the factor by which you would need to multipy your 1987 salary to keep up with inflation over these years. Compare this value with those computed from exercise 7.

Key Concepts

Absolute reference
Collating sequence
Design a worksheet solution
Fill Right/Fill Down
Formula translation from algebra
Operator precedence
Relative reference

Arithmetic operators
Comparison operators
Domain of a function
Formula template
Logical operators
Range of a function
Replication of formulas

SOLVING MORE COMPLEX PROBLEMS WITH SPREADSHEETS

L E A R N I N G O B J E C T I V E S

- To learn the variety of built-in functions defined in the Works spreadsheet module.

- To understand the information that must be provided to invoke a built-in function.

- To use tests within a spreadsheet computation to control the results produced by a spreadsheet.

- To gain experience and confidence in solving more complex problems with a spreadsheet.

I n this chapter you will learn to use some built-in functions that are provided in Works SS and to solve problems of higher complexity than you have previously solved. You will find that a wide selection of built-in functions exists that can be employed to solve many commonly occurring problems. You will learn how to provide the information necessary to invoke a built-in function in a spreadsheet formula and how to control the results of a computation dependent upon intermediate results that are obtained as the computation is carried out. Finally, you will gain additional insight into the overall process of solving problems with a spreadsheet.

12.1 GENERIC SPREADSHEET BUILT-IN FUNCTIONS

In Chapter 11 you learned about the process of constructing formulas using the data-object operators that are provided in a typical spreadsheet package. Spreadsheets also normally provide an extensive group of functions, known as **built-in functions,** that are more complex than those that you would wish to construct directly as spreadsheet formulas. These functions allow the spreadsheet user to develop solutions to a broader range of problems than would be possible without them. The types of functions provided are similar in purpose to those found on advanced scientific and financial calculators. While it is possible for spreadsheet users to create formulas of their own to compute such function values, it is often true that the typical spreadsheet user possesses neither the knowledge, the desire, nor the time to develop such formulas. Hence, the availability of these built-in functions represents a great enhancement in your ability to solve problems.

Typical spreadsheets provide built-in functions to perform such operations as sum a set of values, average a set of values, find the minimum of a set of values, find the maximum of a set of values, find the mean and standard deviation of a set of values, find the future value of an investment, find the slope and intercept of the best line through a set of points (this function is not available in Works), take the logarithm of a value, take the exponential function of a value, find the positive square root of a value, and find the sine, cosine, or tangent of a value. An annotated list of many of the built-in functions provided in Works SS is presented in the next section.

To use a built-in function in a spreadsheet it is necessary to know both the name of the function as defined in that particular spreadsheet package and the information the function requires to compute its value. The syntax required to specify the information to the function is particular to each spreadsheet. However, some general comments will help to illustrate the underlying concepts.

As a model of a function for a computation it is convenient to think of a **black box** into which we place elements of information and receive in return a data-object value. The function is called a black box because we care nothing about how the function computes its value—only that it returns the correct value to us. This concept is illustrated in Figure 12.1. Different elements of information that are required by a function to compute a value are called **function arguments.** Ar-

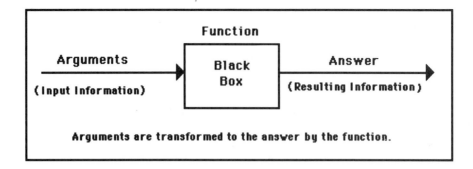

Figure 12.1 Conceptual view of a function as a black box.

guments are used to pass values into the function where they can be acted on to produce the resulting value. Recall the concept of a function from the Chapter 11 discussion.

For example, if a function is used to compute the area of a rectangle, then the function must have two arguments—the length and width of the rectangle. These two elements of information are always necessary to compute the area. Furthermore, they are the only units of information necessary to compute the area. Thus, if a rectangle has a length of 10 units and a width of 20 units, then the rectangle area function would return the value 200 (i.e., the length times the width). Each time you wish to invoke a built-in function, you need only specify its name and give values for the arguments it will use to compute the data-object value.

The **syntax** required to invoke a built-in function is carried over from algebra and includes:

- The name of the function.
- A left parenthesis.
- A list of the arguments, each separated from the next by a comma.
- A right parenthesis.

(In some spreadsheets, such as Lotus 1-2-3, an @ sign must precede the name of the built-in function.) In a built-in function, an argument can be provided as an expression, another built-in function, a cell name, or the actual numerical value that is to be used in the computation.

EXAMPLE FUNCTION.   To illustrate these ideas more fully, let us suppose that we wish to compute the formula $z = \sqrt{b^2 - 4ac}$. That is, we wish to compute the square root of b squared minus 4 times a times c.

To enter this formula using built-in functions, you would consult the manual for a given spreadsheet to see if there is a built-in function for the square root. Let us assume that you have learned from the manual that the built-in function to compute the square root is named SQRT and that it has one argument. (This is, incidentally, the name of the square root function in Works SS. The Works SS manual also indicates that this function requires one argument—the value for which the square root is to be computed.)

As discussed earlier, to invoke a function in a spreadsheet, its name and its arguments must be included as part of a formula entered in the formula object of a cell. Following our method for translating a formula into the worksheet, you must now pair up each variable in the formula with a cell. Assume then that A1 is paired with a, B1 with b, C1 with c, and D1 with z. Because z is to receive the resultant data-object value, we enter the formula =SQRT(B1*B1-4*A1*C1) into cell D1.

Notice in this case that the argument to the built-in function SQRT is an expression. In this case the value of the expression $b^2 - 4ac$, is passed to the square root function, just as in the original algebraic formula. Hence, D1 will display the value that would be computed for z. Recall from algebra that the value of the SQRT function is defined only for arguments that are nonnegative.

BUILT-IN, NONNUMERICAL FUNCTIONS. In most cases where functions are used, numerical values will be passed as arguments and a numerical value will be returned for the answer, just as for the SQRT function. However, functions need not operate only on numerical values or return only numerical values. Furthermore, the data type of the arguments of a function need not match the data type that the function returns.

Consider, for example, a function whose purpose is to take a text string as input and return as its value the number of characters in the string. If such a function received the input string *shoes* it would return the number 5. Similarly, if this function received the input *100*, it would return the number 3. The latter occurs because any number is a valid text string that has as its characters the digits that make up the number. The input argument for this function has a data type of text and the value returned from the function is of type number.

One very important kind of function that spreadsheets invariably contain is the conditional function, uniformly called the **IF function**. It typically has three arguments:

- A logical value (must be *True* or *False*).
- The value to be returned by the function if the first argument is *True*.
- The value to be returned by the function if the first argument is *False*.

Note that the value to be returned can be of type textual, logical, or numerical.

The first argument is called the *conditional part* of the IF function and its value is often assigned by the use of a comparison operator. In general, however, *any* expression that evaluates to a logical value can be used to assign the value to the first argument. The conditional function IF can be used to assign one of two different values to a data object dependent upon whether the first argument is *True* or *False*. A graphical depiction of the operation of the IF function is shown in Figure 12.2. Note that when the condition is *True*, the value of *Expression1* is computed and returned as the data-object value. If the condition is *False*, then the value of *Expression2* is returned as the data-object value. Only one path is followed (either the left side or right side) for a given condition.

Thus, the computational rule for the evaluation of the IF function is stated as follows: If the condition (first argument) is *True*, then return the value in the second argument; otherwise, return the value in the third argument.

Consider the following simple description of *what* we wish to compute. An employer wishes to give a 10 percent bonus to every salesman whose total sales are greater than or equal to $100,000. An English statement of this decision process using the preceding IF syntax would be

IF(sales >= 100000, bonus is salary * 0.10, bonus is 0)

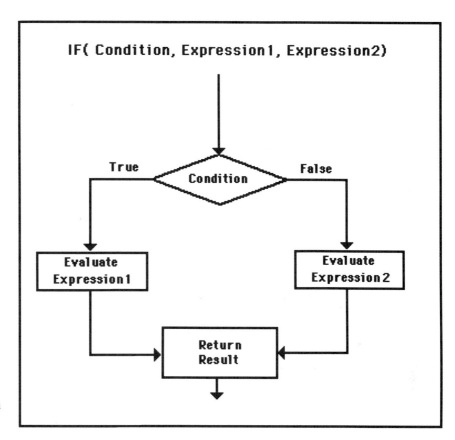

IF(Condition, Expression1, Expression2)

Figure 12.2 Graphical depiction of the operation of the IF function.

Let us see how to enter this formula in a spreadsheet. We assume that cell Q2 contains the total sales for a particular salesman and cell G2 contains his salary. The bonus using the spreadsheet formula is then

$$=IF(Q2>=100000, G2*0.10, 0)$$

The first argument in the IF function is Q2>=100000. Recall from Section 11.2 that a comparison operator, such as >=, requires two arguments and produces a *True* or *False* result. Because Q2 is a cell name, the value of the data object of this cell is one argument that will be used. The other argument is the number 100,000. If the value of cell Q2 is greater than or equal to 100,000, the result of the comparison is *True*; otherwise, the result is *False*. When the value of cell Q2 is greater than or equal to 100,000, the value the IF function returns is 10 percent of the value contained in cell G2 (10 percent of a salesman's salary). Otherwise, the IF function returns a bonus of 0.

Let us consider a slightly more complex example. Suppose that *what* we wish to compute is described by the following statement: A bonus should be awarded to a salesman only if his total sales are greater than $100,000 *and* his current salary is less than or equal to $50,000. Because the result of the computation will be different, depending on a condition, we must again employ an IF function.

The condition itself requires that two subconditions, (Q2>=100000) and (G2<=50000), both be *True* to receive a bonus. If either or both of the subconditions is *False*, then no bonus is to be awarded. Examination of the truth tables of

Chapter 9 shows that the AND function describes exactly the way the two conditions must be combined for this particular example. Consequently, we may use the formula

=IF((Q2>=100000) AND (G2<=50000), G2*0.10, 0)

to describe how to compute the bonus. (Remember that AND must be written as a function in Works SS—see Exercise Set 11.3.)

In writing this formula we note that the first argument of the IF function must be a logical value. Its form is (Q2>=100000) AND (G2<=50000). Recall AND is a logical operator that returns a logical value, the data type required for the first argument of the IF function. The first input to the AND operator is the comparison operator Q2>=100000 that returns a logical value. The second input for the AND operator is G2<=50000 and is also a comparison operator that returns a logical value. It is clear from this formula that for a bonus other than zero to be awarded the total sales for a salesman must be greater than or equal to $100,000 and the salary must be less than or equal to $50,000. For such cases a value of 10 percent of the current salary will be awarded as a bonus. Otherwise the value of 0 will be returned.

Note that in this example there is a hierarchy of evaluations of functions that must be performed to arrive at the IF function's value. Such a hierarchy of evaluations is called **nesting of functions.** Before you can understand the semantic meaning of such a nesting, you must isolate each argument of the IF function from the next. Looking at the commas that separate the different arguments shows how this is to be done. Next the precedence of evaluation for the comparison and logical operators is applied. Finally, when a *True* or *False* result has been computed, a decision can be made about whether the second or third argument of the IF function is to be evaluated and returned.

Often it is a good practice to construct a truth table for a complicated condition to be sure that all possibilities are considered and that the values computed for each possibility are appropriate. You must thoroughly understand logical operators and their use with the IF function if you are going to perform real-world computations.

SPREADSHEET POWER.   Now you should begin to see a hint of the computational power at your command in a spreadsheet. A given cell in the spreadsheet can reference any other cell or any other set of cells through a formula for the computation of the cell's data object. That cell's value can be used in turn by other cells to compute additional information. Thus, a long and complex sequential computation can be constructed with one intermediate step (computational result) following another. One cell's values are fed into another, whose value feeds another, and so on. Thought of in this manner, the formula in a cell of a spreadsheet is similar to an instruction in a programming language. A group of cells can then work together in turn to solve a complex problem just as a program's individual steps can solve a complex problem. The process of constructing a spreadsheet solution is therefore similar to the process of constructing a program. However, although the user of a spreadsheet must do the same kind of thinking about a problem that a programmer would, the spreadsheet environment hides much of the complexity necessary to program the solution in a programming language.

It now should be clear to you that the process of entering even complex formulas into a spreadsheet is intuitively clear to most users because of the direct analogy between the syntax and semantic meaning of spreadsheet formulas and algebraic formulas as discussed earlier. Once you specify *what* you wish to compute as a series of formulas that you write down, this direct translation process allows you to describe *how* to do it in a spreadsheet's specific syntax.

Exercise Set 12.1

1. Give some examples of built-in functions. How do they differ from the kinds of formulas that a user would normally construct?
2. Why is a black box a good model for a built-in function?
3. What information is required before a built-in function can be used in a spreadsheet?
4. Is it possible to nest expressions in a function argument? Explain.
5. For what purpose is the IF built-in function used? Draw a diagram that illustrates how it works.
6. What kind of data type is required for the first argument of the IF function?
7. Why is it often useful to employ the logical operators AND, OR, and NOT when using the IF function?
8. Describe a problem for which the IF function would return a logical result rather than a numerical result.

12.2 BUILT-IN FUNCTIONS IN WORKS SS

Works SS provides 54 different built-in functions that are available to you for problem solving. These functions are too numerous to describe fully or even list completely here. However, you may examine the name of each of the Works SS functions by selecting the *Paste Function* command of the **Edit** menu. (See Figure 10.5 for a list of all menu commands.) As we have previously discussed, you must also know the arguments that are required to use a function in addition to its name. You may determine the arguments required by looking up the function definition in the Works manual or using the following restricted list. In the following compilation of built-in functions you may encounter several functions whose purpose is unfamiliar to you or whose usage you are uncertain about. This is expected, given the sophisticated level of problem solving that is possible in a spreadsheet. Should you be required to use a given built-in function to solve a problem, your instructor will provide sufficient background describing its use in a specified problem area. It is the authors' intention in the following to inform the reader of the existence of these built-in functions in Works SS and to provide sufficient information for the knowledgeable reader to call upon a given function.

SELECTED MATHEMATICAL BUILT-IN FUNCTIONS.   Some **mathematical functions** follow.

EXP(*number*)   computes *e* to the power *number*.

LN(*number*)   computes logarithm, base *e*, of *number*.

LOG10(*number*)	computes logarithm, base 10, of *number*.
MOD(*number, divisor*)	computes remainder after *number* is divided by the *divisor*.
RAND()	computes a random number between 0 and 1; note that this function has no argument.
ROUND(*number, # of digits*)	computes *number* rounded to the number of digits, *# of digits*.
SIGN(*number*)	+1 or -1, dependent on the sign of the *number*— +1 if number >=0, -1 if number < 0.
SQRT(*number*)	computes the square root of *number*.

SELECTED TRIGONOMETRIC FUNCTIONS. Arguments to the **trigonometric functions** sine, cosine, and tangent functions are assumed by Works SS to be expressed in radians. Values returned by the arcsine, arccosine, and arctangent are expressed in radians. The function DEGREES will return the number of degrees, given a value in radians. The function RADIANS will return the number of radians, given a value in degrees.

ACOS(*number*)	Computes arccosine of *number*.
ASIN(*number*)	Computes arcsine of *number*.
ATAN(*number*)	Computes arctangent of *number*.
COS(*number*)	Computes cosine of *number*, where *number* is in radians.
DEGREES(*number*)	Converts *number* in radians to degrees.
RADIANS(*number*)	Converts *number* in degrees to radians.
SIN(*number*)	Computes sine of *number*, where *number* is in radians.
TAN(*number*)	Computes tangent of *number*, where *number* is in radians.

LOGICAL FUNCTIONS. The following are the **logical functions.**

AND(*V1, V2,...,VN*)	1(*True*) if all *V1, ..., VN* are not zero; 0 (*False*) otherwise.
OR(*V1, V2,...,VN*)	1(*True*) if any of *V1, ..., VN* is not zero; 0 (*False*) otherwise.
IF(*value, # if true, # if false*)	*# if true*, if *value* is not zero; *# if false*, if *value* is zero.
NOT(*V1*)	1(*True*) if *V1* is zero; 0 (*False*) otherwise.

FINANCIAL FUNCTIONS. In the following **financial functions,** *rate* is expressed as a decimal value and is the interest rate for the number of periods, *nper. PV* is the present value, *FV* is the future value, and *PMT* is the periodic constant payment amount. *Type* contains a value of 1 or 0 to select, respectively, between payments at the beginning of the payment period or at the end of the payment period. If *type* is not included as an argument, then its value is assumed to be 0. The arguments

PV, *FV*, and *PMT* use the following cash flow convention: cash received is considered positive, and cash paid out is considered negative.

FV(*rate,nper,pmt,pv,type*)	Computes the future value at a compounded interest rate (*rate*), of payment periods (*nper*), payment amount (*pmt*), and present value (*pv*). *Type* is 0 or 1 as discussed earlier.
PV(*rate,nper,pmt,fv,type*)	Computes the present value needed to reach a given future value (*fv*) with compounded interest rate (*rate*) in payment periods (*nper*) with payment amount (*pmt*). *Type* is 0 or 1 as discussed earlier.
NPER(*rate,pmt,pv,fv,type*)	Computes the number of payments necessary to reach a given future value (*fv*) given the present value (*pv*) with periodic payment amount (*pmt*) at a compounded interest rate (*rate*) per period. *Type* is 0 or 1 as discussed earlier.
PMT(*rate,nper,pv,fv,type*)	Computes the periodic payment amount required to reach the future value (*fv*) from the present value (*pv*) in the number of payments (*nper*) with a compounded interest rate (*rate*). *Type* is 0 or 1 as discussed earlier.
RATE(*nper,pmt,pv,fv,type,g*)	Computes the interest rate per period that is required to reach the future value (*fv*) from the present value (*pv*) in the number of payments (*nper*) with periodic payments (*pmt*). *Type* is 0 or 1 as discussed earlier. The argument (*g*) is an initial guess at the expected value for this interest rate. RATE uses an iterative process involving subsequent guesses to arrive at its results. This process may not always converge to a correct value. If not, the function reports an error and you may need to try a different value for *g*.

STATISTICAL FUNCTIONS. For the following **statistical functions** there may be any number of arguments *V1*, ..., *VN*. Often it is desirable to select a range of values for the arguments by clicking on the first member of the range dragging to the last member then releasing the mouse button. Entries entered in this way show in a *range form*. For example, if cells A1 to A10 were selected by dragging, then the argument would appear as A1:A10 and would contain 10 cell references. Arguments that contain text or blank values are ignored for each of the following functions. Hence, for example, if the arguments for the average function include one or more blank cells or cells containing textual data as arguments, these cells are not included in the computation of the average—this means that each such cell contributes neither to the count of the number of cells used for the average nor to the total value for summing all the cells.

AVERAGE(*V1, V2, ..., VN*)	Computes the average value of the list of arguments *V1, ..., VN* by summing each value and dividing by the total number of values.
COUNT(*V1, V2, ..., VN*)	Counts the number of arguments that contain nonblank, nontextual values.
MAX(*V1, V2, ..., VN*)	Finds the largest value in the list of arguments *V1, ..., VN.*
MIN(*V1, V2, ..., VN*)	Finds the smallest value in the list of arguments *V1, ..., VN.*
SUM(*V1, V2, ..., VN*)	Sums the values of the arguments *V1, ...,VN.*
STDEV(*V1, V2, ..., VN*)	Computes the standard deviation of the arguments *V1, ..., VN.*
VAR(*V1, V2, ..., VN*)	Computes the variance of the arguments *V1, ..., VN.*

USING BUILT-IN FUNCTIONS. The use of the built-in functions provides you with considerable power from the perspective of your problem solving, because you need not attempt to develop formulas to compute these functions. In fact, it is necessary only to choose the *Paste Function* operation from the **Edit** menu, select the function name of interest, and specify the arguments to the function.

As an example of this procedure using Works SS, let's suppose that we have created the spreadsheet shown in Figure 12.3. The problem we wish to solve requires the computation of the average value of the monthly sales listed. As shown, this average value will be entered into cell E4. To indicate to Works SS that we wish to enter a formula into E4, we type the = symbol shown in the formula bar.

Then under the **Edit** menu select *Paste Function.* The dialog box in Figure 12.4 will be displayed. Point to the function name AVERAGE and click; this function becomes highlighted as shown in Figure 12.4. Click on the *OK* button and the name AVERAGE() will be inserted into the formula bar. Note that the insertion pointer will be positioned *between* the parentheses. Works is now ready for you to enter the arguments to use in computing the average.

To specify the values to use for the average, we will use range selection. Click on cell B2 and drag to cell G2. Then release the button. A retangular box will

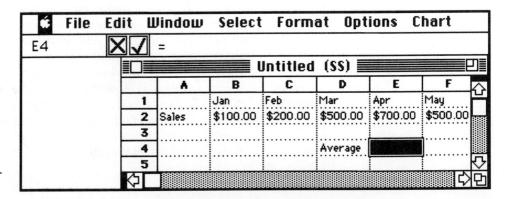

Figure 12.3 Sample worksheet for calculating average values.

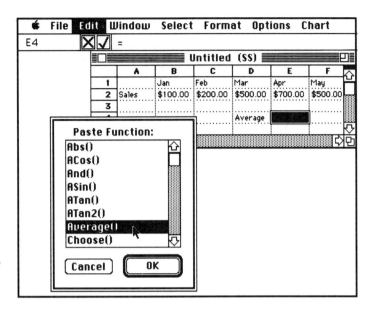

Figure 12.4 Using the *Paste* function under the Edit menu.

appear as shown in Figure 12.5 that surrounds the area actually selected. This range of cells B2:G2 is automatically entered as the arguments for the average function, as is shown in the formula bar in Figure 12.5.

Finally, when the check box is selected to enter the formula, the average value is computed as shown in Figure 12.6. Note that this process would have been the same if a range of 100 or even 1000 cells had been required!

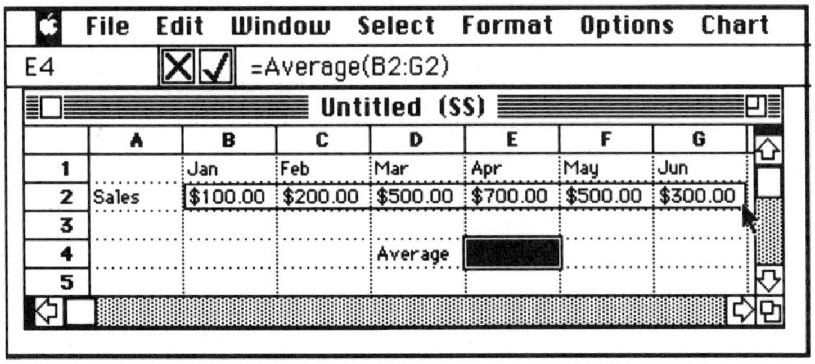

Figure 12.5 Selecting a range of cells for an average by dragging.

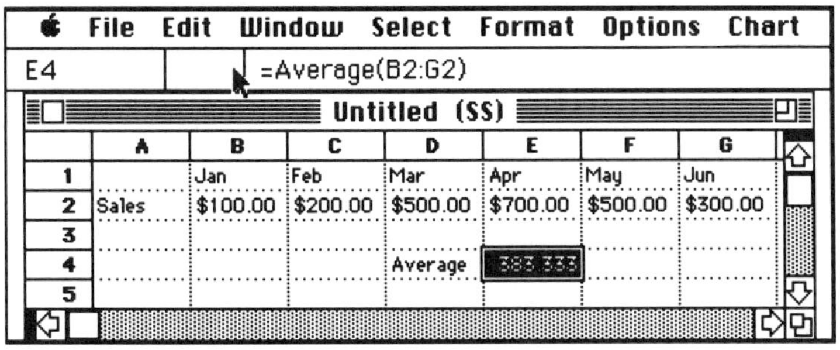

Figure 12.6 Result of computing the average sales value.

	File Edit Window Select Format Options Chart

| C9 | ⊠☑ | =FV(C6,C8*12,−C4,−C3,0) |

Savings (SS)

	A	B	C	D	E
1		Future Value of Savings			
2					
3		Principal	1000		
4		Monthly Payment	100		
5		Yearly Interest Rate	0.06		
6		Interest Rate per Month	0.005		
7					
8		Number of Years	10		
9		Accumulated Savings	$18207.33		
10					

Figure 12.7 Example problem solution using built-in function FV.

As a final example of the use of a built-in function, let us compute the future value of a bank account. Let us assume that we start with the present value of $1000 and that we make monthly payments of $100. Finally, assume that the interest rate paid is 6 percent per year and that the interest is compounded monthly.

Note that the values of $1000, $100, and 6 percent are representative values that we might wish to change for *what if* considerations. These values are then properly termed parameters of this problem as we defined in Chapter 10. Hence, we should reserve places on the spreadsheet where we may place these numbers, labeling them clearly. In the sample spreadsheet of Figure 12.7 we have placed the labels for these values in column B. We have done this by clicking on cell B3 and dragging down to cell B5 and releasing the mouse button. Then we typed the entry *Principal*, pressed the *Tab*, typed *Monthly Payment*, pressed *Tab*, typed *Yearly Interest Rate*, and clicked on the *Check* box. We next entered the actual numerical values in column C using this same method. Note that 6 percent has been entered as the decimal value 0.06.

Next we need to compute the future value. We specify the time at which future value is to be computed—set at 10 years as shown in cell C8. Clearly, this number could be altered for any number of years desired. To compute the future value given this information, we recall that there is a built-in function in Works SS called FV() and that this function has five arguments: interest rate per period, number of periods, payment per period, present value of amount saved, and type.

Because we wish to place the future value under the year for which it is computed, we make cell C9 the active cell. We then type = to indicate to Works SS that a formula is being entered into this cell. Finally, we choose *Paste Function* from the **Edit** menu, and scroll down to find the function FV. Double-click on FV. The function name *FV* will be inserted into cell C9 after the equal sign, and the insertion pointer will be positioned between the parentheses just as in the previous example. We next explain how to set up the values to use for each argument of function FV.

Argument 1—*Interest rate per payment period*. Because the interest will be compounded monthly based on a yearly interest rate of 6 percent, we must compute the interest rate per month or 6 percent/12 = 0.005. We place the formula =C5/12 into cell C6 for this computation. The data-object value in cell C6 will then automatically change if we change the yearly interest rate in cell C5. The label *Interest Rate per Month* has been entered in cell B6. The value of cell C6 should be the value used for argument1 of the function FV. To insert this cell address for the first argument, while the cursor is placed between the parentheses, move the cell pointer to cell C6 and click. Because a formula entry is active, the cell name C6 will be inserted between the parentheses. Type a comma. This completes the entry of the first argument of the function FV.

Argument 2—*Number of payment/compounding periods.* We next will compute the number of periods for the number of years in question. With the insertion pointer positioned just after the comma as earlier, we type C8*12, followed by a comma. This completes entry of the second argument. Because C8 contains the number of years for the computation and the second argument of FV *must* contain the total number of monthly periods in the number of years specified, we have multiplied C8 times 12.

Argument 3—*Periodic payment amount.* Each month we will make a payment of C4 dollars to the savings account. To maintain agreement with the cash flow convention discussed in the financial function section of this chapter, we enter –C4. (Recall that the negative sign indicates this is a payment.) The entry is completed by typing a comma.

Argument 4—*Present value of savings.* We started the account with the amount contained in C3. Because this is money paid *into* the savings account, we must make it negative. Thus, we enter the value -C3 and type a comma to separate the fourth argument from the last argument. This completes the entry of the fourth argument.

Argument 5—*Type.* We assume that the interest will be paid at the end of the month in question; thus, the value 0 is entered here.

This completes the entry of the formula in cell C9; thus, we click on the check box to the left of the formula and out comes the result of the computation for the future value after 10 years.

Actually, to make things look better, we selected *Dollar* under the **Format** menu to format the data object for cell C9. That produced the $ sign. Choosing *Number of Decimals* equal to two under the **Format** menu produced the two decimals after the decimal point shown in C9. Commas could also have been entered if desired. Note the form of the formula that appears in the formula bar.

Exercise Set 12.2

1. Suggest uses for the Works built-in functions in each of the categories listed in this section.

2. What Works SS built-in function would you use to find the average value of a group of 100 contiguous table entries? Why would this function be more convenient to use than developing your own formula for computing the average?

3. Assuming that several entries are empty in the table of exercise 2 above, is there any problem in computing the average value using the built-in function? Explain. Would this be a problem in developing your own formula for computing the average? Explain.

4. Arguments of the trigonometric functions in Works are assumed to be specified in what units?

5. What convention is assumed in Works concerning the sign of argument values that represent dollar amounts in financial functions such as FV, PV, and so on?

6. What is the purpose of the argument g in the financial built-in function RATE?

Computer Practice 12.2

1. Use the Works SS built-in logical functions to evaluate the following two logical functions to see if they are equal. (*Hint*: if the truth tables for each function are the same, then the functions are equal.)

   $f(w, x, y, z) = $ NOT (OR (AND (w, x), AND (y, z))))

   $g(w, x, y, z) = $ AND (OR (NOT (w), NOT (x)), OR (NOT (y), NOT (z))))

2. Use the data in exercise 8 of Computer Practice 11.5 to compute the average and standard deviation of the inflation rate for the year range from 1988 to 2000.

3. Exclude entries for 1989, 1990, 1991 in exercise 2 and see if the average and standard deviation are computed properly. (Recall that because of the way that the average function works, clearing entries for these years will simply exclude them from consideration in the average computation.) Obtain the formula for the standard deviation from your instructor and check the worksheet result using a hand calculator.

4. Find the prices of several automobiles that you would really like to own. Set up a spreadsheet to compute the monthly payment you would have to make assuming that you make a $1000 down payment, need a five-year loan, and can obtain a 10 percent interest rate. (Note that this can be a very depressing problem—but not as depressing as exercise 6!)

5. Alter the worksheet of exercise 4 so that you can perform *what if* analysis by changing the interest rate, number of years, and/or down payment and see the results with each new set of parameters.

6. Find the prices of several houses that you would like to own. Assume that you can make a $10,000 down payment, qualify for a 30-year mortgage payment, and obtain a 10 percent interest rate. Set up a spreadsheet that will allow you to determine your monthly payment. (Don't faint when you see the answers!)

7. Alter the worksheet of exercise 6 so that you can perform *what if* analysis by changing the interest rate, number of years, and/or down payment and see the results with each new set of parameters.

8. Suppose that you currently have $10,000 saved. You would like to turn this amount into $100,000 in 10 years through investment. What rate of interest would you require on your investment?

9. As discussed earlier, the RAND function has a range from 0 to 1. If properly implemented in a spreadsheet, it should uniformly distribute its values over

this range; consequently, its average value for a large number of trials should be close to 1/2. Construct a two-dimensional table to compute the Rand function in which 100 values run down each of 10 columns. Average each column of 100 values and place the average in row 101 under its respective column. Determine the average and standard deviation of the 10 different column average values obtained. What do these results suggest about the Works implementation of the RAND function?

10. Use the charting features of Works SS to graph the function COS(X) for $0 \leq x \leq 2\pi$ radians. Works SS provides the function PI() to compute π.

11. Use the charting features of Works SS to graph the functions COS(X) and SIN(X) for $0 \leq x \leq 2\pi$ radians on the same graph.

12.3 INTEGRATING THE SPREADSHEET CONCEPTS

The discussion of this section will focus on integrating several of the concepts we have presented in this and earlier chapters to **design a worksheet** to solve a useful example problem. As you work through this section, a fundamental decision that must be made repeatedly is the choice of the kind of cell reference to use. The concepts of absolute and relative cell reference for formulas and how to translate an algebraic formula into a spreadsheet formula have been previously discussed in Chapter 11. You may wish to review them before continuing with this section.

Because we usually want sheet-level editing of the worksheet to preserve the relationships of cells, we will often choose relative reference in developing cell formulas. Departures from this convention will be discussed fully. Thus, although we will not state the preceding assumption explicitly when we write down a formula, we are nonetheless making such an implicit decision with each cell we reference in a formula. Recall that this decision can have profound consequences at a later time when we replicate a formula or reposition cells on the worksheet.

It is now time to explore solving a complete problem with Works SS. Let us suppose that you are managing a small company. (We choose a small one so we don't have to show too large a worksheet.) As the manager, you must compute the gross pay, net pay, and deductions for each employee. In addition, some employees work overtime. As such, any hours over 40 per week must be paid at some increased rate; let us assume double time (100 percent *increase* over normal hourly rate). We will also assume for simplicity that deductions for taxes, social security, and so on, are all computed at 40 percent of gross pay. This then describes *what* we want to do in general terms. As we work through this problem we will have to refine some of the preceding discussion to translate it into spreadsheet formulas as we discussed in the last chapter.

Given this general description of the problem, we can now choose the *form* of the worksheet. It would be desirable to have a table organization in which we list the employee name, hourly pay rate, total number of hours worked, gross pay, deductions, and net pay. Thus, six columns having titles similar to the preceding items will be required. Also certain parameters that we are using in the problem are subject to change. These include the overtime hourly rate increase percentage and the percentage deductions to be used. It is good worksheet design to reserve cells to hold each parameter value. If changes in these parameter values occur,

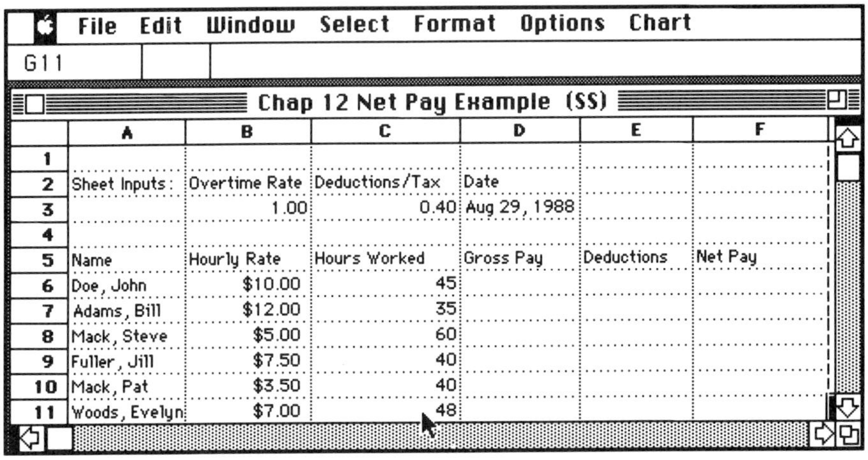

Figure 12.8 Set-up for the net pay worksheet.

because many formulas reference these cells, any changes will automatically propagate to the final answers computed in the worksheet.

Note that it is a dangerous practice to bury parameter values in formulas! It is all too easy to forget which formulas need to be modified to reflect the new assumed values when you haven't used a worksheet for a while. Missing only one formula when you change the assumptions is all it takes for disaster to strike! Important decisions are sometimes based on the results of worksheet computations. *It cannot be overemphasized that care and extreme caution must be exercised in the developing and checking of spreadsheet computations.*

To complete the form of the worksheet we also add the date to allow us to determine to which pay period the worksheet refers. The sample sheet we produce then is shown in Figure 12.8.

To enter the information shown in this worksheet we have simply used the point-and-click method for entries in rows 2, 3, and 5. The *Tab* key was used to move across a row. For the table entries in rows 6 to 11, we have selected the range A6:C11 by pointing and dragging. Then we tabbed between each entry across a row. Remember that the active cell will wrap around within the selected area automatically when the *Tab* key is used! The numbers in the *Hourly Rate* column were formatted using the *Dollar* option under the **Format** menu. Two decimal digits were chosen from the *Number of Digits* option under the **Format** menu. Note that we have entered the overtime percentage increase and percentage deductions using a decimal value in cells B3, and C3. Thus, 100 percent and 40 percent translate to 1.0 and 0.40, respectively, as decimals.

Next, we need to compute the gross pay for each person. To do this we need to write a formula that will compute the correct value in all cases. What are the cases we have to consider?

1. If the number of hours worked is 40 or less, then

$$\text{gross pay} = (\text{hours} * \text{pay rate})$$

2. If the number of hours worked is **not** 40 or less (i.e., number of hours must be greater than 40), then

$$\text{gross pay} = (40 * \text{pay rate}) + (\text{hours} - 40) * (\text{pay rate}) * (1 + \text{overtime rate})$$

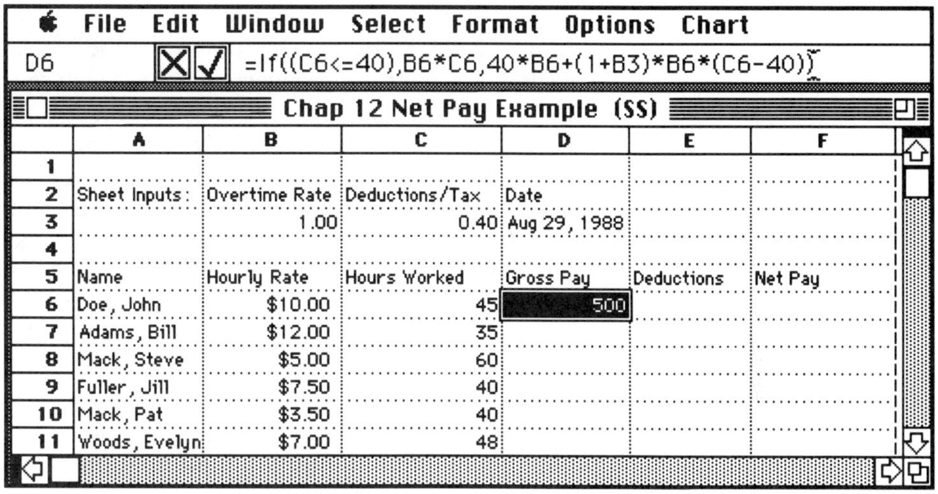

Figure 12.9 Entry of formula to compute gross pay for John Doe.

Clearly, *two* different formulas will be required to compute the gross salary. The one to use will depend upon the answer to the question, "Is the number of hours worked <= 40?" Thus, we need to compare the number of hours worked against the value of 40. We know from Chapters 9 and 11 that the comparison operators are used for that purpose. Based on whether the result of this comparison is *True* or *False*, we use, respectively, the first formula or the second. The condition can then be expressed as

(hours <= 40)

and will result in the value of *True* or *False*.

To select which of the two formulas to use will require the IF built-in function that you learned about earlier in this chapter. The syntax of the Works SS IF function is identical to that presented in the earlier discussion. We show in Figure 12.9 a formula to compute the gross pay for John Doe, the first person in the table.

We entered this formula into the formula bar as follows:

- Cell D6 was selected.
- The = key was pressed—at which time Works SS recognized a formula was being entered.
- IF((was typed.
- Cell C6 was selected, causing the relative reference C6 to be entered into the formula.
- <= 40), was typed.
- Cell B6 was selected, entering a relative reference.
- * was typed.
- Cell C6 was selected, entering a relative reference, and so on.

It is clear that cell B6 is the hourly rate; C6, the hours worked; and B3, the overtime percentage increase for John Doe. Thus, the *True* condition gives the formula B6*C6, and the *False* condition gives the expression 40*B6+(1+B3)*B6*(C6-40).

This formula for John Doe should be replicated into the cells remaining in column D to complete the computation of the gross pay for all employees. This replication is carried out by selecting the range of cells D6:D11 and then selecting *Fill Down* from the **Edit** menu. It produces the results shown in Figure 12.10.

What happened? There is an error in the worksheet cell D8. If you compute the values that should be obtained for the gross pay, you will find that with the exception of the first cell, anyone working more than 40 hours does not get paid enough. (This is not an error you can afford to make if you value your safety!) Clearly, there is something wrong. But what is it?

This is the first example of *many* similar problems you are going to have when using a spreadsheet! *If we had not pointed out this error to you, would you have realized there was an error in this computation?* The way you find the errors is by critically evaluating all the results your worksheet produces. You should never trust spreadsheet results until you have verified them yourself by many simple test computations! The larger the worksheet, the more difficult it is to determine if its results are correct. Scientists doing complex computer modeling have had extensive experience in testing whether or not their models were properly programmed. The rest of us must now learn this difficult process as we too begin to use computers. Validating any computer solution to a problem is a slow, difficult process.

The error in this problem comes from the fact that we used relative reference for *all* cells in the formula. Recall from Chapter 11 that this means a template is formed fixing the position of all cells relative to cell D6. When we shift the formula to cell D8, what cell is used to compute the overtime percentage?

We intended to use cell B3. Unfortunately, if we check the formula for cell D8 we see that because relative reference was employed in the original formula the template has shifted the cell referenced to B5. The formula in cell D8 appears as

IF((40-C6)>=0, B6*C6, 40*B6+(1+B5)*B6*(C6-40))

When we check the contents of cell B5, it contains the textual value *Hourly Rate*. This text value cannot be used for a computation. Unfortunately, Works SS treats this value as zero and proceeds with the computation—subsequently

File Edit Window Select Format Options Chart						
D8		=If((C8<=40),B8*C8,40*B8+(1+B5)*B8*(C8-40))				

Chap 12 Net Pay Example (SS)

	A	B	C	D	E	F
1						
2	Sheet Inputs:	Overtime Rate	Deductions/Tax	Date		
3		1.00	0.40	Aug 29, 1988		
4						
5	Name	Hourly Rate	Hours Worked	Gross Pay	Deductions	Net Pay
6	Doe, John	$10.00	45	500		
7	Adams, Bill	$12.00	35	420		
8	Mack, Steve	$5.00	60	300		
9	Fuller, Jill	$7.50	40	300		
10	Mack, Pat	$3.50	40	140		
11	Woods, Evelyn	$7.00	48	616		

Figure 12.10 Results obtained after replicating cell D6.

	File	Edit	Window	Select	Format	Options	Chart		

D6   `=If((C6<=40),B6*C6,40*B6+(1+$B$3)*B6*(C6-40))`

Chap 12 Net Pay Example (SS)

	A	B	C	D	E	F
1						
2	Sheet Inputs:	Overtime Rate	Deductions/Tax	Date		
3		1.00	0.40	Aug 29, 1988		
4						
5	Name	Hourly Rate	Hours Worked	Gross Pay	Deductions	Net Pay
6	Doe, John	$10.00	45	500		
7	Adams, Bill	$12.00	35	420		
8	Mack, Steve	$5.00	60	400		
9	Fuller, Jill	$7.50	40	300		
10	Mack, Pat	$3.50	40	140		
11	Woods, Evelyn	$7.00	48	392		

Figure 12.11 Corrected absolute reference to cell $B$3 and replication.

giving us the wrong answer. (Excel more appropriately shows an error for this cell's calculation, however!)

Hence, we emphasize again that *the choice of cell reference used in formulas is absolutely critical to the proper function of the worksheet.* To make the replication work correctly we alter the formula in cell D6 to that shown in the formula bar of Figure 12.11. Here we use an absolute reference for cell B3, because all formulas to compute the gross salary must use *this* cell's value and only this cell's value for the percentage increase. Replication of this formula into the cells below it produces a correct computation of the gross salaries.

Next we consider the computation of the deductions for each person. From the problem description, we may set up the following formula to compute each person's deduction:

payroll deduction = (gross salary) * (percent deduction)

	File	Edit	Window	Select	Format	Options	Chart		

E6   `=D6*$C$3`

Chap 12 Net Pay Example (SS)

	A	B	C	D	E	F
1						
2	Sheet Inputs:	Overtime Rate	Deductions/Tax	Date		
3		1.00	0.40	Aug 29, 1988		
4						
5	Name	Hourly Rate	Hours Worked	Gross Pay	Deductions	Net Pay
6	Doe, John	$10.00	45	500	200	
7	Adams, Bill	$12.00	35	420	168	
8	Mack, Steve	$5.00	60	400	160	
9	Fuller, Jill	$7.50	40	300	120	
10	Mack, Pat	$3.50	40	140	56	
11	Woods, Evelyn	$7.00	48	392	156.8	

Figure 12.12 Computation of the payroll deductions.

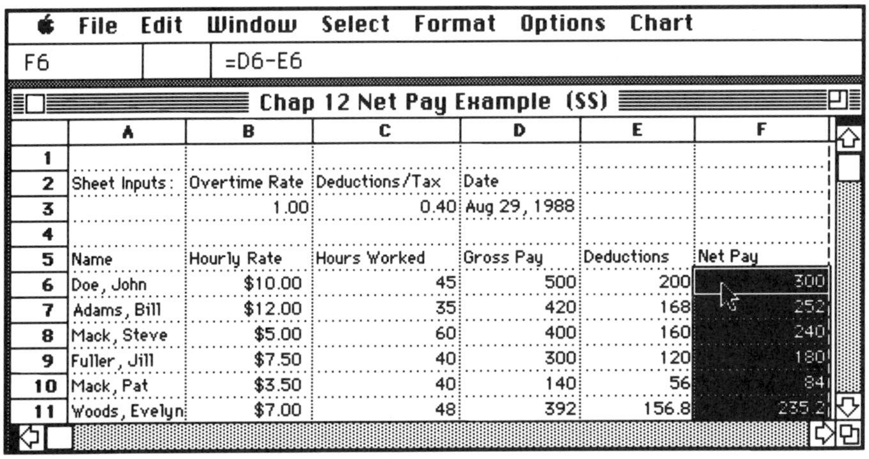

Figure 12.13 Computing the net pay for each employee.

Translating this formula into a worksheet formula to describe John Doe's deductions would then produce =D6*$C$3. We have chosen relative reference for D6 because the gross salary for each person will change. However, learning from our error earlier, we choose absolute reference to the deduction percentage because each person's deduction percentage comes from the same cell. This reference must not change as the formula is replicated. The result of entering and replicating this formula is shown in Figure 12.12.

Finally, we are in a position to compute the net pay for each employee. The formula relating net pay, gross pay, and deductions is given by

$$net\ pay = (gross\ pay) - (deductions)$$

Translating this formula into a worksheet formula for computing John Doe's net pay gives =D6-E6. Note that we use relative reference for each of the cells because they will change for each person in the table. Replicating this formula into each of the remaining cells produces the result shown in Figure 12.13.

With the calculation of the net pay we have completed the basic computations necessary to solve this problem. However, if we examine the worksheet

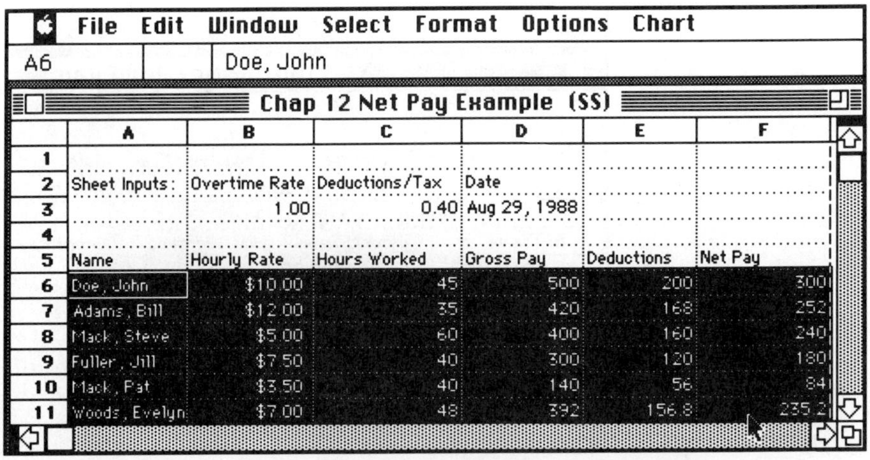

Figure 12.14 Selecting the range for the *Sort* operation.

closely, we notice that the order in which the employees appear is not ideal. It would be more pleasing to list the employees in alphabetical order.

SORT OPERATION. Recall from Chapter 11 that the *Sort* operation for Works SS is found under the **Edit** pull-down menu. To use *Sort* it is first necessary to select the range of items upon which you wish to operate. As noted earlier, this selection must be done carefully because only the group of items you select will be altered as a result of the sort. For example, if only the column of names in Figure 12.13 (column **A**) were selected and then sorted, none of the *other* columns of the table would be altered as a result of the sort. This would mean that the name Bill Adams (the first name alphabetically) would be moved to the top of the list of names in column A. His name would then appear on the same row with John Doe's gross pay, deductions, and net pay. Thus, we would have inadvertently mixed up the names and their correct net pay.

Thus, to sort the table according to employee name we first select all the rows and columns that must be altered by the *Sort* operation. The selection is shown in Figure 12.14. The specification of the column to sort is identical to that performed in Chapter 11 and will not be repeated here. The result of sorting the worksheet by employee name is shown in Figure 12.15.

FORMATTING CELLS. The next operation that you will perform in this example is to format the display of results in cells for the gross pay, net pay, and deductions. If you look closely at the way the results of the last three columns in Figure 12.15 are displayed, you will note that some of the field entries have decimal points in them and some do not. Although the values can be read, they are not uniform in appearance or aesthetically pleasing. Recall that formatting a cell allows you to control the way the information is displayed in that cell. As discussed earlier, Works SS provides an extensive set of formatting options.

To format this worksheet, you first select the range D6:F11. Next select the *Fixed* operation from the **Format** pull-down menu to specify the form of the numbers to be displayed. Then select *Number of Decimals* also under the **Format** menu. Enter 2 in the dialog box that appears to indicate that you wish to display two decimal digits for the cents. These formatting operations will produce the

Figure 12.15 Result of performing the sort.

	File	Edit	Window	Select	Format	Options	Chart
A6			Adams, Bill				

Chap 12 Net Pay Example (SS)

	A	B	C	D	E	F
1						
2	Sheet Inputs:	Overtime Rate	Deductions/Tax	Date		
3		1.00	0.40	Aug 29, 1988		
4						
5	Name	Hourly Rate	Hours Worked	Gross Pay	Deductions	Net Pay
6	Adams, Bill	$12.00	35	420	168	252
7	Doe, John	$10.00	45	500	200	300
8	Fuller, Jill	$7.50	40	300	120	180
9	Mack, Pat	$3.50	40	140	56	84
10	Mack, Steve	$5.00	60	400	160	240
11	Woods, Evelyn	$7.00	48	392	156.8	235.2

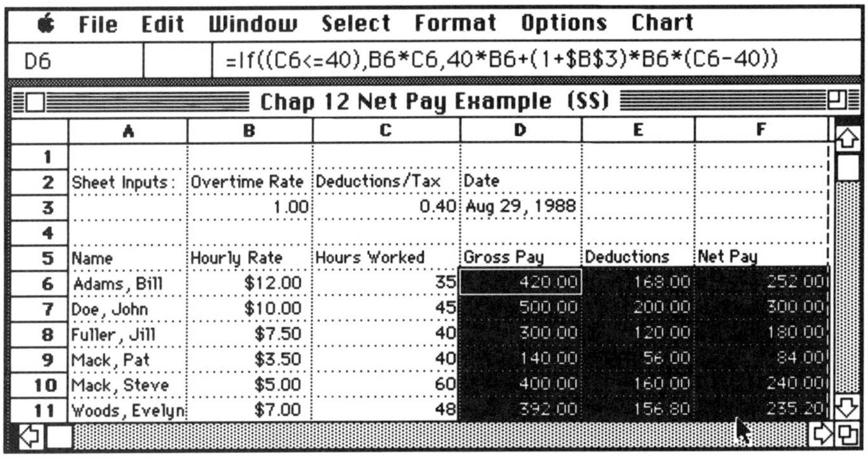

Figure 12.16 Results of formatting the display of data-object values.

form of the worksheet shown in Figure 12.16. Note that this form of the worksheet has a much better appearance and is easier to read and understand.

SUMMING VALUES.   As a final operation on the worksheet, we will compute the sum of the columns for *Gross Pay*, *Deductions*, and *Net Pay*. It is possible to compute these sums by entering a formula referencing each cell in the column. Instead of taking this approach, let us use a built-in function. In the preceding list under statistical functions, we find the function SUM, which totals the values of its arguments. If you select cell D13 as the active cell, activate the **Edit** pull-down menu, choose the *Paste Function* operation, and select SUM() from the list, then the formula =SUM() will be entered into cell D13 as shown in Figure 12.17.

Note that Works SS positions the insertion point in the formula between the parentheses. You are ready, therefore, to enter the arguments for the SUM function.

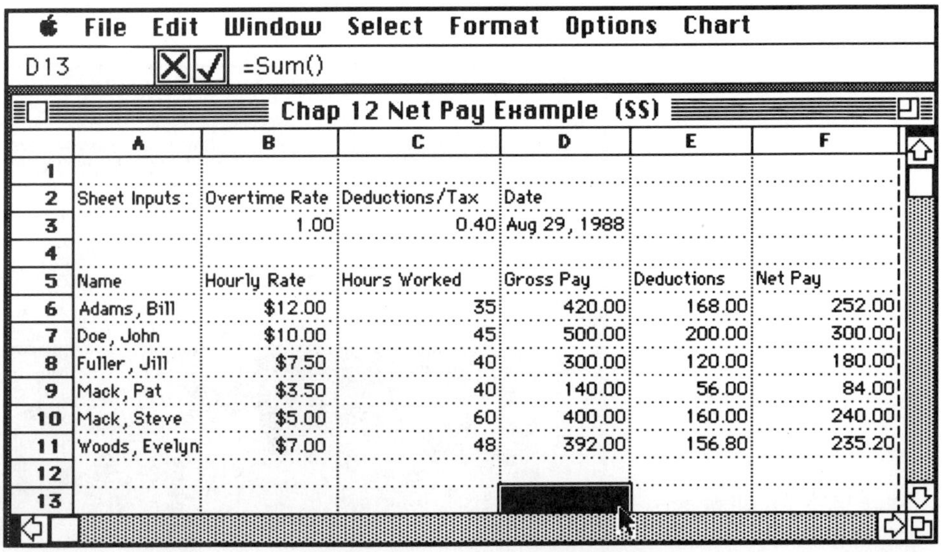

Figure 12.17 Use of the *Paste* function to insert SUM into a cell.

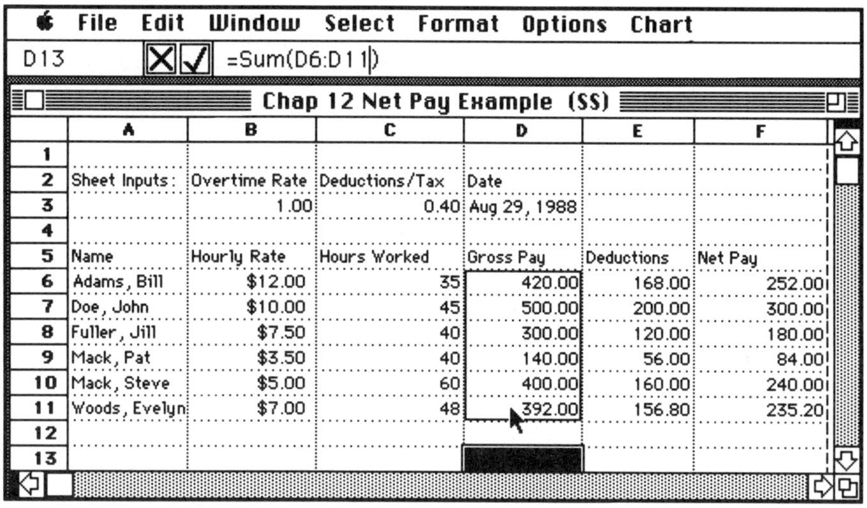

```
 File   Edit   Window   Select   Format   Options   Chart
D13        [X][✓]  =Sum(D6:D11)
```

	A	B	C	D	E	F
1						
2	Sheet Inputs:	Overtime Rate	Deductions/Tax	Date		
3		1.00	0.40	Aug 29, 1988		
4						
5	Name	Hourly Rate	Hours Worked	Gross Pay	Deductions	Net Pay
6	Adams, Bill	$12.00	35	420.00	168.00	252.00
7	Doe, John	$10.00	45	500.00	200.00	300.00
8	Fuller, Jill	$7.50	40	300.00	120.00	180.00
9	Mack, Pat	$3.50	40	140.00	56.00	84.00
10	Mack, Steve	$5.00	60	400.00	160.00	240.00
11	Woods, Evelyn	$7.00	48	392.00	156.80	235.20
12						
13						

Figure 12.18 Selecting the range of cells for the SUM function.

The values for which you wish to compute the sum are those in the range D6:D11. By selecting this range on the worksheet and clicking in the check box, the formula =SUM(D6:D11) will be entered for you. Figure 12.18 shows the result after selection of this range for the SUM function. Selection of this range produces the square box surrounding these cells D6:D11. Clicking the check box causes the computed value to be displayed in cell D13.

Replicating this formula in E13 and F13, by using *Fill Right* under the **Edit** menu, produces the final result shown in Figure 12.19. To make the worksheet nicer to read, the cells holding these totals have been formatted as described earlier. Here we also have used the *Dollar* option under the **Format** menu to produce the forms shown.

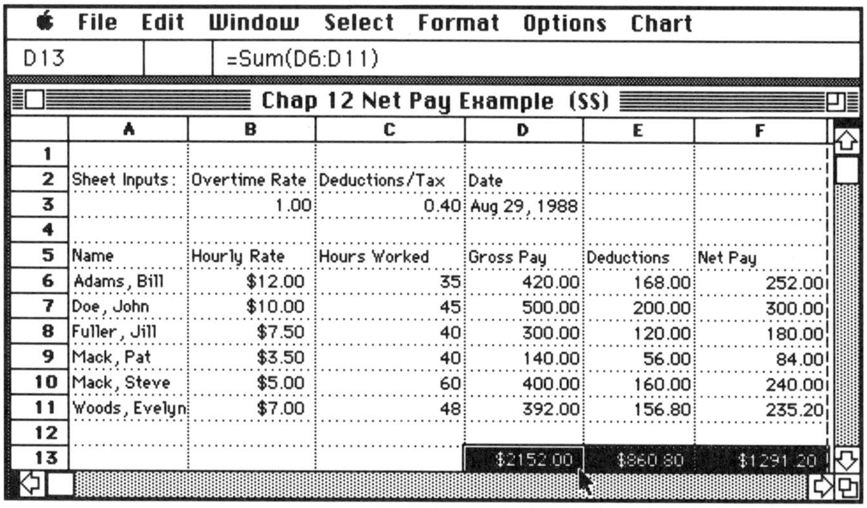

```
 File   Edit   Window   Select   Format   Options   Chart
D13        |  =Sum(D6:D11)
```

	A	B	C	D	E	F
1						
2	Sheet Inputs:	Overtime Rate	Deductions/Tax	Date		
3		1.00	0.40	Aug 29, 1988		
4						
5	Name	Hourly Rate	Hours Worked	Gross Pay	Deductions	Net Pay
6	Adams, Bill	$12.00	35	420.00	168.00	252.00
7	Doe, John	$10.00	45	500.00	200.00	300.00
8	Fuller, Jill	$7.50	40	300.00	120.00	180.00
9	Mack, Pat	$3.50	40	140.00	56.00	84.00
10	Mack, Steve	$5.00	60	400.00	160.00	240.00
11	Woods, Evelyn	$7.00	48	392.00	156.80	235.20
12						
13					$2152.00	$860.80	$1291.20

Figure 12.19 Final worksheet showing totals for each column.

Computer Practice 12.3

1. Using Works SS, construct the *Net Pay Example* worksheet developed in this section.

2. Modify the *Net Pay Example* worksheet to solve the following problem. The employer wishes to reward the workers who have put in overtime with a bonus that is to be added to the employee's salary. The bonus will be awarded based upon the following conditions. If the employee has worked from one to five hours of overtime, the bonus should be $50.00. If the employee has worked more than five hours but 10 or less hours of overtime, the bonus should be $75.00. If the employee has worked more than 10 hours of overtime the bonus should be $100.00. In your solution label the bonus amount and the value computed for it.

3. Suppose you wish to purchase a new home and you want to see how much the payments will be, how fast your equity will increase as you pay off the loan, and what the yearly tax writeoff will be by finding the total amount of interest you paid in a given year. Construct a spreadsheet solution as described in this problem. Print out values of your spreadsheet for years 5, 10, 15, and 20 of the loan.

   Relevant formulas to use are

   a. Monthly payment $= I * A / (1 - V^N)$
   b. Balance after payment number $k = (A / V^k) * ((V^k - V^N) / (1 - V^N))$
   c. Interest amount of payment $k = I *$ Remaining balance for payment k
   d. Principal paid = Monthly payment - Interest for payment k

   In the preceding formulas, I is the interest rate per payment period, A is the amount of the loan, $V = 1 / (1 + I)$, and N is the total number of payment periods. For example, if the yearly interest rate is 12 percent and the length of the loan is 10 years, then $I = 12$ percent$/12 = 1$ percent $= 0.01$ and $N = 120$.

   Set up your spreadsheet as follows to compute the required quantities. Calculate the payment number k shown under the column labeled *Payment Number* so that during the first year the numbers range from 1 to 12, during the second year, from 13 to 24; and so on. These values should be calculated from the number of years elasped since the start of the loan as shown in cell C12. Finally, add a total interest payment for the year in cell C28 to use for income tax purposes. Note the full precision of the calculated values has been used to allow you to check your results. You should format the worksheet cells once you have the correct answers to make the appearance more acceptable.

	A	B	C	D
1				
2			payment schedule	
3				
4	loan amount		80000	
5	interest rate	as decimal	0.16	
6	term in years		20	
7				
8		i	0.0133333333333333	
9		v	0.98684210526316	
10		payment	1113.0047520217	
11		v^n	0.041633322113724	
12		year	1	
13				
14	Payment No.	Balance before payment k	Interest for payment k	Principal for payment k
15	1	80000	1066.6666666667	46.338085355025
16	2	79953.661914645	1066.0488255286	46.955926493092
17	3	79906.705988152	1065.4227465087	47.582005513
18	4	79859.123982639	1064.7883197685	48.216432253173
19	5	79810.907550386	1064.1454340051	48.859318016549
20	6	79762.048232369	1063.4939764316	49.510775590103
21	7	79712.537456779	1062.8338327571	50.170919264638
22	8	79662.366537514	1062.1648871669	50.839864854833
23	9	79611.52667266	1061.4870223021	51.517729719564
24	10	79560.00894294	1060.8001192392	52.204632782491
25	11	79507.804310158	1060.1040574688	52.900694552925
26	12	79454.903615605	1059.3987148747	53.606037146964
27				
28		Total interest this year	12757.354602718	

4. This problem is designed to let you explore a learning curve for psychological experiments. The following formula approximates the probability that an animal or a human subject learns the correct response to a certain stimulus after n trials.

$$L_n = [1 - (1 - C)^{n-1}], n = 1, 2, 3, 4, 5, \ldots$$

Here L_n represents the probability that a subject has learned the correct response before the trial n. C represents the probability that the subject who does not know the correct response to a stimulus learns the correct response on any given trial. (It is assumed that C is independent of the trial number n.) Develop a spreadsheet solution that will allow you to investigate the number of trials necessary for a subject to have a probability of at least 0.95 of learning the correct response to a stimulus. Develop this solution as a table in which the trial number runs down a column of the spreadsheet and various values of C run across the top of the table. Graph your solutions for different values of C as a function of n.

5. In this problem you will investigate population growth. If the population is known to grow at the rate of K percent per year, then the population in the (n+1)st year P_{n+1} can be found from the population in the nth year P_n by the formula

$$P_{n+1} = (1 + K) P_n$$

where K is expressed as a decimal fraction. Different geographical areas have different values of K as shown.

Geographical area	Population (millions)	Growth rate (%)
North America	272	0.7
Latin America	429	2.2
Europe	497	0.3
Africa	623	2.9
Asia	2995	1.8
World	4816	1.7

Develop a spreadsheet solution that will allow you to determine how long it will take each of these different areas to double in their population. Represent your results pictorially as follows. Draw pictures in which each preceding geographical area is represented using MacPaint. Use Works SS to develop a bar chart of the time taken for each area. Cut each bar out of the worksheet and paste it on the proper MacPaint picture.

6. The spread of a disease or a rumor in a population can be approximately modeled by the following formula:

$$I = \frac{n + 1}{1 + ne^{-(k(n+1))\,\text{day}}}$$

Here I is the number of people in the population who are infected (or know the rumor) and are actively spreading the disease/rumor and n = the number of people in the population. Day is the day number since the rumor/disease was started. On day zero the formula becomes:

$$I = \frac{n + 1}{n + 1} = 1$$

Here k is a constant that is determined by the rate at which the disease/rumor spreads. (k is usually a function of n, as you might expect; that is, with more people the rumor/disease tends to spread even faster.) The number e is the base of natural logarithms and is approximately 2.71. Remember that e to a power can be computed using the Works SS function EXP(X). To start, set $n = 100$, $k = 1/200$. Then develop the worksheet to tabulate the number of infected or contacted individuals each day up to 20 days. Next perform *what if* explorations and vary k to see how the contact parameter affects the number of infected people for each of the 20 days. Plot graphs for several examples showing how the number of infected persons changes for different values of k.

Key Concepts

Built-in functions

Financial functions

Design a worksheet

Function arguments

Function as black box
IF function
Mathematical functions
Statistical functions

Function syntax
Logical functions
Nesting of functions
Trigonometric functions

CHAPTER 13

COMMUNICATING USING COMPUTERS

L E A R N I N G   O B J E C T I V E S

- To learn some important computer communication concepts.

- To learn how to create a communications document using the Works communications module.

- To learn to set communication parameters using the Works communications module.

- To learn to capture the text of a communications session using the Works communications module.

- To learn to send and receive files using the Works communications module.

I n this chapter you will learn a number of important communications concepts to be used in a discussion of the Works communications module. You will learn how to use Works to set the parameters for a communications session, to connect your computer to another computer, to transfer information between computers, and to terminate a communications session. If you do not plan to use the Works communications module you can skim this chapter, because it is not essential for the rest of the text.

13.1 SOME USES OF COMPUTER COMMUNICATIONS

Before we begin the study of communications concepts and the details of how to communicate using Works, we will briefly review why people find computer communications valuable. There are, of course, many different reasons for using computer communications.

The information services such as CompuServe, The Source, and Dow Jones provide a vast array of different kinds of information for a fee. News, weather, business, entertainment, travel, and many other kinds of information are available. This information is the latest available, and therefore, exceedingly valuable for some purposes.

Some information services provide electronic mail services that allow users to communicate with each other. In addition, many of these services provide bulletin boards that contain information of special interest for some users. For example, CompuServe has bulletin boards for users of different computers and even particular software packages. If you are a user of a given software package, you can exchange ideas with other users of the package, keep up with the lastest developments with the package, and even transfer software to your computer to improve or enhance the performance of the software package.

To use an information service, you must pay an initial subscription fee, at which time you would be given a password and directions for connecting to the service. Thereafter, the charges are based on how much you use the system.

There are also hundreds of free (or minimal-fee) bulletin board services run by hobbyists. These allow you to communicate with individuals having similar interests. Examples of the kinds of different subjects covered are real estate, genealogy, religion, sports, medicine, humor, games, law, graphics, food, and music. As a user of a bulletin board, in addition to having discussions with other users, you may want to transfer files from the bulletin board to your computer or send one of your files to the bulletin board. Public domain software, which you can copy to your computer, is available from some services and many bulletin boards. With this free software you may be able to use your computer more effectively or to have fun with an interesting game.

You can also use a Macintosh as a terminal to a large mainframe computer. This could, for example, allow you to do some work at home instead of at the office; or if you are a student, you could use your computer as a terminal for working with the college's main computer. These kinds of usage can improve your efficiency.

Information can also be transferred between different kinds of microcomputers. For example, files can be moved between the Macintosh and the IBM PC and compatible personal computers. Because computers of different manufacturers use different formats for writing to disks, direct connection between two computers may be the only convenient way to transfer information from one computer to another.

The preceding list of possible uses of computer communications is only indicative of the kinds of things that you might do. The possibilities are vast, and you will have to become involved to learn how best to use computer communications for your own purposes.

13.2 SOME COMMUNICATIONS CONCEPTS

In this section we will consider several concepts associated with communication between computers using the telephone system. The required components of a communications system is shown in Figure 13.1. The block called *other computer* can be, for example, another Macintosh, a microcomputer of another manufacturer, a mainframe computer, or the computer of an information service. The other computer can be located anywhere that can be reached using the phone system. The line labeled *phone line* represents a connection through the phone system, and it does not imply that there must be a direct line between the computers. (*Note:* Two computers can also be connected directly over an RS-422 or RS-232 common interface without a modem. Recall from Chapter 2 that the Macintosh modem and printer ports are RS-422 common interfaces.)

Let us assume that you are in the process of sending information to the other computer. The **modem** attached to your computer takes digital signals received from your computer and converts them into a form—often tones of different frequencies—suitable for transmission through the telephone system. At the receiving modem the information is converted back into digital signals that can be used by a computer. These processes are called **modulation** and **demodulation**, respectively. This is the origin of the term modem—**mo**dulation and **dem**odulation.

The modems at the two ends of the data transmission link can be of different design, but it must be possible to set various parameters in the modems so that

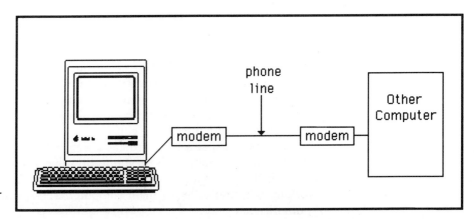

Figure 13.1 Configuration for inter-computer communications.

they behave in the same way. In a later section we will examine the settings allowed by Works. The operation of a modern modem is usually controlled by the computer to which it is attached.

The Works communications module, in turn, controls the computer and its communication with the modem. A similar situation exists at the other computer. Hence, to the users of the computers it appears as though the computers are communicating directly with each other. A hypothetical conversation between the computers using English to represent the control signals might be the following:

Macintosh	*Other Computer*
I am ready to send a file.	
Are you ready to receive?	
	I am ready. Send the file.
Here is the file.	
(Data are relayed.)	
	There was an error in the last block of data. Send it again.
OK. Sending it again.	
(Data are relayed again.)	
	Entire file received without error.
I am finished. Signing off.	
	OK. So long.

As the information is being transmitted between the computers, the machines must agree that an action is allowable. For example, one of the computers may not be able to process the incoming information fast enough and may need to request the other computer to pause temporarily in the communications process to allow it to catch up. Before each significant communications action, the computers signal agreement that the action is permitted. This process is called a **handshake** between the computers. For example, the slower machine, which needs extra time for the processing of the incoming data, does not complete the handshake until it is ready.

The details of how the transmission process will be managed constitute a **protocol**. Although you do not need to know any of the technical details of any protocol, you need to know they exist and when to use a particular protocol. For example, if the communication is between two Macintoshes, a particular protocol is used; if only one of the computers is a Macintosh, a different protocol is used. The number of different protocols supported depends on the communications software. Works supports three protocols: MacBinary, Xmodem text, and Xmodem data. These will be discussed later.

The rate of information transfer over a telephone or telegraph line is called a **baud** in honor of Baudot, a pioneer in telegraph communications. For the purposes of our discussion, you can think of a baud as being equivalent to 1 bit per second. A text character is represented by 7 or 8 bits, depending upon the system being used. A start bit, one or two stop bits, and sometimes a parity bit are also added for the transmission process. Hence, a total of between 9 and 12 bits is required per character transmitted. Baud rates above 110 usually use 10 bits for each character. Thus, dividing the baud rate by 10 gives a reasonable estimate of the number of characters transmitted per second. High baud rates are desirable to reduce transmission times and thus the cost of sending information. A common problem in communications is the failure to set the two modems to the same baud rate, which produces garbled transmissions.

The communications system may be either *half duplex* or *full duplex*. In a half-duplex system information may be transmitted in either direction, but in only one direction at a time. This is analogous to a one-lane bridge on which cars cross in either direction, but in only one direction at a time. A full-duplex system allows simultaneous transmission in both directions, analogous to traffic on a multilane bridge. The system used in a particular situation depends upon both the communications software and the modems. Works supports full-duplex communications.

Echo mode refers to the immediate retransmission of every character by the receiving computer. This has the advantage of allowing the user to verify that the information is being transmitted as planned. If the system is set for echo mode, every character is doubled on the screen of the sending computer. This situation is demonstrated in Figure 13.2 for transmission between two Macintoshes. Works provides an option to accept or reject the echo.

From the user's perspective the communications process can be divided into the following major steps.

- Set the modem parameters for the particular communication.
- Establish a link between the two computers.
- Transfer information in either or both directions. This may involve creating new disk files for received information.
- Break the link between the two computers.

These steps will be discussed in detail for Works, beginning with Section 13.4.

Exercise Set 13.2

1. What is a modem? How many are required for communications between two computers?
2. What are modulation and demodulation?
3. Do the modems used in the communications process have to be of the same design?

JJooee, II aamm rreeaaddyy ttoo ttrraannssffeerr
tthhee ffiillee yyoouu wwaanntteedd. AArree
yyoouu rreeaaddyy??

Figure 13.2 Data transmission with echo.

4. Why is the setting of parameters important for modems?

5. What controls a modem?

6. What is a handshake between computers? Why is it important?

7. What is a communications protocol?

8. Name three communications protocols supported by Works.

9. What is a baud?

10. Approximately how many characters could be transmitted in one second by modems having baud rates of 300, 1200, and 2400, respectively.

11. Suppose you have a file of 100,000 characters. Approximately how long would it take to transfer this file at a rate of 300 baud? Assume 10 bits are used to transmit one character.

12. What is a half-duplex communications system? What is a full-duplex communications system?

13. What is echo mode? Why is it desirable? Why would it be useful to have a modem that can switch the echo mode off?

14. List the major steps in the communications process.

13.3 MODEMS

Modems for the Macintosh are available with a wide range of features at discount prices ranging from approximately $100 to $450. Less expensive modems tend to operate at slower baud rates and to have fewer features. A full-featured modem, known as a **smart modem**, has its own microprocessor and can help with the communications process. Desirable features include:

■ The ability to communicate at a variety of speeds including baud rates of 300, 1200, and 2400. Speed is particularly important for interactions with information services that charge for the time used.

■ The ability to operate in a mode corresponding to the *Hayes AT* standard, a popular modem control language used by many microcomputers. This control language is supported by Works.

■ The ability to dial automatically the modem number of another computer.

■ The ability to answer an incoming call automatically. This allows you to perform other work in Works with your computer while you are waiting for the initiation of communications.

■ The ability to support different communications protocols.

You may encounter modems with few of these features or with all of them. The steps required in Works to connect your computer to another will depend on whether or not your modem has the automatic dialing feature. Without automatic dialing, it will be necessary for you to dial the number manually to establish a link with the other computer. You should determine what features are on any modem available to you.

Exercise Set 13.3

1. What is a smart modem?
2. List the important features of a smart modem.
3. How might an expensive smart modem save a user considerable money relative to the cost of one of the least expensive modems?
4. Why should you determine the features of modems available for your use?

13.4 OVERVIEW OF WORKS COMMUNICATIONS

In this section we look at the Works communications module at an overview level. In addition, the details of how to create and save a communications document are discussed. The sequence of activities involved in communications is presented, but a discussion of the details of each major step is delayed until later sections.

The first step is to start Works using the techniques described earlier. To use the communications module, click the *Communications* icon shown in Figure 13.3. At this point you can open an existing communications document or create a new one. You can have many communications documents, but only one can be open at a time.

CREATING A COMMUNICATIONS DOCUMENT.   To create a new communications document select the *New* command from the **File** menu. When the dialog box of Figure 13.4 is displayed, click the *Communications* icon, and then click the *OK* button.

A Works **communications document** consists of

- A group of stored settings necessary for the communications process.
- A list of telephone numbers that can be dialed automatically.
- An optional document in which all communications will be saved automatically.
- A window for viewing the communications as they occur.

Assuming that you have a Hayes-compatible smart modem, you can have Works dial the telephone number to initiate the communications between the computers. This process is called establishing the physical link between the computers. As you will see later, you can also create a communications document and set the modem to answer when it is contacted.

Figure 13.3 The *Communications* icon.

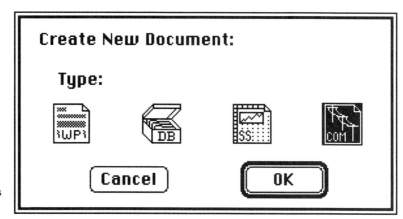

Figure 13.4 Dialog box for creating a communications document.

After the physical link has been established, you may have to perform other actions to ensure that the computers are using the same protocol for the communication process, that they are both using the same baud rate, and so on.

During the communications session you can type messages and you can receive or transmit any number of files. You can use the other Works modules during the communications, letting the communications occur in the background.

SAVING A COMMUNICATIONS DOCUMENT.   The technique for saving a communications document is similar to that for saving other types of documents. Select the *Save* or *Save As* command from the **File** menu. If the *Save As* command is being used, enter a meaningful name in the *Save* dialog box and click the *Save* button.

When a communications document is saved, the settings and telephone numbers are automatically saved. If an optional document has been created to capture the communications text, it will also be saved. The contents of the window for viewing the exchange of information during the communications are not saved.

Finally, when you are finished you may have to break the communication link and then hang up the telephone. The term *break the communication link* means to complete a sequence of steps that tell the other computer that you have finished the communication. This is important for information services that are charging for the time you are connected to them because hanging up the phone may not disconnect you from the service. The procedure is different for the various information services, so you need to learn it for each of the services you are using. In the case of direct communication between Macintoshes or other microcomputers, hanging up the phone is normally sufficient.

Exercise Set 13.4

1.   How do you start the communications module?
2.   What are the components of a communications document?
3.   Give the steps for creating a communications document.

4. During a communications session with Works are the activities restricted to the communications? Explain.

5. Give the steps for saving a communications document.

6. What is saved when a communications document is saved?

Computer Practice 13.4

1. If a folder named *Learning Microsoft Works* is available on your system:

   ■ Find the *Learning Microsoft Works* icon and double-click it.

   ■ Follow the directions given by the program until the main menu appears that contains a series of options in long oval boxes. Click the oval that contains *Communications*.

   (**Communications**)

   ■ Follow the instructions given by the program and you will be led through a simulated communications session that will give you much insight into the discussion in this chapter.

2. In this practice you will start Works' communication module, look at the *Communications Setting* dialog box, and name the communications document. Proceed as follows:

   ■ Open Works and click the *Communications* icon.

   ■ Select the *New* command from the **File** menu.

   ■ Look at the *Communications Settings* dialog box, but do not change any settings. This window will be discussed in detail in the next section.

   ■ Click the *OK* button on the window. A blank communications document name *Untitled (CM)* will be displayed.

   ■ Select the *Save As* command from the **File** menu. Enter the name *practice 13.4* and click the *Save* button. This document will be used in the practice at the end of the next section.

   ■ Quit Works by selecting the *Quit* in the **File** menu.

13.5 THE COMMUNICATIONS SETTINGS DIALOG BOX

As soon as a new communications document is created, the *Communications Settings* dialog box of Figure 13.5 is displayed. (Also, the dialog box can be displayed at any time during a session by selecting the *Settings* command from the **Communications** menu.) This dialog box can also be accessed at any time by selecting the *Settings* command of the **File** menu. The appropriate buttons should be clicked to correspond to the particular communications session. To make the correct settings, you will have to know what the receiving modem and/or computer require. Information services will supply the required settings when you subscribe to them. For other situations ask about the settings if that is possible. Otherwise you will have to experiment by trying the possible choices to find the correct settings.

BAUD RATE.   Select the baud rate that corresponds to that used by the modem of the other computer. This will probably be a value of 300, 1200, or 2400 baud. The higher settings, above 2400, are normally used when the Macintosh is emulating a terminal and is connected directly to a computer without the need for a modem. We note, however, that modems for personal computers that operate at 9600 baud are now available. Remember that failure to select the same rate as that used by the receiving modem will result in garbled transmission.

DATA SIZE.   Characters are represented within the Macintosh using 8 bits per character. However, Works can transmit the characters using either 7 or 8 bits per character. The choice of data size will depend upon the requirements of the receiving computer. Data size will also be affected by whether or not a parity bit (see the following discussion of parity) is used.

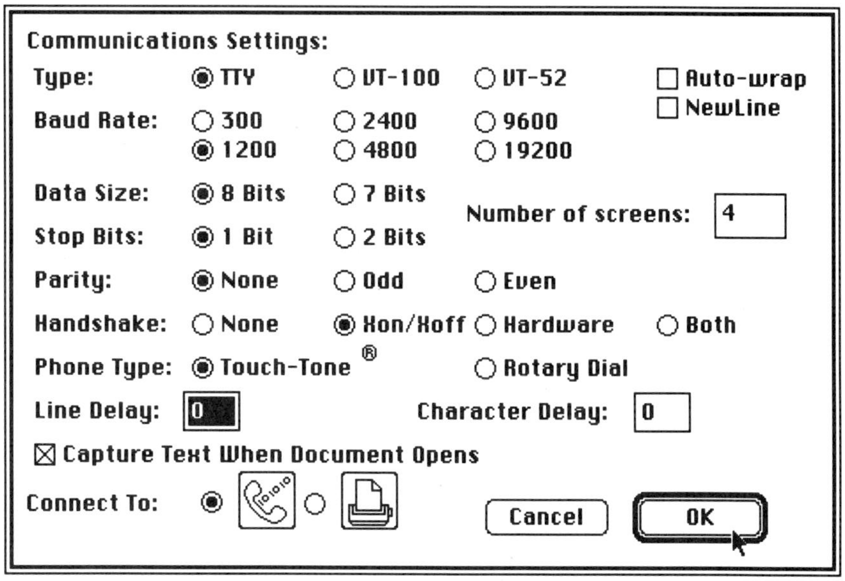

Figure 13.5 The *Communications Settings* dialog box.

STOP BITS. An extra bit, called a stop bit, is attached to the end of each transmitted character. Some computers require two stop bits per character.

PARITY. A **parity** bit is an extra bit attached to the binary representation of a character for error-checking purposes. For odd parity, the parity bit is set to 0 or 1 to make the total number (including the parity bit) of 1 bits odd. For even parity, the parity bit is set to make the total number of 1 bits even. The types of parity are illustrated in Figure 13.6 for the character *A*. Information services tend not to use a parity bit.

For transmissions that use parity, a 0 or 1 is added at the source computer to produce a grouping of bits having, for example, even parity. At the receiving computer each grouping of bits is checked to see if it has the expected parity, in this case even parity. If the parity is wrong, an error has occurred during the transmission that changed one or more bits in the group. The receiving computer can then request that the data be sent again.

HANDSHAKE. Recall that handshaking refers to the way communicating computers synchronize the transmission of data. Again, you will need to know what the other computer is expecting. The handshaking can be done by the software, the hardware, or both. If high data transmission rates, 2400 baud or greater, are to be used, handshaking will be required. The Xon/Xoff handshaking is used by most information services.

LINE DELAY/CHARACTER DELAY. In some cases it is very difficult to send and receive data without errors occurring; for example, one computer can send information when the other computer is not looking for it. It may help to introduce a time delay between each line sent and/or each character sent. The line delay and character delay options are used to introduce these time delays. Integers entered in these blocks correspond to delays in units of 1/60 of a second. For example, entering a 5 in the character delay box produces a delay of 5/60 seconds between each character.

CONNECT TO. Ordinarily the modem should be attached by a cable to a modem port. (See the discussion of Chapter 2.) In some circumstances, the modem port

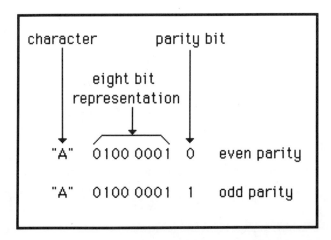

Figure 13.6 Illustration of the types of parity.

may be used already for attaching some other device. In this case, the printer port can be used for attaching the modem. Select the proper port in the *Setting* dialog box by clicking the appropriate button.

TYPE.   The type refers to the kind of terminal that Works is emulating in this session. The default type is TTY, which corresponds to a teletype or dumb terminal. Works can also emulate two other terminals, the Digital Equipment Company terminals VT-100 and VT-52.

NUMBER OF SCREENS.   The *Number of Screens* feature allows a user to save some number of the most recent screens in RAM. The default value of 4 means that the contents of the four most recent screens are saved in RAM and can be examined by scrolling with the scroll arrows or box. As new information is received during a communications session, it is placed at the bottom. A corresponding amount of the oldest information is displaced from the top and is no longer available for viewing. If zero is selected as the number of screens, you will still be able to see information being transferred on the screen, but you will not be able to scroll to see information that has passed off the screen. If you attempt to specify more screens than can be saved in RAM, a warning message will be displayed and Works will use the maximum number of screens that it can save.

CAPTURE TEXT WHEN DOCUMENT OPENS.   In some sessions, it is desirable to save in a disk file a copy of all the text displayed during the communications. Clicking the *Capture Text When Document Opens* box causes Works to enter a capture text mode immediately when a session is started. The name of a file is requested for saving the text. If the box is not checked, no text capture occurs unless the *Capture Text* command is selected under the **Communications** menu. This command is discussed in detail in Section 13.6.

Exercise Set 13.5

1.   What is the purpose of the baud rate setting? What will happen if the baud rate settings are different for the sending and the receiving computers?
2.   What is the purpose of the data size setting?
3.   What is a stop bit? What settings are possible for Works?
4.   What is a parity bit? Do all communications systems use parity bits? Give examples of the two kinds of parity.
5.   What options are provided by Works for handshaking? When should Xon/Xoff handshaking be used?
6.   When should the line and character delay options be used? What is the unit of the line and character delay?
7.   What options are provided for selecting a communications port? Which port should normally be selected?
8.   What does the *Type* option do?
9.   What valuable feature is provided by the *Number of Screens* option? What happens if too many screens are requested?

Computer Practice 13.5

1. Open Works and click the *Communications* icon.
2. Select in the scroll box the document named *practice 13.4.* Open the document. The *Communications Settings* dialog box should be displayed.
3. Make the following settings by clicking the appropriate buttons. In some instances the default value of a feature is the same as the requested setting.
    - Type: TTY
    - Baud Rate: 2400
    - Data Size: 8 bits
    - Stop Bits: 1 bit
    - Parity: none
    - Handshake: Xon/Xoff
    - Phone Type: Touch-tone
    - Line Delay: 0
    - Character Delay: 0
    - Connect To: phone
4. Click the *OK* button on the *Communications Settings* dialog box. The *Communications* window named *practice 13.4* should be displayed.
5. Save the communications document as *practice 13.5* by selecting the *Save As* command from the **File** menu and entering the new name in the *Save* box. Click the *Save* button.
6. Quit Works by selecting the *Quit* command in the **File** menu.

13.6 MAKING THE COMMUNICATIONS CONNECTION

When all the parameters on the *Communications Settings* dialog box have been set, clicking the *OK* button causes the dialog box to disappear and an empty communications window to be opened.

Suppose that we want to connect our computer to the computer at the Universal On-line News and Services information service. Further, suppose we want to save in a disk file all that occurs during the communications session. We must indicate that we want to make a record in a disk file of the text displayed during a communications session (i.e., capture text) and dial the telephone of the other computer.

CAPTURE TEXT COMMAND. If one selects the *Capture Text* command in the **Communications** menu (see Figure 13.7), the dialog box of Figure 13.8 will be displayed. In the *Save Captured Text As* box, the default name *Captured Text* will be displayed. If a different name is not typed into the box, a file will be created called *Captured Text* in which everything received will be saved. In our example, the name *Universal On-line News* has been entered for this particular communications session. You can click the *Capture* button on the dialog box to complete the command to capture text.

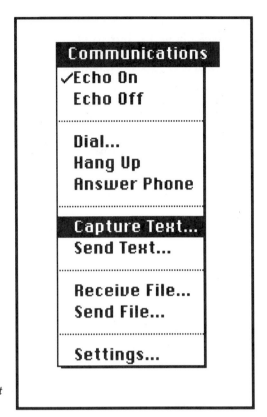

Figure 13.7 The *Capture Text* command.

The *Capture Text* command, which switches with the *End Text Capture* command, can be given at any time during a communications session. For example, *Capture Text* could be used to capture text early in the session; then the *End Text Capture* command could be given to stop the capture of text. These commands can be used repeatedly during the session.

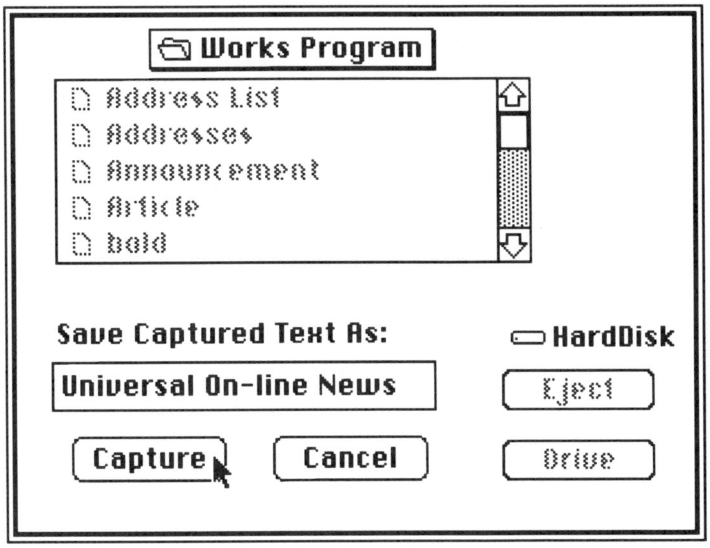

Figure 13.8 The *Capture Text* dialog box.

DIAL COMMAND. Select the *Dial* command from the **Communications** menu. This will cause a telephone list box to be displayed as shown in Figure 13.9. Because this is a new communications document, the telephone list box would be empty. We have typed the name and telephone number of the information service into the telephone list.

A telephone number can consist of 50 or fewer characters, which is long enough for even an international number and a password. Hyphens, spaces, slashes, and parentheses are ignored by Works (if a Hayes compatible modem is used) and can be used to make the numbers more readable. The following are all equivalent:

    12125550001
    1 212 555 0001
    1 (212) 555-0001
    1-(212)-555-0001
    1-212-5550001
    1-212-555-0001

Commas can be used to introduce delays of approximately two seconds per comma. This is useful, for example, when it is necessary to dial 9 to get an outside line. For example, the entry 9,,1-212-555-0001 could be used to dial an outside line, wait four seconds for getting the outside line, and then dial the number of the information service.

To dial the other computer, click the *Dial* button beside the name of the information service. If the modem is a Hayes-compatible smart modem, the telephone number will be dialed. If the modem has a speaker, you will be able to hear the number being dialed. If the modem is not Hayes compatible, the *Dial* command cannot be used. It will be necessary for you to consult the reference manual for your modem to obtain directions about making a connection with another computer.

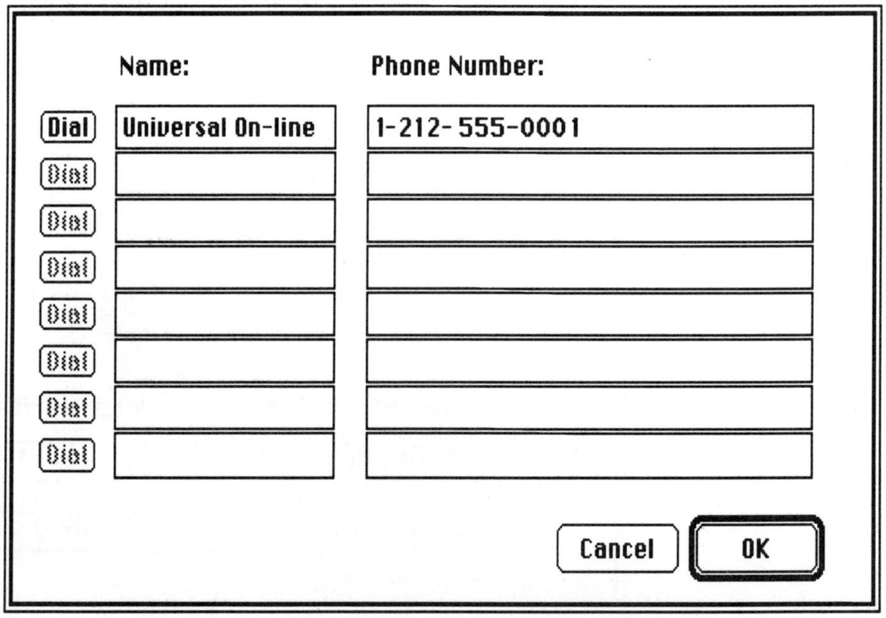

Figure 13.9 The telephone list box.

During the time the dialing is in progress, the message *Dialing* will appear on the screen. When the connection is made between the modems, the message *Connect* will appear on the screen. We are now ready to communicate with the other computer.

ADDING OR CHANGING NUMBERS IN THE TELEPHONE BOOK.   Recall that the telephone book is stored with a communications document. The following steps allow you to add or edit telephone numbers.

- Open the communications document.
- Select the *Dial* command from the **Communications** menu.
- To add a number, move the insertion pointer to the next blank space in the telephone book and type the name and number.
- To edit a number, move the pointer over the appropriate number and edit as you would any word processing text.

Be sure to save the communications document to save the changes made to the telephone book.

ANSWERING THE PHONE AUTOMATICALLY.   You can use Works to answer incoming calls from other computers automatically. Your modem must be Hayes compatible and must have the auto-answer feature. To accomplish this, do the following.

- Open a communications document. This may be an existing document or a new one.
- Examine the communications settings and change them if necessary to agree with the expected calls.
- Select the *Answer Phone* command in the **Communications** menu. The modem will now automatically answer the phone when it rings.

When the communications session is over, select the *Answer Phone* command again. The checkmark beside the command should disappear, indicating that answering the phone has been disabled.

Exercise Set 13.6

1. What appears immediately after the communications settings have been completed? What is the purpose of this?
2. What is the purpose of the *Capture Text* command? When can the command be given? How many times can it be given during a communications session? What command stops the capture of text?
3. What is the default name of the *Capture Text* disk file?
4. Give the steps for the procedure for dialing another computer.
5. What appears on the communications screen as the computer is dialing?
6. How does one know that a successful connection to another computer has been made?
7. How many characters can be used for a telephone number? What is the purpose of spaces and hyphens in a telephone number?

8. Describe the use of commas in a telephone number.

9. Give the procedure for adding a number to the telephone book.

10. Give the procedure for changing a number in the telephone book.

11. What kind of modem is required for automatic answering of the phone?

12. Give the procedure for using the automatic phone answering feature of Works.

13. Give the procedure for ending the automatic phone answering.

Computer Practice 13.6

In this computer practice session you will simulate signing on to the Universal On-line News and Services information service. Of course, this is not as informative as actually signing on to an information service, but it is less expensive.

1. Open Works and click the *Communications* icon.

2. Select the *Open* command from the **File** menu, select and open the communications document *practice 13.5.*

3. Click the *OK* button on the *Communications Settings* dialog box to accept the settings that were made in the previous computer practice. The empty communications window *practice 13.5* (CM) will appear.

4. Select the *Capture Text* command from the **Communications** menu. This will cause a dialog box to be displayed. Type *Universal On-line News* in the box titled *Save Captured Text As.* All communications that appear in the communications window will be saved in this file. (Of course, the file will be empty because we are only simulating the communications session.)

5. Select the *Dial* command from the **Communications** menu. The telephone list box (see Figure 13.9.) will appear.

6. Type the name of the information service, Universal On-line, in the first box under the heading *Name.*

7. Type the phone number, 1-212-555-0001, in the first box under the heading *Phone Number.*

8. Click the *Dial* button that is to the left of the name of the information service. At this time the dialing would occur if the modem were turned on. In our case, the telephone list box disappears, just as it would when the dialing was complete.

9. Select the *End Capture Text* command from the **Communications** menu. In our case, no text was captured because this is only a simulation.

10. Select the *Hang Up* command from the **Communications** menu. If this had been a real communications session, the phone would now be hung up.

11. Click the close box of the communications document *practice 13.5.* Do not save the document.

12. Quit Works.

13.7 SENDING AND RECEIVING INFORMATION

One of the main reasons for communications between computers is to exchange disk files. Works makes a distinction between text files and files that contain graphs or pictures.

SENDING USING THE KEYBOARD.   The simplest way to communicate with the other computer is to use your keyboard. Whatever you type will appear almost simultaneously on the screens of both computers. If you are involved in a conversation, you should pause to give the other person an opportunity to respond. This method is ideal for the round table discussions conducted by some users groups. Each person can type replies as needed.

SEND TEXT COMMAND.   The *Send Text* command is used to send text files to another computer. This can sometimes be used to save money when communicating with an information service that charges for the connect time. For example, to use the electronic mail service of the information service, you could type the text in advance. Then send the mail using the *Send Text* command, which would take much less time than typing the text while connected to the service and would, therefore, cost less.

When the *Send Text* command is used only the text is transmitted; any formatting information is deleted before transmission. Only Works files can be transmitted; any other type of file must be imported by Works before it can be transmitted. The procedure for sending text files follows.

- Select the *Send Text* command in the **Communications** menu. A dialog box of the form shown in Figure 13.10 will be displayed.
- Select the document to be sent in the scroll box of the dialog box.
- Click the *Send* button on the dialog box to start sending the document to the other computer.

During the sending of the text you will not be able to use the communications module for other work. You can use the other Works modules if you wish. When

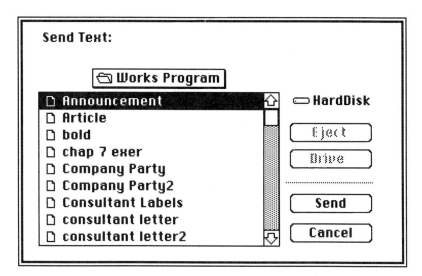

Figure 13.10 The *Send Text* dialog box.

the transmission of the text is complete, a message will be displayed. You can then perform other work with the communications module.

XMODEM PROTOCOL. Works supports the **Xmodem protocol** for transfer of information between computers. Three variations of the Xmodem protocol are used by Works. You will have to select one of them in order to send a file to another computer. The variations are

- **MacBinary**. The **MacBinary** version of Xmodem protocol should be used if the information is being exchanged between two Macintoshes. MacBinary works for any kind of file.

- **Xmodem Text**. The **Xmodem Text** version of Xmodem protocol should be used for exchanging text files (no graphics or pictures) between a Macintosh and any other kind of computer.

- **Xmodem Data**. The **Xmodem Data** version of Xmodem protocol should be used for exchanging complex files (including graphics and pictures) between a Macintosh and any other kind of computer.

Kermit is another popular file transfer protocol. It is not available in Works, however. To use it, you would need a different communications package.

SEND FILE COMMAND. The *Send File* command of the **Communications** menu allows transmission of any Works files, including those that contain graphs and/ or pictures. The procedure for using this command is the same as that for the *Send Text* command except that a protocol must be specified.

As an example of *Send File* command usage, let us send the file *Company Party* (see Figure 5.5), which contains pictorial data, to another Macintosh. Because the file is to be sent to another Macintosh, the MacBinary protocol should be used. The steps follow.

- Select the *Send File* command in the **Communications** menu. A dialog box of the form shown in Figure 13.11 will be displayed.

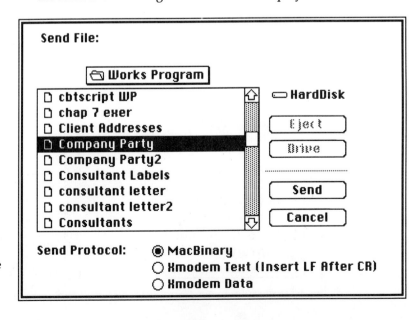

Figure 13.11 The *Send File* dialog box for sending the *Company Party* file to another Macintosh.

- Click the *MacBinary* protocol button.
- Select the document to be sent, *Company Party*, in the scroll box of the dialog box.
- Click the *Send* button on the dialog box to start the sending of the document *Company Party* to the other Macintosh.

After the *Send* button is clicked the message box of Figure 13.12 will be displayed. This box shows the status of the sending of the file to the other Macintosh. Because the transfer is just beginning, the *Blocks Completed* count is zero. As the transfer continues, this count will increase. Also note that a *Retransmissions* count greater than zero means that transmission errors occurred that required retransmitting one or more blocks of the file. If this count is high and more files are to be sent, you could try slowing the transmission by increasing the character and/or line delay in the *Communications Settings* window.

If the file *Company Party* is to be sent to a non-Macintosh computer, the protocol must be selected as Xmodem Data because the file contains pictorial data. (However, this does not mean that the pictorial data can be used in the new system.) The procedure for sending the file is the same as just considered except the *Xmodem Data* button must be clicked.

RECEIVE FILE COMMAND.   Any kind of file can be received using the *Receive File* command. The procedure for receiving a file is almost identical to that for sending a file.

- Select the *Receive File* command in the **Communications** menu. A dialog box of the form shown in Figure 13.13 will be displayed. Notice the default name for the received file is *Xmodem File*. This default name is already selected, so a more meaningful name can be typed immediately if you wish.
- Click the appropriate protocol button. You may know the correct protocol for some reason—for example, if the sending computer is a Macintosh, choose MacBinary. If you do not know, you can always select the *Xmodem Data* option, which assumes the file is as complex as possible.
- Click the *Receive* button on the dialog box to start the receiving of the document from the other computer.

After the *Receive* Button is clicked the transmission information box of Figure 13.14 is displayed. Notice that neither the name of the source file nor its size is known.

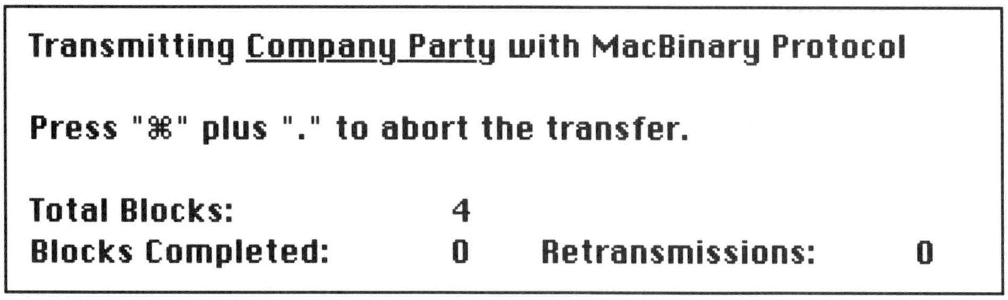

Figure 13.12 Transmission information box for MacBinary.

Transmitting <u>Company Party</u> with MacBinary Protocol

Press "⌘" plus "." to abort the transfer.

Total Blocks: **4**

Blocks Completed: **0**   **Retransmissions:**   **0**

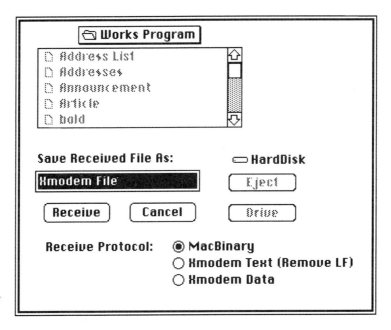

Figure 13.13 The *Receive File* dialog box.

Exercise Set 13.7

1. How can the keyboard be used in the communication process?
2. What is the purpose of the *Send Text* command? What happens to formatting information when this command is used?
3. How can the *Send Text* command be used to reduce the cost of communicating with an information service?
4. Give the procedure for using the *Send Text* command.
5. List the three variations of the Xmodem protocol that are supported by Works.
6. When should the MacBinary protocol be used?
7. When should the Xmodem Text protocol be used?
8. When should the Xmodem Data protocol be used?
9. How does one specify which protocol is to be used in sending or receiving a file?
10. What kinds of files can be sent using the *Send File* command?

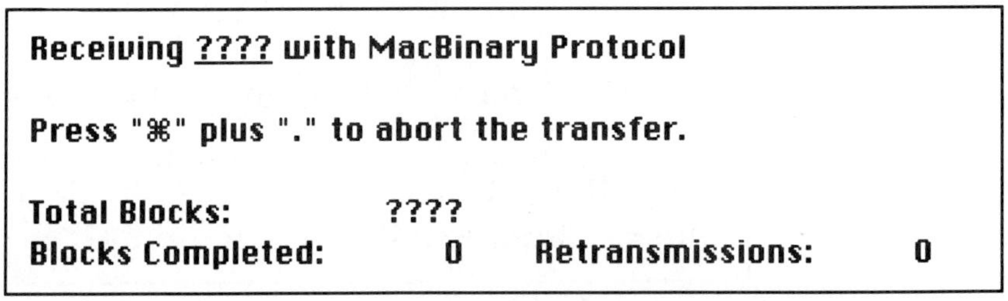

```
Receiving ???? with MacBinary Protocol

Press "⌘" plus "." to abort the transfer.

Total Blocks:            ????
Blocks Completed:        0      Retransmissions:      0
```

Figure 13.14 *Receive Information* box for MacBinary protocol.

11. List the kinds of information found in a transmission information box.

12. What kinds of files can be received using the *Receive File* command?

Computer Practice 13.7

In this computer practice session you will *simulate* sending your document *practice 7.4* to another Macintosh.

1. Open Works and click the *Communications* icon.

2. Create a new communications document by selecting the *New* command of the **File** menu. The *Communications Settings* dialog box should appear.

3. Change the baud rate to 1200 by clicking that button. Click the *OK* button. The *Communications Settings* dialog box should disappear, and an empty communications window should be displayed.

4. Select the *Send File* command from the **Communications** menu. When the *Send File* dialog box is displayed, select the document *practice 7.4* in the scroll box of the dialog box.

5. Click the *MacBinary* button because the document is to be sent to another Macintosh.

6. Click the *Send* button to start the sending of the document. A transmission information box will be displayed.

7. Read the transmission box, which will not change, because this is a simulation. Press simultaneously the *Clover* key and the *Period* key to end the simulated transmission.

8. Quit Works.

13.8 ENDING THE COMMUNICATIONS SESSION

To end a communications session, you should perform the following steps.

- Disconnect from the system if you are using an information service or other system that required you to execute special actions to connect to it. The phone connection between the computers may still exist after you have disconnected from the system.

- Hang up your telephone by selecting the *Hang Up* command of the **Communications** menu. Works directs your modem to hang up.

- Save the communications document if appropriate. In the discussion in this chapter all the work has been done with an untitled document. It should be saved if the communications settings and telephone numbers will be used again. Let us assume that the communications settings are the standard ones for future work. For that reason we save the document with the name *Standard Communications*. Later, when the document is opened, the blank window with the title *Standard Communications (CM)* will be displayed; and the communications settings and the telephone number saved with the document will be available.

- Quit the Works Communications module by selecting the *Quit* command in the **File** menu.

If you conduct different kinds of communications, such as using an information service, participating in a round table discussion with other computer users, or calling non-Macintosh computers, you should create a different communications document for each category of use. Then the communications settings and telephone numbers will be immediately available when you need them. Without these documents, you are likely to forget some important setting and to spend unnecessary time trying to start a session.

Exercise Set 13.8

1. List the three major steps for ending a communications session.
2. Why might it be valuable to have more than one communications document?
3. What is displayed if an existing communications document is opened? Are these parts of the communications document that are not displayed? Explain.

Key Concepts

Baud	Communications document
Demodulation	Handshake
MacBinary protocol	Modem
Modulation	Parity
Protocol	Smart modem
Xmodem Data protocol	Xmodem protocol
Xmodem Text protocol	

INTEGRATING SOLUTIONS WITH THE WORKS MODULES

L E A R N I N G   O B J E C T I V E S

- To gain an understanding of how to approach solving a large information management problem.

- To learn to integrate the use of all the Works modules to solve a large information management problem.

- To learn to transfer information between the Works modules.

T his chapter shows how MacPaint and the Works WP, Works DB, and Works SS modules can be used jointly to solve a significant information management problem that could not be done without integrating the use of such programs. A solution is constructed to a realistic example problem that involves producing graphics-enhanced documents, storing and retrieving database information, merging database information with word processing documents to create individualized forms and letters, moving database data to a spreadsheet to perform calculations and create charts, and copying spreadsheet-generated charts and calculations into a word processing report. The example will demonstrate that integrating the modules makes Works a very powerful problem-solving system.

14.1 DESCRIPTION OF THE PROBLEM

In this section a high-level description of the problem will be given. Details will be discussed in later sections. The problem to be solved with Works is as follows. Ace Consultants, Inc., has been hired to investigate the relationships between various life-style factors and the values of health parameters for males between the ages of 40 and 50. The major steps needed to solve this problem follow.

- Select at random from census data names and addresses for males between the ages of 40 and 50. Store this information in a database.
- Create a survey packet and send a copy to each chosen participant.
- Save the survey results in a database.
- Select information from the database and transfer it to a spreadsheet environment.
- Make calculations in the spreadsheet environment to produce charts of life-style factors versus health factors.
- Repeat the previous two steps as many times as is necessary to complete the analysis.

14.2 THE DATABASE OF NAMES AND ADDRESSES

For our survey, assume that names and addresses for males between the ages of 40 and 50 have been selected at random from census data. (The method used for the random selection is important, but it is not discussed here.) This information is then stored in a database. Figure 14.1 shows the form for records of the database, and Figure 14.2 shows the first seven records in list format.

Computer Practice 14.2

1. Create the form of Figure 14.1 using Works DB.
2. Enter the records shown in Figure 14.2 into the database. This small database will be used in subsequent sections to explore the ideas introduced in this chapter.

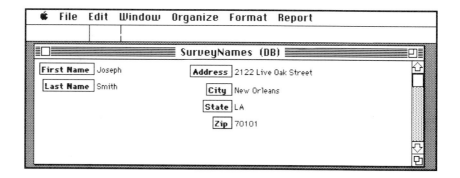

Figure 14.1 Database design for names and addresses.

3. Save the database with the name *SurveyNames*.

14.3 THE SURVEY PACKET

We will mail a packet to all chosen participants and encourage them to participate by offering them a free gift. The packet will consist of

- A form letter briefly describing the survey and asking for participation (Figures 14.3 and 14.4).
- A gift sheet describing (and showing diagrams of) the gifts offered. The participant is to return this sheet, with his choice of gift marked, along with his portion of the survey (Figure 14.5).
- Part A of the survey to be filled out by the participant (Figure 14.6).
- Part B of the survey to be filled out by a physician (Figure 14.7). Attached to this part will be the physician's reimbursement form.

Each of the preceding forms is to be created using Works WP and is to contain graphics to make them more interesting. Appealing, easy-to-read, easy-to-complete documents are essential to obtain a high response level from the chosen participants. The graphics are to be done in MacPaint and pasted into the documents.

The merge feature of Works is to be used with the documents and the *SurveyNames* database to create an inside address and salutation on each copy of the forms. (The merge technique was discussed in Chapter 8.)

First Name	Last Name	Address	City	State	Zip
Joseph	Smith	2122 Live Oak Street	New Orleans	LA	70101
Thomas	Dedmond	1212 Palm Lane	Santa Clara	CA	95050
William	White	1020 Lakeview Way	Jonesville	OH	44444
Paul	Wrangler	1122 Hillside Dr.	Hyatt	NY	10800
George	Belton	1011 Maple Leaf St.	Hazel Green	AL	35820
Clancy	Duggan	105 Park Ave.	New York	NY	10045
Harrison	Matthews	220 Quincy St.	Roaring Spring	PA	16673

Figure 14.2 A portion of the database.

Ace Consultants, Inc.
103 South Elm Street
Nashua, NH 03061

March 12, 1989

Mr. [SurveyNames: First Name] [SurveyNames: Last Name]
[SurveyNames: Address]
[SurveyNames: City] , [SurveyNames: State]   [SurveyNames: Zip]

Dear Mr. [SurveyNames: Last Name]

    Your name has been selected at random by our computer as a participant in a nationwide survey to assess the effects of certain lifestyle factors on important health parameters. As a token of our appreciation for your participation in this survey, we would like to send you one of the gifts shown on the enclosed gift sheet. Just check the gift you would prefer and return the gift sheet with your survey.

    It will take you less than 15 minutes to complete Part A of the survey and place it in the postage–paid return envelope. The completion of Part B of the survey will require you to make a brief visit, at our expense, to your family doctor.

                  Sincerely,

                  John H. Watkins
                  Chief, Survey Division

Figure 14.3 Form letter prepared for the merge process.

Computer Practice 14.3A

The goal of this practice session is to produce the form letter that appears in Figures 14.3 and 14.4. The method suggested is only one of many possibilities. You could do the steps in a different order.

1. Open Works WP and create a new word processing document.

2. Type *Mr.* after spacing down about 10 lines. Type *Dear Mr.* after spacing down several more lines. Type the remainder of the letter as it appears in Figure 14.3.

**Ace Consultants, Inc.
103 South Elm Street
Nashua, NH 03061**

March 12, 1989

Mr. Joseph Smith
2122 Live Oak Street
New Orleans, LA 70101

Dear Mr. Smith:

Your name has been selected at random by our computer as a participant in a nationwide survey to assess the effects of certain lifestyle factors on important health parameters. As a token of our appreciation for your participation in this survey, we would like to send you one of the gifts shown on the enclosed gift sheet. Just check the gift you would prefer and return the gift sheet with your survey.

It will take you less than 15 minutes to complete Part A of the survey and place it in the postage-paid return envelope. The completion of Part B of the survey will require you to make a brief visit, at our expense, to your family doctor.

Sincerely,

John H. Watkins
Chief, Survey Division

Figure 14.4 A form letter after merging.

3. Open the *SurveyNames* database, and then make the form letter the active window by selecting it using the **Window** menu.

4. Enter the database field names into the form letter. Recall that this requires using the *Prepare to Merge* command in the **Edit** menu. The dialog box follows.

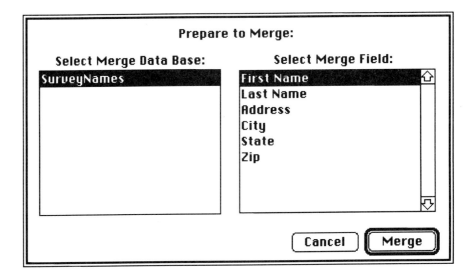

5. Save the document with the name *Form Letter*. Close the document and quit Works so that you can use MacPaint.

6. Create the logo for Ace Consultants, as follows. Alternatively, you may wish to create only the graphics in MacPaint and type the company name and address in Works WP.

7. Copy the graphics created in MacPaint into the Works WP document *Form Letter*.

8. Save the final version of the form letter with the name *Form Letter*.

The gift sheet portion of the mailing packet is shown in Figure 14.5. Notice that it also uses the merge feature and that it contains several figures. To create the gift sheet, perform Computer Practice 14.3B.

Computer Practice 14.3B

The goal of this practice session is to produce the gift sheet that appears in Figure 14.5. The method suggested is only one of many possibilities.

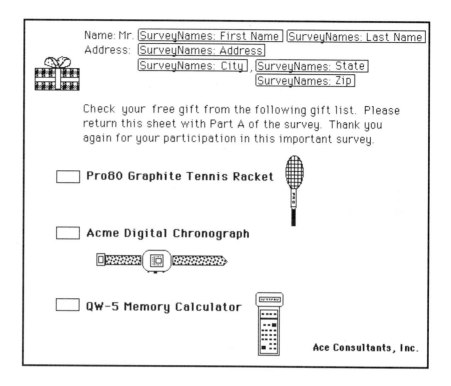

Figure 14.5 The gift sheet.

1. Open Works WP and produce a new empty word processing window.

2. Type *Name: Mr.* after spacing down a few lines. Type *Address:* on the next line. Type the remainder of the text for the gift sheet as it appears in Figure 14.5. Do not concern yourself too much with the line spacing; you can edit the gift sheet to obtain proper spacing after you have added the graphics.

3. Open the *SurveyNames* database and then make the gift sheet the active window by selecting it using the **Window** menu.

4. Enter the database field names into the gift sheet. Recall that this requires using the *Prepare to Merge* command in the **Edit** menu. The dialog box was shown in the previous computer exercise.

5. Draw the boxes for selecting the gift using the Works draw feature. Recall that the *Draw* command in the **Edit** menu is used to select the object to be drawn. It is suggested that you draw one box (e.g., the box before *Pro80 Graphite Tennis Racket*). Then that box can be copied and pasted in other locations. To align the boxes, use the Works hand.

6. Save the document with the name *Gift Sheet*. Close the document and quit Works so that you can use MacPaint.

7. Create the figures for the gift box, tennis racket, chronograph, and calculator, which are shown here, using any method you wish in MacPaint.

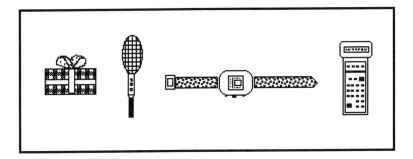

8. Copy the graphics created in MacPaint, one at a time, into the Works WP document *Gift Sheet*.

9. Save the final version of the form letter with the name *Gift Sheet*.

Computer Practice 14.3C

In this computer practice you are to create the survey forms that are shown in Figures 14.6 and 14.7. No new concepts are required to prepare these forms, so the details on how to proceed are being omitted. However, the following suggestions are made.

- Create the drawing of the snake and staff, as shown here, using MacPaint. Paste the figure into the documents.

- Draw all the boxes using the drawing feature of Works WP. Copy a box and paste it to the locations of all boxes of the same size.

- Recall that the large box, which surrounds the "To the doctor" statement in the survey form for doctors, can be created with the draw feature of Works WP after the text has been entered.

Save the documents as *Survey Part A* and *Survey Part B*.

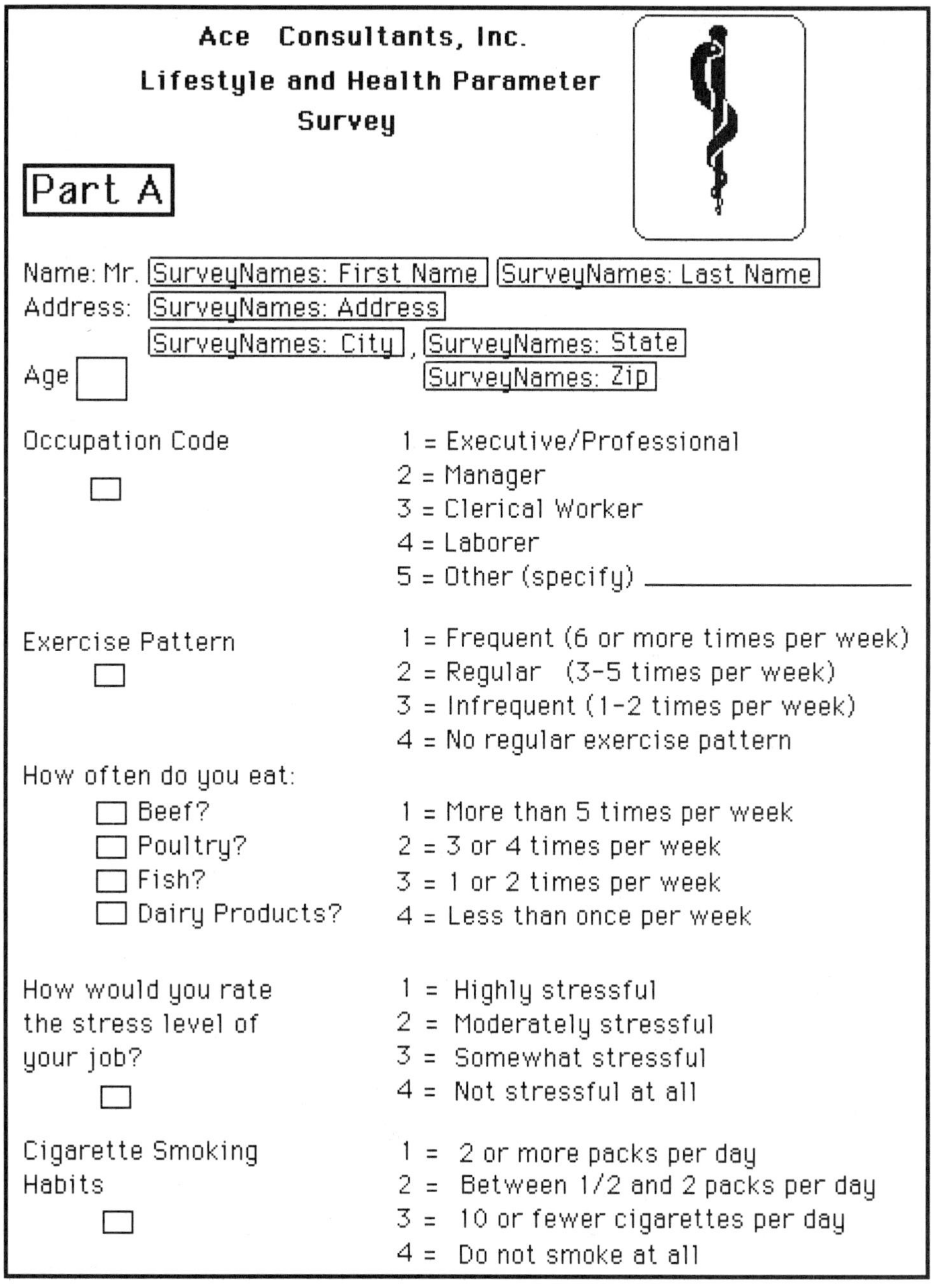

Ace Consultants, Inc.
Lifestyle and Health Parameter Survey

Part A

Name: Mr. SurveyNames: First Name SurveyNames: Last Name
Address: SurveyNames: Address
SurveyNames: City, SurveyNames: State
Age SurveyNames: Zip

Occupation Code
1 = Executive/Professional
2 = Manager
3 = Clerical Worker
4 = Laborer
5 = Other (specify) ________

Exercise Pattern
1 = Frequent (6 or more times per week)
2 = Regular (3-5 times per week)
3 = Infrequent (1-2 times per week)
4 = No regular exercise pattern

How often do you eat:
Beef?
Poultry?
Fish?
Dairy Products?
1 = More than 5 times per week
2 = 3 or 4 times per week
3 = 1 or 2 times per week
4 = Less than once per week

How would you rate the stress level of your job?
1 = Highly stressful
2 = Moderately stressful
3 = Somewhat stressful
4 = Not stressful at all

Cigarette Smoking Habits
1 = 2 or more packs per day
2 = Between 1/2 and 2 packs per day
3 = 10 or fewer cigarettes per day
4 = Do not smoke at all

Figure 14.6 Survey Part A, recipients form.

14.4 THE SURVEY DATABASE

In this section we create a database to hold the results of the survey. The advantage of using a database in this instance is that the selection features of Works DB can be used to isolate sets of records for later analysis.

CREATING THE NEW DATABASE. We can create the new database (Figure 14.8) and import the old database data at the same time by the following steps.

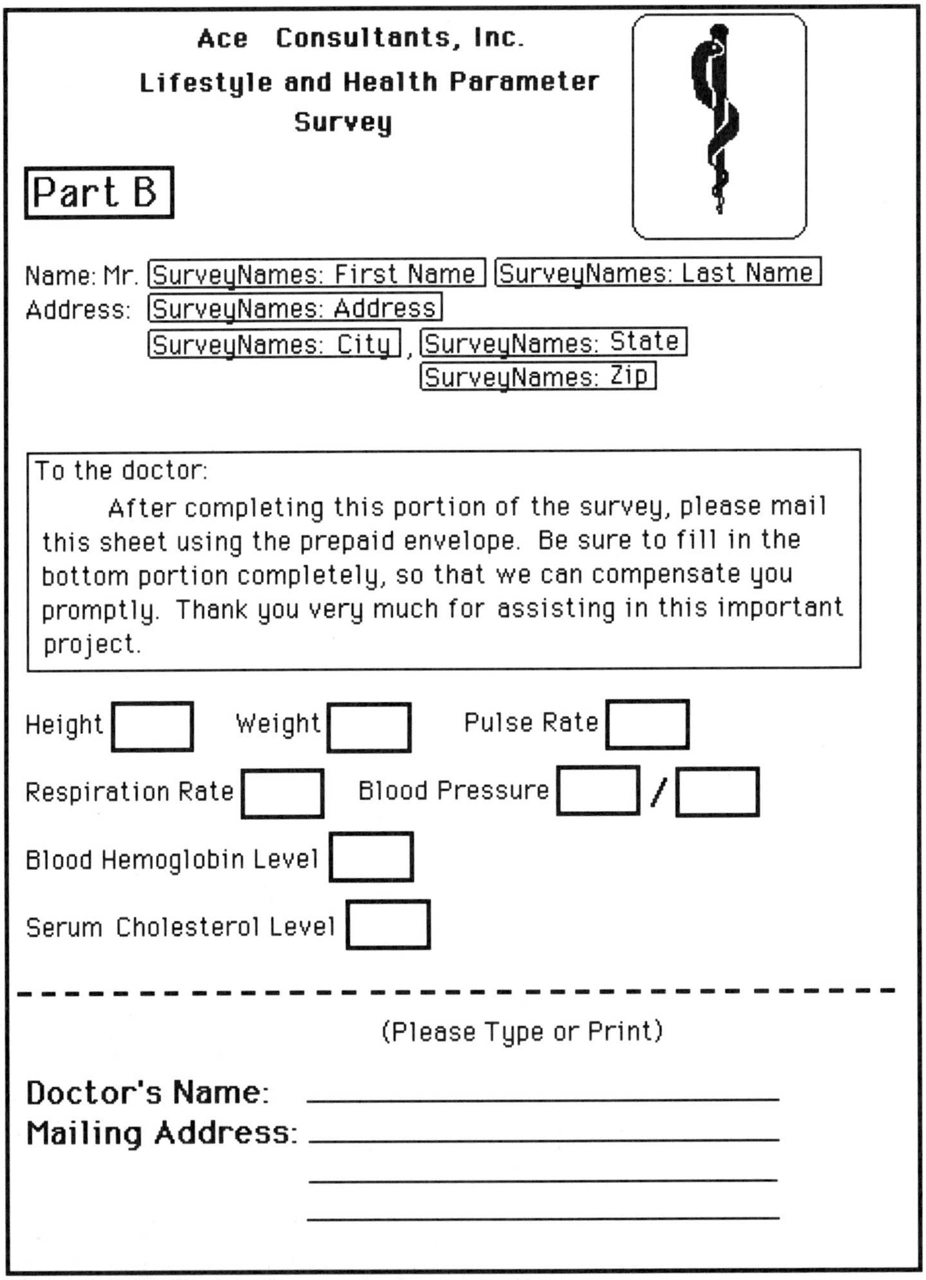

Ace Consultants, Inc.
Lifestyle and Health Parameter Survey

Part B

Name: Mr. [SurveyNames: First Name] [SurveyNames: Last Name]
Address: [SurveyNames: Address]
[SurveyNames: City], [SurveyNames: State]
[SurveyNames: Zip]

To the doctor:
After completing this portion of the survey, please mail this sheet using the prepaid envelope. Be sure to fill in the bottom portion completely, so that we can compensate you promptly. Thank you very much for assisting in this important project.

Height [ ] Weight [ ] Pulse Rate [ ]
Respiration Rate [ ] Blood Pressure [ ] / [ ]
Blood Hemoglobin Level [ ]
Serum Cholesterol Level [ ]

(Please Type or Print)

Doctor's Name: ____________________
Mailing Address: ____________________

Figure 14.7 Survey Part B, doctors form.

- Opening the *SurveyNames* database.
- Adding the new fields.
- Using the *Save As* command to save the database with the name *SurveyResults*.

Notice that the field names are displayed in a manner to mimic the layout of the survey forms. Using the *Tab* key accesses the fields in exactly the same order as they appear in the survey forms. (The *Return* key behaves differently.)

Computer Practice 14.4A

1. Open Works and open the *SurveyNames* database.
2. Add the following new fields to the database:
   - *Survey Returned?*
   - *Age*
   - *Occupation*
   - *Exercise*
   - *Beef*
   - *Poultry*
   - *Fish*
   - *Dairy*
   - *Smoking*
   - *JobStress*
   - *Height*
   - *Weight*
   - *Pulse*
   - *Respiration*
   - *Blood Pressure 1*
   - *Blood Pressure 2*
   - *Hemoglobin*
   - *Cholesterol*
3. Move the fields on the database form to obtain a design that is similar to that shown in Figure 14.8.
4. Enter into the database the data shown in Figure 14.24. Note that some of this data will be added to records already in the database, but the last two records contain completely new data. (Review Section 8.5 if necessary.) This database will be used for future computer practice sessions. Ignore the field *HW Ratio* for now.
5. Save the database with the name *SurveyResults*.
6. Quit Works.

ADDING A CALCULATED FIELD. Database fields whose values are calculated based on other fields in the database are called *calculated fields*. Because we are interested in the weight-to-height ratio (rather than the individual weight and height values), we will add a new field to the database called *HW Ratio*. This will be a calculated field. The steps necessary for this are:

- Open the database.
- Add the field *HW Ratio*.
- Choose the *Set Field Attributes* command in the **Format** menu.
- Set the dialog box as shown in Figure 14.9. It is easy to miss the *Computed* box, so be sure to click it. Finally, click the *OK* button.

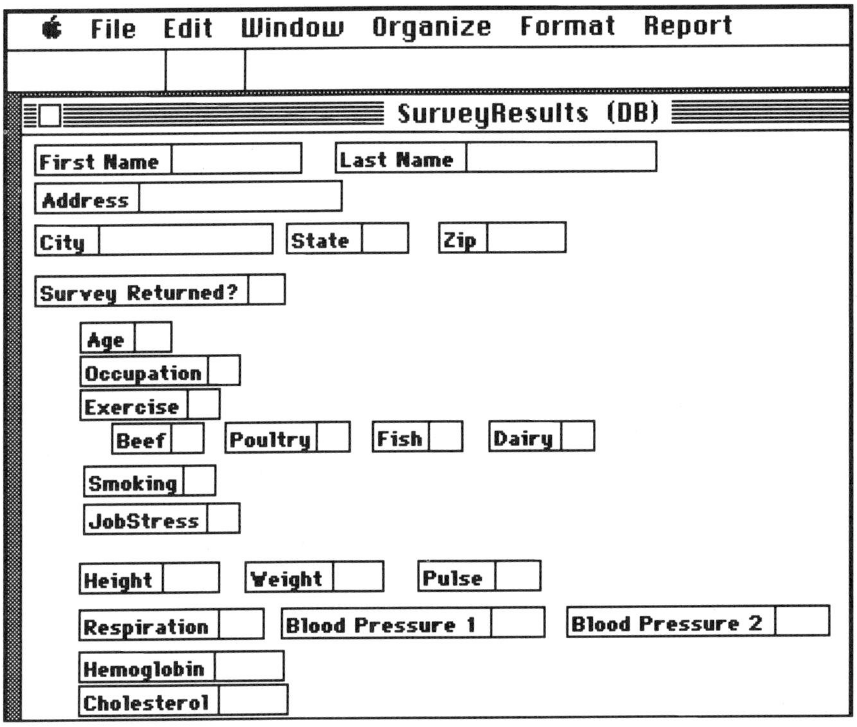

Figure 14.8 Design of the *SurveyResults* database.

To make the computation, you can select the cell of the first record under the heading *HW Ratio*. You would then type the following formula into the formula bar:

$$=Weight/Height$$

When the checkmark in the formula bar is clicked, the computed values shown in Figure 14.10 will be shown.

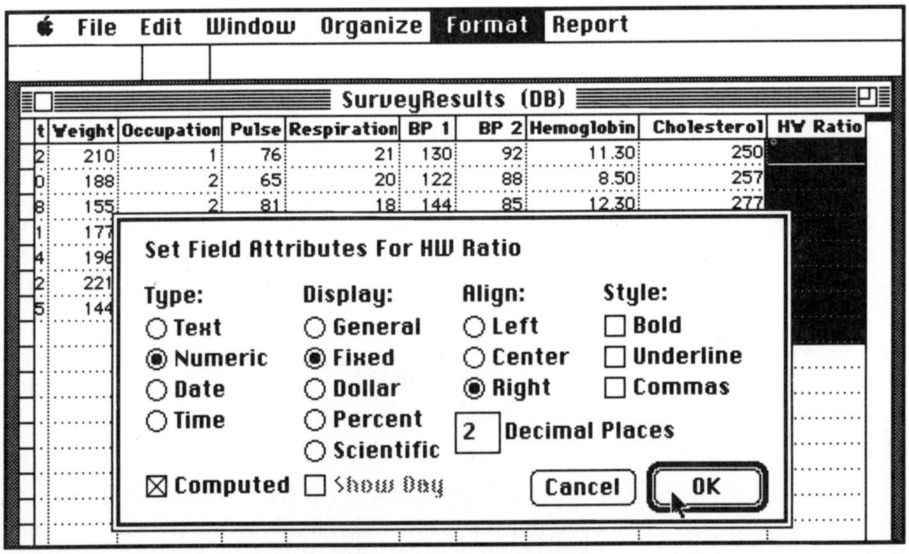

Figure 14.9 Setting parameters for a calculated field.

▉	File	Edit	Window	Organize	Format	Report				

1   =Weight/Height

SurveyResults (DB)

t	Weight	Occupation	Pulse	Respiration	BP 1	BP 2	Hemoglobin	Cholesterol	HV Ratio
2	210	1	76	21	130	92	11.30	250	2.92
0	188	2	65	20	122	88	8.50	257	2.69
8	155	2	81	18	144	85	12.30	277	2.28
1	177	1	55	26	135	94	9.00	303	2.49
4	196	1	76	26	133	78	10.20	177	2.65
2	221	4	65	19	146	81	11.60	183	3.07

Figure 14.10 Part of the database after computing *HV Ratio*.

We are almost ready to begin the analysis of the data. The first step will be to select a set of records of interest. Then the selected set will be transferred to a spreadsheet to allow computations and graphs to be produced. This is discussed in the next section.

Computer Practice 14.4B

The goal of this practice session is to add the calculated field to the database.

1. Open the *SurveyResults* database.
2. Select the *Add New Field* command from the **Edit** menu.
3. Type the new field name, *HW Ratio*, when the following dialog box is displayed:

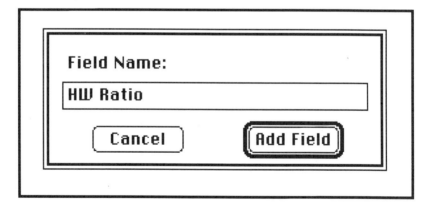

Field Name:

HW Ratio

Cancel   Add Field

4. Once you have added the *HW Ratio* field to the database, select it by pointing at the name of the field and clicking.
5. Select the *Set Field Attributes* command from the **Format** menu. The dialog box of Figure 14.9 will be displayed. Make the entries shown in the figure and click the *OK* button. The dialog box will disappear, the *HW Ratio* field will be filled with zeros, and an equal sign (=) will be entered in the formula bar.
6. Type the remaining part of the formula to obtain

    =Weight/Height

7. Click the check box in the formula bar. The values will appear in the cells.
8. Save the database and quit Works.

	File	Edit	Window	Organize	Format	Report
1			1			

SurveyResults (DB)

t	Weight	Occupation	Pulse	Respiration	BP 1	BP 2	Hemoglobin	Cholesterol	HW Ratio
2	210	1	76	21	130	92	11.30	250	2.92
1	177	1	55	26	135	94	9.00	303	2.49
4	196	1	76	26	133	78	10.20	177	2.65

Figure 14.11 Selection of records with *Occupation* equal to 1.

14.5 ANALYSIS OF DATA

Many analyses can be performed with our data. We make a single analysis to illustrate the approach. In particular, we will determine the relationship between occupations and pulse rates. The steps required for the analysis are not given in detail here, but they are covered in the computer practice for this section.

Because we wish to analyze each occupation separately, we set a record selection rule in the database to choose only those records with *Occupation* = 1. (Later this process will be repeated for other occupation categories.) The screen in Figure 14.11 shows the fields of interest after the selection. The records are selected and can be copied to the Clipboard so they can be transferred to a spreadsheet. Note that we have moved the *Occupation* field to the right of its original position (this won't affect our form) so that it will be next to the health parameters.

To create the spreadsheet to receive the records, select the *New* command from the **File** menu. When the dialog box is displayed, click the *Spreadsheet* icon and click the *OK* button. Save the spreadsheet with the name *Occupation Analysis*. Select an appropriate area on the spreadsheet for the records.

The situation at this time would be:

- The database *SurveyResults* is open but is not active. All the records corresponding to *Occupation* = 1 are highlighted.

- The selected records from the database are on the Clipboard.

- The newly created spreadsheet, *Occupation Analysis*, is active and has an appropriate number of rows and columns for the pasting of the occupation data from the database. This is shown in Figure 14.12. Columns G and H are selected even though they cannot be seen on the screen.

After the *Paste* command is selected from the **Edit** menu, the spreadsheet becomes that shown in Figure 14.13.

	File	Edit	Window	Select	Format	Options	Chart
A1							

Occupation Analysis (SS)

	A	B	C	D	E	F	
1							
2							
3							
4							

Figure 14.12 Spreadsheet with area selected for pasting.

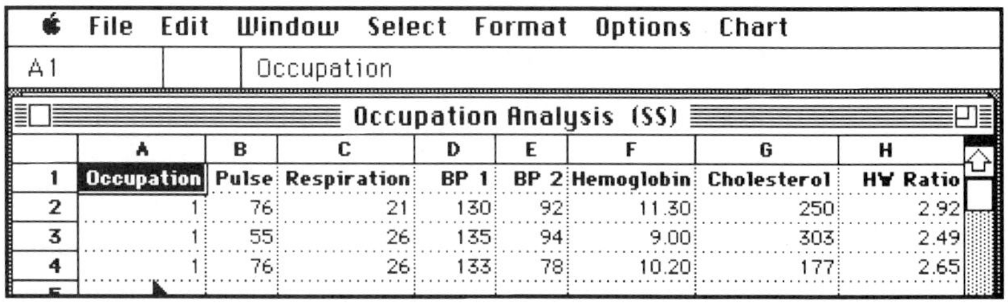

Figure 14.13 The spreadsheet after pasting occupation data.

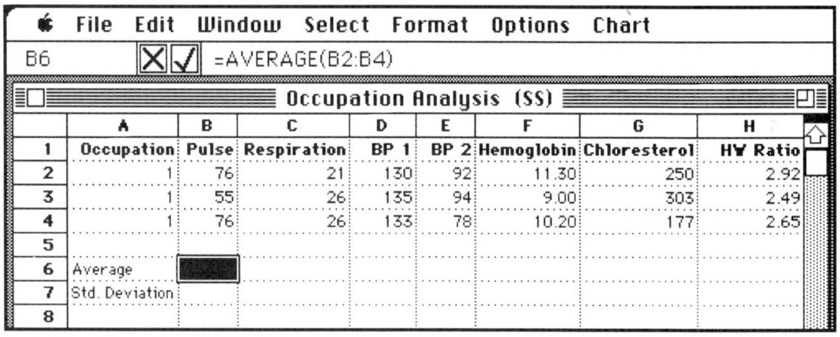

	A	B	C	D	E	F	G	H
	Occupation	**Pulse**	**Respiration**	**BP 1**	**BP 2**	**Hemoglobin**	**Cholesterol**	**HW Ratio**
2	1	76	21	130	92	11.30	250	2.92
3	1	55	26	135	94	9.00	303	2.49
4	1	76	26	133	78	10.20	177	2.65

A1 — Occupation — Occupation Analysis (SS)

Figure 14.14 Entering the formula into cell B6.

B6 =AVERAGE(B2:B4) — Occupation Analysis (SS)

	A	B	C	D	E	F	G	H
1	**Occupation**	**Pulse**	**Respiration**	**BP 1**	**BP 2**	**Hemoglobin**	**Chloresterol**	**HW Ratio**
2	1	76	21	130	92	11.30	250	2.92
3	1	55	26	135	94	9.00	303	2.49
4	1	76	26	133	78	10.20	177	2.65
5								
6	Average							
7	Std. Deviation							
8								

For each of the health factors in the spreadsheet we wish to compute the average and the standard deviation. The labels *Average* and *Std. Deviation* are typed into cells A6 and A7, respectively. Figure 14.14 shows the use of the built-in function AVERAGE to compute the average in cell B6. The built-in function STDEV for standard deviation is being entered in cell B7 in Figure 14.15. Cells B6:H7 are selected and filled right to produce the worksheet of Figure 14.16.

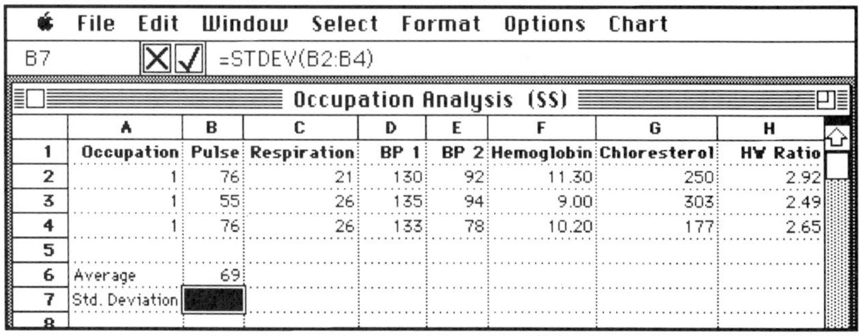

Figure 14.15 Entering the formula into cell B7.

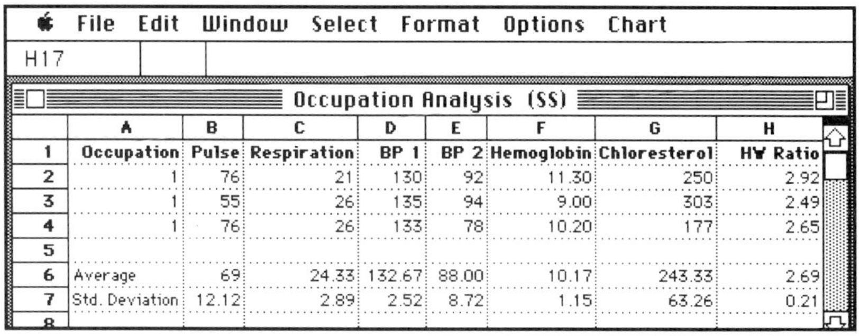

B7 =STDEV(B2:B4) — Occupation Analysis (SS)

	A	B	C	D	E	F	G	H
1	**Occupation**	**Pulse**	**Respiration**	**BP 1**	**BP 2**	**Hemoglobin**	**Chloresterol**	**HW Ratio**
2	1	76	21	130	92	11.30	250	2.92
3	1	55	26	135	94	9.00	303	2.49
4	1	76	26	133	78	10.20	177	2.65
5								
6	Average	69						
7	Std. Deviation							
8								

Figure 14.16 The worksheet after the formulas are filled right.

H17 — Occupation Analysis (SS)

	A	B	C	D	E	F	G	H
1	**Occupation**	**Pulse**	**Respiration**	**BP 1**	**BP 2**	**Hemoglobin**	**Chloresterol**	**HW Ratio**
2	1	76	21	130	92	11.30	250	2.92
3	1	55	26	135	94	9.00	303	2.49
4	1	76	26	133	78	10.20	177	2.65
5								
6	Average	69	24.33	132.67	88.00	10.17	243.33	2.69
7	Std. Deviation	12.12	2.89	2.52	8.72	1.15	63.26	0.21
8								

	A	B	C	D	E	F	G	H
1	Occupation	Pulse	Respiration	BP 1	BP 2	Hemoglobin	Chloresterol	HV Ratio
2	1	76	21	130	92	11.30	250	2.92
3	1	55	26	135	94	9.00	303	2.49
4	1	76	26	133	78	10.20	177	2.65
5								
6	Average	69	24.33	132.67	88.00	10.17	243.33	2.69
7	Std. Deviation	12.12	2.89	2.52	8.72	1.15	63.26	0.21
8								
9								
10								
11	Occupation	Pulse	Respiration	BP 1	BP 2	Hemoglobin	Chloresterol	HV Ratio
12	2	65	20	122	88	8.50	257	2.69
13	2	81	18	144	85	12.30	277	2.28
14								
15	Average	73.00	19.00	133.00	86.50	10.40	267.00	2.48
16	Std. Deviation	11.31	1.41	15.56	2.12	2.69	14.14	0.29
17								

Figure 14.17 The worksheet after calculations for *Occupation* 2.

Because the goal is to produce an analysis of occupations versus pulse rates, information for the second and remaining occupations must be selected from the database and copied to the spreadsheet; calculations are then made. Figure 14.17 shows the result for the second occupation. Results for the remaining occupations are obtained using the same techniques, but they are not shown here.

After the computations have been completed in the worksheet for all the occupations, the screen of Figure 14.18 was produced in preparation for charting *Pulse Rate* versus *Occupation*. Information has been copied from other parts of the spreadsheet to put it in the row form necessary to create a series chart.

Selecting the *New Series Chart* command from the **Chart** menu causes the dialog box of Figure 14.19 to be displayed. Information about the chart to be created is entered and the *Plot It!* button is clicked. The result is the chart shown in Figure 14.20.

Computer Practice 14.5

The goal of this practice session is to reproduce the operations described in the text to produce the analysis of occupations versus pulse rates. This activity should be a valuable aid in mastering the integrative aspects of Works.

	A	B	C	D	E	F	G
25							
26	Occupation	1	2	3	4		
27	Avg Pulse	69.00	73.00	74.50	65.50		
28							
29							

Figure 14.18 Data in row form for series chart creation.

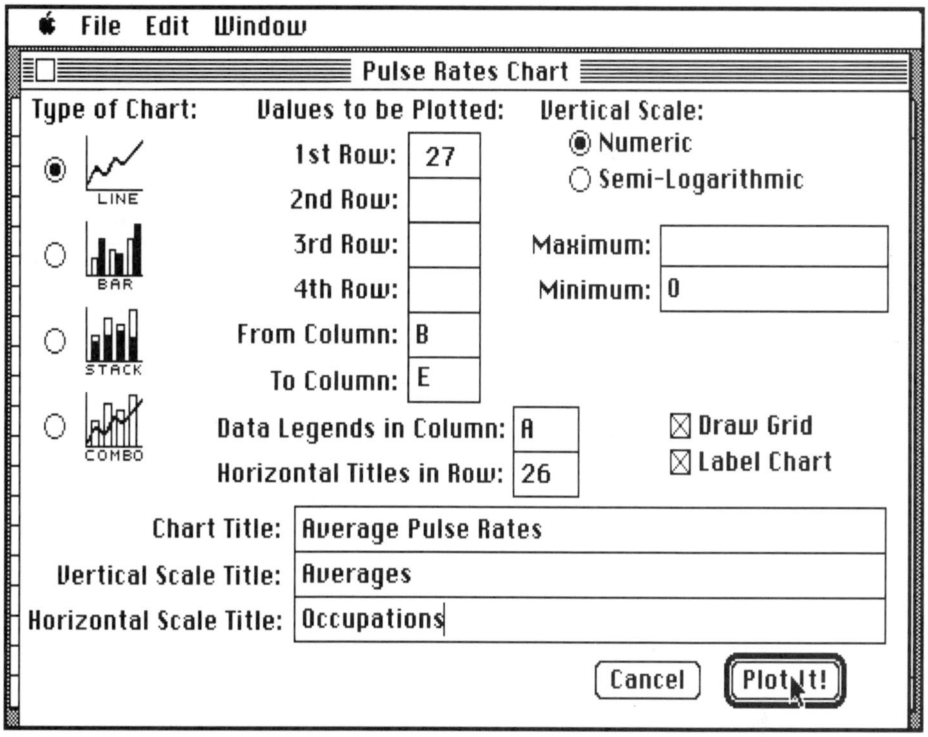

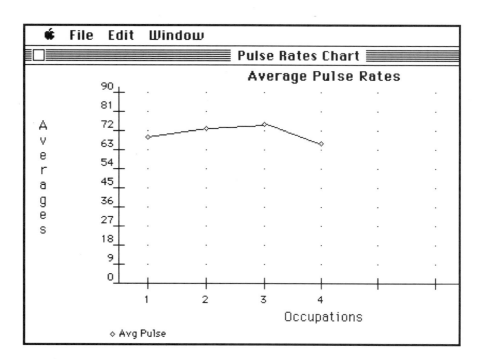

Figure 14.19 Dialog box for creating the series chart.

1. Open the *SurveyResults* database.
2. Select the set of records having *Occupation* = 1. This is accomplished as follows:

Figure 14.20 Series chart for occupations versus pulse averages.

■ Select the *Record Selection* command from the **Organize** menu. The following record selection dialog box will be displayed. (In the dialog box the selections for the next step have already been made.)

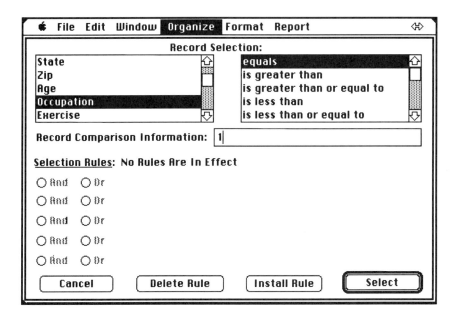

■ In the dialog box select the *Occupation* field in the left box and the equals operator in the right box. Type *1* into the box titled *Record Comparison Information*. Click the *Install Rule* button. Click the *Select* button. A screen will be displayed that is identical to Figure 14.11 except that the records are not highlighted.

■ Select the cells by dragging diagonally from the first cell of the *Occupation* column to the last filled cell of the *HW Ratio column*. The database should now look exactly like Figure 14.11.

3. Transfer the data to a new worksheet by performing the following:

■ Select the *Copy* command from the **Edit** menu. This will place a copy of the data (and the column titles) on the Clipboard.

■ Create a worksheet to receive the information by selecting the *New* command from the **File** menu. Save this worksheet with the name *Occupation Analysis*.

■ Select cells A1 through H3 on the *Occupation Analysis* worksheet to correspond to the database entries selected earlier and stored on the Clipboard.

■ Select the *Paste* command from the **Edit** menu. The result is shown in Figure 14.13.

4. Make the computations for the average and standard deviation on the *Occupation Analysis* worksheet by proceeding as follows:

■ Type *Average* in cell A6, and type *St. Deviation* in cell A7.

■ Compute the value of the average for pulse as follows:

• Select cell B6.

- Select the *Paste Function* command from the **Edit** menu. Find the AVERAGE function in the scroll box, click it, and click the *OK* button. The partial formula will appear in the formula bar.
- Select the range for the computation by pointing to cell B2 and dragging to cell B4.
- Click the check box in the formula bar; the computed average will appear in cell B6.

■ Compute the value of the standard deviation for pulse by performing steps similar to those just completed for the computation of the average.

- Select cell B7.
- Paste the formula =STDEV() in cell B7.
- Select the range B2 through B4.
- Click the check box; the computed standard deviation will appear in B7.

Note: It may be necessary to select the *Fixed* command from the **Format** menu and the *Number of Decimals* command from the **Format** menu to obtain two digits to the right of the decimal.

5. Make the computations for the other health categories by selecting cells B2 through H7 and using the *Fill Right* command of the **Edit** menu.

6. Create entries on the *Occupation Analysis* worksheet for *Occupation* = 2 by repeating steps 2 through 5 with appropriate changes in the locations of the cells used.

7. Copy *Occupation* and average *Pulse* data to rows 26 and 27 of the *Occupation Analysis* worksheet. The simplest method is to type the labels and values. If you wish, you can use edit commands to make the transfer. You should have the data shown in Figure 14.18 when you finish.

8. Create the *Pulse Rates* chart by performing the following:

■ Select the data to be plotted by pointing to cell A26 and dragging to cell E27.

■ Select the *New Series Chart* command from the **Chart** menu. The dialog box of Figure 14.19 will be displayed. By selecting the *Change Chart Name* command from the **Edit** menu, you can give the chart a name of your choosing.

■ Make the entries shown in Figure 14.19.

■ Click the *Plot It!* button. The chart of Figure 14.20 will be displayed.

Additional suggestions for computer practice follow. Do as many as time permits.

1. Repeat analysis described in the text but for *Occupation* versus *Cholesterol*.
2. Do an analysis of *Exercise* (pattern) versus *Pulse*.
3. Do an analysis of *Beef* (consumption) versus *Cholesterol*.
4. Do an analysis of *Stress* versus *Cholesterol*.
5. Do an analysis of *Smoking* (habits) versus *Pulse*.
6. Do an analysis of *Smoking* (habits) versus *Cholesterol*.

14.6 PREPARING A FINAL REPORT

When the report detailing the results of the study is prepared for the agency that requested the study, charts and computations will be included. It is easy to copy any Works SS charts or computations and paste them into the Works WP report. We give an outline of the required steps here.

- Open a new Works WP document and save it as *Survey Report.* Open the Works SS document *Occupation Analysis* and choose the *Select Definition* from the **Chart** menu. Choose the chart *Pulse Rates Chart* and plot it by clicking on the *Plot It!* button in the resulting dialog box (see Figure 14.19).

- Resize the displayed chart to a smaller size, similar to that illustrated in Figure 14.21, by using the grow box in its lower right corner.

- Select *Copy* from the **Edit** menu to copy the chart to the Clipboard. Next, select the window *Survey Report* from the **Window** menu and paste the chart into the WP document.

- Use the Works WP *Draw* command to place a border around the chart in *Survey Report.*

- Select the *Occupation Analysis* Works SS worksheet from the **Window** menu. Select the *No Grid* option from the **Options** menu; then select the data from which the *Pulse Rate Chart* was created. The situation is illustrated in Figure 14.22.

- Copy the selected SS data to the Clipboard, return to the *Survey Report* WP document, and paste the data into the report. Note that you may have to rearrange your graphics (i.e., chart and border—remember, they must be moved separately) and the newly pasted text to get an orderly display. You can also add your own descriptive text if you like. With a little effort, you

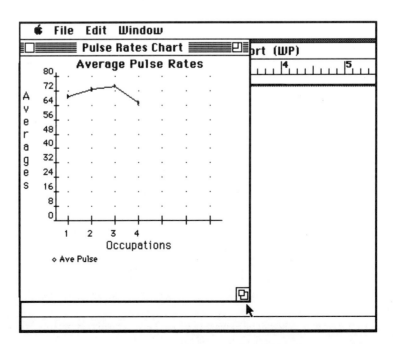

Figure 14.21: Resizing a chart in preparation for copying it.

	A	**B**	**C**	**D**	**E**	**F**	**G**
17	Occupation	Ave	Ave		Ave	Ave	Ave	Ave
18		Pulse	Respiration	BP 1	BP 2	Hemoglobin	Chloresterol
19	1	69.00		24.33	132.67	88.00	10.17	7.30
20	2	73.00		19.00	133.00	86.50	10.40	8.00
21	3	74.50		17.60	145.00	92.00	11.20	7.30
22	4	65.50		21.30	133.00	88.00	9.80	8.20
23							
24							
25	Occupation	1		2	3	4	
26	Ave Pulse	69.00		73.00	74.50	65.50	
27							
28							

Figure 14.22 Preparing to copy Works SS data to the report.

should be able to produce a document with an appearance similar to that shown in Figure 14.23.

By proceeding as described earlier, you can put as many charts and as much spreadsheet data into your report as you like. In fact, in a quite similar way, you could also place information from the database into your report as well. If you desire, the graphics material can be modified or enhanced using MacPaint. As you can see, it is quite easy to generate an interesting and informative Works WP report.

This concludes our discussion of the problem. There are, of course, many more comparisons that could be made based on the data. The goal was, however, to demonstrate how the Works modules could be used jointly to solve a complex

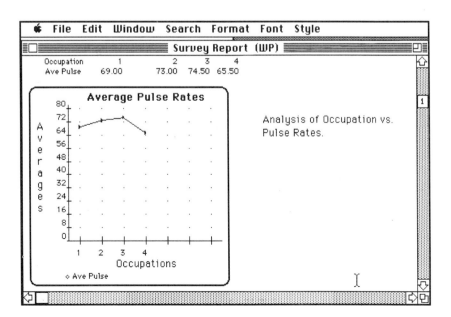

Figure 14.23 A portion of the report with chart and data pasted in.

SurveyResults (DB)

First Name	Last Name	Address	City	State	Zip	Age	Exercise	Beef
Joseph	Smith	2122 Live Oak Street	New Orleans	LA	70101	42	1	1
Thomas	Dedmond	1212 Palm Lane	Santa Clara	CA	95050	45	2	3
William	White	1020 Lakeview Way	Jonesville	OH	44444	48	1	2
Paul	Wrangler	1122 Hillside Dr.	Hyatt	NY	10800	43	3	3
George	Belton	1011 Maple Leaf St.	Hazel Green	AL	35820	44	3	4
Clancy	Duggan	105 Park Ave.	New York	NY	10045	44	4	3
Harrison	Matthews	220 Quincy St.	Roaring Spring	PA	16673	42	1	2
Joel	Harmon	102 E. Main	Taylors	SC	29687	43	2	4
Frank	Walker	339 Wellington St.	New York	NY	10034	47	4	1

SurveyResults (DB)

Beef	Poultry	Fish	Dairy	JobStress	Smoking	Survey Returned?	Height	Weight	Occupa
1	4	4	4	1	4	YES	72	210	
3	2	2	3	2	3	YES	70	188	
2	2	1	3	3	4	YES	68	155	
3	1	2	4	2	1	YES	71	177	
4	4	3	2	2	3	YES	74	196	
3	1	1	3	4	1	YES	72	221	
2	2	2	2	3	4	YES	65	144	
4	3	3	1	4	2	YES	73	188	
1	3	4	1	1	2	YES	66	143	

SurveyResults (DB)

Occupation	Pulse	Respiration	BP 1	BP 2	Hemoglobin	Chloresterol	HW Ratio
1	76	21	130	92	11.30	250	2.92
2	65	20	122	88	8.50	257	2.69
2	81	18	144	85	12.30	277	2.28
1	55	26	135	94	9.00	303	2.49
1	76	26	133	78	10.20	177	2.65
4	65	19	146	81	11.60	183	3.07
3	71	20	131	92	9.50	153	2.22
3	78	23	134	89	9.00	166	2.58
4	66	17	113	76	11.00	177	2.17

Figure 14.24 Sample database used in the examples.

problem. With respect to our goal, there is little to be gained by further discussion of this problem. You should have learned how the modules can be used together to solve involved problems. The integrated nature of the Works modules greatly increases the power of the system.

Computer Practice 14.6

1. Create a Works WP report similar to that described in this section using the *Occupation* versus *Pulse* analysis. Experiment with several different report layouts.

2. Using one of your additional analyses from Computer Practice 14.5, create a report that includes the material used in the previous problem as well as data and some charts from your analysis.

PART III

INVESTIGATING SOME ADVANCED CONCEPTS

PREPARING COMPLEX DOCUMENTS WITH MS WORD

L E A R N I N G   O B J E C T I V E S

- To gain an overview of Microsoft Word.

- To survey several of the advanced word processing features available in Microsoft Word.

- To learn how an advanced word processing program can be used to prepare complex documents.

This chapter describes the document preparation program Microsoft Word, which is one of the most powerful such packages currently available for the Macintosh. Microsoft Word has many features that are very valuable for writing such documents as term papers, large reports, and books. Reading this chapter should give you an appreciation for the ease with which complex documents can be produced with Microsoft Word. If you have access to the package, you should perform the computer practice activities given in the chapter; however, the new ideas discussed here will be valuable even if you cannot practice them.

15.1 SOME FUNDAMENTALS

Microsoft Word, hereafter called Word, is a very powerful word processing program. It can do almost any activity necessary for the preparation of a document. Because Word has so many features, it is impossible to discuss them all in a single chapter. Our coverage will be restricted to a few of the most commonly needed features, and even these will not be covered in depth.

A listing of some of the features found in Word follows. Several of these— including hyphenation, on-line help, and spelling checking—will be useful to you as soon as you start using Word. Do not think, however, that you need immediately to learn them all. At the time that you need to use a feature you can learn it.

- Calculations
- Customized menus
- Footnotes, auto-numbered
- Form letters
- Glossaries
- Help, on-line
- Hidden text
- Hyphenation
- Index generation
- Keyboard commands, comprehensive
- Multiple columns
- Outlining, integrated
- Page preview
- Short and long menus
- Show special symbols,
- Sorting
- Spelling checking
- Split windows
- Table of contents generation
- User-defined styles

Almost all your knowledge of the word processing module of Works transfers to Word. For example, all the techniques that you learned for selecting, cutting, pasting, and other editing activities can be used with Word. Many of the commands in the Works WP pull-down menus are also found in Word. So if you have learned Works, you can start immediately, without further instruction, to use Word. In this chapter we are going to concentrate on surveying some of the additional capabilities provided by Word. We will only briefly discuss those features that are the same as those found in Works.

GETTING STARTED WITH WORD.   To start Word find the icon shown in Figure 15.1 and double-click it (or select the icon and use the *Open* command of the **File** menu). You can create a new document by selecting the *New* command of the **File** menu.

To continue work on a previously created document, double-click the icon for the document. This causes Word to be executed and opens the document. An example Word document icon *Chapter 15* is shown in Figure 15.2.

THE WORD WINDOW. A Word window for a newly created document is shown in Figure 15.3. A horizontal bar, the *End* mark, shows the location of the end of the document. All Word documents have an *End* mark. The location of the insertion point is shown by a blinking vertical line.

The paragraph mark, which is shown in Figure 15.3, is a special symbol that is shown only if the *Show* ¶ command of the **Edit** menu has been selected. (*Note:* Special symbols are discussed in Section 15.4.) This command causes special symbols, such as ¶, that are not ordinarily visible to be displayed. The symbol marks the end of a paragraph and indicates the location of the formatting information that is associated with the paragraph. When the special symbols are not displayed, if you delete the blank space at the end of a paragraph, you also delete the ¶ and the formatting information. This will cause the formatting information of the next paragraph to be applied to the current paragraph, because the current paragraph has then become a part of the next paragraph. Word will not permit you to delete the last paragraph symbol in a document.

The selection bar, which is an invisible bar approximately 0.125 inch wide that forms the left border of the window, is very useful for selecting elements of the document. (Recall that Works WP also had a selection bar.) Whenever the pointer is in the selection bar, it becomes an arrow that points into the document. The following operations are allowed when the pointer is in the selection bar:

- *Click*—selects the entire line.
- *Double-click*—selects the current paragraph.
- *Command click*—selects the entire document.

The lower left-hand corner of the bottom line of the window shows the number of the current page of the document. If this page number is dimmed, it is not accurate because the document needs to be repaginated. In contrast to Works, which automatically repaginates the document as text is appended or edited, Word requires that the *Repaginate* command of the **Document** menu be selected to repaginate the document.

The block to the right of the page number block of the bottom line gives the style being used in the the paragraph containing the insertion point. A *style* is a collection of formatting rules that can be applied to a paragraph. For example, the style *Normal* implies a 6-inch line, first line of the paragraph indented 0.5 half inch, left justification of text, and tabs at all the 0.5-inch and 1-inch marks. *Normal* is an example of one of the 33 automatic styles that are applied by Word. Another

Figure 15.1 The Microsoft Word icon.

Figure 15.2 A Microsoft Word document icon.

automatic style is *Footnote*, which is used automatically when the *Footnote* command is selected in the **Document** menu. Later you will learn to create your own styles to make formatting documents easier.

The final part of the last line of the window is a horizontal scroll bar. A line in Word can be as wide as 22 inches, but the screen displayed by Word is approximately 6 inches wide. Hence, horizontal scrolling is necessary in the case of wide lines. A nice feature is automatic scrolling to the right (and back to the left) as long lines are typed. This allows the user to see all parts of a wide line as it is typed.

SHORT AND FULL MENUS. Word has two forms for some of its menus, a **short menu** and a **full menu**; the full form of a menu contains commands that are not available on the short form. The user can switch between the forms by selecting the available command *Short Menus* (or *Full Menus*) from the **Edit** menu. Figure 15.4 shows the short and full forms of the **Edit** menu. In this chapter we assume that full menus are being used. The full menus are given in Figure 15.46 at the end of the chapter.

SPEED OF OPERATION. Word has been developed to execute very rapidly as you type and edit information. As you edit a document, the document is not actually modified; instead information about the changes is saved in memory. When a *Save* command is given, Word inserts all changes into the document as it is being saved on disk. Inserting these changes can be time-consuming. In effect, the ability to save the document rapidly has been traded for speedy execution

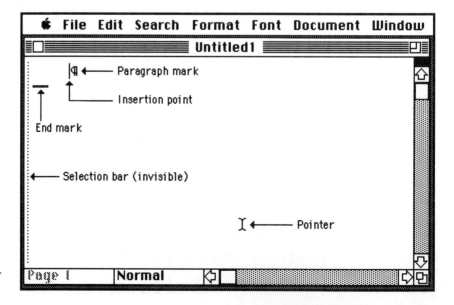

Figure 15.3 The Word window.

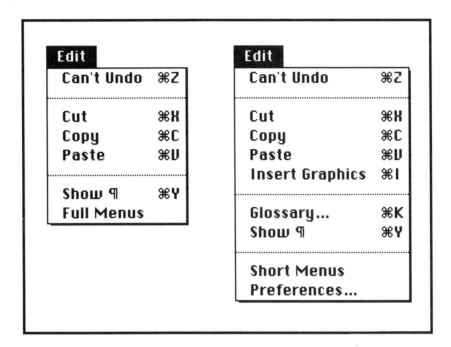

Figure 15.4 Short and full forms of the **Edit** menu.

during the entering and editing of a document. Do not be surprised if saving Word documents is slow.

As a Word document is being saved, the percentage of the document saved so far is displayed in the lower left-hand corner of the window. When 33 percent and 66 percent of the document have been saved, Word pauses to process graphics objects that may have been inserted into the document. These pauses may last for many seconds. Don't panic if the computer appears to be taking a very long time to save a document.

Exercise Set 15.1

1. Why is saving a Word document sometimes quite time-consuming? What advantage results from the choice to make saving a document more time-consuming than editing a document in Word? Why is additional time for saving a document required at 33 percent and 66 percent?
2. Describe the Word window.
3. When are special symbols displayed?
4. What is the selection bar and how is it used?
5. What is a style?
6. Why does Word have a horizontal scroll bar?
7. What is the difference in short and full menus?

15.2 USING THE ON-LINE HELP FEATURE

Word has many features, more than you will need for many jobs. Fortunately, you can learn to use a feature at the time that you need it. It is also likely that after several months of not using a feature, you will forget some of the details of how to use it. Both learning a feature and recalling details are aided significantly by the **on-line help feature** of Word. To use this feature, select the command *About Microsoft Word* from the **Apple** menu. Selecting this command causes the dialog box shown in Figure 15.5 to be displayed. Click the *Help* button to use the on-line help feature.

A window will then be displayed, similar to that shown in Figure 15.6, that contains an alphabetical index of topics for which help can be obtained. Using the scroll box you can find the topic of interest. You then select the topic by clicking it and click the *Help* button. (Alternately, point to the topic and double-click it.) Figure 15.7 shows the first page of the information that is displayed about the Help feature itself. Notice the vertical scroll box, which indicates that more information can be obtained by scrolling.

The index may not contain a topic in the form that seems reasonable to you, and some searching through likely possibilities may be necessary. The same problem exists with the Word manual, but the searching is faster with the on-line Help system. The on-line Help system is not, however, as extensive as that found in the manual.

Computer Practice 15.2

The goal of this practice is to help you become familiar with the features of the Word on-line Help facility.

1. Open Word and select the *About Microsoft Word* command from the **Apple** menu.
2. Click the *Help* button.
3. Scroll through the topics in the *Help* window until you find the *Selecting Text* entry. Double-click on this topic.
4. Determine what Help gives as the methods for selecting a word and selecting a sentence.
5. Click the *Previous* button. What happens?
6. Click the *Next* button twice. What happens?
7. Click the *Topics* button. What happens?
8. Scroll through the topics and select the *Keyboard-Character Formatting* entry. Read this material carefully.
9. Click the *Cancel* button.
10. Quit Word.

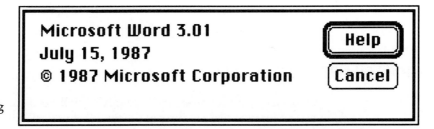

Figure 15.5 The *Help* dialog box.

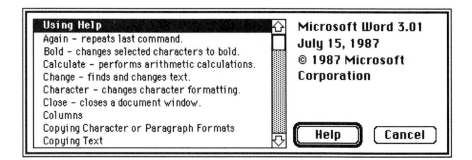

Figure 15.6 Index of Help topics.

15.3 USING THE RULER

Recall that with Works WP you could turn the ruler display on or off. In addition, the ruler always reflected the settings of the paragraph in which the insertion pointer was located. The **ruler** in Word behaves in a similar way. To turn the ruler on or off select the *Show Ruler/Hide Ruler* command from the **Format** menu.

The ruler has a different form, depending on whether short or full menus are being used. In Figure 15.8 the form of the ruler is shown for short menus. Notice that the ruler can be used to set the format for

- Left and right margins.
- Flush left tabs.
- Alignment (flush left, centered, flush right, and justified).
- Line spacing (single space, one-and-a-half space, and double space).

On a ruler, default tabs appear at the 0.5-inch and the 1-inch marks. If the pointer is moved to the ruler and clicked, a flush left tab is inserted at the location of the

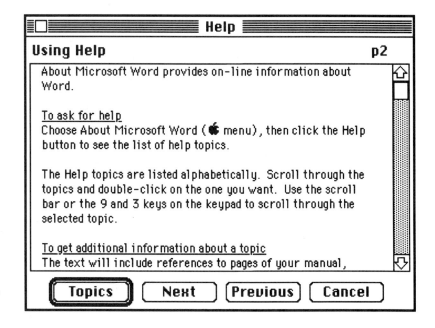

Figure 15.7 Display of information about Help.

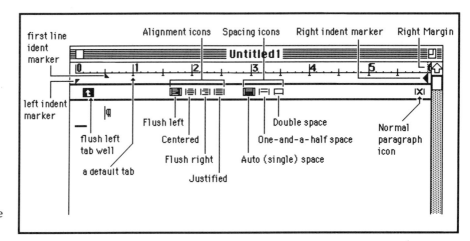

Figure 15.8 The form of the ruler for short menus.

pointer, and all default tabs to the left of the new tab are removed. The process is illustrated in Figure 15.9. To remove a nondefault tab from a ruler, point at the tab and drag it off the ruler.

If the *Full Menus* command has been selected, more icons appear on a ruler, as shown in Figure 15.10. The tab stop icons allow you to position text precisely within a line. Because different characters have different widths, using tabs is the best way to create tables in which the columns are aligned properly. Using the space bar to insert extra spaces to align the information in columns does not usually work satisfactorily. The effects of the tabs are shown in Figure 15.11. The *vertical line* icon creates vertical lines for tables and forms.

Exercise Set 15.3

1. To what part of a document do the settings on a ruler refer?
2. What must be done to display the ruler or remove the ruler from the screen?

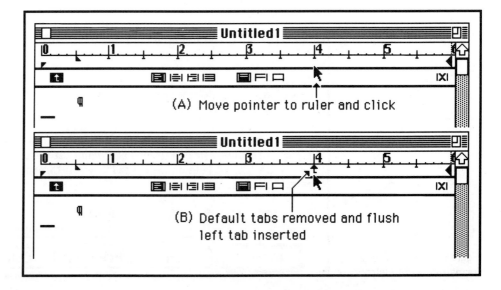

Figure 15.9 Inserting a flush left tab.

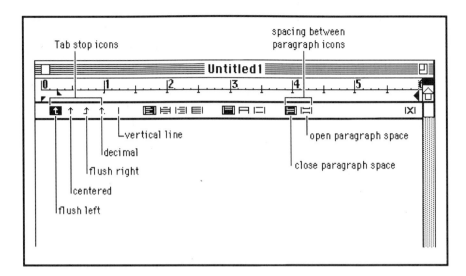

Figure 15.10 The form of the ruler for full menus.

3. List the kinds of alignments supported by Word and describe the appearance of text using each type of alignment.

5. Where are default tab markers in Word?

6. List the kinds of tabs supported by Word.

7. How is a tab inserted on a ruler?

8. How is a tab removed from a ruler?

9. What kind of tab is available on rulers when short menus are being used?

Computer Practice 15.3

1. Open Word and create a new document by selecting *New* from the **File** menu.

2. Select the *Full Menus* command from the **Edit** menu.

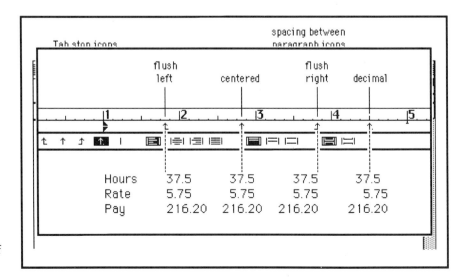

Figure 15.11 Illustration of the use of the Tab icon.

3. Select the *Show Ruler* command from the **Format** menu.
4. Create the table that is displayed in Figure 15.11.
5. Select the *Hide Ruler* command from the **Format** menu.
6. Use the *Save As* command from the **File** menu to save the table as *practice 15.3*.
7. Quit Works.

15.4 SPECIAL SYMBOLS

Word embeds **special symbols** as invisible characters in the text to indicate certain functions to be performed. For example, the paragraph symbol ¶ is inserted in the text at the end of every paragraph, and all the formatting information for a paragraph is stored at the location of the ¶ symbol. Every time the *Tab* key is pressed, the tab symbol ➡ is inserted in the text. A knowledge of these special symbols is useful in creating special formatting effects and in solving formatting problems.

The **Show ¶** /**Hide ¶** **command** of the **Edit** menu switches between showing the special symbols and hiding them. Figure 15.12 shows a portion of text with the *Show ¶* command active.

A list of the special symbols, their meanings, and the actions that produce them is given in Figure 15.13. If you need one of these keystrokes but have forgotten it, you can quickly obtain the needed information by using the Help feature and selecting the *Keyboard-Typing and Editing* topic. The handling of footnotes is covered in detail in Section 15.8.

Special symbols are also used to typeset mathematical formulas. You can obtain more information from the *Formula* topic of the Help feature. When the *Hide ¶* command is active, formulas are displayed in their final form, as shown in the lower half of Figure 15.14. When *Show ¶* is active, the special symbols used to create the formula are displayed, as shown in the upper half of the figure.

As·an·aid·to·the·aspiring·writer,·Flesh·gives·a·number·of·techniques
for·testing·the·readability·of·a·passage.··Three·sample·tables·are·given
below.¶

Average·sentence·length·in·words🔲¶
¶
Very·easy➡   ··8·or·less¶
Easy➡   11¶
Fairly·easy➡   14¶
Standard➡   17¶
Fairly·difficult➡   21¶
Difficult➡   25¶
Very·difficult➡   29·or·more➡ ¶
¶

Figure 15.12 Text showing special symbols.

Symbol	Meaning	Action Required
¶	Paragraph mark	Press the *Return* key
↵	End-of-line mark	Press *Shift-Return* keys
....	Normal spaces	Press the *Space Bar*
~~	Nonbreaking spaces	Press *Command-Space Bar*
✦	Tab mark	Press the *Tab* key
------	Normal hyphens	Press the *Hyphen* key
≈≈≈≈≈	Nonbreaking hyphens	Press *Command-~* keys
------	Optional hyphens	Press *Command-Hyphen* keys
\	Formula character	Press *Command-Option-Backslash* keys
☐	Graphic	Select the *Insert Graphics* command of the **Edit** menu
①	Page number	Click the page number icon in a header or footer
1/16/88	Date	Click the date icon in a header or footer
12:59 PM	Time	Click the time icon in a header or footer
①	Auto-numbered footnote reference mark	Select the *Footnote* command of the **Document** menu and select auto-reference in the dialog box

Figure 15.13 The meaning of the special symbols.

Exercise Set 15.4

1. What actions must be performed to display the special symbols and to hide them.
2. What is the general purpose of the special symbols?
3. What is the purpose of the following special symbols?
   a. ¶
   b. ↵
   c. ......
   d. →
4. Why is a knowledge of special characters useful?
5. How can you get information about special characters for creating formulas?

$$x_{1,2} = \backslash F(-b \pm \backslash R(b^2 - 4ac), 2a) \longleftarrow \text{Special symbols}$$

$$x_{1,2} = \frac{-b \pm \sqrt{b^2 - 4ac}}{2a} \longleftarrow \text{Resulting formula}$$

Figure 15.14 An example of a formula built using special symbols.

Computer Practice 15.4

1. Open Word and then open the document *practice 15.3* that was created and saved in Computer Practice 15.3.
2. Select the *Show ¶* command from the the **Edit** menu.
3. Identify all the special symbols associated with the document.
4. Close the document.
5. Quit Word.

15.5 SPELLING CHECKING

The **spelling checking** feature of Word has a built-in dictionary of 80,000 words. In addition, words not found in the built-in dictionary can be saved easily in specialized dictionaries, called *user dictionaries*, that are created by the user. For example, if you need to check the spelling of a set of technical terms, the words can be saved as they are encountered during the spelling checking.

To use the spelling checker, you first place the insertion pointer at the location where you want the checking to begin. Then you select the *Spelling* command from the **Document** menu as shown in Figure 15.15. Notice that in the third line of the first paragraph of the figure, the word *number* has been misspelled as *nubmer*. We will follow the operation of the spelling checker through the detection and correction of this error.

Selecting the *Spelling* command causes a window named *Spelling* to be opened as shown in Figure 15.16. Clicking the *Start Check* button will begin the process of checking words in the document for incorrect spelling. During the time that the checking is occurring, a small watch will be displayed. When a suspected error is found, the unknown word is highlighted in the text, and the word is placed after the phrase *Unknown Word* in the Spelling window.

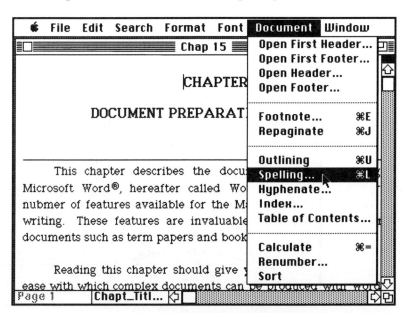

Figure 15.15 Selecting the spelling checking feature.

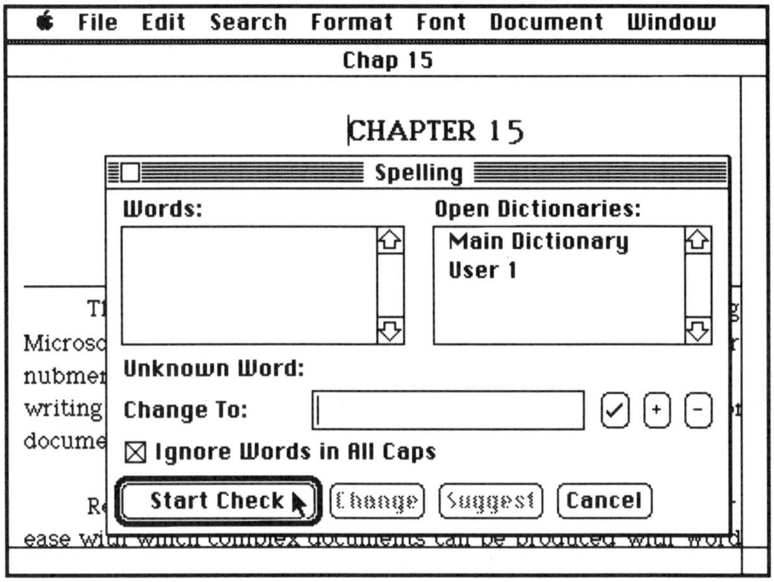

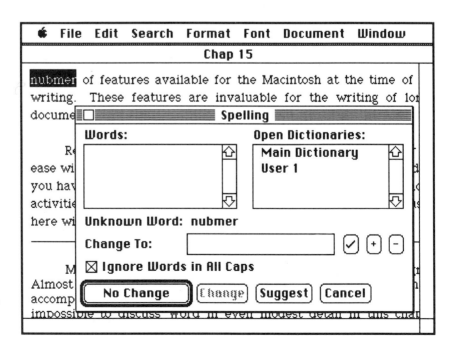

Figure 15.16 The *Spelling* window.

Figure 15.17 shows the situation when the first unknown word is encountered. The highlighted word in this example, *nubmer*, is misspelled, but in other instances the word may be a proper name or a special word not found in the dictionary. Several responses are available.

■ Clicking the *No Change* box causes this occurrence of the word and all future occurrences during your current work session to be treated as correct.

Figure 15.17 Finding of an unknown word by the spelling checker.

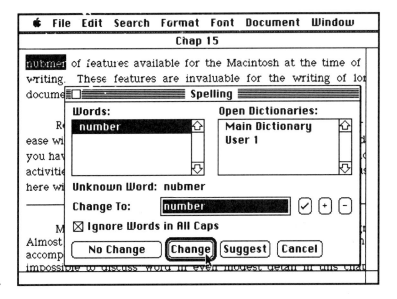

Figure 15.18 Ready to change a misspelled word.

- The word may be one that you would like to save in a dictionary for use in future work. In this case, select a user dictionary in the *Spelling* window by clicking it. Then click the + button.

- The word may be misspelled. Suggestions for the correct spelling can be obtained by clicking the *Suggest* button. To substitute a correctly spelled version of the word, click the correct version, which will then be transferred to the *Change To* box. Finally, click the *Change* button to substitute the correct word. This situation is shown in Figure 15.18 just before the *Change* button is clicked.

- The spelling checker may not have a correct spelling in its list of suggestions. In some cases the spelling may be a variant, such as a plural of one of the suggested words, may have an interchanged pair of letters that the speller did not detect, or may otherwise be misspelled. Click the *No Change* button if the word is correct. If you see that the word is misspelled, click the incorrect version that is after the phrase *Unknown Word* to transfer it to the *Change To* box, edit the incorrect version, and click the *Change* button.

As soon as the spelling has been changed, the search for other unknown words will continue. When the end of the document is reached, you can either stop or continue from the beginning of the document.

Computer Practice 15.5

1. Open Word and select the *New* command from the **File** menu.

2. Type the text, which contains spelling errors, shown in the following box exactly as you see it. Line 1 contains the errors *chech* and *speling*. Line 4 contains the errors *proccess* and *ckeck*. Line 6 contains the errors *begining* and *startign*.

3. Save the incorrect document with the name *practice 15.5*.

4. Perform a spelling check of the incorrect paragraph. Whenever an error is found, click the *Suggest* button; find the correct spelling in the list of suggested words and select it; and click the *Change* button.

> The ability to chech speling is a valuable feature of Microsoft Word. The checking can be done at any time and can be repeated during a session. One approach that speeds the checking proccess is to ckeck only the new text. To perform this activity, place the pointer at the begining of the new text before startign the spelling check.

5. Quit Word. Do not save the corrected document; you will use the document with errors again in Computer Practice 15.6.

15.6 HIDDEN TEXT

Hidden text is information that you do not want to print in your final document. For example, in preparing a long document, you can write notes about work to be done at some future time. Hidden text can be displayed on the screen, printed, or made to disappear.

To create hidden text, select the *Character* command from the **Format** menu. The dialog box shown in Figure 15.19 will then be displayed. Notice in the *Character Formats* portion of the window, the box titled *Hidden*. Clicking this box will cause all text entered thereafter to be treated as hidden text until the *Hidden* box is unchecked. A dotted line is drawn under all hidden text. A short hidden text note is shown in Figure 15.20.

To show or hide the hidden text, select the *Preferences* command of the **Edit** menu. The *Preferences* dialog box is shown in Figure 15.21. Clicking the *Show Hidden*

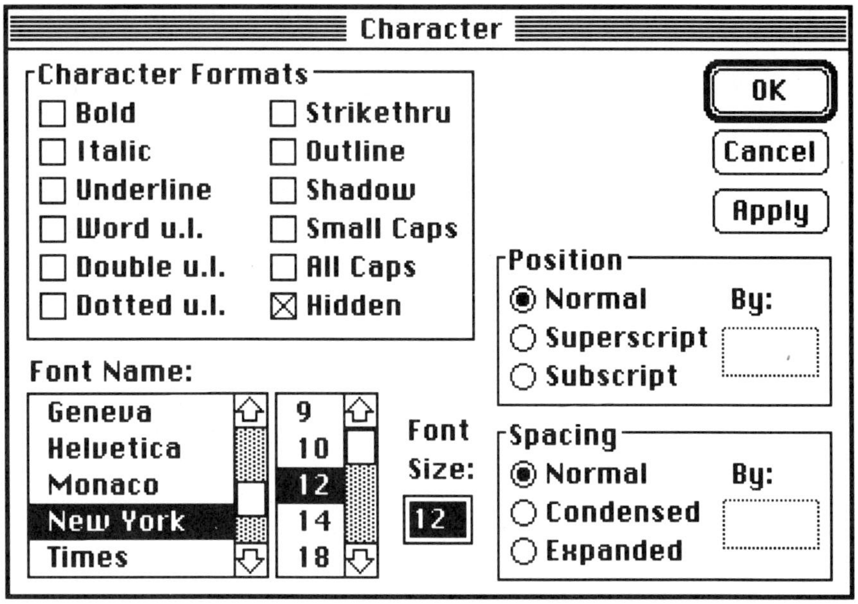

Figure 15.19 Selecting hidden text using the *Character* dialog box.

> ### CHAPTER 15
>
> ### DOCUMENT PREPARATION WITH WORD®
>
> <u>Don't forget to show how to handle footnotes.</u>
>
> ---
>
> This chapter describes the document preparation prog Microsoft Word®, hereafter called Word, which has the lar number of features available for the Macintosh at the time of writing. These features are invaluable for the writing of lo documents such as term papers and books.

Figure 15.20 An example of hidden text.

Text box so that it contains an *x* causes the text to be displayed. Clicking the box again causes the hidden text not to be displayed.

Computer Practice 15.6

1. Open Word and open the document *practice 15.5* that was created in the last section.

2. Enter the following hidden text at the beginning of the document: "This document must be checked for spelling." If you click the *Show Hidden Text* box in the *Preferences* dialog box, the result should be the same as that in the following box.

> <u>This document must be checked for spelling.</u>
>
> The ability to chech speling is a valuable feature of Microsoft Word. The checking can be done at any time and can be repeated during a session. One approach that speeds the checking proccess is to ckeck only the new text. To perform this activity, place the pointer at the begining of the new text before startign the spelling check.

3. Select the *Preferences* command from the **Edit** menu and click the *Show Hidden Text* box in the *Preferences* dialog box to remove the x. Notice that the hidden text disappears.

4. Quit Word.

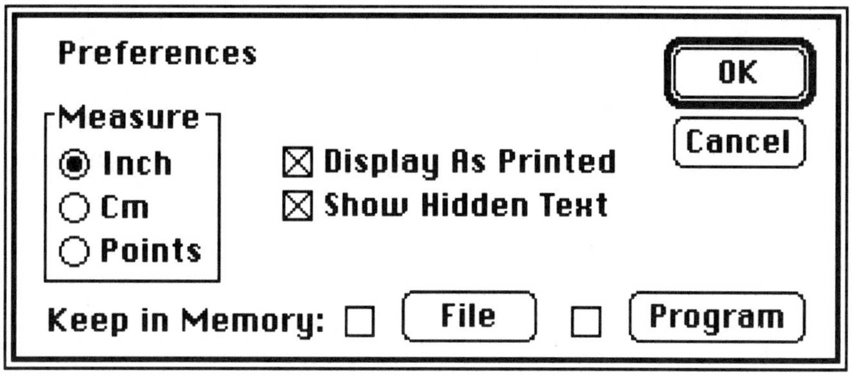

Figure 15.21 The *Preferences* dialog box.

15.7 SPLIT WINDOWS

When full menus are being used, the upper right-hand corner of the Word window contains a small black rectangle, called the split bar. Dragging the split box, as illustrated in Figure 15.22, to a new location in the vertical scroll bar creates a **split window.** As an example, in Figure 15.23 the split bar has been used to create a split window for viewing an early version of this chapter.

We now have two independent windows for viewing a document. Editing can be done in either window. With the scroll bars for a window, any part of the document can be viewed. This is a very valuable feature for long documents because we often need to look at some other part of the document to complete the current work. Notice that in the example in Figure 15.23, the beginning of the chapter appears in the upper window, and page 23 (in dimmed form) appears in the lower window.

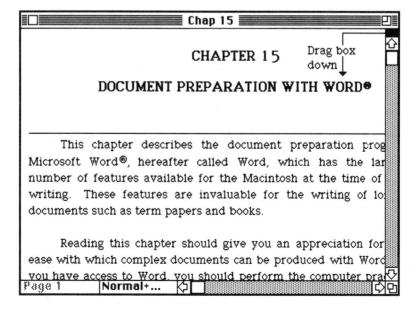

Figure 15.22 Dragging the split bar.

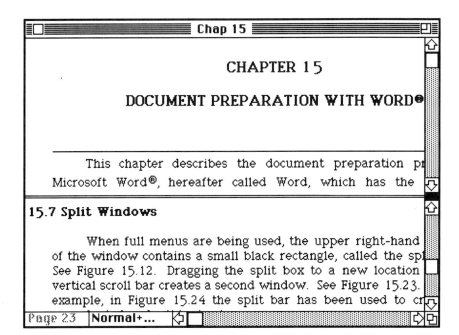

Figure 15.23 An example of a split window.

Computer Practice 15.7

The purpose of this exercise is to experiment with split windows. A short document will be created and manipulated.

1.   Open Word and select the *New* command from the **Edit** menu.

2.   Type the document that appears in the following box.

> When full menus are being used, the upper right-hand window contains a small black rectangle, called the split bar. Dragging the split box to a new location in the vertical scroll bar creates a second window. These windows are independent of each other and either can be used for viewing a document.
>
> With the scroll bars for a window, any part of the document can be viewed. This is a very valuable feature for long documents because we often need to look at some other part of the document to complete the current work.

3.   Select the entire document by pressing the *Command* key and clicking. Move the right indent marker to 4 inches so that the document will need more lines.

4.   Drag the split bar to approximately the middle of the window. Experiment with scrolling the two windows. Your window should look something like the figure on the facing page.

5.   Quit Word.

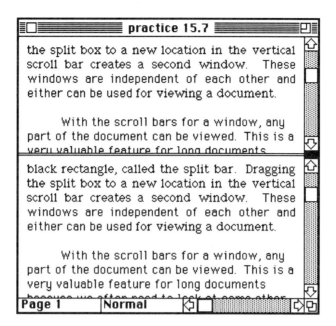

15.8 FOOTNOTES

Word makes the inclusion of **footnotes** in a document easy and convenient. It will number footnotes automatically, renumber footnotes when a footnote is added or deleted, and give a choice for the printing location of the footnotes. Footnotes can be edited at any time using the usual techniques.

To create a footnote, select the *Footnote* command of the **Document** menu. The *Footnote* dialog box shown in Figure 15.24 will be displayed. Notice that the *Auto-numbered Reference* box is checked. This means that an appropriate footnote reference number will be added automatically at the location of the insertion point if the *OK* box is clicked. For example, if four footnotes have been added earlier in the document, the next footnote will be numbered 5. If a footnote is added between footnotes 4 and 5, for example, the new footnote is given the number 5, and all footnotes after it are renumbered.

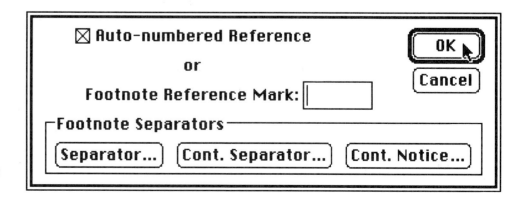

Figure 15.24 The *Footnote* dialog box.

The following actions occur when the *OK* box is clicked.

- A footnote reference number is inserted as a superscript in the location of the insertion point.
- The window splits to reveal a footnote window in the lower part of the original window.
- The reference mark is inserted in the footnote window.
- The insertion point is moved to the new location in the footnote window.

The situation at this stage is shown in Figure 15.25. Considerable work has been done automatically for the user.

After the footnote information has been typed into the footnote window, drag the split bar to either the top or the bottom of the window. The footnote window will disappear and the insertion point will return to the location at which you entered the footnote reference.

The location of the footnotes in the printed document can be selected by clicking the appropriate button in the *Page Setup* dialog box. This box, which is shown in Figure 15.26, is obtained by selecting the *Page Setup* command of the **File** menu.

The footnote window can be opened at any time by pressing the *Shift* key and dragging down the split bar. This is useful, for example, for examining the footnotes and editing them. To close the footnote window proceed as described above.

Computer Practice 15.8

In this practice you will enter text that will be used here for entering a footnote and used in the next section for page preview.

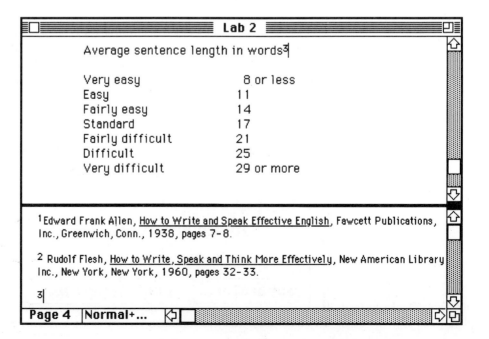

Figure 15.25 Adding a footnote.

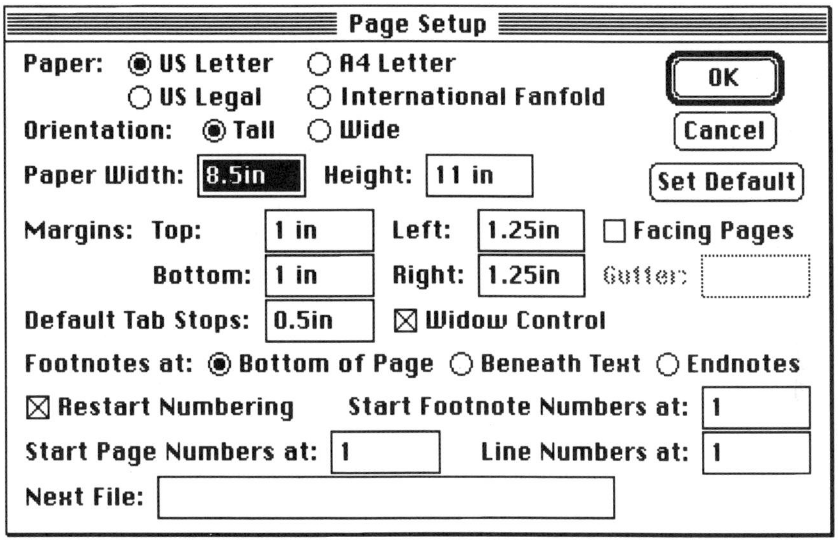

```
┌──────────────────── Page Setup ────────────────────┐
│ Paper:  ⦿ US Letter    ○ A4 Letter            ┌────────┐ │
│         ○ US Legal     ○ International Fanfold │   OK   │ │
│ Orientation:   ⦿ Tall  ○ Wide                 └────────┘ │
│ Paper Width: [8.5in]   Height: [11 in]        [ Cancel ] │
│                                               [Set Default]│
│ Margins: Top:    [1 in]    Left:  [1.25in]   ☐ Facing Pages│
│          Bottom: [1 in]    Right: [1.25in]   Gutter [    ]│
│ Default Tab Stops: [0.5in]    ☒ Widow Control            │
│ Footnotes at: ⦿ Bottom of Page ○ Beneath Text ○ Endnotes │
│ ☒ Restart Numbering    Start Footnote Numbers at: [1]    │
│ Start Page Numbers at: [1]      Line Numbers at: [1]     │
│ Next File: [                                        ]    │
└─────────────────────────────────────────────────────────┘
```

Figure 15.26 Selecting the footnote printing location.

1. Open Word and select the *New* command from the **File** menu.

2. Type the document titled *Writing Using a Word Processor* and found in the box on the next page.

3. Find the words *E. F. Allen* near the end of the second paragraph. Place the insertion pointer immediately after *Allen* and select *Footnote* command of the **Document** menu. If an *x* is not in the *Auto-numbered Reference* box, click it. Click the *OK* button. The footnote reference number 1 will be automatically inserted, and the footnote window will appear in the lower half of the window.

4. Type the following for the footnote:

   Edward Frank Allen, *How to Write and Speak Effective English*, Fawcett Publications, Inc., Greenwich, Conn., 1938, pages 7-8.

5. Select the *Page Setup* command from the **File** menu. Click the *Footnotes at Bottom of Page* button.

6. Drag the split bar to the bottom of the window.

7. Save the document as *practice 15.8*.

15.9 PAGE PREVIEW

The **page preview** feature is one of the most useful of the features available with Word. The Macintosh screen is too small to see an entire page at once; consequently, it is not unusual to print a document and then find that the pages are not properly composed. With the page preview feature, you can quickly examine the layouts of the pages of a document.

To access the page layout feature, select the *Page Preview* command of the **File** menu. Figure 15.27 shows the form of the page preview window. Normally, two adjacent pages are previewed in the window. The *One Page/Two Page* icon can be used to switch between the viewing of one or two pages.

Writing Using a Word Processor

Using a word processor in the writing process has many advantages. A poor typist does not have to worry about mistakes because it is easy to correct them. An error in the design of a document can be eliminated using the cut and paste feature. Spelling can be checked and corrected easily. The list of advantages goes on and on.

But it is a mistake to think that having a word processor will make you a good writer. First you must have something worth saying. Then you must say it in an entertaining and informative way. Such writing is difficult and takes much practice. E. F. Allen gave the following description of the situation.

"Writing is at once the easiest and most difficult of the arts.

"It is the easiest because its tools--paper, pen, and ink--are familiar and accessible to all, and skill in their use may be acquired by any intelligent person.

"It is the most difficult because, in order to excel in the use of tools so familiar to everybody, a person must exercise the same care and diligence practiced by his fellows who write.

"The ability to write well is possible to anyone, whatever his station in life or his formal education. This is given ample proof in the history of literature.

"Shakespeare, greatest genius of letters, was a ne'er-do-well country youth who attended school less than seven years. Robert Burns was a peasant laborer of no formal education. Daniel Defoe was a butcher's son, a brickmaker and jack-of-all-trades. Keats was a stablekeeper's son, who was taken early from grammar school to be made an orderly in a London hospital."

The displayed pages are too small to read (see Figure 15.28) but large enough to show clearly the overall composition of a page. The pages displayed will be those at the current insertion point in the document. Clicking one of the vertical scroll arrows will move the preview one page backward (with the upper arrow) or one page forward (with the lower arrow). The scroll box can be dragged for rapid movement through the document.

Use the *Magnifier* icon to obtain a close-up view of a portion of a document. Click the icon and move it to the location of interest and click again. The indicated portion of the document will be magnified to normal size, as shown in Figure 15.29. Use the scroll arrows and boxes to see other parts of the page. Click the *Magnifier* icon to return to the normal page preview format.

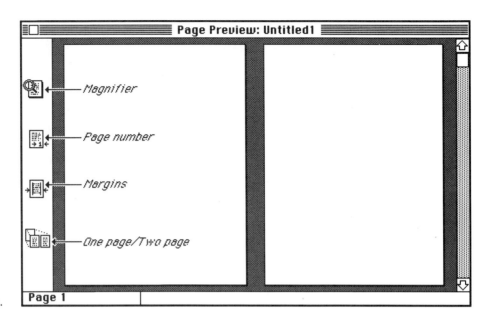

Figure 15.27 The form of the *Page Preview* window.

The *Page Number* icon can be used to position the page number. When this icon is clicked, the pointer changes to the current page number. Moving the pointer to the desired location and clicking places the page number at that position. As the pointer moves, its horizontal and vertical positions are displayed in the bottom line of the window in the page number area.

When the *Margins* icon is clicked, the margins, page breaks, page number, headers, and footers are displayed. These can all be dragged to new locations, and as they are dragged the exact position is displayed in the page number area. If a page break is dragged, the page is redrawn as soon as the button is released. For the other page elements, the page must be double-clicked to cause the page to be redrawn.

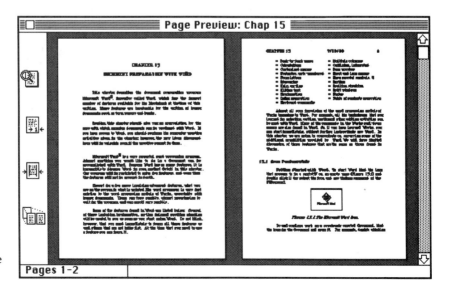

Figure 15.28 A sample page preview.

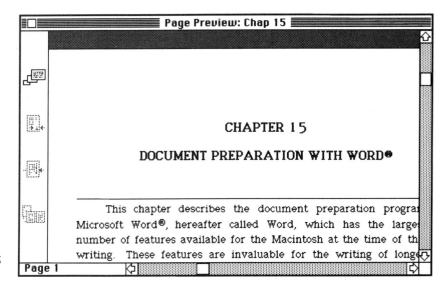

Figure 15.29 Effect of using the magnifier icon.

Changes made using the *Page Number* icon and the *Margins* icon are global changes in the document. Thus, they should not be used to attempt reformatting a single page.

Computer Practice 15.9

1. Open Word and open the document *practice 15.8*.
2. Select the *Page Preview* command of the **File** menu. You should see the footnote at the bottom of the first page and several lines of text at the top of the second page.
3. Use the magnifier icon to examine the contents of the first page.
4. Click the close box.
5. Select the *Page Setup* command of the **File** menu. Click the *Footnotes at Endnote* button.
6. Select the *Page Preview* command of the **File** menu. Notice that the footnote has moved to the end of the text on the second page.
7. Click the close box and close the document.
8. Quit Word.

15.10 MULTIPLE COLUMNS

In this section you will learn how to create **multiple-column documents,** as shown in Figure 15.30. The format shown is that of newspaperlike columns. Formats are also available for side-by-side columns in which the text does not flow from the bottom of one column to the top of the next column, as is done in newspaper columns, and for columns in tables. These formats are not discussed here, so you

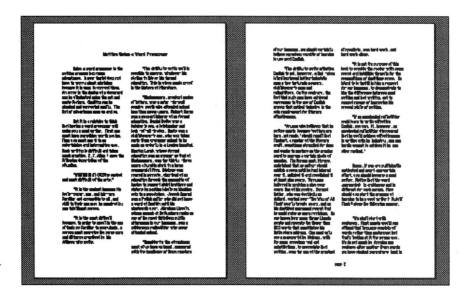

Figure 15.30 Newspaper-like columns as shown by *Page Preview*.

should consult the *Columns* topic of the Help feature if you have a need for one of them.

For the text of the newspaper columns example, the insertion pointer was positioned immediately before the word *Using* of the first paragraph. The *Command* and *Enter* keys were pressed simultaneously to break the document into two sections as shown in Figure 15.31. The break is signaled by a double dotted line. The top section for the title has left and right indents set at 0 inch and 6 inches, respectively.

To create newspaperlike columns, use the *Section* command of the **Format** menu. The window shown in Figure 15.32 will be displayed. A **section** is defined

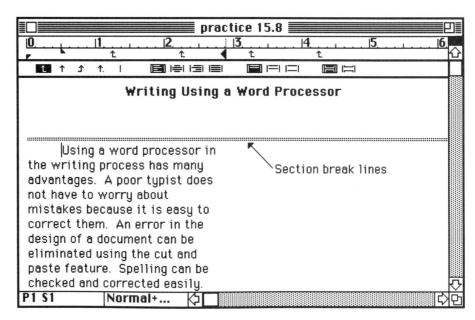

Figure 15.31 Typing of text for newspaperlike columns.

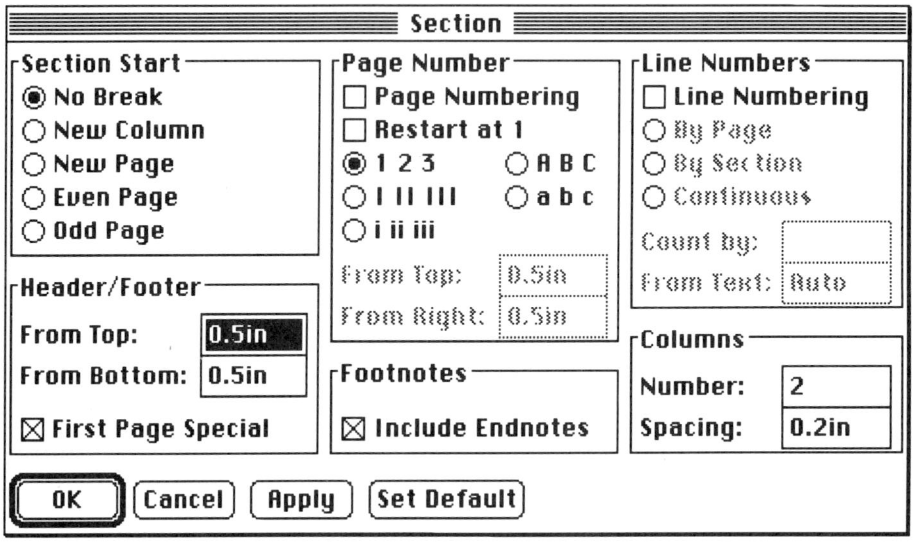

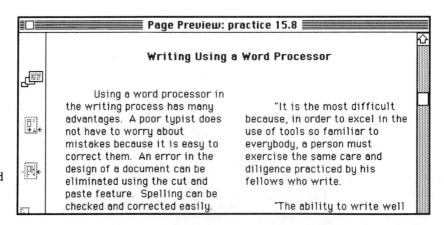

Figure 15.32 The *Section* window with two columns entered.

as a part of a document whose page layouts differ from other parts of the document with respect to any one or more of: page number format; position of page numbers, headers, and footers; location of footnotes; or number of columns.

The lower section was set for multiple columns. This was done by selecting the *Section* command of the **Format** menu. The *No Break* button in the upper left-hand corner of the *Section* dialog box was clicked because there is more than one column layout on the page. If the *No Break* button is not clicked, a break occurs after the title, and all other text moves to the second page. In the *Columns* block found in the lower right hand corner, 2 was entered for the number of columns, and 0.2 was entered for the separation between columns. A narrow single column appeared immediately.

The division of the text into two (or more) columns does not actually occur until the text is printed. To see how the text will appear when it is printed, use the *Page Preview* command. Figure 15.33 uses the magnifier icon of *Page Preview* to show the final newspaperlike columns of this example.

Figure 15.33 The newspaperlike columns displayed in magnified form using *Page Preview*.

Page Preview: practice 15.8

Writing Using a Word Processor

Using a word processor in the writing process has many advantages. A poor typist does not have to worry about mistakes because it is easy to correct them. An error in the design of a document can be eliminated using the cut and paste feature. Spelling can be checked and corrected easily.

"It is the most difficult because, in order to excel in the use of tools so familiar to everybody, a person must exercise the same care and diligence practiced by his fellows who write.

"The ability to write well

Computer Practice 15.10

In this practice you will create the newspaperlike columns described in Section 15.10. Except for the size of the windows, your results should be similar to the figures shown in the section.

1. Open Word and open the document *practice 15.8*.

2. Select the entire document by placing the pointer in the selection bar, pressing the *Command* key, and clicking. If the ruler is not displayed, select the *Show Ruler* command from the **Format** menu.

3. Set the first line indent marker and the left indent marker both to 0 inches. Set the right indent pointer to 6 inches.

4. Move the insertion pointer to immediately before the word *Using* in the first paragraph. Press simultaneously the *Command* and *Enter* keys. A double dotted line should appear above the first line of the paragraph to indicate a section break (see Figure 15.31). The insertion pointer should still be immediately before the word *Using* which is now in the second section.

5. Set the values for the second section by selecting the *Section* command from the **Format** menu. Then click the *No Break* button. Set the *Number of Columns* to 2 and the *Spacing* to 0.2. The text should immediately be displayed as a narrow single column (see Figure 15.31).

6. Use the *Page Preview* command of the **File** menu to see the double columns.

7. Quit Word.

15.11 STYLES AND THE WORK MENU

It highly desirable that the formatting of the parts of a document be consistent throughout the document. In longer documents, obtaining this consistency is very difficult if you depend on your memory to recall the details. The solution provided by Word is to let the user define a collection of paragraph formats, called **styles**, that can be applied with a single command. To make the application of styles easy, a special menu, the **Work** menu, can be used to contain styles of interest. Figure 15.34 shows a **Work** menu that has three installed styles. This section describes how to create a style and install it in the **Work** menu. After a style has been created, formatting changes can be made to all pargraphs using that style by editing the definition of the style.

To define a style, select the *Define Styles* command of the **Format** menu. If no styles have been defined previously, the window shown in Figure 15.35 will be displayed. Notice that the predefined style, *Normal*, is highlighted. For the high-

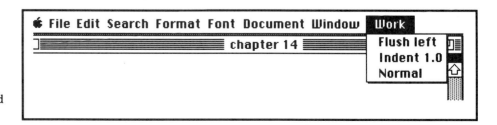

Figure 15.34 The *Work* menu with three installed styles.

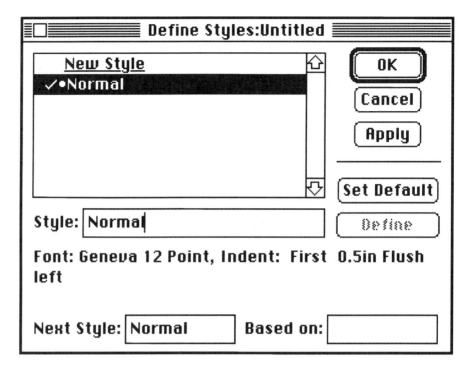

Figure 15.35 The *Define Styles* dialog box.

lighted style, the formatting associated with it is shown below the box titled *Style*. For this example, *Normal* style shown here is Geneva 12 point, with the first line of a paragraph indented 0.5 inches, and with flush left lines. If you do not like this definition for *Normal* style, it can be changed and saved as the default using the *Set Default* button. Notice that the window also contains a line called *New Style*.

Perhaps the simplest way to define a style is to create a paragraph that has the desired format and use it as an example in the defining process. As an illustration, suppose that a paragraph has been created that is like a normal paragraph except that the first line of the paragraph is not indented, that is, the first line is flush left. We will call this *Flush left*.

Place the insertion point anywhere in the example paragraph. Select the *Define Styles* command from the **Format** menu. In the *Define Styles* window click the *New Styles* line. Below the *Style* box the information *Normal + Indent: First 0 in* will be displayed. This means that the new style being defined by the example paragraph is like *Normal* except for the nonindenting of the first line. Type the name of the style, *Flush left*, in the *Style* box. The result is shown in Figure 15.36. Click the *OK* box to complete the creation of the style. Figure 15.37 shows the defining of a style, *Indent 1.0*, that is based on the style *Flush left*.

To add a style to the **Work** menu, select the *Styles* command of the **Format** menu. A *Styles* dialog box of the form shown in Figure 15.38 will be displayed. The number and names of the styles shown will depend upon the definitions made previously. Press simultaneously *Command-Option-+* (plus) and the pointer will change into a plus sign, +. Move the +pointer over the style to be added to the **Work** menu, *Normal* in this case, and click. The style will be added to the **Work** menu, and the **Work** menu will be added to the menu bar if this is the first style added. The **Work** menu now has the form shown in Figure 15.39. This process can be repeated for any number of styles.

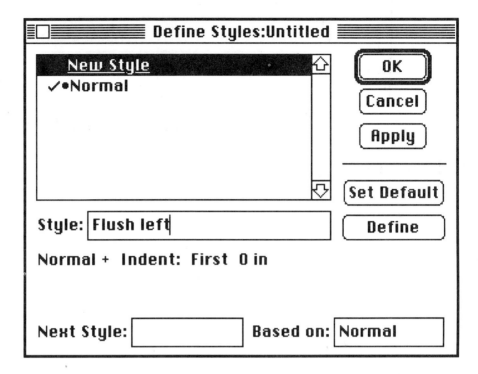

Figure 15.36 Defining the *Flush left* style.

To set a paragraph to a style, place the pointer anywhere within the paragraph. Then select the style from the **Work** menu. All the formatting rules associated with the style will be applied immediately.

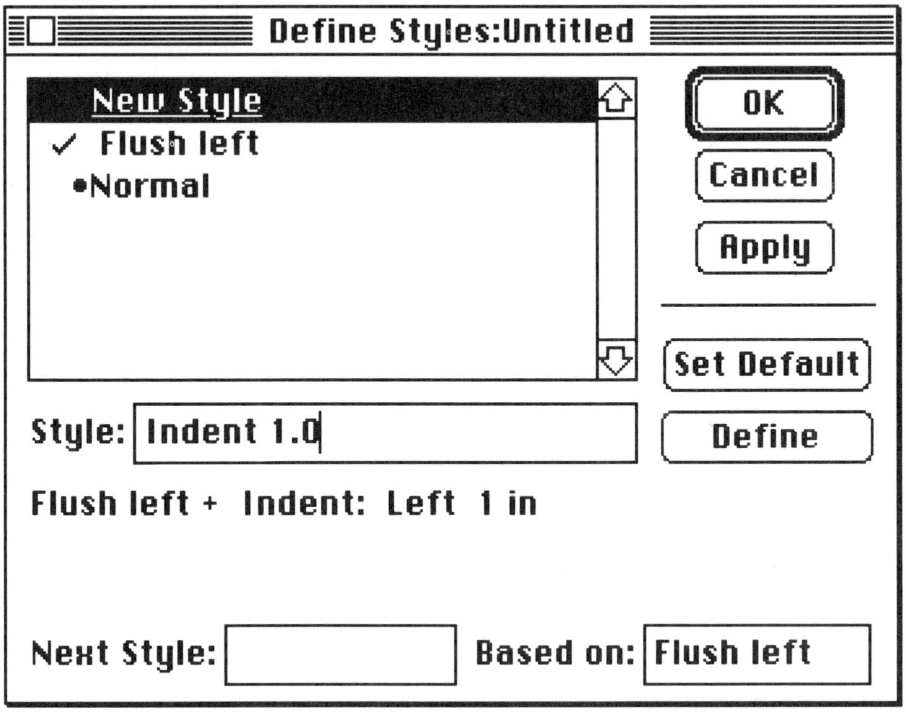

Figure 15.37 Defining the *Indent 1.0* style.

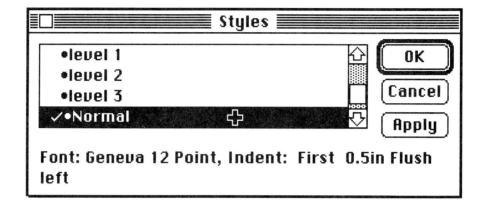

Figure 15.38 Adding the *Normal* style to the **Work** menu.

Computer Practice 15.11

1. Open Word and select the *New* command of the **File** menu.

2. Select the *Show Ruler* command from the **Format** menu, select the *Geneva* command from the **Font** menu, and select the *12 Point* command from the **Font** menu.

3. Select the *Define Styles* command from the **Format** menu. In the resulting dialog box, the entry *New Style* will be highlighted. Click on the style named *Normal*.

4. Select the *Geneva* option from the **Font** menu, and select the *12 Point* command from the **Font** menu.

5. Set the left and right indents to 0 and 6 inches, respectively. Set the first line indent to 0.5 inches.

6. You should see a dialog box exactly like Figure 15.35.

7. Click the *Define* button. At this point the *Normal* style will have been redefined to have the *Geneva* Font, character size *12 point*, and first indent at 0.5 inches with all other lines flush left.

8. Click *New Style*. Type *Flush left* in the *Style* box. On the Ruler, move the first line indent to 0 inches. You should now have a window exactly like Figure 15.36. Click the *Define* button to complete definition of the *Flush left* style.

9. Click *New Style*. Type *Indent 1.0* in the *Style* box. On the Ruler, move the first line indent to 1 inch. You should now have a window exactly like Figure 15.37. Click the *Define* button to complete definition of the *Flush left* style.

10. Press the keys *Command-Option- +* simultaneously to obtain the + pointer. Click the *Normal* style. The name **Work** will be added to the menu bar (if it is not already present) and *Normal* will be added as an option under this menu. Repeat these steps to add the *Flush left* and *Indent 1.0* styles to the **Work** menu.

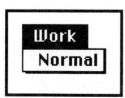

Figure 15.39 The **Work** menu after *Normal* is added as the first style.

11. Click the *OK* button to return to the document. Examine the **Work** menu to see that the styles *Normal, Flush left,* and *Indent 1.0* have been added to it.

12. Type in a short paragraph. Place the selection point anywhere in the paragraph. Successively click on the styles *Normal, Flush left,* and *Indent 1.0* under the **Work** menu to see the effect on your paragraph. Note that *all* paragraphs having a given style will be altered if that style is changed under *Define Style.* Thus, it is very easy to change the form of an entire document if styles have been used.

13. Quit Word.

15.12 FORM LETTERS

Word has a powerful facility for creating mailing labels, **form letters,** or other individualized documents. Word can do all the things Works WP can and many others. Some of the capabilities of Word will be examined in this section by developing a form letter to send to the participants in the Lifestyle and Health Survey described in Chapter 14. The form letter to be sent should notify the participant that his form (Form A) has been received. If his doctor has not returned his form (Form B), the participant should be told, so he can take appropriate action. Finally, the participant should be given information about the mailing of his gift. A sample form letter of each type is shown in Figure 15.40.

Producing the form letters requires the creation of two documents. The data document contains the records from which the variable data is to be taken for printing the letters. The main document is a description of the letter to be sent.

THE DATA DOCUMENT.   Recall that Works WP used information in a database for producing form letters. A Word **form letter data document** is instead another word processing document. Figure 15.41 shows the data document that will be used for the form letters described here. Note that this figure was displayed using the Show ¶ command; consequently, spaces are shown as dots.

In the example, the first line of the data document is a header record that gives the names of the fields in the records that follow in subsequent lines. In this example the header is

First Name,Last Name,Address,City,State,Zip,Form A,Gift,Form B

Notice that commas are used to separate the field names and that there are no blank spaces around the commas. Tabs are also allowed as separators for the field names. There could be up to 256 field names. The end of the header record is signaled by pressing the *Return* key. For the example data document, the *Show* ¶ command has been used to emphasize the role of the *Return* key.

The order and number of the fields in the data records must be the same as the field names in the header record. Each data field for a record must be present, but if no data is available for a field an empty field can be signaled by using a pair of commas (,,) to represent the field. A data record can extend over many lines, and the end of a record is given by pressing the *Return* key.

Ace Consultants, Inc.
103 South Elm Street
Nashua, NH 03061
March 31, 1989

Mr. Joseph Smith
2122 Live Oak Street
New Orleans, LA 70101

Dear Mr. Smith:

Your Lifestyle and Health Parameter Survey form has
been received. Your Pro80 will be mailed within the next
10 days.

Ace Consultants, Inc.
103 South Elm Street
Nashua, NH 03061
March 31, 1989

Mr. Thomas Dedmond
1212 Palm Lane
Santa Clara, CA 95050

Dear Mr. Dedmond:

Your Lifestyle and Health Parameter Survey form has
been received. We have not yet received the survey
form from your doctor. We will be mailing your QW-5 in
about 10 days after the doctor returns his form.

Thank you for participating in our survey.

Sincerely yours,

T. Ken Porter
President

Figure 15.40 Sample form letters.

The data records shown were exported from Works DB by using the *Save As* command with the *Export Text* box clicked. The exported data fields were separated by tabs that were replaced by commas after the records were placed in the data document. Values for the fields named *Form A, Gift,* and *Form B* were typed into the records. The data document was saved with the name *SurveyNames*.

```
First.Name,Last.Name,Address,City,State,Zip,Form.A,Gift,Form.B¶
Joseph,Smith,2122.Live.Oak.Street,New.
Orleans,LA,70101,Yes,Pro80,Yes¶
Thomas,Dedmond,1212.Palm.Lane,Santa.Clara,CA,95050,Yes,QW-5,No¶
William,White,1020.Lakeview.Way,Jonesville,OH,44444,Yes,Acme,No¶
Paul,Wrangler,1122.Hillside.Dr.,Hyatt,NY,10800,Yes,Acme,Yes¶
George,Belton,1011.Maple.Leaf.St.,Hazel.
Green,AL,35820,Yes,Pro80,No¶
Clancy,Duggan,105.Park.Ave.,New.York,NY,10045,Yes,Pro80,No¶
Harrison,Matthews,220.Quincy.St.,Roaring.Spring,PA,16673,Yes,QW-
5,Yes¶
```

Figure 15.41 Data document for a form letter.

THE MAIN DOCUMENT.   The main document contains the description of the form letter. For our letter, the main document is shown in Figure 15.42. The first paragraph must be a DATA statement that contains the name of the data document. It has the form:

«DATA name of data document».

Field names from the data record are enclosed in the special symbols « and ». They can be placed anywhere in the document. These symbols are created in the following ways:

« is produced by pressing *Option - *(backslash).

» is produced by pressing *Option - Shift - *.

The field names must match exactly their appearance in the header record of the data document. For example, in «First Name» the uppercase letters and the space between the words are required. An error message will be displayed during the merge phase if a field name in the main document does not match exactly a field name in the data document. Names from the data document are used to create the inside address and the salutation.

Recall that the letter is to notify the survey participant if the doctor has not returned Form B. Thus, the letter should have different formats, depending upon the status of Form B. This is accomplished with the **IF statement**, which has the following syntax.

«IF *condition*»

text to be printed if the condition is *True*

«ELSE»

text to be printed if the condition is *False*

«ENDIF»

The condition must contain a field name from the data document. The operator = can be used to test for a text string (enclosed in quotes), and the operators =, >, and < can be used to test for numerical values.

The «ELSE» and its corresponding action are optional. The «ENDIF» is always required. Note that the operation of the IF statement is almost identical to the operation of the IF statement described for spreadsheets.

«DATA SurveyNames»

Ace Consultants, Inc.
103 South Elm Street
Nashua, NH 03061
March 31, 1989

Mr. «First Name» «Last Name»
«Address»
«City», «State»   «Zip»

Dear Mr. «Last Name»:

Your Lifestyle and Health Parameter Survey form has
been received. «IF Form B="Yes"»Your «Gift» will be
mailed within the next 10 days.«ELSE» We have not yet
received the survey form from your doctor. We will be
mailing your «Gift» in about 10 days after the doctor
returns his form.«ENDIF»

Thank you for participating in our survey.

Sincerely yours,

T. Ken Porter
President

Figure 15.42 The main document for the form letter.

For the example main document the IF statement has the following form. (The indenting and the word *Print* are intended to make the statement more readable for you. They should not appear in the form letter.)

«IF Form B = "Yes"»

Print: Your «Gift» will be mailed in the next ten days.

«ELSE»

Print: We have not yet received the survey form from your doctor. We will be be mailing your «Gift» in about 10 days after the doctor returns his form.

«ENDIF»

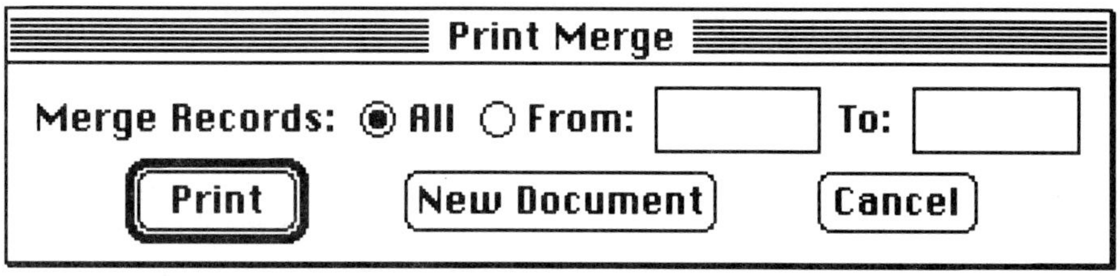

Figure 15.43   The *Print Merge* dialog box.

To produce the form letters select the *Print Merge* command from the **File** menu, thereby causing the dialog box of Figure 15.43 to be displayed. The *New Document* button allows the merged documents to be previewed on the screen instead of printing them.

The form letters shown earlier in Figure 15.40 are for the first two records of the data document. Notice how the IF statement has caused the body of the two letters to be different.

NESTED IF STATEMENTS.   IF statements can be nested, that is, IF statements can contain IF statements. We will use this feature to improve the form letter. Notice that only an abbreviation for the gift is printed on the form letter because the abbreviation was stored in the data document. To store the entire description of the gifts repeatedly would be quite wasteful. We replace the occurrences of «Gift» in the form letter main document with the following IF statement that will be within our original IF statement. (Again the indenting is intended to make the statement more readable, and it should not appear in the main document for the form letter.)

«IF Gift="Pro80"»

Pro80 Graphite Tennis Racket

«ELSE»

«IF Gift="Acme"»

Acme Digital Chronograph

«ELSE»

QW-5 Memory Calculator

«ENDIF»

«ENDIF»

Figure 15.44 shows the main document for the form letter with the new IF statement inserted. Figure 15.45 shows the resulting form letters for the first two records of the data document.

Form letters can also use a SET instruction that updates information that varies from printing to printing, an ASK instruction that asks for information before each printing of a letter, and an INCLUDE instruction that inserts a document into another document. These instructions will not be covered here.

Dear Mr. «Last Name»:

Your Lifestyle and Health Parameter Survey form has been received. «IF Form B="Yes"»Your «IF Gift="Pro80"»Pro80 Graphite Tennis Racket«ELSE»«IF Gift="Acme"»Acme Digital Chronograph«ELSE»QW-5 Memory Calculator «ENDIF» «ENDIF» will be mailed within the next 10 days.«ELSE»We have not yet received the survey form from your doctor. We will be mailing your «IF Gift="Pro80"»Pro80 Graphite Tennis Racket«ELSE»«IF Gift="Acme"»Acme Digital Chronograph«ELSE»QW-5 Memory Calculator«ENDIF» «ENDIF» in about 10 days after the doctor returns his form.«ENDIF»

Thank you for participating in our survey.

Figure 15.44 Body of the revised main document for form letters.

Mr. Joseph Smith
2122 Live Oak Street
New Orleans, LA   70101

Dear Mr. Smith:

Your Lifestyle and Health Parameter Survey form has been received. Your Pro80 Graphite Tennis Racket will be mailed within the next 10 days.

Thank you for participating in our survey.

Mr. Thomas Dedmond
1212 Palm Lane
Santa Clara, CA   95050

Dear Mr. Dedmond:

Your Lifestyle and Health Parameter Survey form has been received. We have not yet received the survey form from your doctor. We will be mailing your QW-5 Memory Calculator in about 10 days after the doctor returns his form.

Thank you for participating in our survey.

Sincerely yours,

Figure 15.45 First two revised form letters.

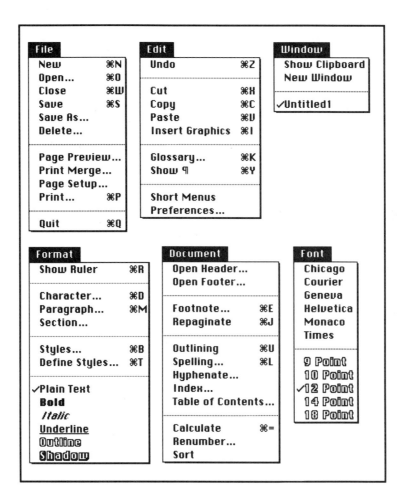

Figure 15.46 Long menus for Microsoft Word.

Computer Practice 15.12

Type the documents shown in Figures 15.41 and 15.44 and use them to reproduce the two versions of the form letter.

Key Concepts

Footnotes

Form letter data document

Hidden text

Multiple-column documents

Page preview

Section

Show ¶ /Hide ¶ command

Spelling checking

Style

Form letter

Full menu

IF statement

On-line help feature

Ruler

Short menu

Special symbols

Split windows

PUBLISHING FROM THE DESKTOP WITH PAGEMAKER

L E A R N I N G O B J E C T I V E S

- To gain an overview of desktop publishing.
- To survey some features of Pagemaker.
- To learn how Pagemaker could be used to prepare publication-quality documents.

This chapter describes desktop publishing and indicates how it can be of value to individuals and organizations. You will be given a survey of the features of the page layout software package PageMaker. Through this brief introduction, you will gain insights into how typical page layout software operates and how it differs from word processing software. A short document is prepared using PageMaker to show how actual page layouts can be produced and to suggest how desktop publishing is accomplished.

16.1 OVERVIEW OF DESKTOP PUBLISHING

Desktop publishing is already an important topic, and its importance is increasing as better and even more cost-effective desktop publishing tools become available. Even if you do not have desktop publishing software readily available, you can read this chapter for general information. Of course, if PageMaker is available, you should complete the computer practice to duplicate the short document produced in the chapter and gain a greater understanding of the concepts presented here.

Desktop publishing is a technological extension of the techniques of publishing to such microcomputers as the Macintosh and IBM personal computers with software like PageMaker. It offers very significant cost reductions: a Macintosh desktop publishing system can be purchased for less than $10,000, but a standard electronic typesetting system costs $100,000 and up. The publishing industry is enormous; annual sales are in excess of $100 billion. Every organization is in some sense a publisher. Consider the needs for advertising copy, brochures, mailing materials, direct mail, postcards, newsletters, internal publications, and annual reports. All these can be done with desktop publishing. Indeed, catalogs and even scientific journals have been produced with desktop publishing software.

Because of the significance of publishing and the power available to those who control publishing, desktop publishing is a very important microcomputer application area. There is no doubt that desktop publishing is particularly valuable to individuals or groups with tight budgets. Desktop publishing currently accounts for production with a value of approximately $1 billion per year. It has been estimated that in two years this amount will increase to approximately $5 billion. It is safe to say that desktop publishing is having a major impact on people and on society.

The availability of a variety of printers for desktop publishing allows very high-quality documents to be produced. Laser printers such as the Apple LaserWriter print at a resolution of 300 dots per inch, which is sufficient for many projects, such as in-house newsletters and classroom handouts. For even higher-quality printing, Linotronic 100/300 printers with a resolution of 1240 to 2740 dots per inch can be used. This resolution is for most purposes as good as standard typesetting, and many books are now published using Linotronic printers.

The quality of a document produced using desktop publishing depends primarily upon the graphic design skills of those doing the work. A poorly designed document looks bad regardless of how well it is printed. You will see that PageMaker is capable of producing a wide variety of page layout designs. Thus, the limitations you face in doing desktop publishing are more likely to be in your own design skills than in the software or hardware. To assist the inexperienced user, PageMaker includes design templates for many common publishing tasks.

The first step in using desktop publishing is to determine in a general way how a publishing problem is to be solved. For example, suppose that you have been assigned the job of producing a newsletter for your company. You need to know the approximate number of pages per issue, the number of copies of each issue to be printed, the number of issues per year, the kinds of topics to be printed, the sources of the information to be printed, the approximate number and kinds of graphics in each issue, the number of photographs to be reproduced per issue, the level of quality expected for the publication, and the budget for the publication.

After these high-level problems have been resolved, you must begin the design of the newsletter. You should determine the size of the pages—small-sized pages, letter-sized pages, tabloid pages, and so on. Assuming that equipment is not already available, certain decisions will determine the kinds of hardware to be purchased. For example, if high-quality printing is required, you must at least have access to a Linotronic printer. You can proof the output from a printer such as the LaserWriter and then send it to be produced with the Linotronic. Or the Laser-Writer may be sufficient for all the work. If considerable art work in the form of photographs and drawings is to be included, you may need a scanner to digitize them for computer manipulation.

After the hardware decisions, or concurrently with the hardware decisions, you must decide on the desktop publishing software that you will use for preparing the newsletter. There are many choices. If you are a novice, you will benefit from software that uses a *what you see is what you get* (known as WYSIWYG) display such as that produced by PageMaker.

PageMaker uses the metaphor of a drawing board containing one or two pages with enough room on the drawing board outside the pages to paste some text or graphics until they are needed in a page. (The drawing board is sometimes called a "pasteboard.") Text and graphics are placed on the pages and moved until a satisfactory layout is obtained. This is the approach that has been used traditionally for preparing page layouts by hand. Thus, many graphics designers will find the operations in PageMaker to be intuitive. For longer documents, graphics designers normally develop a design for the pages before any information is placed on the pages. In an analogous way PageMaker also allows master pages to be designed and used throughout a document.

Next comes the actual design of the pages of the newsletter. It should be attractive and easy to read. Graphics should lead the eye into the proper portion of the text. It would be good to incorporate a pleasing design feature in all issues that readers will associate with the newsletter. If possible, the design should also allow the reader to associate the newsletter with the company.

You may have guessed that good designs are difficult to produce. Most users of computers do not have the graphic design experience required for easily producing a good layout. However, a good desktop publishing software package such as PageMaker will help, because it is easy to alter the design elements and thus allow experimentation with different design possibilities. One of the design templates may even provide a satisfactory design for the planned publication.

16.2 SURVEY OF SOME PAGEMAKER FEATURES

In this section we survey some of the desktop publishing features available in PageMaker. The coverage is not comprehensive and topics are not discussed in detail. The goal is to provide a high-level view of the kinds of things that can be done with PageMaker. In the next section these features will be illustrated when we develop a small document. (For completeness, all the PageMaker menus are given in Figure 16.42 at the end of this chapter.)

PageMaker is a page layout tool, as its name implies. Although PageMaker has some capabilities for editing text, it assumes that the text has already been prepared with a word processor. This text is placed into the document based on the layout of the pages. Either Works WP or MS Word can be used for this purpose.

To start PageMaker double-click its icon (Figure 16.1) or the icon of a Page-Maker document. When PageMaker is opened, a screen containing a picture of the company logo and copyright information is displayed until a command is chosen from the menu bar.

Selecting the *New* command from the **File** menu causes the *Page Setup* dialog box shown in Figure 16.2 to be displayed. You are asked to enter the starting page number and the total number of pages. If the number of pages turns out to be wrong, new pages can be inserted into the document or extra pages can be removed later.

Options for double-sided and facing pages are available. Either or both of these options can be selected by clicking the appropriate box(es). The *Facing pages* option displays two pages on the drawing board and allows work to be switched at will to either page. A graphic can be placed to extend across the border of the facing pages.

DRAWING BOARD.   Clicking the *OK* button causes the **drawing board** to be displayed, as shown in Figure 16.3. The rulers can be switched on and off by selecting the *Rulers* command from the **Options** menu. The position where the zero marks of the rulers intersect forms the upper left-hand corner of the page itself in a single-page display and the upper middle point of a two-page display (see Figure 16.7). This intersection point is called the ruler zero point. You can drag the zero point marker to a new location to reset the zero point. This is similar to moving the rulers on the drawing board. If the rulers are displayed, then moving the pointer on the drawing board causes dotted line indicators on the rulers to move and show the location of the pointer. Thus, rulers allow items placed on the page to be positioned with precision. The space outside the page is known as the **pasteboard** and can hold graphics and text until they are to be placed on the page.

The dashed lines within the page show the locations of the margins as they were defined on the *Page Setup* dialog box. In this particular case they also

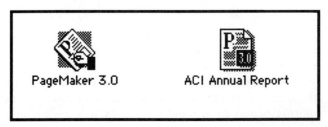

Figure 16.1 PageMaker icons.

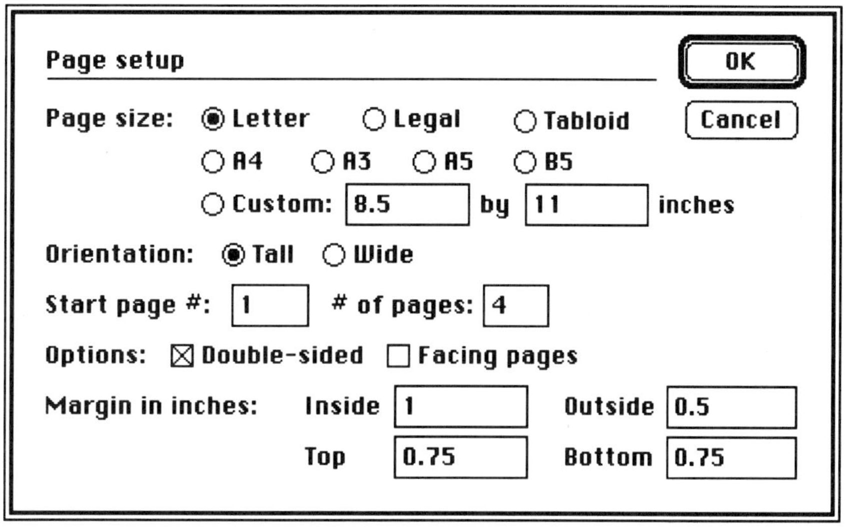

Figure 16.2 The *Page Setup* dialog box for PageMaker.

correspond with the width of the single column defined by default for placing items. Shortly, you will learn how to change the number and positions of the columns.

PAGE ICONS.   The page icons in the lower left-hand corner of the drawing board are of two types: regular and master. The regular page icons, which contain numbers, identify the pages in the document. You may jump to a page by clicking its icon. The page icon of the current page or pages is always highlighted. A PageMaker document can have as many as 128 pages, so icons for all the possible

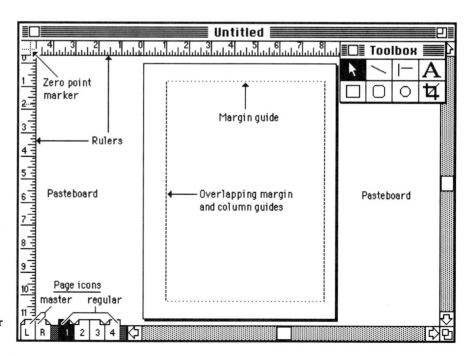

Figure 16.3 The PageMaker drawing board.

pages cannot be displayed at once. Scroll arrows appear at each side of the group of icons whenever there are more icons than can be displayed.

The master page icons in the far left corner (L and R) are very important because they can be used to globally design the left-hand and right-hand pages of the documents. The design of these **master pages** is automatically repeated on each page of the document. This unity of design improves documents. The templates provided by the master icons can be modified on any page for any purpose.

TOOLBOX. The tools in the **toolbox** displayed in the upper right-hand corner of Figure 16.3 are identified in Figure 16.4. With the exception of the cropping tool, the tools have the same meaning and mode of operation as described for MacPaint. Thus, you already know how to use them.

CROPPING TOOL. The *cropping tool* is used to **crop graphics**. For example, suppose that the Ace Consultants logo has been placed on a page and selected by clicking as shown on the page in Figure 16.5. Notice, although it is too small to read, that an address appears to the right as part of the logo. We want to crop the figure to remove the address.

To perform the cropping, select the cropping tool by clicking it. Move the tool so that it is over the middle handle in the right edge of the selected graphic. When the mouse button is pressed, the pointer becomes a double-headed arrow, as shown in part A of Figure 16.6. Dragging the arrow to the left produces the result shown in part B. The cropping tool can be placed over any handle of a graphic and moved to hide part of the graphic. The size of the graphic is not changed by cropping it, and the hidden part can be recovered by reversing the cropping process.

The size of a graphic, whether cropped or not, can be changed. Placing the pointer over a handle and pressing the mouse button causes the pointer to change to a double-headed arrow. The arrow can be dragged to change the size of the graphic. Holding down the *Shift* key and dragging a corner handle causes the graphic to be changed proportionately. Holding down the *Command* key while dragging a corner handle causes the graphic to be resized to print properly according to the printer's resolution. In this case the graphic snaps to the next

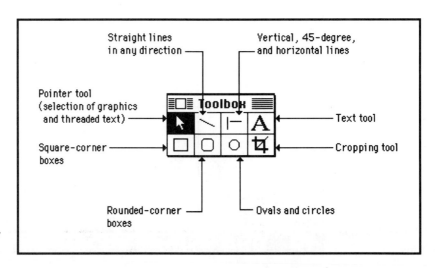

Figure 16.4 The PageMaker tools.

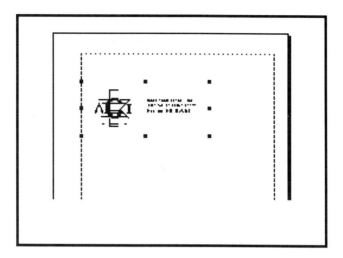

Figure 16.5 The figure to be cropped.

appropriate size for the printer. A resized graphic may look distorted on the screen, but it will print properly. Holding down both the *Shift* and *Command* keys allows a graphic to be resized proportionately and guarantees that it will print properly.

FACING PAGES.   If the *Facing Pages* box is clicked on the *Page Setup* dialog box, two pages will be displayed on the drawing board whenever it is appropriate. On the

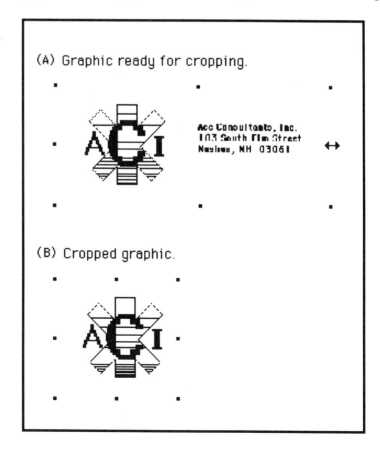

Figure 16.6 Cropping the Ace logo graphic.

left will always be an even-numbered page, and on the right will always be an odd-numbered page, which is true of an open book. This is illustrated in Figure 16.7. Notice that page icons numbered 2 and 3 are highlighted.

With the *Facing Pages* option you are able to see the layouts of the two pages that will be simultaneously visible to readers of the document. Then you can revise the layout of one or both of the pages to achieve a more pleasing effect if that is necessary. If you plan to have a graphic cross the boundary of the pages, this option is essential.

MULTIPLE COLUMNS ON A PAGE.   On many pages it will be desirable to have multiple columns. Selecting the *Column guides* command from the **Options** menu, as shown in Figure 16.8, will cause the dialog box of Figure 16.9 to be displayed.

Let us assume that the number of columns has been entered as 3, and the space between columns as 0.25 inches, as shown in the dialog box. **Column guides** will then be placed on the page as shown in Figure 16.10. If a master page icon were selected before using the *Column guides* command, all pages of the same type (left or right pages) would have three columns with the indicated column separation.

The column widths on any page can be changed to meet the design needs for the page. The procedure involves moving the pointer to a column boundary, which is indicated by the dotted line, and dragging it to the desired width in a way similar to that used to expand spreadsheet column widths.

Figure 16.11 shows the **changing of the column width** of the middle column by dragging the arrow on the left boundary. The moving of the boundary can be repeated until the desired size is obtained. Other column boundaries in the same page can also be moved. You have complete control over the size of the columns even if they were originally produced by a master page template.

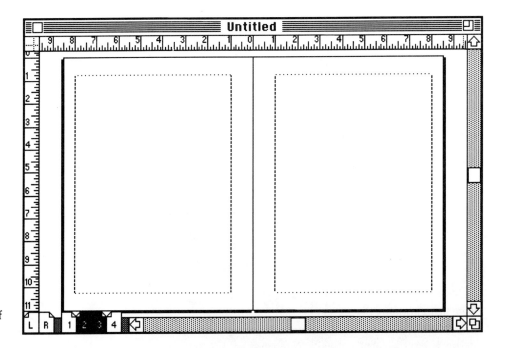

Figure 16.7 An example of facing pages.

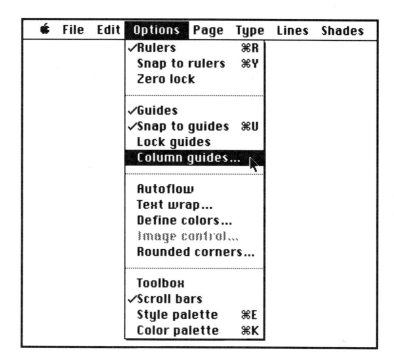

Figure 16.8 The *Column guides* command in the **Options** menu.

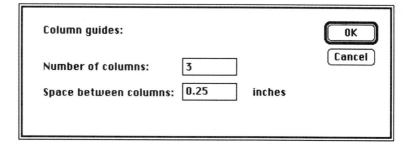

Figure 16.9 The *Column guides* dialog box.

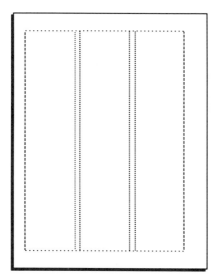

Figure 16.10 Page with column guides.

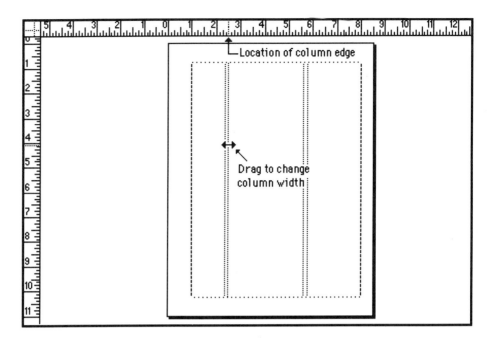

Figure 16.11 Changing the width of a column.

RULER GUIDES. Additional guides can be dragged onto a page to assist with precision placement of text or graphics. These guides, called **ruler guides**, can be horizontal or vertical. Unlike column guides, they do not control the placement of text; instead they serve as visual guides for the manual alignment of text or graphics. The maximum number of ruler guides on a page is 40. The steps for placing the guides follow.

- Point to the horizontal or vertical ruler as appropriate.
- Drag the pointer into the page. A double-headed arrow pointer appears as the ruler is dragged onto the page. A dotted line representing the ruler guide moves with the pointer.
- Release the mouse button when the ruler is in the desired location.

A ruler guide can be moved at any time by pointing to a dotted ruler guide and dragging the guide to a new location. A ruler guide can be removed by dragging it back to a ruler. The placing of a ruler guide is illustrated in Figure 16.12.

PLACING TEXT. After a page layout has been designed, **placing text and graphics** is accomplished using the *Place* command of the **File** menu. This important command initially behaves analogously to the *Open* command. A *Place* dialog box is displayed almost identical to an *Open* command dialog box. A document is selected for placing just as if a document were being opened. A pointer icon whose form indicates the type of placement technique is then displayed. The pointer icon can be moved to any position on the page. When the pointer is in the proper location, clicking will place the document on the page.

TEXT PLACEMENT MODES. There are three kinds of text placement techniques: manual, semi–automatic, and automatic. These techniques are used to **flow text** into a document. Each technique has an associated placement icon, as shown in Figure 16.13.

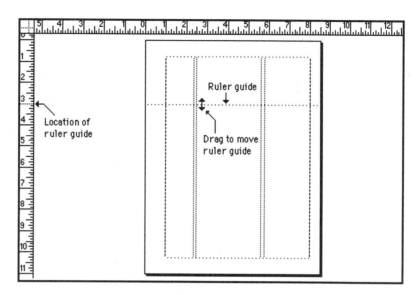

Figure 16.12 Placing a ruler guide.

In manual text placement mode, text stops flowing when it reaches a graphics break or the bottom of a column. A new copy of the icon is then obtained using techniques described later and moved to any location in the publication. This mode gives the greatest control for the placement of text, but it is tedious for long documents.

The semi–automatic option causes text to stop flowing at a graphics break or at the bottom of a column. A new placement icon is produced automatically for moving to a new location.

The automatic text placement mode causes text to flow automatically from column to column until all the document has been placed. Extra pages are added if needed. This option is particularly valuable for long documents.

The *Autoflow* command of the **Options** menu is used to switch between the automatic and the manual placement modes. When the *Autoflow* command is checked, the automatic placement mode applies, and the automatic flow icon is displayed. When the *Autoflow* command is not checked, the manual flow mode applies, and the manual icon is displayed. The semi–automatic placement icon is obtained from the manual or automatic icon by holding down the *Shift* key. Releasing the *Shift* key causes the original placement icon to be displayed.

In Figure 16.14 a text document is about to be placed in the middle column just below the ruler guide. Notice the *Manual Text* icon. Clicking when the icon is in the correct position will cause the text to flow into the document. In this example the manual text flow option will be used, so when the bottom of a column is reached, the flow of text stops.

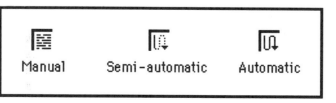

Figure 16.13 Text placement icons used by the *Place* command.

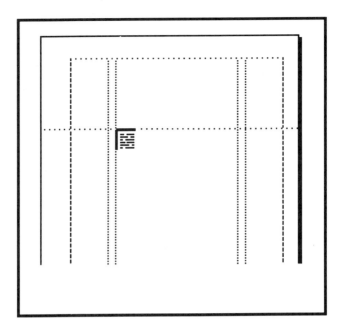

Figure 16.14 Placing the *Manual Text* icon for flowing text.

PAGE SIZE. In Figure 16.15 the text has been placed into the middle column of the page. Notice that simulated text, or **greeking**, is visible in the column. The greeked text is ideal for considering the layout of the page. If the actual text needs to be read, the **Page** menu offers five sizes:

- Fit in window size (which we are using in the example).
- 50% size.
- 75% size.
- Actual size.
- 200% size.

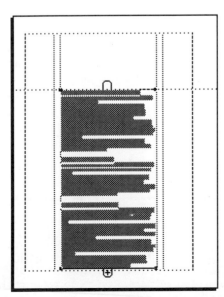

Figure 16.15 Example of flow of text into a document.

Selecting any of these sizes immediately changes the display to the indicated size. It may be necessary to reposition the page after a new size is selected. The smaller sizes are useful for obtaining views of larger portions of a page, but some detail is lost. The larger sizes—actual size and 200% size—are valuable for examining of details and very precise alignment of text or graphics.

WINDOWSHADES.   Notice in Figure 16.15 that the text is enclosed by horizontal lines, each of which has a handle in its middle. Because of their shape, the lines are called *windowshades*, and they bracket the current block of text. An actual-sized example is shown in Figure 16.16. The windowshade handle at the bottom of the text contains a + sign to indicate that there is more text to flow into the document. When all the text for the document has been placed in the document, the handle will contain a # sign. A windowshade handle can be dragged to expose or hide text. Any such change will cause subsequent text to be automatically rearranged.

In the manual text flow option, clicking the + sign in the text handle causes the pointer to change again into the *Manual Text* icon. The icon is then moved to the location where text flow is to begin again. Clicking will start the flow, which will stop when the end of the column is reached. The result of this technique, which is called **threading text**, is shown in Figure 16.17.

THREADED TEXT.   Threaded text is treated as a unit. If a change is made to any part of the unit, the text automatically adjusts. For example, suppose that a sentence is deleted in the publication near the beginning of a block of threaded text. The text will automatically flow up to fill the space previously occupied by the sentence. This could move text in many pages. Earlier it was noted that moving a windowshade handle would cause subsequent text to be moved. This is the result of the threading of the text. Changes in a block of threaded text have no effect on other blocks of threaded text. Text from different documents that are placed in the publication is in different text blocks, and any new text typed within PageMaker outside an existing block forms a new block.

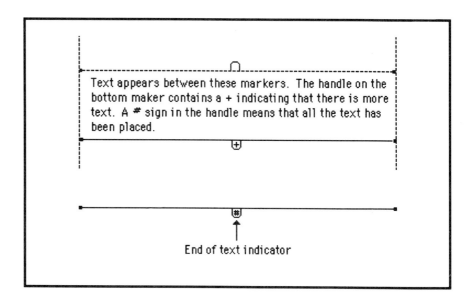

Figure 16.16 Illustration of text handles.

SNAP TO GUIDES   Obtaining the precise alignment of text required in high-quality publications is difficult. The practiced eye can detect tiny misalignments, and individuals who do not know what is wrong often recognize, nevertheless, that something is wrong. The *Snap to guides* command in the **Options** menu is a valuable aid in obtaining precise alignments. When this command is on, all guides act as if they exert a "magnetic" pull on all documents. If a placement icon is near a guide, it will snap to the guide to guarantee that all text and graphics are aligned with the guide.

CHANGING TEXT APPEARANCE.   If you do not like the appearance of the text, many options are available for changing it. You can, for example, resize a text block by selecting it by clicking, pointing at the + sign in the bottom handle, and dragging the handle up the column. This is shown in Figure 16.18. You may also change the width and length of a column by pointing at one of the corner handles and dragging the double-headed arrow as illustrated in Figure 16.19. In this case, the text will rearrange to fit the new shape of the column.

SPECIAL TEXT PLACEMENT.   Text can also be made to flow into any portion of a page for the purpose of producing a special effect such as placing text beside a graphics

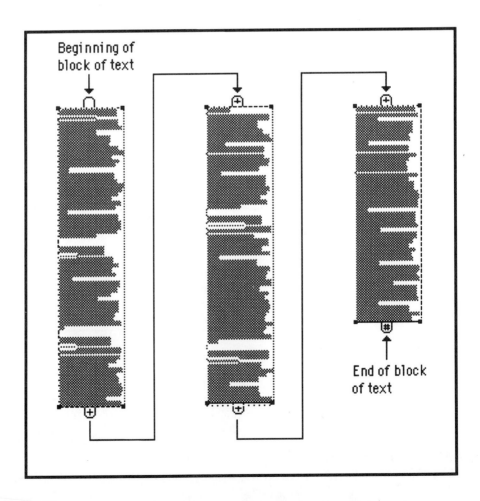

Figure 16.17 A block of threaded text.

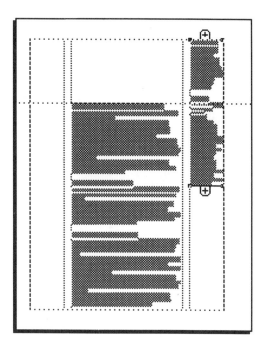

Figure 16.18 Text after dragging the + handle up a column.

object. The area into which the text is to be placed is marked by dragging the *Manual Text* icon to form a rectangle for the text. When the mouse button is released, the text flows into the block. The procedure is illustrated in Figure 16.20. Notice that in this example no part of the rectangle created by dragging the icon is located at a guide. When the rectangle has been filled by text, the flow of text stops.

Other techniques available for manipulating text include inserting another text block anywhere in existing text, moving text, and editing text. Editing text,

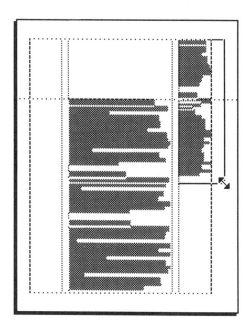

Figure 16.19 Changing the shape of a text block.

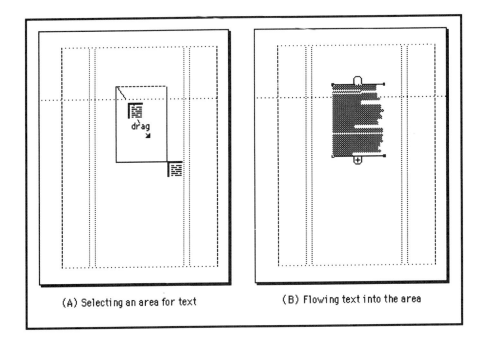

(A) Selecting an area for text   (B) Flowing text into the area

Figure 16.20 Selecting an area for flowing text.

which uses the text tool, is quite similar to editing in Works WP or Word. Help for using these or other techniques can be obtained by selecting the *Guidance* command from the **Apple** menu, provided that the help files have been installed on your system.

PLACING GRAPHICS. The process of placing graphics documents is almost identical to that for placing text. A graphics document selected for placement will have one of the icons shown in Figure 16.21 as the place icon. The icon is placed at the desired location, the mouse button is clicked, and the graphic flows onto the page. The result of pasting the Ace Consultants logo is shown in Figure 16.22. Notice that the form of the drawing is visible, but details are unavailable, as with greeked text.

Selecting the *Actual size* command from the **Page** menu displays the object as shown in Figure 16.23. Because the drawing is larger than the column width, part of the logo extends into the area used to separate columns. If this would be a problem, select the drawing by clicking and using the four-headed arrow. Drag it to the desired location as shown in Figure 16.24.

If a graphic is clicked with the pointer tool, it becomes selected, and eight handles in the form of small boxes are displayed. Clicking anywhere outside the graphic deselects it. A selected graphic can be resized by dragging any of its

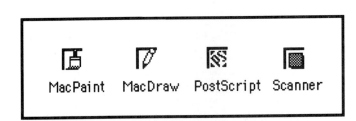

MacPaint   MacDraw   PostScript   Scanner

Figure 16.21 Graphic icons used by the *Place* command.

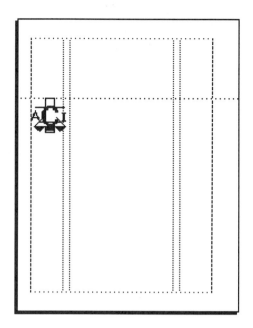

Figure 16.22 Placing a graphics document on a page.

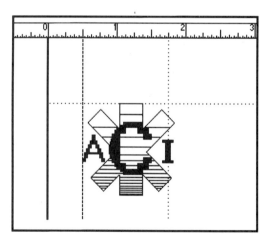

Figure 16.23 Graphics displayed using the *Actual Size* command.

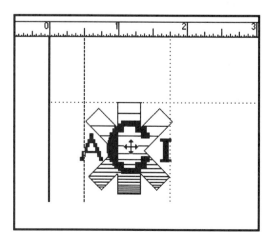

Figure 16.24 Moving graphics with the four-headed arrow.

handles. For MacPaint figures this may result in distortion. Holding down the *Shift* key during the dragging process causes the original proportions of the figure to be retained. Holding down the *Command* key during the dragging causes the resulting figure to be sized for printing without distortion. Because the resolution of the screen and the printer may be different, the graphic may look distorted on the screen, but it will print satisfactorily. Holding down both the *Shift* and *Command* keys causes a graphic to be resized in proportion to the original graphic and adjusts the graphics for the printer. In resizing a MacPaint figure to be printed on a laser printer, the graphic will jump to new sizes that can be printed without distortion. Also, a graphic can be cropped using the techniques described earlier.

TEXT WRAP. The *Text wrap* command of the **Options** menu specifies how text will wrap around a graphic. Selecting the command displays the dialog box shown in Figure 16.25. (Identifying titles have been added for the icons.) The icons under the *Wrap option* control the graphic boundary. The leftmost icon removes the graphic boundary to allow text to flow over a graphic. The middle icon creates a rectangular boundary around a graphic in which the space between the graphic and text is given by the standoff values shown in the boxes at the bottom of the dialog box. The right box cannot be selected unless a nonrectangular boundary has been created, which will be described later. The icons under *Text flow* describe how text is to flow around a graphic. The left icon causes a column break at a graphic so that text flow jumps to the next column. The middle icon causes text to jump over the graphic and continue to flow in the same column. The right icon causes text to wrap all sides of a graphic and continue to flow down the column.

Figure 16.26 shows the result of selecting the Ace logo by clicking it and selecting the *Rectangle* icon in the *Text wrap* dialog box. The graphic is now surrounded by a rectangular box made of dotted lines, which shows the standoff area for the text. The shape of the box can be changed by dragging the diamond-shaped handles at the corners of the box. Standoff handles can be added by pointing to the dotted line and clicking. Additional handles allow complex standoff shapes to be drawn around a graphic.

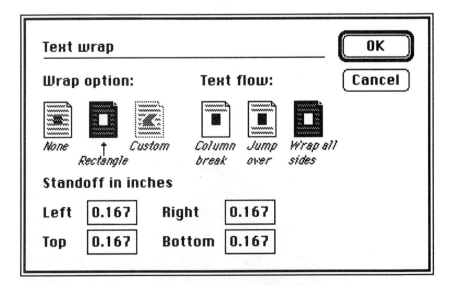

Figure 16.25 The *Text wrap* dialog box.

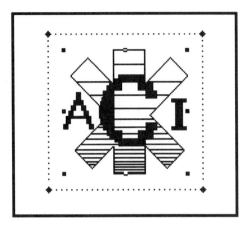

Figure 16.26 Standoff rectangle around a graphic.

Figure 16.27 shows the standoff handles dragged to new positions so that the Ace logo is within a diamond. Text flowing around this graphic will assume the diamond shape, as illustrated in Figure 16.28.

CHARACTER AND PARAGRAPH SPECIFICATIONS. After text has been placed in a document, it can be manipulated by PageMaker to improve its appearance. Some possibilities follow.

- Change the font.
- Change the size of the font.
- Change the style of the font.
- Hyphenate automatically or with prompting.
- Change tabs and paragraph indents.
- Change line spacing.
- Change alignment.
- Kern pairs of characters. (This will be explained later.)

Figure 16.27 A rearranged graphics standoff box.

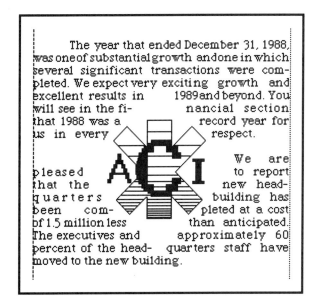

The year that ended December 31, 1988, was one of substantial growth and one in which several significant transactions were completed. We expect very exciting growth and excellent results in 1989 and beyond. You will see in the financial section that 1988 was a record year for us in every respect.

We are pleased to report that the new headquarters building has been completed at a cost of 1.5 million less than anticipated. The executives and approximately 60 percent of the headquarters staff have moved to the new building.

Figure 16.28 Text flowing around the standoff box.

Almost any change that can be made within a word processor can be made with PageMaker. As changes are made the text automatically rearranges throughout the document. Figure 16.29 shows text in greeked form that was justified after the text had been placed. The justification process involved selecting text by dragging the text tool through the paragraphs, selecting the *Paragraph* command from the **Type** menu, and clicking the *Justify* button on the resulting dialog box.

For some fonts, especially with larger sizes of character, some pairs of characters appear to be too far apart. For example, the pairs Ta, Te, To, Tu, Wa, Wo, and Yo may have separations that are not aesthetically pleasing. For high-quality

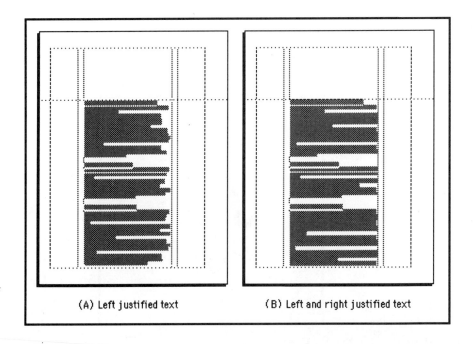

Figure 16.29 Illustration of the PageMaker justification feature.

(A) Left justified text   (B) Left and right justified text

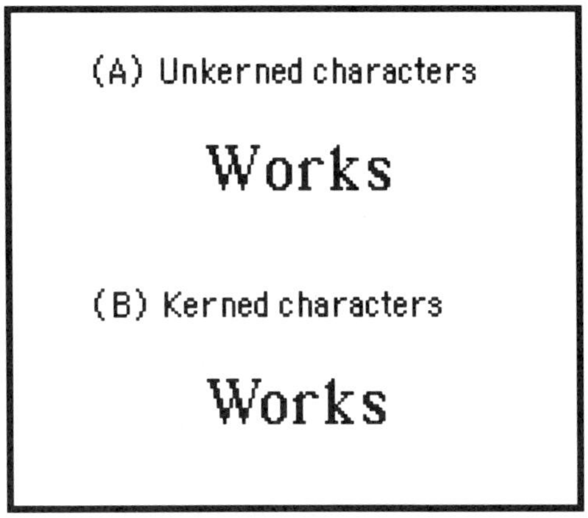

```
┌─────────────────────────────────┐
│                                 │
│  (A) Unkerned characters        │
│                                 │
│           Works                 │
│                                 │
│  (B) Kerned characters          │
│                                 │
│           Works                 │
│                                 │
└─────────────────────────────────┘
```

Figure 16.30 Kerning the characters *Wo*.

publications the extra space between the characters is removed, a process called *kerning*. Kerning may result in characters overlapping. In the *Paragraph specifications* dialog box, obtained by selecting the *Paragraph* command from the **Type** menu, is an option for automatic kerning of those pairs of characters that were specified for kerning by the designer of the font. Figure 16.30 shows an example of kerning.

Exercise Set 16.2

1. Describe the PageMaker drawing board.
2. How are the drawing board and the pasteboard related? What is the purpose of the pasteboard?
3. What is the zero point? How can it be reset?
4. What is the purpose of master page icons and regular page icons?
5. How is the cropping tool used?
6. When should the *Facing Pages* option be used?
7. How do we get multiple columns on a page?
8. How does one change column widths?
9. What are ruler guides? How are ruler guides set?
10. How is text placed on a page? How is a drawing placed on a page?
11. What is greeking? How is it useful?
12. What is a windowshade? What are text handles?
13. How can the amount of text displayed in a block be changed?
14. How can text be made to fit in an area not at a column guide?
15. What is threading of text?
16. What is the purpose of the *Snap to guides* command?
17. How can the shape of a text block be changed?
18. How can a graphics document be moved for more precise positioning?
19. What is kerning? How is it done in PageMaker?

16.3 WORKING WITH PAGEMAKER

In this section we will use two different methods to create the first two pages of a hypothetical annual report for Ace Consultants, Incorporated. The first method demonstrates the flexibility associated with manual placement of documents. This method can be used at any time. The second method shows how the text wrap feature makes the placement of documents more efficient. You may wish to use PageMaker to create the document yourself in the computer practice at the end of the section.

16.3.1 Method I—Using Manual Methods

The first step in preparing the document is to create a tentative design for its pages. This is the most difficult and important part of the work. PageMaker will make implementing the design fairly easy, but a poor design will produce an unappealing document regardless of the tools available for implementation. The design can be done with pencil and paper and then tested using PageMaker. If the first attempt is not satisfactory, it is easy to rearrange the design elements with the computer and try again. Here we will assume that the design has been completed and is to result in the pages of Figures 16.40 and 16.41 at the end of the chapter. You should look at these figures now to see what we are trying to produce.

The design of a page is concerned with the relative positions of the elements on a page and not with the particular text or graphics objects on a page. The relative

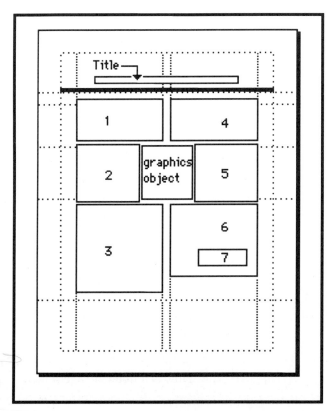

Figure 16.31 Design of page 1 of the Annual Report.

positions of the elements for page 1 are shown in Figure 16.31. The information in the tentative design is essential for setting up columns and ruler guides. We also assume that before we start using PageMaker that all text has been prepared with a word processor such as Word and that all graphics objects have been prepared with a suitable program.

Notice in the design for page 1 that the title extends across two columns and is underlined with a heavy mark. The numbered blocks (except 7) represent areas into which text will be placed. The width of the text will have to be narrower in the vicinity of the graphics object than elsewhere. If the amount of text does not fill the designated areas, it will be necessary to make the columns narrower, shorten the part of the page, or both. The area numbered 7 is to be filled with a signature—a graphics object. Now we begin the implementing of the design.

First we open PageMaker and create a new document. When the *Page Setup* dialog box is displayed, set all the margins to 0.75 inches. We set the number of pages to two and click the *OK* button. At this time the PageMaker drawing board is displayed.

Although the sample document has only two pages, in a real situation an annual report would have many pages. For that reason we are going to set up master pages for the document. These will then be used for working with the actual pages.

We click the right master page icon (page 1 is a right-hand page because it is odd-numbered) in the bottom left corner of the drawing board. Choose the *Rulers* command from the **Options** menu. Select the *Columns guides* command from the **Options** menu. In the resulting dialog box we enter 2 for the number of columns, 0.25 inches for the space between columns, and click the *OK* button. Column guides will now be displayed on the page. The columns are too wide, so we move (with the double-headed arrow) the leftmost column guide from 0.75 inches to 1.25

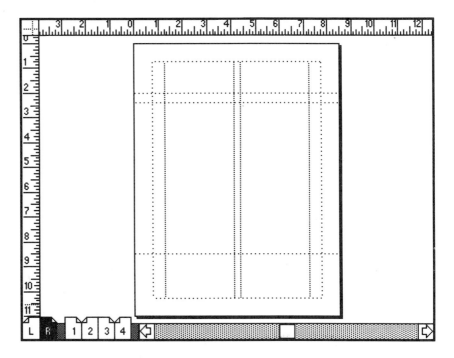

Figure 16.32 The right master page.

inches and the rightmost column guide from 7.75 inches to 7.25 inches. In this move the dotted lines on the ruler, which move as the pointer changes position, help in setting the positions of the column guides. Ruler guides are also dragged to positions at 2.0 inches, 2.375 inches, and 8.5 inches. The ruler at 2.0 inches serves as a lower boundary for the title and its underline. The one at 2.375 inches marks the bottom of the first line of text. The ruler at 8.5 inches is an approximate boundary for the bottom of the text. The final result is shown in Figure 16.32.

We now click the icon for left master page and enter information about it. When the *Column guides* command is selected, we type 3 for the number of columns and 0.25 inches for the separation of columns. Rulers are dragged to 2.0 inches and 8.5 inches. Figure 16.33 shows the final result.

To produce the actual page 1, we click the *Page 1* icon. A page display will appear that is identical to the right master page. Now we must place the information in the page. We start with the title by entering the bold underline. We use the horizontal line tool, starting at the left margin and dragging to the right margin. The line width was set to 8 points using the **Lines** menu. The *Place* command of the **File** menu is used to select the document containing the title. (In this example, only the title is in the document, and the title already has the desired font size and style.) The resulting *Manual Text* icon is placed at the left margin above the bold line, clicked, and dragged diagonally to the right margin, forming a long, narrow rectangle. The title will flow into the rectangle with the same font size and style it had in the document, but it is likely to be improperly placed. We point to within the title, press the mouse button to obtain the four-headed arrow, and move the title until we are satisfied with its position.

Next we place the Ace logo drawing near the middle of the page. First we drag a horizontal ruler to 3.75 inches to mark the approximate top of the graphics object.

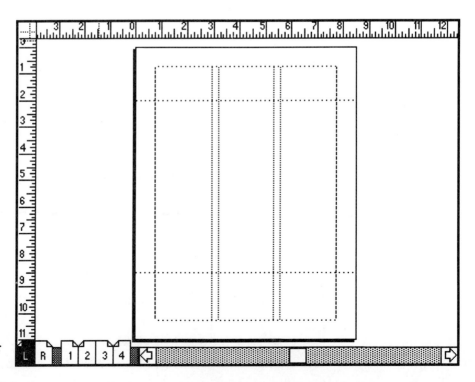

Figure 16.33 The left master page.

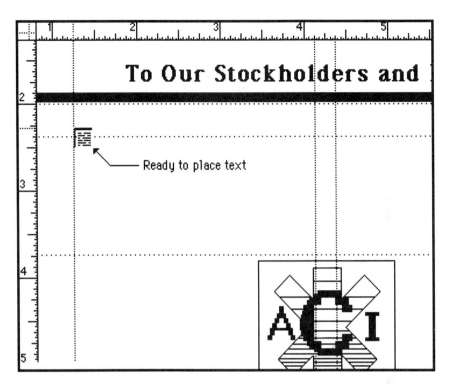

Figure 16.34 Page 1 ready for flowing of text.

We use the *Place* command again to select the drawing. The MacPaint icon is positioned below the ruler guide to the left of center and clicked. The position of the drawing is adjusted using the four-headed arrow. Figure 16.34 shows the result just before text is placed on the page.

We are now ready to place text on the page, so we use the *Place* command to select the document containing the text. (In this example only the text for the first page, excluding the title, is in the document.) The *Text* icon is placed on the left margin slightly above the ruler guide at 2.375 inches and clicked as illustrated in Figure 16.34. The text begins flowing into the document, and the flow stops when the top of the drawing is encountered because the default for text flow is to break the flow at a graphic. It is likely that the top line of the text is not in the proper position, but this can be corrected by dragging the text with the four-headed arrow. When we place the next text block, the current windowshades will disappear. So we drag a ruler guide to 3.75 inches to mark the location of the bottom window-shade bar to assist in aligning the next text block. The final result is shown in Figure 16.35.

To place the next block of text beside the drawing, we first click the + in the bottom handle of the windowshade. The windowshades for the previously placed text disappear and a new *Manual Text* icon is displayed. Then we move the *Manual Text* icon to the left margin with the icon touching the ruler guide at 3.75 inches. We press the mouse button and drag to produce the outline of a rectangle beside the drawing. When the button is released, text flows into the rectangle. The top line of the new block of text will have correct vertical placement, called *leading* (pronounced "ledding"), relative to the preceding line. This was the purpose of the ruler guide at 3.75 inches. The last line of the text may not be the one desired. The double-headed arrow can be used to drag the bottom handle until the desired last line is displayed.

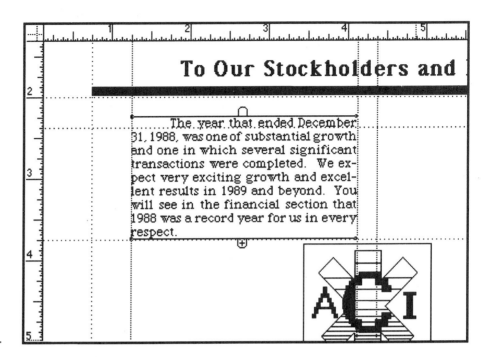

Figure 16.35 Page 1 after placing the first text block.

For placing the text beside the drawing: if the outline of a rectangle is not drawn before the mouse button is released, the text flows to the bottom of the column and covers the edge of the drawing. This appears to be a disaster, but we can recover by dragging the bottom windowshade handle back up the column to near the bottom of the graphic. Then the corner of the text can be dragged to the left to make the text fit beside the drawing.

Figure 16.36 shows the situation just before flowing the text into the column below the drawing. Before the + in the handle was clicked to display the *Text* icon,

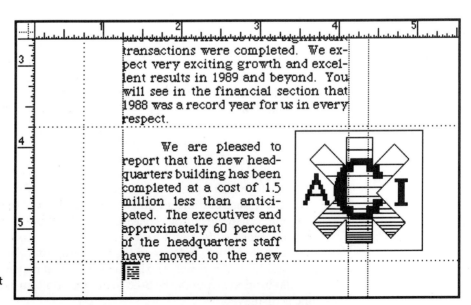

Figure 16.36 *Manual Text* icon in position to flow text down the column.

a ruler guide was dragged to the bar for the bottom windowshade. If the *Text* icon touches both the margin guide and the ruler guide as shown in the figure, the new text block will have proper leading. Without the ruler guide it is difficult to obtain the exact leading for the new text.

To stop the text before it reaches the bottom of the column, the *Text* icon is dragged to form the outline of a rectangle. The bottom handle is dragged if necessary to obtain the desired last line. The resulting situation is shown in Figure 16.37. Clicking the + in the bottom handle will change the pointer into the *Manual Text* icon, which can then be moved anywhere in the document.

We move the *Text* icon to the top margin of the second column and make it touch the left column guide. Clicking causes the text to flow until it is stopped again by the logo graphic. The situation is shown in Figure 16.38.

The remaining part of the text can be flowed down the page in a manner similar to that for the left column. The text should be flowed into the outline of a rectangle beside the drawing. Then the remaining text is flowed into the regular-width column. If the appearance of the complimentary close used in the document is jumbled, we select the text tool and edit that part of the text. Finally, the signature, which is a graphic document, is placed in the complimentary close.

Except for the construction of the graphs, page 2 is easier to fill than page 1 because text does not have to be flowed around a graphic. Assume that the graphs have already been prepared from a spreadsheet package or some other graphics software package. We click the icon for page 2, and a page layout is displayed exactly like the left master page. We place the title and its bold line on the page in the same way as for page 1. The graphs should then be placed on the page in the three columns in the locations shown in Figure 16.41. Now we are ready to place the text.

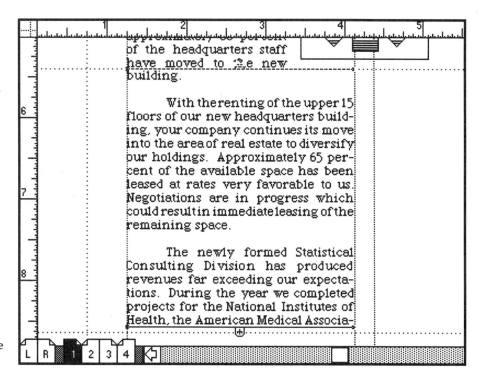

Figure 16.37 Last text in the first column.

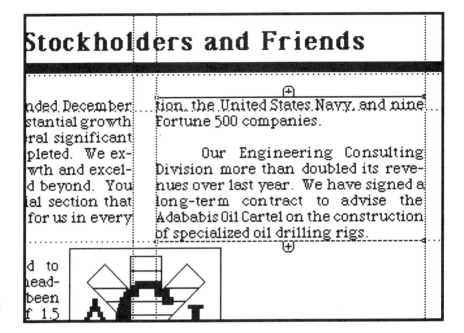

Figure 16.38 Text stopped by the logo graphic.

After selecting the text document for the page by using the *Place* command, we place the *Text* icon at the top left corner of the left column and click. The text flows until it is stopped by the *Revenues* graph. The *Manual Text* icon is obtained by clicking the bottom handle. The *Text* icon is placed below the *Revenues* graph and a small rectangle is outlined by dragging to receive the next paragraph.

The *Manual Text* icon is obtained again and placed in the second column below the *Net Earnings* graph, and a paragraph is flowed into it. A *Manual Text* icon is placed at the top of the third column and clicked. We have finished except for possible adjustments of the locations of text blocks or graphs. Any of these can be moved by pointing to it, pressing to get the four-headed arrow, and dragging to the desired location.

16.3.2   Method II—Using Automatic Methods

We visualize a design for page 1 similar to that shown in Figure 16.39. This design has only two blocks for flowing text instead of the six blocks shown in the design of Figure 16.31. This reduction in the effort required for placing the text will be made possible by the text wrap feature. Master pages are created as before. The title for page 1, its underline, and the Ace logo graphic are placed on page 1 exactly as in method I.

The Ace logo is selected by clicking it. Then we select the *Wrap text* command in the **Options** menu. In the dialog box we click the *rectangular* text wrap icon and the *wrap all sides* text flow icon, and accept the suggested standoff values that appear in the dialog box. The resulting dialog box is identical to that of Figure 16.25. After the *OK* button is clicked, the Ace logo graphic is enclosed by the standoff box shown in Figure 16.26.

The *Place* command is used as before to obtain the *Manual Text* icon for the document for the first page. The icon is placed slightly above the ruler guide at

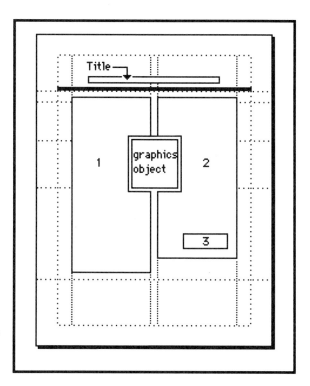

Figure 16.39 New design of page 1 of the Annual Report.

2.375 inches and clicked. The text flows down the column, around the graphic to the bottom of the column. We use the top windowshade handle to adjust the location of the first line of the text. We drag the handle of the bottom windowshade upward to display the appropriate amount of text.

The second column of text is obtained by clicking the + in the bottom windowshade of the first column, placing the *Manual Text* icon at the appropriate location at the top of the second column, and clicking. The text flows down the column, flows around the Ace logo graphic, and stops when the text is exhausted. All remaining work is the same as for method I.

Computer Practice 16.3

In this practice you will create the two pages just described except that the preparation of graphs will be simplified.

1. Open Works WP or Word and get a new document. Type the title of the first page—"To Our Stockholders and Friends"—in bold 18-point type. Save the document. Repeat this for the title of the second page.

2. Type the text of the first page and save it in a document.

3. Type the text of the second page and save it in a document. (Note: All text could have been typed into a single document to be used for creating both pages. (However, this involves slightly different techniques from that described in this section.)

4. Create graphics documents for the pages. You may create the actual documents displayed in Figures 16.40 and 16.41, which could be time-consuming,

or you can use MacPaint to create simplified versions of the graphics. If you choose the latter, use approximately the following dimensions within MacPaint:

ACI logo,   1.5 x 1.5 inches

All graphs,   2.25 inches wide x 2.375 inches high

The graphics can be resized in PageMaker if necessary.

5. Open PageMaker and select the *New* command from the **File** menu.

6. In the *Page Setup* dialog box, place an *x* in the *Double-sided* box, remove the *x* in the *Facing pages* box, and set all margins to 0.75 inches.

7. Create the master pages by following the directions given in the section.

8. Click the page 1 icon and place the ACI logo document in the middle of the page as described in this section.

9. Place the text on page 1. See the discussion in this section for details.

10. Click the page 2 icon and place the graphs on the page.

11. Place the text on the page.

12. Print the document and save it if you desire. Select the *Save As* command of the **File** menu for saving the document. Select the *Print* command of the **File** menu to print the document.

Figure 16.40 The first page of the sample document.

Financial Summary

In 1988, Ace Consultants Incorporated continued its unbroken string of record setting years. Records were made in each profit center of the company. Revenues increased 21.8% to $39 million for the greatest rate of growth in the history of the company.

The increase in net earnings at $1.1 million surpassed the million dollar

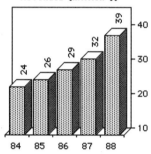

mark for the first time. A strong emphasis on cost control and improved efficiencies in computer activities contributed to the strong improvement in net profit.

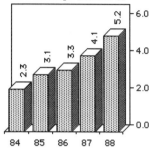

Net earnings were reduced by extraordinary expenses for the new company headquarters. In the absence of these expenses our net earnings would have been a remarkable $6.8 million. Not only will these expenses not occur in 1989, but the company should experience a profit from the leases signed for space in the building.

Earnings per share increased 27 percent despite

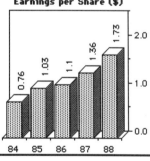

a 5 percent increase in shares of common stock. This strong showing places our company at the top of the comprehensive consulting industry.

The price of a share of the common stock of Ace Consultants continued its upward march. On October 2, 1988, the price of a share reached an all time high of $31.87. Despite the stock market rollback in October 1988, the low price for a share in the fourth quarter was $27.75.

To enhance the marketability of the common stock of the company, we plan to begin offering the stock on the New York Stock Exchange in the third quarter of 1989. This change is also necessary to emphasize the significance of company growth in the last five years.

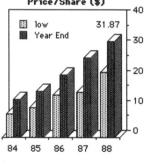

Figure 16.41 The second page of the sample document.

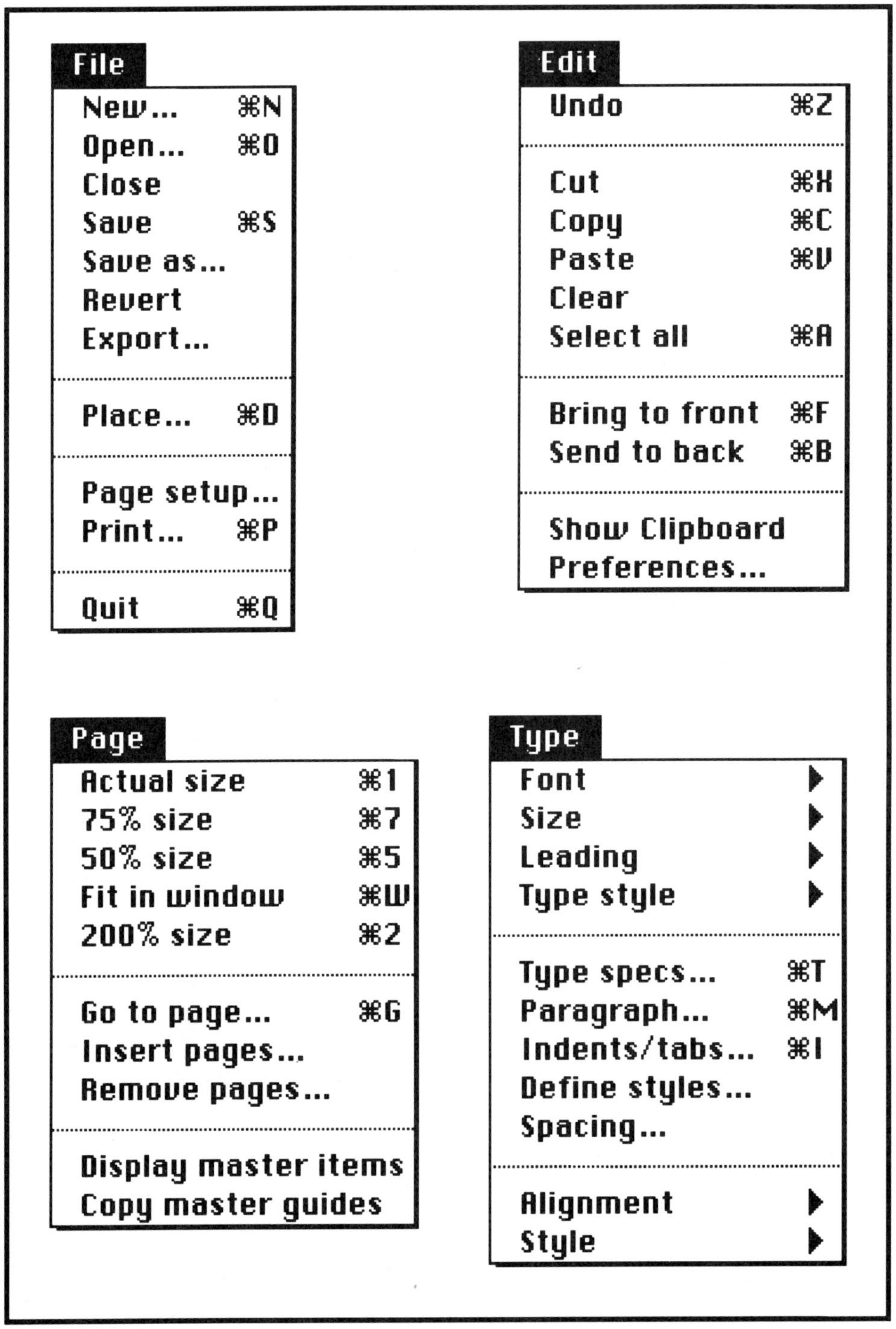

File	
New...	⌘N
Open...	⌘O
Close	
Save	⌘S
Save as...	
Revert	
Export...	
Place...	⌘D
Page setup...	
Print...	⌘P
Quit	⌘Q

Edit	
Undo	⌘Z
Cut	⌘X
Copy	⌘C
Paste	⌘V
Clear	
Select all	⌘A
Bring to front	⌘F
Send to back	⌘B
Show Clipboard	
Preferences...	

Page	
Actual size	⌘1
75% size	⌘7
50% size	⌘5
Fit in window	⌘W
200% size	⌘2
Go to page...	⌘G
Insert pages...	
Remove pages...	
Display master items	
Copy master guides	

Type	
Font	▶
Size	▶
Leading	▶
Type style	▶
Type specs...	⌘T
Paragraph...	⌘M
Indents/tabs...	⌘I
Define styles...	
Spacing...	
Alignment	▶
Style	▶

Figure 16.42A PageMaker menus.

Options		Lines	Shades
Rulers	⌘R	None	None
Snap to rulers	⌘Y	Hairline	Paper
Zero lock		.5 pt ————	Solid
		1 pt ————	10%
Guides		2 pt ————	20%
Snap to guides	⌘U	4 pt ————	30%
Lock guides		6 pt ————	40%
Column guides...		8 pt ————	60%
		12 pt ————	80%
Autoflow			
Text wrap...			
Define colors...			
Image control...			
Rounded corners...			
Toolbox			
Scroll bars			
Style palette	⌘E		
Color palette	⌘K	Reverse line	

Figure 16.42B PageMaker menus.

Key Concepts

Changing column widths	Column guides
Cropping graphics	Drawing board
Flowing text	Greeking text
Master page	Pasteboard
Placing text and graphics	Ruler guides
Threading text	Toolbox

EXTENDING THE RELATIONAL DATABASE MODEL

L E A R N I N G   O B J E C T I V E S

- To gain an understanding of the fundamental operators of relational algebra.

- To learn to use the information retrieval power contained in relational algebra.

- To understand the three basic types of relationships that can exist between database relations.

- To learn how implementations of the relational database model can be structured based on link attributes.

- To learn how to design relational databases that model data relationships accurately and efficiently.

In this chapter you will significantly extend your knowledge of the relational database model. The three remaining relational algebra operators not introduced in Chapter 9 will be defined, and the retrieval capabilities of relational algebra will be explored through a number of example retrievals. One of the common methods for commercially implementing the relational database model will be presented and illustrated with a detailed example database design. You will gain insight into why different relational database systems present quite different appearances to their users, and you will gain the knowledge necessary to learn to use various of these systems.

17.1 RELATIONAL ALGEBRA

You will recall from the discussion in Chapters 8 and 9 that an essential part of the relational database model is the concept of a relational retrieval language. Remember that the language **relational algebra** is the language whose retrieval capabilities form the set of basic capabilities against which other relational retrieval languages are measured. Further recall that in Chapter 9 you were introduced to the **select** and **project** operators—two of the five basic relational algebra operators. In this section we complete the definiton of the relational algebra retrieval language and begin to explore its information retrieval capabilities.

BASIC RELATIONAL OPERATORS.   Relational algebra is defined by five basic operators that are applied to existing relations to produce new relations. There are also other relational algebra operators, called derived operators, that can be written as combinations of the basic five. The basic operators are **select**, **project**, **union**, **minus**, and **cross** (sometimes called the **Cartesian product** operator).

The definitions of the **select** and **project** operators are given in Chapter 9. The other three basic operators will now be defined and some examples given to illustrate the definitions. Then the most important of the derived operators—the **natural join** operator—will be defined.

Note that in the definitions and some of the examples that follow (where there is no semantic context) the convention of naming relations with capital letters from the last half of the alphabet and attribute names with letters from the first half of the alphabet will be followed. In later examples, where appropriate, both relations and attributes will be given more semantically meaningful names.

For the purpose of the definitions that follow, let R and S be two relations of k-tuples that have equivalent relational schemes, and let T be any relation of n-tuples. (Remember that by saying that two relations have equivalent relational schemes, we mean they have exactly the same attributes in their schemes, though not necessarily in the same order.)

The relation R **union** S is defined to be the set of k-tuples that is formed by appending (or adding) the tuples of S to the tuples of R *after* rearranging the attribute order of the tuples from S (if necessary) so that the order of the attributes in S matches the order in which those attributes appear in the relational scheme for R. Note that it is required that R and S have equivalent relational schemes for the union to be defined.

The relation R **minus** S is defined to be the set of tuples in R not found in S. When a tuple from R is tested for membership in S, components will be tested by attribute name and not position. Again, it is essential that the relational schemes for R and S be equivalent.

The relation R **cross** T, written R x T, is defined to be the usual Cartesian product of the sets R and T. If R and T happen to have common attribute names, these attribute names will be modified in the relational scheme for R x T by a prefix denoting from which of the sets R and T the attribute values come. For example, if both R and T have the attribute *Name*, these attributes would be renamed *R.Name* and *S.Name* , respectively, in the scheme for R x T.

Some simple examples will illustrate these definitions. Suppose relations R(*Name, Position*), S(*Position, Name*), and T(*Name, Salary, Department*) contain the following data:

R:	Name	Position
	Smith, J. P.	Manager
	Jones, L. T.	Salesman
	Kline, H. F.	Clerk

S:	Position	Name
	Manager	Clark, B. C.
	Clerk	Kline, H. F.

T:	Name	Salary	Department
	Smith, J. P.	33,000	Sales
	Kline, H. F.	14,000	Sales

Let us now construct some new relations using the previously defined operators.

R *union* S:	Name	Position
	Smith, J. P.	Manager
	Jones, L. T.	Salesman
	Kline, H. F.	Clerk
	Clark, B. C.	Manager

R *minus* S:	Name	Position
	Smith, J. P.	Manager
	Jones, L.T.	Salesman

S *minus* R:	Position	Name
	Manager	Clark, B. C.

R x T:	*R.Name*	*Position*	*T.Name*	*Salary*	*Department*
	Smith, J. P.	manager	Smith, J. P.	33,000	Sales
	Smith, J. P.	manager	Kline, H. F.	14,000	Sales
	Jones, L. T.	salesman	Smith, J. P.	33,000	Sales
	Jones, L. T.	salesman	Kline, H. F.	14,000	Sales
	Kline, H. F.	clerk	Smith, J. P.	33,000	Sales
	Kline, H. F.	Clerk	Kline, H. F.	14,000	Sales

Note that not all the tuples in R x T are semantically meaningful, that is, they do not contain related information. The second tuple, for example, contains a *Position* value that belongs to Smith and *Salary* and *Department* values that describe Kline. It would make sense to consider only tuples 1 and 6, where *R.Name* and *T.Name* match. This can easily be done using the **select** operator as follows:

$$N = \textbf{select from } R \times T \textbf{ where } R.Name = T.Name$$

Then N has the following data:

N:	*R.Name*	*Position*	*T.Name*	*Salary*	*Department*
	Smith, J. P.	manager	Smith, J. P.	33,000	Sales
	Kline, H. F.	clerk	Kline, H. F.	14,000	Sales

The preceding combination of the **cross** and **select** operators occurs so frequently that it is considered a derived operator and is given the special name *natural join.* The notation R<x>T is used to denote the natural join of R with T. Formally, it is defined as follows:

R<x>T = **select from** R x T **where** (Tuple values match for *all* pairs of common attribute names from R and T.)

Since the common attribute names in R< x >T have *matching* values, there is no need to keep both names (and qualify them by using the relation name as a prefix) in the **natural join** as was done in R x T. A second **natural join** example will illustrate further.

Consider relational schemes R(A,B,C,D) and S(B,D,E,F), with instance relations given by

R:	*A*	*B*	*C*	*D*
	1	2	3	6
	3	2	7	4
	1	2	9	4
	7	1	7	1

S:	*B*	*D*	*E*	*F*
	2	4	5	7
	5	3	2	9
	1	1	8	8

Then R< x>S is

A	B	C	D	E	F
3	2	7	4	5	7
1	2	9	4	5	7
7	1	7	1	8	8

Look at this last example carefully to make sure you understand exactly how R<x>S is formed, because the **natural join** is used quite frequently in information retrieval from relational databases. Notice how the common attribute names B and D appear only *once* in the resulting relational scheme. Also notice how each of tuples 2 and 3 of R is matched (or joined) to tuple 1 of S because both the B and D attribute values match for those tuples. Likewise tuple 4 of R is joined to tuple 3 of S. Tuple 1 of R and tuple 2 of S have no matching tuples in the other relation and hence are excluded from the **natural join**.

Exercise Set 17.1

Consider the relations N(*Name, ID#*), S(*ID#, Salary, Dept#*), and D(*Dept#, Manager*), with instances given as follows.

N:	Name	ID#
	Smith	101
	King	102
	Clark	103
	Black	104

S:	ID#	Salary	Dept#
	103	20000	A1
	101	22000	A1
	102	30000	B2
	104	27000	A3

D:	Dept#	Manager
	A1	Jones
	B2	Thomas
	A3	Hill

1. Display the relation R = N<x>S.
2. Display the relation T = S<x>D.
3. Display the relation U = **select from** S **where** *Salary* GT 20000.
    (Note that GT means "greater than.")
4. Display the relation V = N<x>U, where U is defined in exercise 3.
5. Display the relation W = **project** *Name, Salary* **from** V, where V is defined in exercise 4.
6. Describe the contents of relation W in exercise 5 as an English command in the form "Find ... ".
7. Display the relation X = N< x>S< x>D.
8. Referring to relation X from exercise 7, display the relation M = **select from** X **where** *Dept#* EQ B2.
9. Referring to relation M from exercise 8, display the relation P = **project** *Name, Manager* from M.
10. Repeat exercise 6 for relation P from exercise 9.
11. Referring to relation X from exercise 7, display the relation Q = **project** *Name, Manager* **from** X.
12. Referring to relation Q from exercise 11 and relation P from exercise 9, display the relation L = Q **minus** P.
13. Repeat exercise 6 for relation L from exercise 12.

17.2 RETRIEVALS USING RELATIONAL ALGEBRA

In this section you will see how the relational algebra operators can be used to retrieve information from an example database. Our example database is designed to allow an insurance company to keep track of all the policies it sells. In addition to information about the policies, the database can store information about the buyers of the policies, the salesmen for the policies, the districts in which the salesmen work, and the regions in which the districts reside. With this information, the company can not only retrieve information about particular policies, but also organize various kinds of summary information and reports about its sales.

EXAMPLE DATABASE STRUCTURE.   The database will consist of five relations: POL-ICY, BUYER, SALESMAN, DISTRICT, and REGION. The database organization itself is realistic, but the number of attributes in each relational scheme has been limited for simplification. Also attribute names have been abbreviated to simplify the display of relational schemes and diagrams. The full names and associated abbreviations are given in Figure 17.1. These relations have the following relational schemes:

POLICY(*SS#, Pol#, SID#, Type, Date, Amount*)
BUYER(*SS#, Bname, Occ-code, Baddress, Bphone*)
SALESMAN(*SID#, Sname, Saddress, Sphone, District#, Comm-rate*)

Full Name	Abbreviation
social security	SS#
policy number	Pol#
policy type	Type
policy date	Date
policy amount	Amount
buyer's name	Bname
occupation code	Occ-code
buyer's address	Baddress
buyer's phone	Bphone
salesman's identification number	SID#
salesman's name	Sname
salesman's address	Saddress
salesman's phone	Sphone
commission rate	Comm-rate
district number	District#
district manager	Dmanager
district location	Dlocation
district phone	Dphone
region number	Region#
region manager	Rmanager
region location	Rlocation
region phone	Rphone

Figure 17.1 Attribute names and abbreviations for the insurance database.

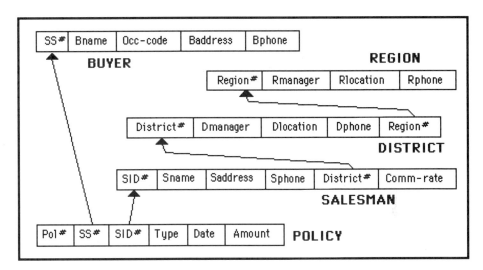

Figure 17.2 Diagram of the insurance database.

DISTRICT(*District#, Dmanager, Dlocation, Dphone, Region#*)
REGION(*Region#, Rmanager, Rlocation, Rphone*).

It is often useful to represent a database and the "natural" relationships between relations with a diagram, as in Figure 17.2. Although the relationships shown are not the only ones possible, they represent the ones that would be formed using the **natural join** operator.

Note the use of lines to connect like attributes in the diagram and the use of arrows on one end of the lines. These directed lines are used to represent the fact that the relationships depicted are *many-to-one* in the direction of the arrows. This means, for example, that there may be many tuples in POLICY that correspond to one tuple in SALESMAN. In other words, a salesman can sell (we hope) many policies. Similarly, the relationship from POLICY to BUYER is many-to-one, because a buyer can buy more than one policy as well. Test the other many-to-one relationships depicted in a similar way and convince yourself that the interpretations are reasonable. *One-to-one* and *many-to-many* relationships are also possible in a database design. More will be said about these relationships a little later in this chapter.

EXAMPLE DATABASE CONTENTS. To illustrate the relational algebra operators, the example database should contain enough data to make the results of retrievals meaningful. In the example retrievals that follow, it is assumed that the database contains the data shown in Figure 17.3.

EXAMPLE RETRIEVALS. We examine now the use of relational algebra for retrieving information from this database. A number of retrievals designed to illustrate the various categories of information that might be requested from such a database design are presented. Use the database contents shown in Figure 17.3 to calculate each relation as you read.

Retrieval 17.1: Find the buyer social security number, the policy number, and the salesman identification number for all policies written for more than $100,000.

BUYER

SS#	Bname	Occ-code	Baddress	Bphone
111-11-1111	Jack Smith	CL	1 Oak St., Dallas, GA	414-444-5555
222-22-2222	Joan Clark	P	2 Elm St., Rome, GA	414-333-6666
333-33-3333	Bill Jones	CL	Box 323, Greer, SC	803-555-2222
444-44-4444	Jane Bell	P	Box 441, Berea, SC	803-999-5555
555-55-5555	Sue Dixon	M	101 Main St., Flay, NC	704-888-4343

POLICY

Pol#	SS#	SID#	Type	Date	Amount
123456	111-11-1111	103	whole	3-1-85	90,000
123666	222-22-2222	103	whole	4-6-86	160,000
234567	333-33-3333	102	term1	5-6-84	290,000
876541	333-33-3333	102	term1	6-7-87	1,200,000
435671	444-44-4444	101	term1	6-9-83	2,000,000
123123	444-44-4444	101	term2	5-1-80	30,000
221112	555-55-5555	102	term2	1-1-78	45,000

SALESMAN

SID#	Sname	Saddress	Sphone	District#	Comm-rate
101	Joe Hill	12 Oak St., Berea, SC	803-333-4421	A12	10%
102	Beth Dell	1 E. Main St., Flay, NC	704-777-8787	A13	12%
103	Lou Gray	Box 22, Rome, GA	414-888-6543	B14	10%

DISTRICT

District#	Dmanager	Dlocation	Dphone	Region#
A12	Dick Buff	Greenville, SC	803-987-8765	22
A13	Bob Jones	Asheville, NC	704-777-7765	22
B14	Lisa Quinn	Rome, GA	414-111-2312	33

REGION

Region#	Rmanager	Rlocation	Rphone
22	Mary Black	Charlotte, NC	704-331-1131
33	Sam Long	Atlanta, GA	414-822-8765

Figure 17.3 Contents of the example insurance database.

The information requested and the attribute qualified on (*Amount*), are all found in the single relation POLICY. This retrieval can be accomplished by a **select** followed by a **project.** In the following, the relation N contains the desired information.

M = **select from** POLICY **where** *Amount* GT 100,000 (*note*: GT means *greater than*, GE means *greater than or equal to*, LT means *less than*, and so on)

N = **project** *SS#, Pol#, SID#* **from** M

Retrieval.17.2: Find the buyer social security number and the policy number for all policies for more than $100,000 that were sold by the salesman with identification number 101.

Again both the information required and the attributes on which the retrieval is qualified are from the same relation, so a **select** followed by a **project** will produce the desired result. However, for this retrieval an AND is needed in the **where** clause of the **select** operator.

M = **select from** POLICY **where** *Amount* GT 100,000 AND *SID#* EQ 101

N = **project** *SS#*, *Pol#* **from** M

Retrieval 17.3: Find the buyer social security number and date for all policies that are for over $200,000 or that were sold by salesman number 102.

Once more the information needed and the information qualified on are both in the single relation POLICY. As a consequence, a **select** followed by a **project** should produce the desired retrieval. The only difference in this retrieval and the previous one is the use of an OR in the **select** operator **where** clause. Both M and N are displayed in Figure 17.4.

M = **select from** POLICY **where** *Amount* GT 200,000 OR *SID#* EQ 102

N = **project** *SS#*, *Date* **from** M

Retrieval 17.4: Find the buyer social security number and date for all policies that were sold by salesman 102 or that were for over $100,000 and sold by salesman 103.

Here both an AND and an OR are needed. It will be assumed that AND takes precedence over OR. Parentheses will be used to override this precedence rule when that is needed. You should keep in mind that among commercially available database management systems, there are no standard rules for handling mixed AND/OR expressions. Consequently, it is important to check any particular system you are using to see what rules are applicable. If the system allows parentheses (and not all do) in such expressions, you can use parentheses in any expression to be certain of the interpretation. Assuming an AND over OR precedence rule, the preceding retrieval can be written as:

M = **select from** POLICY **where** *SID#* EQ 102 OR *Amount* GT 100,000 AND *SID#* EQ 103

N = **project** *SS#*, *Date* **from** M

Note that to minimize a reader's possible misinterpretation, the where clause could be written in the equivalent form: **where** *SID#* EQ 102 OR (*Amount* GT 100,000 AND *SID#* EQ 103).

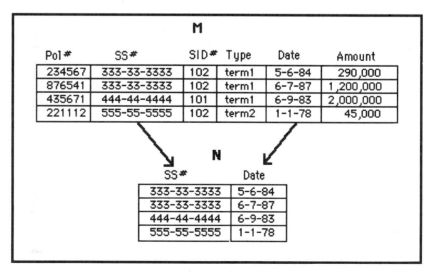

Figure 17.4 Relations M and N of Retrieval 17.3.

So far, all the example retrievals have involved only the one relation POLICY. The following retrievals will call for information that can only be retrieved using several relations at once.

Retrieval 17.5: Find the policy number and the salesman's name for all policies written for more than $200,000.

This looks very similar to Retrieval 17.1, except that the salesman's name rather than his identification number is being asked for. It is necessary to access relation SALESMAN to report this information. (Look back at our database diagram in Figure 17.2 and confirm this.) This access is accomplished using the **natural join** operator. First use a **select** operator on POLICY to qualify the policies of interest, then use the **natural join** to put the information about those policies together with the corresponding salesman information. Finally, a **project** operator will produce the desired result. The entire sequence of operators is given first, then all the involved relations are displayed in Figure 17.5.

M = **select from** POLICY **where** *Amount* GT 200,000

N = M<x>SALESMAN

P = **project** *Pol#*, *Sname* **from** N

Notice that the **natural join** of M and SALESMAN is formed by matching rows in each relation based on the common attribute *SID#*. In other words, the rows in POLICY representing policies sold by a particular salesman are matched with the row representing that salesman in SALESMAN. In this way, all the information about the salesman for a particular policy is appended to the row for that policy.

You should write down each intermediate relation (as was done in Figure 17.5) for Retrievals 17.6 and 17.7, which are quite similar to Retrieval 17.5. In this way, you will begin to gain some intuition relative to the **select-join-project** sequence of operators that occurs in one form or another in a great many relational algebra retrievals.

Retrieval 17.6: Find the names and phone numbers of all salesmen who work in region number 22.

M = **select from** DISTRICT **where** *Region#* EQ 22

N = M<x>SALESMAN

P = **project** *Sname*, *Sphone* **from** N

Retrieval 17.7: Find the names and occupation codes of all buyers of policies of type term1.

M = **select from** POLICY **where** *Type* EQ term1

N = M<x>BUYER

P = **project** *Bname*, *Occ-code* **from** N

In the following retrieval you will notice that the qualification of rows (sold by Joe Hill) occurs in SALESMAN and the information asked for (buyers' names and addresses) is located in BUYER. There is no direct connection between these two relations, but they are indirectly related through their mutual connection to POLICY. (Again, it would be helpful for you to look back at the database diagram in Figure 17.2 and confirm this claim.) Two **natural joins** will be required to put this information within reach.

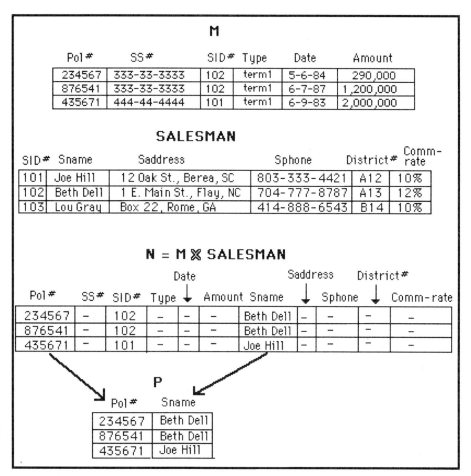

Figure 17.5 Relations of Retrieval 17.5. Some of the actual data contents of relation N have been omitted to allow display of the entire relation on one line.

Retrieval 17.8: Find the names and addresses of all buyers of policies sold by Joe Hill.

First **select** the row from SALESMAN containing information about salesman Joe Hill, then form the **natural join** of this relation with POLICY, putting together information about those policies sold by Joe Hill and the data about Hill from SALESMAN. Now this relation will be **joined** with BUYER to add the relevant information about the buyers of these policies. Finally, a **project** operator extracts the particular information desired. You should again construct the intermediate relations to see exactly how this sequence of operators produces what we want.

M = **select from** SALESMAN **where** *Sname* EQ "Joe Hill"

(Note the use of quotes. Quotes are generally needed for any text value that contains embedded blank spaces.)

N = M<x>POLICY

P = N<x>BUYER

Q = **project** *Bname, Baddress* **from** P

The technique of forming multiple **natural joins** to connect related information in a database is extended to four **natural joins** in the next example retrieval. Notice how each **natural join** is formed. For example, the **natural join** of M and BUYERS is matched on the attribute *SS#*; the **natural join** of N and SALESMAN, on the attribute *SID#*; and so on. Consult the database diagram given in Figure 17.2 and display for yourself the intermediate relations M, N, P, Q, and R.

Retrieval 17.9: Find the buyer's name, policy number, policy amount, salesman's name, region manager's name, and the region office phone number for any policies that have been written for more than $1 million.

M = **select from** POLICY **where** *Amount* GT 1,000,000

N = M<x>BUYERS

P = N<x>SALESMAN

Q = P<x>DISTRICT

R = Q<x>REGION

S = **project** *Bname, Pol#, Amount, Sname, Rmanager, Rphone* **from** R

Retrieval 17.10: Find the names of all salesmen who have sold *no* policies to buyers with occupation code CL.

This retrieval can best be written using the **minus** operator on relations. First, get the names of *all* salesmen into one relation (M); then subtract the names of those who have sold policies to buyers with occupation code CL (relation R). The last two steps are shown in Figure 17.6. You should verify for yourself that the relation R given there is produced by the following sequence of relations N, P, Q, and R.

M = **project** *Sname* **from** SALESMAN

N = **select from** BUYER **where** *Occ-code* EQ CL

P = N<x>POLICY

Q = P<x>SALESMAN

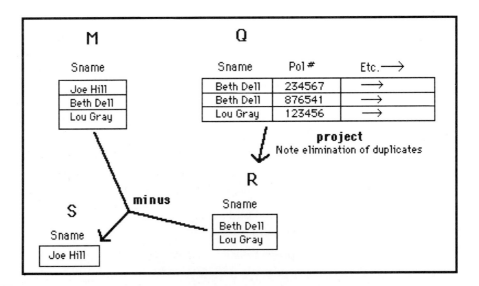

Figure 17.6 Last two steps of Retrieval 17.10.

R = **project** *Sname* **from** Q

(Recall that the **project** operator eliminates duplicate tuples.)

S = M **minus** R

Exercise Set 17.2

Using the insurance database described in this section, write relational algebra commands that perform the following retrievals:

1. Find the names, phone numbers, and commission rates for all salesmen who work in district A13.
2. Find the names of all salesmen in district A13 with a commission rate of 10 percent or more.
3. Find the social security number for buyers of policies that are for more than $100,000 and that were sold by salesman 102.
4. Find the social security number for buyers of policies that are for more than $100,000 or that both were for less than $100,000 and were sold by salesman 103.
5. Find buyers' names and phone numbers for all policies for more than $250,000.
6. Find buyers' names and addresses for buyers with occupation code = P who have bought policies from salesman 101.
7. Find buyers' names for all policies sold by salesmen in district A13.
8. Find names of all salesmen who have never sold a policy for more than $200,000.
9. Find the responsible region managers' names for all policies of over $1 million.
10. Find the district managers' names and phone numbers for those districts that have salesmen with a commission rate below 12 percent but that have no salesman with a commission rate above 15 percent.
11. Find the district managers' names for districts in which policies for over $500,000 have been written.
12. Find the district managers' names for districts in which no policies for over $500,000 have been written.

17.3 RELATIONAL DATABASE IMPLEMENTATION

In the previous section ideas were presented that provide a strong conceptual framework for understanding relational database management systems. With several modern relational database systems, these concepts are implemented in a way that allows direct access to the system for a user possessing this conceptual knowledge. However, this situation is the exception rather than the rule, and to use most relational database management systems requires some translation of the underlying concepts we have discussed to the particular system of interest.

There are two major reasons for the lack of standardization in implementing the relational database model. First, the importance of the relational model approach to database management system design has only recently been fully realized. As a consequence, a large number of database management systems are using many different design approaches that were in place before the standardizing structure of the relational model was available. This lack of standardization has been particularly noticeable in the microcomputer area because of the large number of software vendors who are producing database management software.

For the past several years any new database software that has been introduced has been called a *relational* system by its creators; however, the term *relational* has been badly misused in this context, and many of these systems have few if any of the characteristics of a true relational database management system as we have defined it (based on the relational data model and retrieval language).

A second reason that the many "relational" database management systems vary widely is that there is no standard way of implementing the relational concepts. By *implementation* we mean the methods and techniques used to provide, at the file and record manipulation level, the functionality expressed in the relational model. These implementation methods and techniques are not generally of critical importance to a database management system user, because ideally, they are completely hidden at the user level. However, in most current database management systems, some implementation details are still visible in certain areas, because to hide them completely would adversely affect the efficiency of operation. Of particular concern for implementation purposes is the question of what techniques are used to perform relational **natural joins**.

As the retrievals from our example insurance database have clearly demonstrated, use of the **natural join** is required for the retrieval of related information in separate relations. The way in which the **natural join** is implemented is a central implementation consideration. In this section some possible ways are examined in which the **natural join** (which essentially models the way our database relations are related to one another) might be implemented. Hence, you will gain some insight into why various database management systems can present quite different interfaces to their users. Once you see the considerations behind the way the relationships between relations are implemented, you will be much more able to move from one relational database system to another and to assimilate their particular implementation strategies.

TYPES OF RELATIONSHIPS BETWEEN RELATIONS.   Recall that relationships between relations can be one of several different types: **one-to-one, many-to-one,** or **many-to-many.** A clear understanding of each of these types of relationships is essential for our discussion. We therefore begin with an example database that illustrates each type. Consider the relations and associated relational schemes for a task management database defined in the following discussion. Just as in the insurance example database, abbreviations are used for the attribute names. These are given in Figure 17.7.

Rather than start with the task management database fully designed (as we did with the insurance database), let us work through some of the considerations involved in creating such a design. Suppose the attributes in Figure 17.7 are organized into relations as follows:

TASK(*Task#, Tcomp_date*)
EMPLOYEE(*Emp#, Emp_name*)

CONTRACT(*Contract#, Amount, Comp_date*)
MANAGER(*Mgr_name, Office_loc*)

Notice that as these relations are presently constructed, there are no apparent relationships among them at all. Now suppose the following relationships and constraints must be incorporated into this database design.

- A contract is broken down into various tasks. No task is associated with more than one contract.
- Each task has one manager, and no manager manages more than one task.
- Each task has a number of employees assigned to it, and an employee may be assigned to split time between several tasks at once.

Verify for yourself that the preceding conditions imply the following kinds of relationships among our database relations.

TASK	<———	one-to-one	———>	MANAGER
TASK	———	many-to-one	———>	CONTRACT
TASK	———	many-to-many	———	EMPLOYEE

MODELING DIFFERENT RELATIONSHIP TYPES. We now consider how these relationships can be designed into our conceptual relational model by adding the appropriate attributes to the relational schemes. Then we examine how retrievals using these relationships might actually be accomplished in terms of file and record lookups. These considerations lead to an examination of some alternative ways of "building in" these relationships within the database definition for the sake of efficiency.

To include the one-to-one relationship between TASK and MANAGER in the database design, the attribute *Mgr_name* could be added to the relation TASK (or the attribute *Task#* could be added to the relation MANAGER). Alternatively, the two relations could be combined into a single relation, because the records are paired in a one-to-one manner.

This last course of action may be desirable in some cases but undesirable in others. For example, the MANAGER relation may contain a number of attributes about managers which are independent of the task to which the manager happens

Full Name	Abbreviation
task number	Task#
task completion date	Tcomp_date
employee number	Emp#
employee name	Emp_name
contract number	Contract#
contract amount	Amount
contract completion date	Comp_date
task manager name	Mgr_name
manager office location	Office_loc

Figure 17.7 Attribute names/abbreviations for the task management example database.

to be assigned at the present time. Indeed, that information must be stored even if the manager is not currently assigned to a task. Hence it would be desirable to keep the MANAGER relation separate from the TASK relation. So the first action described will be taken, that is, attribute *Mgr_name* will be added to the relation TASK. This action clearly allows us to associate a unique manager with each task.

To incorporate the many-to-one relationship between TASK and CON-TRACT, attribute *Contract#* could be added to relation TASK. The only difference between this arrangement and the preceding one for the one-to-one relationship between TASK and MANAGER is that there would be several tuples (records) in TASK containing a given *Contract#* value (one for each of the tasks contained within the contract), whereas for a given *Mgr_name* value, there would be only one tuple in the relation TASK containing that value. In other words, the ways in which we incorporate one-to-one and many-to-one relationships into a relational database design are identical. The difference in these two kinds of relationships only shows up in the data itself, not in the database design.

Finally, the many-to-many relationship between TASK and EMPLOYEE could be structured by adding the attribute *Task#* to relation EMPLOYEE, but there is an additional complication here. Because an employee can be assigned to several tasks at once, we must either add *several* attributes to EMPLOYEE for recording the *Task#* values for all the tasks to which an employee is assigned or else expect to *repeat* rows in EMPLOYEE, one row each time an employee is assigned to a task. Both of these approaches have drawbacks.

Because the number of tasks to which an employee may be assigned may be unknown in advance of setting up the database, it is impossible to know how many attributes to include for holding such information. On the other hand, if a row in EMPLOYEE is stored for each employee-task assignment, much information about each employee will be repeated a number of times (once for each task to which the employee is assigned).

A better method than either of those previously described for modeling a many-to-many relationship is to create a new relation for this purpose, ASSIGN(*Emp#,Task#*), to hold the information about which employees are assigned to which tasks. In this way, information can be stored and retrieved for any number of task assignments per employee with no difficulty, yet employee-specific information is still stored only once per employee in relation EM-PLOYEE. The following example instance of the ASSIGN relation illustrates. Notice how employees with employee numbers 1001 and 1256 are each assigned to more than one task and that task numbers 124 and 165 each have several employees assigned to them.

Task#	Emp#
124	1001
124	1256
165	1001
165	1344
177	1256

A graphical interpretation of the new database design will help clarify what has been created and will demonstrate why the added attributes were included in existing relations and why the new relation ASSIGN was created. The new database design is summarized in the diagram in Figure 17.8. After you study this diagram carefully, you may want to reread the previous few paragraphs. Using the diagram as you read, you should gain a much better understanding of these techniques.

Note in Figure 17.8 that arrows have been added to indicate what kind of relationships (many-to-one, including the direction, or one-to-one) is *expected*, but remember that there is no actual difference in the design for one-to-one and many-to-one relationships. On the other hand, the many-to-many relationship requires a new relation for its incorporation, and the relationships between this new relation and the existing ones are then many-to-one.

INEFFICIENCY OF SOME INFORMATION RETRIEVALS.   Let us now consider how certain information retrievals would be processed using the previously modeled database structure and the relational operators. Some information is now contained explicitly in the individual relations. For example, to find the unique *Contract#* associated with a task, simply **select** the appropriate row in TASK and use the **project** operator to get the *Contract#*. On the other hand, to find the contractor for the contract for a particular task would require a **natural join** (we could first select only the row from TASK we are interested in) of TASK with CONTRACT. This would amount to looking up the unique row in CONTRACT that has a *Contract#* that matches the *Contract#* in our selected row from TASK.

This same relationship can be used in the opposite direction. Suppose we want to find the *Task#* for all the tasks that are a part of a given contract. First **select** the appropriate row from CONTRACT, then do a **natural join** with TASK. This process is entirely symmetric to that of the previous retrieval. However, the join will now be more difficult to accomplish, because TASK will have to be searched to find *all* the rows (not the unique one as before) there that match the given row in *Contract#*.

The last retrieval described will require a search through the entire relation TASK unless that relation has been indexed in a way that allows the direct

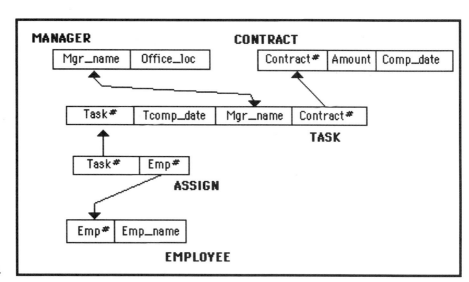

Figure 17.8 The task management example database after restructuring to include relationships among the relations.

retrieval of rows that have *Contract#* matching the *Contract#* in the selected row from CONTRACT. In other words, if it is known in advance what information requests are likely, **indices** can be built to aid in looking up the required information. Otherwise, the retrieval proceeds by the inefficient method of searching all rows in a relation to find the desired information. This inefficiency can be quite troublesome when relations are large.

It is precisely this efficiency problem that causes the most concern when implementing a database management system, and there is no ideal solution to it. Building indices and keeping them up to date as data is entered and deleted from a database is very expensive in terms of use of computer resources. Consequently, it is unwise to have an index for all, or even most, of the attributes in each relation in our database. On the other hand, without such indices, retrieval times for certain information can be unacceptably large. Many microcomputer database management systems resolve this problem by restricting somewhat the flexibility of the relational retrieval language, and it is this method that we discuss in the next section.

Exercise Set 17.3

1. Give two reasons that there is no standard implementation strategy for commercial relational database systems.

2. Are all "relational" database systems based on the relational model you have studied?

3. Identify the three basic types of relationships that can exist between database relations.

4. What is the purpose of the relation ASSIGN in Figure 17.8? What type of relationship between the TASK and EMPLOYEE relations does ASSIGN implement?

5. Explain why the database structure shown in Figure 17.8 makes certain information retrievals less efficient than others that would appear to be completely symmetric.

17.4 IMPLEMENTING DIFFERENT TYPES OF RELATIONSHIPS

In the true relational model, **joins** more general than **natural joins** are used. For example, **joins** can be formed using any attributes desired for matching, not just those with the same names, as long as they have the same data types. Furthermore, these more general **joins** can be created *dynamically*, meaning that they are created as needed. In other words, there is no requirement that these **joins** be anticipated at the time the database structure is created, because they can simply be defined whenever the need arises. All attributes are available at any time for use in **joins**. In practice, this flexibility is generally compromised in some ways in order to eleviate the inefficiency problems we discussed earlier. We discuss one of the most frequently used implementation methods in the context of our task management example database.

KEY ATTRIBUTES. The concept of a **key** for a relation is central in the implementation method we discuss. Essentially, a key for a relation R is an attribute (or set of attributes) within the relational scheme whose value (set of values) within any particular row uniquely determines the values within that same row for all the other attributes. Put another way, a key is an attribute (or attributes) that allows us to distinguish among rows in a relation. The definition of *key* can be stated more precisely, but this intuitive description suffices for our purposes.

The concept of a key can be illustrated with a simple example. Consider the following relation that contains employee information:

$$E(SS\#, Name, Address, Phone, Salary, Department)$$

Making the reasonable assumption that once an employee's social security number is known, all the other information within a row with that *SS#* value will be uniquely determined, the attribute *SS#* is a key. In other words, no two employees will have the same social security number, and so a particular social security number can occur in only one row within the relation E.

On the other hand, the attribute *Name* would probably not serve as a key for the preceding relation E, because two employees might have the same name. Similarly, none of the other single attributes would be keys for E, although probably *Name* and *Address* together would serve as a key, because presumably there would never be two employees by the same name living at the same address. Whatever attribute or combination of attributes is chosen for a relation's key, it must be true that any particular value for the key can be associated with no more than one row in the relation.

We adopt the convention of underlining the key attribute(s) in relational schemes. Using this convention (and making some assumptions), the task management example database would be represented as follows:

EMPLOYEE(*Emp#*, Emp_name)
MANAGER(*Mgr-name*, Office_loc)
TASK(*Task#*, Tcomp_date, Mgr_name, Contract#)
CONTRACT(*Contract#*, Amount, Comp_date)
ASSIGN(*Task#*, *Emp#*)

Consider for a moment the relation ASSIGN. Neither of its two attributes taken individually can serve as a key; both attributes are required. To see why this is the case, look at our previous example instance of that relation.

Task#	Emp#
124	1001
124	1256
165	1001
165	1344
177	1256

Because each task generally has many employees assigned to it, the attribute *Task#* does not uniquely determine the value of the remaining attribute, *Emp#*. This is clearly seen in the preceding instance of ASSIGN, because several rows have the same task number but different employee numbers. Similarly, several rows have the same employee number but different task numbers, reflecting the fact that an employee can be assigned to several tasks at the same time. Hence neither *Emp#* nor *Task#* forms a key for ASSIGN. In other words, the values of *both* attributes must be known before a *unique* row has been determined. Hence, the two attributes taken together form a key.

LINK ATTRIBUTES.   As you saw in our design of the task management database in the previous section, one technique that allows you to relate two relations is to place into one of the relations an attribute whose values enable you to search out related information in the other. You also saw that even though this scheme gives the retrieval power desired from a conceptual perspective, it does not necessarily allow efficient retrieval of related information.

One of the most common techniques for achieving the desired information retrieval efficiency is to add a *variable-length attribute* to a relation and to place in it all the *key values* for the related rows in another relation. A variable-length attribute is an attribute that can have *multiple values*, thereby allowing the storage of many key values relating many rows in one relation to a row in another relation. This arrangement permits a direct lookup of related information, provided that we have indices for searching out key values. An example from the task management database will illustrate.

Variable-length attributes are placed in the relations CONTRACT and TASK that will allow the implementation of the many-to-one relationship from TASK to CONTRACT. These new attributes are called **link attributes**, since it is through them that information from two related relations is linked together. With these link attributes defined, the relational schemes will appear as follows (note that we have removed the attributes that we added in the conceptual database design of Figure 17.8—the link attributes now serve the function for which those attributes were introduced):

TASK(*Task#*, *Tcomp_date*, *Contract_link*)
CONTRACT(*Contract#*, *Amount*, *Comp_date*, *Task_link*)

Notice that new link attributes have been placed in *both* relations, in contrast to the addition of just a single attribute in the conceptual design. The reason for this is to make the access of related information equally efficient, regardless of which direction of the relationship is used.

An example instance of the two relations, given in Figure 17.9, will help you visualize the effect of the link attributes. The arrows are drawn to emphasize the linking effect of the two link attributes. Notice how having *both* link attributes allows easy access in either direction.

Carefully observe that because the TASK-to-CONTRACT relationship is many-to-one, the link attribute *Contract_link* in TASK is actually a single-valued attribute, because a task can be linked to only one contract. However, the attribute *Task_link* in CONTRACT is multiple-valued, because each contract can be linked to many constituent tasks.

Using the technique of multiple-valued link attributes (also sometimes called *pointer* attributes), the many-to-many relationship between EMPLOYEE and TASK can be implemented directly and the need for the ASSIGN relation can be eliminated. However, it is important to note that if there were some information that was *specific* to the employee-task assignment (e.g., percentage of the employee's time allotted to the task), then the ASSIGN relation would still be

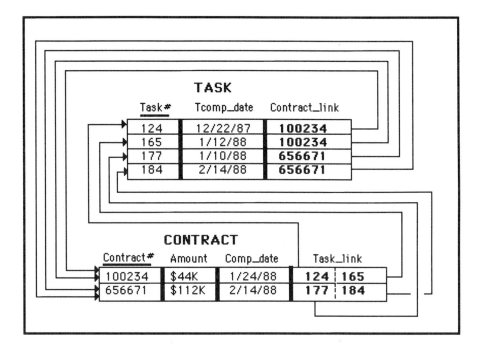

Figure 17.9 An example showing the effect of adding link attributes to the database relations TASK and CONTRACT.

necesary to hold that information, since it would not naturally belong to either EMPLOYEE or TASK, but rather to the relationship between them. If ASSIGN were to be kept, the *Emp#* and *Task#* attributes would be replaced by link attributes.

The required relational schemes for applying the link attribute technique to the entire example database are

> EMPLOYEE(*Emp#*, Emp_name, Task_link1)
> TASK(*Task#*, Tcomp_date, Contract_link, Employee_link, Mgr_link)
> CONTRACT(*Contract#*, Amount, Comp_date, Task_link2)
> MANAGER(*Mgr-name*, Office_loc, Task_link3)

You should be aware of the limitation placed upon the conceptual relational model by the link attribute technique. With these attributes, the only **joins** that are to be allowed are those implied by the presence of the link attributes themselves. These **joins** correspond to the **natural joins** that would be possible in the conceptual design for this database given in the previous section. No other **joins** are possible. In most cases this limitation does not impose a large burden, and if you discover a need for additional **join** capabilities after your database is designed, most systems allow a modification of the design to include the appropriate link attributes. What has been lost is the flexibility to accomplish ad hoc **joins**, but this has been compensated for in greatly increased information retrieval efficiency.

There are probably as many variations on the preceding technique as there are database management software vendors, but if you have a clear understanding of the ideas presented, you should have little difficulty in picking up the particular language and nuances of any of the currently available relational database management systems. In the next chapter, we discuss the Reflex Plus system at length, and you will see how some of these techniques are used.

Exercise Set 17.4

1. What are key attributes?

2. What are link attributes? How are they related to key attributes?

3. Use the example instance of employee-task assignments given for the AS-SIGN relation in this chapter to construct an instance, similar to Figure 17.9, of the two relations TASK and EMPLOYEE that includes the *Employee_link* and *Task_link* attributes.

4. Draw a diagram, similar to Figure 17.8, illustrating the task management database with link attributes included. Draw lines to connect the link attributes to their keys and indicate what type of relationship they represent.

5. Use the following information to construct an instance for the entire task management database using the link attribute structure. (Note: The results of this exercise will be used in the next chapter when you implement the task management database in Reflex Plus.)

   - Contract number 1000 is for $55,000 and has a completion date of 4/24/90.

   - It consists of three tasks numbered 101, 202, and 303 that have completion dates of 2/1/90, 2/23/90, and 4/24/90, respectively.

   - Jones, whose office is 106 Bldg A, has been assigned to manage task 101; Smith, whose office is 108 Bldg B, has been assigned to manage task 202; Williams, whose office is 300 Bldg G, is the manager for task 303.

   - Employees Allen (*Emp*#=198), Glenn (*Emp*#=177), and Hill (*Emp*#=132) have been assigned to task 101.

   - Employees Allen and Roberts (*Emp*#=145) have been assigned to task 202.

   - Employees Roberts, Glenn, and Hill have been assigned to task 303.

6. Give the relational schemes for the relations of the insurance database described in earlier sections of this chapter using the link attribute technique to model all the relationships.

7. Draw a diagram illustrating the insurance database with link attributes as constructed in exercise 6. Draw lines to connect link attributes to their keys.

17.5 DATABASE STORAGE REQUIREMENTS

When a multiple-file database is stored on disk, the disk space requirements can become an important consideration as the database is actually filled with data. In this section, you will see how to do some simple calculations to get a rough estimate of the disk space requirements for storing a database.

Recall that the disks the Macintosh uses hold either 800K bytes or 400K bytes (K = 1024), depending upon whether the disk drive can read/write both sides or only one side of the disk. Remember that a byte is the amount of space required to store one character of text; hence, a double-sided floppy disk stores approximately 800,000 characters of text, assuming none of the disk is used for other purposes.

Let us now estimate space requirements for the insurance example database. The first step is to estimate how much storage is required for a record of each type. A BUYER record might have the following layout:

SS#	——	11 characters (bytes)
Bname	——	30 characters
Occ-code	——	3 characters
Baddress	——	40 characters
Bphone	——	12 characters
	Total	96 characters (bytes)

Similarly, the requirements for the other record types can be estimated. Suppose those estimates are

REGION	——	65 bytes
DISTRICT	——	68 bytes
SALESMAN	——	91 bytes
POLICY	——	50 bytes.

Now suppose the following requirements for the data to be stored are anticipated.

- There are four regions to be represented in the database.
- Each region consists of eight districts.
- On the average, a district has 20 salesmen.
- Each salesman to expected to service an average of about 100 policies.
- It is expected that there will be approximately seven different buyers for each 10 policies sold.

What are the disk space requirements for the storage of this information? The database will contain approximately the following numbers of records (and hence bytes of data) of each record type:

REGION	—	4 records @ 65 bytes each = 260 bytes
DISTRICT	—	32 records @ 68 bytes each = 2,176 bytes
SALESMAN	—	640 records @ 91 bytes each = 58,240 bytes
POLICY	—	64,000 records @ 50 bytes each = 3,200,000 bytes
BUYER	—	44,800 records (64,000 * .7) @ 96 bytes each = 4,300,800 bytes
	Total	7,561,476 bytes

Hence, this database should not be stored on floppy disks (it would require 10 double-sided ones to hold the data), because it would require an inordinate amount of disk switching to do even the simplest kinds of data retrievals. A hard disk drive is required for databases of this size. In this case, a 10 megabyte (recall that a megabyte is 1 million bytes) capacity drive would be the minimum requirement, and a 20-megabyte drive would be preferable, to allow for database expansion. Note that although the insurance database structure is a realistic one, the number of attributes was purposely limited to make the database easier to display as an example, so the actual requirements for such a database may be even larger.

It should be clear that database disk storage requirements cannot be ignored when planning a microcomputer database. And even though most small-business and individual databases may not be as large as our insurance database example, it is still true that a hard disk drive is a necessity for most practical database applications. Fortunately, the prices of hard disk drives have dropped significantly over the past few years, and the performance parameters of the drives have increased. It is now possible to purchase drives with 40-megabyte capacity (or more) at moderate prices. Thus, it can be quite cost effective for a small business or even an individual to organize and use sizable databases for information management requirements.

Exercise Set 17.5

Make some estimates about attribute field sizes (assume link attributes require 5 bytes for each value) and use the following estimates about relation sizes to estimate the total disk space requirements for the task management database described in the text. Assume that the database will contain information about 50 contracts, each consisting of about 25 tasks, with each task having approximately 10 people assigned to it. Assume further that the average employee is assigned to two tasks.

Key Concepts

Cross operator	Indices
Key	Link attribute
Many-to-many relationship	Many-to-one relationship
Minus operator	Natural join operator
One-to-one relationship	Relational algebra
Union operator	

CHAPTER 18

USING RELATIONAL DATABASE POWER WITH REFLEX PLUS

LEARNING OBJECTIVES

- To learn how to create Reflex Plus databases.

- To learn how to load data into a Reflex Plus database using Reflex Plus default data entry forms or custom-designed entry forms.

- To learn how to retrieve information from Reflex Plus using simple one-file selection criteria.

- To learn how to use Reflex Plus reports to retrieve related information from multiple files and format the information display.

I n this chapter you will see how the relational database model is implemented in the commercial database system Reflex Plus. You will learn how to define a Reflex Plus database and how to load data into the database using either Relex Plus default entry forms or your own custom-designed entry forms. You will learn how to select data from a single file in the database using simple selection criteria. In addition, you will learn how to construct Reflex Plus reports to choose only those attributes you wish to display and to extract related information from multiple files.

18.1 CREATING REFLEX PLUS DATABASES

Reflex Plus is a fully relational database management system produced and marketed by Borland International. It has a high-level user interface that allows easy database definition, data input form creation, database information selection, and database report specification. In fact, you will notice that many of these functions are implemented in Reflex Plus in ways that are quite similar to the ways the corresponding functions are implemented in Works DB.

In this chapter you will work through all of Reflex Plus' basic functions using the task management example database from the previous chapter. The chapter is written in a tutorial style that can easily be used with the Reflex Plus software itself. However, even if you do not have the Reflex Plus package available, the chapter may still be read with profit, and it will provide you with a detailed example of a representative fully relational database management system.

Reflex Plus provides a graphical method for defining databases. You create and modify a database design in the *Database Overview* **window.** Relational schemes will appear as tables in this window. Reflex Plus uses a link attribute scheme quite similar to that described in Chapter 17 for establishing relationships among relations, and relationships will be represented on the screen by lines connecting relations by way of the appropriate link attributes. You will see that Reflex Plus provides for automatic link attribute update whenever possible. Through the link attributes, you will be able to perform the equivalent of the **natural join** operator.

Reflex Plus automatically generates data entry forms, which you can then easily modify on screen using MacPaint-type operations. Once a relation is created, whenever it is opened by double-clicking on its name bar in the *Database Overview* window, the default entry form (which can be modified if you choose) is displayed.

Reflex Plus reports can be generated in default table format or you can custom-design them. Again the custom-designed reports are created on the screen using a combination of MacPaint-type features and other capabilities. The construction of complex information retrievals is accomplished using the logical operators OR, AND, and NOT. These queries can be constructed when they are needed, or they can be saved and automatically incorporated into reports in a manner quite similar to that seen in Works DB reports.

In this section you will see how to define a database structure within the *Database Overview* window. The example used will be the design we developed for the task management database in Chapter 17. Glance ahead to Figure 18.3 to see how this design looks once its definition has been completed in the *Database Overview* window. In addition to entering the information shown in that screen, you will also set the data types of all the attributes of the database and the types (e.g., many-to-one) of each of the links (shown as the connecting lines in Figure 18.3).

ENTERING THE FIRST RELATION DEFINITION.   Open the Reflex Plus database system by double-clicking on the Reflex Plus icon. You will be presented with a blank window titled *Database Overview*. Pull down the **File** menu and select *New*. You will then be given the dialog box shown in Figure 18.1, in which you are prompted to name and create a database (relation). Begin with the TASK relation by typing in the name *TASK* and selecting *Database,* as shown in Figure 18.1.

A box should now appear within the *Database Overview* window into which you will type the attribute names for TASK. The file name *TASK* is at the top of this box and the first attribute position selected (highlighted). Recall that the relational scheme for TASK is (using our link attributes):

TASK(*Task#, Tcomp_date, Mgr_link, Emp_link, Contract_link*)

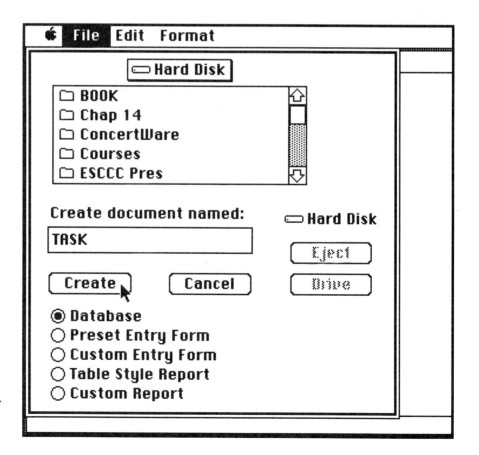

Figure 18.1 Dialog box for defining a database relation.

Type the first attribute name, *Task#*, into the selected attribute position. To complete your definition of the attribute *Task#*, pull down the **Describe** menu. *Task#* is to be an integer, so select *Integer Field* from the **Describe** menu. Additionally, *Task#* is the key attribute for TASK, so you should select *Key Field* from the **Describe** menu. Notice that *Task#* is now underlined to indicate that it has been designated as a key. You have now completed the definition of attribute *Task#*. Press the *Return* key and you will automatically be given space for another attribute.

Type in the next attribute name, *Tcomp_date*, and select *Date Field* as its data type from the **Describe** menu. Press *Return* and type in the *Mgr_link* attribute name. For now this attribute will be a text field; thus, it is not necessary to access the **Describe** menu, because *Text Field* is the default data type. Later you will see that Reflex Plus will automatically give this and the other link attributes the appropriate data types to contain the appropriate key values once the actual links have been established. Complete the definition of TASK by entering the attribute names *Emp_link* and *Contract_link*.

ENTERING MORE RELATION DEFINITIONS.   After entering the last attribute name for TASK, pull down the **File** menu and select *New*. Repeat the previously described process to create the relations MANAGER, EMPLOYEE, and CONTRACT using the following relational schemes:

> MANAGER(*Mgr_name*, *Office_loc*, *Task_link1*)
>
> EMPLOYEE(*Emp#*, *Emp_name*, *Task_link2*)
>
> CONTRACT(*Contract#*, *Amount*, *Comp_date*, *Task_link3*)

All these attributes will be text fields, except that *Emp#* and *Contract#* will be integers and *Comp_date* will be a date field. Don't forget to designate the key attribute in each relation.

CONFIGURING THE DATABASE DESIGN IN ITS WINDOW.   Note that the file (relation) definition boxes can be moved around on the screen by selecting the file name at the top of a box and then dragging the box by the thin strip at the top of the selected box. The file rectangles themselves can be resized by selecting the rectangle and then dragging the grow box (the small square at the bottom right corner of the file rectangle). Configure your boxes so that your final screen looks something like Figure 18.2.

ENTERING LINK INFORMATION.   You are now ready to establish the actual links that will implement the relationships that exist between the relations of the database. Recall that these relationships are

TASK	<——	one-to-one	——>	MANAGER
TASK	——	many-to-one	——>	CONTRACT
TASK	——	many-to-many	——	EMPLOYEE

To implement the one-to-one relationship between TASK and MANAGER, select the *Mgr_link* attribute from TASK and hold and drag the mouse over the *Task_link1* attribute in MANAGER. When you release the mouse, you will see that

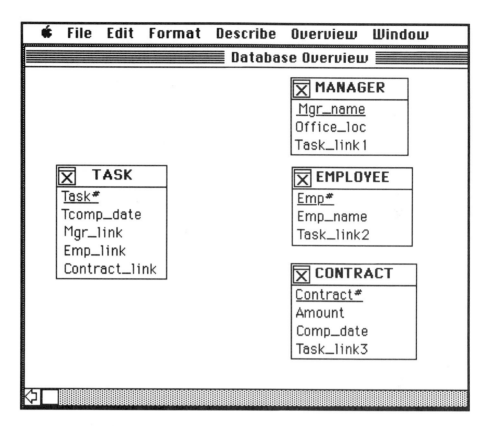

Figure 18.2 Task management database relations entered and repositioned in the *Database Overview* window.

a line (or link) now connects the two attributes. Next you need to describe the kind of relationship you wish to establish (one-to-one in this case). *Mgr_link* should still be the selected attribute. Pull down the **Describe** menu and you will see two possibilities for this "end" of your link:

A Link to One MANAGER Record

A Collection of Links to MANAGER Records.

Because a task has only one manager, select *A Link to One ... .* Now select the *Task_link1* attribute from MANAGER and pull down the **Describe** menu again. Because it is also true that a manager can manage only one task, again select *A Link to One ... .* These steps complete the definiton of the one-to-one relationship between TASK and MANAGER.

The many-to-many relationship between TASK and EMPLOYEE is established in the same way, except for the type of links you select. Select *Emp_link* in TASK and drag the mouse, releasing it over the attribute *Task_link2* in EMPLOYEE. Select *A Collection of Links ...* for both ends of this link because it is a many-to-many relationship. In other words, each TASK row can be connected to many EMPLOYEE rows and vice versa.

Finally, to establish the many-to-one link from TASK to CONTRACT, choose *A Collection of Links ...* for attribute *Task_link3* CONTRACT because a given contract will have many tasks associated with it. On the other hand, select *A Link to One ...* for attribute *Contract_link* in TASK, since a given task is associated with only one contract. You should be especially careful with many-to-one links so that the different link types are set on the correct ends of the link.

Your screen should now look similar to Figure 18.3. Notice how easily Reflex Plus handles the different types of relationships. You will see in a moment that all the link attributes have been given new data types. First, you should complete your database definiton by selecting *Save Design* from the **File** menu.

QUITTING AND RESTARTING A SESSION.   If you are using this chapter as a hands-on tutorial with Reflex Plus, you will probably need to stop your session at various points and continue the tutorial later. To do this now, select *Quit* from the **File** menu (if you had not already saved your design, you would have been given the option to do this before quitting the session). To return to the database at the preceding point at a later time, simply start Reflex Plus and then select *Show Database File* from the **Overview** menu. Next select TASK from the list of files offered. Once TASK is displayed, select *Show Linked Files* from the **Overview** menu. Click the mouse at any clear spot on the screen and you will be back to the point at which you left earlier (the screen of Figure 18.3).

Computer Practice 18.1

1.   Using this section as a guide, enter the definition of the task management database into Reflex Plus.

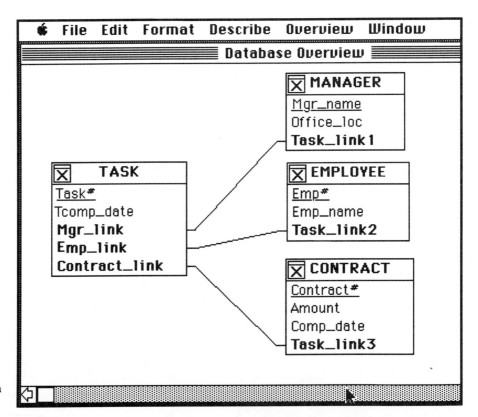

Figure 18.3 Task management database design with links defined.

2. Redesign the relational schemes for the insurance database relations of Chapter 17, converting them to the link attribute form for use in Reflex Plus.

3. Implement the insurance database, as configured in exercise 2 in Reflex Plus. Be sure to designate a key attribute for each relation.

18.2 REFLEX PLUS DATA ENTRY

As mentioned before, Reflex Plus provides default **data entry forms** for all the files (relations) in a database. In this section you will see how to access the default entry forms and use them for data entry. In addition, you will learn how to browse through the database contents using the **Search** menu and how to modify the default entry forms.

USING A DEFAULT DATA ENTRY FORM.   You can access a default data entry form for a relation by simply opening that relation in the *Database Overview* window by double-clicking in the file name box. If you want to change the appearance of the data entry form, you can modify it and save your modified form to be used when you next open the relation. We begin this portion of our tutorial by entering some data into the EMPLOYEE relation. You will not enter any information into the *Task_link2* attribute until data entry for linked files is discussed later in this section. The data to be entered is the instance data of exercise 5 in Exercise Set 17.4,

EMPLOYEE

Emp#	Emp_name
198	Allen
177	Glenn
132	Hill
145	Roberts

MANAGER

Mgr_name	Office_loc
Jones	106 Bldg A
Smith	108 Bldg B
Williams	300 Bldg G

TASK

Task#	Tcomp_date	Mgr_name	Contract#
101	2/1/91	Jones	1000
202	2/23/91	Smith	1000
303	4/24/91	Williams	1000

CONTRACT

Contract#	Amount	Comp_date
1000	55,000	4/24/91

ASSIGN

Task#	Emp#
101	198
101	177
101	132
202	198
202	145
303	145
303	177
303	132

Figure 18.4 Data for the task management example database.

which is reproduced in Figure 18.4. Of course, the information contained in the ASSIGN relation in that figure will be represented as link attributes.

From the *Database Overview* window, open the EMPLOYEE relation for data input by double-clicking the relation name in the EMPLOYEE box. You should then see the default EMPLOYEE data entry form shown in Figure 18.5.

Type in your first *Emp#* value, 198, and press *Tab*. Next type in the *Emp_name* value, Allen, and again press *Tab*. Since you do not wish to enter a *Task_link2* value at this time, you are ready to enter this record into your database by selecting *Enter Record* from the **Entry** menu. Now select *Blank Record* from that same menu and you are ready to enter data for the next record. Type in the second *Emp#* = 177 and *Emp_name* = Glenn; then select *Enter Record* from the **Entry** menu.

MODIFYING ENTRY FORMS.   Before entering more data, we will change the data entry form. To do this, select *Entry Design* from the **Entry** menu. You will be presented with a form layout screen on which you can redesign the entry form. Select the *Emp_name* data entry field , then drag it to the right an inch or so using the thin strip at its top, as illustrated in Figure 18.6.

Next select the text field currently labeled *Emp_name* by clicking anywhere over the text and drag it in the same manner to the right, so that it is again positioned next to its data field. Now move the cursor inside this highlighted text field (until it becomes an I-beam) and click. You can now edit the text in this field as you would text in a word processing document. Change the text to read "employee name." Reposition the *Task_link2* data field (drag it by one of the side handle bars after selecting it) and its label so that your screen looks somewhat like the one displayed in Figure 18.7.

This completes the modifications to be made to this entry form. Close the layout screen by selecting *Entry* from the **EntryDesign** menu. You can now continue your data entry with the new entry form. Enter *Emp#* = 132, *Emp_name* (or employee name)= Hill and *Emp#* = 145, *Emp_name* = Roberts.

VIEWING THE CONTENTS OF A RELATION.   Before leaving this form, you can check to see that your data has actually been entered using commands from the **Search** menu. Select *First Record* from this menu and you should see displayed one of the records that you entered into the database. By repeatedly selecting *Next Record*

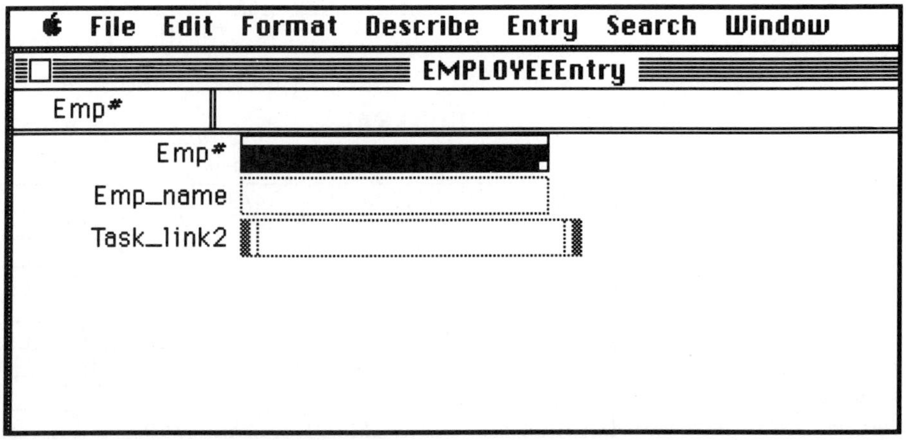

Figure 18.5 Default data entry form for relation *EMPLOYEE*.

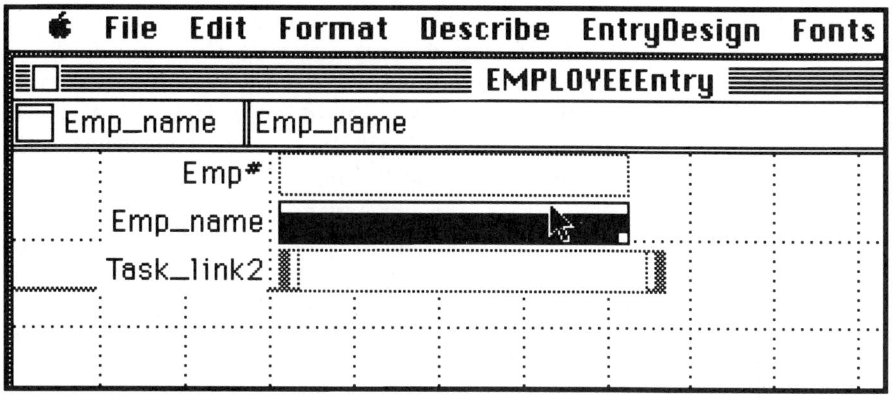

Figure 18.6 Preparing to move the *Emp_name* data field.

from the **Search** menu, you can walk through all the records stored in the relation. Note that the records are not stored in the order that you entered them, but are instead listed in order by key value (*Emp#*, in this case).

If some of the records you just "entered" are missing, you probably forgot to select *Enter Record* before you selected *Blank Record* for the next record in the process previously described. You can reenter those records missing using this form by first selecting *Blank Record* from the **Entry** menu and proceeding as before, remembering to select *Enter Record* after each record's data is completed and then *Blank Record* to enter the next record.

EDITING RECORDS.   You can also edit any of the records in the relation. First find the record to be edited using the **Search** menu commands. Then simply select and retype or edit any incorrect fields. When you finish editing the record, select *Enter Record* from the **Entry** menu to replace the old record with the updated one.

ENTERING RELATED RECORDS AND LINK ATTRIBUTES.   Leave the EMPLOYEE data entry form window by choosing *Database Overview* from the **Window** menu. Once you are back in the *Database Overview* window, open the default data entry form for the TASK relation by double-clicking on the name TASK..

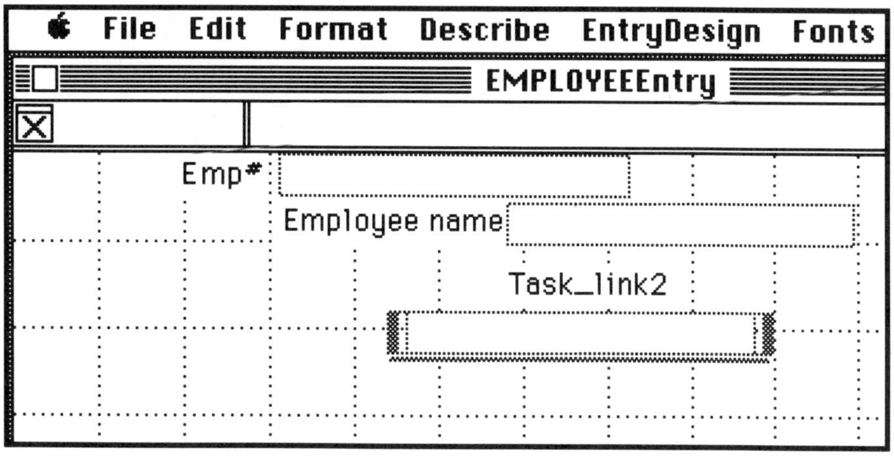

Figure 18.7 Modified EM-PLOYEE data entry form.

When you are presented with the TASK data entry form type in the value *101* for *Task#* and press *Tab*. Enter *2/1/91* into the *Tcomp_date* data field and then *Jones* into the *Mgr_link* data field. Now you are ready to enter the link attribute values for the employees assigned to this task. Recall that these link values are the key attribute values (*Emp#*) for the relevant EMPLOYEE records—in this case, 198, 177, and 132. Type *198* into the *Emp_link* data field and press *Return* (*note:* not *Tab*). Notice that *Emp_link* expands to receive another *Emp#* value. Type in *177*, press *Return*, and type in *132*. Now instead of pressing *Return*, press the *Tab* key. Pressing *Return* would cause Reflex Plus to expand the *Emp_link* data area for another *Emp#,* whereas pressing *Tab* advances to the next attribute *Contract_link*. Enter the value *1000* for this attribute, then select *Enter Record* from the **Entry** menu to enter this record into the database.

Before entering any more data, look at the records that you previously entered into EMPLOYEE. Return to the EMPLOYEE data entry form by choosing it from the **Window** menu. Use the commands from the **Search** menu to look at the EMPLOYEE records. Notice, as is illustrated in Figure 18.8, the presence of the *Task#* value for those employees whose employee numbers were included in the TASK record that you entered a moment ago. Reflex Plus has automatically placed these values in the appropriate EMPLOYEE records.

Recall that you have not yet entered any records into MANAGER or CON-TRACT. When Reflex Plus attempts to enter link attribute key values automatically for records (related to the record into which data is being entered) that are not found in the database, it will create the necessary records. In this case MANAGER and CONTRACT records will be automatically created with key values *Jones* and *1000*, respectively. To check this, return to the *Database Overview* window and open the default data entry form for relation MANAGER. You will see displayed the record shown in Figure 18.9

Return to the TASK entry form and enter the remaining two records. Next go to the MANAGER entry form and complete the data entry for that relation. Do this by using the *First Record* and *Next Record* commands from the **Search** menu and editing the records already created by Reflex Plus. Don't forget to select *Enter Record* for each record after you edit. Repeat this process to complete the data entry for the CONTRACT relation.

When you have completed entering the data from Figure 18.4, open each of the relations TASK, EMPLOYEE, MANAGER, and CONTRACT and use the *First*

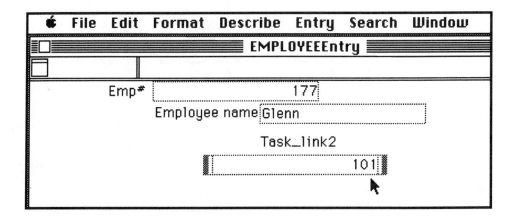

Figure 18.8 Reflex Plus automatically updates link attribute data when it becomes available.

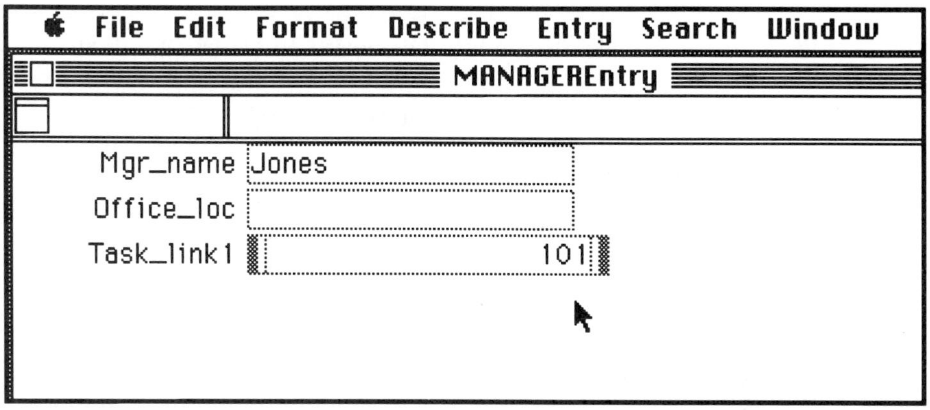

```
 🍎   File   Edit   Format   Describe   Entry   Search   Window
┌──────────────────────────────────────────────────────────────┐
│▤□═════════════════════ MANAGEREntry ═══════════════════════   │
├──┬─┬───────────────────────────────────────────────────────── │
│□ │ │                                                           │
├──┴─┴───────────────────────────────────────────────────────── │
│        Mgr_name  Jones                                         │
│        Office_loc                                              │
│        Task_link1                              101             │
│                                                                │
│                                      ▶                         │
│                                                                │
└──────────────────────────────────────────────────────────────┘
```

Figure 18.9 New records corresponding to link attribute key values are created automatically.

Record and *Next Record* selections to check that all the necessary data has in fact been stored. If you find errors, they can be corrected by simply reentering the correct data or editing the existing values and then selecting *Enter Record*.

Computer Practice 18.2

1. Enter the data given in Figure 18.4 into the Reflex Plus task management database that you defined in Computer Practice 18.1.

2. Enter the data of Figure 17.3 into the insurance database that you defined in Computer Practice 18.1. Note that you will need to translate the data into a link attribute format.

18.3 DATA RETRIEVAL USING SELECTION CRITERIA

In the previous section, you used one of Reflex Plus' data retrieval and display methods, namely, the **Search** menu functions within a data entry window. Of course, there are many occasions when you want to retrieve information in different formats and use more sophisticated **selection criteria** than "first record," "next record," and so on. The Reflex Plus implementation method for the **select** operator of relational algebra is quite similar to the method used in Works DB.

SELECT OPERATOR RETRIEVALS. The **select** operator will first be illustrated with some example retrievals from the EMPLOYEE relation. Open EMPLOYEE for data entry. Select *Search On* from the **Search** menu; you will be given a record qualification screen. Notice on this screen that you can qualify the records to be retrieved using any of the nonlink attributes in EMPLOYEE (in this case, there are only two: *Emp#* and *Emp_name*). Select the attribute *Emp#* (it is actually already preselected, since it is the first attribute in EMPLOYEE), then choose the *Less Or Equal* operator and type in the value *150*. Click *Enter* and notice that the selection criterion is written out in the box at the bottom of the screen, as illustrated in Figure 18.10.

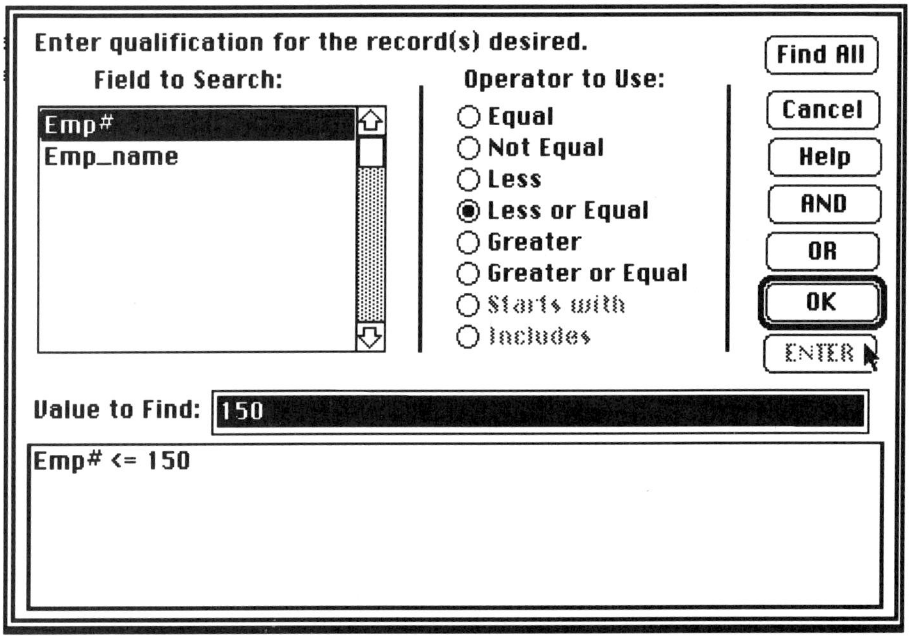

Figure 18.10 Reflex Plus record selection dialog box.

Click *OK*; you will be returned to the EMPLOYEE data entry window, where you can observe your selection criterion entered into the right-hand box at the top of the window. If you want to modify the criterion, you can edit it directly in this box (in fact, you could have typed it directly into this box initially), as you would any Works WP text. Try changing the value from 150 to 160.

To display the newly qualified records, we again go to the **Search** menu and use the *First Record* and *Next Record* selections. This time *First* and *Next* refer to records *within* the set of qualified records. Try these commands; you should find that two records (of the four you entered) satisfy the given qualification. Notice that what you have done is equivalent to the relational algebra command

select EMPLOYEE **where** *Emp*# <= 160

You have seen how to edit the record qualification criterion directly. You can also go back to the record qualification screen and replace the current criterion with a new one. The next example illustrates the use of an OR condition to retrieve records for employees whose name starts with the letter "H" or the letter "A."

Choose *Search On* again from the **Search** menu. Select the attribute *Emp_name*, the operator *Starts With*, and the value "H." (It does not matter in such retrievals whether letters are capitalized or not.) Click *Enter* and then select *OR*. Now select *Emp_name*, *Starts With*, and the value "A." Click *Enter* and then *OK*. Figure 18.11 displays the EMPLOYEE data entry window that is returned. In this window, use *First Record* and *Next Record* to view the records that now qualify for retrieval. Notice that the conditions are expressed in terms of a built-in Reflex Plus function STARTS, which takes two arguments (a text string variable and a character) and returns *True* or *False*.

In Reflex Plus you can use multiple ORs and ANDs together in a single record selection. However, *parentheses are not allowed, and neither operator takes precedence over the other*. In other words, these operators are always evaluated

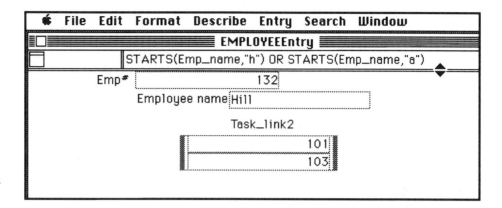

Figure 18.11 EMPLOYEE data entry window with record selection criterion applied.

from *left to right*. Hence, a great deal of caution should be exercised when writing selection criteria that involve multiple OR/AND usage.

If your record selection criterion gets too large to fit in the data entry window box reserved for it, the box can be expanded. Place the cursor at the bottom of the box so that it appears as a double arrowhead (as shown in the upper right of Figure 18.11). By dragging the mouse, you can resize the selection criterion display box.

Computer Practice 18.3

Select the following information from the task management database you implemented in Computer Practices 18.1 and 18.2.

1. All TASK records for tasks with completion dates before 3/25/91.
2. All TASK records for tasks with completion dates between 2/1/91 and 2/18/91 (inclusive).
3. All EMPLOYEE records for employees whose names begin with "A" and whose employee numbers are greater than 150.
4. All EMPLOYEE records for employees with employee numbers larger than 180 or with employee numbers between 100 and 150 (inclusive).

Select the following information from the insurance database you implemented in Computer Practices 18.1 and 18.2.

5. All POLICY records for policies sold by agent number 101 or agent number 103.
6. All POLICY records for policies sold by agent 101 for over $150,000.
7. All BUYER records for buyers with occupation code = CL or M.
8. All BUYER records for buyers with social security numbers between 100-00-0000 and 300-00-0000 (inclusive).

18.4 CONSTRUCTING REFLEX PLUS REPORTS

In this section you will generate some example reports using the TASK relation. You will see that with **Reflex Plus reports** it is easy to add the capability of the

project relational operator to the **select … where** capability you used in the previous section. In addition, you may format the output in various ways.

CREATING A REPORT.   Open Reflex Plus, and from the **File** menu, select *New*. You will now be given a dialog box like that in Figure 18.12. Choose a *Table Style Report* and name your report *Task Report 1* (note that as you enter a name, Reflex Plus replaces spaces with underscores) as shown in Figure 18.12.

Once you click *Create*, you will be given another dialog box in which you can choose the attributes to include in the report. (See Figure 18.13.) Notice that this process is equivalent to issuing the relational algebra command

project attribute name(s) **from** TASK

The link attributes are not available for display in reports. These attributes exist only to give a "join" capability for multiple-relation data retrieval. You will see how they can be used to construct such retrievals in the next section. For the present report, select *Include All* and then *OK*.

The next window displayed allows you to define the **select** operator command for this report. It is identical to the record qualification window you used in the previous section. For now, select *Find All* and then *Select*. You should see the report that is displayed in Figure 18.14. If the report is printed, the gray bars and grid are not shown.

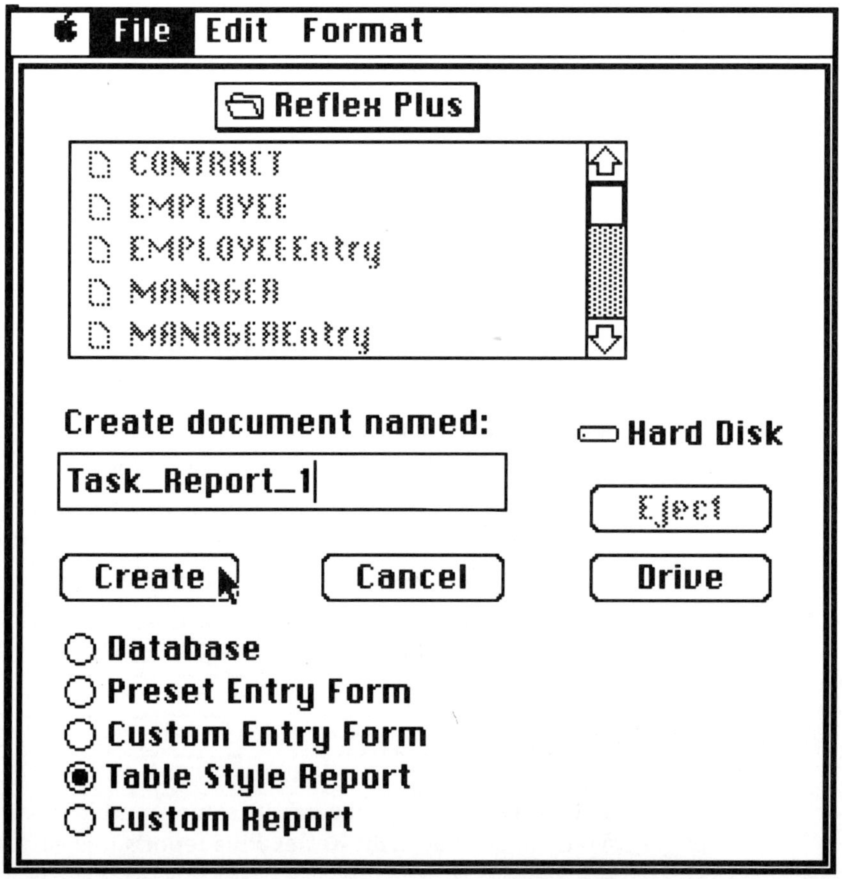

Figure 18.12 Dialog box for creating a new report.

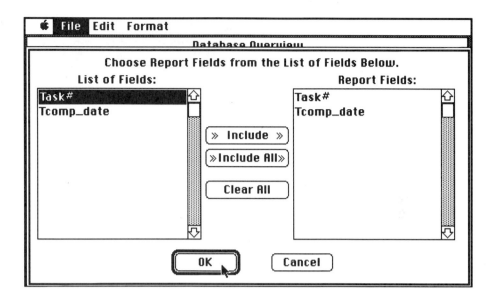

Figure 18.13 Dialog box for defining a **project** operator for a report.

MODIFYING A REPORT LAYOUT.   You can change the default report layout in a manner almost identical to the one you used to change data entry forms. For example, to alter your current report format, select *Report Design* from the **Report** menu. You will be presented with a report layout window. Select and drag the *Tcomp_date* data and text fields to the line below the line they are currently on, so that your screen looks something like the one in Figure 18.15. Note that if you select the gray side bars and drag, both data fields are moved. Do not do this now. You will see the purpose of such an action shortly. For now, make sure you point and click *inside the field* you wish to move to select it and then drag by the thin white bar at the top of the field area.

REPEATING COLLECTIONS.   The gray sidebars on the middle row of the report format outline the **repeating part** of the report (or a **repeating collection** in Reflex Plus terms). The fields inside the repeating collection will be "repeated" in the sense that data for these fields from each row qualified for the report will be displayed. In other words, you get a repetition of values, depending upon the

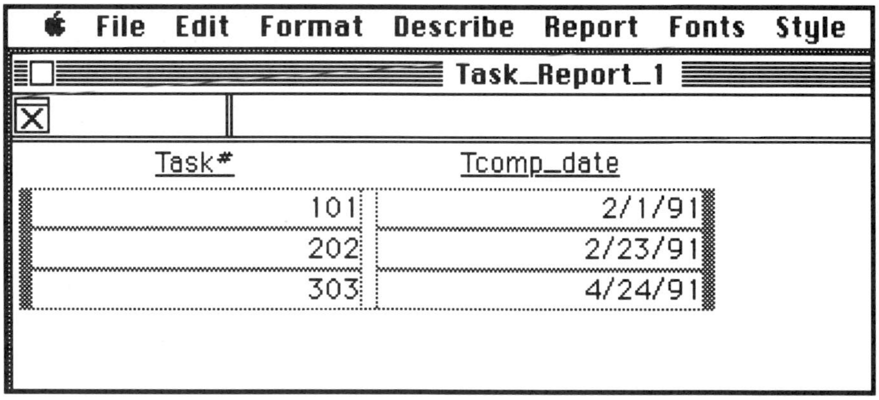

Figure 18.14 Reflex Plus report displayed.

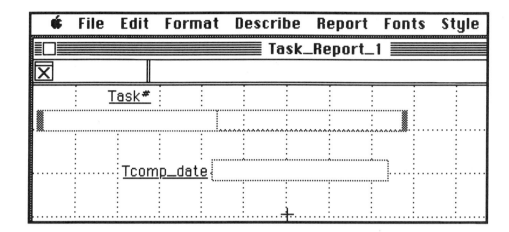

Figure 18.15 Repositioning data fields on a report layout screen.

number of qualified rows you have for the report. Repeating collections will play a central role in the reports involving retrievals of related information in multiple files.

With the current report configuration, the *Tcomp_date* text and data fields are outside the repeating collection for the report. Because you want a *Tcomp_date* value for each task, you need to include these fields (at least the data field) within the repeating collection. To do this, first select the repeating collection by clicking while the cursor is over one of the two gray sidebars. Then resize the repeating collection using the small grow rectangle in the lower right corner of the repeating collection area. You can also move the entire repeating collection around on the screen by dragging one of the selected sidebars.

Also, recall how you altered the position and contents of the label field in the customized data entry form you created. Use these techniques to reformat your report to look like that given in Figure 18.16. You will have to resize the label field for *Tcomp_date*.

DISPLAYING A REPORT. Now select *Report* from the **Report** menu and you will see the TASK data displayed in the revised format. Look at the choices in the **File**

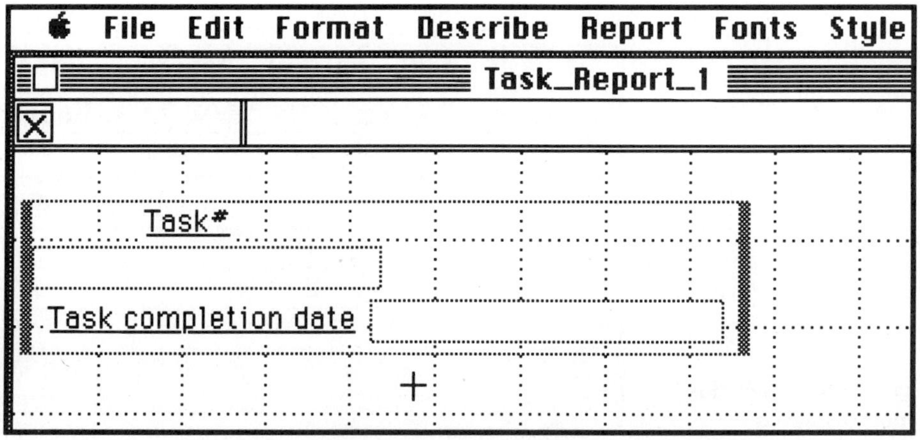

Figure 18.16 Reformatted report layout.

menu. You can now save the new report or you can abort the current changes and revert to the last previously saved version. Select *Save Report*.

You can sort the report for presentation by selecting *Sort On Fields* from the **Report** menu and then choosing the attributes on which we wish to sort and the order in which they are be sorted. For example, choose to sort on *Task#* in reverse order (Z...A, 9...0) and click *OK*. However, when the report screen is returned, you will notice that the order of the displayed records is the same as it was before you specified the sort order. To display the newly sorted report, you must recalculate the report by selecting *Calculate* from the **Report** menu. Do this and observe the report as it is displayed.

CHANGING A REPORT'S RECORD SELECTION CRITERION.   It is very easy to change your record selection criterion for a report (actually for a repeating collection). Select *Report Design* from the **Report** menu to get to the report layout window. Next select the repeating collection by clicking on one of the gray sidebars. Selection criteria are actually associated with repeating collections rather than with entire reports. The reason for this is that you can have several different repeating collections within a report, and these collections can repeat on different selection criteria. For example, in the next section you will construct a report that has a repeating collection embedded within a repeating collection, and the inner collection will derive its repeated rows from a relation different from the one the outside collection uses.

Having selected the repeating collection (the gray bars should now be black), select *Paste Formula* from the **Edit** menu. Select TASK as the source relation from the next screen. You will now be presented with a record qualification screen, where you can configure the selection criterion you desire for the associated repeating collection. As an example, select the attribute *Task#*, the comparison operator *Less Or Equal*, and the value *250*. These choices are displayed in Figure 18.17. Now select *Enter* followed by *OK*.

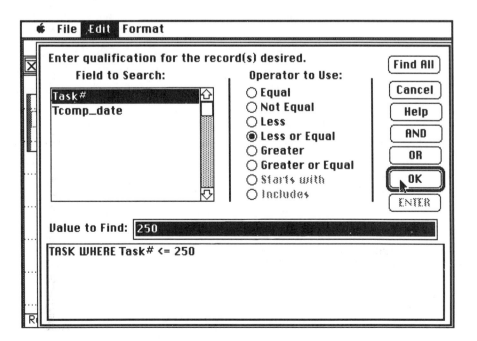

Figure 18.17 Record selection dialog box for report.

To see your new report, select *Report* from the **Report** menu; the selected records should appear. By returning to the layout window (select *Report Design* from the **Report** menu), you can edit the selection criterion directly in its display box at the top of the window. To do this, select the repeating collection first, then simply move the cursor inside the selection criterion display box and edit as you would any word processing text. Try changing the selection value from 250 to 303 and then return to the report by selecting *Report* from the **Report** menu.

In addition to direct editing of a selection criterion, you can return to the record qualfication dialog box and configure a new selection criterion. To do this, simply select the repeating collection (within the layout window) and again choose *Paste Formula* from the **Edit** menu.

In summary, the Reflex Plus report capabilities include all those available with the relational algebra operators **project** and **select**, plus a number of additional capabilities, such as formatting, sorting, and multiple repeating collections. In the next section you will see how this latter capability together with link attributes can be used to provide the function of a **natural join** operator. There you will construct more complex reports that require the retrieval of related information from multiple relations.

Computer Practice 18.4

Create Reflex Plus reports to display the following information from the task management database you implemented in Computer Practices 18.1 and 18.2.

1. Task numbers for tasks with completion dates before 3/25/91.
2. Task numbers and completion dates for tasks with completion dates between 2/1/91 and 2/18/91 (inclusive).
3. Employee names and employee numbers for employees whose names begin with "A" and whose employee numbers are greater than 150.
4. Employee names for employees with employee numbers larger than 180 or with employee numbers between 100 and 150 (inclusive).

Create Reflex Plus reports to display the following information from the insurance database you implemented in Computer Practices 18.1 and 18.2.

5. Policy numbers and amounts for policies sold by agent number 101 or agent number 103.
6. Policy numbers and social security numbers of the buyers for policies sold by agent 101 for over $150,000.
7. Buyer names and social security numbers for buyers with occupation code = CL or M.
8. Buyer names and phone numbers for buyers with social security numbers between 100-00-0000 and 300-00-0000 (inclusive).

18.5 DATA RETRIEVAL FROM MULTIPLE RELATIONS

The basic method in Reflex Plus for retrieving information from related relations is the use of nested repeating collections. Recall that repeating collections are associated with particular relations and have their own selection criteria. To gain the function of the **natural join** operator, a nested repeating collection arrangement is used, with the inner collection being qualified on link attributes. Some example retrievals (reports) from the task management database will illustrate the technique.

Retrieval 18.1.   Construct a report listing each task manager's name, office location, the task number he/she is assigned to, and the task's completion date.

Notice that the information required is contained in the two relations MANAGER and TASK as illustrated in Figure 18.18. To produce the desired retrieval, you will create a report with MANAGER as the source relation and then pull into that report the linked information from TASK.

In relational algebra this would require using the **natural join** operator, but remember that you have already built a **join** of MANAGER and TASK into your database design through link attributes. Hence you need only to exploit the presence of that link, rather than being concerned with the **join** explicitly.

To construct a report for this retrieval, select *New* from the **File** menu. Next choose *Custom Report* in the next window, name the report *Manager_Report_1*, and click *Create*. You should then be presented with a report layout screen.

You will now lay out the basic information that comes from our source relation MANAGER. To enter any item (data or text) into a custom report, you must first create a box on the layout screen to contain the item. To do this, place the cursor at the upper left-hand corner of where you want the box to be positioned; then holding the mouse button down, drag open a box of the size you desire and release the button. Once a box has been positioned, you must go to the **Describe** menu and define the data type for that box. After doing this, you can enter the appropriate data field in the formula box.

Create a layout screen box to hold *Mgr_name* values, and select *Text Field* from the **Describe** menu. Then type *Mgr_name* into the formula box, the top right-

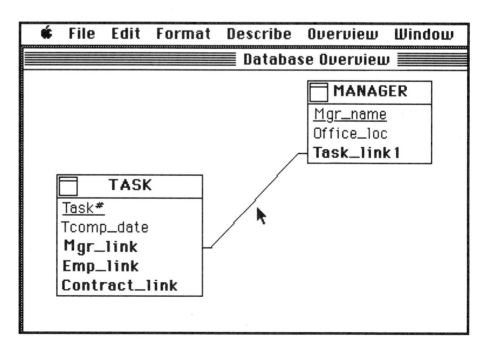

Figure 18.18 Relations needed for Retrieval 18.1.

hand box in the window—not the data field box you just created. Repeat this process to create a data field for the *Office_loc* attribute, located under the *Mgr_name* field. You now need to include these fields in a repeating collection.

Create a box that includes the two fields and then select *Repeating Collection* from the **Describe** menu. To complete the repeating collection definition, you must define the selection criterion associated with the collection. The criterion you want will select all the records from MANAGER. To define this criterion, with the repeating collection selected, select *Paste Formula* from the **Edit** menu. Select MANAGER in the next window. From the record selection qualification dialog box that is now displayed, select *Find All* and you will be returned to the report layout window.

Notice the selection criterion (in this case, just the name of the relation, since you have selected all records) displayed in the criterion display box. This is the same formula box that was used for displaying and entering data field names previously, and whenever a repeating collection is selected, the associated selection criterion will appear in this box. As an alternative to the preceding steps, you could have typed the criterion directly into the criterion display box in the report layout window, once you selected the repeating collection.

Check to see that the current report works, by selecting *Report* from the **Report** menu. The information for Jones, Smith, and Williams should be displayed as in Figure 18.19. If this is not the case, go to the **File** menu and select *Revert to Old Report*. This action will erase your report changes since the last version saved (the entire report will be erased, in this case) and give the last saved

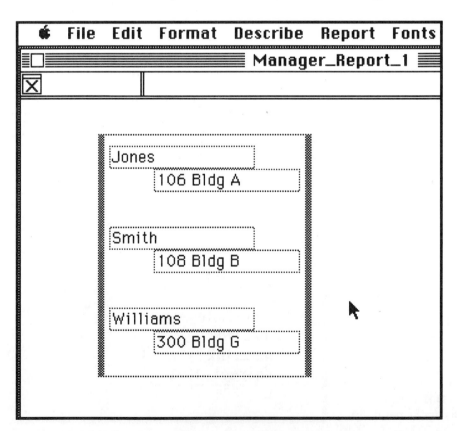

Figure 18.19 First phase of report for Retrieval 18.1 displayed.

report specification (the starting window, in this case). From this window you can then reenter the report specification. When the report functions as it is supposed to, select *Save Report* from the **File** menu. This action will allow you to revert to this point later if necessary.

Select *Report Design* from the **Report** menu to return to the report layout window. Next, bring the linked information from TASK into your report. Expand the repeating collection downward and to the right to accommodate the additional information (look ahead at Figure 18.20). Now create two more fields directly below the *Office_loc* field (leave a line between, for our second repeating collection border) to hold the *Task#* and *Tcomp_date* data. For the first of these fields, select *Integer Field* as the data type from the **Describe** menu, and then type *Task#* into the formula box. For the second field, select *Date Field* and type *Tcomp_date* into the formula box.

To complete the report you must tell Reflex Plus where to find these last two fields. Do this by enclosing them in a repeating collection and then defining a selection criterion for that repeating collection. Enclose the two fields with a box and select *Repeating Collection* from the **Describe** menu. Make sure that the border of the repeating collection does not touch any field borders; if it does, an error message will inform you that report areas may not overlap. If you get this message, go back and resize (you may have to move some data fields) the box you are using to define the repeating collection. Your screen should now look something like Figure 18.20 (without the associated identifiers that are added for emphasis).

With the inner repeating collection selected, you can now specify its associated selection criterion by typing *Task_link1* into the criterion display window (see Figure 18.21). This tells Reflex Plus that you want all records referenced by the key attribute values in *Task_link1* for the *presently selected* record in the outer repeating collection. In other words, you wish to retrieve the information from

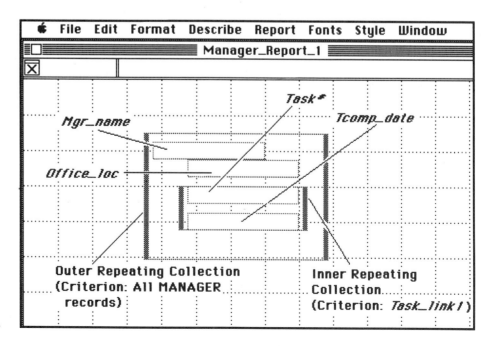

Figure 18.20 Report specification for Retrieval 18.1.

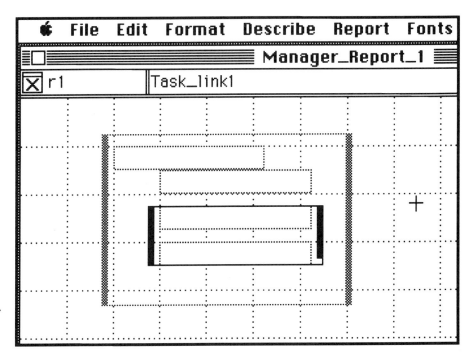

Figure 18.21 Defining inner repeating collection selection criterion.

the joined records of MANAGER and TASK. Once a record has been selected for inclusion in the outer repeating collection, the criterion (*Task_link1*) for the inner collection will retrieve *all* the records in TASK whose key values are given in the *Task_link1* attribute for the selected outer collection record.

Select *Report* to see how the report functions. You should see the data for Jones (task 102), Smith (task 101), and Williams (task 303) correctly displayed as in Figure 18.22. (Note that to display the information for Williams will require you to scroll.) If you do not obtain this display, you can select *Revert to Old Report* from the **File** menu and go back through the steps of the second phase of the report specification. Once the report is functioning correctly, select *Save Report* from the **File** menu.

This report could be formatted in various ways by returning to the report layout window and moving the repeating collections and data fields around and by inserting descriptive label fields. No matter what format is chosen, the repeating collections must contain the same fields as before. To add a descriptive label field, draw a box for the field, select *Label* from the **Describe** menu, and type the label directly into the label box area—not in the formula box as before for data fields. Try adding several descriptive labels and repositioning items, so that your report appears similar to Figure 18.23.

Suppose now there is a manager who is not currently assigned to a task. Let us enter data for such a manager into our database. Save your report and return to the *Database Overview* window. Open the MANAGER data entry form, select *Blank Record* from the **Entry** menu, and type in the name *Jackson* for our new manager and *106 Bldg B* for the office location. Do not enter a *Task_link1* value. Select *Enter Record* from the **Entry** menu and then return to the *Task_Report_1* window.

Examine the report using the scroll bar and notice that Reflex Plus has not displayed any information for manager Williams. To get that information dis-

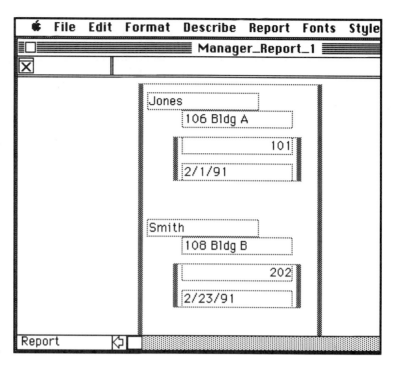

Figure 18.22 Partial display of report for Retrieval 18.1.

played, you must select *Calculate* from the **Report** menu. After you do this, you will find information about Jackson displayed as shown in Figure 18.24. Of course, there is no task data reported for Jackson, because there is none in the database.

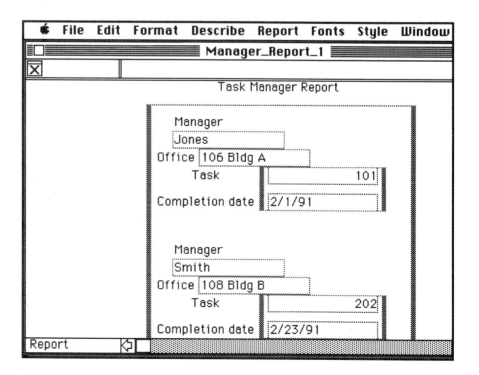

Figure 18.23 Report for Retrieval 18.1 with labels added.

Suppose that you would prefer to have displayed information about *only* those managers who have a task assignment. You can accomplish this by changing the selection criterion associated with your outer repeating collection, selecting only those managers that have entries in the *Task_link1* attribute.

To do this, go to the *Report Layout* window and select the outer repeating collection. In the criterion display box, add the phrase "where EXISTS(*Task_link1*)" after MANAGER, then calculate and display the report. You should find that the record for Williams is not included. Save your report.

Retrieval 18.2 Construct a report that for each contract lists the contract number, contract amount, completion date, and all the constituent task numbers along with the names of all employees assigned to each task.

Note that this retrieval uses information from the three relations shown in Figure 18.25. Using relational algebra, we would expect to execute two **natural joins** to accomplish this retrieval. In Reflex Plus this translates into a report with *triple* nested repeating collections whose selection criteria are formulated using the built-in join link attributes. The outer repeating collection will select all the records from CONTRACT, the middle one will select records in TASK accessed through the *Task_link3* attribute in each CONTRACT record, and the inner one will select records in EMPLOYEE accessed through the *Emp_link* attribute in the associated TASK records. This isn't as hard to set up as it sounds.

The report specification for this retrieval is actually very similar to that of Retrieval 18.1, so its construction is left to the reader. The resulting report layout window, with label fields included to help document it, is shown in Figure 18.26. The attribute names for the data fields (top to bottom) are *Contract#*, *Comp_date*,

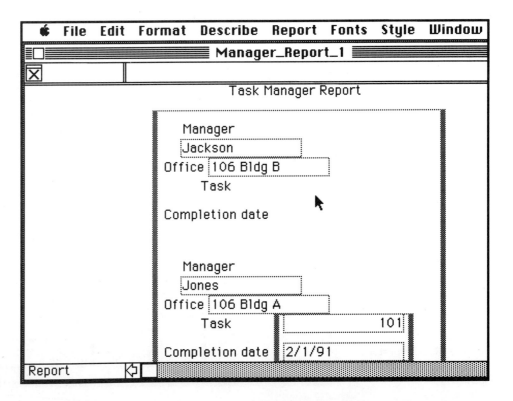

Figure 18.24 Report includes data for managers with no task assignment.

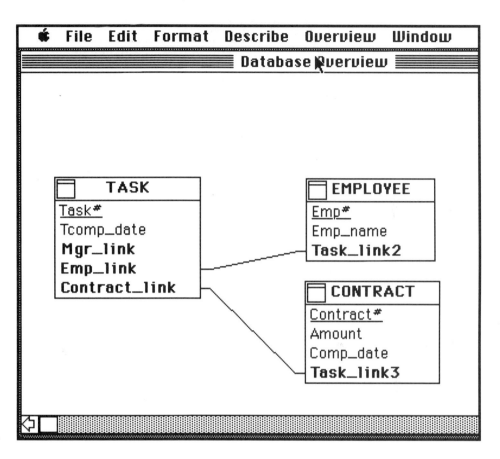

Figure 18.25 Relations
needed for Retrieval 18.2.

Amount, Task#, and *Emp_name.* Recall that both *Contract#* and *Task#* are *Integer Fields, Comp_date* is a *Date Field,* and the other two attributes are *Text Fields.* The selection criteria associated with the repeating collections are

Outer collection:	CONTRACT where EXISTS(*Task_link3*)
Middle collection:	*Task_link3*
Inner collection:	*Emp_link*

Computer Practice 18.5

Create Reflex Plus reports to display the following information from the task management database you implemented in Computer Practices 18.1 and 18.2.

1. The names of employees who are assigned to task 303.
2. The name of the manager and the employees assigned to task 202.
3. The names of all managers together with the names of the employees that work on the task that the manager manages.
4. For each contract the amount of the contract and its consituent task numbers and their completion dates.

Create Reflex Plus reports to display the following information from the insurance database you implemented in Computer Practices 18.1 and 18.2.

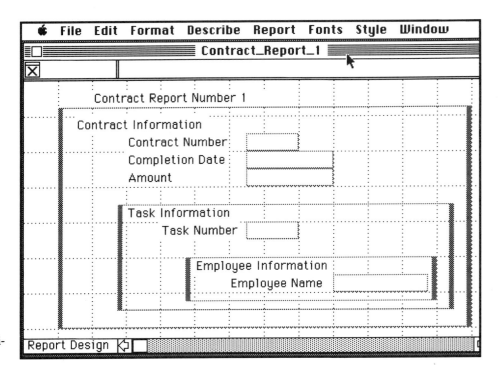

Figure 18.26 Report specification for Retrieval 18.2.

5. The salesman names for all policies sold for more than $500,000.

6. All district manager names and the names of the salesmen who work in the district.

7. All salesman names together with the names and phone numbers of buyers to whom they have sold policies.

8. The region manager names for all regions in which policies of more than $1 million have been sold.

18.6 MORE COMPLEX REFLEX PLUS RETRIEVALS

To generate some slightly more complex reports and to demonstrate how easy it is to **expand a database definition** in Reflex Plus, you will now add a new relation DEPARTMENT to your task management database. DEPARTMENT will contain information about the various departments that employees can belong to, and hence will be linked to EMPLOYEE as follows:

EMPLOYEE —— many-to-one ——> DEPARTMENT

Starting with the *Database Overview* window, select *New* from the **File** menu and then choose to define a *Database* named DEPARTMENT in the dialog box that is presented. Click *Create;* you will see a new file box with the title DEPARTMENT placed in the *Database Overview* window. DEPARTMENT will contain three attributes: *Dept#* (an *Integer Field* and the key attribute), *Dept_mgr* (a *Text Field*), and *Employ_link* (this is a link attribute field, so we allow it to be a *Text Field* for now). Once you have defined DEPARTMENT in the *Database Overview* window, move its file box to the far right of the window. Move the CONTRACT box down a little so that there is room for the EMPLOYEE box to expand by one attribute. Your Database Overview window should look like the one depicted in Figure 18.27.

Select the relation *EMPLOYEE* and select *Insert Field* from the **Overview** menu, then type in the attribute name *Dept_link*, which will be a *Text Field* for now. Now select *Dept_link*, hold and drag the mouse over *Employ_link*, then release it to establish the EMPLOYEE - DEPARTMENT link. Now with *Dept_link* selected, select *A Link to One ...* from the **Describe** menu. Select the attribute *Employ_link* and then select *A Collection of Links ...* from the **Describe** menu. You have now completed the definition of the many-to-one relationship from EMPLOYEE to DEPARTMENT, and your screen should look similar to Figure 18.28. From the **File** menu, select *Save Design* to make these changes to the database permanent.

Open DEPARTMENT for data entry, and using the *Enter Record* and *Blank Record* selections from the **Enter** menu, enter data for two departments. The first department has department number 510, department manager Hobarth, and employee numbers 198, 177, and 132. The second department has number 610, manager Quincy, and employee number 145.

The following retrievals should be studied carefully, as they illustrate some of the more commonly used Reflex Plus retrieval capabilities. Keep Figure 18.28 clearly in mind as you read and study the selection criteria associated with various repeating collections. These criteria will be difficult to understand unless the database structure (especially the link attributes) is kept clearly in mind.

Retrieval 18.3.   Construct a report listing the employee names and task numbers to which the employees are assigned for all employees of department number 510.

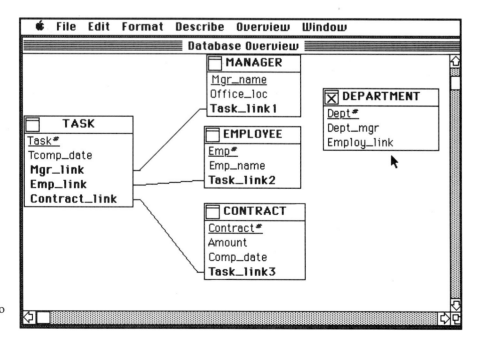

Figure 18.27 Adding the relation *DEPARTMENT* to the database.

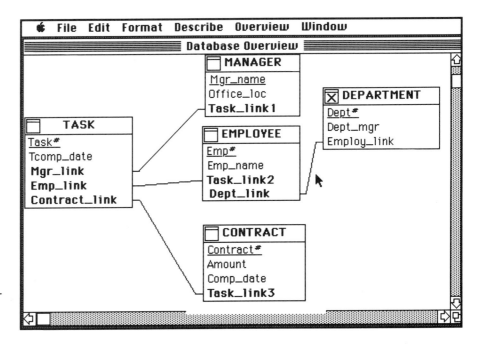

Figure 18.28 Task management database with DEPARTMENT added.

The report specification is given in Figure 18.29. Notice the use of the outer repeating collection whose criterion qualifies the DEPARTMENT relation, even though no data for the report is taken from that relation. The repeating collection selection criteria are:

Outer collection: DEPARTMENT where *Dept#* = 510
Middle collection: *Employ_link*
Inner collection: *Task_link2*.

The report produced by the preceding specification is shown in Figure 18.30.

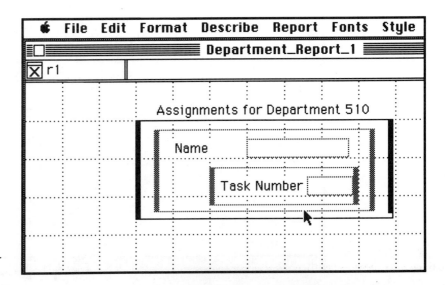

Figure 18.29 Report specification for Retrieval 18.3.

Retrieval 18.4. Construct a report listing the names of the employees in department number 610 who are assigned to task 202.

The report specification is given in Figure 18.31. Note the use of the EXISTS function. If the EXISTS function returns a value of *False,* no data will be displayed for that EMPLOYEE record. The selection criteria are

Outer Collection: DEPARTMENT where *Dept#* = 610
Inner Collection: *Employ_link* where EXISTS(*Task_link2* where *Task#* =202)

Computer Practice 18.6

Construct Reflex Plus reports for the following retrievals from the task management database.

1. The manager names for tasks that have employees assigned from department 510.
2. The names of employees of department 610 who are assigned to a task within contract 1000.

Construct Reflex Plus reports for the following retrievals, given in Chapter 17 in relational algebra, from the insurance database.

3. (Retrieval 17.1) Find the buyer social security number, the policy number, and the salesman identification number for all policies written for more than $100,000.

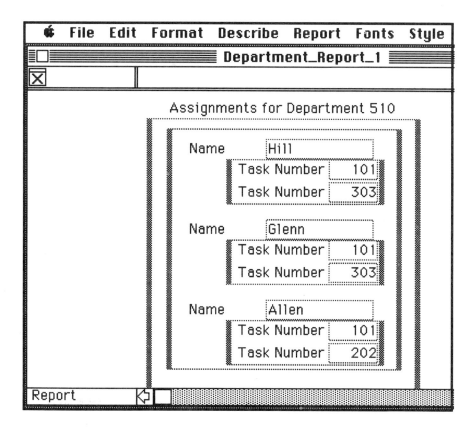

Figure 18.30 Example report for Retrieval 18.3.

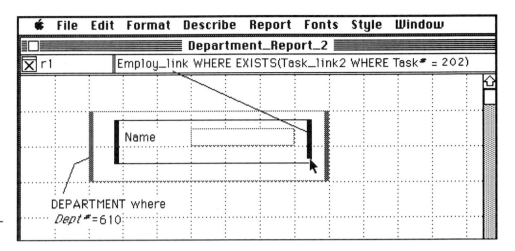

Figure 18.31 Report specification for Retrieval 18.4.

4. (Retrieval 17.2) Find the buyer social security number and the policy number for all policies for more than $100,000 that were sold by the salesman with identification number 101.

5. (Retrieval 17.5) Find the policy numbers and the salesman's name for all policies written for more than $200,000. (Compare with Retrieval 18.1.)

6. (Retrieval 17.6) Find the names and phone numbers of all salesmen who work in region 22. (Compare with Retrieval 18.1.)

7. (Retrieval 17.8) Find the names and addresses of all buyers of policies sold by Joe Hill. (Compare with Retrieval 18.2.)

8. (Retrieval 17.9) Find the buyer's name, policy number, policy amount, salesman's name, region manager's name, and the region office phone number for any policies that have been written for more than $1 million. (Compare with Retrieval 18.2.)

Key Concepts

Database Overview window
Reflex Plus data entry form
Repeating collections

Expand a database definition
Reflex Plus reports
Selection criteria

CHAPTER 19

EXAMINING ADVANCED SPREADSHEET FEATURES WITH EXCEL

L E A R N I N G   O B J E C T I V E S

- To understand structured objects such as arrays, tables, and databases that are available for problem solving in advanced spreadsheet environments.

- To learn to apply the basic spreadsheet problem solving methods you learned in Works to the Excel spreadsheet.

- To extend your experience with advanced spreadsheet features by using the array, table, and database structures of Excel.

- To learn about the charting and macro features of Excel.

I n this chapter you will learn to use the Excel spreadsheet package and examine some advanced features within Excel. The discussion assumes that you are familiar with concepts from Chapters 8 - 12. However, the chapter is sufficiently self-contained that the reader already familiar with spreadsheets could learn Excel by reading this chapter and only occasionally referencing the indicated sections from the earlier chapters. You will see that Excel contains all the Works SS features and a number of additional powerful features. In particular, you will learn about groupings of worksheet cells called arrays and tables. Additionally, you will learn to use the Excel database facility and how to write macro functions using the Excel macro language. Finally, you will learn to use some of Excel's built-in functions and graphical features to extend your problem-solving capabilities.

19.1 STRUCTURED OBJECTS IN SPREADSHEETS

In addition to manipulation of data objects and formula objects, which we discussed in connection with Works SS, advanced spreadsheets allow manipulation of **structured objects.** Although a simple object exists in only one cell in a spreadsheet, a structured object consists of a collection of cells that have a single name and that can be operated on as a unit. Examples of spreadsheet structured objects include arrays, tables, and databases. As you will see, structured objects apply to a number of different kinds of problem-solving activities.

19.1.1 Arrays

The simplest grouping of cells that can be formed in a spreadsheet is the **array**. A spreadsheet array is a contiguous rectangular grouping of cells of the *same* data type. By general convention in most spreadsheets a rectangular array of cells is specified by giving the location of the upper left-hand corner cell in the rectangle followed by the location of the lower right-hand corner cell—just as you did previously with range notation in Works SS. The respective corner locations are separated by a colon, so that A1:B2 defines a contiguous rectangular grouping of four cells whose locations are A1, A2, B1, and B2. Likewise, A1:A10 defines a single column of 10 cells whose locations are A1, A2, . . ., A10. (If you are not familiar with the use of range notation in a spreadsheet, read Chapter 10, Section 5.) Arrays such as the latter in which the cells are either *all* in one row or all in one column are sometimes referred to as *vectors*.

You can define operations on an entire array of cells, just as you defined operations on a single cell. One of the most natural kinds of operations is to take as input one array of cells and produce as output a new array with exactly the same structure. The data objects of the resulting output array are often obtained by operating on the corresponding data objects of the original array. For example, suppose that the 50 values contained in cells A1:E10 form an array and that we want to produce a corresponding new group of 50 numbers, by multiplying each one by 75 and adding 100 to the result. First you must specify where the new array of 50 new numbers is to be located. Let us choose to locate the new array of 50 cells in the range F1:J10. Then you would define a formula with the range A1:E10 as its input and the range F1:J10 as its output.

Note the distinction between performing this computation as an operation on arrays and the way you would perform this computation in a spreadsheet like Works SS that does not allow the use of arrays. In the latter case, you would define a formula to operate on each cell and replicate this formula through all cells in the range of interest. Generally, this will be less convenient than viewing A1:E10 as a unit (a collection of 50 cells) that you operate on only once.

Actually, the input and output arrays need not have the same structure (arrangement in rows and columns) or even the same number of cells. For example, suppose we want to compute the sum of each cell's value for each of the 50 cells in the preceding example. In this case we would have a formula with an array of 50 numbers as input and produce only one number as the result.

To summarize, to use arrays in formulas, two elements of information are always required. First, the collection of cells to be operated on by the formula must be specified. A natural syntax to specify the input array would be *range* notation. Thus, if a formula contains a range descriptor, it will execute the operation for *all* cells in the specified range. To illustrate an example of this usage, consider the computation of the sum of all 50 cells in the array A1:E10. Most spreadsheets provide a built-in function for this purpose whose name is SUM. Consequently, the formula =SUM(A1:E10) means sum the values contained in the 50 cells located in the array whose upper left-hand corner is at A1 and whose lower right-hand corner is located at E10. Thus, the array of 50 items input produces one item output.

Second, if the application of the formula is to produce an array as a result, then to distinguish this situation from the usual one of computing just a single value, some additional syntax must be added to the usual formula syntax to indicate it. Let us choose braces surrounding a formula to indicate that an array result is to be produced. By entering the formula {=(A1:E10*75)+100} we mean that each of 50 *new* cells will have its value calculated according to the formula and its relative position in the array. Thus, if the new array were defined over F1:J10, then the value in cell F1 would be computed from the formula =(A1*75)+100, F2 would be computed from the formula =(A2*75)+100, and so forth, and cell J10 would have its value computed from the formula =(E10*75)+100. An example worksheet produced for this latter computation is shown in Figure 19.1.

19.1.2 Tables

Another simple but versatile grouping of cells in a spreadsheet is a table. Whereas in an array all the elements must have the same data type, in a table we may group cells of differing data types, provided that each of the rows or each of the columns contains cells of the same data type. Thus, groups of records, such as the databases discussed in Chapters 8, 9, 17, and 18, are examples of tables. Databases are one type of table used in Excel and are discussed later in this section.

Note, however, that a table need not have different data types among its elements. You have seen that tables in spreadsheets form a convenient way to

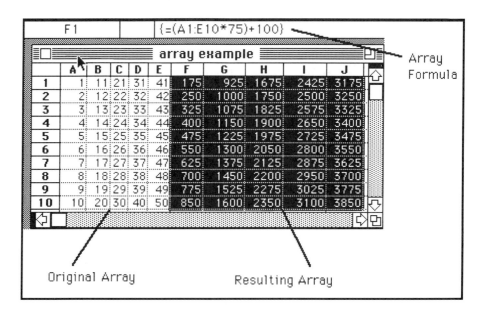

Figure 19.1 Example of an array computation.

organize information for studying *what if* scenarios. Excel provides two particularly useful table structures for such *what if* scenarios, called *one-input* tables and *two-input* tables. These table forms are also very useful for developing charts.

Excel table forms have significant advantages over the more common use of formula replication to develop a table, because the functions being studied require only an implicit dependence on the independent variables of the table. Consequently, for an Excel table the function may depend on the contents of a cell; we need not, however, specify this dependence as a formula. In contrast, to use formula replication to generate a table, it is necessary to know the explicit dependence of the function being studied on the table-independent variables; that is, the formula to be replicated must be written directly in terms of the table-independent variables.

To illustrate this idea more clearly, consider the example worksheet shown in Figure 19.2. The labels of cells shown are chosen to show part of an income tax calculation. The *what if* scenario being studied is to determine if money should be borrowed using a home equity loan to invest in tax-free bonds. Because interest paid on the home equity loan is tax deductible, any interest paid will lower the *Taxable Income* shown in row 15 of the spreadsheet. The amount of the deduction actually obtained depends in a complex manner on the other deductions appearing on an IRS Schedule A–Itemized Deduction form, but it can be easily computed using a worksheet, named *Schedule A,* that follows the steps listed on the *Itemized Deduction* form and transferred to the *Itemized Deduction* line, row 13. Note also that the amount of interest paid during the year depends upon the amount borrowed, the length of time taken to pay off the loan, the total interest paid during the current year of the loan, and the interest rate at which the loan is made. These elements appear in rows 3 - 6 of the worksheet, and the *Current Yearly Total Interest Payment*, row 7, that results is transferred to *Schedule A* to compute the total itemized deductions. Note that the values entered into the table in column B of Figure 19.2 are for display purposes only; they have not actually been computed using an actual tax table.

	A	B	C
1	Income Tax Table Example		
2			
3	Duration of Home Equity Loan	3	years
4	Amount Borrowed	$10,000	
5	Current Year of Loan	1st	year
6	Interest Rate	10	percent
7	Current Yearly Total Interest Payment	$1,000	
8			
9	Wages from W2 Form	$38,000	
10	Taxable Interest Earned	$2,000	
11	Non-Taxable Interest Earned	$600	
12			
13	Itemized Deductions	$8,000	
14			
15	Taxable Income	$32,000	
16	Tax to be Paid	$8,500	
17	Net Income	$32,100	
18			
19			
20	"What if Table"		
21	Equity Loan Amount	Net Income	
22	5000	$31,800	
23	10000	$32,100	
24	15000	$32,600	
25	20000	$33,100	
26	25000	$33,700	

Figure 19.2 Example Excel one-input table computation.

Income generated by tax-free bonds appears as *Non-Taxable Interest Earned* in row 11 of the spreadsheet and does not add to the *Taxable Income* shown in row 15. The final result to be computed is the *Net Income*, row 17 of the example calculation. We may express this formula as

Net Income = Wages + Taxable Interest Earned + Non-Taxable Interest Earned - Tax to Be Paid

Finally in rows 22 - 26 are entered different equity loan amounts borrowed and their associated *Net Income* as computed from the preceding formula. This table allows the *what if* study to be performed. Note that by inserting each of the *Equity Loan Amounts* in rows 22 - 26 into *Amount Borrowed*, row 4, a corresponding *Net Income* can be computed. Excel automates this process, as we shall describe shortly.

Before leaving this example, we note that the dependence of *Net Income* on the *Amount Borrowed* for the home equity loan is a very complicated function. It is not one that can be easily expressed as a formula. Hence, formula replication to create the table shown in rows 22 - 26 is not an option available to generate the table. One must therefore have recourse to the one-input table of Excel for this *what if* analysis.

ONE-INPUT TABLES. An Excel **one-input table** consists of one column (or row) of input data and one or more columns (or rows) of functions that depend on this vector of input values. The use of an Excel one-input table is particularly desirable for a *what if* scenario if you have a formula or several formulas whose results are to be studied as a function of some single set of changing input values—the input vector.

These formulas may be the result of a very complex computation involving hundreds of intermediate results or a single formula in a cell. Formula replication, such as you used earlier in Works SS to construct a table, required that you be able to express in a formula the explicit dependence on the independent variable. One-input table structures do not require this. In fact, it is only necessary to identify an input cell in an existing spreadsheet computation where the independent variable values of the table are to be inserted and then specify the location of an existing function in your worksheet that depends on the value of this input cell. In our earlier example of Figure 19.2, the cell labeled *Amount Borrowed*, cell B4, is the input cell for the table, and the cell labeled *Net Income*, cell B17, is the location of the function computed. The spreadsheet will then automatically enter each of the independent values into the input cell, compute the value that results, and copy the result into the corresponding position in the table.

If a group of formulas uses the same input cell, a one-input table will allow you to perform *what if* analysis with this group of formulas—each formula's values in each new row (or column) of the table. If the table is constructed around the independent variable, arranged, say, with its values listed down one column, then a reference to each different formula that depends (implicitly or explicitly) on this variable is placed in separate columns across the table.

TWO-INPUT TABLES. A **two-input table** is one in which the function that we wish to study depends upon two independent variables. For such a function, it would be convenient to arrange one of the independent variables along a row and the other along a column, as was done for exercises 2 and 4 in Computer Practice 12.3. The one-input table concept discussed earlier can easily be extended to allow *two* input cells to be defined along with the location of the function being studied. At the intersection of the rows and columns containing the independent variables we could place a reference to the function to be computed and evaluate this function for each possible pair of the independent variables in which one member of the pair is taken from the input row vector and the other is taken from the input column vector. Excel provides such a structure, and we will study it shortly. Again, as for the one-input table, you need not write the explicit dependence of the function on the two input cells. As long as you have a computed result that depends on these cells you can study this result in a two-input table.

DATABASES. We have seen that the concept of a database is fundamental to many information-processing activities. In essence, database programs allow a user to store structured information and then update and selectively retrieve that information. Many advanced spreadsheet programs allow database operations on groups of cells; however, the functionality of the **spreadsheet database** is somewhat reduced from that available in the fully relational database systems. In practice, current spreadsheet databases are limited to a single relation (table) for information retrieval. Advanced spreadsheet programs provide many of the database features that you have learned in Chapters 8 and 9 with Works DB but do not provide report generation that is as flexible as Works DB.

A database *within* a spreadsheet environment is defined by specifying the group of cells that you wish to include in the database. You can then use analogs to the relational algebra **select** and **project** operators to operate on the database cells collectively. In addition, you can apply the *full computational power* of spreadsheet operations to the results obtained from the database operations. However, only *one* contiguous group of cells can be considered as a spreadsheet database at any time using the current generation of spreadsheet software.

An example spreadsheet database is shown in Figure 19.3. This structure is by now very familiar to you. The first row of the table defines the fields or attributes of the database. Note that this first row, row 5, *is* a part of the database and must be included when describing the group of cells that comprise the database. Each subsequent row of the table contains *instances* or *actual values* for the attributes. Rows of the database are often called records of the database—as in our earlier discussions.

Note that the records in the spreadsheet database are identically structured. This structural uniformity makes it possible to create operators that manipulate records of the spreadsheet database just as we have operators that manipulate individual cells. Spreadsheet database operators typically include the ability to insert records, delete records, select records, project records, and sort records according to major and minor fields. Selection criteria can be made quite complex in spreadsheet databases because the arithmetic, logical, and relational operators for the spreadsheet all can be employed to develop the selection criteria for record retrieval. Thus, for example, you can easily select only those salesmen in the database whose salary exceeded $50,000 and whose total yearly sales exceeded $100,000. You will see how to do such operations when we explore the use of Excel database operations.

Exercise Set 19.1

1. Explain the difference in approach between computing an array of values using an array operation and formula replication. Which appears easier and why?

2. Use the sample syntax of Section 19.1.1 to construct an array formula to add the value 35 to each of the 25 cells in the range B1:F5. Contrast the effort in entering this formula with that of cell replication that you used with Works SS.

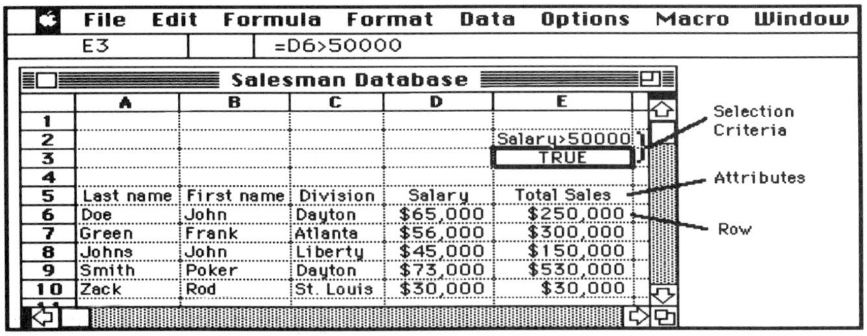

Figure 19.3 Example Excel spreadsheet database.

3. How does the computation of a one-input table differ from both an array operation and formula replication?

4. Explain why, in a long computation that involves many different formulas whose results are intermediate to the final result, it could be difficult to develop one formula that shows the explicit dependence of a given input on the final result.

5. Describe why a two-input table can be viewed as an extension of the concept of a one-input table.

19.2 EXCEL OVERVIEW

In analogy with Works, you can cause the Excel program to execute by double-clicking on the Excel *program* icon, the *Resume Excel* icon, or on one of the icons of the several kinds of documents that can be produced by Excel. The form of the Excel *program* icon is shown at the left of Figure 19.4. To its right is the form of the *Resume Excel* icon.

The Excel program is best viewed as being composed of three separate subsystems that pass information back and forth so naturally and intuitively that they operate as one system. These systems are the *Worksheet* subsystem, the *Chart* subsystem, and the *Macro* subsystem. Each subsystem produces a different kind of document. Document icons produced by each subsystem are shown as the third, fourth, and fifth icons, respectively, in Figure 19.4. A different main menu will be displayed dependent upon which subsystem is activated, and the options within a given menu name will also change. Many of the operations that can be performed in the Worksheet and Chart subsystems already are familiar to you from Works SS.

The *Macro* subsystem in Excel, however, is a new kind of subsystem. In it you can construct *macro worksheets* that are special kinds of worksheets in which instructions similar to those in a third-generation programming language can be entered. (In future discussion we will call macro worksheets simply *macrosheets*.)

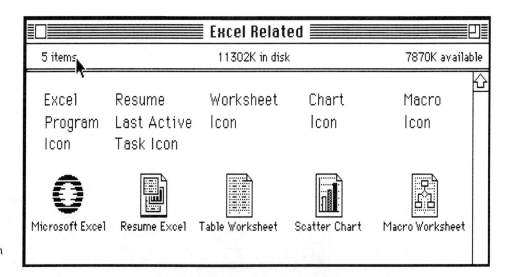

Figure 19.4 Excel program and application icons.

These special sheets allow advanced problem solving in a spreadsheet, because *you can define* functions that can be called on by worksheets and macrosheets in much the same way that built-in functions can be used in Works SS worksheets. These macro functions form a library upon which you can draw for your problem-solving needs.

The Excel *Worksheet* and *Chart* icons are well chosen because they suggest a worksheet and a chart, respectively. The *Macro* icon displays symbols that appear on a flow chart (a diagrammatic technique used in programming) and therefore suggests programming. Each of these three closely connected subsystems will be discussed in the following sections of this chapter.

19.3 EXCEL WORKSHEET SUBSYSTEM

On opening the Excel *program* icon, the screen will appear as shown in Figure 19.5. Alternately, if a worksheet icon is used to enter Excel, then that worksheet will be displayed. Most aspects of the worksheet subsystem function like those of Works SS. In fact, Excel pull-down menus will have within them many operations that are already familiar to you. In some instances, however, operations with which you are familiar in Works SS are placed in different menus in Excel. For example, the *Paste Function* operation appears in the **Formula** menu in Excel rather than in the **Edit** menu as in Works SS. Both the semantics and syntax of using a given operation are usually the same for the two programs. A few operations perform differently and are discussed later.

In Excel there are 16,384 rows and 256 columns available for use in a single worksheet. In addition, an Excel worksheet may reference cells on other worksheets and macrosheets to obtain values or function results. A problem may extend onto more than one sheet, but there is also the capability to solve individual parts of a problem on separate worksheets and bring each part together on a

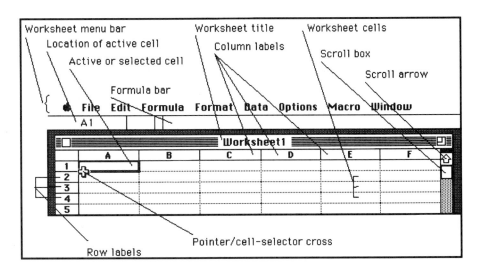

Figure 19.5 Excel worksheet.

summary worksheet. This feature is of obvious benefit to structuring the solution to a problem.

We imagine, as with other application programs, that the screen is a window through which we view only a portion of a worksheet. The scroll box and scroll arrows are used to move the window about on the spreadsheet just as you have learned in other applications.

WORKSHEET MENUS.   To give you a quick overview of the commands in Excel and to provide a convenient reference, we show in Figure 19.6 the pull-down menus for the worksheet subsystem. Recall that different menus and selections appear, depending upon whether a worksheet, chart, or macrosheet is the active window. We will discuss in greater detail later in this chapter many of the commands that are shown in Figure 19.6.

FILE MENU.   With the exception of *Links*, each of the operations in Figure 19.6 under the **File** menu should be familiar from your experience with Works SS. Consequently, we do not discuss them in great detail. However, some differences should be pointed out. Because Excel can create any one of the three kinds of documents—a worksheet, chart, or macrosheet—if *New* is selected, you must tell

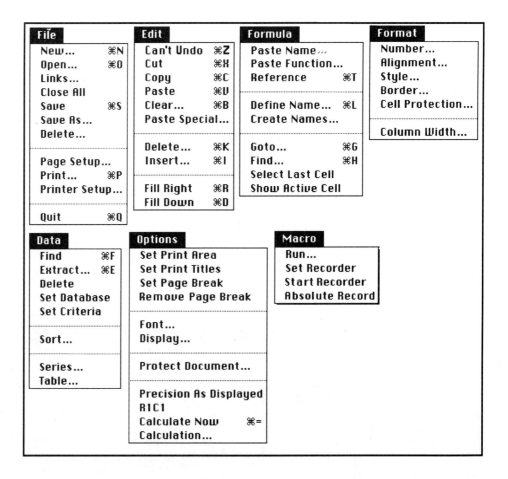

Figure 19.6 Excel worksheet menus.

Excel which kind of document you want to create. When *New* is selected, a submenu such as that shown in Figure 19.7 will appear. By clicking on the appropriate button you will be selecting both the kind of document that you want to create and the Excel subsystem with which you will be working.

A new operation is *Links*. As was mentioned earlier, in Excel, formulas on one worksheet can reference cells on another worksheet. However, before a worksheet's data can be used by another worksheet, the former worksheet must be opened. The purpose of the *Links* command is to display the name of each of the worksheets that is referenced by the active worksheet. When *Links* is selected, a dialog box will appear that displays the list of worksheets referenced. These worksheets can then be opened by pointing and double-clicking on each name displayed.

The final operation in the **File** pull-down menu that we will discuss is *Page Setup*. A display of this menu (when the ImageWriter is the selected printer) is shown in Figure 19.8, where we see a number of interesting features. The function is similar to that in Works SS. It allows the user to adjust the printed output from Excel to a variety of different physical paper sizes, format the size of the output (e.g., a 50% reduction of the worksheet size), and select the orientation of the output on the page (either portrait or landscape printing mode). Also printing of row and column headings for the worksheet cells or the grid lines showing the cell boundaries can be turned on or off as desired. Finally, title information on the top of each page and on the bottom can be chosen. Thus, you have considerable control over the appearance of a worksheet in Excel as in Works SS.

Computer Practice 19.3

1. Execute the Excel program by locating and opening the Excel *program* icon as shown in Figure 19.4. Observe the menu bar presented. This is the menu bar associated with the worksheet subsystem. Select *New* from the **File** menu. When the dialog box of Figure 19.7 is displayed, select *Macro Sheet* and click *OK*. You will observe a new worksheet is open on the screen. Also note that there is no change in appearance of the menu bar. However, although the menu bar appears the same, there are changes within the menu options available in these subsystems. For example, the built-in functions available under *Paste Function* differ between these two subsystems. Finally, drag down the **File** menu to *New* and then double-click *Chart*. Note that in addition to a *Chart* window appearing, the menu bar also changes. Close all the windows and select *Quit* under the **File** menu. This should return you to the desktop.

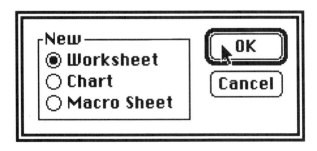

Figure 19.7 The different applications you create with Excel.

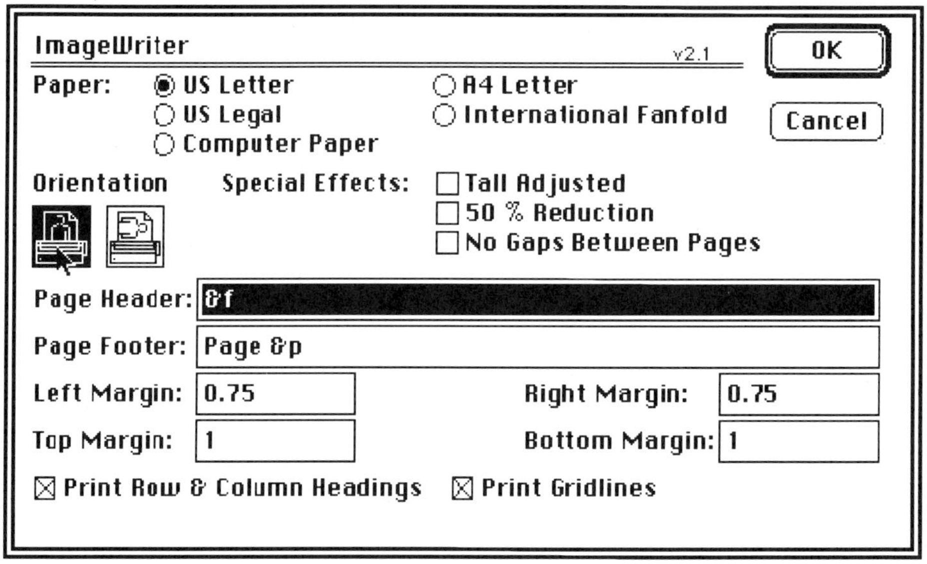

Figure 19.8 Options for printing worksheets.

19.3.1 Cell-level Editing Operations in Excel

As discussed in Chapter 10, the most basic editing operations that can be performed on the worksheet are cell-level editing operations—operations to enter and/or edit the contents of *one* cell. The point-and-click philosophy that is used in Excel for cell-level editing is essentially identical to that you learned with Works SS.

DATA OBJECTS VERSUS FORMULA OBJECTS. In Excel, as in Works SS, cell-level editing commands are used to manipulate either the data object or the formula object of a cell. Formula objects have an equals sign (=) as the first character of a sequence of characters to distinguish them from data objects.

THE ACTIVE CELL. As in Works SS, in Excel only one cell at a time can be active when performing cell-level editing operations. In Excel, the active cell is easily distinguishable from the other cells because it is enclosed by double lines. The location of the active cell is always displayed in the active cell location descriptor area, shown in Figure 19.5 just below the menu bar and above the upper left-hand corner of the worksheet. For example, cell A1 is the active cell in Figure 19.5.

SELECTION OF THE ACTIVE CELL. The active cell in Excel is selected with the mouse, just as in Works SS. Excel uses a different form for the *cell pointer/cell-selector cross*. (See Figure 19.5.) By positioning the center of the cell-selector cross over a cell and clicking, the cell under the cross is selected as the active cell and its location is displayed in the active cell location indicator area. Just as in Works SS, any information typed in from the keyboard or pasted using the **Edit** pull-down menu will be entered into the active cell and will be displayed in the formula bar. The active cell will continue to take information typed from the keyboard until you terminate data entry (or you have entered 255 characters).

TERMINATION OF DATA ENTRY. Data entry in Excel is terminated in the same manner as that in Works SS. By way of review, these operations include pressing the *Tab* key, pressing the *Return* key, selecting a new active cell, selecting the *Check* button that appears in the space just left of the formula bar, and, if you have a keyboard with cursor control keys, moving the cursor to a new cell using one of these keys. If you decide that the information you entered is *not* what you intended, then you can restore a cell to its original state by selecting the *Undo* command from the **Edit** menu or selecting the *x button* that appears in the area just left of the formula bar when a cell is open and data is entered.

As in Works SS, *while entering a formula object*, clicking on a new cell causes corresponding cell references to be inserted into the cell and the cell containing the formula to remain active. This feature is provided to simplify the entry of formulas. Thus, you must use one of the other means to terminate the entry of a formula.

FORMULA-BAR EDITING. All the editing commands you learned for Works SS are available in the formula bar. Recall in this connection the function of the insertion pointer and the I-beam pointer. To invoke the I-beam pointer it is only necessary to move the cell-selector cross into the area of the formula bar by suitable manipulation of the mouse. The cell-selection cross then changes into the I-beam pointer and all the Works SS actions, such as *Cut, Copy, or Paste*, are now available for use.

REFERENCING CELLS OF OTHER WORKSHEETS. Excel permits formulas to reference cells located on *other* worksheets. Thus, *when a cell formula is being entered*, by accessing the **Window** menu, you can select the name of the worksheet whose cell you wish to reference, if it has been previously opened. (If the file is not already opened, you can open it by selecting *Open* from the **File** menu.) This different worksheet then becomes the active worksheet. Selecting a cell in this worksheet by pointing with the cell-selector cross and clicking causes the reference to this worksheet's *name and cell location* to be inserted in the formula of the original sheet. The old worksheet then can be reactivated by selecting its name in the **Window** menu and entry of the formula can be continued. Of course, it is possible to enter the cell reference by typing it in the correct syntax; however, in view of the complexity of this syntax, it is often better to let Excel enter it for you.

RANGE SELECTION. Recall from Chapter 10, Section 5, that the process of marking out contiguous groups of cells by clicking and dragging is familiar from Works SS and is called *range selection*. Range selection is also useful for defining a *one-input* or *two-input table, database,* or an *array*—new kinds of spreadsheet structures.

FORMATTING CELLS. Excel provides a broader range of options to format cells than is available in Works SS. To format a cell or range of cells in Excel, you first select the cell or range of interest. You next pull down the **Format** menu, where you will see the options shown in Figure 19.6. If, for example, the *Number* option is selected, the dialog box of Figure 19.9 is displayed. Note the wide range of number formats available and that additional choices are available by scrolling. Click on the format desired, then select the *OK* button; the data objects selected will be formatted according to your choice.For the example format highlighted in

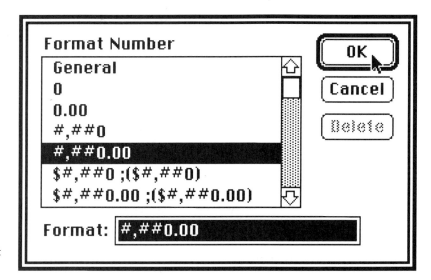

Figure 19.9 Some choices within the number format operation in Excel.

For the example format highlighted in Figure 19.9, the number will be displayed with two decimal places to the right of the decimal point. Also commas will be inserted. For the format below that shown highlighted, the output would contain a dollar sign preceding the number and display no decimal places to the right of the decimal point. You may experiment with any of the formats shown to see their effect on the actual form of the numbers displayed.

Computer Practice 19.3.1

1. Execute the Excel program by opening the Excel *program* icon.
2. Select the range of cells A1:C5.
3. Type in the phrase *Now is the time for all good men to come to the aid of their*. Do this by typing each word then pressing *Tab*. Note that Excel moves the active cell through the selected range in the same way Works SS does.
4. Under the **Format** menu select the option *Alignment*. In the dialog box displayed select *Center*. Note that the text is now repositioned into the center of each cell. Alter the width of a cell by moving the cell selection cross into the column label area and dragging a column delimiter right or left, just as you would do in Works SS. What effect does this have on the text?
5. Select the range A6:C10.
6. Retype the phrase in step 3, but use the *Return* key to terminate each entry. How does the appearance of this phrase differ from that discussed earlier?
7. Repeat step 4, but select *Right* from the dialog box. Watch what effect this has on the appearance of the text.
8. Select cell B3 of the worksheet.
9. Move the cell selection cross into the formula bar. (Note that it changes into an I-beam pointer.) Insert *wo* in front of *men*.

10. This completes a simple illustration of cell-level editing features in Excel. Save your document as *Exercise 19.3.1*. You will use it in the computer practice of the next section.

19.3.2 Sheet-level editing commands

Sheet-level editing operations, as discussed in Chapter 11, cause a restructuring (repositioning of cells) of the worksheet and/or affect the contents of more than one cell at a time. These operations are often performed after some information already has been entered into the worksheet. You then might discover either that cells need to be rearranged to make room for additional information or that a formula needs to be replicated among a number of cells. Most sheet-level operations in Excel are found under the **Edit** pull-down menu as shown in Figure 19.6. Most of these operations have been discussed in detail in Chapter 11, Section 5, and that discussion will not be repeated here. However, a few of these operations behave differently from those in Works SS or have no direct analog and are discussed below.

Recall that if the effect of an operation performed inside the **Edit** menu was not what you intended and you haven't as yet entered another operation, selection of the *Undo* operation will restore the worksheet to the state that it had prior to your action. *Undo* can save you a lot of typing; that is, trying to restore part of a worksheet that was inadvertently altered. Note, however, that *Undo* reverses only those operations that are performed *under* the **Edit** menu.

INSERT AND DELETE.   *The Excel* Insert *operation behaves differently from the operation* Insert *in Works SS. Be very careful in its use until you become thoroughly familiar with it.* In Excel, *Insert* can be used to insert one or more cells into the middle of rows or columns of the worksheet. Alternatively, the Excel *Insert* can enter an *entire* column or row at one time, just as the Works SS *Insert* does. There is no command named Delete in Works SS. *Delete* in Excel functions somewhat like *Cut* in Works when an entire row or column has been selected. However, *Delete* in Excel can remove a selected range of cells in the middle of the worksheet, just as *Insert* can add them.

We show in Figures 19.10 and 19.11 examples of selecting a group of cells in the worksheet, shown by the highlighted area, and deleting them. Because other cells will have to fill in the area vacated by the deleted cells, Excel responds by asking whether the area vacated is to be filled by shifting cells left (moving the cells to the right of the vacated area into the hole) or shifting cells up (moving the cells below the vacated area into the hole). One can easily see from these examples that inserting or deleting cells in the middle of the worksheet (not possible in Works SS) can cause a major restructuring of the entire worksheet.

Excel, like Works SS, provides a simple means to add or delete an entire row or column of the worksheet. By moving the cell-selector cross into either the column *label* area or the row *label* area and clicking, the respective column or row becomes highlighted. If *Insert* (*Delete*) is selected now, then an entire row or column of the worksheet will be added (removed) as requested. When entire columns or rows are selected, Excel knows that it must shift cells left, for deleting columns, or up, for deleting rows, respectively, and it does not prompt you in this case. In many circumstances a full row or column operation will be what you

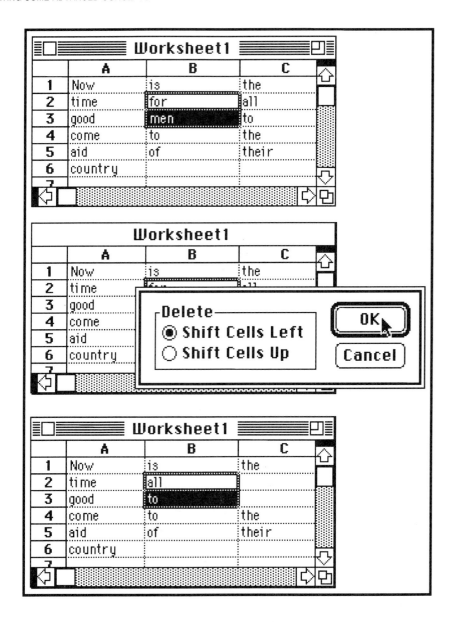

Figure 19.10 Example of deleting, then filling by shifting cells left.

desire, and it is much safer to use because it does not mix up the alignment of rows and columns that already exist within the worksheet.

COPY AND PASTE.   As we learned in Chapter 11, the process of copying (replicating) the formula object of a cell into other cells is very important. One way that Excel provides this facility is through the *Copy* and *Paste* sequence accessed through the **Edit** menu. Unlike Works SS, a *Copy* operation on one cell in Excel will *Paste* into a range of cells. However, the Excel *Fill Right* and *Fill Down* operations, which are identical in function to those operations in Works SS, are generally preferable in most instances. Note that for either the *Copy* and *Paste* or *Fill Right* and *Fill Down* operations in Excel a formula template is formed for each relative cell reference.

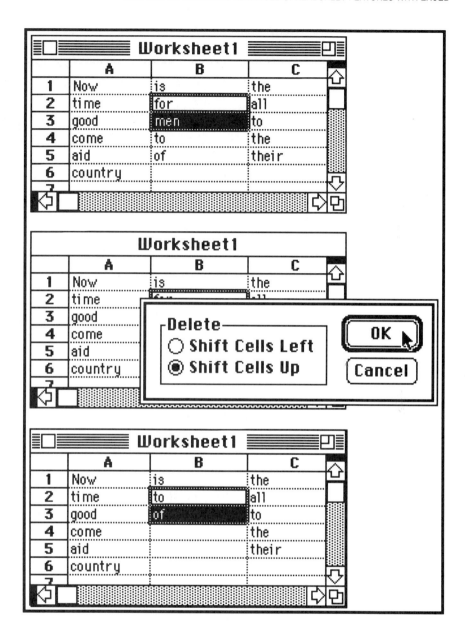

Figure 19.11 Example of deleting, then filling by shifting cells up.

CUT. Note that the *Cut* operation is not identical to *Copy* when used in Excel. First and most important, a *Paste* operation that follows a *Cut* operation retains the *original* cell references in formulas. Thus, in this one instance, *no* template is formed for determining cell references, no matter what kind of cell reference is used in the formula. The formula placed in the new cell is the same as that in the original cell.

Second, unlike the usual *Cut* after which you can *Paste* any number of times, in Excel, *Cut* places its information in a temporary buffer that can be used only once. *Clearly, then, the purpose of* Cut *in Excel is for moving information from one place to another in the worksheet and not for replicating formulas.* In fact, the operation of *Cut* in Excel is identical to the *Move* operation of Works SS.

FILL RIGHT AND FILL DOWN.   Excel provides a more convenient operation than *Copy* and *Paste* for replicating cells when blocks of cells are to be replicated. For this organization, *Fill Right* or *Fill Down* should be used. The operation of *Fill Right* or *Fill Down* is identical to that discussed for Works SS in Chapter 11; the discussion will not be repeated here.

The following general point should be noted. In replicating formulas, Excel does a much better job of checking for errors than does Works SS. For example, if the computation in Section 4 of Chapter 12 is carried out in Excel, when the replication shown in Figure 12.11 occurs, an error in value is displayed as shown in Figure 19.12. In contrast, Works SS simply computed an incorrect value and indicated nothing. Excel will do data type checking to see if the data object type being referenced in a formula is consistent with how it is used. Textual data objects clearly cannot be multiplied times a number in Excel!

SORT.   The *Sort* operation for Excel is found under the **Data** menu, although its function is that of a sheet-level operation. It is similar in function to the *Sort* operation found under the **Edit** menu in Works SS. To use *Sort*, it is first necessary to select the range of cells you wish to sort. As mentioned in the Works SS discussion of sorting, this selection must be done carefully, because *only* the group of items you choose will be repositioned. Next you select *Sort* from the **Data** menu. This produces the dialog box shown in Figure 19.13.

Note that the Excel *Sort* operation allows sorting either by rows, rearranging the order of the rows in the table, *or* by columns, rearranging the order of the columns—depending upon which button you click. Next you must enter, by clicking on a cell or typing a cell address into the *1st Key* box, the location of the primary field in the table that contains the values on which you are sorting.

As in Works SS, the *2nd Key* box in Figure 19.13 refers to sorting *within* those items that have the same first key value. The *3rd Key* box is used to order those items that have the same first *and* second key values. The sort will choose either alphabetic order or numerical order, depending on the data type in the field. The order within either can be chosen as ascending or descending.

Computer Practice 19.3.2

1.   Open the Excel worksheet named *Exercise 19.3.1* from the last section.

2.   Select cells B2:B3 by dragging.

Figure 19.12 Excel results after replicating the formula in cell D6 in the example of Chapter 12. Compare with Figure 12.11 for Works SS.

🍎 File Edit Formula Format Data Options Macro Window					
D8		=IF((C6<=40),B6*C6,40*B6+(1+B3)*B6*(C6−40))			
		Net Pay Example			
	A	B	C	D	E	F
1						
2	Sheet Inputs:	Overtime Rate	Deductions/Tax	Date		
3		100%	40%	Aug. 28, 1987		
4						
5	Name	Hourly Rate	Hours worked	Gross Pay	Deductions	Net Pay
6	Doe, John	$10.00	45	500		
7	Adams, Bill	$12.00	35	420		
8	Mack, Steve	$5.00	60	#VALUE!		
9	Fuller, Jill	$7.50	40	300		
10	Mack, Pat	$3.50	40	140		
11	Woods, Evelyn	$7.00	48	616		

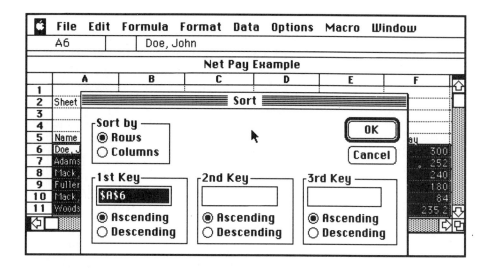

Figure 19.13 Sort dialog box.

3. Select *Delete* from the **Edit** menu.

4. When the dialog box appears, select *Shift Cells Left* and click *OK*. You should now observe the arrangement of cells A1:C5 as shown in Figure 19.10.

5. With the range B2:B3 still highlighted, select *Insert* from the **Edit** menu.

6. When the dialog box appears, select *Shift Cells Right* and click *OK*. You should now find that two blank cells have been added in locations B2:B3 and that the cells containing *all* and *to* are repositioned to their locations at the beginning of this exercise. Note that *Insert* and *Delete* literally add cells to or delete cells from the middle of the worksheet. *Clear*, on the other hand, removes the contents of cells without restructuring the worksheet.

7. Obtain a new worksheet. In cells A1 and A2, enter the values *1* and *2*, respectively.

8. In cell A3, enter the value =A1+A2.

9. Select cell A3 and choose *Cut* from the **Edit** menu. Then click on cell A4 and select *Paste* from under the **Edit** menu.

10. Look at the form of the formula in cell A4. Note that the formula is identical in form to that which was entered in step 8. You have verified that *Cut* does not create a formula template. Also note that the entry in A3 has been erased. Consequently, in Excel *Cut* followed by *Paste* is identical to the *Move* operation of Works SS.

11. Click on cell A5. Click on the **Edit** menu. Note that *Paste* is now dimmed and cannot be selected. This demonstrates that *Cut* can be followed by only one *Paste* operation.

12. Repeat steps 9 through 11, replacing *Cut* with *Copy*. Note in step 10 that a formula template is formed and a new formula is produced.

13. Note that any number of successive *Paste* operations can be performed, because *Paste* is still bold in the **Edit** menu after the *Copy* operation. Verify this by selecting the range of cells A6:A15. Choose *Paste* from the **Edit** menu. Observe that a *Paste* following a *Copy* in Excel will fill the number of cells selected for *Paste* and is therefore unlike the Works SS *Copy* operation. Note

also that a formula template has been formed and that a new formula is shown in each of the cells A6:A15.

14. Obtain a new worksheet and enter the last names (in column A), first names (in column B), and telephone numbers (in column C) of five persons you know. Make up several additional persons that have the same last name but different first names and telephone numbers and add these to your list.

15. Drag over all the entries. Select *Sort* from the **Data** menu. Enter appropriate selections in the dialog box to sort the listing according to last name, and within the same last name according to first names. Each sort should be performed in ascending alphabetical order.

16. Repeat step 15, but now sort the entries on the telephone numbers, such that the person having the largest telephone number comes first in the list and the person having the smallest telephone number is last.

19.3.3 Excel Data Object Operators and Built-in Functions.

Excel provides a superset of data object operators and functions described for Works SS. The precedence of the Excel data object operators is identical to Works SS. Table 9.7 summarizes this precedence, with the exception that AND and OR have the same precedence level in Excel, just as in Works SS.

ARITHMETIC OPERATORS.   Excel provides a set of arithmetic operators identical to those discussed in Works SS. These operators are shown in Table 9.2.

COMPARISON OPERATORS.   The comparison operators for Excel are identical in form to the comparison operators that were discussed in Chapter 11 for Works SS. These operators are listed in Table 9.3. However, they differ from those in Works SS in two ways. First, the Excel comparison operators produce a value of *True* or *False* rather than the numerical value of 1 or 0 produced in Works SS. Second, in Excel, comparison operators can be used to compare like data types of any kind, not just numbers, as in Works SS. For example, comparison between two text objects or two logical objects can be made if desired.

LOGICAL OPERATORS.   The logical operators in Excel are the functions AND(*V1,V2, ... ,VN*), OR(*V1,V2, ... ,VN*), and NOT(*V1*). These functions are identical in concept to those previously discussed in Chapter 11, with two exceptions. First, Excel logical functions return a value of *True* or *False* rather than the 1 or 0 for the Works logical functions. Second, unlike the Works SS logical functions, in which any *number* can be input as an argument, the arguments input to the logical functions in Excel must contain only the values of *True* or *False*. This data type consistency helps reduce in Excel worksheets some errors that might accidentally arise in using Works SS logical functions.

BUILT-IN FUNCTIONS.   As was discussed in Chapter 12, spreadsheets provide an extensive set of **built-in functions** that can be used to compute results that cannot be easily constructed using only the simple arithmetic, logical, and comparison operators. You saw some examples of the various kinds of worksheet built-in functions in the Works SS discussion of Chapter 12.

Excel provides over 90 different such built-in functions—almost double the number found in Works SS. The name of each Excel built-in function can be found under the *Paste Function* option of the **Formula** pull-down menu. Also, many of these function names are identical to their Works SS counterparts. Those Excel functions that have the same name as a Works SS function also have identical arguments and semantic meaning to those discussed in Chapter 12. Thus, you can read Chapter 12, Section 3 to obtain information about many Excel functions not included here.

In the following discussion we list a few functions in Excel that have no counterpart in Works SS. These additional functions will broaden the range of problems you can solve easily using a spreadsheet.

ADDITIONAL STATISTICAL FUNCTIONS.   One category in which additional functions are provided is in the group of functions called statistical functions. In addition to the statistical functions discussed in Chapter 12 for Works SS, Excel provides, among others, the following functions.

LINEST(*Y-array, X-array*). This function has two arguments for input. Each is an *array*, as discussed in Section 1 of this chapter. The second argument, X-array, of the function contains a list of the independent variable values. The first argument, Y-array, of the function is a list of the dependent variable values that correspond to values in X-array. This function returns an *array* of two values, *m* and *b*. These values are, respectively, the slope and intercept of the best line passing through the ordered pairs drawn from the X-array and Y-array values. Recall that the equation for a line is given by

$$y = m * x + b$$

The method used by Excel to find *m* and *b* is a well-known method called *least squares*. Your instructor can provide additional information about the method of least squares. The name of this function, LINEST, is an acronym of its purpose, LINear ESTimation.

To show how we would use this function, consider the example worksheet shown in Figure 19.14, where an arbitrary set of *x* values has been entered into the cells B1:F1. To obtain a *y* value from its corresponding *x* value, we have simply mentally multiplied each *x* by 2 and placed the result below its *x* value. Note, however, that Excel does not know how we computed the *y* values from the *x* values.

To compute *m* and *b* for this "made-up" data, we first choose the location where the two-element array containing *m* and *b* is to be placed. Choose the range B3:C3 for this purpose by clicking and dragging. Then, to insert the function,

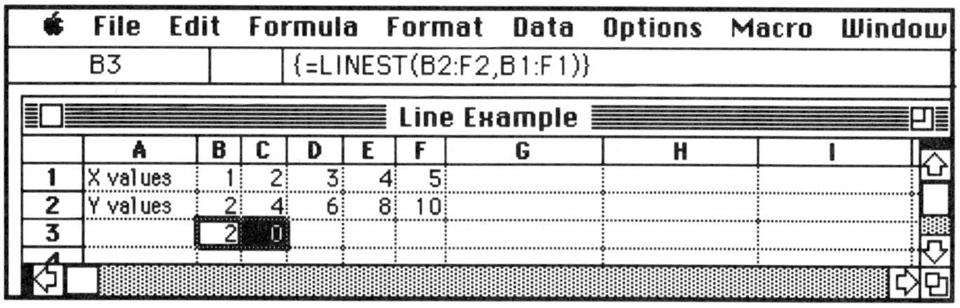

Figure 19.14 Example computation from the LINEST function.

select *Paste Function* from the **Formula** menu and scroll down until the function LINEST appears. Double-click on this function and its name will appear in the formula bar. To enter the arguments of the function, first select the range B2:F2 (Y-array) by clicking and dragging; type a comma to separate the first argument from the second; and finally drag over the range B1:F1 to enter X-array. To complete the function entry, hold down the *Command* (*Clover*) key, and while this key is down, press *Return*. This latter operation is the syntax used in Excel to indicate that the output is an array. Note that the braces are added to the formula by Excel in the formula bar. These indicate an array formula, as discussed in Section 1. The range of the array output is the range selected at the time the formula was being entered, in this case B3:C3.

When the array formula is entered, the values output for *m* (in cell B3) and *b* (in cell C3) are 2 for *m* and 0 for *b*, respectively. Hence, Excel has determined that the best line (in the sense of least squares) through this set of data is of the form

$$y = 2 * x$$

Note the equation of this line is exactly the function that was used to compute the initial data. Normally, you will not know the best line necessary for the data in question. Thus, in this instance our example is somewhat contrived. In many instances the data will not even be linear (i.e., obtained exactly from the equation of a line), but a line may be a reasonable approximation to it and can be conveniently used.

TREND(*Y-array, X-array, new-x-array*). This function has three arrays as input. The arrays Y-array and X-array are used as in LINEST to compute, using least squares methods, values for *m* and *b* to be used in the equation of a line. The third array, new-x-array contains a set of *x* values for which the equation of the line

$$y = m * x + b$$

is to be computed. The TREND function returns an array of *y* values calculated from the line equation and corresponding to the entries in new-x-array.

As a simple example, suppose that you have followed the cost of energy usage in your house over the last 10 years. When you plot the cost as a function of year using the spreadsheet you notice that it is approximately a straight line. We shall call such uniformity in the data a trend. Observing this trend, you want to learn what the approximate cost of your energy usage will be five and 10 years from today.

The TREND function allows you to make this estimate very easily. Input as X-array the list of years for which you have energy usage data. Input as Y-array the corresponding values for the cost of the energy. Input as new-x-array, the years for which you want approximate cost values to be calculated. TREND will compute from the best straight line through your data an array whose values are the costs corresponding to the years specified in new-x-array.

Note that the actual data may not be adequately approximated by a straight line. This may be the case for a number of reasons, one being that the data is nonlinear—quadratic or cubic, for example. In such instances it is not appropriate to use the TREND function for approximation or extrapolation. For completeness we note that some software packages (typically not spreadsheet packages) provide the capability to fit a wide variety of different functions and polynomials to data.

LOGEST(*Y-array*, *X-array*). This function is analogous to LINEST except that it computes values of *m* and *b* for the growth function defined by

$$y = b * m \wedge x$$

Solutions to many equations describing processes in physics, biology, economics, and so forth, are similar in dependence to the growth function; thus, it is convenient to determine *m* and *b* for these processes, just as it is useful to determine a line using LINEST. The use of this function is completely analogous to the use of LINEST. Define the location of input arrays and select the location for the array of two cells in which *m* and *b* will be output.

If the logarithm of this equation is taken, the form of the equation will be a line when considered as a function of LOG(x), and hence the name LOGEST. This transformation should also give you some insight into how the values of *m* and *b* are computed.

GROWTH(*Y-array*, *X-array*, *new-x-array*). This function is analogous to TREND. In this case, Y-array and X-array hold the values used to compute *m* and *b*, as done by LOGEST. GROWTH then returns an array of *y* values, where each *y* is computed from the equation

$$y = b * m \wedge x$$

using its corresponding *x* in new-x-array. Thus, if you know a given set of data should follow a growth function, then by placing the *x* and *y* values for the data into X-array and Y-array, respectively, you can compute estimated growth values for the *x*s you have specified in new-x-array.

LOGICAL FUNCTIONS.   In addition to the logical functions AND(), OR(), and NOT(), Excel contains the built-in function IF(). This function is identical to the Works SS IF function and will not be further discussed.

TEXT FUNCTIONS.   Because Excel is a very general-purpose problem-solving environment, it contains an entire class of functions not found in Works SS. These functions are available to be used on data objects of the text data type or to return values of text data type.

DOLLAR(*number, number of digits*). This function rounds a number to a given number of digits and writes out the number as a text value in currency format. For example, DOLLAR(23456.1467, 2) would return the value $23,456.15.

LEN(*V1*). This function returns the number of characters in the argument *V1*. For example, LEN("hello") would return the value 5 because there are five letters in *hello*. Here quotation marks are not counted as part of the text, but are used instead to indicate a text value for the argument.

MID(*V1*, *start-position*, *number-of-characters*). This function returns the number of characters specified by the argument, *number-of-characters*, starting at the position *start-position* in the text value *V1*. For example, MID("Now is the time for", 5, 6) would return "is the." The 5 indicates to start the text string at the fifth letter ("i" in "is") and the six indicates that the next six characters are to be returned.

Computer Practice 19.3.3

1. Work through the example computation given for the LINEST function in this section.

2. Given the following data, determine, using the TREND function, the estimated values for x = 20, 30, and 40.

$x = 0$	2.5	5	7.5	10
$y = 5$	11	14	22	23

3. Given the following data, determine using the LOGEST function what the values of *m* and *b* are.

$x = 1$	2	3	4	5
$y = 2$	4	8	16	32

4. Given the data in exercise 3, using the GROWTH function, determine what the values for x = 8, 16, 32, and 48 will be. Note that the values computed are just 2 raised to the power of *x* and indicate how many distinct choices there are for a pattern of bits that can appear in a cell of computer memory that is *x* bits long.

19.4   STRUCTURED OBJECTS IN EXCEL WORKSHEETS

We have defined the spreadsheet data structures of *arrays*, *tables*, and *databases* in Section 1 of this chapter. The Excel worksheet subsystem can operate on each of these kinds of structures. Each is examined in turn in the following section.

19.4.1 Excel Arrays

As an example of the use of an array in Excel, let us examine how to set up an array to compute the logarithm, base 10, for each of 16 entries. We already know at least one way to solve this problem. We could enter the 16 values as one range of cells and then replicate the function LOG10 into 16 new cells referencing each of the input cells separately through a formula template. An array structure, however, is somewhat easier to use to construct this same computation.

First, we decide on the organization we want to use for the input data. For example, suppose that the rectangle A1:B8 (containing 16 cells) holds the 16 different values for which the LOG10 is to be computed. Note these inputs could be arranged in any convenient rectangular form, not just the one preceding.

Next, we decide on the organization to be used for the 16 computed values. Suppose we want the output values to be placed in the rectangular area C1:D8 so that C1 contains the value LOG10(A1), C2 contains the value LOG10(A2), and so on, until D8 contains the last value LOG10(B8).

You can cause Excel to perform this computation by selecting for output the rectangle C1:D8 by dragging, entering the formula =LOG10(A1:B8), and selecting the check box *while holding down the Command key*. Immediately, *all* values in the output array are computed and displayed. Recall from the last section that terminating any formula entry with the *Command* key depressed indicates to Excel that an array value is to be output.

Through these simple steps we have indicated to Excel that all 16 values in the range A1:B8 are inputs and that the 16 values in the rectangle C1:D8 are output values. If *any* of the cells in C1:D8 is selected, the formula bar will show {=LOG10(A1:B8)}, where Excel has added the braces to indicate that an array formula is being used. (Do not type the braces! They are added by Excel automatically whenever the *Command* key is held down while *a formula entry is terminated*.) From now on this entire group of cells must be edited as a group. You cannot change a single cell's formula without changing the group.

Computer Practice 19.4.1

1. The array example in Section 1 of this chapter was generated using Excel. Reproduce the array of values shown in Figure 19.1 using the methods discussed in this section. Use the form of the formula shown in the formula bar of Figure 19.1 to help you obtain the results.

2. Place the following 10 values for x in cells A11 to A20 of the worksheet: 0, 10, 20, ... ,90. Using the array method discussed in this section, compute the function

$$y = 10 * x + 5$$

    Place the array results in the cells B11 to B20. Note that the function syntax will be similar to exercise 1. After the function values have been calculated, select cells C8 and D8. While these cells are selected, type the formula

$$= LINEST(B11:B20, A11:A20)$$

    and as you depress the *Command* key click in the *Check* box to enter the formula. Recall that the built-in function LINEST computes the slope and intercept of the best line through a set of data. Compare the value obtained in cells C8 and D8 with the form of the formula used to compute the data entered into function LINEST. Note that you are using arrays to compute the initial y values and to return the value of the slope and intercept from the LINEST function.

3. Choose a series of 10 values of x that range from 5 to 20. Use these values to compute the function

$$y = 5.0 * (2.0 \wedge x)$$

    using the array method discussed in this section. Place the x values arranged in order from smallest to largest in cell A11 and extending down this column to A20. Start the y array of computed values in cell B11 and let them continue to B20. After the y values have been computed, select the two cells C8 and D8 by dragging. While selected, type the formula

$$=LOGEST(B11:B20, A11:A20)$$

    hold down the *Command* key, and click in the *Check* box. Recall that the built-in function LOGEST computes the parameters m and b for an exponential growth function. Compare the values in C8 and D8 with the corresponding form of the formula used to generate the y data values.

4. Modify exercise 2 so that you extrapolate the results for this line out to values of $x = 200, 250, 300, 350$, and 400, using the Excel function TREND. Do the new values of y computed using TREND agree with the original formula at the xs? Test using hand calculations.

5. Modify exercise 3 so that you extrapolate the results of this growth curve to values of $x = 22, 24, 26, 28$, and 30, using the Excel function GROWTH.

19.4.2 Excel One-Input Tables

One-input and two-input tables are particularly useful for investigating how changes in the value of an input for a calculation influence the results. Recall from Section 1 of this chapter that the use of these Excel table structures requires only that you be able to define implicitly the dependence of a result on an input value. Use of a one-input table in Excel requires three steps:

1. Set up a sample calculation that defines the implicit dependence on the input value.

2. Enter the independent variables to be used in the table calculation and specify the *locations of the functions* whose values are to computed in the table.

3. Define for Excel the location and extent of the table and the location of the *table input cell.*

We will illustrate the construction of a one-input table with an example.

ONE-INPUT TABLE EXAMPLE.   To illustrate the use of the one-input table structure in Excel, let us consider again the calculation of the accumulated savings amount that we studied in Chapter 12. The elements of this example calculation are shown by cells B1:C9 of Figure 19.15. To obtain this worksheet, we have entered the calculation shown in Figure 12.7 into an Excel worksheet. The steps that were used were almost identical to those used in Works SS. Note that in Excel it is permissible to enter percentage values, such as for cell C5. Excel automatically converts each percentage value to a decimal fraction when required for a computation.

SAMPLE CALCULATION.   The section of the worksheet in the range B1:C9 comprises the *sample calculation* described for step 1 for a one-input table. In this case, we would like to extend the sample calculation by studying the accumulated savings amount as a function of different interest rates. We will summarize the study as a table in which the interest rate runs down one column and the associated saving earned appears in the adjacent column, as shown in Figure 19.15.

Note that we have all the pieces to solve this problem *already* present in the sample calculation. If we successively insert into cell C5 (which contains the yearly interest rate), each new interest rate, Excel will compute in cell C10 an associated total savings amount. (Thus, all we have to do manually to generate the table is collect each of the values obtained. Fortunately, we won't have to do this, however! Excel can automate this process for us.) We emphasize that cell C5 serves a *special* role in our calculation and is called the *table input cell* for the sample calculation. By altering its values we get each new result desired.

INDEPENDENT VARIABLE AND FUNCTION LOCATIONS.   To define the table independent variable values as in step 2, we enter into the range A12:A15 values of the interest from 5% to 10% in 1% increments. To complete step 2, we must enter the location of each function whose values are to appear in the table. According to Excel table syntax, function locations must be placed into the cells in the row above the first independent variable value and in successive columns to the right of the column containing the independent variable. Thus, in our example B10 is the cell into which the location of the first table function is to be entered. Note for this sample calculation that the value of the accumulated savings amount appears in cell C9. Thus, we enter the formula =C9 into cell B10 to define the location of the formula, thus completing step 2.

In this example there is only one function being computed. Note, however, that if other function values we wished to study had also depended upon cell C5, we could have entered their locations in cells C10, D10, and so on, across the row.

DEFINING THE TABLE EXTENT AND TABLE INPUT CELL.   To perform step 3, defining the table extent, we now select cells A10:B16 by dragging. This defines the physical location of the table on the worksheet to Excel. With this range highlighted, select the *Table* operation from the **Data** menu. The dialog box in Figure 19.16 will appear. Now it is necessary to define the location of the *table input cell.* Enter $C$5, the absolute coordinates of the *table input cell,* into the *Column Input Cell* box. (Alternatively, you can simply click in the *Column Input Cell* box to select it and then move the cell selection cross to cell C5 and click. Its coordinates will automatically be entered for you.) The *Column Input Cell* box is selected because the independent variable values are located in a column of the table. Excel one-input tables can also be organized with the independent variable values entered

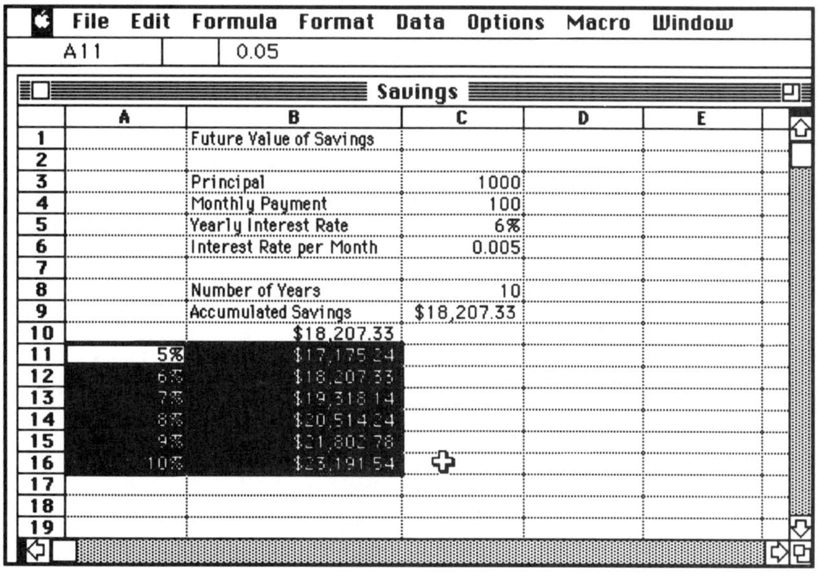

Figure 19.15 A sample calculation and a one-input table.

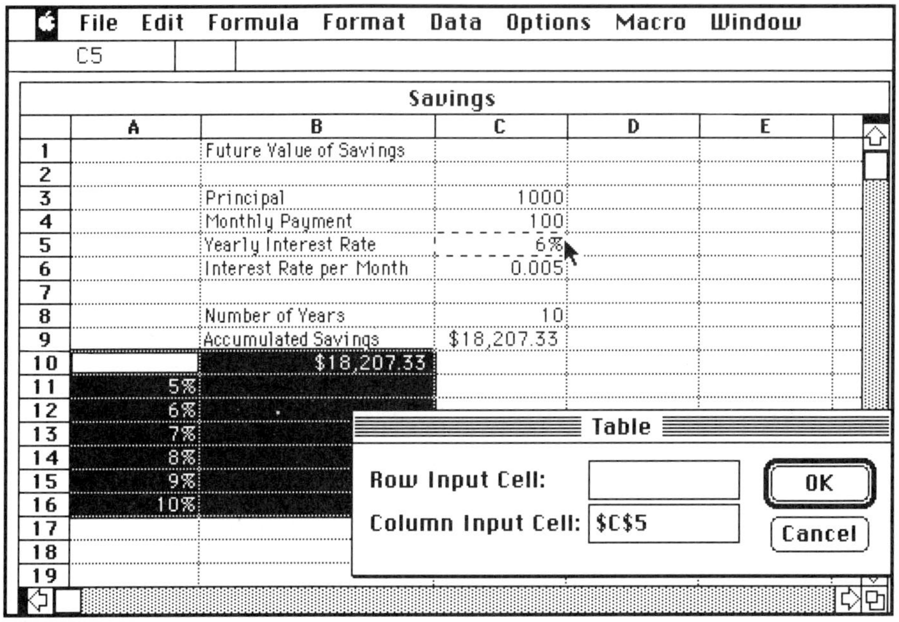

Figure 19.16 Selection of the table input cell by clicking.

in a row. Finally, click *OK*; the table values shown in Figure 19.15 will appear. Note that the table cells have been formatted to make the table appearance more pleasing.

Computer Practice 19.4.2

1. Work through the construction of the one-input table example presented in this section. First, set up the sample calculation as described in Chapter 12, Section 3. You will see that entry of the worksheet is very similar to that of Works SS. Next, enter the independent variable values in cells A11:A16, and enter the function location in cell B10. Finally, drag over the table extent and define the *Column Input Cell* as $C$5. Your table entries should then be computed automatically.

2. Modify the problem as follows. Instead of studying the accumulated savings amount as a function of the interest rate for a fixed length of 10 years, fix the interest rate at 8% and study how the accumulated saving depends upon the number of years saved. In this case your table should have years as its independent variable. Note that cell C8 now becomes the *table input cell* because this cell contains the number of years used in the sample calculation. Let the number of years vary from 2 to 40 in steps of two. To enter these, first enter a 2 into cell A11, using the *Check* box to terminate the data entry. While A11 is still the active cell, select the *Series* option in the **Data** menu. In the dialog box presented click on *Columns* and *Linear*. Set the *Step Value* to 2 and the *Stop Value* to 40 and click *OK*. Excel will automatically generate the desired year values for you.

3. Set up a sample calculation for SIN(X), COS(X), and TAN(X) so that each function references the same cell for its X value. Construct a one-input table

with X down a column and the three functions above listed across successive columns. Compute each function for 16 values of X over the range $0 <= X <= 2\pi$.

19.4.3 Excel Two-Input Tables

Excel has a second kind of table called a *two-input table* that allows the values of a given function to be studied as a function of two different variables (inputs). In the following we will briefly describe how a two-input table is set up. The method is a direct extension of the one-input table and follows the same three steps with a few minor variations.

As discussed in the last section, in step 1 of the process for defining a one-input table, the sample calculation is set up. For our two-input table example, let us combine the results computed in exercises 1 and 2 of Computer Practice 19.4.2. Thus, we will compute a table that shows the accumulated savings as a function of years held and interest rate arranged as a two-dimensional grid of values. Because the sample calculation used in the last section has both of these inputs already considered, we can use it with no modifications.

Clearly, in a two-input table there will be *two* table input cells—one for each independent variable. Thus, C5 is one of table input cells and C8 is the other because these cells hold the interest rate and the number of years, respectively, in the sample calculation. This completes step 1 of the two-input table definition.

We now consider step 2. Recall that this step requires specification of the independent variable values and the location of the functions to be used. For a two-input table, one independent variable vector is placed down a column, the second independent variable vector is placed across a row. Enter the function location into the cell at the intersection of the row and column vectors forming the table. Note that only one function at a time can be studied in a two-input table.

We enter one independent variable vector, the interest rate, into cells A11:A16. Across the table in cells B10:E10 we enter the number of years the savings account is held. (See Figure 19.17.) We enter into cell A10 (the intersection of the column and row vectors forming the table) the location of the function whose result we wish to study—in this case, =C9. This completes step 2.

Finally, we perform step 3, in which the physical position of the table and the two-table input cells are defined. Select the range of cells A10:E16 for the table by dragging. The table range must include the cell containing the table function location and all the row and column vector entries. The *Table* operation is now selected from the **Data** menu. Next the absolute cell references for *both* the *Column Input Cell* and the *Row Input Cell* must be entered in the dialog box. Click on cell C8 to enter the *Row Input Cell* location. Move the cell pointer to the *Column Input Cell* box and click to select this box. Then move the cell pointer to cell C5 and click to enter the location. Once *OK* is clicked, the table is automatically computed.

Note that we must be careful to match the column vector of values with the location where these values enter the sample calculation as defined by the column input cell. This is also true for the row vector. The interest rates appear in column A (A11:A16) of the table in Figure 19.17 and enter into the calculation in cell C5. Likewise, the numbers of years over which the savings are held appear in row 10 (B10:E10) and enter into the computation in cell C8.

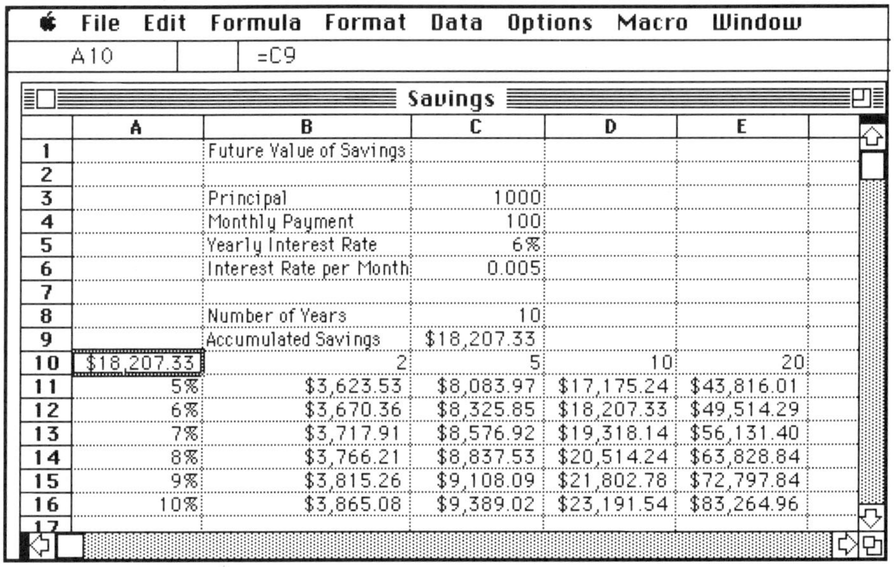

	A	B	C	D	E
1		Future Value of Savings			
2					
3		Principal	1000		
4		Monthly Payment	100		
5		Yearly Interest Rate	6%		
6		Interest Rate per Month	0.005		
7					
8		Number of Years	10		
9		Accumulated Savings	$18,207.33		
10	$18,207.33	2	5	10	20
11	5%	$3,623.53	$8,083.97	$17,175.24	$43,816.01
12	6%	$3,670.36	$8,325.85	$18,207.33	$49,514.29
13	7%	$3,717.91	$8,576.92	$19,318.14	$56,131.40
14	8%	$3,766.21	$8,837.53	$20,514.24	$63,828.84
15	9%	$3,815.26	$9,108.09	$21,802.78	$72,797.84
16	10%	$3,865.08	$9,389.02	$23,191.54	$83,264.96

Figure 19.17 A two-input table in Excel.

In using a sample calculation that has more than two parameters, it is a simple matter to study a wide variety of dependences for pairs of the independent variables by developing two-input tables on different combinations of independent variable pairings. No new work needs to be done for such studies except to generate the independent variable values and to select the new row and column input cells!

Finally, note that although our example calculations have been fairly simple, there is nothing to prevent a long and complex worksheet computation involving numerous intermediate steps to be used to construct one-input or two-input tables in exactly the same manner as we have done here. You need only identify the table input cell or cells and the location of the result you wish to study. For such complex computations it would be impractical to employ formula replication methods.

Computer Practice 19.4.3

1. Work through the example two-input table presented in this section.
2. Redo exercise 2 of Computer Practice 12.4 using a two-input table.
3. Redo exercise 4 of Computer Practice 12.4 using a two-input table.
4. Study the monthly payments required to buy a car as a function of the amount borrowed and the interest rate. Employ a sample calculation to set up all the variables in the problem and assume a five-year loan. Use a two-input table for the solution. The function PMT defined in Chapter 12, Section 2 can be used to compute the payments.
5. Modify exercise 4 to allow you to study the monthly payments as a function of the interest rate and the number of months of the loan for a fixed amount borrowed. Note how easy it is to solve this problem once the sample calculation has already been performed.

19.4.4 Excel Databases

Another impressive feature of Excel is the database. You have already learned a substantial amount about database systems. The Excel database provides very sophisticated selection and projection operations on a single table. Just as in Works SS, the name for each different attribute is placed along the top row of the table. These attribute names, you will recall, are termed field names.

For example, in the Excel *Accounts Payable Database* in Figure 19.18 the names of the attribute are *Date, Item Purchased, Cost, Payee's Name, Payee's City,* and *Payee's State*. Each row below the top row of the table is called a record or *n*-tuple. A record will be entered into the table for each item that has been purchased.

Spreadsheet databases allow you to *Find* or *Extract* information stored in the spreadsheet database. Both of these operations are found under the **Data** menu of Excel. *Find* is analogous to selectively retrieving records as controlled by the current selection criteria. It is similar in function to the **select** operator of relational algebra. *Extract* corresponds to the projecting records in the database that meet some selection criteria. Thus, *Extract* in Excel is similar to the combination of the **select** and **project** operators of relational algebra.

In Excel, a record of the database is shown highlighted if it is selected through a *Find* as shown in Figure 19.19. *Extract* causes a new set of entries to appear in the Excel spreadsheet outside the range of the database. The Excel database operations are located in the **Data** menu and will be discussed in more detail later in this section.

DEFINING AN EXCEL DATABASE.   Any rectangular area of a worksheet can be defined as a database, although to be useful, a database should be organized as a table having field names and record entries, such as shown in Figure 19.18. It is, however, important to realize that the act of entering the attribute names and entering rows of information does not by itself identify the region as a database to Excel.

To define a range of cells as a database you first select the range of cells desired. Note that you *must* also include in the range the attribute row containing the field names. Then select the *Set Database* **operation** from the **Data** menu.

Having defined a database to Excel, a wide range of operations is possible. These include powerful operations, such as finding all records that meet a given selection criteria and using the data extracted from the database for other desired spreadsheet computations. It is this latter capability that makes a spreadsheet database particularly desirable for certain problem areas. Although some computational features are built into database management systems, currently those

🍎	File	Edit	Formula	Format	Data	Options	Macro	Window

A5		7/10/1987

Accounts Payable Database

	A	B	C	D	E	Paye
1	Date	Item Purchased	Cost	Payee's Name	Payee's City	Paye
2	6/2/87	water pump	$34.65	Yissage Auto	Greenville	SC
3	6/12/87	computer paper	$142.25	ComputersRus	Atlanta	GA
4	6/30/87	paper clips	$0.40	Walmart	Spartanburg	SC
5	7/10/87	midi interface	$285.00	Opcode Systems	Palo Alto	CA
6						

Figure 19.18 Example Excel database.

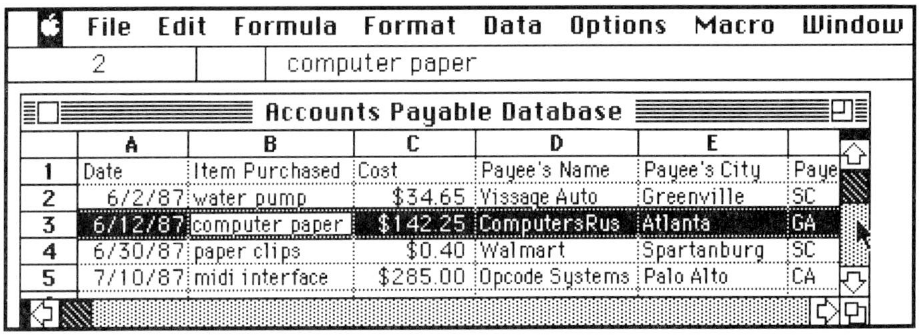

Figure 19.19 Example of the *Find* operation on an Excel database.

features do not rival the computational power available in a spreadsheet. You must also keep in mind, however, that the database features of spreadsheets are somewhat limited relative to those found in most relational database systems.

EDITING. Because the spreadsheet database is just a collection of cells, all the editing commands that you learned earlier can be applied to manipulate the information in the spreadsheet database. Both cell-level and sheet-level commands are operative. Thus, for example, to add a record to the database you need only to select the entire row in front of which you wish the record to be added. Then by selecting *Insert* from the **Edit** menu, a blank row will appear.

When such a procedure is used, Excel will automatically extend the range of the database to include any new rows added, provided that these rows were inserted *above* the last row of the database range. If a new row is typed *after* the last row of the database, the entire database including this new row must be reselected and the *Set Database* operation must be performed again.

SELECTION CRITERIA. To retrieve information from the spreadsheet database it is necessary to specify the criteria that are to be used to select the records of interest; this is done with the **Set Criteria operation**. Once the selection criteria have been set, operations such as *Find* or *Extract* can be performed.

In Excel, each set of criteria that is to be used for a database selection must be given a name. Any cell *outside* the database range can be used to define a name for a set of criteria. The name is entered into the cell data object. There are two methods that are used to specify record selection criteria, *Comparison Criteria* and *Computed Criteria*.

SELECTION USING COMPARISON CRITERIA. **Comparison criteria** are the simpler of the two record selection criteria to use and will meet many of your needs. Our discussion will begin by considering the specification of just one set of criteria. As we will see shortly, more than one set of comparison criteria can be specified at one time. Each set of comparison criteria used *requires* that the name chosen for the set be the name of a *field* in the database. This name is entered into a cell that we shall call the *criteria name* cell.

Immediately below the cell containing the criteria name (in the same column) are entered the actual comparisons that are performed to decide if a record in the database is selected. If *any* of the comparisons performed in the column evaluate to *True* for a record, its contents are returned in a *Find* or *Extract* operation.

The form of a comparison entry is either a value or a relational operator and a value. If a value alone is entered for a comparison, then the contents of the field name for each record are tested for equality against the value. Alternately, if a relational operator and a value are both entered, then the contents of the field name for each record are tested against the value according to the relation specified.

Let us use our *Accounts Payable Database* of Figure 19.18 to illustrate these ideas. Suppose that you wished to find all payments that were made to ComputersRus. You could define a criteria name to be *Payee's Name*, the name of the field you will use for selecting records. You can choose a cell to hold this name, say, K6, and enter *Payee's Name* into the cell.

Next, you need to define the comparison criteria to be used on this field. In the cell below the criteria name, K7, you enter the value ComputersRus. This value will then be compared with the actual contents of the *Payee's Name* field for each record in the database. Only those records whose *Payee's Name* field equals the ComputersRus value will be selected.

Note, however, that Excel does not yet know that these cells are to be used as criteria when searching the database. To inform Excel, you must select these two cells as a range, K6:K7, and then select *Set Criteria* from the **Data** menu. Now if you execute the *Find* command from the **Data** menu, only those records that have the value ComputersRus for their *Payee's Name* field will be selected.

COMPARISONS USING OR.   Excel allows you to chain comparison criteria together. If you wish to find all the transactions that involve either ComputersRus or Vissage Auto, then an additional cell in this column, say K8, could be given the value Vissage Auto. The range of three cells, K6:K8, would then be selected and defined as the selection criteria using the *Set Criteria* operation as described earlier. The rule to remember is that entries in a column below the criteria name are combined using an OR for selection purposes—thus, a match with *any* value in the list is selected.

One word of warning about comparison criteria is that if the cell range chosen for *Set Criteria* includes an empty cell, then *all* records are selected. Because all entries in a column are combined using OR, an extra blank cell at the end selects everything. Thus, be very cautious about dragging to ensure that only the range you desire is specified as the criteria range.

Rather than choose equality as the comparison operation, we could ask for those records having the value of the *Cost* field greater than 20. Because this example is for comparison criteria, you again must choose the criteria name to be the name of the relevant field. Suppose that you choose cell L6 to hold the name *Cost*. The actual comparison is defined by placing >20 into cell L7. This entry in cell L7 indicates that the value of the *Cost* field for each record is to be compared to see if it exceeds 20. If the *Cost* entry does exceed 20, then the record is selected. If the value of the *Cost* field for a record is less than or equal to 20, however, the record is not selected. Any of the comparison operators can be used to set comparison criteria on a field value.

Excel does not limit the database criteria to one column. You can enter several field names across a row of cells if you choose to and list under each column entries for comparison. Any number of these different field-name criteria can be chosen *at the same time* as the criteria to use for selecting records. To use more than one set of comparison criteria at once, select the range of cells for the criteria you desire and then choose the *Set Criteria* operation.

The rule for using multiple comparison criteria is that the separate columns are combined using AND. Thus, for a record to be selected where multiple field names are considered simultaneously (multiple columns), *all* field comparisons in a given row must evaluate to *True*.

To illustrate this idea, suppose that you wish to retrieve only those records containing payments to either ComputersRus or Vissage Auto AND that have a payment amount that exceeds $20. To solve this problem you must AND together the two examples of the comparison criteria we developed earlier. To select the database criteria for this problem, you would need to select the range K6:L8. But note that the blank cell L8 *cannot* be included in the criteria range, otherwise the *Cost* selection will accept every record.

To correct this situation you should enter >20 into cell L8 as well. Because this comparison is combined using OR with itself in this column, it produces the same comparison as before, but we have removed the blank cell in the criteria range. Reselect the range K6:L8 and choose *Set Criteria* from the **Data** menu. The criteria range now includes both the *Payee's Name* and the *Cost* field comparisons. Because these comparison criteria are in different columns and are simultaneously selected, Excel combines the criteria using an AND. The only records selected now are those that meet both criteria.

SELECTION USING COMPUTED CRITERIA. Excel also provides for much more complex selections than are possible with the comparison method discussed earlier. If the criteria you desire employ computations based on the values of database fields or other operations more complex than the simple comparisons discussed earlier, computed criteria must be used. Computed criteria require you to set up *logical* expressions that evaluate to *True* or *False*. Thus, you must create logical formulas using the comparison and logical operators, as discussed in Chapter 11.

Analogous to the comparison criteria discussed earlier, Excel requires a name to be given to each computed criteria you wish to use. You enter this name into a cell that must be located outside the range of the database. Note that computed criteria names may *not* be the names of fields. You then enter, using standard Excel syntax, a logical formula into the cell immediately below the cell that contains the computed comparison's name. By selecting these two cells and choosing *Set Criteria* from the **Data** menu, they become the set of criteria employed for the database record selection.

To illustrate the use of computed criteria, consider the following example. You want to find all records whose item cost is greater than or equal to $100 and is less than or equal to $200. Thus, if X is the item cost, then $X <= \$200$ AND $X >= \$100$. This expression is almost identical to the actual formula you need to use to compute the logical value that determines whether to select a record. *Formulas used in a set of computed criteria must use relative reference to cells in the first record of the database to obtain values for fields.*

For this example, the value required is located in the *Cost* field. According to Figure 19.18, the cell in the first record that contains a *Cost* value has relative reference C2. Hence, the formula

$$=AND((C2>=100), (C2<=200))$$

is the formula that computes the *True* or *False* result you desire for record selection. Because relative reference is chosen for cell C2, as each new record is tested, Excel uses the *Cost* value to determine the answer to the logical formula.

To complete this example, you need to choose the cell where the computed criteria will be named. Then insert the preceding formula into the cell below the cell chosen for the name. Finally, select these two cells and choose the *Set Criteria* operation from the **Data** menu. Any *Find* operation will now use this computed criteria for the selection of records. Note that, as for comparison criteria discussed earlier, multiple-row (same-column) computed criteria selections are combined using OR together, whereas multiple-column (same-row) computed criteria selections are combined using AND.

USE OF FIND AND EXTRACT.   Once the selection criteria have been specified with *Set Criteria* you can retrieve the records of interest. The *Find* operation is found under the **Data** menu. When *Find* is executed, the first record meeting the selection criteria is highlighted. If no record meets the criteria, you will be so informed. To retrieve other records simply click in the scroll area to the right of the screen. Note that when *Find* is active, the scroll box shows a cross-hatched appearance. You can move forward or backward in the selection by using the up- or down-pointing scroll arrows. Be careful not to let the selections of interest scroll by without your seeing them, however. To deactivate the *Find* operation you need only click on any cell in the spreadsheet area.

To use *Extract* you must specify an area outside the database area in which to place the data extracted from the database. To tell Excel which field values to report you need to list the field names of the data you wish to extract. The order of the field names need not follow their order in the database, but they must appear along a row. Once the field names desired have been entered, select them by dragging across them. Then choose *Extract* from the **Data** menu. A dialog box will be presented. Click *OK*. Under the field names you highlighted will appear values for each of the records in the database that meet the selection criteria currently active. As an option, you can choose the button *Delete Duplicate Records* in the *Extract* dialog box to obtain only unique values in the **project** operation.

DATABASE BUILT-IN FUNCTIONS.   In addition to the built-in functions discussed earlier, Excel provides a set of **database built-in functions** that can be used to operate on database records *selected* by the currently active criteria. These functions each have three arguments:

Argument 1: Name of the database.

Argument 2: Name of the field in which the operation is to be performed.

Argument 3: Name of the criteria to use.

In simple usage you can use the *Paste Name* operation found under the **Formula** menu to paste the names *Database* and *Criteria* into the first and third arguments, respectively, for a built-in database function. These names will always hold the currently active database range and criteria range for the Excel worksheet. You should enter the field name surrounded by quotation marks to define the field of interest.

Examples of the built-in database functions in Excel are

DSUM(*Database*, *"field"*, *Criteria*). Sums up the values in the specified field of each record of the current database as selected by the current criteria.

DAVERAGE(*Database,"field",Criteria*). Averages the numerical values in the specified field for the records selected by the current criteria. Items with text or blank values in field are not counted or totaled in computation of the average.

DSTDEV(*Database*, *"field"*, *Criteria*). Computes the standard deviation of the specified field for all records selected by the current criteria. Text or blank values are not counted or summed.

DVAR(*Database*, *"field"*, *Criteria*). Computes the variance in a manner analogous to DSTDEV.

As a simple example, if we wished to compute, using the sample database in Figure 19.18, the total of all costs associated with ComputersRus, then we would develop criteria as previously outlined to select the records having *Payee's Name* = ComputersRus and enter in some cell outside of the database the formula

$$= \text{DSUM(Database, ``Cost'', Criteria)}$$

The resulting data object computed for this cell would be the total of all expenditures to ComputersRus.

Exercise Set 19.4.4

1. What is the purpose of the *Set Database* operation?
2. What is the purpose of the *Set Criteria* operation?
3. What process is necessary to define a database area to Excel?
4. What does the *Find* operation do?
5. What does the *Extract* operation do?
6. What is the form of the comparison criteria in Excel? What happens when several rows and columns are selected together in the *Set Criteria* operation?
7. What is the form of the computed criteria in Excel? Why would you choose to use a computed criteria rather than a comparison criteria?
8. Explain how you would set up selection criteria and use Excel built-in database functions to compute the average amount owed to you for all clients whose total purchases minus amount owed is less than $1000. Assume that you are using a spreadsheet database for clients that has attribute names *Total Purchases* and *Amount Owed* in cells C10 and D10, respectively.

Computer Practice 19.4.4

1. Work through Chapter 9, Section 3, of this book developing an Excel database for the WINN radio station. Set up selection criteria in Excel to perform each of the information retrievals discussed in that section.
2. Set up an Excel database to develop a simple budget management system in which you can determine the totals of expenditures in each budget category as well as extract all expenditures in a given category.
3. Develop an Excel database system that could be used to do the bookkeeping for a small company having only two or three employees and whose main

activity is the sale of merchandise by mail order. Assume that only a small number of different items are marketed. Your system should keep track of inventory, accounts receivable, accounts payable, salaries, and so on. Use a separate worksheet for each separate function of your system. This process will modularize your system and make it easier to understand and modify.

19.5 THE EXCEL CHARTING SUBSYSTEM.

Another powerful feature of many of the advanced spreadsheets such as Excel or Lotus 1-2-3 is the ability to produce sophisticated graphical displays to simplify the presentation of calculations performed in the spreadsheet environment. Excel provides a wider variety of charts than is available in Works SS. One major advantage is the ability to produce graphs in which the independent variable values need not be evenly spaced, as was required for Works SS. In addition, it is possible to perform more flexible labeling of the charts using Excel. Finally, Excel allows the chart data to be either row or column organized. Recall that in Works SS, the data for line and bar charts was required to be row organized, whereas the data for pie charts had to be column organized.

EXCEL CHARTS.   To perform the **chart operation,** it is first necessary to select all the elements of a table of values to be plotted. (The term *table* in this section refers to the generic usage as range and is not restricted to the one-input or two-input table structures of Excel. The latter, however, can easily provide values for a chart.) Next, the *Copy* option is selected in the **Edit** menu. Then *New* option is selected from the **File** menu. It will display an option of *Chart* that should be selected. (See Figure 19.20.)

A blank chart will now appear as the active window. By selecting the *Paste Special* option in the **Edit** menu, you can define for Excel the organization of the data. This is illustrated by Figure 19.21. Note that the *Copy* and *Paste Special* sequence is one way to pass information from the worksheet subsystem to the chart subsystem.

The button *Columns* in Figure 19.21 means the selected table is column organized and the independent variable values are in the first column of the table

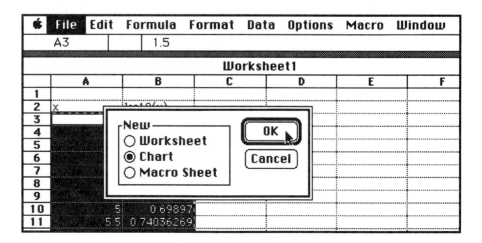

Figure 19.20 Selecting a chart.

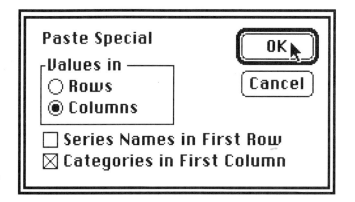

Figure 19.21 Selecting the type of organization used for the table.

(if the table is column organized, the independent variable *must* be in the first column). The button *Rows* means row organization for the data and the independent variable values must be along the top row of the table. As soon as the *OK* button is selected a graph will be generated. The type of graph produced will be controlled by the default chart type that is currently in effect.

When a chart is the active window in Excel one of the menu options available on the menu bar is **Gallery**. (See the menu bar in Figure 19.22.) This allows the user to select from a wide variety of different chart types. There are many options within a type of chart. For a scatter-plot graph the forms are as shown in Figure 19.22. Here we have selected a graph in which each axis employs a logarithmic scale. Such plots are useful for growth and trend analysis.

Figure 19.23 shows a sample graph. For completeness we have also added a chart title, label for the independent variable, and label for the dependent variable. To create the chart title *Plot of Log10*, the option *Attach Text* was selected from

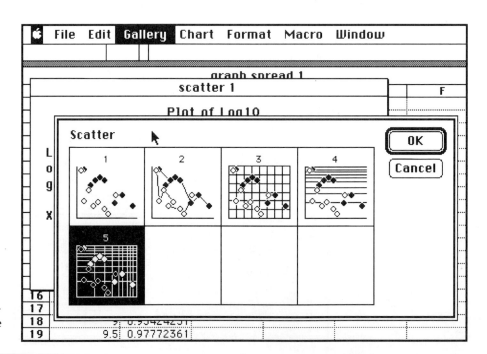

Figure 19.22 Sample selection of formats within the *Scatter Chart* option.

the **Chart** menu. This produces a dialog box in which *Chart Title*, *Category Axis*, *Value Axis*, and *Series or Data Point* appear as click buttons. The *Chart Title* option was selected and the title *Plot of Log10* was then typed. The data typed appeared in a formula bar just under the **Chart** menu. Editing of the title data is possible inside the formula bar using all the text editing commands. When the check box was clicked, the chart title appeared but was not in boldface type. To make the text bold, the *Text* option was selected under the **Format** menu. The *Bold* option was then clicked in the dialog box presented. This completed the entry of the chart title.

The category axis title was then entered in a manner identical to the steps described earlier for the chart title. To complete the labeling of the chart, the *Value Axis* option was selected after *Attach Text* option was chosen from the **Chart** menu. The value axis title *Log X* was typed into the formula bar, and when the check box was clicked, the value axis title subsequently appeared as characters arranged along a horizontal line at the left edge of the chart. To correct the appearance, *Text* was again selected from the **Format** menu and both the *Bold* and *Vertical* buttons were clicked in the dialog box presented. This produced the vertical value axis label shown in Figure 19.23. Note that individual points on the graph can also be labeled using the *Series or Data Point* option under the **Chart** menu.

Excel provides a large number of chart operations. The best way to learn about them is by direct experimentation with the available menu selections. This concludes the brief overview of charting operations available in Excel.

Computer Practice 19.5

1. Reconstruct the chart displayed in this section. Use *Series* to generate 30 values of *x* in the interval $2 <= x <= 50$. Develop an array formula to compute LOG10(x) for these values. Select the table area where your calculations are and choose *Copy* from the **Edit** menu. Follow the description in this section to complete the chart.

2. Using your database results of exercise 2 from Computer Practice 19.4.4, develop a pie chart that displays the distribution of expenditures for your budget categories.

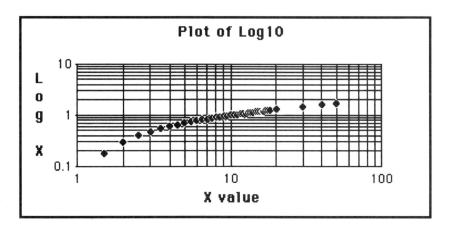

Figure 19.23 Graph of LOG10 (x) using logarithmic scales on each axis.

3. Use the table of trigonometric functions developed for exercise 3 of Computer Practice 19.4.2 to chart values of the sine, cosine, and tangent on the same chart. What problems do you face?

4. Choose one of the exercises from Computer Practice 19.4.3 and experiment with different ways of charting a two-input table.

19.6 THE EXCEL MACRO SUBSYSTEM

Earlier chapters of this book as well as earlier sections of this chapter have demonstrated that once certain details are mastered, spreadsheets can provide an extremely flexible problem-solving environment. This section discusses how a macro language can be used in spreadsheets to provide even more problem-solving power. In fact, using the macro language features of Excel will allow you the option to create *entire applications* that would have required a comprehensive knowledge of a programming language such as COBOL, FORTRAN or PL1, prior to the development of the advanced spreadsheet. We attempt in the remainder of this section to provide an overview of concepts necessary for you to write an application in a macro language. Novice computer users may wish to skip the remainder of this section.

After completing this section you are *not* expected to be able to write complex macros. However, you will be expected to have an overview of what kinds of things will be possible using macros and the steps that are necessary to produce a macro procedure. Entire books are written about the concepts presented in this section, so do not feel surprised if you do not grasp everything discussed here on the first reading.

MACRO SUBSYSTEM. In Excel a special kind of sheet is provided for writing macros. This sheet is called a **macrosheet**. To obtain a macrosheet you must transfer to the macro subsystem. This is accomplished through selecting the option *New* in the **File** menu. A dialog box will appear that includes the option *Macro Sheet*. Selection of this button causes Excel to open a new macrosheet into which instructions can be inserted describing *how* to solve specific subproblems. The functions available on the macrosheet are different from those available on the worksheet.

Advanced spreadsheets other than Excel allow creation of solutions to subproblems, but currently they do not allow separate macrosheets to be created. The existence of separate macrosheets is an advantage of Excel because it allows better organization of problem solutions. As a result, a macro need be defined only once on a macrosheet. It then can be called on to perform its function from *any* other worksheet or macrosheet. Hence, the macro development philosophy in Excel is one of building general-purpose tools that solve specific subproblems for you once and for all. Once these tools are built, they can be used again and again. We will term the set of instructions necessary to solve a subproblem a **macro procedure**. The term *procedure* is commonly used in connection with programming languages to have this same meaning.

Associated with each macro procedure is a *name* that can be used to call up the sequence of steps that are necessary to solve that subproblem. Thus, the use of a macro procedure is very like calling on a built-in function. The macro name serves two very important purposes: to help *you* remember the purpose of the procedure (i.e., which subproblem it solves) and to tell Excel *where* the first statement for the procedure can be found.

Instructions in a procedure are normally interpreted sequentially down a column. Thus, once the location of the first instruction has been identified (through the name of the procedure), the location of the next one is known. Because of this sequential nature of processing instructions, macro procedures are normally written one statement after another down the sheet. There are also control structures such as the IF statement that allow the order of execution of the statements to be changed.

As an example of a subproblem for which a procedure (macro) might be written, suppose that we want to find the shipping charges for sending a package of a given weight by land, sea, or air. Clearly, this is the kind of subproblem that would occur again and again in dealing with costs in a shipping department. Consequently, it makes sense to write a macro and thus be able to call on this macro whenever shipping costs need to be found. Before considering this more difficult problem, we will develop a simple macro to compute the area of a rectangle.

MACRO REQUIREMENTS.   With any macro we will always need to define two elements: the purpose of the procedure (i.e., what the macro computes) and the information the procedure requires to compute the desired result. This is the same information we would require to use a built-in function. Let us now examine the construction of a simple macro to compute the area of a rectangle. We will therefore call this macro *AreaofRectangle*. The purpose of this macro procedure is clear—to calculate the area of a rectangle.

To compute the area of a rectangle we require information. Each separate piece of information that we need to know about the subproblem before we can solve it will become an argument of the procedure. The two arguments that are required for this problem are the length and the width of the rectangle. Once these values are known, the area can be calculated.

MACRO INTERFACE.   The name and arguments discussed earlier can be thought of as an interface section that must exist for each macro procedure we create. To produce this interface in the macrosheet will always require the same considerations we now describe. We can think of this as a syntax that must always be used for defining a macro procedure.

In Figure 19.24, on the right-hand side, we show a macrosheet named *Macro* that was obtained through the **File** menu as discussed earlier. In the cells of this macrosheet we have entered sequentially down a column the instructions to define the name and arguments of this macro. In cell A1 we entered the macro name.

In the next two rows in this column we define the two arguments of the macro procedure. Excel provides a special macrosheet function, =ARGUMENT, that must be used to define each argument of a macro procedure. The function =ARGUMENT has two parameters: a *name* (entered within double quotation marks) that Excel will use to refer to the argument and the data type of the argument. Note that the first argument of *AreaofRectangle* has been given the name *length*. Its data type has been defined as 1—meaning its value must be a

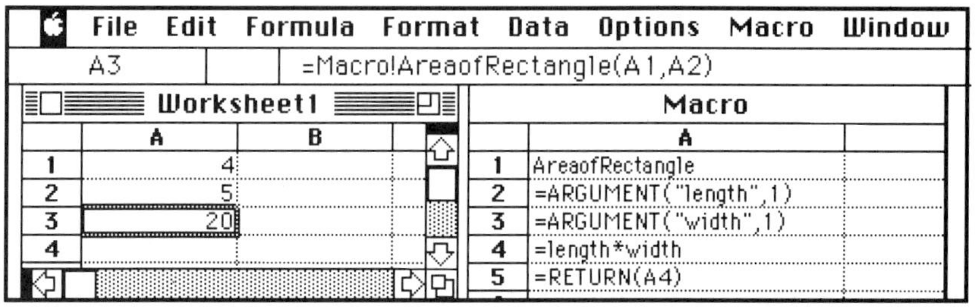

Figure 19.24 Sample *Areaof-Rectangle* macro procedure.

number. The second parameter of *AreaofRectangle* has been given the name *width*. It also has a data type of 1, meaning its value must also be a number. These three cells complete the specification of the interface section of the macro.

MACRO BODY. The cell entries between the macro interface discussed earlier and the macro return described next form the macro body. Entries appearing in the macro body describe how to solve the subproblem. They may also call on other macro procedures. In our example there is only one entry. Entry A4 defines the formula used to compute the area of a rectangle expressed in terms of the parameters *length* and *width* (i.e., *=length*width*).

MACRO RETURN. The final entry in cell A5 in the *AreaofRectangle* procedure is required for each macro procedure definition. This cell contains the RETURN function. The RETURN function tells Excel that all the statements in this procedure have been completed. Because a cell reference of A4 is contained as an argument of the RETURN function, the value computed from length*width will become the data object value of the cell invoking the *AreaofRectangle* procedure.

DEFINING MACRO NAMES. Before any macro procedure can be executed, it is necessary to define its name to Excel as being a macro procedure name. The *Define Name* option of the **Formula** menu is used for this purpose.

The actual form of the dialog box is shown in Figure 19.25. Note that there are two options available, a function macro and command macro. Any macro that returns a value as its purpose should be defined as a function macro. In this example, cell A1 of the macrosheet was selected before the *Define Name* option was chosen. Excel shows the macro procedure name and the absolute address of the cell containing this name. It is now only necessary to choose *OK*.

Once the name of the function macro has been defined it appears as one of the possible functions available in the *Paste Function* option of the **Formula** menu. Note that macro defined functions appear at the end of the list after the Excel built-in functions.

INVOKING A MACRO. The formula bar of Figure 19.24 shows how cell A3 of the worksheet entitled *Worksheet1* calls upon the previously defined macro procedure *AreaofRectangle* to compute a value. Note here that the name of the macro procedure is referenced in the worksheet. However, the name of the procedure is preceded by *Macro!*, as shown in the formula bar.

As discussed earlier, whenever a spreadsheet references cells from another spreadsheet or macrosheet it is necessary to indicate the name of the different

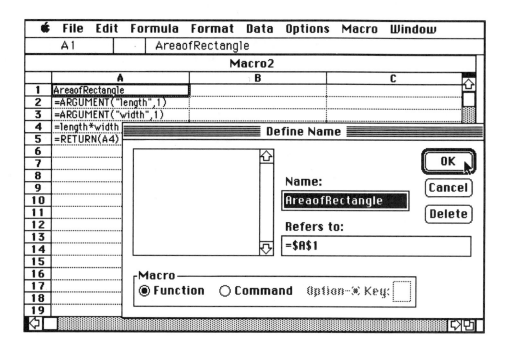

Figure 19.25 Defining a macro name to Excel.

spreadsheet and the location of the cell of interest. In Excel this is done by typing the sheet name, followed by an exclamation point, followed by the name of the cell or its cell coordinates. We also have provided values for the two arguments of the *Areaofrectangle* procedure values in its invocation in the spreadsheet.

Thus, the value associated with the first parameter named *length* is 4 and the value of the second parameter named *width* is 5. Consequently, we find the value of 20 displayed by cell A3 of the worksheet, as expected.

SHIPPING COST EXAMPLE. The purpose of this example procedure is to compute shipping cost. Let's call this macro *Shippingcost*. The choice of name is *yours* to determine.

To compute the shipping charges we require information. We know that the shipping charges depend upon the weight (say in pounds) of the package. This will be one argument. The charges also depend upon the carrier to be used for shipping, whether by land, sea, or air. Let us define, as per Paul Revere, 1 to mean by land, 2 to mean by sea, and 3 to mean by air. Then the second argument for this macro procedure will be a number—1, 2, or 3—to indicate which means of shipping is to be used. (Let us assume here for simplicity that the charges are independent of the distance shipped.) Once values for both the weight and carrier have been specified, we can compute the shipping cost.

Again we must construct the interface section for this new macro. In Figure 19.26 we show a macrosheet named *Macro1* that was obtained as discussed in our earlier example. In cell A1 we again enter the macro name. In the next two rows in this column we define the arguments of the procedure. Note that the first argument of *Shippingcost* has been given the name *weightinpounds*. Its data type has been defined as 1—meaning its value must be a number. The second argument of *Shippingcost* has been given the name *carriertype* and has a data type of 1. These cells complete the interface section of the macro procedure.

Cell A4 in the body of this macro calls on a built-in function of Excel that performs a look-up on a column-organized table. The information given to this function consists of the value we wish to find in the first column of the table, the location of the table expressed as an array reference, and the column number whose contents are associated with the value in the first column and whose value is to be returned. Thus, in our example because the name *weightinpounds* has a value that is being used as the independent variable with which to look up an associated shipping cost, this name is made the first parameter of the VLOOKUP function.

A table has been entered in the locations B3:E10 on the macrosheet, and it becomes the second parameter. The last parameter of the VLOOKUP function specifies which column the associated value is to be selected from. The columns are counted, with 1 being the independent variable column. The column number to be used clearly depends upon the *carriertype* argument of the *Shippingcost* procedure. When the carrier type is 1, 2, or 3, the value selected from the table should be in column 2, 3, or 4, respectively, because, as noted, the independent variable column is always counted as 1 in the VLOOKUP function. After the VLOOKUP function has found the value in the table, we can imagine that cell A4 of the *macro1* sheet contains the value.

The final statement in the *Shippingcost* procedure serves the same purpose as in our previous example. Because a cell reference to A4 is contained as a parameter of the RETURN function, the value found in looking up in the table becomes the value of the cell calling up the *Shippingcost* procedure. As in the earlier example, it is necessary to define the name as being a macro procedure name. To perform this operation, we follow the same steps as discussed for the *AreaofRectangle* macro.

Finally, the upper part of Figure 19.26 shows how cell A1 of the worksheet entitled *worksheet macro call example* calls upon the previously defined macro procedure *Shippingcost* to compute a value. The value associated with the first parameter, named *weightinpounds*, is 3, and the value of the second parameter, named *carriertype*, is also 3. When the table look-up is performed, we should look down the column containing the weight until we find the value 3. Then we should read across this row until we find the cost column for air shipping. We should then return this value of 3.5 to the cell A1 in the worksheet. You will note that the value contained in cell A1 of the worksheet is indeed 3.5.

We make the following observations in closing this section. Not only can worksheet cells invoke procedures in a macrosheet just as they can invoke built-in functions in Excel, but *macrosheet cells* can also call on other procedures. Thus, one procedure can call upon any other procedure or group of procedures to solve its required subproblems. Consequently, a very complicated problem can be solved by building up the solution using many simple independent procedures working together.

This is exactly the way programmers solve complicated problems in a programming language. Thus, many of the concepts that must be learned to write macros are the same as those required to write solutions to problems in a programming language. As soon as you begin to tell the computer *how* to solve the problem, the level of complexity becomes substantially greater. With this additional control comes much greater complexity that requires a deeper understanding of how the computer operates.

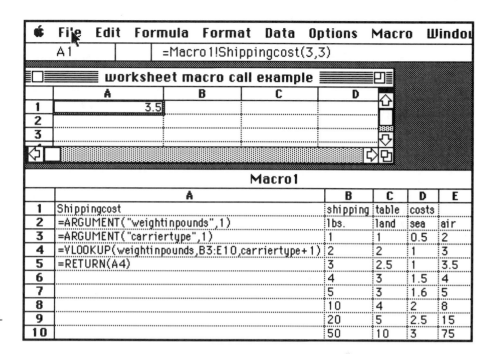

Figure 19.26 Example *Shippingcost* macro.

Exercise Set 19.5

1. Define the term *macro procedure*.
2. How does a macrosheet differ from a worksheet in Excel?
3. Explain why you would want to define a macro procedure.
4. What steps are necessary to create a macro procedure in Excel?
5. Write down the instructions that you would need to use to define a macro procedure to compute the area of a square.

Computer Practice 19.5

1. Construct the *AreaofRectangle* macro procedure.
2. Construct the *Shippingcost* macro procedure.
3. Develop your own macro procedure to compute the volume of a cylinder.

Key Concepts

Array	Built-in function
Chart operations	Comparison criteria
Computed criteria	Database built-in functions
Extract operation	Find operation
Macro procedure	Macrosheet
One-input table	Paste Formula operation
Paste Name operation	Set Criteria operation
Set Database operation	Spreadsheet database
Structured object	Table operation
Two-input table	

EXPLORING COMPUTER GENERATED SOUND, MUSIC, AND ANIMATION

L E A R N I N G   O B J E C T I V E S

- To discover that today's microcomputers can process information so rapidly that they can record and play back sounds, including speech and music, take pictures, and produce graphical animation.

- To gain insight into how computer interfaces convert information sensed in the real world into digitized values that can be processed by the computer.

- To gain insight into the process by which digital information processed by the computer can be output in a form that can be sensed by a human being.

- To learn about the concept of a virtual world in which the computer generates the sensory data received by the human being, thus supplementing the normal environment as a source of sensory information.

I n this chapter you will learn that computers can be used to process information other than the textual, pictorial, or numerical types that we have previously discussed. In effect, computers can simulate for presentation to the human senses certain elements of the natural environment itself. You will learn about the process of analog-to-digital conversion that is used to convert information from the real world into digital values that the computer can process. Through this process the computer can sense and interpret its environment. The inverse process, digital-to-analog conversion, allows digital values within the computer to control elements directly in the physical environment surrounding the computer. You will examine some activities, such as speech or music generation and animation, where real-time computation, using both analog-to-digital and digital-to-analog conversion processes, is important. You will gain an overview of how several different software packages have been constructed to allow you to participate in these activities.

20.1 VIRTUAL COMPUTER WORLDS

As you have learned, the computer provides the user with a variety of language contexts, each of which promotes the illusion that the computer *is that context*. By coupling outputs of the computer to the human sensory perceptors, it is possible to create the illusion of worlds that simulate aspects of the physical environment. Indeed, it is possible to simulate environments that have *no physical analog outside of the computer*.

The degree of the coupling to the human senses may be very primitive, such as when CRT screens supply visual stimuli and stereo speakers provide auditory stimuli. In the future the interface may be much more sophisticated, with more direct coupling between the computer and the sensory centers of the brain.

Today it is possible to have a computer generate stereoscopic views of a scene that when observed by the viewer give the impression of being inside the scene, similar to that obtained in a 3D movie. However, these scenes are interactive in that they change as the viewer's head turns or as the viewer "walks" about in the scene. In addition, the viewer can "reach" into the perceived three-dimensional scene and "touch," receiving tactile feedback about objects in the scene through special gloves controlled by the computer. In other words, the viewer can explore the world created by the computer in ways similar to those used to explore the *real* world.

Worlds having their existence only in a computer are called **virtual worlds**. Clearly, the "realness" of such virtual worlds will increase as technology improves, and they will become increasingly difficult to distinguish from the real world. Through such simulations we increasingly will be able to treat the imagined as real. The ramifications of such virtual worlds are of considerable philosophical interest, but a discussion of them is beyond the scope of this text. You are encouraged to read more about this concept. In this chapter, we examine the elements of producing some very primitive virtual worlds that interact with our visual and auditory senses.

Exercise Set 20.1

1. Write an essay about the differences between the real world and virtual worlds discussed in this section. Try to imagine some thought experiments that would let you determine if your brain's sensory center was directly wired to a computer, or if the world you are currently experiencing is the real world rather than an imagined world.

2. Read Plato's *Allegory of the Man and the Cave* and contrast with the virtual-world concept as discussed earlier.

20.2 CONVERTING INFORMATION BETWEEN ANALOG AND DIGITAL FORM

TRANSDUCERS. Information about the environment is sensed by the human nervous system through **transducers**. Transducers transform energy in one form into another form. For example, when we hear sounds, the form of this information comes to us from pressure variations in the air around us. Our ears convert these pressure variations into neural signals that are processed by the brain. Thus, our ears are transducers that convert the pressure variations, one form of energy, into electrical potentials, another form of energy, used by the brain. In a similar manner, light intensity is converted to neural signals by our eyes. Thus, our eyes are transducers for converting light energy into electrical potentials used by the brain. Each different human neural sense receptor behaves as a transducer converting a given type of energy into a neural signal that can be processed by the brain.

Man-made transducers also exist to convert many of the forms of energy as sensed by the human sensual receptors into electrical signals that can be used by a variety of devices including a computer. For example, a microphone is a transducer that converts pressure variations such as sound into electrical potentials that can be sent along a telephone wire or into a computer. A television camera is a transducer that converts light intensity into electrical potentials that can be used by a television set or by a computer. In fact, there are transducers that convert information such as temperature and even chemical structure (smell and taste to the human senses) to electrical potentials.

ANALOG-TO-DIGITAL CONVERSION. Before any electrical potential can be used by a computer it must be converted into a digital value, that is, a grouping of bits that collectively represents the value of the electrical signal. The number of bits taken together to represent the value determines how accurately a given value can be represented. This point is important for the following reason. Electrical potentials that are produced by a **transducer**, such as a microphone, are continuous. Thus, an electrical potential can assume any value between its minimum and maximum values. In contrast, as soon as the number of bits to represent a value is specified, only a finite number of different values is possible. The transformation between a continuous range, such as the electrical potentials output from a microphone to a discrete set of values, such as those used by a computer, is called **analog-to-digital conversion**. Devices to perform this transformation are called *analog-to-digital converters* (ADCs).

Consider, for example, using 2 bits of information to represent the electrical potential produced from a microphone - amplifier unit. (Microphones generally produce very small electrical potentials and are coupled with amplifiers to increase [amplify] the range of electrical potentials they produce.) Because 2 bits are grouped together, four different patterns of 1s and 0s are possible. We can assign each distinct pattern of 2 bits to a given range of the electrical potential.

To illustrate the preceding concept further, assume that the electrical potential from the microphone/amplifier unit can vary from -5 volts to 5 volts. (Volts are units used to measure electrical potential.) Using 2 bits, the interval from -5 to 5 volts can be broken down into four ranges, where each range is (5-(-5))/4 = 2.5 volts in extent. Assignment of these ranges is arbitrary but could be chosen as shown in Figure 20.1. Here bit pattern 00 is used to indicate a voltage from -5 to less than -2.5; bit pattern 01 indicates a voltage from -2.5 to less than 0, and so on. Note, then, that when the 2-bit ADC gives a value of 00, we know that the voltage is between -5.0 and -2.5 volts, but we cannot tell more precisely than that what it was! Once the analog-to-digital conversion has been completed, we are left only with the bit pattern of the result. Thus, the *precision* with which the voltage is represented by our bit pattern is determined by the number of bits grouped together.

In the preceding example, we could improve the precision of our digital result by using more bits to represent each voltage value. Typical ADCs use from 8 to 12 bits. For an 8-bit ADC, 256 different bit patterns would be possible, and in our earlier example, each interval would represent approximately 0.0391 volts, as opposed to the preceding 2.5-volt intervals. For a 12-bit ADC, 4096 bit patterns would be possible, and each interval would be approximately 0.00244 volts. Choice of the precision to be used depends upon the cost of the ADC interface and

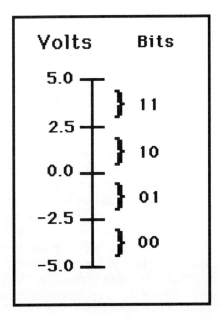

Figure 20.1 Four voltage ranges from a 2-bit ADC.

amount of memory. The larger the number of bits, the higher the cost of the ADC. Also, as we shall see shortly, processing speech and music can require very large amounts of memory.

Current versions of the Macintosh do not contain ADCs. However, a number of companies manufacture interfaces consisting of hardware and software systems that will allow the Macintosh owner to convert analog signals to digital values for computer processing. In the next section we discuss the MacRecorder™ hardware and software system, which allows speech and music to be converted into digital form and subsequently processed.

SAMPLING RATE. Another aspect of analog-to-digital conversion is the rate at which measurements of time-varying analog signals are taken. This rate is called the **sampling rate** and is expressed as the number of measurements (of a quantity such as pressure) per second. To illustrate this point clearly, consider that the sounds that we hear as music are variations in pressure as a function of time. The pressure increases for a time and then decreases, moving our ear drum back and forth in sequence. The precise nature of the variation with time allows us to distinguish different instruments, voices, and so forth. To reproduce an instrument or a voice accurately it is necessary not only to have values digitized precisely, as discussed earlier, but also to have enough values to allow the time variation of the phenomenon being sampled to be faithfully reproduced.

In the upper curve of Figure 20.2 is shown an example of the way a parameter such as pressure (as transduced by a microphone) might vary with time over a short interval. Note that the variation with time is continuous. There are no jumps from one value to the next. The digitally sampled curve is shown in the middle graph of Figure 20.2 superimposed on top of the original signal.

Over the time interval shown, 13 samples of the signal have been taken. The times at which the sampling has been performed are shown by the dark vertical lines in the figure. When a time-varying signal is sampled, the continuous variation is "frozen" at a particular time and converted into a bit pattern to represent the value at the time of the sample. The horizontal line at each sample time indicates a digitized value that is constant *over the sample time interval*. Then at a later time the signal value is again frozen and converted into another bit pattern. Consequently, the continuous signal is ultimately represented by a list of bit patterns, each representing a value of the signal at a selected time.

We emphasize that the digital values that represent the signal are constant over the duration of a sample interval. Thus, in Figure 20.2, the short, horizontal lines are the constant digital value assigned for the duration of the sample time. Therefore, the continuous variation of the signal is replaced by discrete jumps in value in the digital representation of the signal, as shown in Figure 20.2. Note, however, that as the sampling rate is increased, the time between samples becomes shorter (the vertical lines in Figure 20.2 become closer together) and the digital representation more closely approximates the original signal.

Analog-to-digital converters not only have a given number of bits of precision associated with them, but also have a maximum sampling rate. Typical ADCs take from 1000 to 250,000 samples per second. Some can sample over a 100 million times a second. As both the sampling speed and number of bits of precision increases, so does the cost of the ADC. Also note that at a sampling rate of 250,000 samples per second if the size of each sample is 1 byte, then the *entire*

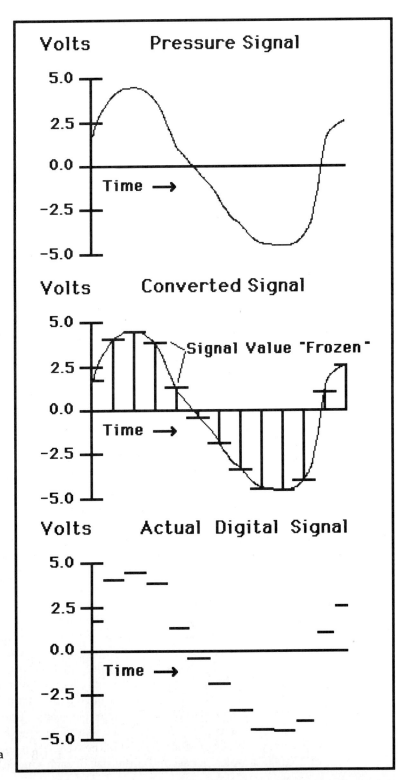

Figure 20.2 Digitization of a pressure signal.

memory of a standard Macintosh Plus or SE is used in only four seconds of sampling. This is not very much music or speech information. In general, then, digital sampling represents a compromise between the number of bits used for each sample and the number of samples taken per second.

FREQUENCY.   A natural question to ask is, "What is the slowest sampling rate that can be used?" Clearly, the slowest rate at which sampling can be performed depends upon how fast the signal changes. Considered from the perspective of a signal, a note or tone is simply a repeating or cyclical variation of the pressure as a function of time. Figure 20.2 shows an example of one cycle of a variation of a given note. If our ear was acted on by the pressure variation produced by repeating this signal over and over again, it would sound very much like a single note struck on a piano. The *pitch* of the note would be determined by how many repetitions of this cycle occurred in one second. For example, A above middle C on the piano is equivalent to having 440 of these cycles occur in one second. Humans can hear as high as approximately 20,000 such cycles per second. The number of cycles per second is called the **frequency**. Frequency is measured in units of Hertz, where a Hertz is one cycle per second. Thus, the A note discussed earlier has a frequency of 440 Hertz.

NYQUIST FREQUENCY.   To obtain reasonable fidelity it is necessary to sample at a frequency that is at least twice as large as the highest frequency present in the signal to be sampled. The sample frequency (measured in the units of number of samples taken per second) that is twice as high as the highest frequency present in the signal is called the **Nyquist frequency**. Thus, if a music piece had no notes higher than A above middle C, then sampling at a rate of 880 times per second should produce reasonable fidelity. Increasing the sample rate could of course improve the fidelity, however, by making the digital approximation follow the actual signal more closely. Sampling at the Nyquist frequency removes a kind of distortion called **aliasing**. If a given signal is sampled at a rate below its Nyquist frequency, aliasing causes those frequencies present in the actual signal that are *above* half the sample frequency to be included improperly as lower-frequency components in the digitized signal, thus distorting it.

A well-used example of aliasing is observed in western movies, where wagon wheels often appear to rotate opposite to the direction of the wagon motion. This occurs because the rate at which the movie camera shutter operates is slower than twice the rate at which the spokes in a wagon wheel pass a given point. In other words, the camera samples at a frequency below the Nyquist frequency for the spokes in the wheel and produces distortion in the frequency at which the spokes appear to be moving.

FILTERING.   To avoid the effects of aliasing while at the same time providing a slower sample rate, it is often possible to remove the higher-frequency components from a given signal. The process of transforming a signal such as that just described, where certain frequency components are selectively altered, is called **filtering**. Filters can be attached to microphones or other sources of electronic signals to alter the resultant signal output. When using an ADC it is often necessary to apply a *low-pass* filter—a filter that has the property of attenuating (removing) frequencies higher than a given value from the signal. This upper-limit frequency is often called the *cutoff frequency*. By removing the frequencies higher than the cutoff frequency, the signal can be sampled at a lower rate and not produce the distortion associated with aliasing. However, if the cutoff frequency is set too low, then important information in the signal also can be attenuated and the signal will no longer have good fidelity.

DIGITAL-TO-ANALOG CONVERSION.   The process of converting digital values back into analog signals is called **digital-to-analog conversion**. Through this process the computer can directly control or modify its environment. Devices to perform this conversion are called digital-to-analog converters (DACs). Built into all the Macintosh computers except the Mac II is a single 8-bit DAC. This DAC controls the internal speaker in the Macintosh and can also be connected to an external amplifier and speaker system through a plug located on the back of the computer. (The Mac II contains two 8-bit DACs and can be used to produce stereo sounds with an external stereo system.) Thus, digital information contained in the computer can be manipulated and "played back" by the computer. In this sense, then, any signal that can be acquired by an ADC can be edited much as text might be edited in a word processing document and then played back using the built-in DAC in the Macintosh. If the signal output by the computer is to represent faithfully the signal originally digitized, then the rate of sampling and the rate of playing back must be the same.

The DAC built into the Macintosh can be written to at a maximum frequency of approximately 22 kiloHertz. (*Kilo* means "thousand"; thus, there are about 22,000 sample values written out per second to the DAC.) Because of the Nyquist frequency limitation, this means that sounds having a frequency of up to about 11,000 cycles per second can be generated. Although this frequency is substantially below the upper range of 20,000 Hertz that humans can hear, some very impressive music and voice can be generated by the Macintosh.

We note in closing this section that the human ear is capable of resolving music within about 12 bits of precision. This is the same precision used by digital audio compact disk players for audio recording. Although the Macintosh DAC has only 8 bits of precision, the sounds emitted generally have good fidelity.

Exercise Set 20.2

1.   If a signal is sampled by an ADC at 10,000 samples per second, at what rate should the digital values be output to a DAC to reproduce the same signal? What is the highest frequency that can be present in the signal and not produce aliasing? Explain.

2.   If a human voice is sampled by an ADC at 10,000 samples per second and then subsequently written back to a DAC at 20,000 values per second, describe the change in the sound of the voice that would occur.

3.   If an 8-bit ADC is used to sample a given signal will it improve the fidelity of the output if a 12-bit DAC is used to play the signal back? Explain.

4.   Given that the human ear can hear frequencies as high as 20,000 Hertz, what would be the lowest sample rate needed for an ADC used to create compact disks for your musical enjoyment? Do research to find out what sample rate actually is used in making compact disks.

5.   Using the values shown in Figure 20.2 for a hypothetical pressure signal, construct the result that would be produced by a 2-bit ADC at the same sample rate as shown in the figure.

6. Double the sample rate over that shown in Figure 20.2 and see what effect this would have on the digital approximation to the original signal. Assume that you have a 4-bit ADC. Show your result by constructing a graph similar to that shown in the lower part of Figure 20.2

7. How many bytes would be required to store on a compact disk an entire rock concert that lasts three hours when the ADC used has a sample rate of 30,000 samples per second with 12 bits of precision? How many Macintosh floppy disks would this require?

20.3 USING MACRECORDER

In this section we describe briefly a hardware and software product called MacRecorder that will illustrate many of the concepts we have discussed earlier in this chapter. We note that our brief discussion cannot cover all the features found in MacRecorder. To appreciate fully the advantages that derive from sound processing, you need to experience firsthand a software package such as that we describe here.

MacRecorder contains as hardware a microphone, a low-pass filter, an amplifier, and an 8-bit ADC. In addition, the tape output signal from an external amplifier can be plugged into the ADC interface. The MacRecorder hardware itself plugs into the modem port or printer port of the Macintosh. A wide variety of input signals ranging from voice to music can be sampled easily. (Other signals properly amplified can also input to this inexpensive ADC as well. Future scientists take note!)

The low-pass filter has a cutoff frequency of 11,000 Hertz to prevent aliasing, as discussed earlier. The sample rate from the ADC can be set at 22,000, 11,000, 7000, or 5000 samples per second. (Note that a sample from the MacRecorder ADC is 1 byte; thus, samples per second translate to bytes per second.) To avoid aliasing at the lower sampling rates, software filtering of the signal is applied. The maximum sample rate of 22,000 bytes per second matches the maximum rate obtainable from the DAC installed already in the Macintosh as discussed earlier. The DAC output rate can be controlled by the software to match the slower sample rates as required.

Two software components are available in MacRecorder—HyperSound™ and SoundEdit™. HyperSound is designed to allow voice and music output when executing inside the Macintosh HyperCard system. SoundEdit is a stand-alone component used without the HyperCard system. We shall focus on it in the following discussion. SoundEdit provides a wide variety of options to allow you to input digitized information into the computer, manipulate it, and play it back.

The use of a computer to control the motion of a loudspeaker to generate music is an example of real-time computing. **Real-time computing** refers to the processing of information so that the results can be used to control events as they occur in the surrounding environment. In many instances of real-time computing, the speed at which the computer operates is critical. Clearly, if a computer takes one second to compute each value of a group of successive values, it will not be very useful for generating music when several tens of thousands of computations of these values are required per second!

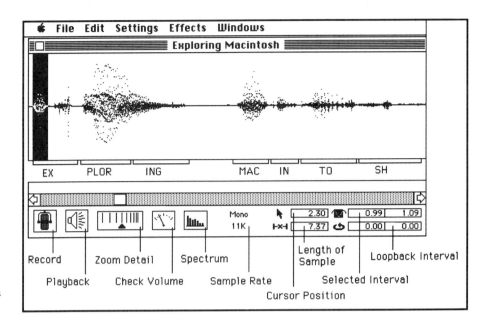

Figure 20.3 Sample screen from SoundEdit.

A sample screen of SoundEdit is shown in Figure 20.3. At the bottom of the screen a number of different icons appear that allow you to select several different options for interacting with the MacRecorder system.

The *Microphone* icon in the bottom left of the figure is selected when you want to convert a signal into digital form. The length of time that is available for recording depends upon the amount of free memory available in your computer. Once the operating system, Finder, and SoundEdit have been loaded into the RAM of a 1-Megabyte Macintosh, there is enough memory for approximately a 30-second recording when using the 22,000-byte-per-second sample rate. Proportionally greater durations of time are available at the lower sample rates, although at a sacrifice in fidelity, as discussed earlier.

The upper portion of Figure 20.3 shows an actual signal recorded using the MacRecorder digitizer hardware and SoundEdit. The signal was produced by speaking the words *Exploring Macintosh* into the microphone. The sample rate employed was 11,000 bytes per second. This sample rate was found to reproduce a very-high-fidelity rendition of the words *Exploring Macintosh* when played back. The form used for displaying this signal is analogous to that in Figure 20.2. The vertical axis represents the pressure (i.e., its digital value) as measured by the microphone, and the horizontal axis is time.

Below the signal we have added annotations to the figure that show the actual letter combinations that correspond to each part of the signal. SoundEdit allows the user to select by dragging any contiguous group of digitized values and then to play them back. The highlighted part at the left side of the figure was chosen in this way. If the *Speaker* icon is clicked with the portion of the signal selected as shown in Figure 20.3, then the sound of EX in EXPLORING will be heard. If no region is selected then the entire recorded signal is played back.

Actually, a very large number of points is shown in this graph. The density of the points obscures the underlying variations that are actually present in the signal. To expand the scale so that the full detail of the signal can be seen, use is

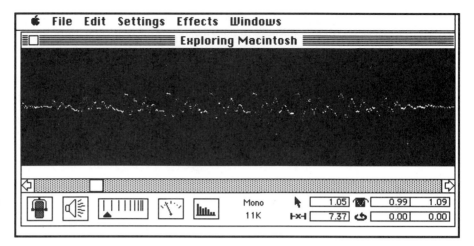

Figure 20.4 Expanded view of the selected portion of the signal in Figure 20.3.

made of the *Zoom Detail* icon. By dragging the Zoom pointer to the left, the scale can be expanded. In Figure 20.4 we show the result of expanding the scale so that the highlighted area in Figure 20.3 fills the screen horizontally. Examination of this figure shows the actual form of the digitized signal. Any portion of the signal can be so examined.

Note that editing of the sound signal is performed just as you would with text. By dragging over an area you can select *Copy* or *Cut* operations from the **Edit** menu. Either will place the selected data on the Clipboard. You can then position the insertion pointer anywhere in the signal and select *Paste*. The data will be inserted at that position. In this way you can construct a wide variety of special sounds of interest to you.

Other features available are the *Check Volume* icon and the *Spectrum* icon. The *Check Volume* icon allows you to monitor the level of the sound and to adjust the level until appropriate. The *Spectrum* icon can be selected to show how large a contribution different frequency intervals make to the signal being monitored. One use of this latter feature is to show you what sample rate you need to use for a given signal.

As indicated earlier, the sample rate can be selected from four different values. By clicking in the sample rate area a dialog box will be presented that allows a choice of the sample rate. Also shown will be an indication of the length of time available to record at that sample rate. It is also possible to select a special data compression mode for storage of sampled data. In this mode some fidelity is lost but only one eighth as much data is stored, and thus much longer samples can be obtained. This mode is primarily used for speech signals.

Available from the menu bar are some additional features that are too numerous to discuss fully here. However, to give you some indication about what can be done, we will mention several. There are options to reverse the signal (play it backward), add an echo, pass the signal through a filter you specify (just like a stereo equalizer), and mix up to four different signals together.

In this section we have discussed sound at a relatively primitive level—that associated directly with the acquisition and manipulation of digital values that represent the actual air pressure variations produced. In the next section we examine a higher-level view of sound in which we consider sheet music editing, the defining of instrument sounds, and the playing of musical works by groups of instruments.

20.4 USING CONCERTWARE+MIDI FOR MUSIC COMPOSING AND PERFORMANCE

It is our purpose in this section to describe briefly one of a number of different programs that allow the user to compose and edit music. These programs make composing and editing music as accessible as a word processor makes composing and editing written materials. The example program discussed is ConcertWare+MIDI. This software package consists of three components: the Music Player, the Music Writer, and the InstrumentMaker. Each component has a function that can be deduced easily from its name. Note that our discussion by necessity must be brief. ConcertWare+MIDI has many more features than we can possibly discuss in one section of one chapter. Finally, although we discuss many concepts in this section, you must hear the music generated by the computer to fully appreciate working in this medium.

Output of music from ConcertWare+MIDI can use the DAC built into the Macintosh as discussed in previous sections of this chapter. Thus, music can be played on the internal speaker or, alternatively, on headphones or an amplifier system plugged into the DAC output jack on the back of the Macintosh case. These latter two options are preferable for achieving high fidelity. In addition, a MIDI interface can be connected to either the modem or printer ports and the music output to a wide variety of music synthesizers and drum machines that accept MIDI-compatible signals. (Recall from Chapter 2 that MIDI is a standard interface that allows electronic instruments to be connected together.)

Input of notes can come directly from a MIDI-compatible keyboard instrument or from the Macintosh keyboard or the mouse, as we shall see later. Note that unlike the MacRecorder system, ConcertWare+MIDI does not perform direct analog-to-digital conversion of the pressure variations of the sound for input purposes. Instead, parameters such as the pitch, duration, and key-press velocity are associated with each note as it is played, and these parameters are digitally encoded for use by the computer. Such encoding of the music allows very long pieces of music to be stored in a very small amount of RAM or disk space as compared with the direct digitization of the pressure variations.

MUSIC WRITER.   The Music Writer component of ConcertWare+MIDI allows you to enter, edit, play, and print music. A sample screen for Music Writer is shown in Figure 20.5. The piece of music is *The Entertainer* by Scott Joplin. This screen allows the entry of music notation conveniently using the mouse. In the center of the screen are shown measures 19 - 21 of the piece. Four voices are shown and can be played simultaneously using the built-in DAC. If a MIDI interface is used, up to eight voices can be played simultaneously, dependent on the MIDI synthesizer. Editing takes place one voice at a time. The voice currently active is shown by the highlighted number in the upper left part of the screen. In Figure 20.5, voice 1 is the one being edited. Clicking in a voice number box makes that voice active.

Below the current voice selection area is a box labeled *Show Voice Above*. When selected, this option will cause the active voice to be displayed on a staff

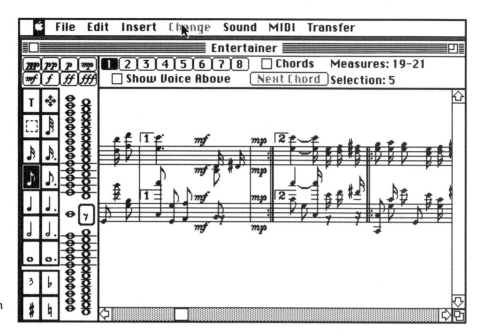

Figure 20.5 Example screen from Music Writer.

directly above the full-display the current score shown. Note in the full score display that repeats with first and second endings are entered in the score. These are shown in standard music notation with the colon and repeat bars. In addition, loudness indicators, such as *pp, mf, ff,* and so on, can be entered directly in the score and influence its playing. Looking closely at Figure 20.5, you will see the presence of slurs shown as a curved line connecting two notes and accidentals with a sharp (#) symbol preceding them. Although it is not our intention to teach musical notation, it is important to see from this display that a very full range of music composition features are present in the Music Writer component.

The active voice is edited in a variety of ways. In the simplest but most time-consuming mode, the user can use the mouse to enter notes and chords. Editing on the music staff functions just like word processing. The insertion pointer can be positioned by clicking. Where notes are to be replaced, dragging can be used to indicate the range selected. The length of note to be entered can be selected from the palette of notes on the left edge of the screen by clicking over the desired length. The pitch of the note is selected on the desired position within the staff palette just to the right of the length of notes. Accidental sharps, flats, or natural indications can also be selected from the palette in the lower left-hand corner. Lyrics can be added where desired using the *T* option in the upper left-hand corner. In beginning a piece the key signature can be set, as well as the tempo. Tempo changes can be set throughout the piece.

More elegant entry and editing of the score is possible for accomplished musicians. Under the **Sound** menu is the option *Record* that allows music to be entered directly from a keyboard attached to the MIDI interface. Consequently, the user can play the piece and have the computer produce the music score *in sheet music form* from the performance. Before entering the notes input in this way into the score, the user can hear the captured notes by selecting the *Play* option under the **Sound** menu. While useful for some purposes, the editing by *Record* option is not a panacea for all music entry, largely because timing for note intervals is not captured as accurately as would be desirable. Also under the **Sound** menu is the option to *Set Instruments*. Thus, a given voice can be associated with a particular instrument available either in the instrument library to be discussed later or on your MIDI synthesizer.

MUSIC PLAYER.   Once a score has been constructed, the Music Player component of ConcertWare+MIDI can be used to play the completed score. Figure 20.6 shows the form of the Music Player screen.

The Music Player in ConcertWare+MIDI provides an option to play the composition either on the DAC contained within the Macintosh or on a MIDI synthesizer connected to the modem or printer ports of the computer. When the *MIDI* option is checked under the **MIDI** menu, the output is directed to the MIDI interface; this is the default mode. By clicking on the *MIDI* option the checkmark will disappear and the output will be directed to the DAC. Clicking in this manner switches back and forth between these output modes.

When the DAC is used, only four voices can be played simultaneously. For this reason voices numbered 5 to 8 are shown dimmed in Figure 20.6. An X in a voice box indicates that that voice is to be played. By clicking in the box the voice can be turned on or off. Thus, any combination of voices can be heard. The tempo is selected by scrolling in the scroll bar showing the tortoise (slower) and the hare (faster). To the left of the tempo scroll bar is shown the current part of the piece being played. The form of the information presented is analogous to a player piano roll, in which the vertical position of a line shows the pitch of the note and the length of the line is the duration. The vertical line shows the current position of the music as it is played. The loudness of the sound when using the DAC is controlled by the scroll bar showing different-sized notes. The larger note is loudest; the smaller is most quiet.

In the middle of the screen is shown information about the instruments used in playing the piece. To the left and right are shown icons of pianos each outlined

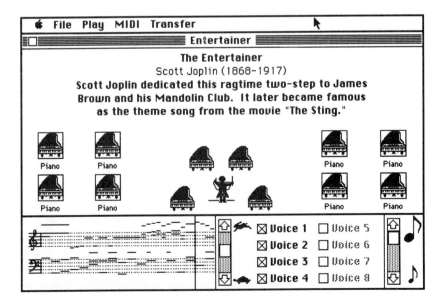

Figure 20.6 Sample screen from the Music Player.

in a square. These icons show the type of instruments that are defined in the score for the eight different possible voices. For the Entertainer only four voices are used in the score, and each one is a piano. For a symphonic piece, the instrument mix might include a violin, oboe, flute, and so forth. Surrounding the conductor are the distinct four voices that can be played on the DAC or certain other synthesizers at one time, even though more than four voices appear in the piece. Some synthesizers allow all eight voices to be played simultaneously.

The instruments actually used for playing the composition can be altered from those initially specified in Music Writer. By double-clicking in the square surrounding the icon of the instrument you wish to change, a dialog box will appear that shows the list of instruments available in the instrument library. You can scroll through this list to find the appropriate instrument. By double-clicking on this instrument its sound will replace the sound of the original instrument in the piece. One of the instruments available in the ConcertWare instrument library is the faucet drip. (It is certainly interesting, if not abhorrent, to hear one of Bach's fugues played on a dripping faucet—or the conga drum, for that matter!)

INSTRUMENTMAKER.   The final component of ConcertWare+MIDI that we discuss is the InstrumentMaker. This component allows the user to define new instruments that can be output on the DAC of the Macintosh. Many music synthesizers provide a similar capability. Reproduction of music sounds differs from general sound because instruments produce their sound by vibration (i.e., a repetition of a given set of pressure variations). As a result it is somewhat easier to characterize an instrument than to characterize general sounds. In fact, as we noted earlier, the basic elements are the pitch, duration, and keyboard velocity (loudness). There are a number of more subtle parameters that can change from one instrument to another, however, and these are the parameters that we can control in the InstrumentMaker.

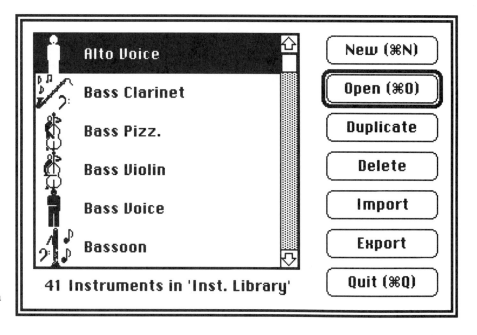

Figure 20.7 Opening screen of the InstrumentMaker.

An example screen when the InstrumentMaker is started is shown in Figure 20.7. The options are to create a new instrument, edit an existing instrument's parameters, duplicate an instrument to experiment with its parameters, import an instrument from another disk, and export an existing instrument to an instrument file. For this example we will open an existing instrument, the alto voice shown highlighted in the figure.

Opening the *Alto Voice* instrument produces the screen shown in Figure 20.8. In this screen the mouse can be used to choose a wide variety of parameters to alter the sounds produced when the instrument is played.

DESIGNING INSTRUMENT TIMBRE. At the right of Figure 10.8 is a graph of the pressure variation as a function of time that the instrument produces. Because musical instruments produce sounds that are periodic in time (i.e., they are vibrating objects that repeat their motion over and over again), the pressure variation shown can be repeatedly written out to the DAC to produce the sound of an instrument. By changing the speed at which the graph is cycled through, the pitch of the sound can be varied. (In actual fact, however, to move through the curve faster on the Macintosh, some of the points are simply skipped.) The shape of this pressure variation graph is what produces the **timbre** (tonal quality) of each different instrument. The shape can be defined by directly drawing using the pencil tool. The pencil will appear automatically if the cursor is moved into this area. Note that the function of this curve is to control the pressure variations produced by a speaker in exactly the same way that the MacRecorder system does. In fact, the MacRecorder system could be used to obtain the pressure variation of an instrument such as a trumpet. By drawing one cycle of the same pressure curve here in the InstrumentMaker and playing it, the instrument sound would become a trumpet.

There is another way to define the pressure variation curve to be used for a given instrument. In the upper left-hand corner of the screen is a box labeled

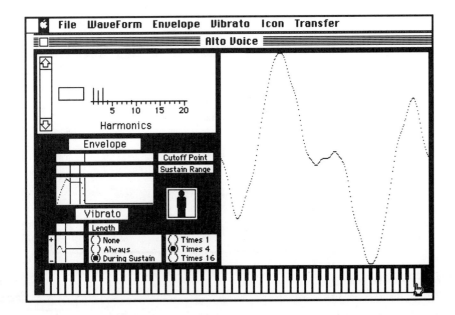

Figure 20.8 Instrument design screen for InstrumentMaker.

Harmonics. Harmonics are tones that are spaced at integer multiples of the base frequency (fundamental) of a tone. The fundamental tone for A above middle C on the piano is 440 Hertz. The first harmonic is twice the base frequency (880 Hertz), the second harmonic is three times the base frequency (1320 Hertz), and so on. It is well known from mathematics that any continuous pressure variation as a function of time for an instrument can be produced by adding together tones at different harmonic frequencies, each with a specified loudness (also called amplitude). By entering the amplitudes for each harmonic frequency, any given pressure variation curve can be constructed.

ENVELOPE DEFINITION. If the instrument as defined earlier was played with no other alteration, its sound would not be very realistic. The reason is that the intensity of the sound produced by an instrument should change through the course of time. For example, when a note is struck on a piano it first increases in loudness and then sustains the loudness at essentially a constant level until the key is released; after the key is released, the loudness level decreases. The pressure variations we have described in the previous discussion repeat in exactly the same manner each time; thus, they always have the same loudness. For this reason, to increase the realism of the sound created by the instruments we create, it is necessary to define an *envelope* that determines the loudness of the note at each instant of time as the note is played.

The loudness-controlling envelope is defined in the area of the screen labeled *Envelope*. Here three regions are defined: the attack, the sustain, and the decay of the note. The middle bar under *Envelope* is labeled *Sustain Range*. Two vertical lines appear in this bar. The position of these bars specifies where the three regions occur. The interval to the left of the first line is the attack region of the envelope. Here the sound normally increases in loudness. By drawing the shape of this portion of the envelope using the pencil tool, you can control how the loudness level increases. The interval between the two lines is the sustain region. Normally, the loudness is approximately the same in this region. Finally, to the right of the second line is the decay region for the note. Normally, the loudness level gradually lowers until no sound can be heard at all.

You can draw the way you want the loudness level to behave in each of these regions by moving the cursor into the wide bar below the *Sustain Range* bar. The cursor will then change into a pencil that will allow you to draw the desired shapes. You can also reposition the length of each region by moving the selection pointer to a line in the *Sustain Range* bar and dragging it to the left or right of its current position. Finally, the *Cutoff Point* bar is used to define when the note can no longer be heard. Position the vertical line displayed here by dragging, as done previously in the *Sustain Range* bar.

VIBRATO. As a final parameter that can be used to change an instrument's sound, InstrumentMaker provides the ability to add **vibrato** to the note. Vibrato refers to a slight wavering change in pitch that is often used in performance with wind or stringed instruments. Vibrato is added using the area of the screen labeled *Vibrato*. The + and - indicate, respectively, an increase or decrease in pitch. The *Length* bar allows the user to specify how long the vibrato duration is to be.

Experimenting with the various parameters can be very interesting. To hear the sounds produced by your instrument, you can move the cursor over the keyboard at the bottom of the screen. The cursor will change into a hand with an outstretched finger, as shown in the bottom right-hand corner of Figure 20.8. By appropriately clicking the mouse you can experience the three ranges of the note selected. Pressing down the mouse button demonstrates the attack region. Keeping the button down demonstrates the sustain region. Releasing the button demonstrates the decay and cutoff regions.

Exercise Set 20.4

1. ConcertWare+MIDI uses a different method for storing music from that of MacRecorder. Explain the nature of this difference fully and its impact on how one would use each package.

2. Explain the terms *attack*, *sustain*, and *decay* with reference to the envelope of a musical note. Why is the specification of an envelope necessary in addition to describing the pressure variation of the note?

3. If you have ConcertWare+MIDI available, contrast the envelope of the the the conga drum with that of the piano. Explain in terms of the shapes of the two different envelopes the differences in the sound obtained.

4. Explain the term *vibrato*. What aspect of a musical note does this term represent? Would you expect vibrato to be a characteristic present in the human voice? Explain.

20.5 COMPUTER IMAGING AND ANIMATION

We have discussed in Chapter 1 examples of the importance of computer graphics in visually oriented computing. We have observed in Part II that graphs and charts of data can be easily drawn using spreadsheets. In this section we want to extend the notion of computer graphics to include the production of images and the animation of images. As noted in Chapter 2, with the exception of the Macintosh II, all the members of the Macintosh line have only a single bit to control each pixel on the screen. Consequently, a pixel must be either fully white ("on") or fully dark ("off"). In a black-and-white picture of an object the brightness at a given point in the image can be drawn from a wide range of intensity values. As a result, the kinds of images that can be produced on Macintoshes other than the Mac II are somewhat limited.

In contrast, the Mac II currently uses up to 8 bits of information to determine the color and brightness (for black and white display) of a pixel. There are therefore up to 256 levels of brightness (for black and white) or 256 shades and brightnesses of color that can be displayed at each pixel location on the screen. Consequently, truer images can be produced on the Mac II screen. In fact, there are three 8-bit DACs in the Mac II that control the red, blue, and green electron guns that fire electrons into the colored phosphors on the screen and create the individual pixels on the screen. Consequently, the Mac II hardware is capable of displaying one of 256*256*256 or approximately 16 million colors at any pixel location. However, to reduce the amount of memory required to display an image on the screen, only 8 bits of information are used to control each pixel. This allows any 256 of the 16 million possible colors to be displayed at a given pixel. Many software packages for the Mac II allow the user to select the color table and thus specify which 256 colors are to be displayed at a given time.

Although images in which individual pixels change brightness are not possible on the other types of Macintoshes, it is possible to simulate brightness variations in an image on them by grouping together several pixels (say a square 4 pixels by 4 pixels in size) and turning some number of these on or off in proportion to the brightness that should appear in that area of the image. The larger the number of pixels in a square that are turned on, the brighter the region appears. Using groups of these pixels together for this purpose, however, causes some loss in the spatial resolution of the image (i.e., the image appears somewhat fuzzy). Newspapers use a similar technique called half-toning to create pictures. If you look closely at a newspaper picture, you will observe ink dots of varying sizes and densities. An example of this process is shown in Figure 20.9.

Just as music can be converted to digital form by using analog-to-digital conversion methods, image information can be captured as well. Devices such as television cameras or optical scanners are transducers that convert light intensity and/or color into electrical potentials. These electrical signals can then be converted to digital signals using ADCs. However, the sampling rate at which such converters must operate is extremely high. In fact, it takes only about 68 microseconds (a microsecond is a millionth of a second) for an electron beam to make one horizontal pass across a television screen. One complete picture is formed by scanning the beam horizontally across the screen one row at a time. Approximately 350 rows are scanned for each full image.

To avoid flicker on the screen and to make the images appear continuous to the human eye, the image must be redrawn approximately 30 times per second. If we imagine that one row of a picture is broken up into 512 pixels, each of which has 8 bits of information, then the ADC would have to be able to sample at a rate in excess of 7 million bytes per second! This sample rate is nearly 1000 times faster

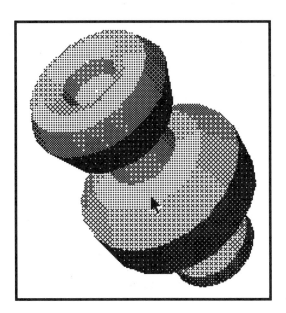

Figure 20.9 An image produced by grouping pixels to form brightness variations.

than that required for sound. Nonetheless interfaces are available that allow computers to take video pictures, and all the kinds of editing features we have discussed for sound and more can be used to manipulate computer digital images. By writing the digital values back to a DAC that controls the electron beam of a CRT, the pixels are reconstructed on the screen and the image appears.

Not only can pictures be taken, but motion of objects in a scene can occur. As noted earlier, the human eye cannot detect events that occur more rapidly than about 1/30 of a second. Consequently if a scene containing an object, such as a ball, is first drawn and then erased and redrawn in a position slightly altered from the initial position at a rate fast enough, the brain will perceive this object as moving continuously across the scene. Because the computer can modify the contents of a memory cell at an extremely high speed (several million times per second) it is possible to create real time **animation** of simple objects on the computer screen.

However, the more complex the animation, the more computer time is taken to alter the image and the slower the rate at which the objects will be able to move. Today's computers, as fast as they are, are no where near fast enough to allow animation of realistic complex scenes in real time. Computer-animated movies, such as those discussed in Chapter 1, take weeks to months of computer time to produce and are created by taking individual pictures frame by frame of computer-generated images, just as cartoons are generated by taking pictures frame by frame of hand-drawn images.

Realistic visual images involving animation are an important element in creating the virtual worlds discussed in the first section of this chapter. Today software exists to bring together images, animation, and sound on personal computers and thus allows you to experiment with creating your own virtual worlds. In this vein, it is important to note that the computer is providing the creative artist with the opportunity to work in a variety of different media at the same time. In the next section we discuss an example software package, VideoWorks II™, that provides the user with the ability to create animated images and to orchestrate animation, sound, and text together into a presentation.

Exercise Set 20.5

1. Suppose that the Macintosh II used only 4 bits to describe each pixel. How many different colors could appear at a given pixel location? Assuming that memory costs $500 per Megabyte and that the screen has a resolution of 480 X 640 pixels, how much less would it cost to store the entire screen image when compared with using 8 bits per pixel?

2. Assume that a computer screen has a resolution of 1024 X 1024 pixels and that each pixel requires 24 bits of information. At what rate, expressed in terms of bytes per second, would values have to be written to a DAC to display a new image each 1/30 of a second?

3. Estimate the rate of sampling, expressed as bytes per second, that the human visual system achieves. Assume that the resolution of the eye is 8 bits for each of the three primary colors and that there is a grid of pixels 4096 X 4096 in size in each image sampled.

4. How long would it take to fill up one 400-million-byte laser disk using the sample rate found for exercise 3? If the human brain stores its images directly,

what does this suggest to you about the storage capacity of the human brain? Do you think this is the way the brain stores images? Can you think of some alternatives?

20.6 USING VIDEOWORKS II

In the final section of this chapter we examine the software package VideoWorks II. This package can be used to develop animated presentations. VideoWorks II consists of two subsystems, called *Overview* and *VideoWorks*. The Overview subsystem can be used much like a slide show to orchestrate the presentation of text and graphics displays. In Overview, music or sound can be selected as a backdrop to slides. The VideoWorks subsystem provides tools to create animation. Animation created in VideoWorks can be merged with the general presentation scheme developed in the Overview subsystem. Thus, VideoWorks II is both a scripting tool that allows the time sequence of the presentation of information to be organized and modified and an animation construction set to produce individual animated elements that can be used alone or merged with the overall presentation sequence developed in Overview.

We note that we cannot describe fully the VideoWorks II software package in the space available. Our description, by necessity, is an overview, providing only a glimpse of what is possible. Furthermore, as noted in our discussion of sound and music, experiencing the medium directly is a must. It is simply not possible to convey the impact of animation through a text description. You should experience this medium directly, if at all possible.

The VideoWorks II software package has an excellent guided tour that uses animation (written using the VideoWorks II system) to guide the user through the use of the system. If you have access to this tour, we strongly advise you to experience it now firsthand. It will make more clear the relation of the various components available in the package.

OVERVIEW SUBSYSTEM.   Overview is an information presentation manager. In essence, it is used to create a script that describes the time sequence for the presentation of information, much in the way you would stack slides into a carrousel for a presentation. However, not only can you display computer-generated slides on the computer screen by prescribing the length of time each is displayed and designating their sequence, but you also can choose to insert electronic movie clips at any point, add existing animated elements (created using the VideoWorks subsystem discussed later) to each of the slides you are presenting, and add sound effects and a music backdrop. All of this is accomplished by simply dragging the icons of the kinds of objects you wish to display on to a line that describes the order of presentation. We subsequently shall call this line the *time line*. Construction and editing of this line is the fundamental act the user performs in the Overview subsystem. The time line always plays from left to right. Thus, the document corresponding to the icon on the left end of the line is displayed first and the document corresponding to the icon on the right end of the line is displayed last in the presentation.

An example of an Overview time line is shown in Figure 20.10. It is shown as the dimmed line across the center of the figure. On this time line is also shown the icon of a clock, called the *Timer*, and three *MacPaint File* icons. The Timer is an Overview tool that sets the length of time that each slide will be displayed on the screen. Multiple Timers can be used in an Overview, as we discuss later. The *MacPaint File* icons are also Overview tools, each indicating that the MacPaint document whose name is displayed below the icon will be displayed on the screen for the number of seconds indicated above the icon. Thus, for the time line of Figure 20.10, the pictures of a boat, a plane, and a train, respectively, would be shown on the computer screen when this Overview document is executed. Each picture would appear for three seconds as set by the initial Timer. You will also note the small square surrounding the number 3 over the first icon. This square is called the *Playback Head*. The Playback Head indicates the position of the time line that currently is being played.

Execution of an Overview document is accomplished using the *Panel*. The Panel is a small window that has button options that look like the buttons on a tape or a video recorder. A picture of the Panel is shown in Figure 20.11. By pressing *PLAY*, the entire Overview time line will be played back. *REWind*, step *BACK*, *STOP*, *STEP* forward, and *LOOP* all have their intuitive meanings with respect to the time line of the Overview document and the current position of the Playback Head within the time line. By using the **Window** menu, shown in Figure 20.10, you can choose whether or not to display the Panel.

Scenes from Overview are drawn on the *Stage*. The *Stage* is another window accessible from the **Window** menu. To see a presentation you will normally want to make *Stage* the active window or at least clear away most of the other windows on the screen. VideoWorks II windows can be easily managed using the **Window** menu.

CONSTRUCTING AN OVERVIEW TIME LINE.   The *tool* icons that can be used to create time lines in the Overview subsystem are shown in Figure 20.11. To construct an Overview, the *Overview* window in VideoWorks II is made the active subsystem after opening the VideoWorks II icon—a picture of a video camera. Movement between the Overview and VideoWorks subsystems is carried out by selecting *To Overview* or *To VideoWorks* options found under the **File** menu.

When a new *Overview* window is opened, the overview tools (shown annotated in Figure 20.12) are displayed, as well as a window similar to that of Figure 20.10, except that only the portion of the time line between the left edge of the window and the *Timer* icon will appear. The rest of the window will be empty.

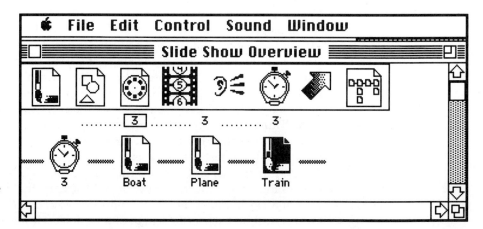

Figure 20.10 Example time line from the Overview subsystem.

Figure 20.11 The Panel window used to play a presentation.

The tool icons can be dragged from the tool area into a position on the time line in the *Overview* window. When a tool is dragged into position in the overview window, it will be opened to reveal different documents of its type that are available for display on the screen. For example, the first tool shown in Figure 20.10 is a *MacPaint File* tool. Dragging this tool into the overview window and attaching it to the time line would allow the user to select an existing MacPaint document to appear at that point on the time line. The tools *Pict File* and *Glue File* are used to display text or pictures that have been created using these Macintosh file formats.

The next icon tool is that of a *Movie* and indicates that animation frame sequences that can be constructed using the VideoWorks subsystem can also be inserted on the time line. As with other tools, available Movie documents are displayed by opening the icon. The *Ear* icon tool indicates that sound effects, including music, can be added to the time line and will begin during the presentation at the point chosen on the time line. Opening the *Ear* icon displays the different sound documents that can be used. You can, of course, navigate through the file system to locate all such documents available.

The arrow or *Transition* icon indicates that a special effect is to be used as the next slide is shown. For example, you might specify that an image is to slide slowly off of the screen to the right to reveal the next image. Alternatively, an image can dissolve bit by bit to reveal the next image. The *Overview* icon is the tool used to add an existing Overview to the current Overview being constructed. Thus, a previously constructed Overview can be embedded into a new Overview, saving the effort of re-creating the earlier Overview. The entire previously constructed Overview will be played before the next slide is shown in the current Overview. Finally, as discussed earlier, the *Timer* icon is used to determine how long a given document is to be displayed. Editing operations, such as *Cut*, *Copy*, and *Paste*, can be performed on the time line and its objects in exactly the same manner as you have done with text items in word processing packages.

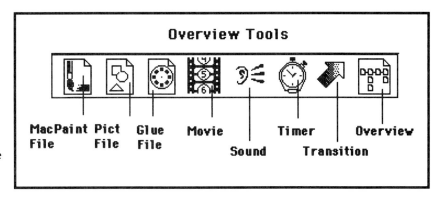

Figure 20.12 Tools available in the Overview subsystem.

Somewhat more advanced features are also possible within Overview. For example, more than one tool can appear at a given time on the time line. Thus, a Movie, Ear, or Timer tool, or some combination of these, might appear below one of the file type icons. The effect of placing such a tool below an existing tool is to add the elements of that tool to the existing events that happen at that time. For example, a *Movie* icon could be dragged to a position immediately below the MacPaint tool for the boat in Figure 20.10. The purpose of this Movie tool might be to add moving waves and/or a moving background to the stationary image of the boat. In addition, an Ear tool might be dragged under the Movie tool, thus creating a column containing three tools. The purpose of adding the Ear tool could be to add the sound of sea gulls and ocean waves to the scene.

You should now have some sense of the problem-solving power available in VideoWorks II. Here again you see the development of a problem solution by breaking the solution into a series of steps, each of which solves a part of the entire problem. The time line shows visually the order of the steps that must be taken to solve the problem. Note that embedding existing Overviews in a time line is identical in concept to calling on Macro functions that you had previously defined in a spreadsheet.

Finally, we note that in VideoWorks II more than one Movie tool may appear in a given column. Let us call the operation of placing multiple Movie tools in a column be "adding" Movie tools. (This process of "adding" is formally termed *overlaying clip animations*.) When Movie tools are "added," an order of drawing must be considered.

Movie tools are composed of a collection of frames. A **frame** is a snapshot of a scene at a given time. The animation of a Movie tool is produced by rapidly displaying and erasing each frame in sequence, as described in the last section. We shall define the term *current frame* to mean the frame being drawn. The current frame of the Movie tool closest to the top in a column of tools is drawn on top of any document file (if present and produced using the MacPaint, Pict, or Glue formats). Next, the current frame of the Movie tool positioned next lowest in the column is drawn over the top picture produced up to that point. This process is continued until the last Movie tool's current frame is drawn. The entire composite frame is then displayed on the screen. Then the next composite frame for the entire picture is composed using the same process, the old frame is erased, and the new frame is displayed. This sequence continues until the duration set for this element of the time line has elapsed. Then the tools in the next column to the right on the time line are executed.

An example of a slightly more complex presentation is shown in Figure 20.13. The first screen displayed is a picture of the VideoWorks II logo. Directly below the MacPaint File tool named *VideoWorks II logo* is seen a Movie tool. The purpose of this tool is to display an animation sequence on top of the VideoWorks II logo. The Movie tool causes the spelling out of the word *presentation* letter by letter drawn in real time. Recall that both the picture and the animation sequence are displayed at the same time, as shown by their same position on the time line.

The next screen image to appear is a slide created in a Glue File format. As this slide is displayed it is accompanied by a sound sequence. Similarly, the next slide presented was created using a Pict File format and displays another image accompanied by another sound sequence. This image disappears by dissolving. This action is initiated by selecting a transition tool, as shown highlighted in the

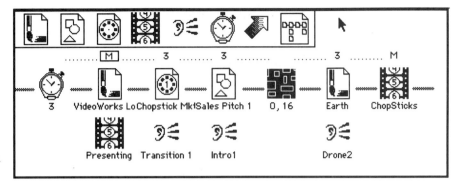

Figure 20.13 A more complex example Overview created using multiple Overview tools in the same column.

figure. It dissolves to reveal a slide of the earth accompanied again by a sound sequence. Finally, the presentation ends with a short animation sequence. Note that the duration for which each slide is displayed is determined by the *Timer* icon at its time line position (if one is defined) or by the *Timer* icon nearest to the slide tool but located to the left of the slide tool. The exception to this rule occurs when a Movie tool is added to a time line. In such instances the default condition is to have the duration be the length of the Movie tool. The M indicates this default duration.

VIDEOWORKS ANIMATION SUBSYSTEM.   The VideoWorks subsystem provides animation tools that allow the user conveniently and quickly to develop movie sequences that can be individually saved and executed alone or pieced together with other sequences to form more complex animation sequences. Owing to the wide range of options available for using this subsystem, we are forced in our discussion to focus on a conceptual overview of its elements. We shall not describe in full detail how to carry out the different operations discussed. Our presentation provides an overview that will make using this package much easier to understand for the first-time user, however.

THE SCORE.   Just as the time line served as the main organizational element for learning about the Overview subsystem, the *Score* Window serves as the organizational element for the discussion of the VideoWorks subsystem. Your familiarity with the time line in Overview will help you understand how to work with the VideoWorks subsystem. The Score is organized as a two-dimensional array of cells that has 24 numbered rows and a sufficient number of columns from which to construct the *frames* that make up the whole movie. An entire column of cells in the Score is termed a frame because a frame is constructed by drawing a column of cells. (See Figure 20.14.) Recall that a frame is one snapshot used to make a Movie. Conceptually, frames are played from left to right to form animation in the VideoWorks subsystem, just as the time line is played from left to right to form a presentation in the Overview subsystem.

An entire row of cells in the Score is called a *channel*. (See Figure 20.14.) Channels allow a given animation sequence to be broken down into subunits. As a simple example of this concept, you might wish to construct a movie in which a dog walks from left to right across the screen while a car moves across from right to left. Each event can be viewed as being distinct from the other. That is, animation of the dog walking need not be complicated by having to consider the

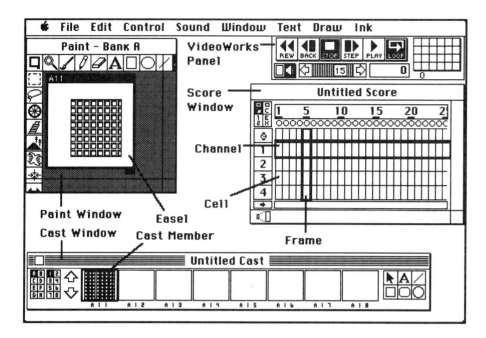

Figure 20.14 Several windows in the VideoWorks subsystem.

moving car. By treating each action as a separate channel in the Score, its animation can be constructed independently. (This is another example of dividing a complex problem into smaller problems to make it easier to solve.)

To obtain a frame to be displayed on the screen, VideoWorks "adds" together the entire column of picture components, one from each channel. Here the term *add* is used precisely as we discussed earlier in connection with the Overview subsystem. Hence, higher-numbered channel cells are drawn *over* (on top of and hence obscuring) lower-numbered channels. This drawing hierarchy gives a three-dimensional effect to the scene, because objects that obscure other objects are interpreted by the viewer to be closer. Note also that it can be convenient to exchange the roles of several channels as a scene progresses. For example, in part of the movie it might be desirable to have the dog pass in front of the car, whereas in another part the dog might need to pass across behind the car. The channel labeled with the clock icon is special and may be used to add sound to the animation. It is not counted as one of the 24 possible channels.

The VideoWorks Panel, shown in the upper right-hand corner of Figure 20.14, has a function similar to that of the Overview Panel. For example, the Panel may be use to *Play* the Score just as it was used to *Play* an Overview time line. Frames are ultimately displayed on the *Stage*, as was discussed in connection with Overview. The grid of boxes on the right of the Panel are used for editing purposes and can be used to select which channel is to be used. The scroll box with a number in it is used to set the speed at which the frames are drawn, that is, it controls the speed at which the Movie is played.

Note that when several Movies are added in Overview, their respective channels are simply copied into a new Score for the entire display. For this reason there is a limit of 24 channels that can be used in displaying any Overview scene. The first Movie uses the first set of channels in the new Score, then the next Movie's channels fill in starting at the next available channel in the new Score. This process is continued until channel 24 of the new Score is finally filled or all the Movies have been added. Any channels needed above this number simply are not displayed. This process explains why Movies farther down in a column have their frames draw over those higher up in an Overview column.

The elements that make up one cell of one channel of a given frame of a Movie reside in the *Cast*. These elements, called *Easels*, are the basic parts of pictures from which a given movie is composed. No part of a Movie can appear that does not come from an Easel. The Cast contains a maximum of 512 different Easels. The *Cast* Window is shown at the bottom of Figure 20.14. The *Cast* Window displays a miniature image of eight different Easels at a time.

To understand an Easel name, such as A13, you should think of the *Cast* as being organized as a stack of pages in a picture album. The top page is called A, the next B, and so forth, down to H. There are eight such pages in the stack. Each page contains 64 pockets into which a part of a picture (Easel) can be inserted. Pockets are arranged in a grid eight rows by eight columns on a page. In naming an Easel, the letter of the page is given, followed by the number of the row followed by the number of the column. The name A13 would therefore describe an Easel located on the first page of the stack of pages. On the first page, the particular Easel to be chosen is located at the intersection of the first row and the third column. By clicking on the grid of letters and numbers at the left of the *Cast* Window you can select the page letter and row number of the eight Easels that will be displayed in the window.

USING EASELS AND CHANNELS FOR ANIMATION.   Animation in VideoWorks can be constructed using a variety of methods. In each method part of what you are to do is to assign an Easel name to a channel cell. There is never more than one Easel in a given channel cell in the Score. Note, however, adjacent channel cells can have different Easels. As we will see shortly, an Easel may be a picture that is simple or very complex, and it may be created in a variety of ways. In addition to the Easel's name, other information, such as its position on the Stage, is also stored in the Score. As a consequence, to animate a car moving across a scene, you need not create a succession of different Easels in which the car is drawn slightly displaced from one Easel to the next.

In fact, it is only necessary for you to select a channel where the car sequence will appear. You can do this by clicking in a channel box of the Panel. Alternately, VideoWorks will choose a free channel automatically for you if you don't do it yourself. Next select the Easel that shows the car by finding and clicking on its picture in the *Cast* Window. Finally, move to the location on the Stage that you would like the car to start from; click and drag the car smoothly across the Stage in the direction you wish it to move. (Once you have selected the Easel, you may wish to close the *Cast* Window to better see the Stage for this last operation.) This simple sequence of actions alone is sufficient to create a moving car, by directly assigning positions and Easel names to a contiguous group of cells in a channel. The process just described is called *Real-Time Recording* in VideoWorks. (VideoWorks has simply sampled the coordinates of the car in real time as you moved it and plays them back for you whenever you desire!)

Note that the recording will begin in a channel at the frame indicated by the current position of the Playback Head. The Playback Head moves from one column to the next automatically during the operation. The position of the Playback Head is indicated by a small black square located in the area just to the right of the arrow appearing under the channel numbers of the *Score* Window. You can drag the Playback Head to any desired position by selecting it and dragging.

Other methods allow you to place each Easel and its position directly into a cell of a channel. For example, suppose that you wished to create a movie segment that had the earth rotating about its axis. Assume for our discussion that the earth is being viewed from the moon. In VideoWorks this kind of animation requires many different Easels appearing one after another in cells of the same channel. For example the Earth could be drawn with the continents of the Americas showing centered on the sphere in the first Easel; then an Easel showing the earth with the Americas displaced slightly to the right and the Pacific ocean in a position more central on the sphere would be assigned to the next cell; and so on. By playing back this sequence of Easels for the channel, the picture of the earth would appear to rotate when displayed on the Stage. This method of approach is called *frame-by-frame animation* in the VideoWorks subsystem. Movement from one place to another on the Score can also be achieved using this method. Thus, you could easily create an Earth that both spins and moves around on the Stage.

Note that many different kinds of editing operations are possible within the Score. It is possible to position an Easel at some start location, select the final position at which you wish to have the Easel finish, and have VideoWorks determine all the cell positions in between. You can *Copy* any sequence of Score cells and *Paste* them somewhere else, thus adding an animation sequence in another channel if desired. You can insert a sequence anywhere in a channel. You can literally redraw a scene while it is moving if desired. You can also step through the scene displayed on the Stage step by step. At any point, you can click on any object in the scene and the *Cast* window containing that object will be displayed, allowing editing if desired. The object can also be dragged to a new position if desired.

CONSTRUCTING EASELS.   To conclude the discussion for this section, we describe briefly how to construct an Easel. An Easel is the basic element of the VideoWorks animation. Easels can be constructed in a variety of ways. For example, many Macintosh drawing programs can be used to create art work that can be pasted into an Easel from the Clipboard. Pictures taken from a scanner or television camera can be pasted into an Easel. An Easel can also be constructed using *Paint* tools available in the VideoWorks subsystem. Painting in VideoWorks is performed by first opening the *Paint* Window by clicking on *Paint* in the **Window** menu. A portion of the *Paint* Window is shown in the upper left-hand corner of Figure 20.15. Note that on the Macintosh II full color and gray level display is possible when painting in VideoWorks. Thus, some very realistic animation becomes possible.

To obtain an Easel on which to work, it is necessary to drag an *Easel* icon out of the border square located in the upper left-hand corner of the *Paint* window and into the work area in the center of the window. The size of the Easel can then be altered by dragging on the tab at the lower right corner. Painting in VideoWorks is very similar to MacPaint. Around the border of the *Paint* window are seen various tools whose effects are already familiar to you from MacPaint. There also are a number of additional tools that allow you to perform new operations on pictures such as a tool to rotate, one to create the impression of perspective in a drawing, a slant tool, a distortion tool and so on. You can also select special inks in drawing pictures, such as transparent ink that will allow other channels below a given channel to show through.

As we conclude this section it should be clear that systems such as VideoWorks II provide a wide range of features to produce and edit short animated presentations. Experience with this system or a system of its type will help you begin to appreciate the concept of the virtual computer world that is essential to understand if you wish to have insight into the increasingly important role computers will play in the future for multimedia information management and display.

Key Concepts

Aliasing	Analog-to-digital conversion
Animation	Digital-to-analog conversion
Envelope	Frame
Filtering	Frequency
Nyquist frequency	Real-time computing
Sampling rate	Timbre
Transducer	Vibrato
Virtual worlds	

ORGANIZING HYPERTEXT INFORMATION WITH HYPERCARD

L E A R N I N G   O B J E C T I V E S

- To understand the fundamental concepts of hypertext.
- To learn to use HyperCard hypertext documents.
- To explore how to create your own HyperCard hypertext documents.
- To gain insight into the use of HyperCard for creating multimedia hypertext documents.

I n this chapter you will be introduced to the idea of hypertext, a concept that promises to provide a new perspective on the way we use computers for many kinds of information storage and presentation. After a brief survey of the history of hypertext, you will explore some of its fundamental concepts using the hypertext system HyperCard. Using HyperCard, you will see how to create your own hypertext information storage and presentation documents. Such documents can use text, graphics, digitized photographs, and sound to produce multimedia information stores. You will gain an understanding of how such information can be accessed in highly flexible ways using HyperCard as the underlying organizing system. Once you have this understanding, you will have access to an innovative and exciting new way of communicating information using computers.

21.1 BASIC IDEAS OF HYPERTEXT

In its most basic form, **hypertext** is an extension of some very commonly used writing devices—such as footnoting, cross-referencing, and inclusion of parenthetical remarks—for organizing the display of information in nonsequential or **nonlinear documents.** However, hypertext provides many capabilities that far exceed those available in such writing devices. The reference material accessed using hypertext ideas can contain digitized photographs and drawings, as well as audio information such as recorded speeches and music. It is this ability to organize a multimedia information display that is accessed according to the "reader's" own desires that has created much of the excitement surrounding hypertext ideas. We are indeed at the beginning of a new age in information presentation and organization!

It is often the case that when we write we would like to mention topics or information related to our main theme that would become a distraction if included directly in the text itself. The writing devices mentioned earlier give us some capability of including such material without sacrificing the linear flow of the main thoughts of the topic being developed.

By referring a reader to a different chapter, page number, or another book, for example, the writer of a book can provide the reader an opportunity to explore related material at the reader's convenience. If the referenced material is brief, the writer might choose to include it as a footnote or as parenthetical text. However, if too much such complete reference material is included, it becomes very difficult for the reader to maintain the proper level of concentration on the central theme being developed. On the other hand, if references only are given, for the reader to benefit at all, it is necessary to obtain the relevant materials before the actual reference information can be accessed. If a writer uses such material frequently, it imposes a burdensome material management overhead on the reader. How many times have you wished to check a reference but did not have the time and/or the necessary reference material? Or worse yet, how many times have you expended considerable effort to check a reference, only to discover that it wasn't worth the effort at all?

Of course a writer is aware of the limitations that must be considered when referencing material that is related but not central to the main writing topic. As a consequence, the writer is constantly making decisions about which related material or references should be included. The result is that the reader is often given a very selected set of reference material that can be quite a bit smaller than the writer would actually have preferred but that was restricted to keep the main writing theme uncluttered.

READER PARTICIPATION.   Unfortunately, the reader has no participation in deciding which reference material is included or excluded; the writer must make these decisions for all readers. Although some readers may be intensely interested in a subject's historical background, the writer must remember that not every reader will have such a perspective. Hence, some compromise position must be taken relative to historical background references. In a similar way, the writer must restrict reference material in other possible directions.

If a separate edition could be produced for each reader and that reader could participate in the production of that edition, then the reference material would be ideally suited for that reader's interests. Of course, if these interests change at a later date, then another, different tailored edition would have to be produced. As ideal as this sounds, it appears to be absurdly impractical. In fact, it is absolutely impractical as long as traditional methods for publishing material are followed. However, the concept of hypertext opens doors to exactly the kind of tailoring of material to a reader's needs that we have described.

Using hypertext ideas, many different references can be included in an electronic document *without disturbing* the linear flow of the main document theme. The reader can choose to explore any number of these references or none at all. The key to these capabilities is that links to these references are embedded in the document in very nonintrusive ways. If a reader wishes to ignore them, they do not interfere with the reading of the main text. Because a hypertext document is presented in electronic form, it is very easy to include multimedia document components, such as digitized pictures or sound, as part of the document itself or as reference material. Furthermore, the order in which this material is accessed is primarily determined *by the reader* and not by its writer or creator. Using a well-designed and implemented hypertext document is like having an entire library and resource center at your fingertips—with exploration of related topics in various directions and media available almost instantaneously!

IMPLEMENTING HYPERTEXT.   How is hypertext accomplished? The fundamental concept of hypertext is the inclusion within a document of **electronic links** to related information that can be accessed or called directly from within that document. These links can be thought of as extended electronic footnotes that can be accessed and displayed or not as the reader desires. They are accessed in an active mode rather than a passive mode. That is, they must be called into the document by the reader, otherwise they are not seen and do not interfere with the main document's presentation.

The links can be represented within the document in many different ways. For example, key words might be in bold or highlighted in some different way to indicate that they have related material linked to them. By moving a mouse pointer over those words and clicking, or otherwise indicating an interest by means of special keys (most hypertext systems use the mouse in integral ways), the reader can cause the linked information to be retrieved and automatically displayed. Return to the original document, or even the previous most recent reference material, is accomplished by clicking a *Return* button or some similar activity.

There are other ways that material might be linked. For example, menus might be displayed at the bottom of the screen indicating when additional material is available. Or buttons might be provided on the screen so that when they are clicked, certain additional material or options are presented. In fact, there are many ways to implement the links physically, but however they are implemented, they should be easily accessible and nonintrusive. You will see later in this chapter that HyperCard allows considerable flexibility in constructing links for moving among the information stored in one of its linked documents.

A BRIEF HISTORY OF HYPERTEXT.   The first published description of the concepts underlying a hypertext system is generally credited to Vannevar Bush in 1945. Bush, who was President Franklin Roosevelt's science advisor, wrote an article to encourage a major post - World War II effort to mechanize and automate a system for tracking and using scientific literature. His vision was a machine called a memex that would contain a large library of articles, sketches, and photographs. The memex would have used microfilm and several viewing screens. The links would have been implemented by way of photo-cell-readable dot codes. Of course, in 1945 the digital computer was still in its early infancy, so Bush can be excused for not anticipating the power his memex and a computer might realize together.

Actually, this combination was not explored seriously until nearly 20 years later. In the 1960s two men, Douglas Engelbart, at Stanford Research Institute, and Ted Nelson, at Brown University, set out independently to implement hypertext systems. Engelbart's system made use of his own new invention—the mouse. Nelson actually coined the term *hypertext*. Since these beginnings, hypertext research has proceeded in many directions. Andrew van Dam and others at Brown have created a highly acclaimed and successful system that allows professors to author course notes in multimedia hypertext. This project, called Intermedia, not only allows professors to create their own hypertext lessons, but also allows students to add to the system their own annotations and reports. Rooms are available where students can go and explore multimedia information presentations. To experience the same degree of information exploration using traditional methods would require impossible amounts of time and energy on the part of the information seeker!

As you can see from the preceding outline, the ideas inherent in hypertext are not really new. Full hypertext systems have been under development for several decades. Why, then, do we claim that hypertext supplies you with a *new* capability for information storage and display? The reason is that until quite recently, there were no hypertext systems available on relatively inexpensive and widely available personal computers. The major advances in computer hardware capabilities over the past few years have opened up new possibilities for making hypertext widely accessible. While the ideas in HyperCard have been around for quite some time, the fact that HyperCard is implemented on the Macintosh and is thus available to a very large audience enhances the use of hypertext immensely. Recently, hypertext systems have become available for the IBM personal computer and its compatibles as well. You will be hearing much about hypertext in the future, because such packages will greatly increase the general awareness of the innovative nature of hypertext as an information presentation tool.

Exercise Set 21.1

1. Describe in your own words the idea of hypertext.
2. Do you think a hypertext document could be implemented without using computers? Explain.
3. What is meant when it is said that hypertext provides for a nonlinear (or nonsequential) document construction? Why is this capability important? Can you think of any disadvantages it might have for a user?
4. What traditional writing conventions are used to attempt to achieve some of the same goals as hypertext has?
5. In what ways does hypertext allow the reader to participate in the "construction" of the document to be read?
6. Give your reaction to the statement that hypertext is an exciting *new* concept.
7. What is the importance of HyperCard in the history of hypertext? Was it the first hypertext system?

21.2 USING HYPERCARD STACKS

In this section you will explore the use of the Macintosh hypertext software package HyperCard. By working with HyperCard, you will gain additional insight into the meaning and importance of the ideas discussed in the previous section. Our purpose here is not to learn to build a HyperCard application, but to see how to use an existing HyperCard application. In the next section, you will learn how to build an application of your own.

STARTING HYPERCARD.   To open HyperCard, find and double-click on the Hyper-Card icon shown in Figure 21.1.

When you open HyperCard you will see displayed a screen that is called the *Home Card.* A typical Home Card is shown in Figure 21.2. HyperCard documents are called **stacks**. These documents can be thought of as collections or stacks of **cards**, where each card is the size of a single Macintosh screen. Any information that can be displayed on, or accessed from (such as sound and music), a Macintosh screen can be placed on a card.

HyperCard cannot run without a Home Card, and that Home Card is unique, because there can be only one Home Card for a particular running copy of the HyperCard software. However, the software user can configure the Home Card in

Figure 21.1 The HyperCard icon.

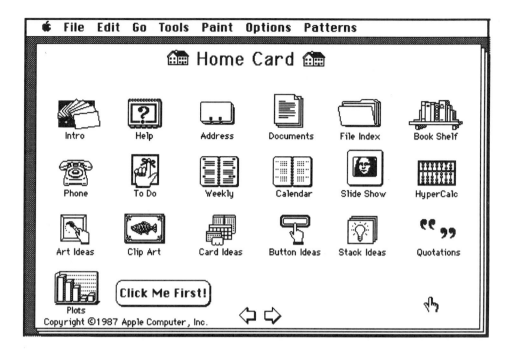

Figure 21.2 An example HyperCard Home Card.

many different ways, allowing access to only some chosen set of stacks. Hence, the Home Card shown in Figure 21.2 is only one of many different forms a particular Home Card could take.

The HyperCard Home Card provides access to a number of different card stacks. Notice in Figure 21.2 that the mouse pointer has the shape a pointing finger (in the lower right corner of the screen). This icon represents the HyperCard *browse* tool, which is used to select and click on buttons that provide automatic links to other cards and stacks.

Notice the **Tools** pull-down menu (actually, it is a pull-down palette of tools) in the menu bar of the Home Card. By accessing this palette menu, you can access various tools with which HyperCard cards can be constructed. The palette contains some familiar MacPaint tools and some important new tools; we will investigate it thoroughly a little later. It is also the case that as you move the mouse cursor around on certain cards, its shape (and hence its function and the tool it represents) will change automatically. Shortly, you will see that this context-sensitive tool selection technique is used extensively in HyperCard.

MOVING AROUND IN HYPERCARD STACKS.   The icons shown in Figure 21.2 are actually buttons that form links to various HyperCard stacks, and clicking one of them will cause the first card of the appropriate stack to be automatically displayed. For example, if you click on the *Intro* icon (upper left), the first card of the *Intro* stack, shown in Figure 21.3, will be displayed.

By placing the browse tool over the *What is HyperCard?* button and clicking, the card in Figure 21.4 will be displayed. This card gives an informative graphical representation of one of the basic ideas in HyperCard. The arrows represent the links that allow you to move easily from card to card by clicking buttons. Note that the cards being linked need not be in the same stack—or even on the same disk.

Figure 21.3 The firstcard of the *Intro* HyperCard stack.

As you will see in the next section, such HyperCard link buttons are easy to create, and they can be placed anywhere on a card and have many different appearances. In fact, the form of HyperCard buttons can range from predefined radio buttons and rounded-corner rectangle buttons with the button name inside to icons that you design and construct yourself. About the only limitation on a link button is that it can link to only one other card. This is not a serious limitation because you can have a great many buttons (and hence access to a great many other cards and stacks) on a given card.

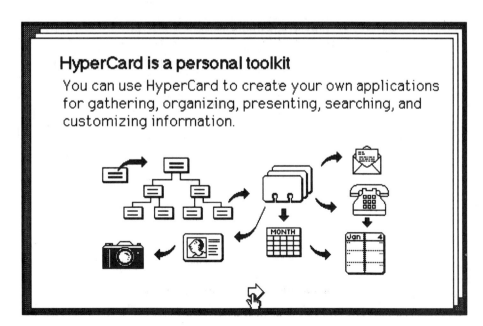

Figure 21.4 Card accessed by clicking the *What is HyperCard?* button of the card of Figure 21.3.

Take note of the arrow button at the bottom of the card shown in Figure 21.4. (The browse tool is partially over it.) This is a standard HyperCard button that takes you to the next card in the current stack (to the initial card in the stack, if the current card happens to be the last one of the stack). Clicking it now causes the card in Figure 21.5 to be displayed for the particular stack being used for this example.

At the bottom center of the card of Figure 21.5, you will notice two arrow buttons. The arrow pointing to the right advances you to the next card in the same stack when it is clicked; the one pointing to the left returns you to the previous card in the same stack when it is clicked.

These same two functions of advancing or retracing cards in the current stack can also be accessed by selecting the commands *Next* and *Prev*, respectively, from the **Go** pull-down menu. In addition, choosing the *Home* selection from that menu will always return you to the HyperCard Home Card.

SETTING THE USER LEVEL IN HYPERCARD.   Let us choose the *Home* command under the **Go** menu and return to the Home Card to see how to set the *user level*. There are five categories of HyperCard user capabilities, or user levels. The number of HyperCard options and activities that are available to you will depend upon which of these levels has been selected. The five user levels follow. Each level provides capabilities that include all the capabilities of all the levels that precede it in the list.

- Browsing
- Typing
- Painting
- Authoring
- Scripting

Briefly, the brow*sing* level allows a user to look at cards in a stack and navigate freely from card to card using buttons; the *typing* level adds the capability to enter

Figure 21.5 Card accessed by clicking the *Next Card* button of the card shown in Figure 21.4.

text within certain fields that can be predefined on cards; the *painting* level adds the capability to use MacPaint-like tools to create graphics on cards; the *authoring* level adds the capability to create stacks and cards with fields and buttons of your own; the *scripting* level adds the capability to write commands or programs (scripts) in the language HyperTalk.

The menus displayed and the choices available within those menus will depend upon what user level has been set. For the rest of this chapter, we assume that the user level is *authoring*. The user level can be set and changed easily by accessing the card at the end of the *Home Card* stack and selecting the appropriate radio button. To access this card, you select the previous card button from the Home Card.

AN EXAMPLE HYPERCARD EXCURSION.   Before examining some of the authoring capabilities in HyperCard, let us make one more stack excursion. From the Home Card, clicking on the *Address* icon (see Figure 21.2) causes the card in Figure 21.6 to be displayed. Note that this card has the standard *next card* and *previous card* arrow buttons. It also has another standard button in the lower right corner. This button allows you to return to the beginning of the stack of which the current card is a member. Note that this is different from returning to the Home Card from which you access various stacks.

You will also notice six **icon/buttons** on the left of the card of Figure 21.6. These icon/buttons were placed there by the card's creator, and they have various functions. The house-shaped icon is a button that returns you to the Home Card. The next two icons represent buttons that provide links to two kinds of calendar stacks. Clicking on the first of these causes a calendar similar to that shown in Figure 21.7 to be displayed, with the current week highlighted (the week of July 11-17, 1988, in the figure). The fourth icon represents a button linked to a note card (things-to-do) stack.

The last two icons are not buttons that are linked to other cards or stacks; they are used to initiate actions to be taken on the current stack. The first of these gives

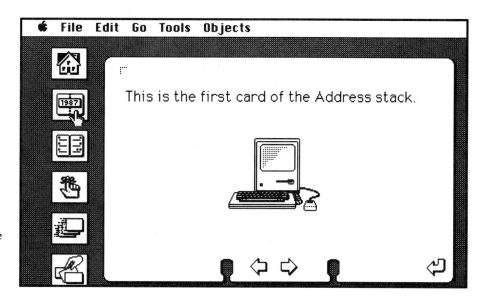

Figure 21.6 First card in the *Address* stack accessed from the Home Card of Figure 21.2.

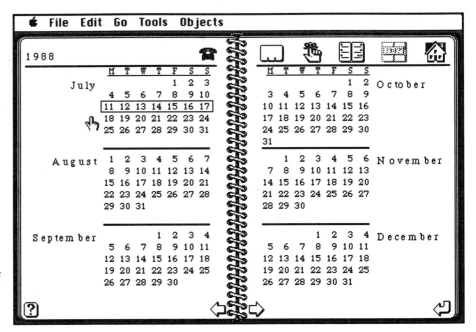

Figure 21.7 A card in one of the *Calendar* stacks accessed from the card of Figure 21.6.

you a rapid tour of the current stack by accessing and displaying its cards in rapid succession. The final icon/button allows you to sort the current stack according to the name field on each address card. The icons used are the ones commonly used for these actions within HyperCard stacks.

The particular *Calendar* stacks in this example are also linked together. If you use the browse tool to select a given week as shown in Figure 21.7, an appointment calendar for that week will be displayed as shown in Figure 21.8. If you move the browse tool to one of the text areas (or *fields* as they are called in HyperCard), it will change to the *text* tool and you can click and then enter appointments or notes. Notice that several such entries have been made in the calendar shown in Figure 21.8.

By clicking on the icon shaped like an address card at the top middle of the appointment calendar card, you can return to the *Address* stack. Then clicking the *next card* arrow button will cause a card like the one shown in Figure 21.9 to be displayed. Notice the similarities between the cards in Figures 21.2 and 21.9. The common features of the cards in a stack are usually stored as a part of a card's *background*. Each card has two display areas called the **background** and **foreground areas**. These two areas are defined and manipulated independently, but they are displayed simultaneously. Although quite frequently it is desirable for all of a given stack's cards to have the same background, it is possible for different cards within the same stack to have different backgrounds. It is convenient to place information that is common to many cards in the background display area and then simply to copy the background to all new cards created. We explore this idea in more detail in the next section. For example, for the cards in the *Address* stack, it would make sense to place the column of icons/buttons to the left of the addresses as well as the arrow buttons at the bottom of the cards in the background area, because these features appear on all the cards in the stack.

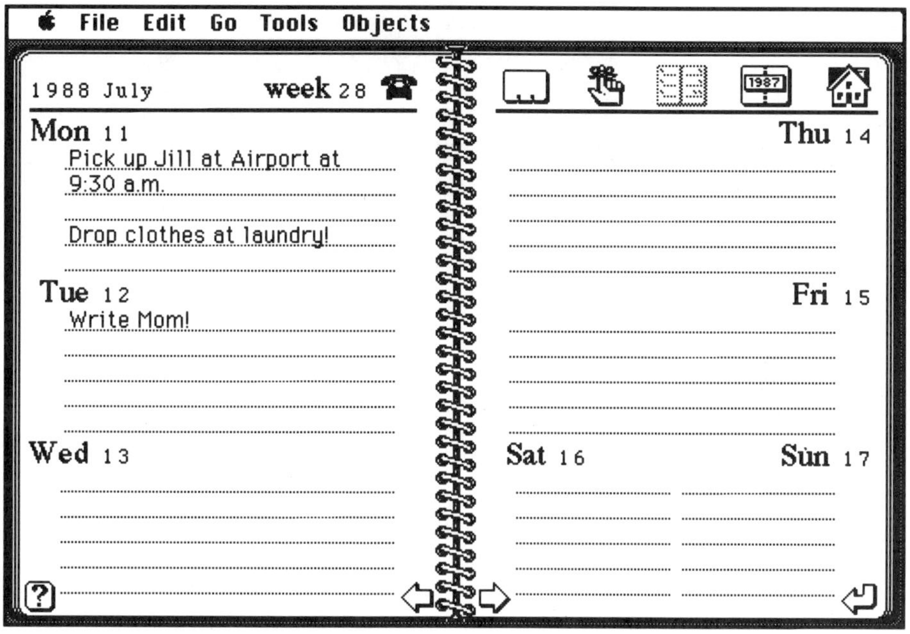

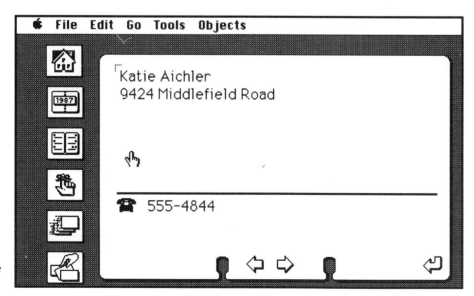

Figure 21.8 A card from the *Appointment Calendar* stack accessed from the card of Figure 21.7.

STAYING ORIENTED IN HYPERCARD STACKS. One of the potential disadvantages of using HyperCard stacks (and other hypertext documents) to access and display information is the ease with which you can lose track of the information path you have followed to get to the card you are presently viewing. For example, you may wish to review a card you have previously examined. How will you find it? You might be able to use the *next card* and *previous card* buttons, but remember that they only provide access to the next and previous cards in the current stack. You may have accessed the current card from another stack. How do you return to that stack?

Figure 21.9 A card from the *Address* example stack.

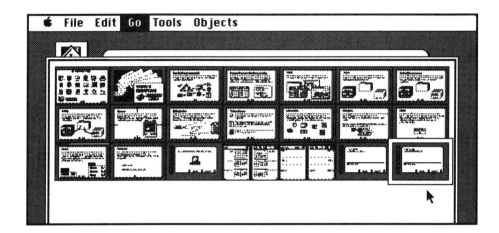

Figure 21.10 An example
Recent display screen.

HyperCard provides two methods for doing this kind of backtracking and an additional method for finding particular textual information in a stack. Each of these **stack navigation methods** is designed to help you avoid becoming disoriented as you move from stack to stack.

The two backtracking methods are provided through the *Back* and *Recent* commands in the **Go** menu. The *Back* command returns you to the most recently visited previous card. By repeatedly using this command, you can retrace your entire hypertext session. The *Recent* command allows you to view the last 42 different cards you have viewed in compact form. An example is shown in Figure 21.10 for a HyperCard session (which has not yet visited 42 cards). From this display you can go to any card represented by pointing to its representation and clicking. The card you were viewing when you selected the *Recent* command is highlighted by an outlined box. Even though the form of the *Recent* display does not allow you to see the details on any of the cards, you can usually pick out the card you are looking for by its outlined features. For example, see if you can pick out the Home Card, the first card of the *Intro* stack (shown in detail in Figure 21.3), and the

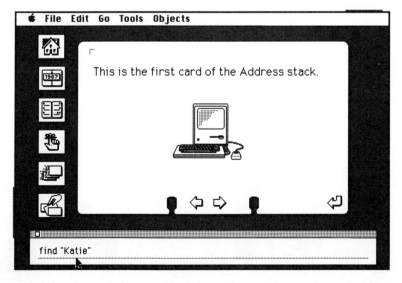

Figure 21.11 Example of
Find command dialog box.

first *Address* stack card (shown in detail in Figure 21.6) from the *Recent* display of Figure 21.10.

A third method for navigating through a HyperCard stack is accessed through the *Find* command in the **Go** menu. When the *Find* command is selected, a small dialog box is displayed over the bottom of the current card, as shown in Figure 21.11. In this box you type in a text string that you would like to locate within the current stack (the quotes are supplied automatically by HyperCard, and the cursor is positioned between them for text insertion when the dialog box is presented).

When the *Return* key is pressed, HyperCard will find and highlight with a rectangle the first occurrence of the text string that is found anywhere within a text field (you will learn about text fields in the next section) on a card within the current stack. By pressing the *Return* key again, the next occurrence of the string will be located. The first occurrence of the string asked for in Figure 21.11 is shown highlighted in Figure 21.12.

Exercise Set 21.2

1. Describe the organization of HyperCard documents.
2. How are HyperCard links accessed? Can cards in different stacks be linked?
3. Describe the methods available in HyperCard to review a card that you have previously visited in a session.
4. What is the function of a Home Card? How many Home Cards can a given application of HyperCard use? Is a Home Card required?

Computer Practice 21.2

1. Open HyperCard and access the *Intro* stack. You should have displayed the card shown in Figure 21.3. Click the *What is HyperCard?* button. Access all the cards in this stack sequentially by using the *next card* button. When you reach the last card (shown here), select the *Home to explore on my own button.*

What next?

Click Help cards to find out more about exploring HyperCard and making stacks of your own.
Or click Home and rely on serendipity to uncover the unexpected.

- Help cards

- Home to explore on my own

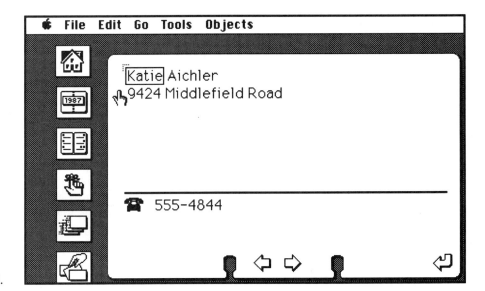

Figure 21.12 Text string specified in Figure 21.11 found and highlighted using the *Find* command.

2. Next, from the Home Card, access the *Address* stack. You should have displayed the card shown in Figure 21.6. Choose the *rapid view* icon (next to the last icon/button on the left-hand side of the card). Next choose the *Recent* command from the **Go** menu. You should get a display like the one shown next. Notice that the *rapid view* cards do not appear on a *Recent* screen.

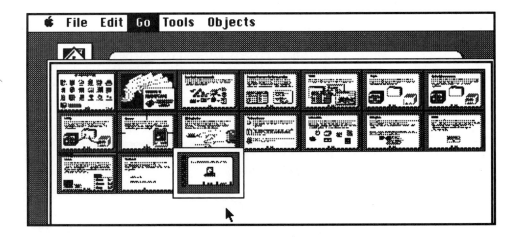

3. From the *Recent* screen display of step 2, try selecting one of the cards in the *Intro* stack. Next choose the *Back* command from the **Go** menu to return to the initial card of the *Address* stack. Follow the link to the *Appointment Calendar* stack (third icon/button from the top on the left side of the card). Move the browse tool (pointing finger) over a text area until it is changed into the I-beam text tool. Click the mouse button and then enter some text. Return to the Home Card (icon/button in the upper right corner of the card).

21.3 CREATING HYPERCARD STACKS

In this section we will go through an outline of the steps required for you to create your own HyperCard stack. At the end of the section you will be asked to create the example stack. The stack we will create will be small and incomplete; we will put in only enough cards to illustrate the major ideas. It will be named *Literature* and will contain information about major literary personalities and works.

To begin, open HyperCard. You should now have the Home Card displayed. Before you proceed, it will be instructive for you to see what information is in the background area of the Home Card. To do this, select *Background* from the **Edit** menu. You will then see a screen like the one in Figure 21.13 (provided the original HyperCard Home Card has not had its background area modified). Notice that the only objects in the Home Card background area are the *next card* and *previous card* buttons. Also notice that the menu bar has a different lower border; this border indicates that you are viewing the background of the card only. To return to a view of both background and foreground areas for the card, select *Background* again from the **Edit** menu.

With the full Home Card displayed, select *New Stack* from the **File** menu. You will then be given the dialog box shown in Figure 21.14. Type in the name of the stack, *Literature*. You will notice that you are offered the option of copying the current background as the default background for the cards of your new stack. Select this option so that each of the cards in your new stack will inherit the *next card* and *previous card* buttons from the Home Card background. The actions of these buttons will be automatically adjusted to reference cards in your new stack. To complete the definition of the new stack, click the *New* button.

When the definition of the new stack has been completed, the first card (and currently the only card) of the new stack will be displayed. It will look like the card shown in Figure 21.13 except that the menu bar will not be bordered as it is in that figure. Before we place buttons on the present card and create additional cards for the stack, we will add some information to the card background. To begin this activity, select the *Background* command from the **Edit** menu.

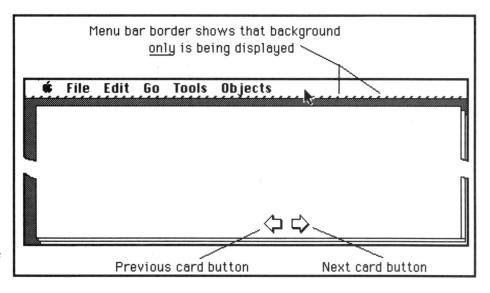

Figure 21.13 Background of the Home Card displayed.

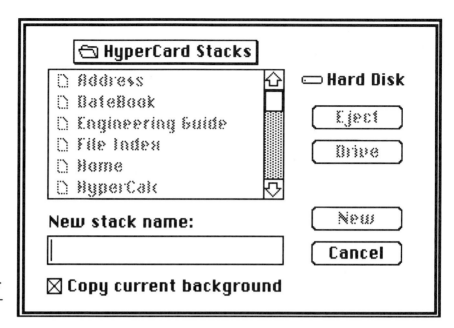

Figure 21.14 Dialog box for definition of a new Hyper-Card stack.

The tools available for creating card displays are found under the **Tools** pull-down menu and are shown in Figure 21.15. You will recognize many of the tool icons from your work with MacPaint. These HyperCard tools have functions almost identical to their MacPaint counterparts. Some of these tools have enhancements and additional capabilities in HyperCard, but we will not need those capabilities for our example and so we will not discuss them here.

The three tools in the first row of the HyperCard tool palette have functions quite different from those of the drawing tools. You have already seen that the primary functions of the browse tool are to select and follow button links and to access and choose commands from pull-down menus. The *button* tool is used to define and set the characteristics of link buttons. Similarly, the *text field* tool is used to define areas on cards called text fields. As the name suggests, **text fields** are areas

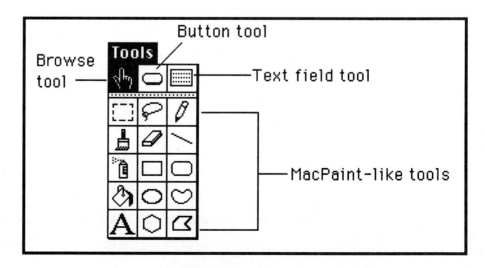

Figure 21.15 HyperCard tools palette.

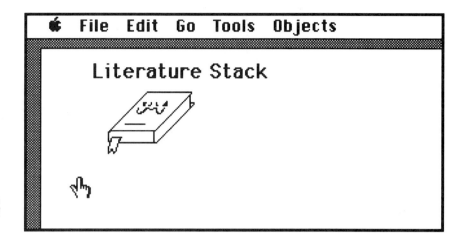

Figure 21.16 New background information added to the first card of the new stack.

on a card where text can be entered. You have seen an example of the use of a text field in the *Appointment Calendar* stack of the previous section. In contrast to textual information entered using the MacPaint type of text drawing tool, textual information in text fields can be edited using common word processing techniques. As in MacPaint, text entered with the drawing text tool must be edited as a graphics object using the eraser, lasso, and so on.

With the background area for your first card accessed (as illustrated in Figure 21.13), you can use the HyperCard drawing tools to create additional background display information. Figure 21.16 shows the card after a graphics object and some text have been so entered. Once this information has been placed in the background area, the *Background* command should be selected once again from the **Edit** menu to return the display to both background and foreground, as shown in the figure. Once this is done, any information entered with the HyperCard tools or by pasting from the Clipboard will be entered to the foreground of the card. New cards are created by choosing the *New Card* command from the **Edit** menu. A new card inherits the background information (but not the foreground information) of the card that is displayed when it is created.

Next, we will add a link button to the first card of our new stack. First, we will copy a graphics object to serve as the icon for our button from a card of the *Art Ideas* stack provided with HyperCard. (Alternatively, we could create such an icon directly on the card using the drawing tools.) To access the *Art Ideas* stack, choose *Home* from the **Go** menu, then select the *Art Ideas* stack icon.

From the first card of the *Art Ideas* stack. click on the *People, Humans* button. Near the middle of the card that is subsequently displayed, you will find the human bust figure (which we will use to represent the class of English poets) seen in Figure 21.17. Select this object with either the marquee or lasso tool and copy it to the Clipboard by selecting the *Copy Picture* command from the **Edit** menu.

Select the *Back* command from the **Go** menu several times until you are returned to the first card of your new stack (or select the *Recent* command and click on the representation of this card). Now select *Paste* from the **Edit** menu; the graphics object will be placed on your card. It can then be moved to the position shown in Figure 21.17.

We intend for the bust graphic to serve as an icon for a button that will link this card to a card representing English poets. To create the button, first select the

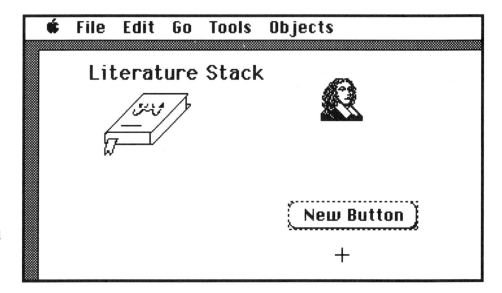

Figure 21.17 The first card of the new stack with an icon pasted and a button created.

button tool from the **Tools** menu. Next choose the *New Button* command from the **Objects** menu. Your card should now look something like the one pictured in Figure 21.17. By moving the pointer to the lower right corner of the button and then dragging, you can resize the button rectangle. By moving the pointer inside the button area and then dragging, you can move the entire button on the card. Using these techniques, it is easy to position the button so that it covers the *bust* icon as illustrated in Figure 21.18.

To complete the definition of the button, select the button (if it is not already selected) by clicking on it. Once the button is selected, choose the *Button Info* command from the **Objects** menu. The dialog box shown in Figure 21.19 will be presented. In this box you can name the button and set some of its properties. The settings selected in the figure will make the button transparent (so that its icon can be seen through it) and cause the button to be highlighted (by inverting the pixels inside it) whenever the pointer is clicked and held inside it. When you have finished making the desired settings, click *OK*. Figure 21.20 illustrates how the button should then appear.

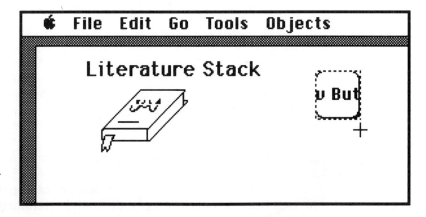

Figure 21.18 The card of Figure 21.17 with the button resized and moved to cover the *bust* icon.

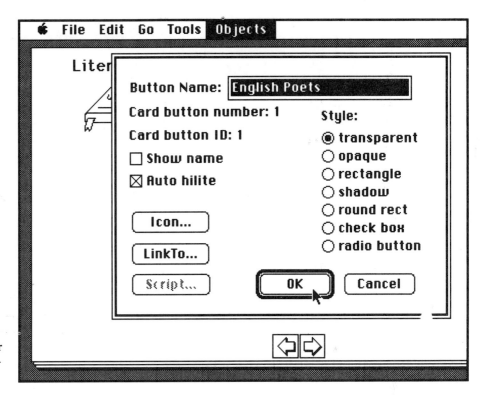

Figure 21.19 Dialog box for setting button characteristics.

Next we will place a text field under our button to identify its purpose further. To do this, you select the field tool from the **Tools** menu and then select the *New Field* command from the **Objects** menu. The new field can be sized and moved analogous to the way those activities were done for the button earlier. Using these techniques, you can position the field as shown in Figure 21.20.

The characteristics of text fields can be set in a manner similar to that used for buttons. To do this the field is selected (first the field tool must be selected if it is not

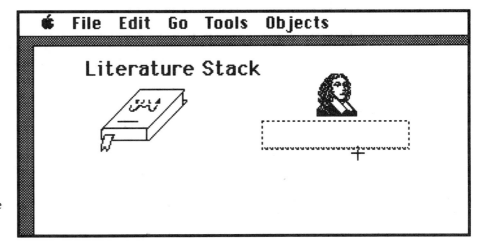

Figure 21.20 Positioning the new field under the button.

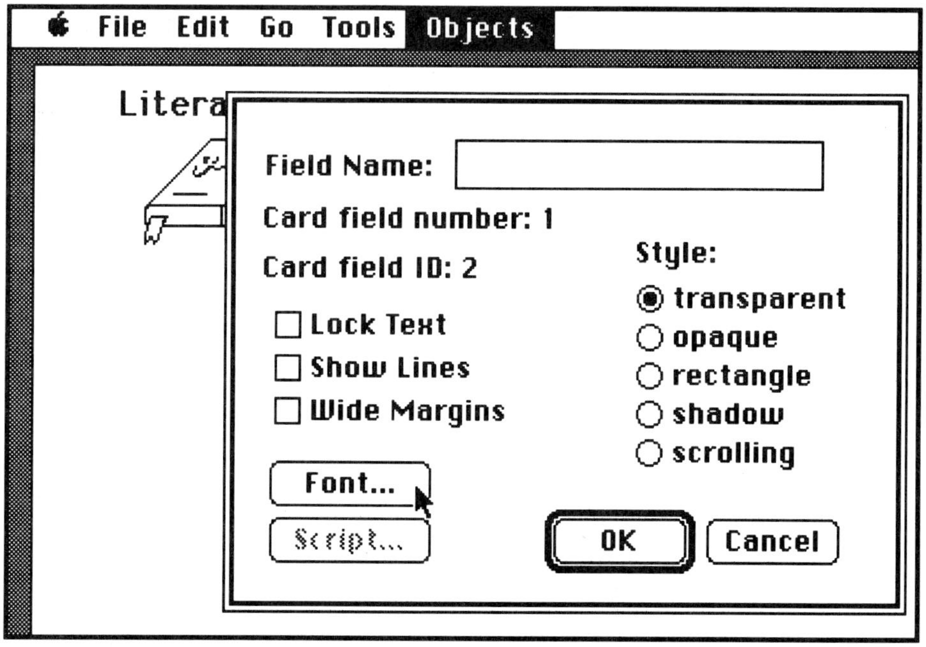

Figure 21.21 Dialog box for setting field characteristics.

already active) by clicking within its area and then choosing the *Field Info* command from the **Objects** menu. When this is done, a dialog box like the one shown in Figure 21.21 will be displayed, and the field's characteristics can then be set.

By clicking the *Font* button in the *Field Info* dialog box, you can access the dialog box shown in Figure 21.22. Using this dialog box, you can make various settings familiar to you from your word processing experience to affect the appearance of text entered into a field. Note that these settings are global for the

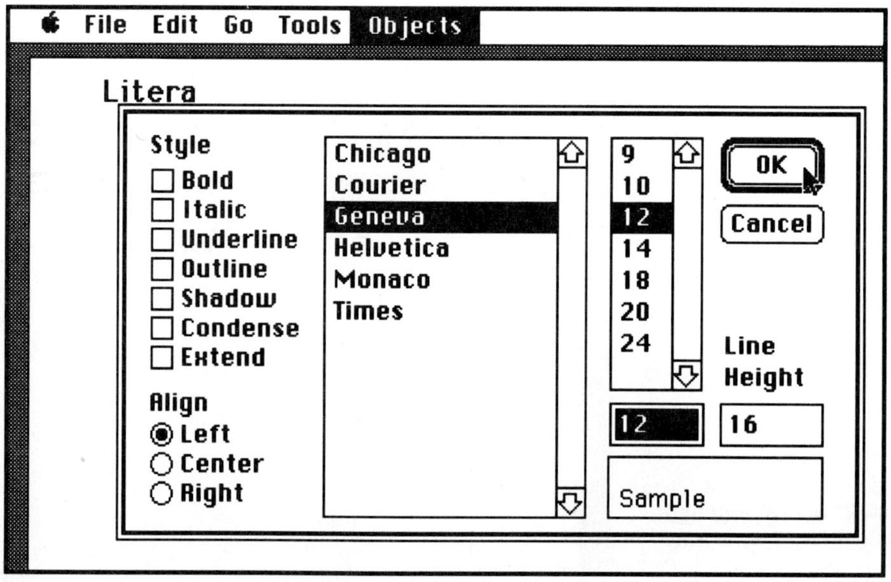

Figure 21.22 Dialog box for setting a field's font characteristics.

field. Hence, you cannot change settings for particular words or characters, only for the field as a whole.

After completing the field characteristic settings, you are returned to the card. If you now select the browse tool and move the tool over the new text field area, it will change to an I-beam. After clicking, the pointer will change to a text insertion pointer (blinking vertical line) and you can enter text into the field. Because we have set the field to be transparent, it may be difficult to place text in multiline fields correctly. If this is the case, the field characteristic could be changed to *rectangle* while text is being entered and then reset to *transparent* later. Figure 21.23 shows the card with text entered and the browse tool active. You are now ready to define the link that this button will implement.

To **define a link** (or later to change the link) for a button, first select the button tool from the **Tools** menu. Next, select the button of interest by clicking anywhere within the button area. When the button is selected, an outline of the button area will be visible, even though the button itself may have been previously set to transparent. Once the button is selected, choose the *Button Info* command from the **Objects** menu. Once again this will result in a dialog box as shown in Figure 21.19. In the box displayed, click the *LinkTo* button; the dialog box shown in Figure 21.24 will be presented.

With the *Link Definition* dialog box on the screen, you can use any of the **Go** menu commands or other card link buttons to locate the card to which you wish to link. While you navigate through various cards and stacks, the dialog box will remain on the screen, except when you choose the *Recent* command from the **Go** menu. In that case, the *Recent* screen will temporarily cover the dialog box until you choose a card from it. Note that you can move the dialog box, by dragging on its upper border, to examine a card more completely.

You can also define a new card to which you wish to link by selecting the *New Card* command from the **Edit** menu. In fact, that is what we want to do here. Once a new card has been created and is displayed, complete the link definition by clicking the *This Card* button. When you do this you will be returned to the card on which the button resides. The link has now been implemented. To move to the new card to place information on it, you simply select the browse tool and click the newly linked button. Figure 21.25 shows the new card with four text fields added

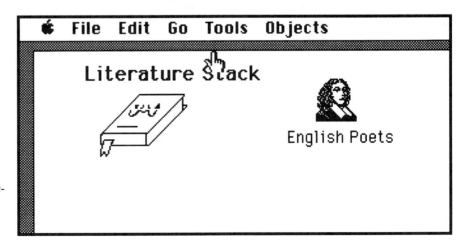

Figure 21.23 The first *Literature* stack card after placing the button and text fields on it.

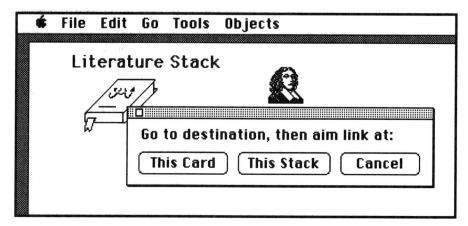

Figure 21.24 Dialog box for defining a button link destination.

to it. Note that the background from the card that was active when the new card was created is copied automatically to the new card.

In Figure 21.26, text has been entered into the text fields by first selecting the browse tool and then moving it over the text fields and clicking to access the text entry tool. The text fields have also been made transparent, which means that the boundaries do not show. The title *English Poets* was added using the drawing text tool.

Figure 21.27 shows new buttons placed over the text fields. Note that each button has been sized appropriately to cover its associated text field. The buttons next should be selected in turn and their characteristics (*transparent* and *auto hilite*) set in dialog boxes obtained using the *Button Info* command in the **Objects** menu (see Figure 21.19).

Using the techniques described earlier, you can create new cards to which each of these buttons will be linked. We will illustrate briefly for the *18th Century* button. Suppose we decide to put a card for the poet William Blake as the first card

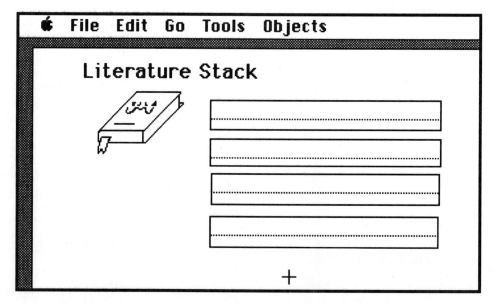

Figure 21.25 New card with text fields added.

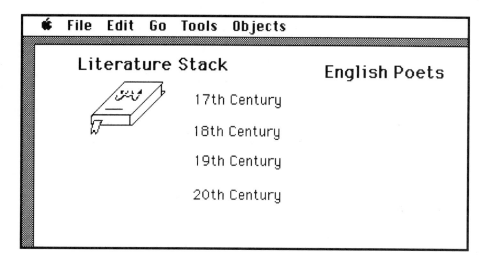

Figure 21.26 The new card with text fields entered and a title added to the foreground.

in the group of cards for this category. Figure 21.28 shows a possible configuration of fields for such a card.

The larger field shown on the card in Figure 21.28 is to be set to be a *scrolling* field (see Figure 21.21). Additionally, two buttons, *Major Poems* and *Contemporaries*, are be added to the card as illustrated in Figure 21.29. Note that these buttons have been named and the buttons and names are displayed instead of button icons. To accomplish this, the buttons are set to *Round rect*, and the *Show name* feature is selected (see Figure 21.19). Using these buttons, a *Literature* stack user could view more information about William Blake.

We would place information in the stack about another eighteenth-century poet by linking the *next card* button to a new card and then placing that information on the new card. Continuing this process, we would define a sequence of cards containing introductory information about all the eighteenth-century poets to be placed in the stack.

Figure 21.30 shows the first card to be linked to the *Major Poems* button. Note the use of the scrolling field and the digitized image that has been pasted on the

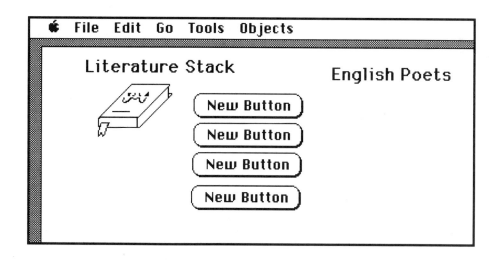

Figure 21.27 Placing buttons over the text fields.

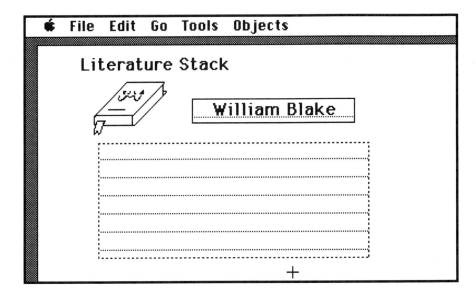

Figure 21.28 Defining a card for the *18th Century* button link.

card. (This image was copied to the Clipboard from the *Slide Show* stack included as a demonstration stack with HyperCard and then pasted onto the card shown.)

With the use of a scanner device, images can be digitized and copied into drawing/paint programs. These images can then be modified if desired and copied to other documents, such as HyperCard stacks. It is also possible to call other applications directly using HyperCard links. Hence, programs like

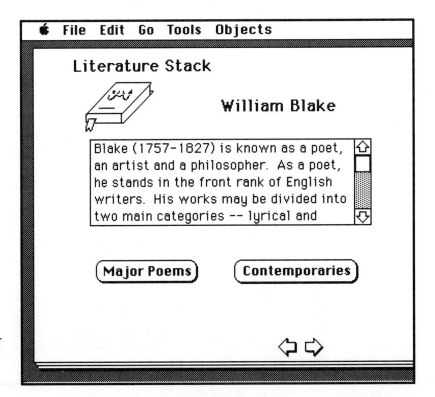

Figure 21.29 The card of Figure 21.28 with a scrolling field and *Major Poems* and *Contemporaries* buttons.

Figure 21.30 An additional *Literature* card using a digitized image.

ConcertWare+MIDI and MacRecorder could be called to include audio components within a HyperCard stack. Programs like Video Works II could provide easily constructed animation. There are many exciting possibilities for innovative **multimedia** information presentation using HyperCard. Although some of these ideas are beyond the scope of the introductory overview in this chapter, with what you have learned here and in Chapter 20, you have all the necessary tools to begin an exploration of these ideas on your own!

Computer Practice 21.3

1. Construct your own version of the *Literature* stack described in this section. Include all the components whose construction is outlined here.

2. Add several more eighteenth-century poets to the *Literature* stack you constructed in step 1. Include cards for several major poems for each of them.

3. Add several nineteenth-century poets and some of their major poems to the *Literature* stack of step 2. Create some *Contemporaries* button links among these poets.

4. If you have access to a scanner device, digitize some appropriate images and place them on cards in your *Literature* stack.

Key Concepts

Background card area	Defining links
Electronic links	Foreground card area
HyperCard cards	HyperCard stacks
Hypertext	Icon/button
Multimedia stacks	Nonlinear documents
Stack navigation methods	Text fields

INDEX